RIA's Complete Analysis of the Job Creation and Worker Assistance Act of 2002

With Code Sections as Amended and Joint Committee Explanation

Thank you for your purchase of RIA's industry-leading complete analysis
of the "Job Creation and Worker Assistance Act of 2002".
We value your business.

Here's a list of handy reference numbers:
1-800-950-1216—To place an order for this or other publications
1-800-431-9025—If you have questions about a previously placed order
or a customer service issue
1-800-742-3348—If you have a question about product content

RIA's Complete Analysis of the Job Creation and Worker Assistance Act of 2002

A THOMSON COMPANY

Denise Marshall
Elizabeth Schademann

Christopher DiMenna,
Supervisor
Christopher Barbieri
Geneva John
Rebecca Nam
Xiomara Tejeda
Samara Washington

Gregg Reed Harris,
Supervisor
Greg Chow
Helen McFarlane
Katie Morton
Michael Paci
Irina Resnikoff
Marcia Sam
Lisa Sarracino

Kim PeGan,
Data Analyst
Young Sone,
Data Analyst

Citator
Janie Davis
Ivette Terry

Paralegals
Catherine Daleo
Monica Grier
Danny Wang

Indexing
David Thompson,
Manager
Janet Mazefsky,
Assistant Manager
Cathy Fisher,
Supervisor
Tom Adewolu
Oslin Busby
George Flynn
Linda Lao
Andrea Leal
Jean Marie Tracy
Arlene Verderber

Legal Resource Center
Peter Durham,
Manager
Lissette Belliard
Agueda Boone
Pierre Calixte
Sandra Crowder
Mustapha Husseini
Patricia Link
Ed Mack
Theresa Scherne
Bernadette Stanton
Michael Stanton
Yevgeniya Uvakina
Karen Wolley Williams
Holly Yue
Velma Goodwine-
McDermon,
Supervisor
Charyn Johnson

**End-User Technical
Services**
Matt Freeman,
Manager
Steven McGill,
Manager
Eric Bauer
Jose Fiol
Jay Loyola
Tanya McDonald
Joseph Oliveri
Raymond Santiago
Valencia Singleton
Dominic Smith

Product Technology
Perry Townes,
Senior Director
Todd Gordon,
Director
Brian McNamara,
Director
David Levine,
Manager

John Melazzo,
Manager
Jay Liu,
Manager
Steve Wisniewski,
Manager
Gene Wojna,
Manager
Eileen Wood,
Information Manager
Ellen Moran,
Supervisor
Daryl Alexander
David Bantel
Geoff Braine
Erick Carrera
Kim Chirls
Resa Cirrincione
Tracey Cruz
Olga Davidov
Alanna Dixon
Romain Eastman
Alan Eldridge
Tatyana Fersht
Terri Ganssley
Michelle Harmon
Jay Kwon
Cynthia Lewis
Shon Lindsay
Yan Liu
David McInerney
Scott Murphy
Pamela J. Otruba
Michelle Paulin
Genevie Peters
Steve Pitamber
Luc Quirion
Jason Rapaccuiolo
Alfred Sehayek
Jason Shen
Esme Smartt
Pisa Sone

Margaret Taylor
Alana Trafford
Vivian Turner
Christian Velez
Rhonda Waller
Dennis Wendell
Linda Wiseman
Chris Yourch
Hongtu Zhang
Teresa Zhang

**Manufacturing
Services
& Fulfillment**

Rick Bivona,
Director
Anthony Scribano,
*Scheduling and
Fulfillment Manager*
Gail Gneiding,
*Manufacturing and
Outside Composition
Manager*
Rachel Hassenbein,
Fulfillment Coordinator
John Disposti,
*Senior Manufacturing
Coordinator*
Greg Miller,
*Associate Production
Manager*
Enid Skolnik,
Fulfillment Coordinator
Anthony Lovari,
Inventory Manager
Bryan Gardner,
*Manufacturing
Coordinator*
Donna Smith,
*Fulfillment Manager
(Carrollton)*

Table of Contents

RIA Research Institute of America

RIA Research Institute of America

¶ 1. Organization of the Book

Organization of RIA's Complete Analysis of the Job Creation and Worker Assistance Act of 2002

This book contains RIA's Complete Analysis of H.R. 3090, the Job Creation and Worker Assistance Act of 2002 (the 2002 Act), which was signed into law on Mar. 9, 2002 (PL 107-147, 3/9/2002). The 2002 Act is a combination of business economic stimulus provisions, relief provisions for lower-Manhattan businesses affected by the 9/11 terrorist attacks, a 13-week extension of unemployment benefits, extensions for expired or soon-to-expire tax breaks, and technical corrections.

Business economic stimulus provisions in the 2002 Act include:

• 30% additional first-year depreciation for most types of new nonrealty property acquired after Sept. 10, 2001 and before Sept. 11, 2004. In general, the property must be placed in service by the taxpayer before 2005 (before 2006 for certain property with longer production periods). The additional depreciation allowance applies for qualifying property placed in service after Sept. 10, 2001. For analysis, see ¶ 101.

• An increase in net operating loss (NOL) carryback periods to five years, for NOLs arising in tax years ending in 2001 or 2002. For analysis, see ¶ 103

• A temporary waiver of the limitation on use of NOLs against the alternative minimum tax (AMT). Under the Act, an alternative tax net operating loss deduction (ATNOL) arising in years ending in 2001 or 2002, or NOL carryforwards to the 2001 and 2002 tax years, may offset 100% of a taxpayer's alternative minimum taxable income. For analysis, see ¶ 104.

Relief provisions for lower Manhattan businesses impacted by the 9/11 terrorist attacks include:

• Additional 30% first-year depreciation for eligible nonresidential or residential realty (to the extent it rehabilitates realty damaged, or replaces realty destroyed or condemned, as a result of the Sept. 11, 2001 terrorist attack) in the New York Liberty Zone (essentially, lower Manhattan). For analysis, see ¶ 501.

• A $35,000 increase in the regular maximum expensing allowance under Code Sec. 179 for qualified Liberty Zone property, the original use of which commences with the taxpayer after Sept. 10, 2001 and that is acquired by the taxpayer by purchase after that date and placed in service before 2007. For analysis, see ¶ 502.

• Straight line depreciation over 5 years (9 years under the alternative depreciation system, or ADS) for qualified leasehold improvement property (generally a non-structural, non-expansion improvement to an interior portion of an existing nonresidential building, provided certain requirements are met) that is in the Liberty Zone, and placed in service after Sept. 10, 2001, and before 2007. For analysis, see ¶ 503.

• The Code Sec. 1033 replacement period for property involuntarily converted in the Liberty Zone as a result of the 9/11 terrorist attack is extended from two years to five years, but only if substantially all of the replacement property is in New York City. For analysis, see ¶ 504.

• A new targeted group of work opportunity credit (WOTC) eligible individuals is created for those who work for smaller businesses in the Liberty Zone (or elsewhere in New York City, if their business was forced to relocate because of the 9/11 terrorist attack). For analysis, see ¶ 505.

Tax breaks extended for two years by the 2002 Act include:

• The ability to use personal nonrefundable credits to offset both regular and AMT liability (for analysis, see ¶ 401).

• The work opportunity tax credit (for analysis, see ¶ 202).

• The welfare to work credit (for analysis, see ¶ 201).

• The Code Sec. 45 credit for production of energy from alternative sources (for analysis, see ¶ 205).

• The suspension of the 100% of taxable income limit on percentage depletion from marginal oil and gas wells (for analysis, see ¶ 206).

The technical corrections relating to five previous tax laws include corrections that affect 2001 returns filed in 2002.

Contents A complete list of topics discussed, arranged by paragraph title and number ¶ 2

Analysis of the Tax Provisions. The analysis of the 2002 Act is arranged in topical order. Each analysis paragraph starts with a boldface title. That is followed by a list of the Code sections substantively affected by the change, the Act section that caused the change, and the generally effective date for the change. Each analysis paragraph discusses the background for the change, the new law change, and the effective date for that change. Analysis paragraphs may include (1) illustrations and observations providing practical insight into the effects of the change, (2) recommendations explaining how to take advantage of opportunities presented by the law change, (3) cautions detailing how to avoid pitfalls created by the law change, and (4) action alert items showing actions that must be taken by a certain date under the new law. Cites in the analysis paragraphs to the appropriate Committee reports (in this case, the Joint Committee on Taxation Explanation) are cited as Com Rept. The Analysis of the 2002 Act is reproduced at ¶ 100 *et seq.* . . . . . p. 1

Client Letters Client letters are included that explain (1) the overall impact of the 2002 Act (¶ 801), (2) the retroactively effective depreciation changes in the 2002 Act (¶ 802), (3) NOL carryback changes in the 2002 Act (¶ 803), (4) how the 2002 Act afects 2001 returns (¶ 804), (5) extender provisions in the 2002 Act (¶ 805), and (6) New York City tax incentives in the 2002 Act (¶ 806) . . . p. 195

RIA **Research Institute of America**

Code as Amended. All Code sections that were amended, added, repealed, or redesignated by the 2002 Act, appear in Code order as amended, added, repealed, or redesignated. New matter is shown in italics. Deleted material and effective dates are shown in footnotes. The Code as Amended is reproduced at ¶ 3000 *et seq.*...p. 301

Act Sections Not Amending Code. This section reproduces in Act section order, all 2002 Act sections, or portions thereof that do not amend specific Code sections. The Act Sections Not Amending Code are reproduced at ¶ 4000 *et seq.* ....p. 401

Committee Reports. No official Committee Reports for the 2002 Act, as passed by the House and Senate, have been issued. Thus, this dataset reproduces all relevant parts of the Joint Committee on Taxation Technical explanation of the 2002 Act. The material comes from the Joint Committee on Taxation Technical Explanation of the Job Creation and Worker Assistance Act of 2002, as passed by the House on Mar. 7, 2002 and by the Senate on Mar. 8, 2002 (JCX-12-02, 3/6/02)

The relevant Committee Reports (in this case, Joint Committee on Taxation Technical Explanations) are reproduced at ¶ 5000 *et seq.* ....p. 501

Act Section Cross Reference Table. Arranged in Act section order, this table shows substantive Code section(s) amended, added, or repealed, the topic involved, the generally effective date of the amendment, the relevant paragraph number for the Analysis and the paragraph where the relevant Committee Reports (in this case, Joint Committee Explanation) are reproduced. The table is reproduced at ¶ 6000 ....p. 601

Code Section Cross Reference Table. Arranged in Code section order, this table shows the amending Act section(s), the topic involved, the generally effective date of the amendment, the relevant paragraph number for the Analysis and the paragraph where the relevant Committee Reports (in this case, Joint Committee Explanation) are reproduced. The table is reproduced at ¶ 6001 ....p. 621

Act Section ERISA Cross Reference Table. Arranged in Act section order, this table shows substantive ERISA section(s) amended, added, or repealed, the topic involved, the generally effective date of the amendment, the relevant paragraph number for the Analysis and the paragraph where the relevant Committee Reports (in this case, Joint Committee Explanation) are reproduced. The table is reproduced at ¶ 6002 ....p. 639

ERISA Section Cross Reference Table. Arranged in ERISA section order, this table shows the amending Act section(s), the topic involved, the generally effective date of the amendment, the relevant paragraph number for the Analysis and the paragraph where the relevant Committee Reports (in this case, Joint Committee Explanation) are reproduced. The table is reproduced at ¶ 6003 ....p. 641

Code Sections Amended by the 2002 Act Table. Arranged in Code section order, this table shows all changes to the Internal Revenue Code made by the Act,

RIA Research Institute of America

Index. A detailed index, which directs the reader to the appropriate Analysis paragraph, is reproduced immediately after the aforementioned Tables for the

¶ 2. Contents

RIA Research Institute of America

CLIENT LETTERS　　　　　　　　　　　**800**

RIA Research Institute of America

¶ 100. Business Provisions

¶ 101. 30% additional first-year depreciation is allowed for, and the AMT depreciation adjustment is not required for, most new tangible personal property and computer software and certain leasehold improvements acquired after Sept. 10, 2001, if acquired or contracted for before Sept. 11, 2004 and placed in service within certain time limits

Code Sec. 168(k), as amended by 2002 Act § 101(a)
Generally effective: Property placed in service after Sept. 10, 2001, in tax years ending after Sept. 10, 2001
Committee Reports, see ¶ 5001

Code Sec. 167(a) allows taxpayers a depreciation deduction for the exhaustion of property used in a trade or business or for the production of income, see FTC 2d/FIN ¶ L-7501; USTR ¶ 1674; TaxDesk ¶ 264,501. For most tangible property, the deduction is determined under the modified accelerated cost recovery system (MACRS), see FTC 2d/FIN ¶ L-8101; USTR ¶ 1684; TaxDesk ¶ 266,001.

Depreciable computer software, unless it must be amortized over 15 years under Code Sec. 197, is generally depreciated under Code Sec. 167 using the straight-line method and a 36-month useful life. (FTC 2d/FIN ¶ L-7935; USTR ¶ 1674.033; TaxDesk ¶ 265,434)

For most property (other than buildings) depreciated under MACRS, Code Sec. 56 requires that depreciation deductions are calculated, for purposes of determining alternative minimum taxable income (AMTI) under Code Sec. 55, on the 150% declining balance method. This adjustment is required for alternative minimum tax (AMT) purposes whether or not the property is depreciated on the 150% declining balance method for regular tax purposes. (FTC 2d/FIN ¶ A-8220; USTR ¶ 564.01; TaxDesk ¶ 696,513)

New Law. The 2002 Act provides that, for "qualified property" (defined below), (Code Sec. 168(k)(1) as amended by 2002 Act §101(a))

... the depreciation deduction under Code Sec. 167(a) for the tax year in which the property is placed in service includes an allowance equal to 30% of the adjusted basis of the qualified property, and (Code Sec. 168(k)(1)(A))

...the adjusted basis of the qualified property is reduced by the amount of that deduction before computing the amount otherwise allowable as a depreciation deduction for the tax year and any later tax year. (Code Sec. 168(k)(1)(B))

> **☮️ observation:** Congress has indicated that allowing additional first-year depreciation will accelerate purchases of equipment, promote capital investment, modernization and growth, and will help to spur an economic recovery.

For a taxpayer's right *not* to claim the 30% additional first-year depreciation discussed above, see "Election-out" below.

For discussion of the 2002 Act provision that, for a passenger automobile that is qualified property, raises the first-year dollar limit on the depreciation allowable for passenger automobiles, see ¶ 102.

For discussion of the 2002 Act provision that provides additional first-year depreciation for certain property to which the above rule in Code Sec. 168(k)(1) doesn't apply and that is located in the "New York Liberty Zone," see ¶ 501.

> **☮️ observation:** Code Sec. 168(k)(1) (above) doesn't specify whether the half-year, mid-quarter or mid-month depreciation conventions, see FTC 2d/FIN ¶ L-8103; USTR ¶ 1684.01; TaxDesk ¶ 266,701, apply to the 30% additional first-year depreciation. However, examples in the Technical Explanation of the 2002 Act, reflected in Illustrations (1) and (2) below, indicate that the depreciation conventions *don't* apply; i.e., in each example, the 30% additional first-year depreciation is *not* reduced below 30% (as the use of either convention would have required).

> **☮️ caution:** Although, as discussed immediately above, it appears that depreciation conventions don't apply to the 30% additional first-year depreciation itself, the conventions apply to the other first-year depreciation deductions allowed with respect to qualified property. Further, the placement of qualified property into service during the last quarter of a tax year may, in some circumstances, cause the taxpayer to be required to use a mid-quarter convention, rather than a half-year convention, for all of the taxpayer's MACRS property (other than buildings and railroad gradings or tunnel bores) placed into service during that tax year, see FTC 2d/FIN ¶ L-8103; USTR ¶ 1684.01; TaxDesk ¶ 266,701.

> *Illustration (1):* On Mar. 1, 2002, T, a calendar year taxpayer, acquires and places in service "qualified property" that costs $1 million. Assuming that T doesn't make an "election-out" (see below), T is allowed an additional first-year depreciation deduction of $300,000. The remaining $700,000 of adjusted basis is recovered in 2002 and later years under the other depreciation rules of pre-2002 Act law (which are not affected by the 2002 Act). (Com Rept, see ¶ 5001)

observation: Illustration (2) (immediately below) shows that amounts "expensed" under Code Sec. 179 reduce the basis of an asset before the additional first-year depreciation is calculated for the asset and before other depreciation is calculated for the asset.

Illustration (2): On Mar. 1, 2002, W, a calendar year taxpayer, acquires and places in service qualified property that costs $50,000. Assume that the property qualifies for the expensing election under Code Sec. 179, see FTC 2d/FIN ¶ L-9901; USTR ¶ 1794.01; TaxDesk ¶ 268,401. W is first allowed a $24,000 deduction under Code Sec. 179. W is then allowed an additional first-year depreciation deduction of $7,800 based on an adjusted basis of $26,000 ($50,000 original cost, less the $24,000 deduction). The remaining adjusted basis of $18,200 ($26,000 less $7,800) is recovered in 2002 and later years under the other depreciation rules of pre-2002 Act law (which are not affected by the 2002 Act). (Com Rept, see ¶ 5001)

The additional first-year depreciation deduction is subject to the general rules regarding whether an item is deductible under Code Sec. 162 or subject to capitalization under Code Sec. 263 (the regular capitalization rules, see FTC 2d/FIN ¶ L-5601; USTR ¶ 2634; TaxDesk ¶ 256,201) or Code Sec. 263A (the uniform capitalization, or UNICAP, rules, see FTC 2d/FIN ¶ G-5450; USTR ¶ 263A4; TaxDesk ¶ 456,000). (Com Rept, see ¶ 5001)

"Qualified property" defined. The 2002 Act defines "qualified property" as property which satisfies four specified requirements (which are discussed under the four italicized subheadings below). (Code Sec. 168(k)(2))

caution: There are certain types of property which are ineligible to be qualified property even if they satisfy the four requirements of the definition of qualified property, see "Property not eligible for additional first-year depreciation" below.

Requirement that property be of a certain type. To be "qualified property," property must be either: (Code Sec. 168(k)(2)(A)(i))

(1) property to which Code Sec. 168 (which provides the MACRS rules) applies, and which has a recovery period of 20 years or less; (Code Sec. 168(k)(2)(A)(i)(I))

(2) computer software (as defined in Code Sec. 167(f)(1)(B)) for which a deduction is allowable under Code Sec. 167(a) without regard to Code Sec. 168(k)

FTC 2d References are to Federal Tax Coordinator 2d
FIN References are to RIA's Analysis of Federal Taxes: Income
USTR References are to United States Tax Reporter: Income, Estate & Gift, and Excise
PCA References are to the Pension Analysis on Checkpoint and CD-ROM, and in Pension Coordinator
PE References are to the Pension Explanations in Pension and Profit Sharing 2nd
EP References are to the Estate Planning Analysis on Checkpoint and CD-ROM, and in Estate Planning & Taxation Coordinator

(i.e., the rules for additional first year depreciation). (Code Sec. 168(k)(2)(A)(i)(II)) Thus, additional first-year depreciation isn't available for computer software amortized under Code Sec. 197 (see FTC 2d/FIN ¶ L-7958; USTR ¶ 1974; TaxDesk ¶ 265,434). (Com Rept, see ¶ 5001)

(3) "water utility property" (which is a class of MACRS property defined in Code Sec. 168(e)(5), see FTC 2d/FIN ¶ L-8209.1; USTR ¶ 1684.01; TaxDesk ¶ 266,210) or; (Code Sec. 168(k)(2)(A)(i)(III))

(4) "qualified leasehold improvement property" (defined below). (Code Sec. 168(k)(2)(A)(i)(IV)) For a rule excluding "qualified New York Liberty Zone leasehold improvement property" from being "qualified property," see "Property not eligible for additional first-year depreciation" below.

> ⒭*observation:* The property included in item (1) on the above list is MACRS property that is included in the 3-year, 5-year, 7-year, 10-year, 15-year or 20-year MACRS classes.

Requirement of original use. To be qualified property, the original use of the property must begin with the taxpayer after Sept. 10, 2001. (Code Sec. 168(k)(2)(A)(ii)) For purposes of this requirement, "original use" means the first use to which the property is put, whether or not that use corresponds to the use of the property *by the taxpayer.* (Com Rept, see ¶ 5001)

The Technical Explanation says that it is intended that, when evaluating whether property qualifies as "original use" property, the factors used to determine whether property qualified as "new section 38 property" for purposes of the pre-'86 investment tax credit apply, see Reg § 1.48-2. Thus, it is intended that additional capital expenditures incurred to recondition or rebuild acquired property (or owned property) would satisfy the "original use" requirement. However, the cost of reconditioned or rebuilt property acquired by the taxpayer would not satisfy the "original use" requirement, see FTC 2d/FIN ¶ L-17101; FTC 2d/FIN ¶ L-17107; FTC 2d/FIN ¶ P-1603; USTR ¶ 484.09. (Com Rept, see ¶ 5001)

> *Illustration (3):* On Feb. 1, 2002, G buys from F for $20,000 a machine that had been previously used by F. G makes an expenditure on the property of $5,000 of the type that must be capitalized. Whether the $5,000 is added to the basis of the property or is capitalized as a separate asset, that amount is treated as satisfying the "original use" requirement and is qualified property (assuming all other conditions are met). No part of the $20,000 purchase price qualifies for the 30% additional first year depreciation. (Com Rept, see ¶ 5001)

Also, for purposes of the original use requirement, if property (1) is originally placed in service after Sept. 10, 2001, by a person, and (2) is sold and leased back by that person within three months after the date that property was originally placed in service, the property is treated as originally placed in service not earlier than the date on which the property is used under the leaseback. (Code Sec.

168(k)(2)(D)(ii)) Thus, in the case of any property that is originally placed in service by a person and that is sold to the taxpayer and leased back to that person by the taxpayer within three months after the date that the property was placed in service, the property is treated as originally placed in service by the taxpayer not earlier than the date that the property is used under the leaseback. (Com Rept, see ¶ 5001)

> *observation:* As confirmed by the Technical Explanation's identification of "the taxpayer" as the buyer-lessor, the main effect of the sale-leaseback original use rule is to shift eligibility for additional first-year depreciation from the seller-lessee to the buyer-lessor.

> *illustration (4):* On Oct. 15, 2001, X, a calendar year taxpayer, buys a newly manufactured machine from manufacturer M, and begins to use the machine in X's business. On Jan. 10, 2002, X sells the machine to Y, which is a company in the equipment leasing business and is a calendar-year taxpayer. Also, on Jan. 10, 2002, X leases the machine back from Y under a lease, the term of which begins on Jan. 10, 2002. X continues to use the machine in X's business. Thus, Jan. 10, 2002 is the date that the machine is first used under the leaseback, and, thus, first satisfies the original use requirement. Therefore, if the machine meets the other requirements for being qualified property, and if Y doesn't make an "election-out" (see below), Y is allowed additional first-year depreciation for the machine in 2002. X is not allowed additional first-year depreciation for the machine in either 2001 or 2002.

> *illustration (5):* The facts are the same as in Illustration (4), except that (1) X acquires the machine and begins to use the machine on Sept. 5, 2001, and (2) the sale and leaseback of the machine occurs on Dec. 1, 2001. The sale and leaseback of the machine occurs within the three-month time period required under Code Sec. 168(k)(2)(D)(ii). However, the machine fails the requirement, under Code Sec. 168(k)(2)(D)(ii), that property be originally placed in service after Sept. 10, 2001. Thus, Y isn't allowed additional first-year depreciation for the machine. With respect to X, the machine fails the requirement, in Code Sec. 168(k)(2)(A)(ii) (above), that the original use of the machine must begin with the taxpayer after Sept. 10, 2001. Thus, X also isn't allowed additional first-year depreciation for the machine.

FTC 2d References are to Federal Tax Coordinator 2d
FIN References are to RIA's Analysis of Federal Taxes: Income
USTR References are to United States Tax Reporter: Income, Estate & Gift, and Excise
PCA References are to the Pension Analysis on Checkpoint and CD-ROM, and in Pension Coordinator
PE References are to the Pension Explanations in Pension and Profit Sharing 2nd
EP References are to the Estate Planning Analysis on Checkpoint and CD-ROM, and in Estate Planning & Taxation Coordinator

Requirement of timely acquisition or commitment to buy. To be qualified property, property must be: (Code Sec. 168(k)(2)(A)(iii))

(A) acquired by the taxpayer after Sept. 10, 2001, and before Sept. 11, 2004, but only if no written binding contract for the acquisition was in effect before Sept. 11, 2001, or (Code Sec. 168(k)(2)(A)(iii)(I))

(B) acquired by the taxpayer under a written binding contract which was entered into after Sept. 10, 2001, and before Sept. 11, 2004. (Code Sec. 168(k)(2)(A)(iii)(II))

For a taxpayer manufacturing, constructing or producing property for the taxpayer's own use, the requirements of Code Sec. 168(k)(2)(A)(iii) (immediately above) are treated as met if the taxpayer begins manufacturing, constructing, or producing the property after Sept. 10, 2001 and before Sept. 11, 2004. (Code Sec. 168(k)(2)(D)(i))

> **observation:** Congress had indicated that this property is qualified property if all of the other requirements for qualified property are also met.

> **illustration (6):** On Aug. 20, 2004, Q, a computer hardware manufacturer and calendar year taxpayer, begins manufacturing 150 desk-top computers for use in Q's business by Q's employees. Assuming that Q doesn't make an "election-out" (see below), Q is allowed first-year 30% additional depreciation for any of the 150 computers that are placed in service before Jan. 1, 2005 (see below) and that meet the other requirements for being "qualified property."

> **illustration (7):** The facts are the same as in Illustration (6), except that Q begins manufacturing the 150 computers on Aug. 20, 2001. None of the computers are qualified property.

Property is considered manufactured, constructed or produced *by* the taxpayer if it is manufactured, constructed or produced *for* the taxpayer by another person under a contract that is entered into before the manufacture, construction or production of the property. (Com Rept, see ¶ 5001)

Requirement of timely placement into service. To be qualified property, the property must be placed in service by the taxpayer before Jan. 1, 2005, except that property which meets the requirements discussed immediately below is qualified property if it is placed in service before Jan. 1, 2006. (Code Sec. 168(k)(2)(A)(iv))

"Qualified property" includes property which (Code Sec. 168(k)(2)(B)(i))

(1) meets the requirements of Code Sec. 168(k)(2)(A)(i) (that property be of a certain type, see above), Code Sec. 168(k)(2)(A)(ii) (the original use requirement, see above) and Code Sec. 168(k)(2)(A)(iii) (requirement of timely acquisition or commitment to buy, see above), (Code Sec. 168(k)(2)(B)(i)(I))

(2) has a recovery period of at least 10 years or is "transportation property" (see below), and (Code Sec. 168(k)(2)(B)(i)(II))

(3) which is subject to Code Sec. 263A (i.e., the uniform capitalization rules (UNICAP), see above) by reason of Code Sec. 263A(f)(1)(B)(ii) (which requires that property have an estimated production period exceeding two years, see FTC 2d/FIN ¶ L-5920; USTR ¶ 263A4.11; TaxDesk ¶ 456,020) or Code Sec. 263A(f)(1)(B)(iii) (which requires that property have an estimated production period exceeding 1 year and a cost exceeding $1,000,000, see FTC 2d/FIN ¶ L-5920; USTR ¶ 263A4.11; TaxDesk ¶ 456,020). (Code Sec. 168(k)(2)(B)(i)(III))

Where property is "qualified property" solely because it qualifies under Code Sec. 168(k)(2)(B)(i) (immediately above), the property (pre-2006 property) is eligible for 30% additional first-year depreciation only to the extent of the adjusted basis attributable to manufacture, construction, or production before Sept. 11, 2004. (Code Sec. 168(k)(2)(B)(ii)) Thus, for pre-2006 property, the costs eligible for additional first-year depreciation are limited to the portion of the basis that is properly attributable to costs incurred before Sept. 11, 2004. To determine these "eligible progress expenditures," the Technical Explanation intends that rules similar to the rules in Code Sec. 46(d)(3), before its repeal by the Tax Reform Act of '86 (PL 99-514) apply, see FTC 2d/FIN ¶ L-17126; USTR ¶ 464.10. (Com Rept, see ¶ 5001).

"Transportation property" means tangible personal property used in the trade or business of transporting persons or property. (Code Sec. 168(k)(2)(B)(iii))

Property not eligible for additional first-year depreciation. The property described below isn't eligible for the 30% additional first-year depreciation.

Alternative depreciation system property. "Qualified property" doesn't include any property to which the alternative depreciation system ("ADS") under Code Sec. 168(g) applies. (Code Sec. 168(k)(2)(C)(i)) Thus, the additional first year depreciation deduction is precluded for property that is required to be depreciated under ADS. (Com Rept, see ¶ 5001) For a discussion of the ADS, see FTC 2d/FIN ¶ L-9401; USTR ¶ 1684.03; TaxDesk ¶ 267,501.

FTC 2d References are to Federal Tax Coordinator 2d
FIN References are to RIA's Analysis of Federal Taxes: Income
USTR References are to United States Tax Reporter: Income, Estate & Gift, and Excise
PCA References are to the Pension Analysis on Checkpoint and CD-ROM, and in Pension Coordinator
PE References are to the Pension Explanations in Pension and Profit Sharing 2nd
EP References are to the Estate Planning Analysis on Checkpoint and CD-ROM, and in Estate Planning & Taxation Coordinator

For this purpose, the determination of whether the ADS applies is made: (Code Sec. 168(k)(2)(C)(i))

(1) without regard to Code Sec. 168(g)(7) (relating to elections to have the ADS system apply), and (Code Sec. 168(k)(2)(C)(i)(I))

(2) after application of Code Sec. 280F(b) (relating to "listed property" with limited business use, see the second observation below). (Code Sec. 168(k)(2)(C)(i)(II))

> *observation:* The effect of Code Sec. 168(k)(2)(C)(i)(I) (item (1) listed above) is that property that is subject to the ADS only because the tax-payer elected to have the ADS apply *is eligible* to be qualified property if it meets all of the other requirements for being qualified property. Thus, property doesn't become ineligible merely because the taxpayer elected ADS under Code Sec. 168(g)(7).

> *observation:* Presumably, the purpose of Code Sec. 168(k)(2)(C)(i)(II) (item (2) listed above) is to clarify that property that isn't mentioned in Code Sec. 168(g)(1), which provides a list of property that is subject to the ADS, is, nevertheless, subject to the ADS, and, thus, *isn't eligible* to be qualified property, if it is property that is covered by the rule in Code Sec. 280F(b). That rule, see FTC 2d/FIN ¶ L-10018; USTR ¶ 280F4; TaxDesk ¶ 267,615, requires that passenger automobiles and certain other types of "listed property," see FTC 2d/FIN ¶ L-10002; USTR ¶ 280F4; TaxDesk ¶ 267,616, be depreciated under the ADS if not used more than 50% of the time in a "qualified business use," see FTC 2d/FIN ¶ L-10025; USTR ¶ 280F4; TaxDesk ¶ 267,621. The rule in Code Sec. 280F(b) is referred to below as the "more-than-50%-test."

Qualified New York Liberty Zone leasehold improvement property. Qualified property doesn't include any "qualified New York Liberty Zone leasehold improvement property" (as defined in Code Sec. 1400L(c)(2), which is discussed in the observation immediately below). (Code Sec. 168(k)(2)(C)(ii))

> *observation:* In a provision (2002 Act § 301(a)) separate from the 2002 Act section providing for additional first-year depreciation, the 2002 Act added to the Code, in Code Sec. 1400L(c)(2), the category of "qualified New York Liberty Zone leasehold improvement property," referred to in the rule immediately above, for the purpose of permitting the cost of that property to be depreciated, generally, over a 5-year period on the straight-line method, see ¶ 503. Thus, it can be presumed that Congress made "qualified New York Liberty Zone leasehold improvement property" inel-igible for additional first-year depreciation because it believed that quali-fied leasehold improvement property shouldn't receive both the benefit of being depreciated over 5 years *and* the benefit of 30% additional first-year depreciation.

Election-out. Taxpayers are permitted, for any class of property for any tax year, to elect to have Code Sec. 168(k) not apply to all property in that class placed in service during the tax year. (Code Sec. 168(k)(2)(C)(iii)) Thus, taxpayers are allowed to elect out of the 30% additional first-year depreciation for any class of property for any tax year. (Com Rept, see ¶ 5001)

> *observation:* Presumably, property for which the election is made also won't receive the benefit of not being subject to a depreciation adjustment for alternative minimum tax purposes, see "Alternative minimum tax" below.

> *observation:* Presumably there are nine separate "classes" referred to in the election-out rule, i.e., the 3-year, 5-year, 7-year, 10-year, 15-year and 20-year MACRS classes; the water utility property MACRS class; a class consisting of most depreciable computer software and a class consisting of qualified leasehold improvement property, see "Requirement that property be of a certain type" under "Qualified property" above. Thus, for example, if a taxpayer makes an election-out with respect to the class consisting of 15-year MACRS property, items of 15-year MACRS property will be ineligible for 30% additional first-year depreciation (and for exemption from the alternative minimum tax depreciation adjustment) even if the ineligibility rules discussed under "Property not eligible for additional first-year depreciation" (above) don't apply to the items.

> *observation:* Two situations in which a taxpayer might, for a tax year, consider making an election-out for one or more classes, are (1) where the taxpayer has about-to-expire net operating losses and (2) where the taxpayer anticipates being in a higher tax bracket in future years.

Listed property recapture. The 30% additional first-year depreciation is taken into account in computing any recapture amount under Code Sec. 280F(b)(2). (Code Sec. 168(k)(2)(E)(ii))

> *observation:* Where an item of "listed property" passes the "more-than-50%-test" (see "Alternative depreciation system property" under "Property not eligible for additional first-year depreciation" above) in the year that it is first placed in service, but, in a later year, fails the test, the taxpayer must, under Code Sec. 280F(b)(2), in the later year, recapture (i.e., add to his income and to the adjusted basis of the listed property) the excess of (1) the amount of depreciation allowable for the item in earlier

FTC 2d References are to Federal Tax Coordinator 2d
FIN References are to RIA's Analysis of Federal Taxes: Income
USTR References are to United States Tax Reporter: Income, Estate & Gift, and Excise
PCA References are to the Pension Analysis on Checkpoint and CD-ROM, and in Pension Coordinator
PE References are to the Pension Explanations in Pension and Profit Sharing 2nd
EP References are to the Estate Planning Analysis on Checkpoint and CD-ROM, and in Estate Planning & Taxation Coordinator

tax years over (2) the amount that would have been allowable had the property not passed the more-than-50% test in the year that it was first placed in service, see FTC 2d/FIN ¶ L-10032; USTR ¶ 280F4; TaxDesk ¶ 223,113.

illustration (8): On Nov. 15, 2002, V, a calendar year taxpayer, places into service in his business a new car costing $15,000. Assume further that (1) the car is qualified property, (2) V doesn't "elect-out" (see above), (3) in 2002, V's use of the car is, exclusively, in a "qualified business use" (and thus passes the more-than-50%-test, see "Alternative depreciation system property" under "Property not eligible for additional first-year depreciation" above), (4) in 2002, V depreciated the car, which has a five-year recovery period, on the 200% declining balance method (switching to the straight-line method in the first year that the straight-line method yields larger deductions), using a half-year convention (which causes the car to be depreciated over six tax years, see FTC 2d/FIN ¶ L-8702; USTR ¶ 1684.01; TaxDesk ¶ 266,702), and (5) in 2003, V's use of the car fails the more-than-50%-test.

The result is that, in 2002, V is entitled to a depreciation deduction for the car of $6,600 (additional first-year depreciation of $4,500 [$15,000 × 30%] *plus* regular depreciation of $2,100 [($15,000 minus $4,500) × 20%]). However, in 2003, V, before calculating depreciation for the car for that year, must increase his income, and his adjusted basis in the car, by $5,100, which is the excess of $6,600 over $1,500. ($1,500 is the amount of depreciation that V would have been entitled to had V failed the more-than-50% test in 2002 because, in that case, the car would have been subject to the alternative depreciation system and ineligible for additional first-year depreciation, see "Alternative depreciation system property" under "Property not eligible for additional first-year depreciation" above, and V's regular depreciation would have been restricted to the $1,500 [10% × $15,000] that would have been permitted under the alternative depreciation system. Under the alternative depreciation system, V would have been restricted to a 10%, rather than a 20%, depreciation deduction in 2002 because, under the alternative depreciation system, V would have been required to depreciate the car on the straight line method, see FTC 2d/FIN ¶ L-9401; USTR ¶ 1684.03; TaxDesk ¶ 267,501.)

"Qualified leasehold improvement property" defined. For purposes of the 30% additional first-year depreciation rules, qualified leasehold improvement property is any improvement to an interior portion of a building which is nonresidential real property, if (Code Sec. 168(k)(3)(A))

...the improvement is made under or pursuant to a lease (as defined in Code Sec. 168(h)(7), see FTC 2d/FIN ¶ L-9607; USTR ¶ 1684.06), either by the lessee, sublessee or lessor of the building portion, (Code Sec. 168(k)(3)(A)(i))

... the portion of the building is to be occupied exclusively by the lessee (or any sublessee) of the portion, and (Code Sec. 168(k)(3)(A)(ii))

... the improvement is placed in service more than 3 years after the date the building was first placed in service. (Code Sec. 168(k)(3)(A)(iii))

> **recommendation:** Taxpayers who want to take advantage of 30% additional first-year depreciation for improvements being made in relatively new buildings, i.e., buildings placed in service within the last three years, should, if possible, avoid placing the improvements in service within that three-year period.

Qualified leasehold improvement property does not include any improvement for which the expenditure is attributable to: (Code Sec. 168(k)(3)(B))

... enlargement of the building, (Code Sec. 168(k)(3)(B)(i))

... any elevator or escalator, (Code Sec. 168(k)(3)(B)(ii))

... any structural component benefiting a common area, and (Code Sec. 168(k)(3)(B)(iii))

... the internal structural framework of the building. (Code Sec. 168(k)(3)(B)(iv))

For purposes of the above definition of qualified leasehold improvement property, a commitment (i.e., a *binding* commitment (Com Rept, see ¶ 5001)) to enter into a lease is treated as a lease, and the parties to the commitment are treated as lessor and lessee, respectively. (Code Sec. 168(k)(3)(C)(i))

Also, for purposes of the above definition, a lease between related persons is *not* considered a lease. For this purpose, the following are related persons: (Code Sec. 168(k)(3)(C)(ii))

... members of an affiliated group (as defined in Code Sec. 1504, see FTC 2d/FIN ¶ E-7601; USTR ¶ 15,024.17; TaxDesk ¶ 240,808) and (Code Sec. 168(k)(3)(C)(ii)(I))

... persons having a relationship described in Code Sec. 267(b), see FTC 2d/FIN ¶ G-2707; USTR ¶ 2674.03; TaxDesk ¶ 227,904, but substituting the phrase "80 percent or more" for "more than 50 percent" each place the phrase "more than 50 percent" appears in Code Sec. 267(b). (Code Sec. 168(k)(3)(C)(ii)(II))

FTC 2d References are to Federal Tax Coordinator 2d
FIN References are to RIA's Analysis of Federal Taxes: Income
USTR References are to United States Tax Reporter: Income, Estate & Gift, and Excise
PCA References are to the Pension Analysis on Checkpoint and CD-ROM, and in Pension Coordinator
PE References are to the Pension Explanations in Pension and Profit Sharing 2nd
EP References are to the Estate Planning Analysis on Checkpoint and CD-ROM, and in Estate Planning & Taxation Coordinator

Alternative minimum tax. For purposes of determining alternative minimum taxable income under Code Sec. 55, the deduction under Code Sec. 168(a) for qualified property is determined under Code Sec. 168 without regard to any adjustment under Code Sec. 56. (Code Sec. 168(k)(2)(F)) Thus, the 30% additional first-year depreciation is allowed for both regular tax and alternative minimum tax purposes for the tax year in which the property is placed in service. In addition, there is no adjustment to the allowable amount of depreciation for purposes of computing a taxpayer's alternative minimum taxable income for property to which Code Sec. 168(k) applies. (Com Rept, see ¶ 5001)

> *observation:* Thus, presumably, if property is "qualified property" (defined as discussed above), neither the 30% additional first-year depreciation deductions allowable for the property nor any of the other depreciation deductions allowable for the property (in the first year or in later years) are subject to adjustment for alternative minimum tax purposes. This is a significant tax benefit for "qualified property" that is distinct from, and in addition to, the benefit of 30% additional first-year depreciation.

> *illustration (9):* The facts are the same as in Illustration (1) above. The $300,000 of additional first-year depreciation is fully allowable in 2002 for regular tax and alternative minimum tax purposes. *Additionally,* any other depreciation allowable for regular tax purposes in 2002 or later years is not subject to adjustment for alternative minimum tax purposes.

☐ **Effective:** Property placed in service after Sept. 10, 2001, in tax years ending after Sept. 10, 2001. (2002 Act § 101(b))

> *recommendation:* Taxpayers eligible for the additional first-year depreciation, but who didn't claim it on a tax return already filed, should consider filing an amended return.

¶ 102. First-year depreciation limit for passenger automobiles is raised by $4,600 for most new automobiles that are predominantly used in a business and acquired after Sept. 10, 2001, if acquired or contracted for before Sept. 11, 2004 and placed in service before Jan. 1, 2005

Code Sec. 168(k)(2)(E)(i), as amended by 2002 Act § 101(a)
Generally effective: Property placed in service after Sept. 10, 2001, in tax years ending after Sept. 10, 2001
Committee Reports, see ¶ 5001

Code Sec. 280F(a) imposes dollar limits on the amount of depreciation that can be claimed with respect to "passenger automobiles," as defined in Code Sec. 280F(d)(5), see FTC 2d/FIN ¶ L-10003; USTR ¶ 280F4; TaxDesk ¶ 267,603. Code Sec. 280F(a)(1)(A)(i) provides that the dollar limit for the first tax year in the automobile's recovery period is $2,560. Code Sec. 280F(d)(7) states that, in applying Code Sec. 280F(a), any dollar limits provided by Code Sec. 280F(a) must be adjusted annually to reflect changes in the automobile component of the Consumer Price Index (CPI), using Oct. '87 as the base period. For automobiles placed in service in 2001 and 2002, the $2,560 limit for the first tax year in the automobile's recovery period, as adjusted to reflect the automobile component of the CPI, is $3,060. (FTC 2d/FIN ¶ L-10004; USTR ¶ 280F4; TaxDesk ¶ 267,601)

New Law. The 2002 Act directs IRS to increase, by $4,600, the first-year limitation under Code Sec. 280F(a)(1)(A)(i) on depreciation deductions for a "passenger automobile," as defined in Code Sec. 280F(d)(5), if the automobile is "qualified property," as defined under the rules, discussed at ¶ 101, that determine eligibility for the 30% additional first-year depreciation made available by Code Sec. 168(k). (Code Sec. 168(k)(2)(E)(i) as amended by 2002 Act §101(a)) The $4,600 increase doesn't apply to taxpayers who "elect-out" (see ¶ 101) of 30% additional first-year depreciation. (Com Rept, see ¶ 5001)

⚫ *observation:* Property is "qualified property" if the property (1) satisfies the four requirements discussed under "Qualified property" at ¶ 101, and (2) is not made ineligible for status as "qualified property" by any of the rules discussed under "Property not eligible for additional first-year depreciation" at ¶ 101. As applied to passenger automobiles, the effect of these requirements and ineligibility rules is that *in most, but not all, in-*

FTC 2d References are to Federal Tax Coordinator 2d
FIN References are to RIA's Analysis of Federal Taxes: Income
USTR References are to United States Tax Reporter: Income, Estate & Gift, and Excise
PCA References are to the Pension Analysis on Checkpoint and CD-ROM, and in Pension Coordinator
PE References are to the Pension Explanations in Pension and Profit Sharing 2nd
EP References are to the Estate Planning Analysis on Checkpoint and CD-ROM, and in Estate Planning & Taxation Coordinator

stances, a passenger automobile will be eligible for the $4,600 first-year depreciation limit increase, if (1) the taxpayer doesn't make an "election-out" (with respect to the "class" of property that includes the automobile, see ¶ 101), (2) the automobile's original use begins with the taxpayer after Sept. 10, 2001, (3) the automobile is predominantly used by the taxpayer in his business, (4) the automobile is acquired by the taxpayer after Sept. 10, 2001, (5) the automobile is acquired or contracted for by the taxpayer before Sept. 11, 2004, and (6) the automobile is placed in service by the taxpayer before Jan. 1, 2005, see ¶ 101.

The $4,600 increase is not indexed for inflation. (Com Rept, see ¶ 5001)

    observation: Presumably, Congress intends that IRS will continue to make annual CPI adjustments of the $2,560 limit stated in Code Sec. 280F(a)(1)(A)(i) (see above), but will not make annual CPI adjustments in 2001, 2002 or any later year, of the $4,600 increase.

    observation: IRS announced (in Rev Proc 2001-19 and Rev Proc 2002-14, see FTC 2d/FIN ¶ L-10004; USTR ¶ 280F4; TaxDesk ¶ 267,601) the annual depreciation limits for passenger automobiles placed in service in calendar years 2001 and 2002, see above. Presumably, however, IRS will announce an adjustment of the already announced first-year limit, which, for both 2001 and 2002, is $3,060, to reflect the $4,600 increase.

    illustration: On Oct. 15, 2002, T, a calendar year taxpayer, places a new car into service in his business. Assume that the car is qualified property. Assuming that T doesn't make an "election-out" that would make the car ineligible for 30% additional first-year depreciation, T is allowed first-year depreciation for 2002 of no more than $7,660 ($3,060 plus $4,600).

    observation: Code Sec. 280F(a)(1)(C)(ii) states that the annual dollar limitations under Code Sec. 280F(a)(1)(A) "shall be tripled" for "purpose built passenger vehicles," i.e., electric automobiles, see FTC 2d/FIN ¶ L-10003.1; USTR ¶ 280F4; TaxDesk ¶ 267,602. Thus, it is possible, though not certain, that IRS will interpret the direction to increase by $4,600 the first-year limitation on depreciation for passenger automobiles that are qualified property as a direction to increase *by $13,800* ($4,600 × 3) the first-year limitation on depreciation for purpose built passenger vehicles.

    observation: Both Code Sec. 168(k) as amended by the 2002 Act (see ¶ 101) *and* Code Sec. 1400L as added by the 2002 Act (see ¶ 501) provide for 30% additional first-year depreciation. However, Code Sec. 1400L, which applies only to certain property in New York City to which Code Sec. 168(k), as amended, does not apply, does *not* provide any increase in the first-year limitation under Code Sec. 280F(a)(1)(A)(i) on depreciation deductions for passenger automobiles. Presumably, this is because few, if any, passenger automobiles will meet the requirement for additional first-year depreciation under Code Sec. 1400L that substantially all of the use of the property occur within the "New York Liberty Zone," see ¶ 501.

☐ **Effective:** Property placed in service after Sept. 10, 2001, in tax years ending after Sept. 10, 2001. (2002 Act § 101(b))

recommendation: Taxpayers who have automobiles that qualify for the higher first-year depreciation, but who didn't claim it on a tax return already filed, should consider filing an amended return.

¶ 103. NOL carryback period extended to five years for NOLs in 2001 and 2002

Code Sec. 172(b)(1)(H), as amended by 2002 Act § 102(a)
Code Sec. 172(j), as amended by 2002 Act § 102(b)
Generally effective: NOLs for tax years ending after Dec. 31, 2000
Committee Reports, see ¶ 5002

Under pre-2002 Act law, a net operating loss (NOL) generally could be carried back two years and forward 20 years. For certain eligible losses, such as casualty losses of an individual, small business losses attributable to a Presidentially declared disaster, and NOLs incurred by farmers attributable to a Presidentially declared disaster, the carryback period was three years. Unless the taxpayer made an election to forgo the carryback, the entire amount of the NOL for a tax year was carried first to the earliest tax year to which (under the carryover rules) it could be carried, then to the next earliest, and so on in chronological order until it was absorbed. (FTC 2d/FIN ¶ M-4300, ¶ M-4301, ¶ M-4305.1, ¶ M-4305.2; USTR ¶ 1724, ¶ 1724.30; TaxDesk ¶ 356,000, ¶ 356,001, ¶ 356,010, ¶ 356,011)

New Law. The 2002 Act extends the general two-year carryback period to five years for NOLs for tax years ending in 2001 and 2002. (Code Sec. 172(b)(1)(H) as amended by 2002 Act §102(a)) The five-year carryback period also applies to eligible losses that were previously eligible for the three-year carryback period. (Code Sec. 172(b)(1)(H))

observation: Thus, the 2002 Act does not affect losses that could previously not be carried back.

FTC 2d References are to Federal Tax Coordinator 2d
FIN References are to RIA's Analysis of Federal Taxes: Income
USTR References are to United States Tax Reporter: Income, Estate & Gift, and Excise
PCA References are to the Pension Analysis on Checkpoint and CD-ROM, and in Pension Coordinator
PE References are to the Pension Explanations in Pension and Profit Sharing 2nd
EP References are to the Estate Planning Analysis on Checkpoint and CD-ROM, and in Estate Planning & Taxation Coordinator

observation: A corporation can use either Form 1139, Corporate Application for Tentative Refund, or Form 1120X, Amended U.S. Corporation Income Tax Return to receive a refund due to an NOL carryback. An individual can use either Form 1045, Application for Tentative Refund, or Form 1040X, Amended U.S. Individual Income Tax Return, to get a refund from an NOL carryback. The refund will be faster if the taxpayer uses Form 1139 or Form 1045. However, a taxpayer cannot file Form 1139 or Form 1045 before filing the return for the NOL year. Form 1139 or Form 1045 must be filed no later than one year after the year the taxpayer sustains the NOL. If a taxpayer does not file Form 1139 or Form 1045, it must file Form 1120X or Form 1040X within three years of the due date, plus extensions, for filing the return for the year in which it sustains the NOL.

The 2002 Act also doesn't affect the conditions that IRS may impose on a taxpayer seeking approval for a change in accounting method, e.g., a NOL in a short year necessary to effect the change, which IRS may require to be carried forward. (Com Rept, see ¶ 5002)

illustration: G had taxable income of $50,000 for the tax year ending Dec. 31, '95, $90,000 for the tax year ending Dec. 31, '96, $60,000 for the tax year ending Dec. 31, '97, $40,000 for the tax year ending Dec. 31, '98, $50,000 for the tax year ending Dec. 31, '99, and $60,000 for the tax year ending Dec. 31, 2000. G has a $350,000 NOL for the tax year ending Dec. 31, 2001. The NOL is carried back as follows: $90,000 to the tax year ending Dec. 31, '96, $60,000 to the tax year ending Dec. 31, '97, $40,000 to the tax year ending Dec. 31, '98, $50,000 to the tax year ending Dec. 31, '99, and $60,000 to the tax year ending Dec. 31, 2000. The remaining NOL of $50,000 may be carried forward to future years.

A taxpayer may elect to have the carryback period for the loss year determined without regard to the temporary five-year carryback period rule. The election must be made in the manner determined by IRS, by the due date (including extensions of time) for filing the taxpayer's return for the tax year of the NOL. Once the election is made for a tax year, the election is irrevocable for that year. (Code Sec. 172(j) as amended by 2002 Act §102(b))

If a taxpayer elects to forgo the five-year carryback period, the losses are subject to the rules that otherwise would have applied without the five-year rule. (Com Rept, see ¶ 5002)

observation: Whether to waive the five-year carryback will depend on the taxpayer's past and expected future tax brackets. Taxpayers should be aware that a waiver of the carryback period also applies for alternative minimum tax purposes.

☐ **Effective:** NOLs for tax years ending after Dec. 31, 2000. (2002 Act § 102(d))

¶ 104. Alternative tax net operating loss (NOL) deduction increased from 90% to 100% for NOL carrybacks from and NOL carryforwards to tax years ending during 2001 and 2002

Code Sec. 56(d)(1)(A), as amended by 2002 Act § 102(c)(1)
Generally effective: Tax years ending before Jan. 1, 2003
Committee Reports, see ¶ 5002

Under pre-2002 Act law, alternative minimum taxable income (AMTI) could be reduced by the alternative tax net operating loss deduction (ATNOLD), but only up to 90% of AMTI calculated without regard to the ATNOLD. (FTC 2d/FIN ¶ A-8212; USTR ¶ 564.01; TaxDesk ¶ 696,001)

New Law. The 2002 Act allows NOL carrybacks attributable to tax years ending in 2001 and 2002 plus NOL carryforwards to those years to offset 100% of a taxpayer's AMTI. (Com Rept, see ¶ 5002) Thus, the ATNOLD limitation provides that the deduction may not exceed the sum of:

(1) the lesser of:

(A) the ATNOLD (other than the amount of the ATNOLD attributable to NOL carryovers to tax years ending during 2001 and 2002) (Code Sec. 56(d)(1)(A)(i)(I) as amended by 2002 Act §102(c)(1)) , or

(B) 90% of AMTI determined without regard to the ATNOLD (Code Sec. 56(d)(1)(A)(i)(II)) ,
plus

(2) the lesser of:

(A) the amount of the ATNOLD attributable to the sum of the NOL carrybacks from tax years ending in 2001 and 2002 plus the NOL carryforwards to tax years ending in 2001 and 2002 (Code Sec. 56(d)(1)(A)(ii)(I)) , or

(B) the AMTI determined without regard to the ATNOLD minus the amount determined under (1) above. (Code Sec. 56(d)(1)(A)(ii)(II))

In determining AMTI under the above rules, the NOL carryforwards and carrybacks are taken into account as provided under Code Sec. 172(b)(2). (Com Rept, see ¶ 5002)

FTC 2d References are to Federal Tax Coordinator 2d
FIN References are to RIA's Analysis of Federal Taxes: Income
USTR References are to United States Tax Reporter: Income, Estate & Gift, and Excise
PCA References are to the Pension Analysis on Checkpoint and CD-ROM, and in Pension
    Coordinator
PE References are to the Pension Explanations in Pension and Profit Sharing 2nd
EP References are to the Estate Planning Analysis on Checkpoint and CD-ROM, and in
    Estate Planning & Taxation Coordinator

⊘ *observation:* This means that NOL carryovers and carrybacks from the earliest years are used first.

⊘ *illustration:* G had AMTI of $300,000 for the tax year ending Dec. 31, 2000. G had an NOL carryover (as calculated for ATNOLD purposes) of $270,000 for the tax year ending Dec. 31, '99 and an NOL carryback of $20,000 from the tax year ending Dec. 31, 2001. The NOL carryover from '99 will only offset $270,000 of G's AMTI for 2000 and the $20,000 NOL carryback from the tax year ending Dec. 31, 2001 will increase the amount of the ATNOLD to $290,000. This will result in G having AMTI of $10,000 ($300,000 − 290,000) for the tax year ending Dec. 31, 2000.

☐ **Effective:** Tax years ending before Jan. 1, 2003. (2002 Act § 102(c)(2))

¶ 105. S corporation cancellation of indebtedness income doesn't increase shareholder basis

Code Sec. 108(d)(7)(A), as amended by 2002 Act § 402(a)
Generally effective: Discharges of debt after Oct. 11, 2001
Committee Reports, see ¶ 5022

An S corporation is a pass-through entity whose income and loss items are passed through by the S corporation to its shareholders. Thus, income items, including tax-exempt income items, are taken into account by the shareholders and increase the shareholders' bases in their shares of the corporation. Nevertheless, if an S corporation excludes cancellation of indebtedness income under the bankruptcy or insolvency exception, the S corporation, and not the shareholders, is required to reduce its tax attributes.

The Supreme Court held in *Gitlitz v. Com.* that cancellation of indebtedness income of an S corporation that was excluded from income under the Code Sec. 108 cancellation of indebtedness rules was an item of tax-exempt income that increased the shareholders' bases in their S corporation stock and that the Code Sec. 108 rules that reduced the tax attributes of the S corporation applied after the cancellation of indebtedness income was passed through to the shareholders. As a result, shareholders were able to increase their bases in the S corporation before the corporation reduced its tax attributes; thus, they could deduct losses passed through to them from the S corporation before the reduction in the losses took place. (FTC 2d/FIN ¶ D-1765, ¶ D-1863, ¶ J-7416; USTR ¶ 1084.03, ¶ 13,664; TaxDesk ¶ 188,028, ¶ 614,704, ¶ 617,001)

New Law. Under the 2002 Act, the cancellation of indebtedness income of an S corporation that is excluded from income under the Code Sec. 108 cancellation of indebtedness rules is not passed through to the shareholders. (Code Sec. 108(d)(7)(A) as amended by 2002 Act §402(a)) Thus, the shareholders do not increase their bases for the excluded cancellation of indebtedness income. (Com Rept, see ¶ 5022)

⊘ *illustration:* A, the sole shareholder of X, an S corporation, has a basis of $20 in his X stock. During Year 1, X has a $100 loss and $80 of cancellation of indebtedness income. A does not receive any step up in the basis of his X stock, with the result that he can only deduct $20 of X's loss.

☐ **Effective:** Discharges of debt after Oct. 11, 2001 in tax years ending after that date. (2002 Act § 402(b)(1)) However, the above rule does not apply to any discharge of debt before Mar. 1, 2002, under a reorganization plan filed with a bankruptcy court before Oct. 12, 2001. (2002 Act § 402(b)(2))

¶ 106. Use of nonaccrual experience method of accounting is available only for amounts received for performing certain qualified personal services, or for amounts received for services by taxpayers with average annual gross receipts of $5 million or less

Code Sec. 448(d)(5), as amended by 2002 Act § 403(a)
Generally effective: Tax years ending after Mar. 9, 2002
Committee Reports, see ¶ 5023

Certain taxpayers, including many corporations, are prohibited from using the cash receipts and disbursements method of accounting and instead are required to use the accrual method of accounting, see FTC 2d/FIN ¶ G-2054; USTR ¶ 4484; TaxDesk ¶ 440,806. The accrual method often requires the recognition of income before it is received, see FTC 2d/FIN ¶ G-2471; USTR ¶ 4514.011; TaxDesk ¶ 441,700. There are several exceptions to the requirement that corporations use the accrual method: two of those exceptions are for qualified personal service corporations, see FTC 2d/FIN ¶ G-2058; USTR ¶ 4484; TaxDesk ¶ 440,809, and for corporations that meet a $5 million or less gross receipts test (which is an average of gross receipts over a three-year period), see FTC 2d/FIN ¶ G-2069; USTR ¶ 4484; TaxDesk ¶ 440,807. In addition, under pre-2002 Act law, any taxpayer who uses the accrual method of accounting did not have to accrue income due from the performance of services that, on the basis of the taxpayer's experience, would not be collected. (FTC 2d/FIN ¶ G-2502; USTR ¶ 4484; TaxDesk ¶ 440,823) Taxpayers were required to use a six-year moving average to estimate their uncollectible accounts. (FTC 2d/FIN ¶ G-2503; USTR ¶ 4484)

FTC 2d References are to Federal Tax Coordinator 2d
FIN References are to RIA's Analysis of Federal Taxes: Income
USTR References are to United States Tax Reporter: Income, Estate & Gift, and Excise
PCA References are to the Pension Analysis on Checkpoint and CD-ROM, and in Pension
   Coordinator
PE References are to the Pension Explanations in Pension and Profit Sharing 2nd
EP References are to the Estate Planning Analysis on Checkpoint and CD-ROM, and in
   Estate Planning & Taxation Coordinator

New Law. The 2002 Act limits the use of the nonaccrual experience method of accounting to amounts to be received by a person for services, but only if:

• the services are in the fields of health, law, engineering, architecture, accounting, actuarial science, performing arts, or consulting (Code Sec. 448(d)(5)(A)(i) as amended by 2002 Act §403(a)) , or

• the person that was to receive the amounts meets the $5 million or less gross receipts test of Code Sec. 448(c) for all prior tax years. (Code Sec. 448(d)(5)(A)(ii))

> *observation:* Under pre-2002 Act law, any accrual-basis taxpayer could use the nonaccrual experience method to account for receivables for personal services performed by the taxpayer that were unlikely to be collected. Congress, perceiving this provision as unnecessarily favoring service providers over other accrual-basis taxpayers, has limited the availability of this method to service providers in a small number of fields—health, law, engineering, architecture, accounting, actuarial science, performing arts, or consulting. Congress has justified retaining the nonaccrual method for providers of qualified personal services who use the accrual method but must compete with providers of those services who are on the cash method, and thus are not required to report receivables in income until collected. Many providers of the qualified personal services listed above are cash-basis taxpayers because that is one of the few situations in which corporate taxpayers are permitted to use the cash basis. (See FTC 2d/FIN ¶ G-2058; USTR ¶ 4484; TaxDesk ¶ 440,809) Therefore, Congress presumably wanted to help those taxpayers who may be at a disadvantage using the accrual method while at the same time closing what it perceived to be a loophole that allowed taxpayers that provided services to defer recognizing income that they would otherwise be required to recognize under the accrual method of accounting.

The nonaccrual experience method of accounting continues to be available under 2002 Act law for the performance of *nonqualified* services if the average annual gross receipts (as defined in Code Sec. 448(c)) of the taxpayer (or any predecessor) does not exceed $5 million. (Com Rept, see ¶ 5023)

Amounts to be received for all other services (i.e., other than for the qualified personal services listed above or for amounts received by taxpayers who pass the average annual gross receipts test) are subject to the general rule regarding inclusion in income. (Com Rept, see ¶ 5023)

The rules of Code Sec. 448(c)(2) and Code Sec. 448(c)(3) apply for purposes of determining the average annual gross receipts test. Those rules:

(1) require the aggregation of related taxpayers,

(2) define gross receipts,

(3) determine the treatment of taxpayers not in existence for the entire three-year period,

(4) determine the treatment of short tax years, and

(5) determine the treatment of predecessors. (Com Rept, see ¶ 5023)

> **⚡️** *observation:* The Technical Explanation of the 2002 Act states that the rules of Code Sec. 448(c)(3) determining the treatment, for purposes of figuring gross receipts, of taxpayers in existence for less than the three-year period, apply to the determination of average annual gross receipts. However, the 2002 Act amendment to Code Sec. 448(d)(5) requires taxpayers to meet the gross receipts test for all prior tax years.

As under pre-2002 Act law, the availability of the nonaccrual experience method is conditioned on the taxpayer not charging interest or a penalty for failure to timely pay the amount charged. (Code Sec. 448(d)(5)(B))

IRS must issue regs that permit taxpayers to determine amounts to be received for services using computations or formulas which, based on experience, accurately reflect the amount of income (i.e., year-end receivables (Com Rept, see ¶ 5023)) that the taxpayers will not collect. A taxpayer may adopt, or request IRS consent to change to, a computation or formula that clearly reflects the taxpayer's experience. A request under the preceding sentence will be approved only if the computation or formula clearly reflects the taxpayer's experience. (Code Sec. 448(d)(5)(C))

The Technical Explanation says that Congress anticipates that IRS will consider providing safe harbors in the regs that may be relied upon by taxpayers. (Com Rept, see ¶ 5023)

> **⚡️** *observation:* Congress has indicated that it believes that the formula contained in Reg §1.448-2T (FTC 2d/FIN ¶ G-2503; USTR ¶ 4484) may not clearly reflect the amount of income that, based on experience, will not be collected for many qualified services providers, especially for taxpayers who have a significant time lapse between rendering the service and finally determining that the account will not be collected. Congress has indicated that providers of qualified services should not be subject to a formula that requires the payment of taxes on receivables that will not be collected.

> **⚡️** *observation:* Reg §1.448-2T, issued under Code Sec. 448(d)(5) (as in effect before the 2002 Act), requires taxpayers to use a six-year moving

---

FTC 2d References are to Federal Tax Coordinator 2d
FIN References are to RIA's Analysis of Federal Taxes: Income
USTR References are to United States Tax Reporter: Income, Estate & Gift, and Excise
PCA References are to the Pension Analysis on Checkpoint and CD-ROM, and in Pension
  Coordinator
PE References are to the Pension Explanations in Pension and Profit Sharing 2nd
EP References are to the Estate Planning Analysis on Checkpoint and CD-ROM, and in
  Estate Planning & Taxation Coordinator

average to estimate their experience of uncollectible amounts. It appears that Congress intends Code Sec. 448(d)(5)(C) to give taxpayers more lee-way in calculating uncollectible amounts than IRS has permitted to date.

If a taxpayer is required by the 2002 Act amendments to Code Sec. 448(d)(5), discussed above, to change its accounting method and must do so for the tax-payer's first tax year ending after Mar. 9, 2002 (2002 Act § 403(b)(2)), then:

• the change is treated as initiated by the taxpayer (2002 Act § 403(b)(2)(A));

• the change is treated as made with IRS's consent (2002 Act § 403(b)(2)(B)); and

• the taxpayer must take into account the net amount of any adjustments re-quired under Code Sec. 481 over a period of 4 years (or if less, the number of tax years that the taxpayer used the method permitted under Code Sec. 448(d)(5) as in effect before Mar. 9, 2002), beginning with its first tax year ending after Mar. 9, 2002 (2002 Act § 403(b)(2)(C)), under principles consistent with those in Rev Proc 99-49. (Com Rept, see ¶ 5023) (See FTC 2d/FIN ¶ G-2370.1; USTR ¶ 4814; TaxDesk ¶ 443,305 for the rules governing adjustments required by Rev Proc 99-49 under Code Sec. 481.)

observation: Rev Proc 99-49 has been superseded by Rev Proc 2002-9. The rules in Rev Proc 2002-9 concerning adjustments under Code Sec. 481 are the same as those in Rev Proc 99-49.

illustration: Magna Cleaning Corp., which is an office cleaning com-pany with more than $5 million in average annual gross receipts, uses the accrual method of accounting and, for more than five years, has been ac-counting for uncollectible amounts due for services using the nonaccrual experience method. Although Magna, a calendar year taxpayer, met the pre-2002 Act requirements to use the nonaccrual experience method, it does *not* meet the 2002 Act requirements to use that method because it has gross receipts of more than $5 million and the services it performs are not in health, law, engineering, architecture, accounting, actuarial science, performing arts, or consulting. Magna will be required to change its method of accounting for uncollectible amounts, making the necessary ad-justments over a four-year period beginning with its tax year ending after Mar. 9, 2002.

☐ **Effective:** Tax years ending after Mar. 9, 2002. (2002 Act § 403(b)(1))

¶ 107. Commercial revitalization deduction for renewal communities is given a higher priority under the rule that determines the order in which deductions and credits are applied against the up-to-$25,000 of passive losses (or credit equivalents) permitted for certain real estate activities

Code Sec. 469(i)(3)(E), as amended by 2002 Act § 412(a)
Generally effective: Buildings placed in service in renewal communities after
    Dec. 31, 2001 and before Jan. 1, 2010
Committee Reports, see ¶ 5054

Generally, under Code Sec. 469, a taxpayer's losses (or equivalent amount of credits) from passive activities are limited to the taxpayer's income from these activities, see FTC 2d/FIN ¶ M-4601; USTR ¶ 4694; TaxDesk ¶ 411,001. However, under an exception applicable to certain taxpayers for certain real estate activities, eligible taxpayers are allowed up to $25,000 of passive losses (or an equivalent amount of credits) per year ($12,500 for married taxpayers filing separately and living apart, $0 if they aren't living apart), see FTC 2d/FIN ¶ M-5131; USTR ¶ 4694.60; TaxDesk ¶ 413,601.

Under pre-2002 Act law, under the ordering rules which determine the order in which the up-to-$25,000 exception amount is applied against passive losses and credits, the exception amount was applied against all other passive losses and credits (except for the low-income housing credit) before it was applied against passive losses attributable to the "commercial revitalization deduction" available under Code Sec. 1400I, see FTC 2d/FIN ¶ L-12701; USTR ¶ 14,00I4; TaxDesk ¶ 269,301, for the costs of acquiring or constructing certain real estate in renewal communities. (FTC 2d/FIN ¶ M-5144; USTR ¶ 4694.60; TaxDesk ¶ 413,614)

New Law. The 2002 Act moves the position of passive losses attributable to the commercial revitalization deduction under the ordering rule (discussed above) from the position behind all other passive losses and credits (except for the low-income housing credit) to a position in which *all* tax credits are behind the commercial revitalization deduction. (Code Sec. 469(i)(3)(E) as amended by 2002 Act §412(a))

☐ **Effective:** Buildings placed in service in renewal communities after Dec. 31, 2001 and before Jan. 1, 2010. (2002 Act § 412(e))

FTC 2d References are to Federal Tax Coordinator 2d
FIN References are to RIA's Analysis of Federal Taxes: Income
USTR References are to United States Tax Reporter: Income, Estate & Gift, and Excise
PCA References are to the Pension Analysis on Checkpoint and CD-ROM, and in Pension
    Coordinator
PE References are to the Pension Explanations in Pension and Profit Sharing 2nd
EP References are to the Estate Planning Analysis on Checkpoint and CD-ROM, and in
    Estate Planning & Taxation Coordinator

observation: 2002 Act §412(e) states that the above amendment to Code Sec. 469(i)(3)(E), concerning the qualified revitalization deduction, takes effect as if included in the provisions of the 2000 Community Renewal Act to which it relates. The 2000 Community Renewal Act doesn't provide an effective date for 2000 Community Renewal Act §101(b)(2), which is the 2000 Community Renewal Act provision to which the above amendment relates. The effective date stated above is instead derived from the fact that, to qualify as buildings eligible for a qualified revitalization deduction, buildings must be placed in service in a renewal community, and the designations of areas as renewal communities didn't become effective until Jan. 1, 2001, and will end on Dec. 31, 2009, see FTC 2d/FIN ¶ L-12702; USTR ¶ 14,00I4; TaxDesk ¶ 269,302.

¶ 108. Treatment of the employer-provided child care assistance credit recapture "tax" as not being a tax is confirmed and clarified

Code Sec. 45F(d)(4)(B), as amended by 2002 Act § 411(d)(1)
Generally effective: Tax years beginning after Dec. 31, 2001
Committee Reports, see ¶ 5034

Code Sec. 45F provides a tax credit to employers for certain of their costs of providing child care assistance to their employees (the Credit), see FTC 2d/FIN ¶ L-17871; USTR ¶ 45F4; TaxDesk ¶ 382,101.

Under pre-2002 Act law, Code Sec. 45F(d)(4)(B) provided that any increase in tax because of recapture of the Credit "shall not be treated as a tax imposed by this chapter for the purposes of determining the amount of any credit under subpart A, B, or D of this part." (FTC 2d/FIN ¶ L-17878; USTR ¶ 45F4.01; TaxDesk ¶ 382,108)

New Law. The 2002 Act substitutes the phrase "this chapter or for purposes of section 55" for the phrase "subpart A, B or D of this part" in Code Sec. 45F(d)(4)(B) (see above). (Code Sec. 45F(d)(4)(B) as amended by 2002 Act §411(d)(1))

The change clarifies that recapture tax with respect to the Credit is treated like recapture taxes with respect to other credits under chapter 1 of the Code (income tax provisions other than employment taxes and foreign withholding). Thus, it is not treated as a tax for purposes of determining the amounts of other credits or determining the amount of alternative minimum tax. (Com Rept, see ¶ 5034)

observation: Because the recapture tax isn't treated as a tax for purposes of determining the amounts of other credits or determining the amount of the alternative minimum tax, other credits can't be used to reduce the recapture tax. Also, the recapture tax doesn't decrease the taxpayer's alternative minimum tax (AMT), as it would were it included in the calculation of regular tax liability.

 *observation:* Based on its pre-2002 Act language (see above), Code Sec. 45F(d)(4)(B), even before the 2002 Act, presumably had the effect of preventing other credits from being used to reduce any recapture tax arising from the Credit. However, the language substituted by the 2002 Act is the clearer language used elsewhere in the Code regarding the status, as a non-tax, of *other* recapture taxes (see, for example, Code Sec. 45D(g)(4)(B), concerning the new markets tax credit). Thus, this substitution confirms the status of the Credit's recapture tax as a non-tax for purposes of other credits, and clarifies this non-tax status for alternative minimum tax purposes.

☐ **Effective:** Tax years beginning after Dec. 31, 2001. (2002 Act § 411(x))

¶ 109. Mark-to-market election for assets held on Jan. 1, 2001 doesn't trigger deduction of suspended passive losses

Code Sec. None, 2002 Act § 414(a)(2)
Generally effective: Tax years ending after May 6, '97
Committee Reports, see ¶ 5059

Taxpayers other than corporations may elect to mark to market any capital asset or property used in a trade or business (as defined in Code Sec. 1231(b)), and held by the taxpayer on Jan. 1, 2001. The asset is treated as having been sold on Jan. 1, 2001, for an amount equal to its fair market value on that date, and reacquired on that date for an amount equal to its fair market value. Any gain resulting from the above election is treated as received or accrued on the date the asset is treated and is recognized notwithstanding any provision of the Code. (FTC 2d/FIN ¶ I-5110.5; USTR ¶ 14.08; TaxDesk ¶ 223,314)

For taxpayers who are subject to the passive activity rules, a special rule allows the current deduction of suspended passive losses when the taxpayer disposes of his entire interest in a passive activity in a fully taxable transaction. (FTC 2d/FIN ¶ M-5701; USTR ¶ 4694.32; TaxDesk ¶ 417,501)

New Law. The 2002 Act provides that the rule allowing the deduction of suspended losses on the disposition of the taxpayer's entire interest in a passive activ-

FTC 2d References are to Federal Tax Coordinator 2d
FIN References are to RIA's Analysis of Federal Taxes: Income
USTR References are to United States Tax Reporter: Income, Estate & Gift, and Excise
PCA References are to the Pension Analysis on Checkpoint and CD-ROM, and in Pension Coordinator
PE References are to the Pension Explanations in Pension and Profit Sharing 2nd
EP References are to the Estate Planning Analysis on Checkpoint and CD-ROM, and in Estate Planning & Taxation Coordinator

ity won't apply by reason of an election to mark to market an asset held on Jan. 1, 2001. ('97 Taxpayer Relief Act §311(e)(5) as amended by 2002 Act §414(a)(2))

Any gain taken into account by reason of a mark-to-market election with respect to any interest in a passive activity is taken into account in determining the passive activity loss for the tax year. (Com Rept, see ¶ 5059)

The deduction of suspended losses may apply to a subsequent disposition of the interest in the activity by the taxpayer. (Com Rept, see ¶ 5059)

> *illustration:* On Jan. 1, 2001, Taxpayer X owned an interest in a partnership that is a passive activity. The interest had a fair market value of $100,000 and X's basis in the interest was $30,000. X made the mark-to-market election with respect to the interest.
>
> For 2001, X must include in income $70,000 of gain ($100,000 – $30,000) as a result of the mark-to market election. This gain is taken into account in determining X's passive activity loss for 2001. However, X can't deduct any suspended passive losses from the partnership as a result of the election.
>
> If X disposes of the interest in a later tax year in a fully taxable transaction, he will be able to deduct his suspended losses in that year.

For the effect of the mark-to-market election on sales of principal residences, see ¶ 418.

☐ **Effective:** Tax years ending after May 6, '97. (2002 Act § 414(b))

¶ 200. Extenders

¶ 201. Welfare-to-work credit is extended for two years through Dec. 31, 2003 and retroactively restored to Jan. 1, 2002

Code Sec. 51A(f), as amended by 2002 Act § 605(a)
Generally effective: Individuals who begin work for an employer after Dec. 31, 2001
Committee Reports, see ¶ 5073

A welfare-to-work credit is available on an elective basis to an employer for eligible wages paid or incurred by the employer to qualified long-term family assistance recipients during the first two years of employment. Under pre-2002 Act law, the welfare-to-work credit was not available for wages paid or incurred by an employer to individuals who began work for the employer after Dec. 31, 2001. (FTC 2d/FIN ¶ L-17835; USTR ¶ 51A4; TaxDesk ¶ 381,300)

New Law. The 2002 Act provides that the welfare-to-work credit does not apply to individuals who begin work for the employer after Dec. 31, 2003. (Code Sec. 51A(f) as amended by 2002 Act §605(a)) Thus, the 2002 Act extends the welfare-to-work credit for two years (through Dec. 31, 2003). (Com Rept, see ¶ 5073)

> *observation:* The last day a taxpayer can employ a qualifying individual and be eligible to get a credit for wages paid to that individual is Dec. 31, 2003.

> *illustration:* An employer (E) had consistently elected to take the welfare-to-work credit for 2000 and 2001. E hired qualified long-term family assistance recipients in Jan. and Feb. of 2002. E will now be able to take the credit for these employees if E elects to take the credit on its 2002 return and if E employs them for at least 180 days or they complete 400 hours of service for E.

☐ **Effective:** Individuals who begin work for the employer after Dec. 31, 2001. (2002 Act § 605(b))

FTC 2d References are to Federal Tax Coordinator 2d
FIN References are to RIA's Analysis of Federal Taxes: Income
USTR References are to United States Tax Reporter: Income, Estate & Gift, and Excise
PCA References are to the Pension Analysis on Checkpoint and CD-ROM, and in Pension Coordinator
PE References are to the Pension Explanations in Pension and Profit Sharing 2nd
EP References are to the Estate Planning Analysis on Checkpoint and CD-ROM, and in Estate Planning & Taxation Coordinator

¶ 202. Work opportunity credit is extended for two years through Dec. 31, 2003 and retroactively restored to Jan. 1, 2002

Code Sec. 51(c)(4)(B), as amended by 2002 Act § 604(a)
Generally effective: Individuals who begin work for an employer after Dec. 31, 2001
Committee Reports, see ¶ 5072

A work opportunity tax credit (WOTC) is available on an elective basis to an employer for a percentage of first-year wages (subject to a per-employee dollar limitation) paid or incurred by the employer to individuals who belong to one of eight "targeted groups" (e.g., qualified veterans, qualified ex-felons and high-risk youths). Under pre-2002 Act law, the WOTC was not available for wages paid or incurred by an employer to individuals who began work for the employer after Dec. 31, 2001. (FTC 2d/FIN ¶ L-17775; USTR ¶ 514; TaxDesk ¶ 380,700)

New Law. The 2002 Act extends the WOTC by providing that the term "wages" (for purposes of determining the amount of the WOTC) doesn't include any amount paid or incurred to an individual who begins work for the employer after Dec. 31, 2003. (Code Sec. 51(c)(4)(B) as amended by 2002 Act §604(a)) Thus, the 2002 Act extends the WOTC for two years (through Dec. 31, 2003). (Com Rept, see ¶ 5072)

> *observation:* The last day a taxpayer can employ a qualifying individual and be eligible to get a credit for wages paid to that individual is Dec. 31, 2003.

> *illustration:* An employer (E) had consistently elected to take the WOTC for 2000 and 2001. E hired qualified veterans, and high-risk youths in Jan. and Feb. of 2002. E will now be able to take the WOTC for these employees if they complete 120 hours of service for E and if E elects to take the WOTC on its 2002 return.

☐ **Effective:** Individuals who begin work for the employer after Dec. 31, 2001. (2002 Act § 604(b))

¶ 203. Exceptions under Subpart F for active banking, financing and insurance income expiring in 2001 extended through 2006

Code Sec. 953(e)(10), as amended by 2002 Act § 614(a)(1)
Code Sec. 954(h)(9), as amended by 2002 Act § 614(a)(2)
Generally effective: Tax years beginning after Dec. 31, 2001
Committee Reports, see ¶ 5082

Under Subpart F, U.S. persons who are 10% shareholders of a controlled foreign corporation (CFC) are required to include in income their pro rata share of the CFC's insurance income and adjusted net foreign base company income (FBCI) whether or not this income is distributed to the shareholders. Insurance income generally includes income of a CFC attributable to the issuing and reinsuring of any insurance or annuity contract in connection with risks located in a country other than the CFC's country of organization. FBCI includes foreign personal holding income (FPHCI) and foreign base company services income (FBCSI). FPHCI includes dividends, interest, income equivalent to interest, rents, royalties, and annuities. FBCSI income generally includes income from technical, managerial, engineering, architectural, scientific, skilled, industrial, commercial or similar services performed outside the country of incorporation of the CFC, see FTC 2d/FIN ¶s O-2401, O-2404, O-2424, O-2432, O-2494; USTR ¶s 9534.01, 9544.02.

Under pre-2002 Act law, certain income from the active conduct of a banking, financing or similar business, or from the conduct of an insurance business (collectively referred to as "active financing income") was temporarily excluded from the definition of Subpart F income. The exclusion applied only for tax years of a CFC beginning after Dec. 31, '98 and before Jan. 1, 2002, and for tax years of U.S. shareholders with or within which any such tax year of the CFC ended. (FTC 2d/FIN ¶ O-2423.1, ¶ O-2480.3, ¶ O-2480.16, ¶ O-2480.18, ¶ O-2494; USTR ¶ 9534.01, ¶ 9544.02)

New Law. The 2002 Act extends the temporary exclusions for active financing income for five years. Thus, the above rules apply to tax years of a foreign corporation beginning before Jan. 1, 2007. (Code Sec. 953(e)(10) as amended by 2002 Act §614(a)(1)) and (Code Sec. 954(h)(9) as amended by 2002 Act §614(a)(2))

For the determination of life insurance and annuity contract reserves of a qualifying insurance company or branch, see ¶ 204.

☐ **Effective:** Tax years beginning after Dec. 31, 2001. (2002 Act § 614(c))

🔵 *observation:* Making the effective date retroactive to tax years beginning after Dec. 31, 2001 eliminates any problem resulting from the fact that the new extension was enacted after Dec. 31, 2001, the date the old extension expired.

FTC 2d References are to Federal Tax Coordinator 2d
FIN References are to RIA's Analysis of Federal Taxes: Income
USTR References are to United States Tax Reporter: Income, Estate & Gift, and Excise
PCA References are to the Pension Analysis on Checkpoint and CD-ROM, and in Pension Coordinator
PE References are to the Pension Explanations in Pension and Profit Sharing 2nd
EP References are to the Estate Planning Analysis on Checkpoint and CD-ROM, and in Estate Planning & Taxation Coordinator

¶ 204. Special rule for determining life insurance and annuity contract reserves of a qualifying insurance company or branch modified and extended through 2006

Code Sec. 953(e)(10), as amended by 2002 Act § 614(a)(1)
Code Sec. 954(i)(4)(B), as amended by 2002 Act § 614(b)
Generally effective: Tax years beginning after Dec. 31, 2001
Committee Reports, see ¶ 5082

Under pre-2002 Act law, for Subpart F purposes, the reserves of a qualifying insurance company or qualifying insurance company branch for any life insurance or annuity contract ("contract reserves") were determined by taking the greater of: (i) the net surrender value of the contract or (ii) the amount of the tax reserve determined under Subchapter L of the Code by applying the tax reserve method with certain modifications. The determination of these reserves however applied only for tax years of a foreign corporation beginning after Dec. 31, '98 and before Jan. 1, 2002 and for tax years of U.S. shareholders with or within any such tax year of such foreign corporation ended. (FTC 2d/FIN ¶ O-2480.19; USTR ¶ 9534.01)

New Law. The 2002 Act extends the use of the special rule for determining life insurance and annuity contract reserves described above by five years. Thus, the above rules apply to tax years of a foreign corporation beginning before Jan. 1, 2007. (Code Sec. 953(e)(10) as amended by 2002 Act §614(a)(1)) The 2002 Act also allows a taxpayer to determine the value of those reserves using the foreign statement reserve (less any catastrophe, deficiency, equalization, or similar reserves), but only if: (i) the taxpayer submits a ruling request to IRS or IRS provides published guidance, and (ii) IRS determines that the factors considered in determining the foreign statement reserve provide a proper means of measuring income. (Code Sec. 954(i)(4)(B) as amended by 2002 Act §614(b))

In seeking a ruling, a taxpayer is required to provide IRS with necessary and appropriate information as to the method, interest rate, the mortality and morbidity assumptions, and any other factors taken into account in determining foreign statement reserve to allow a comparison of the reserve calculated by applying the tax reserve method of Subchapter L of the Code. The ruling request is subject to IRS user fees. IRS may also publish guidance indicating its approval. Pre-2002 Act law would continue to apply to reserve determinations for any life insurance or annuity contracts for which IRS does not approve the use of the foreign statement reserve. (Com Rept, see ¶ 5082)

For the five year extension of the exception under Subpart F of active banking, financing, and insurance income, see ¶ 203.

☐ **Effective:** Tax years beginning after Dec. 31, 2001. (2002 Act § 614(c))

> *observation:* Making the effective date retroactive to tax years beginning after Dec. 31, 2001 eliminates any problem resulting from the fact

that the new extension was enacted after Dec. 31, 2001, the date the old extension expired.

¶ 205. Credit for electricity produced from renewable resources is extended for two years to include qualified facilities placed in service before Jan. 1, 2004

Code Sec. 45(c)(3), as amended by 2002 Act § 603(a)
Generally effective: Facilities placed in service after Dec. 31, 2001
Committee Reports, see ¶ 5071

An income tax credit is allowed for the production of electricity from either qualified wind energy, qualified "closed-loop" biomass, or qualified poultry waste facilities.

The credit applies to electricity produced by a wind energy facility placed in service after Dec. 31, '93, and before Jan. 1, 2002; to electricity produced by a closed-loop biomass facility placed in service after Dec. 31, '92 and before Jan. 1, 2002; and to electricity produced by a poultry waste facility placed in service after Dec. 31, '99 and before Jan. 1, 2002. The credit is allowable for production during the 10-year period after a facility is originally placed in service. The credit is part of the general business credit. (FTC 2d/FIN ¶ L-17752, ¶ L-17753; USTR ¶ 454; TaxDesk ¶ 384,054).

New Law. The placed-in-service date for qualified wind, closed-loop biomass, and poultry waste facilities is extended to include those facilities placed in service before Jan. 1, 2004. (Code Sec. 45(c)(3) as amended by 2002 Act §603(a)) Thus, the 2002 Act extends the placed-in-service date for qualified facilities by two years. (Com Rept, see ¶ 5071)

> *illustration:* Taxpayer places a qualified poultry waste facility in service on Jan. 1, 2002. Taxpayer may claim a credit for the production of electricity from the facility.

☐ **Effective:** Facilities placed in service after Dec. 31, 2001.
(2002 Act § 603(b))

FTC 2d References are to Federal Tax Coordinator 2d
FIN References are to RIA's Analysis of Federal Taxes: Income
USTR References are to United States Tax Reporter: Income, Estate & Gift, and Excise
PCA References are to the Pension Analysis on Checkpoint and CD-ROM, and in Pension
   Coordinator
PE References are to the Pension Explanations in Pension and Profit Sharing 2nd
EP References are to the Estate Planning Analysis on Checkpoint and CD-ROM, and in
   Estate Planning & Taxation Coordinator

¶ 206. Suspension of taxable income limitation on percentage depletion from marginal oil and gas wells is extended for two years to include tax years beginning before 2004

Code Sec. 613A(c)(6)(H), as amended by 2002 Act § 607(a)
Generally effective: Tax years beginning after Dec. 31, 2001
Committee Reports, see ¶ 5075

Taxpayers are permitted to recover their oil and gas well investments through depletion deductions, which may in certain cases be determined using the percentage depletion method. One limitation that applies in calculating percentage depletion deductions is a restriction that, for oil and gas properties, the amount deducted may not exceed 100% of the taxable income from that property in any year. See FTC 2d ¶ N-2701; USTR ¶ 6134.009; TaxDesk ¶ 271,001.

Special percentage depletion rules apply to oil and gas produced from "marginal" properties. Marginal production is defined as domestic crude oil and natural gas production from stripper well property or from heavy oil property. One special rule under pre-2002 Act law provides that the 100%-of-taxable-income limitation doesn't apply to domestic oil and gas production from marginal properties during tax years beginning after Dec. 31, '97, and *before Jan. 1, 2002.* (FTC 2d ¶ N-2729; USTR ¶ 613A4, ¶ 6134.009; TaxDesk ¶ 271,001)

New Law. The 2002 Act extends the rule suspending the 100%-of-taxable-income limitation with respect to oil and gas production from marginal properties to include any tax year beginning *before Jan. 1, 2004.* (Code Sec. 613A(c)(6)(H) as amended by 2002 Act §607(a))

> *observation:* Congress has indicated that it believes that extension of the waiver of the 100% of income limit will contribute to investment in domestic oil and gas production.

☐ **Effective:** Tax years beginning after Dec. 31, 2001. (2002 Act § 607(b)) Thus, the suspension of the 100%-of-taxable-income limitation with respect to oil and gas production from marginal properties is extended to include tax years beginning after Dec. 31, 2001 and before Jan. 1, 2004. (Com Rept, see ¶ 5075)

¶ 207. Exemption for qualified clean-fuel vehicle property from the depreciation and expense deduction limits is extended for two years to property placed in service before Jan. 1, 2007

Code Sec. 280F(a)(1)(C)(iii), as amended by 2002 Act § 602(b)(1)
Generally effective: Property placed in service after Dec. 31, 2001
Committee Reports, see ¶ 5070

Under pre-2002 Act law, the dollar limits on depreciation and expense deductions (see FTC 2d/FIN ¶ L-10004; USTR ¶ 280F4; TaxDesk ¶ 267,601) don't apply to "qualified clean-fuel vehicle property," if the property is placed in service *before Jan. 1, 2005.* (FTC 2d/FIN ¶ L-10003.1; USTR ¶ 280F4; TaxDesk ¶ 267,604)

"Qualified clean-fuel vehicle property" is property which has the following characteristics:

. . . the property is acquired for use by the taxpayer, and not for resale;

. . . the original use of the property begins with the taxpayer;

. . . the motor vehicle of which the property is a part meets any applicable federal or state emission standards for each fuel by which the vehicle is designed to be propelled;

. . . the property meets applicable federal and state emissions-related certification, testing, and warranty requirements;

. . . the property ("retrofit parts and components") is an engine (or modification of an engine) which may use a "clean-burning fuel" *or* is used in the storage or delivery to the engine of "clean-burning fuel" (defined below) or in the exhaust of gases from combustion of "clean-burning fuel." See FTC 2d/FIN ¶ L-10003.1; USTR ¶ 280F4; TaxDesk ¶ 267,604.

"Clean-burning fuel" is either: (1) natural gas, (2) liquefied natural gas, (3) liquefied petroleum gas, (4) hydrogen, (5) electricity or (6) any other fuel at least 85% of which is one or more of the following: methanol, ethanol, any other alcohol, or ether. See FTC 2d/FIN ¶ L-10003.1; USTR ¶ 280F4; TaxDesk ¶ 267,604.

New Law. The 2002 Act provides that the exemption for qualified clean-fuel vehicle property from the depreciation and expense deduction limits applies to property placed in service after Aug. 5, '97 and *before Jan. 1, 2007.* (Code Sec. 280F(a)(1)(C)(iii) as amended by 2002 Act §602(b)(1)) This change to Code Sec. 280F conforms to the 2002 Act changes that (1) extend the availability of the deduction for qualified clean-fuel vehicle property and defer the phaseout of the deduction for two years, and (2) provide for the unavailability of the deduction for purchases after Dec. 31, 2006 (see ¶ 209). (Com Rept, see ¶ 5070)

☐ **Effective:** Property placed in service after Dec. 31, 2001. (2002 Act § 602(c))

FTC 2d References are to Federal Tax Coordinator 2d
FIN References are to RIA's Analysis of Federal Taxes: Income
USTR References are to United States Tax Reporter: Income, Estate & Gift, and Excise
PCA References are to the Pension Analysis on Checkpoint and CD-ROM, and in Pension Coordinator
PE References are to the Pension Explanations in Pension and Profit Sharing 2nd
EP References are to the Estate Planning Analysis on Checkpoint and CD-ROM, and in Estate Planning & Taxation Coordinator

¶ 208. Tripling of automobile depreciation and expense deduction limits for electric vehicles is extended for two years to vehicles placed in service before Jan. 1, 2007

Code Sec. 280F(a)(1)(C)(iii), as amended by 2002 Act § 602(b)(1)
Generally effective: Property placed in service after Dec. 31, 2001
Committee Reports, see ¶ 5070

Pre-2002 Act law provides for the tripling of the annual limitations for passenger automobile depreciation for a "purpose built passenger vehicle," i.e., a passenger vehicle produced by an original equipment manufacturer and designed so that the vehicle may be propelled primarily *by electricity*, if the vehicle is placed in service *before Jan. 1, 2005.* (FTC 2d/FIN ¶ L-10004.1; USTR ¶ 280F4; TaxDesk ¶ 267,602)

These rules apply to:

(1) the annual depreciation limitations for the years during the passenger automobile's normal recovery period (see FTC 2d/FIN ¶ L-10004; USTR ¶ 280F4; TaxDesk ¶ 267,601),

(2) the limitation for passenger automobiles on the Code Sec. 179 expense election (see FTC 2d/FIN ¶ L-10004; USTR ¶ 1794; TaxDesk ¶ 268,400), and

(3) the annual depreciation limitation for the years after a passenger automobile's normal recovery period (see FTC 2d/FIN ¶ L-10008; USTR ¶ 280F4; TaxDesk ¶ 267,601).

> 🅁🄸🄰 *observation:* Because of rounding in calculating the tripled limitations for purpose built passenger vehicles and in calculating the limitations for other passenger automobiles, the limitations for purpose built passenger vehicles aren't always *exactly* triple the limitations for other passenger vehicles.

> 🅁🄸🄰 *observation:* In addition to the tripling of the dollar limits on depreciation deductions, there are two tax benefits specifically available for electric vehicles. Specifically, there is a credit of 10% of an electric vehicle's cost up to maximum of $4,000 (see ¶ 211 and FTC 2d/FIN ¶ L-18010; USTR ¶ 304; TaxDesk ¶ 397,001), and there is a 50% higher cost threshold for applying the luxury excise tax (see FTC 2d/FIN ¶ W-2971.1; USTR ¶ 40,014).

New Law. The 2002 Act provides that the tripling of the limitations described in (1) through (3) above applies to property (i.e., an electric vehicle) placed in service *before Jan. 1, 2007.* (Code Sec. 280F(a)(1)(C)(iii) as amended by 2002 Act §602(b)(1)) This change to Code Sec. 280F conforms to the 2002 Act changes that (1) extend the availability of the electric vehicle credit and defer the phaseout rules that apply for purposes of the credit for two years, and (2) provide for the unavailability of the credit for purchases after Dec. 31, 2006 (see ¶ 211). (Com Rept, see ¶ 5070)

☐ **Effective:** Property placed in service after Dec. 31, 2001 (2002 Act § 602(c))

¶ 209. Phaseout of maximum deduction for cost of qualified clean-fuel vehicles is deferred for two years so that a full deduction is available for cost of qualified vehicles placed in service in 2002 and 2003; deduction is extended to apply to property placed in service before Jan. 1, 2007

Code Sec. 179A(b)(1)(B), as amended by 2002 Act § 606(a)(1)(A)
Code Sec. 179A(b)(1)(B)(i), as amended by 2002 Act § 606(a)(1)(B)
Code Sec. 179A(b)(1)(B)(ii), as amended by 2002 Act § 606(a)(1)(B)
Code Sec. 179A(b)(1)(B)(iii), as amended by 2002 Act § 606(a)(1)(B)
Code Sec. 179A(f), as amended by 2002 Act § 606(a)(2)
Generally effective: Property placed in service after Dec. 31, 2001
Committee Reports, see ¶ 5074

Certain costs of qualified clean-fuel vehicle property may be expensed and deducted for the tax year in which the property is placed in service. See FTC 2d/FIN ¶ K-7012; USTR ¶ 179A4; TaxDesk ¶ 307,001.

> *observation:* The deduction is not a miscellaneous itemized deduction and is not subject to the 2% floor for those deductions.

Qualified clean-fuel vehicle property includes motor vehicles that use certain clean-burning fuels (natural gas, liquefied natural gas, liquefied petroleum gas, hydrogen, electricity and any other fuel at least 85% of which is methanol, ethanol, any other alcohol or ether). However, qualified clean-fuel vehicle property does not include any qualified electric vehicle. See ¶ 211 and FTC 2d/FIN ¶ K-7012; USTR ¶ 179A4; TaxDesk ¶ 307,004.

> *observation:* A motor vehicle need not be used in a trade or business or for the production of income in order to be a qualified clean-fuel vehicle. Thus, a personal use motor vehicle may qualify for the deduction.

FTC 2d References are to Federal Tax Coordinator 2d
FIN References are to RIA's Analysis of Federal Taxes: Income
USTR References are to United States Tax Reporter: Income, Estate & Gift, and Excise
PCA References are to the Pension Analysis on Checkpoint and CD-ROM, and in Pension Coordinator
PE References are to the Pension Explanations in Pension and Profit Sharing 2nd
EP References are to the Estate Planning Analysis on Checkpoint and CD-ROM, and in Estate Planning & Taxation Coordinator

The maximum amount of the deduction is $50,000 for a truck or van with a gross vehicle weight over 26,000 pounds or a bus with seating capacity of at least 20 adults (not including the driver); $5,000 for a truck or van with a gross vehicle weight over 10,000 but not over 26,000 pounds; and $2,000 for any other motor vehicle. See FTC 2d/FIN ¶ K-7004; USTR ¶ 179A4; TaxDesk ¶ 307,006.

> *observation:* The deduction for the costs of qualified clean-fuel vehicle property is available on a per vehicle basis. That is, each qualified vehicle purchased in 2001 could generate up to the maximum deduction amount available for that type of vehicle. There is no limitation on the number of qualified vehicles that may be purchased in any given year.

> *observation:* The deduction for qualified clean-fuel vehicles is not available for the portion of the cost of any vehicle taken into account under the Code Sec. 179 expense election. See FTC 2d/FIN ¶ K-7003; USTR ¶ 179A4; TaxDesk ¶ 307,001. Thus, if a taxpayer buys a vehicle eligible for deduction under Code Sec. 179A and Code Sec. 179 and pays more than the maximum deduction amount under Code Sec. 179A for that vehicle, that taxpayer cannot deduct the same cost twice but can, for example, take the maximum deduction under Code Sec. 179A for that type of vehicle and deduct under Code Sec. 179 the remainder of the cost up to the amount allowed under the Code Sec. 179 expense election.

> *illustration:* In 2001, T, a small business owner, bought a truck weighing more than 26,000 pounds and costing $60,000 for use in T's business. Assuming the truck qualifies for the clean-fuel vehicle property deduction and is eligible for expensing under Code Sec. 179, and that T is not expensing the cost of any other property under Code Sec. 179, which expense would reduce the amount of any available deduction under Code Sec. 179, T can deduct $50,000 of the cost of the truck under Code Sec. 179A and deduct the remaining $10,000 cost under Code Sec. 179.

Under pre-2002 Act law, the deduction for clean-fuel vehicle property phases out in the years 2002 through 2004, and is unavailable for purchases after Dec. 31, 2004. Specifically, under the phaseout rules, the maximum deduction is reduced by:

. . . 25% for property placed in service in *2002*;

. . . 50% for property placed in service in *2003*; and

. . . 75% for property placed in service in *2004*. (FTC 2d/FIN ¶ K-7005; USTR ¶ 179A4; TaxDesk ¶ 307,001)

New Law. The 2002 Act defers the phaseout of the deduction for clean-fuel vehicle property by two years so that taxpayers can claim the full amount of the deduction for qualified vehicles placed in service in 2002 and 2003. (Com Rept, see ¶ 5074)

♥ *observation:* Under the 2002 Act, a maximum deduction is available for *any* qualified vehicle placed in service in 2002 or 2003, if the qualified vehicle costs at least

... $50,000 for a truck or van with a gross vehicle weight over 26,000 pounds or a bus with a seating capacity of at least 20 adults;

... $5,000 for a truck or van with a gross vehicle weight over 10,000 pounds but not over 26,000 pounds; and

... $2,000 for any other motor vehicle.

♥ *illustration:* In 2002, T buys (1) a qualified clean-fuel truck weighing more than 26,000 pounds and costing $95,000, (2) a qualified clean-fuel van weighing over 10,000 pounds but not over 26,000 pounds and costing $25,000, and (3) a qualified clean-fuel vehicle weighing 10,000 pounds or less and costing $13,000. T's maximum clean-fuel vehicle property deduction for 2002 would be $57,000 [i.e., $50,000 + $5,000 + $2,000].

Specifically, the 2002 Act provides that for any qualified clean-fuel vehicle property placed in service after Dec. 31, 2003, the maximum limit of the deduction will be reduced by: (Code Sec. 179A(b)(1)(B) as amended by 2002 Act §606(a)(1)(A))

... 25% for property placed in service in calendar year *2004*, (Code Sec. 179A(b)(1)(B)(i) as amended by 2002 Act §606(a)(1)(B))

... 50% for property placed in service in calendar year *2005*, (Code Sec. 179A(b)(1)(B)(ii)) and

... 75% for property placed in service in calendar year *2006*. (Code Sec. 179A(b)(1)(B)(iii))

♥ *observation:* Thus, the maximum amount of the deduction for a *truck or van with a gross vehicle weight over 26,000 pounds or a bus with a seating capacity of at least 20 adults (but not including the driver)* placed in service in:

... 2004 will be $37,500,

... 2005 will be $25,000, and

... 2006 will be $12,500.

FTC 2d References are to Federal Tax Coordinator 2d
FIN References are to RIA's Analysis of Federal Taxes: Income
USTR References are to United States Tax Reporter: Income, Estate & Gift, and Excise
PCA References are to the Pension Analysis on Checkpoint and CD-ROM, and in Pension Coordinator
PE References are to the Pension Explanations in Pension and Profit Sharing 2nd
EP References are to the Estate Planning Analysis on Checkpoint and CD-ROM, and in Estate Planning & Taxation Coordinator

illustration: In 2004, T places in service a truck or van with a gross vehicle weight over 26,000 pounds that costs $50,000. Under the 2002 Act, if the same $50,000 truck or van had been placed in service in 2002 or 2003, T could deduct the full $50,000 cost for the tax year in which the truck or van is placed in service. However, as a result of the application of the phaseout rules, T's deduction for his 2004 tax year would be reduced by $12,500 [$50,000 × 25%] to $37,500 [$50,000 − $12,500].

observation: The maximum amount of the deduction for a qualified clean-fuel *truck or van with a gross vehicle weight over 10,000 pounds but not over 26,000 pounds* placed in service in:

. . . 2004 will be $3,750,

. . . 2005 will be $2,500, and

. . . 2006 will be $1,250.

illustration: In 2005, T places in service a qualified clean-fuel truck or van with a gross vehicle weight over 10,000 pounds but not over 26,000 pounds that costs $20,000. Under the 2002 Act, if the same $20,000 truck or van had been placed in service in 2002 or 2003, T could deduct $5,000 of the cost for the tax year in which the truck or van is placed in service. However, as a result of the application of the phaseout rules for clean-fuel vehicle property placed in service in 2005, T's deduction for his 2005 tax year would be further reduced by $2,500 [$5,000 × 50%] to $2,500 [$5,000 − $2,500].

observation: The maximum amount of the deduction for *any other motor vehicle* placed in service in:

. . . 2004 will be $1,500,

. . . 2005 will be $1,000, and

. . . 2006 will be $500.

illustration: In 2006, T places in service a qualified clean-fuel motor vehicle weighing 10,000 pounds or less that costs $20,000. Under the 2002 Act, if the same $20,000 vehicle had been placed in service in 2002 or 2003, T could deduct $2,000 of the cost for the tax year in which the vehicle is placed in service. However, as a result of the application of the phaseout rules for clean-fuel vehicle property placed in service in 2006, T's deduction for his 2006 tax year would be further reduced by $1,500 [$2,000 × 75%] to $500 [$2,000 − $1,500].

The deduction for the cost of clean-fuel vehicle property will not apply to property placed in service after Dec. 31, 2006. (Code Sec. 179A(f) as amended by 2002 Act §606(a)(2)) Thus, the deduction will be unavailable for purchases after Dec. 31, 2006. (Com Rept, see ¶ 5074)

For application of this termination rule to the deduction for qualified clean-fuel vehicle refueling property, see ¶ 210.

☐ **Effective:** Property placed in service after Dec. 31, 2001. (2002 Act § 606(b))

¶ 210. Deduction for cost of clean-fuel vehicle refueling property is extended two years to property placed in service before Jan. 1, 2007

Code Sec. 179A(f), as amended by 2002 Act § 606(a)(2)
Generally effective: Property placed in service after Dec. 31, 2001
Committee Reports, see ¶ 5074

Certain costs of qualified clean-fuel vehicle property and clean-fuel vehicle refueling property may be expensed and deducted for the tax year in which the property is placed in service. See FTC 2d/FIN ¶ K-7012; USTR ¶ 179A4; TaxDesk ¶ 307,001.

> *observation:* The deduction is not a miscellaneous itemized deduction and is not subject to the 2% floor for those deductions.

Clean-fuel vehicle refueling property includes property for the storage or dispensing of a clean-burning fuel, if the storage or dispensing is the point at which the fuel is delivered into the fuel tank of a motor vehicle. Clean-fuel vehicle refueling property also includes property for the recharging of electric vehicles, but only if the property is located at a point where the electric vehicle is recharged. See FTC 2d/FIN ¶ K-7017; USTR ¶ 179A4; TaxDesk ¶ 307,005.

> *observation:* The property does not have to be used in taxpayer's trade or business but may be used for the production of income. However, from a practical perspective, it is difficult to see how the property could only be used as investment property.

Up to $100,000 of the cost of property at each location owned by the taxpayer may be expensed with respect to that location. See FTC 2d/FIN ¶ K-7006; USTR ¶ 179A4; TaxDesk ¶ 307,007.

> *observation:* A taxpayer can claim an aggregate $100,000 deduction for all qualified clean-fuel vehicle refueling property placed in service at any single location. If a taxpayer places qualified refueling property in service

---

FTC 2d References are to Federal Tax Coordinator 2d
FIN References are to RIA's Analysis of Federal Taxes: Income
USTR References are to United States Tax Reporter: Income, Estate & Gift, and Excise
PCA References are to the Pension Analysis on Checkpoint and CD-ROM, and in Pension
    Coordinator
PE References are to the Pension Explanations in Pension and Profit Sharing 2nd
EP References are to the Estate Planning Analysis on Checkpoint and CD-ROM, and in
    Estate Planning & Taxation Coordinator

at multiple locations, he can claim a deduction of up to $100,000 for *each* of those locations.

Under pre-2002 Act law, the deduction for the cost of clean-fuel vehicle refueling property is unavailable for property placed in service *after Dec. 31, 2004.* (FTC 2d/FIN ¶ K-7001; USTR ¶ 179A4; TaxDesk ¶ 307,001)

New Law. In addition to the two-year deferral of the phaseout of the deduction for the cost of qualified clean-fuel vehicle property discussed at ¶ 209, the 2002 Act extends the placed-in-service date for clean-fuel vehicle refueling property. (Com Rept, see ¶ 5074) Specifically, the deduction for the cost of clean-fuel vehicle refueling property will not apply to property placed in service after Dec. 31, 2006. (Code Sec. 179A(f) as amended by 2002 Act §606(a)(2)) Thus, the deduction for clean-fuel vehicle refueling property would be available for property placed in service before Jan. 1, 2007. (Com Rept, see ¶ 5074)

> *observation:* That is, under the 2002 Act, the deduction of up to $100,000 of the cost of clean-fuel vehicle refueling property at each location owned by the taxpayer is available for two years longer than it would have been under pre-2002 Act law. Thus, the deduction will be available for clean-fuel vehicle refueling property placed in service in 2005 or 2006.

For extension of the deduction for the cost of qualified clean-fuel vehicles, see ¶ 209.

☐ **Effective:** Property placed in service after Dec. 31, 2001. (2002 Act § 606(b))

¶ 211. Two-year deferral of the phaseout of the qualified electric vehicle credit permits taxpayers to claim a full credit in 2002 and 2003; credit is extended to apply to property placed in service before Jan. 1, 2007

Code Sec. 30(b)(2), as amended by 2002 Act § 602(a)(1)(A)
Code Sec. 30(b)(2)(A), as amended by 2002 Act § 602(a)(1)(B)
Code Sec. 30(b)(2)(B), as amended by 2002 Act § 602(a)(1)(B)
Code Sec. 30(b)(2)(C), as amended by 2002 Act § 602(a)(1)(B)
Code Sec. 30(e), as amended by 2002 Act § 602(a)(2)
Generally effective: Property placed in service after Dec. 31, 2001
Committee Reports, see ¶ 5070

Under pre-2002 Act law, a tax credit is available for a portion of the cost of a qualified electric vehicle placed in service *before Jan. 1, 2005.* (FTC 2d/FIN ¶ L-18011; USTR ¶ 304; TaxDesk ¶ 397,001)

> *observation:* In addition to this credit, there are two tax benefits specifically available for electric vehicles. The dollar limits on depreciation deductions are about three times higher than the dollar limits that apply to

non-electric vehicles (see ¶ 208 and FTC 2d/FIN ¶ L-10004.1; USTR ¶ 280F4; TaxDesk ¶ 267,601), and there is a 50% higher cost threshold for applying the luxury automobile excise tax, see FTC 2d/FIN ¶ W-2971.1; USTR ¶ 40,014.

A qualified electric vehicle is a motor vehicle that is powered primarily by an electric motor drawing current from rechargeable batteries, fuel cells, or other portable sources of electrical current, the original use of which commences with the taxpayer, and that is acquired for use by the taxpayer and not for resale. See FTC 2d ¶ L-18017; USTR ¶ 304; TaxDesk ¶ 397,009.

> *observation:* Thus, the motor vehicle does not have to be used in taxpayer's trade or business or for the production of income in order for the taxpayer to qualify for the credit. A personal use motor vehicle may qualify the taxpayer for the credit.

The amount of the credit is 10% of the vehicle's cost, limited to a maximum credit of $4,000. See FTC 2d/FIN ¶ L-18011; USTR ¶ 304; TaxDesk ¶ 397,001.

> *observation:* The qualified electric vehicle credit is available on a *per vehicle basis.* That is, *each* qualified vehicle purchased in 2001 can generate up to a $4,000 credit. Although there is no limitation on the number of qualified vehicles that may be purchased in any given year, in no event may the qualified electric vehicle credit exceed the excess, if any, of (1) the regular tax for the tax year, reduced by the sum of the following allowable credits: (a) household and dependent care services credit, (b) credit for the elderly and disabled, (c) credit for interest on certain home mortgages, (d) foreign tax credit and possessions tax credit, and (e) nonconventional fuels credit, over (2) the tentative minimum tax for the tax year (see FTC 2d/FIN ¶ L-18012; USTR ¶ 304; TaxDesk ¶ 397,001).

Under pre-2002 Act law, the full amount of the credit is available for purchases of qualified electric vehicles for purchases before 2002. However, under pre-2002 Act law, the credit is phased out in the years 2002 through 2004. Specifically, for any qualified electric vehicle placed in service after Dec. 31, 2001, the credit is reduced by:

. . . 25% for property placed in service in the year *2002,*

. . . 50% for property placed in service in the year *2003,*

FTC 2d References are to Federal Tax Coordinator 2d
FIN References are to RIA's Analysis of Federal Taxes: Income
USTR References are to United States Tax Reporter: Income, Estate & Gift, and Excise
PCA References are to the Pension Analysis on Checkpoint and CD-ROM, and in Pension Coordinator
PE References are to the Pension Explanations in Pension and Profit Sharing 2nd
EP References are to the Estate Planning Analysis on Checkpoint and CD-ROM, and in Estate Planning & Taxation Coordinator

. . . 75% for property placed in service in the year *2004.* (FTC 2d/FIN ¶ L-18013; USTR ¶ 304; TaxDesk ¶ 397,003)

New Law. The 2002 Act defers the phaseout of the credit by two years and thereby permits taxpayers to claim the full amount of the credit for qualified purchases made in 2002 and 2003. (Com Rept, see ¶ 5070)

> *observation:* Under the 2002 Act, a credit of $4,000 would be available for any qualified vehicle purchased in 2002 or 2003 and costing $40,000 or more, since the credit is 10% of the vehicle's cost and the maximum credit *per vehicle* is $4,000.

Specifically, the 2002 Act provides that for any qualified electric vehicle placed in service after Dec. 31, 2003, the credit will be reduced after the $4,000 limitation is applied by: (Code Sec. 30(b)(2) as amended by 2002 Act §602(a)(1)(A))

. . . 25% for property placed in service in the year *2004,* (Code Sec. 30(b)(2)(A) as amended by 2002 Act §602(a)(1)(B))

. . . 50% for property placed in service in the year *2005,* (Code Sec. 30(b)(2)(B))

. . . 75% for property placed in service in the year *2006.* (Code Sec. 30(b)(2)(C))

Thus, the phasedown of the credit begins in 2004. (Com Rept, see ¶ 5070)

> *observation:* Thus, the *maximum* amount of the credit for a vehicle placed in service in:
>
> . . . 2004 will be $3,000,
>
> . . . 2005 will be $2,000, and
>
> . . . 2006 will be $1,000.

> *illustration:* In 2004, T buys a qualified electric vehicle that costs $30,000. If the phaseout rules didn't apply, T's credit would be $3,000 [$30,000 × 10%]. However, as a result of the application of the phaseout rules, T's credit would be reduced by $750 [$3,000 × 25%] and T would be able to claim a credit of $2,250 [$3,000 − $750] for his 2004 tax year.

For the extension of the tripling of the automobile depreciation and expense deduction limits for electric vehicles, see ¶ 208.

The electric vehicle credit will not apply to any property placed in service after Dec. 31, 2006. (Code Sec. 30(e) as amended by 2002 Act §602(a)(2)) Thus, the credit is unavailable for purchases after Dec. 31, 2006. (Com Rept, see ¶ 5070)

☐ **Effective:** Property placed in service after Dec. 31, 2001. (2002 Act § 602(c))

¶ 212. Reduction of deductions for mutual life insurance companies is suspended for tax years beginning in 2001, 2002, or 2003

Code Sec. 809(j), as amended by 2002 Act § 611(a)
Generally effective: Tax years beginning after Dec. 31, 2000
Committee Reports, see ¶ 5079

In general, a corporation may not deduct amounts distributed to shareholders with respect to the corporation's stock. Code Sec. 809, which was added by the '84 Tax Reform Act, was intended to remedy the failure of prior law to distinguish between amounts returned by mutual life insurance companies to policyholders as customers, and amounts distributed to them as owners of the mutual company. Under Code Sec. 809, a mutual life insurance company is required to reduce its deduction for policyholder dividends by the company's "differential earnings amount." If the company's differential earnings amount exceeds the amount of its deductible policyholder dividends, the company is required to reduce its deduction for changes in its reserves by the excess of its differential earnings amount over the amount of its deductible policyholder dividends. The differential earnings amount is the product of the "differential earnings rate" and the average equity base of a mutual life insurance company.

Under pre-2002 Act law, the "differential earnings rate" was based on the difference between the average earnings rate of the 50 largest stock life insurance companies and the earnings rate of all mutual life insurance companies. The mutual earnings rate applied for this purpose was the rate for the second calendar year preceding the calendar year in which the tax year begins.

A recomputation or "true-up" in the succeeding year is required if the differential earnings amount for the tax year either exceeds, or is less than, the "recomputed differential earnings amount." Under pre-2002 Act law, the "recomputed differential earnings amount" was calculated taking into account the average mutual earnings rate for the calendar year (rather than the second preceding calendar year, as above). The amount of the true-up for any tax year is added to, or deducted from, the mutual life insurance company's income for the succeeding tax year. See FTC 2d/FIN ¶ E-5201; USTR ¶ 8094.

New Law. For a mutual life insurance company's tax years beginning in 2001, 2002, or 2003, the "differential earnings rate" is treated as zero for purposes of

FTC 2d References are to Federal Tax Coordinator 2d
FIN References are to RIA's Analysis of Federal Taxes: Income
USTR References are to United States Tax Reporter: Income, Estate & Gift, and Excise
PCA References are to the Pension Analysis on Checkpoint and CD-ROM, and in Pension Coordinator
PE References are to the Pension Explanations in Pension and Profit Sharing 2nd
EP References are to the Estate Planning Analysis on Checkpoint and CD-ROM, and in Estate Planning & Taxation Coordinator

computing both the "differential earnings amount" and the "recomputed differential earnings amount." (Code Sec. 809(j) as amended by 2002 Act §611(a))

> ⓡ *observation:* If the "differential earnings rate" is zero, then both the "differential earnings amount" and the "recomputed differential earnings amount" are also zero. Thus, the Code Sec. 809 rule requiring a mutual life insurance company to reduce its deductions by its "differential earnings amount" is effectively suspended for tax years beginning in 2001, 2002, or 2003, since the reduction amount is zero. Similarly, the rule requiring a mutual life insurance company to add or deduct a "true-up" to or from its income for a tax year, if the differential earnings amount for the previous tax year either exceeded, or was less than, the "recomputed differential earnings amount," is also suspended for tax years beginning in 2001, 2002, or 2003.

> ⓡ *observation:* Under the 2002 Act, the Code Sec. 809 rule requiring the reduction of a mutual life insurance company's deductions is only suspended, and is scheduled to become effective again for tax years beginning after 2003. Similarly, the requirement that a "true-up" be added to or deducted from a mutual life insurance company's income, where appropriate, is only suspended, and is scheduled to become effective again for tax years beginning after 2003.

☐ **Effective:** Applies to tax years beginning after Dec. 31, 2000. (2002 Act § 611(b))

¶ 213. Authorization for issuance of qualified zone academy bonds of up to $400 million per year is extended for two years to include calendar years 2002 and 2003

Code Sec. 1397E(e)(1), as amended by 2002 Act § 608(a)
Generally effective: Obligations issued after Mar. 9, 2002
Committee Reports, see ¶ 5076

Under pre-2002 Act law, qualified zone academy bonds were authorized to be issued for '98, '99, 2000, and 2001, up to an annual limitation of $400 million nationally. (FTC 2d/FIN ¶ L-15645.12; USTR ¶ 13,97E4.01)

The credit for qualified zone academy bonds is available to banks, insurance companies, and other corporations in the business of lending money ("eligible taxpayers"). The credit is nonrefundable and equal to a percentage of the bonds held by an eligible taxpayer. The credit is in lieu of periodic interest payments, compensates the eligible taxpayer for lending money to the issuer, and functions as payment of interest on the bonds.

The $400 million national limit is allocated among the states based on the proportion of each state's population below the poverty line. The bonds are issued for qualified purposes, which are defined as rehabilitating or repairing the facility in which the academy is located, providing equipment, developing course materials, and training teachers and other school personnel.

A qualified zone academy is defined, in part, as a public school or program below the post-secondary level that is designed with business input to better prepare students for college and the workforce. The school itself must be located in an empowerment zone or enterprise community or, if the school isn't in such a zone or community, then, at the time the bonds are issued, there has to be a reasonable expectation that, of students attending the school or program, at least 35% will be eligible for free or reduced-cost lunches under the school lunch program. See FTC 2d/FIN ¶ L-15645; USTR ¶ 13,97E4; 13,97E4.01.

New Law. The 2002 Act extends the authorization of the issuance of qualified zone academy bonds up to the national limitation of $400 million per year to calendar years 2002 and 2003. (Code Sec. 1397E(e)(1) as amended by 2002 Act §608(a))

> **☯ observation:** Thus, the 2002 Act extends for two years authorization for the issuance of qualified zone academy bonds.

☐ **Effective:** Obligations issued after Mar. 9, 2002. (2002 Act § 608(b))

¶ 214. Archer MSA program is extended through 2003

Code Sec. 220(i)(2), as amended by 2002 Act § 612(a)
Generally effective: Jan. 1, 2002
Committee Reports, see ¶ 5080

Medical savings accounts (MSAs) provide a tax-favored way to save for and pay medical expenses. Code Sec. 220 authorized MSAs as a "pilot project" that was originally scheduled to end in the year 2000. The ability to use MSAs would have ended earlier if the number of taxpayers contributing (or receiving employer contributions) to an MSA exceeded certain statutory limits (also referred to as a "threshold level" or "numerical limitation" or "cap") for '97, '98, or '99.

Section 201(c) of the 2000 Community Renewal Act renamed MSAs as "Archer MSAs" and extended the MSA program through 2002. That Act also clarified that the cap and reporting requirements did not apply for 2000. Moreover, the ability to use Archer MSAs would have ended earlier than 2002 if the number of taxpayers contributing (or receiving employer contributions) to an Archer MSA exceeded certain statutory limits (generally, 750,000 taxpayers) for 2001.

Under pre-2002 Act law, "cut-off year" was defined as the earlier of—

• calendar year 2002, or

• the first calendar year before 2002 for which IRS could have determined, under Code Sec. 220(j), that the numerical limitation for the year had been exceeded.

To date, the number of Archer MSAs established has not exceeded the threshold level. (Com Rept, see ¶ 5080)

Under pre-2002 Act law, no new contributions could be made to Archer MSAs after 2002, except by or on behalf of individuals (including self-employed individuals) who previously had Archer MSA contributions, and employees who were employed by a participating employer. (FTC 2d/FIN ¶ H-1342.2; USTR ¶ 2204.02; TaxDesk ¶ 288,147)

New Law. The 2002 Act amends the definition of "cut-off year" by replacing "2002" with "2003" in each place that it appeared. (Code Sec. 220(i)(2) as amended by 2002 Act §612(a)) Thus, the Archer MSA program is extended for another year, through Dec. 31, 2003. (Com Rept, see ¶ 5080)

> *observation:* Archer MSAs were enacted to provide additional health insurance options and to give individuals more control over their health care dollars by providing incentives for individuals to be more cost-conscious consumers of health care. By extending the Archer MSA program, Congress saw merit in continuing to pursue these objectives.

☐ **Effective:** Jan. 1, 2002 (2002 Act § 612(c))

¶ 215. Indian employment credit for wages paid to qualified Indians is extended through 2004

Code Sec. 45A(f), as amended by 2002 Act § 613(a)
Generally effective: Mar. 9, 2002
Committee Reports, see ¶ 5081

As an incentive for businesses to be located on Indian reservations, employers are eligible for a credit equal to 20% of the first $20,000 of qualified wages and insurance costs paid to a qualified Indian employee for tax years beginning after Dec. 31, '93 and before Jan. 1, 2004. The credit generally applies to services performed on Indian reservations by members of Indian tribes who live on the reservation. (FTC 2d/FIN ¶ L-15671; USTR ¶ 45A4; TaxDesk ¶ 384,039)

New Law. The 2002 Act extends the Indian employment credit for one year to tax years beginning before Jan. 1, 2005. (Code Sec. 45A(f) as amended by 2002 Act §613(a))

☐ **Effective:** Mar. 9, 2002

¶ 216. Depreciation tax breaks for qualified Indian reservation property are extended through 2004

Code Sec. 168(j)(8), as amended by 2002 Act § 613(b)
Generally effective: Mar. 9, 2002
Committee Reports, see ¶ 5081

Under pre-2002 Act law, shortened depreciation recovery periods can be used for qualified Indian reservation property placed in service after Dec. 31, '93 and before Jan. 1, 2004. For example, property normally depreciable over a 5-year period may be depreciated over a 3-year period if it is qualified Indian reservation property. Also, the depreciation deduction allowed for regular tax purposes with respect to qualified Indian reservation property is also allowed for purposes of the alternative minimum tax. Generally speaking, qualified Indian reservation property is MACRS property used predominantly in the active conduct of a trade or business on an Indian reservation. (FTC 2d/FIN ¶ L-8202, ¶ L-8806, ¶ L-8807; USTR ¶ 1684.01; TaxDesk ¶ 267,007)

New Law. The 2002 Act extends the use of the above-described depreciation tax breaks for qualified Indian reservation property by one year. Thus, the above rules apply to property placed in service before Jan. 1, 2005. (Code Sec. 168(j)(8) as amended by 2002 Act §613(b))

☐ **Effective:** Mar. 9, 2002

FTC 2d References are to Federal Tax Coordinator 2d
FIN References are to RIA's Analysis of Federal Taxes: Income
USTR References are to United States Tax Reporter: Income, Estate & Gift, and Excise
PCA References are to the Pension Analysis on Checkpoint and CD-ROM, and in Pension Coordinator
PE References are to the Pension Explanations in Pension and Profit Sharing 2nd
EP References are to the Estate Planning Analysis on Checkpoint and CD-ROM, and in Estate Planning & Taxation Coordinator

¶ 300. Pension & Benefits

¶ 301. Limitation on deductible contributions to SEPs increased from 15% to 25% of compensation

Code Sec. 402(h)(2)(A), as amended by 2002 Act § 411(l)(3)
Generally effective: For years beginning after Dec. 31, 2001
Committee Reports, see ¶ 5042

A simplified employee pension (SEP) is an individual retirement arrangement established by an employer, which can make contributions to the SEP on behalf of its employees, subject to certain contribution and deduction limits.

SEP contribution limits. Employer contributions to a SEP on behalf of an employee are treated as distributed or made available to the employee (and thus taxable to the employee) to the extent the contribution exceeds the lesser of:

(1) 15% of the compensation from the employer includible in the employee's gross income for the year (determined without regard to the employer's contributions to the SEP); or

(2) the dollar limit for a defined contribution plan ($40,000 for 2002).

Under pre-2002 Act law, the percentage of compensation limit (item 1, above) was 15% of compensation. (FTC 2d/FIN ¶ H-12319.1; USTR ¶ 4044.15; TaxDesk ¶ 282,307; PCA ¶ 35,520.1; PE ¶ 404-4.15)

SEP deduction limits. Employer contributions are deductible for a tax year only to the extent they don't exceed 25% of compensation paid to employees. Excess contributions can be carried over and deducted in later years, subject to the 25% of compensation limit. The 2001 Economic Growth and Tax Relief Reconciliation Act (EGTRRA §616(a)) had increased the deductible limit from 15% of compensation to 25% of compensation. (FTC 2d/FIN ¶ H-12315; USTR ¶ 4044.15; TaxDesk ¶ 282,309; PCA ¶ 35,516; PE ¶ 404-4.15)

> **observation:** For changes made to the definition of "compensation" for purposes of determining the percentage of compensation limit on SEP deductions, see ¶ 304.

New Law. The 2002 Act increases the percentage of compensation limit on the SEP contribution limit (item 1, above) from 15% of compensation to 25% of

---

FTC 2d References are to Federal Tax Coordinator 2d
FIN References are to RIA's Analysis of Federal Taxes: Income
USTR References are to United States Tax Reporter: Income, Estate & Gift, and Excise
PCA References are to the Pension Analysis on Checkpoint and CD-ROM, and in Pension Coordinator
PE References are to the Pension Explanations in Pension and Profit Sharing 2nd
EP References are to the Estate Planning Analysis on Checkpoint and CD-ROM, and in Estate Planning & Taxation Coordinator

compensation. (Code Sec. 402(h)(2)(A) as amended by 2002 Act §411(l)(3)) Thus, contributions made by an employer to a SEP on behalf of an employee are included in the employee's income to the extent they exceed the lesser of 25% of compensation or $40,000 (for 2002). (Com Rept, see ¶ 5042)

> **observation:** The increase in the contribution limit from 15% to 25% of compensation conforms the contribution limit to the deduction limit. Thus, after the 2002 Act, the percentage of compensation limit for both the contribution limit and the deduction limit is 25% of compensation.

> **illustration:** Suzette is a participant in her company's SEP. Her compensation from the company is $100,000 per year. Under pre-2002 Act law, the company could contribute up to $15,000 to her SEP account in a plan year without it being taxable to her in that year (15% x $100,000). Any amount contributed to her SEP account over $15,000 in the same plan year would have been taxable to her in that year.

> After the 2002 Act, Suzette is entitled to receive up to $25,000 in company contributions to the SEP in a plan year, without it being taxable to her in that year (25% x $100,000).

☐ **Effective:** For years beginning after Dec. 31, 2001. (2002 Act § 411(x))

¶ 302. Dollar limits for SEP eligibility, and for determining the distribution period from an ESOP, are increased to permit proper inflation indexing

Code Sec. 408(k), as amended by 2002 Act § 411(j)(1)
Code Sec. 409(o)(1)(C)(ii), as amended by 2002 Act § 411(j)(2)
Generally effective: Years beginning after Dec. 31, 2001
Committee Reports, see ¶ 5040

SEPs. Annual employer contributions to a simplified employee pension (SEP) must be made on behalf of each employee who has (1) reached age 21; (2) performed service for the employer during at least three of the five preceding years; and (3) received at least $300 (as adjusted for inflation) in compensation. The cost-of-living adjustments (COLAs) for 2002 raised this $300 amount to $450. (FTC 2d/FIN ¶ H-12305; USTR ¶ 4084.05; TaxDesk ¶ 282,302; PCA ¶ 35,506; PE ¶ 408-4.05)

ESOPs. The distribution requirement for an employee stock ownership plan (ESOP) provides that, unless the participant elects otherwise, distribution of the participant's account balance must be made not longer than: (1) five years, or; (2) for participants with account balances greater than $500,000, five years plus one additional year for each $100,000, or fraction thereof, by which the account balance exceeds $500,000. The $500,000 and $100,000 amounts are subject to CO-

LAs. The COLAs for 2002 made these amounts $800,000 and $160,000, respectively. (FTC 2d/FIN ¶ H-9327; USTR ¶ 4094.11; PCA ¶ 28,628; PE ¶ 409-4.11)

New Law. The 2001 Economic Growth and Tax Relief Reconciliation Act (EGTRRA §611) increased the benefit and contribution limits applicable to qualified retirement plans. In connection with this, EGTRRA also changed the base period applicable to indexing the 2002 dollar amounts (to July 1, 2001) for future COLAs. (Com Rept, see ¶ 5040)

Under the 2002 Act, the same COLA indexing method that applies to pension plan contribution limits also applies to the dollar amount that determines eligibility to participate in a SEP and to determine the proper distribution period for an ESOP. Thus, the Technical Explanation indicates that Congress is changing these amounts to the 2002 indexed amounts so that future indexing will "operate properly." (Com Rept, see ¶ 5040)

> *observation:* The term "operate properly" isn't defined. Presumably, an improper adjustment results from adjusting the original SEP and ESOP amounts only for inflation that's occurred since the July 1, 2001 quarter, which yields a smaller number than that which is indexed for 2002.

SEPs. Under the 2002 Act, the $300 eligibility dollar amount is increased to $450 (the 2002 indexed amount). (Code Sec. 408(k) as amended by 2002 Act §411(j)(1))

ESOPs. Under the 2002 Act, the $500,000 and $100,000 amounts used to calculate the ESOP distribution periods are increased to $800,000 and $160,000, respectively (the 2002 indexed amounts). (Code Sec. 409(o)(1)(C)(ii) as amended by 2002 Act §411(j)(2))

☐ **Effective:** For years beginning after Dec. 31, 2001. (2002 Act § 411(x))

¶ 303. Elective deferrals are no longer taken into account in applying SEP deduction limits for employer contributions

Code Sec. 404(n), as amended by 2002 Act § 411(l)(2)
Generally effective: For years beginning after Dec. 31, 2001
Committee Reports, see ¶ 5042

FTC 2d References are to Federal Tax Coordinator 2d
FIN References are to RIA's Analysis of Federal Taxes: Income
USTR References are to United States Tax Reporter: Income, Estate & Gift, and Excise
PCA References are to the Pension Analysis on Checkpoint and CD-ROM, and in Pension Coordinator
PE References are to the Pension Explanations in Pension and Profit Sharing 2nd
EP References are to the Estate Planning Analysis on Checkpoint and CD-ROM, and in Estate Planning & Taxation Coordinator

An employer contribution to a simplified employee pension (SEP) must be under a specific ceiling to be fully deductible in any year. An employer may deduct contributions paid to a SEP in an amount not in excess of 25% of the compensation paid to employees during the calendar year ending with or within the tax year (during the tax year, in the case of a SEP maintained on the basis of the tax year). (FTC 2d/FIN ¶ H-12315; USTR ¶ 4044.15; TaxDesk ¶ 282,309; PCA ¶ 35,516; PE ¶ 404-4.15)

In applying the 25% ceiling on the employer's deduction for SEP contributions, the annual compensation of each employee that is taken into account under the plan for any year can be no more than $200,000 (for 2002), as adjusted under Code Sec. 401(a)(17).

For purposes of the SEP deduction limit, under pre-2002 Act law, employee elective deferral contributions (as defined by Code Sec. 402(g)(3), see below) were treated as employer contributions and, thus, were subject to the generally applicable deduction limit discussed above. (FTC 2d/FIN ¶ H-12311; USTR ¶ 4144.22; TaxDesk ¶ 282,007; PCA ¶ 35,512; PE ¶ 414-4.22)

An employee's elective deferrals under Code Sec. 402(g)(3) are the sum of the following:

(1) elective contributions under a 401(k) plan, to the extent not includible in gross income;

(2) employer contributions to a salary reduction SEP to the extent not includible in gross income;

(3) employer contributions to a 403(b) annuity contract under a salary reduction agreement, to the extent not includible in gross income;

(4) elective employer contributions under a "qualified salary reduction arrangement" that is part of a SIMPLE retirement plan; and

(5) employee contributions designated as deductible under a Code Sec. 501(c)(18) tax-exempt pension plan trust created before June 25, '59, to the extent deductible from income. (FTC 2d/FIN ¶ H-9152; USTR ¶ 4024; TaxDesk ¶ 284,026; PCA ¶ 28,403; PE ¶ 402-4)

New Law. Under the 2002 Act, elective deferrals made to a SEP are not subject to the deduction limits and are not taken into account in applying the limits to other SEP contributions. (Code Sec. 404(n) as amended by 2002 Act §411(l)(2)) (Com Rept, see ¶ 5042)

> *observation:* The elimination of elective deferrals from the SEP deduction limitation calculation may encourage employers to make larger contributions to SEPs, and may alleviate employer restrictions on the amount of elective contributions an employee can make.

> *illustration:* The Acme Company has a total payroll of $100,000. It sponsors a SEP, under which all employees have elected to contribute 15% of their salaries, and Acme makes a 15% matching contribution.

Thus, employees' elective deferrals to the SEP equal $15,000, and the company's matching contribution equals $15,000, providing $30,000 in total contributions to the SEP. Under the 2002 Act, Acme is entitled to deduct up to $25,000 in employer contributions made to the SEP (25% of the $100,000 of total compensation paid).

Under pre-2002 Act law, the employees' elective deferrals were treated as employer contributions, so they counted towards the $25,000 deduction limit. Thus, under pre-2002 Act law, Acme could deduct only $10,000 of its $15,000 matching contribution (since the employees' elective deferrals were also $15,000 and $25,000 - $15,000 = $10,000).

After the 2002 Act, none of the employees' elective deferrals count as employer contributions. Thus, Acme can deduct all of its $15,000 matching contribution to the SEP, since the total employer contribution is equal to $15,000, and Acme is entitled to deduct up to $25,000.

☐ **Effective:** For years beginning after Dec. 31, 2001. (2002 Act § 411(x))

¶ 304. "Compensation" for purposes of determining deduction limits for contributions to SEPs includes salary reduction amounts

Code Sec. 404(a)(12), as amended by 2002 Act § 411(l)(1)
Generally effective: Years beginning after Dec. 31, 2001
Committee Reports, see ¶ 5042

An employer contribution to a simplified employee pension (SEP) must be under a specific ceiling to be fully deductible in any year. An employer may deduct contributions paid to a SEP in an amount not in excess of 25% of the compensation paid to employees during the calendar year ending with or within the tax year (*during* the tax year, in the case of a SEP maintained on the basis of the tax year). (FTC 2d/FIN ¶ H-12315; USTR ¶ 4044.15; TaxDesk ¶ 282,309; PCA ¶ 35,516; PE ¶ 404-4.15)

In applying the 25% ceiling on the employer's deduction for SEP contributions, the annual compensation of each employee that is taken into account under the plan for any year can be no more than $200,000 (for 2002), as adjusted under Code Sec. 401(a)(17).

FTC 2d References are to Federal Tax Coordinator 2d
FIN References are to RIA's Analysis of Federal Taxes: Income
USTR References are to United States Tax Reporter: Income, Estate & Gift, and Excise
PCA References are to the Pension Analysis on Checkpoint and CD-ROM, and in Pension Coordinator
PE References are to the Pension Explanations in Pension and Profit Sharing 2nd
EP References are to the Estate Planning Analysis on Checkpoint and CD-ROM, and in Estate Planning & Taxation Coordinator

Under pre-2002 Act law, for purposes of the *deduction rules*, compensation generally included only taxable compensation, and thus did not include salary reduction amounts such as elective deferrals under a 401(k) plan or a tax-sheltered annuity ("403(b) annuity"), elective contributions under a deferred compensation plan of a tax-exempt organization or a state or local government (a "section 457 plan"), salary reduction contributions under a Code Sec. 125 cafeteria plan, or qualified transportation fringe benefits under Code Sec. 132(f)(4). In contrast, for purposes of the *contribution limits* under Code Sec. 415, compensation *does* include these salary reduction amounts. (FTC 2d/FIN ¶ H-12311; USTR ¶ 4144.22; TaxDesk ¶ 282,007; PCA ¶ 35,512; PE ¶ 414-4.22)

> ⟨RIA⟩ *observation:* In another change made by the 2002 Act, elective deferral contributions are no longer taken into account in applying the SEP contribution deduction limits, see ¶ 303.

New Law. Under the 2002 Act, the definition of "compensation" for purposes of the limitation on deductions for contributions to SEPs includes amounts treated as a participant's compensation under Code Sec. 415(c)(3)(C) or Code Sec. 415(c)(3)(D) (see observation below). (Code Sec. 404(a)(12) as amended by 2002 Act §411(l)(1))

> ⟨RIA⟩ *observation:* Thus, for purposes of applying the contribution deduction limitation to SEPs, the 2002 Act definition of "compensation" includes any:
>
> (1) amount of compensation which a participant would have received for the year if he were paid at the rate of compensation paid immediately before becoming permanently and totally disabled—as provided in Code Sec. 415(c)(3)(C); and
>
> (2) (a) elective deferrals under Code Sec. 402(g)(3), and (b) amounts contributed or deferred by an employer at an employee's election under a Code Sec. 125 cafeteria plan, Code Sec. 132(f)(4) (relating to qualified transportation fringe benefits), or a section 457 eligible deferred compensation plan, even though these amounts are not includible in the employee's income under Code Sec. 125, Code Sec. 132(f)(4), or Code Sec. 457—as provided in Code Sec. 415(c)(3)(D).
>
> Thus, under the 2002 Act, the definition of compensation, for purposes of the SEP deduction rules, includes salary reduction amounts treated as compensation under Code Sec. 415.

> ⟨RIA⟩ *observation:* As a result, both the SEP deduction rules and the SEP contribution limits use a definition of compensation that includes salary reduction amounts.

☐ **Effective:** For years beginning after Dec. 31, 2001. (2002 Act § 411(x))

¶ 305. Deduction limit for combined plans doesn't apply if defined contribution plan receives only elective deferrals

Code Sec. 404(a)(7)(C), as amended by 2002 Act § 411(l)(4)
Generally effective: For years beginning after Dec. 31, 2001
Committee Reports, see ¶ 5042

Subject to certain limits, employer contributions to qualified retirement plans are deductible. Under Code Sec. 404(a)(7)(A), there is a specific deductible limit where the employer maintains both a defined benefit plan and a defined contribution plan. This limit is the greater of (1) 25% of total pay to participants, or (2) the defined benefit contribution that is necessary to satisfy the minimum funding obligation of Code Sec. 412.

Under pre-2002 Act law, where an employer maintained both a defined benefit plan and a defined contribution plan, the combined limit on deductions (described above) applied, even though the only amounts contributed to the defined contribution plan were employee elective deferrals (as defined by Code Sec. 402(g)(3), see below). (FTC 2d/FIN ¶ H-10120; USTR ¶ 4044.09; TaxDesk ¶ 281,015; PCA ¶ 30,221; PE ¶ 404-4.09)

An employee's elective deferrals under Code Sec. 402(g)(3) are the sum of the following:

(1) elective contributions under a 401(k) plan, to the extent not includible in gross income;

(2) employer contributions to a salary reduction SEP to the extent not includible in gross income;

(3) employer contributions to a 403(b) annuity contract under a salary reduction agreement, to the extent not includible in gross income;

(4) elective employer contributions under a "qualified salary reduction arrangement" that is part of a SIMPLE retirement plan; and

(5) employee contributions designated as deductible under a Code Sec. 501(c)(18) tax-exempt pension plan trust created before June 25, '59, to the extent deductible from income. (FTC 2d/FIN ¶ H-9152; USTR ¶ 4024; TaxDesk ¶ 284,026; PCA ¶ 28,403; PE ¶ 402-4)

New Law. Under the 2002 Act, the deduction limit on combinations of defined benefit and defined contribution plans does not apply where no amounts (except for elective deferrals) are contributed to any of the defined contribution plans

---

FTC 2d References are to Federal Tax Coordinator 2d
FIN References are to RIA's Analysis of Federal Taxes: Income
USTR References are to United States Tax Reporter: Income, Estate & Gift, and Excise
PCA References are to the Pension Analysis on Checkpoint and CD-ROM, and in Pension Coordinator
PE References are to the Pension Explanations in Pension and Profit Sharing 2nd
EP References are to the Estate Planning Analysis on Checkpoint and CD-ROM, and in Estate Planning & Taxation Coordinator

for the taxable year. (Code Sec. 404(a)(7)(C)(ii) as amended by 2002 Act §411(l)(4))

The combined deduction limit of 25% of compensation for qualified defined benefit and defined contribution plans does not apply if the only amounts contributed to the defined contribution plan are elective deferrals. (Com Rept, see ¶ 5042)

> 🅁🄸🄰 *illustration:* Acme Corporation sponsors two qualified retirement plans: a defined benefit pension plan and a defined contribution profit sharing plan with a cash or deferred arrangement (a 401(k) plan). For the 2002 plan year, Acme does not make profit sharing contributions to the defined contribution plan. The only contributions made to that plan in 2002 are elective deferrals under employee salary reduction agreements. Thus, the combined plan deduction limit of 25% of compensation does not apply for 2002. Instead, each plan is subject only to the deduction limits applicable to that plan.

> 🅁🄸🄰 *observation:* Elective deferrals are also no longer taken into account under the 2002 Act in applying the simplified employee pension (SEP) contribution deduction limits, see ¶ 303.

☐ **Effective:** For years beginning after Dec. 31, 2001. (2002 Act § 411(x))

¶ 306. Temporary relief from low yields on 30-year bonds provided for additional funding requirements and for determining PBGC variable rate premiums

Code Sec. 412(l)(7)(C)(i)(III), as amended by 2002 Act § 405(a)(1)
Code Sec. 412(m)(7), as amended by 2002 Act § 405(a)(2)
ERISA §302(d)(7)(C)(i)(III), as amended by 2002 Act §405(b)(1)
ERISA §302(e)(7), as amended by 2002 Act §405(b)(2)
ERISA §4006(a)(3)(E)(iii)(IV), as amended by 2002 Act §405(c)
Generally effective: Plan years beginning after Dec. 31, 2001 and before Jan. 1, 2004
Committee Reports, see ¶ 5025

To be tax-qualified, defined benefit plans and money purchase plans must meet minimum funding requirements. The minimum funding rules require that defined benefit plans and money purchase plans conform to a minimum "funding standard," which is a formula or calculation that determines the minimum contribution the employer must make to its plan each year.

ERISA has similar minimum funding provisions that apply to qualified, as well as nonqualified plans.

Additional contributions are required under a special funding rule for certain single-employer defined benefit pension plans that are underfunded. Under this special rule, a plan is considered underfunded for a plan year if the value of the plan assets is less than 90% of the plan's current liability. The value of plan assets as a percentage of current liability is the "funded current liability percentage."

However, the amount of additional contributions cannot exceed the amount needed to increase the plan's funded current liability percentage to 100%. (FTC 2d ¶ H-7632, ¶ H-7634; USTR ¶ 4124.10; PCA ¶ 25,633, ¶ 25,635; PE ¶ 412-4.10)

The maximum funding requirement for a defined benefit plan is referred to as the full funding limitation. Additional contributions are not required if a plan has reached the full funding limitation. (FTC 2d ¶ H-7629.1; USTR ¶ 4124.07; PCA ¶ 25,630.1; PE ¶ 412-4.07)

For purposes of determining a plan's current liability, and for purposes of determining a plan's required contribution under the additional funding requirements for any plan year, the interest rate used to determine cost must be within the "permissible range." This is a rate of interest which isn't more than 10% above, and not more than 10% below, the "weighted average" of the rates of interest on 30-year Treasury securities during the four-year period ending on the last day before the beginning of the plan year.

Because of the reduction in the nation's outstanding debt, the Treasury does not currently issue 30-year Treasury securities.

> **RIA** *observation:* Due to the reduction in the national debt, and the decision to discontinue the 30-year bond, the rates on these bonds are very low when compared to corporate bonds of similar maturities. This low yield has required employers to contribute more to their plans to meet their funding obligations.

> **RIA** *observation:* A bond's yield moves in the opposite direction of its price. For example, if a $10,000 bond is issued with an interest rate of 5%, and interest rates for similar bonds subsequently rise to 7%, the amount someone would pay for that $10,000 bond would be less than its $10,000 face value. That is, the price of the bond would fall to a level that, when combined with its 5% coupon rate, would yield a 7% return. Conversely, if a $10,000 bond is issued with a coupon rate of 7% and interest rates fall to 5% a purchaser of that bond would have to pay more than its $10,000 face value. That is, the price of the bond would rise to a level that, when combined with its 7% coupon rate, would yield a 5% return.

FTC 2d References are to Federal Tax Coordinator 2d
FIN References are to RIA's Analysis of Federal Taxes: Income
USTR References are to United States Tax Reporter: Income, Estate & Gift, and Excise
PCA References are to the Pension Analysis on Checkpoint and CD-ROM, and in Pension
    Coordinator
PE References are to the Pension Explanations in Pension and Profit Sharing 2nd
EP References are to the Estate Planning Analysis on Checkpoint and CD-ROM, and in
    Estate Planning & Taxation Coordinator

So, as 30-year Treasury bonds have become more scarce, and demand for them has increased, the price investors are willing to pay for these bonds has increased. This has had the effect of driving down their yields.

As a further limitation, the highest rate in the permissible range may not exceed the "specified percentage" of the weighted average of the interest rates. The specified percentage depends on the calendar year in which the plan year begins; for plan years beginning in '99 and thereafter, the specified percentage is 105%. (FTC 2d ¶ H-7635; USTR ¶ 4124.10; PCA ¶ 25,636; PE ¶ 412-4.10)

In some instances, a limiting amount called the "full funding limitation" may be smaller than the minimum funding requirement otherwise determined for the year. This may occur, for example, where plan assets have increased substantially and unexpectedly in value. In this case, the amount to be charged to the funding standard account (and to be contributed) is limited to the amount of the full funding limitation.

For plans with a funded current liability percentage of less than 100% for the preceding plan year, estimated contributions for the current plan year must be made in quarterly installments during the current plan year. The amount of each required installment is 25% of the lesser of (1) 90% of the amount required to be contributed for the current plan year or (2) 100% of the amount required to be contributed for the preceding plan year.

Quarterly contributions are not required once the plan's funded current liability percentage for the plan year reaches 100%.

The Pension Benefit Guaranty Corporation (PBGC) generally insures the benefits owed under defined benefit pension plans. Employers must pay premiums to the PBGC for this insurance coverage. For underfunded plans, additional PBGC premiums are required based on the amount of unfunded vested benefits. These premiums are referred to as variable rate premiums. In determining the amount of unfunded vested benefits, the interest rate used is 85% of the interest rate on 30-year Treasury securities (which are no longer issued) for the month preceding the month in which the plan year begins. (PCA ¶ 58,307; PE ¶ ER4006-4.01)

> *observation:* Due to the reduction in the national debt, and the decision to discontinue the 30-year bond, the rates on these bonds are very low when compared to corporate bonds of similar maturities. This low yield has the effect of increasing the amount of a plan's unfunded vested benefits, subjecting more plans to higher PBGC premiums than would be the case if a higher rate of interest were used in determining unfunded vested benefits.

New Law. To provide relief from some of the consequences of the low yield on 30-year bonds, the 2002 Act amends the determination of current liability for both the Code and ERISA by expanding the permissible range of the statutory interest rate used in calculating a plan's current liability, for purposes of applying the additional contribution requirements for plan years beginning after 2001 and before 2004.

Under this amendment, for plan years beginning in 2002 or 2003, notwithstanding the 105% specified percentage figure set out in Code Sec. 412(l)(7)(C)(i)(I) and ERISA §302(d)(7)(C)(i)(I) , if the rate of interest used for purposes of the funding standard account under Code Sec. 412(b)(5) and ERISA §302(b)(5) exceeds 105%, the rate of interest used to determine current liability may exceed the rate of interest otherwise permitted, up to 120% of the weighted average. (Code Sec. 412(l)(7)(C)(i)(III) as amended by 2002 Act §405(a)(1)) (ERISA §302(d)(7)(C)(i)(III) as amended by 2002 Act §405(b)(1))

Thus, under the 2002 Act, the permissible range is 90% to 120% of the weighted average rate for plan years beginning in 2002 and 2003. (Com Rept, see ¶ 5025)

Using a higher interest rate under the expanded permissible range of 90% to 120% will affect the plan's current liability, which may require the plan to make additional contributions and may affect the amount of any additional contributions. (Com Rept, see ¶ 5025) To address this issue, the 2002 Act provides that, for plan years beginning in 2002 (when the expanded range first applies), in applying the quarterly contribution requirement and in determining the amount of the required installment, the current liability for the preceding plan year must be redetermined using 120%, not 105%, as the specified percentage determined under Code Sec. 412(l)(7)(C)(i)(II). (Code Sec. 412(m)(7)(A) as amended by 2002 Act §405(a)(2)) (ERISA §302(e)(7)(A) as amended by 2002 Act §405(b)(2))

For plan years beginning in 2004 (when the expanded range no longer applies), the 2002 Act provides that in applying the quarterly contribution requirement and in determining the amount of the required installment, the current liability for the preceding plan year must be redetermined using 105% as the specified percentage determined under Code Sec. 412(l)(7)(C)(i)(II) and ERISA §302(d)(7)(C)(i)(II) . (Code Sec. 412(m)(7)(B) as amended by 2002 Act §405(a)(2)) (ERISA §302(e)(7)(B) as amended by 2002 Act §405(b)(2))

Thus, for 2002 and 2004 (but not 2003), the current liability for the preceding year is redetermined, using the permissible range applicable to the present year. (Com Rept, see ¶ 5025)

Finally, the 2002 Act addresses changes to the PBGC's variable rate premiums. For plan years beginning after Dec. 31, 2001, and before Jan. 1, 2004, the interest rate used in determining the amount of unfunded vested benefits for variable rate

---

FTC 2d References are to Federal Tax Coordinator 2d
FIN References are to RIA's Analysis of Federal Taxes: Income
USTR References are to United States Tax Reporter: Income, Estate & Gift, and Excise
PCA References are to the Pension Analysis on Checkpoint and CD-ROM, and in Pension Coordinator
PE References are to the Pension Explanations in Pension and Profit Sharing 2nd
EP References are to the Estate Planning Analysis on Checkpoint and CD-ROM, and in Estate Planning & Taxation Coordinator

premium purposes increases to 100% of the interest rate on existing 30-year Treasury securities for the month preceding the month in which the plan year begins, from 85%. (ERISA §4006(a)(3)(E)(iii)(IV) as amended by 2002 Act §405(c))

ERISA §4006(a)(3)(E)(iii)(III) provides that when the interest rate used in valuing vested benefits rises to 100% of the interest rate on 30-year securities, the value of a plan's assets used in determining unfunded current liability is their fair market value. For plan years beginning after Dec. 31, 2001, and before Jan. 1, 2004, this provision is applied without regard to the increase in valuing vested benefits made by the 2002 Act. Further, any references elsewhere in ERISA to ERISA §4006(a)(3)(E)(iii) are to be treated without regard to ERISA §4006(a)(3)(E)(iii)(IV) (above). (ERISA §4006(a)(3)(E)(iii)(IV) as amended by 2002 Act §405(c))

> **observation:** Thus, other than for purposes of valuing vested benefits for plan years beginning in 2002 and 2003, subclause (IV) has no other effect, and is to be ignored when ERISA §4006(a)(3)(E)(iii) is referred to in other sections or subsections of ERISA.

> **observation:** After the 2003 plan year, the interest rate used in determining the amount of unfunded vested benefits for variable rate premium purposes reverts to 85% of the interest rate on 30-year Treasury securities for the month preceding the month in which the plan year begins.

> **observation:** The two year window is apparently designed to provide employers with some interest rate relief while the Treasury searches for a replacement interest benchmark for the 30-year bond.

☐ **Effective:** For additional plan contributions and PBGC variable rate premiums for plan years beginning after Dec. 31, 2001, and before Jan. 1, 2004. (Com Rept, see ¶ 5025)

¶ 307. Individuals who reach age 50 by the end of the tax year are eligible to make catch-up contributions as of the beginning of the year

Code Sec. 414(v)(5), as amended by 2002 Act § 411(o)(7)
Generally effective: For contributions made in tax years beginning after Dec. 31, 2001
Committee Reports, see ¶ 5045

After 2001, under the 2001 Economic Growth and Tax Relief Reconciliation Act (EGTRRA §631), applicable employer plans can allow individuals who have reached age 50 to make additional "catch-up" elective contributions, up to the "applicable dollar amount" (see ¶ 309). A plan can allow eligible participants to make catch-up contributions without regard to various qualification requirements or limitations that ordinarily apply to "elective deferrals," and without having those catch-up contributions taken into account in applying certain requirements (see ¶ 311).

Under the Code, employees eligible to make catch-up contributions include only those for whom no other elective deferrals may be made to the plan for the plan year (but for the application of the catch-up contribution rule) because of the application of any limitation or restriction contained in either Code Sec. 414(v)(3) or the plan.

But under Prop Reg §1.414(v)-1 (on which taxpayers may rely), a participant who may be allowed to make "catch-up contributions" is an employee who:

(1) is eligible to make "elective deferrals" during the plan year, and

(2) has reached the age of 50 *before the close of the plan year.*

Thus, under the proposed regs, an employee who is *projected* to reach age 50 before the end of the calendar year is considered to be age 50 as of Jan. 1 of that year. Thus, all participants whose 50th birthday occurs in a calendar year are treated the same beginning on Jan. 1 of that year, *regardless* of:

- whether the participant survives to his 50th birthday,
- whether the participant terminates employment during the year, or
- the employer's choice of plan year.

(FTC 2d/FIN ¶ H-9240, ¶ H-9241; USTR ¶ 4144.26; TaxDesk ¶ 284,043; PCA ¶ 28,423; PE ¶ 414-4.26)

New Law. The 2002 Act provides that an eligible participant (who can be allowed to make catch-up contributions) is a plan participant who would attain age 50 by the end of the tax year. (Code Sec. 414(v)(5)(A) as amended by 2002 Act §411(o)(7)(B)) Thus, an individual who will reach age 50 by the end of the tax year can be an eligible participant as of the beginning of the tax year, rather than only at his 50th birthday. (Com Rept, see ¶ 5045)

> *observation:* Thus, the 2002 Act supports the approach taken in the proposed regs regarding the age requirement for catch-up contributions.

> *illustration:* John, a participant in a plan that allows catch-up contributions to eligible participants, is 49 years old and will be 50 on Dec. 31, 2002. John can make catch-up contributions in 2002.

FTC 2d References are to Federal Tax Coordinator 2d
FIN References are to RIA's Analysis of Federal Taxes: Income
USTR References are to United States Tax Reporter: Income, Estate & Gift, and Excise
PCA References are to the Pension Analysis on Checkpoint and CD-ROM, and in Pension Coordinator
PE References are to the Pension Explanations in Pension and Profit Sharing 2nd
EP References are to the Estate Planning Analysis on Checkpoint and CD-ROM, and in Estate Planning & Taxation Coordinator

Also, under the 2002 Act, an eligible participant is a plan participant for whom, because of specified limitations, no other elective deferrals may be made (but for the catch-up contribution rules) for the plan year *or other applicable year.* (Code Sec. 414(v)(5)(B) as amended by 2002 Act §411(o)(7)(C))

> **✔️** *observation:* This provision reflects the fact (not addressed in the proposed regs) that the limitations that may be exceeded under the catch-up contribution rules are respectively based on the plan year and other years, e.g., a calendar year.

☐ **Effective:** For contributions made in tax years beginning after Dec. 31, 2001. (2002 Act § 411(x))

¶ 308. Additional elective deferrals that don't exceed catch-up contribution limit are excludable from eligible participant's income

Code Sec. 402(g)(1)(C), as amended by 2002 Act § 411(o)(1)
Generally effective: For contributions made in tax years beginning after Dec. 31, 2001
Committee Reports, see ¶ 5045

Under certain salary reduction arrangements (i.e., a Code Sec. 401(k) cash or deferred arrangement, a Code Sec. 403(b) tax-sheltered annuity, a salary reduction simplified employee pension, and/or a SIMPLE IRA plan), in lieu of receiving cash, an employee may elect to receive compensation as plan contributions—i.e., as "elective deferrals."

Under Code Sec. 402(g), the maximum annual amount of *excludable* elective deferrals that an individual can make is $11,000 (for 2002). This amount increases annually, to $15,000 in 2006, after which it will be increased based on increases in the cost-of-living. (FTC 2d/FIN ¶ H-9151; USTR ¶ 4024; TaxDesk ¶ 284,025; PCA ¶ 28,402; PE ¶ 402-4)

After 2001, under the 2001 Economic Growth and Tax Relief Reconciliation Act (EGTRRA §631), applicable employer plans can allow individuals who have reached age 50 to make additional "catch-up" elective contributions (without regard to the qualification requirements or limitations that ordinarily apply to "elective deferrals"), up to the "applicable dollar amount." The applicable dollar amount under the catch-up contribution rules is $1,000 for 2002 ($500 for elective deferrals under SIMPLE 401(k) plans and SIMPLE IRA plans). The applicable dollar amounts are scheduled to increase annually until they reach $5,000 and $2,500, respectively, in 2006. These amounts will be adjusted for increases in the cost-of-living after 2006. (FTC 2d/FIN ¶ H-9240; USTR ¶ 4144.26; TaxDesk ¶ 284,043; PCA ¶ 28,423; PE ¶ 414-4.26)

Before the 2002 Act, the catch-up contribution rules in Code Sec. 414(v) did *not* specify that catch-up contributions are excludable from income. But Prop Reg

§1.414(v)-1 (on which taxpayers may rely), provided that catch-up contributions are excludable from income if they don't exceed the applicable dollar amount for catch-up contributions (under Code Sec. 414(v)(2)). Under the proposed regs, the amount of an eligible participant's elective deferrals—under *all* applicable employer plans in which the participant participates for a tax year—that is excludable from gross income cannot exceed the applicable dollar amount for the tax year. Under the proposed regs, an eligible participant can exclude elective deferrals under plans of two or more employers if the total amount of the elective deferrals doesn't exceed the Code Sec. 402(g) limits by more than the applicable dollar amount limiting catch-up contributions. This exclusion applies even if, taken separately, the participant's elective deferrals don't exceed the Code Sec. 402(g) limits under any of the plans, so that none of the plans treat the elective deferrals as catch-up contributions. (FTC 2d/FIN ¶ H-9240; USTR ¶ 4144.26; TaxDesk ¶ 284,043; PCA ¶ 28,423; PE ¶ 414-4.26)

New Law. The 2002 Act provides that elective deferrals that exceed the otherwise applicable Code Sec. 402(g) limit ($11,000 for 2002) are excludable from income to the extent that they don't exceed the applicable dollar amount under the catch-up contribution rules for the tax year. (Code Sec. 402(g)(1)(C) as amended by 2002 Act §411(o)(1))

> *observation:* Thus, the 2002 Act adopts the position taken in the prop regs providing for the exclusion of catch-up contributions.

> *observation:* As a result, the excludable amount of elective deferrals for a tax year is the Code Sec. 402(g) limit plus the year's applicable dollar amount under the catch-up contribution rules.

> *illustration (1):* Ally, who has reached age 50, participates in a 401(k) plan that allows participants who have reached age 50 to make catch-up contributions, up to the applicable dollar amount for the year. The 401(k) plan is not a SIMPLE 401(k) plan. In 2002, Ally elects to have $12,000 of salary reduced and contributed to the plan. Ally doesn't make any other elective deferrals in 2002. Because $12,000, the sum of the Code Sec. 402(g) limit for 2002 ($11,000) and the 2002 applicable dollar amount under the catch-up contribution rules ($1,000), doesn't exceed Ally's $12,000 of elective deferrals for 2002, none of these elective deferrals are includible in Ally's income.

FTC 2d References are to Federal Tax Coordinator 2d
FIN References are to RIA's Analysis of Federal Taxes: Income
USTR References are to United States Tax Reporter: Income, Estate & Gift, and Excise
PCA References are to the Pension Analysis on Checkpoint and CD-ROM, and in Pension Coordinator
PE References are to the Pension Explanations in Pension and Profit Sharing 2nd
EP References are to the Estate Planning Analysis on Checkpoint and CD-ROM, and in Estate Planning & Taxation Coordinator

The exclusion from income for catch-up contributions applies regardless of the treatment of the elective deferrals by the applicable employer plan under the catch-up contribution rules. (Code Sec. 402(g)(1)(C))

> *observation:* This Code change reflects the rule provided under the proposed regs (see above). Thus, if an employee who is over age 50 makes elective deferrals under plans maintained by more than one employer, the amount of the employee's elective deferrals that exceeds the Code Sec. 402(g) limit for the year may be excludable under the catch-up contribution rules—even if none of the elective deferrals under any one of the employers' plans (separately considered) exceeded the Code Sec. 402(g) limit for the year.

Thus, the exclusion limit applies without regard to whether an individual made catch-up contributions under plans maintained by more than one employer. (Com Rept, see ¶ 5045)

> *illustration (2):* A catch-up eligible participant (P) participates in 401(k) plans of two different employers, X Corp and Y Corp. P is 52 years of age. For 2002, the Code Sec. 402(g) limit is $11,000 and the applicable dollar catch-up limit is $1,000 (a $12,000 combined limit). No other limits apply. P elects to defer $7,000 under the X Corp plan, and $5,000 under the Y Corp plan, so that P's total elective deferrals for the year are $12,000. Because the individual amount deferred under each plan is less than the Code Sec. 402(g) limit, neither plan treats any part of these amounts as catch-up contributions. Nevertheless, none of the $12,000 of elective deferrals is includible in P's gross income, because the combined Code Sec. 402(g) and catch-up contribution limit ($12,000) has not been exceeded.

> *observation:* Ordinarily, catch-up contributions are subtracted from elective deferrals in applying the plan's actual deferral percentage (ADP) test (i.e., the nondiscrimination test for elective deferrals under a Code Sec. 401(k) cash or deferred arrangement). But the plan's ADP test would not have to be rerun to disregard elective deferrals that an individual (but not the plan) treats as catch-up contributions, as in illustration (2) above.

☐ **Effective:** For contributions made in tax years beginning after Dec. 31, 2001. (2002 Act § 411(x))

¶ 309. Plan's catch-up contribution limit must be applied on an aggregate basis, applying the controlled group rules

Code Sec. 414(v)(2)(D), as amended by 2002 Act § 411(o)(3)
Generally effective: For contributions made in tax years beginning after Dec. 31, 2001
Committee Reports, see ¶ 5045

After 2001, under the 2001 Economic Growth and Tax Relief Reconciliation Act (EGTRRA §631), applicable employer plans can allow individuals who have reached age 50 to make additional "catch-up" elective contributions (without regard to the qualification requirements or limitations that ordinarily apply to "elective deferrals"). A plan must not permit catch-up contributions for any year in an amount greater than the "applicable dollar amount." The applicable dollar amount under the catch-up contribution rules is $1,000 for 2002 ($500 for elective deferrals under simple 401(k) plans and SIMPLE IRA plans). The applicable dollar amounts are scheduled to increase annually until they reach $5,000 and $2,500, respectively, in 2006. These amounts will be adjusted for increases in the cost-of-living, after 2006.

According to Prop Reg §1.414(v)-1 (on which taxpayers may rely), if elective deferrals under more than one applicable employer plan of an employer are aggregated for purposes of applying a statutory limit, then the aggregate of the elective deferrals treated as catch-up contributions by reason of exceeding that statutory limit under all of these applicable employer plans, must not exceed the applicable dollar limit for the tax year. (FTC 2d/FIN ¶ H-9240, ¶ H-9244; USTR ¶ 4144.26; TaxDesk ¶ 284,043; PCA ¶ 28,423; PE ¶ 414-4.26)

New Law. Under the 2002 Act, for purposes of determining the limitation on the amount of catch-up contributions that a plan can permit, the following plans maintained by the same "employer" (see below) are treated as a single plan:

(1) a Code Sec. 401(a) qualified plan;

(2) a Code Sec. 403(b) tax-sheltered annuity;

(3) a Code Sec. 408(k) simplified employer pension (SEP); and

(4) a Code Sec. 408(p) SIMPLE IRA plan.

For this purpose, an "employer" is determined under the controlled group rules under Code Sec. 414(b) (for a controlled group of corporations), Code Sec. 414(c) (for a group of partnerships, etc., under common control), and affiliated service groups (under Code Sec. 414(m)), and regs IRS issues under Code Sec. 414(o).

All governmental Code Sec. 457 eligible deferred compensation plans maintained by the same employer are treated as a single plan. (Code Sec. 414(v)(2)(D) as amended by 2002 Act §411(o)(3))

> *observation:* Thus, the *total* of an individual's elective deferrals under all of an employer's 401(k) plans, 403(b) contracts, and SEPs, or an employer's SIMPLE IRA plan—including plans maintained by members of

---

FTC 2d References are to Federal Tax Coordinator 2d

FIN References are to RIA's Analysis of Federal Taxes: Income

USTR References are to United States Tax Reporter: Income, Estate & Gift, and Excise

PCA References are to the Pension Analysis on Checkpoint and CD-ROM, and in Pension Coordinator

PE References are to the Pension Explanations in Pension and Profit Sharing 2nd

EP References are to the Estate Planning Analysis on Checkpoint and CD-ROM, and in Estate Planning & Taxation Coordinator

the employer's controlled group—must be taken into account by the plan in determining whether the amount of an individual's catch-up contributions exceeds the applicable dollar amount for the tax year.

⚫️*observation:* If an individual is allowed to make elective deferrals in excess of the applicable dollar amount, then this will be taken into account in applying Code Sec. 401(a)(30), and could cause the plan to be disqualified (see ¶ 311). Thus, the failure of an employer's plan to restrict, to the applicable dollar amount, an employee's elective deferrals under *all* plans that must be aggregated and that are maintained by *any member* of the employer's controlled group, could jeopardize the plan's qualification.

⚫️*observation:* Thus, the 2002 Act adopts the approach taken in the proposed regs.

☐ **Effective:** For contributions made in tax years beginning after Dec. 31, 2001. (2002 Act § 411(x))

¶ 310. Governmental section 457 plan participants can make catch-up contributions equal to the greater of the amount allowed under Code Sec. 414(v) or under Code Sec. 457

Code Sec. 414(v)(6)(C), as amended by 2002 Act § 411(o)(8)
Code Sec. 457(e)(18), as amended by 2002 Act § 411(o)(9)
Generally effective: For contributions made in tax years beginning after Dec. 31, 2001
Committee Reports, see ¶ 5045

After 2001, under the 2001 Economic Growth and Tax Relief Reconciliation Act (EGTRRA §631), "applicable employer plans" can allow individuals who have reached age 50 to make additional "catch-up" elective contributions, up to the "applicable dollar amount" (see ¶ 309). A plan can allow eligible participants to make catch-up contributions without regard to various qualification requirements or limitations that ordinarily apply to "elective deferrals," and without having those catch-up contributions taken into account in applying certain requirements (see ¶ 311). A governmental Code Sec. 457 eligible deferred compensation plan is an "applicable employer plan" that can allow eligible participants to make additional catch-up contributions. (FTC 2d/FIN ¶ H-9240; USTR ¶ 4144.26; TaxDesk ¶ 284,043; PCA ¶ 28,423; PE ¶ 414-4.26)

Under Code Sec. 457(b)(2), a Code Sec. 457 eligible deferred compensation plan must provide that the maximum amount which may be deferred under the plan for a tax year may not exceed the lesser of:

(1) the "applicable dollar amount" ($11,000 in 2002, increasing annually until it reaches $15,000 in 2006, after which it will be adjusted for increases in the cost-of-living), or

(2) 100% of the participant's "includible compensation."

Under Code Sec. 457(b)(3), as a catch-up rule for one or more of a participant's last three tax years ending before the participant reaches normal retirement age, an eligible Code Sec. 457 plan can provide that the plan ceiling is the lesser of:

(1) twice the applicable dollar amount in effect for that tax year, or

(2) the sum of:

(a) the regular plan ceiling for the tax year, plus

(b) the regular plan ceiling that has not been used under the regular plan ceiling or under this catch-up provision for "prior tax years."

> *illustration:* In 2002, P is a participant in a governmental section 457 plan in which the ceiling on deferrals is $11,000 (or 100% of compensation, if less). P is 64 years old in 2002. Normal retirement age under the plan is 65. The plan contains a limited catch-up provision. In the ten years of his participation in the plan, P has deferred a total of $500 less than the aggregate annual maximums allowed. P elects to defer up to the maximum permitted for 2002 under the limited catch-up provision. For 2002, P had includible compensation of $60,000 (so that the deferral ceiling without limited catch-up was $11,000). P may elect to defer the *lesser of* (i) $22,000 (i.e., twice the sum of the applicable dollar amount for 2002), or (ii) the sum of: (a) $11,000, and (b) $500. Thus, for 2002, P may defer $11,500.

Under Code Sec. 457(c), the maximum amount of any individual's compensation which may be deferred under a Code Sec. 457 plan during any tax year must not exceed the maximum under the Code Sec. 457(b)(2) applicable dollar amount (see above), or the catch-up amount under Code Sec. 457(b)(3) (see above). (FTC 2d/FIN ¶ H-3320; USTR ¶ 4574; TaxDesk ¶ 135,516; PCA ¶ 40,421; PE ¶ 457-4)

For a governmental Code Sec. 457 plan, the pre-2002 Act rules that otherwise allow catch-up contributions (under Code Sec. 414(v)) would not have applied to any eligible participant for any tax year for which catch-up contributions were permitted under the Code Sec. 457 rules (i.e., during the three final tax years ending

---

FTC 2d References are to Federal Tax Coordinator 2d
FIN References are to RIA's Analysis of Federal Taxes: Income
USTR References are to United States Tax Reporter: Income, Estate & Gift, and Excise
PCA References are to the Pension Analysis on Checkpoint and CD-ROM, and in Pension
    Coordinator
PE References are to the Pension Explanations in Pension and Profit Sharing 2nd
EP References are to the Estate Planning Analysis on Checkpoint and CD-ROM, and in
    Estate Planning & Taxation Coordinator

before an individual attains normal retirement age). (FTC 2d/FIN ¶ H-9240; USTR ¶ 4144.26; TaxDesk ¶ 284,043; PCA ¶ 28,423; PE ¶ 414-4.26)

> **⊘ observation:** Thus, under pre-2002 Act law, during the three final tax years ending before an individual reached normal retirement age, he would not have been allowed to make catch-up contributions under Code Sec. 414(v) under a governmental Code Sec. 457 plan—even in a year when the Code Sec. 414(v) catch-up rules would have allowed a greater amount of elective deferrals than the Code Sec. 457(b)(3) catch-up rules.

New Law. Under the 2002 Act, the Code Sec. 414(v) catch-up contribution rules don't apply to a participant for any year for which a higher limitation applies to the participant under the governmental Code Sec. 457 plan catch-up provisions, under Code Sec. 457(b)(3) (see below). (Code Sec. 414(v)(6)(C) as amended by 2002 Act §411(o)(8))

For a Code Sec. 414(v) eligible participant who is a participant in a governmental Code Sec. 457 plan, the Code Sec. 457(b)(3) and Code Sec. 457(c) limits on elective deferrals during one or more of the participant's last three years before reaching normal retirement age is the *greater of:*

(1) the sum of—

(a) the plan ceiling established for purposes of the elective deferral limit under Code Sec. 457 *without regard* to the Code Sec. 457(b)(3) catch-up rules, plus

(b) the "applicable dollar amount" (i.e., the catch-up contribution limit) for the tax year under Code Sec. 414(v)(2)(B)(i); *or*

(2) the amount determined under the Code Sec. 457(b)(3) or Code Sec. 457(c) (without regard to this provision, i.e, Code Sec. 457(e)(18)). (Code Sec. 457(e)(18) as amended by 2002 Act §411(o)(9))

Thus, the 2002 Act provides that a participant in a governmental Code Sec. 457 plan can make catch-up contributions in an amount equal to the greater of the amount permitted under the Code Sec. 414(v) rules and the amount permitted under the Code Sec. 457 plan rules. (Com Rept, see ¶ 5045)

> **⊘ illustration:** In 2002, P is a participant in a governmental section 457 plan in which the ceiling on deferrals is $11,000 (or 100% of compensation, if less). P is 64 years old in 2002. Normal retirement age under the plan is 65. The plan contains a limited catch-up provision. In the ten years of his participation in the plan, P has deferred a total of $500 less than the aggregate annual maximums allowed. P elects to defer up to the maximum amount permitted for 2002 under the limited catch-up provision. For 2002, P had includible compensation of $60,000. P is also an eligible participant for purposes of the Code Sec. 414(v) catch-up contribution rules. Thus, as provided in the 2002 Act, for 2002, under Code Sec. 457(e)(18), P would be able to elect deferrals of *the greater of :*

(1) $12,000 (which is the sum of (i) $11,000 (the plan ceiling without regard to the 457 catch-up rules) and (ii) $1,000, P's applicable dollar amount under Code Sec. 414(v); *or*

(2) $11,500, which is the amount that P could defer under Code Sec. 457(b)(3) and (c) without regard to the 457(e)(18) (see Illustration above). Thus, under 414(v)(6)(C), P can elect to defer $12,000 in 2002 (rather than $11,500, as under Code Sec. 457(b)(3)).

☐ **Effective:** For contributions made in tax years beginning after Dec. 31, 2001. (2002 Act § 411(x))

¶ 311. List of qualification requirements that don't apply to catch-up contribution is revised

Code Sec. 414(v)(3)(A)(i), as amended by 2002 Act § 411(o)(4)
Code Sec. 414(v)(3)(B), as amended by 2002 Act § 411(o)(5)
Generally effective: For contributions made in tax years beginning after Dec. 31, 2001
Committee Reports, see ¶ 5045

After 2001, under the 2001 Economic Growth and Tax Relief Reconciliation Act (EGTRRA §631), applicable employer plans can allow individuals who have reached age 50 to make additional "catch-up" elective contributions, up to the "applicable dollar amount" (see ¶ 309). A plan can allow eligible participants to make catch-up contributions without regard to various qualification requirements or limitations that ordinarily apply to "elective deferrals," and without having those catch-up contributions taken into account in applying certain requirements.

Thus, the amount of catch-up contributions that an eligible participant can make for a year (i) is not subject to specified contribution limits under the Code, and (ii) is not taken into account in applying other contribution limits.

Also (except for the rules on the availability of the rules for catch-up contributions to all of an employer's eligible participants, see ¶ 312), just because an applicable employer plan allows a catch-up eligible participant to make catch-up contributions, doesn't mean the plan will be treated as failing specified nondiscrimination requirements. (FTC 2d/FIN ¶ H-9240, ¶ H-9247, ¶ H-9247.1; USTR ¶ 4144.26; TaxDesk ¶ 284,043, ¶ 284,045; PCA ¶ 28,423, ¶ 28,425; PE ¶ 414-4.26)

FTC 2d References are to Federal Tax Coordinator 2d
FIN References are to RIA's Analysis of Federal Taxes: Income
USTR References are to United States Tax Reporter: Income, Estate & Gift, and Excise
PCA References are to the Pension Analysis on Checkpoint and CD-ROM, and in Pension Coordinator
PE References are to the Pension Explanations in Pension and Profit Sharing 2nd
EP References are to the Estate Planning Analysis on Checkpoint and CD-ROM, and in Estate Planning & Taxation Coordinator

New Law. The 2002 Act revises the list of requirements that don't apply to catch-up contributions, as follows, to include requirements for:

... the exclusion for elective deferrals (under Code Sec. 401(a)(30));

... contributions to SEPs (under Code Sec. 402(h));

... tax-sheltered annuities (under Code Sec. 403(b));

... IRAs, SEPs, and SIMPLE plans (under Code Sec. 408);

... plan contributions (under Code Sec. 415(c)); and

... deferrals under section 457 plans (under Code Sec. 457(b)(2), determined without regard to Code Sec. 457(b)(3)). (Code Sec. 414(v)(3)(A)(i) as amended by 2002 Act §411(o)(4))

> *observation:* The above requirements also don't take into account catch-up contributions in applying these limitations to other contributions or benefits.

> *observation:* Thus, under the 2002 Act, the otherwise applicable limitations to which catch-up contributions are not subject has been revised to include:
>
> ... Code Sec. 401(a)(30) instead of Code Sec. 402(g);
>
> ... Code Sec. 408 instead of Code Sec. 408(k) and Code Sec. 408(p);
>
> ... Code Sec. 415(c) instead of Code Sec. 415; and
>
> ... Code Sec. 457(b)(2) (determined without regard to Code Sec. 457(b)(3), the catch-up provision for Code Sec. 457 eligible deferred compensation plans), instead of Code Sec. 457.

> *observation:* The limitations to which catch-up contributions are not subject no longer include the deduction provisions of Code Sec. 404(a) and Code Sec. 404(h).

The Technical Explanation of the 2002 Act says that the changes reflect the fact that catch-up contributions can be made only to a defined contribution plan, not a defined benefit plan. (Com Rept, see ¶ 5045)

> *observation:* Thus, only Code Sec. 415(c) (the limitation on contributions under defined contribution plans) is relevant to catch-up contributions, and not all of Code Sec. 415.

The Technical Explanation of the 2002 Act also says that the changes reflect statutory changes made by the 2002 Act. (Com Rept, see ¶ 5045) *observation:* Thus, it is the qualification requirement under Code Sec. 401(a)(30) to which catch-up contributions are not subject. The Code Sec. 402(g) exclusion provision is refined elsewhere (see ¶ 308), as is the limitation on the amount of allowable deferrals under a Code Sec. 457 eligible deferred compensation plan (see ¶ 310).

observation: Under Prop Regs §1.414(v)-1 (on which taxpayers may rely), catch-up contributions "won't be taken into account" in applying Code Sec. 401(a)(30). But the proposed regs define catch-up contributions to not exceed the applicable dollar amount. Thus, if an individual *is* allowed to make elective deferrals in excess of the applicable dollar amount, then these elective deferrals are not catch-up contributions, and they *will* be taken into account in applying Code Sec. 401(a)(30), and thus could cause the plan to be disqualified.

The 2002 Act seems to have the same effect, even though, under the 2002 Act, catch-up contributions are not subject to Code Sec. 401(a)(30). Thus, if a plan allows participants to make elective deferrals *in excess of* the applicable dollar limit, apparently Code Sec. 401(a)(30) *would* apply to this excess, and thus could jeopardize the plan's qualification.

Inapplicable nondiscrimination requirements. The 2002 Act also revises the list of nondiscrimination rules that a plan won't be treated as failing to meet because of allowing catch-up contributions to include:

. . . the Code Sec. 401(a)(4) nondiscrimination rules;

. . . the actual deferral percentage (ADP) test for CODAs (under Code Sec. 401(k)(3));

. . . the SIMPLE 401(k) plan rules (under Code Sec. 401(k)(11));

. . . the nondiscrimination test for tax-sheltered annuities (under Code Sec. 403(b)(12));

. . . the SEP rules (under Code Sec. 408(k));

. . . the minimum coverage requirements (under Code Sec. 410(b)); and

. . . the top-heavy plan rules (under Code Sec. 416). (Code Sec. 414(v)(3)(B) as amended by 2002 Act §411(o)(5))

observation: But a plan that allows catch-up contributions must still satisfy the requirement to allow all of an employer's eligible participants

---

FTC 2d References are to Federal Tax Coordinator 2d
FIN References are to RIA's Analysis of Federal Taxes: Income
USTR References are to United States Tax Reporter: Income, Estate & Gift, and Excise
PCA References are to the Pension Analysis on Checkpoint and CD-ROM, and in Pension
   Coordinator
PE References are to the Pension Explanations in Pension and Profit Sharing 2nd
EP References are to the Estate Planning Analysis on Checkpoint and CD-ROM, and in
   Estate Planning & Taxation Coordinator

to make catch-up contributions (i.e., the universal availability requirement).

observation: The 2002 Act eliminates the following nondiscrimination requirements from the list above, and thus, these rules *can* apply to catch-up contributions:

. . . the minimum participation requirements (under Code Sec. 401(a)(26)),

. . . the alternative nondiscrimination rules for CODAs (under Code Sec. 401(k)(12)), and

. . . the SIMPLE plan rules (under Code Sec. 408(p)).

☐ **Effective:** For contributions made in tax years beginning after Dec. 31, 2001. (2002 Act § 411(x))

¶ 312. Plans in transition period under nondiscrimination rules for certain dispositions and acquisitions are not subject to universal availability requirement for catch-up contributions

Code Sec. 414(v)(4)(B), as amended by 2002 Act § 411(o)(6)
Generally effective: For contributions made in tax years beginning after Dec. 31, 2001
Committee Reports, see ¶ 5045

After 2001, under the 2001 Economic Growth and Tax Relief Reconciliation Act (EGTRRA §631), applicable employer plans can allow individuals who have reached age 50 to make additional "catch-up" elective contributions, up to the "applicable dollar amount" (see ¶ 309). A plan can allow eligible participants to make catch-up contributions without regard to various qualification requirements or limitations that ordinarily apply to "elective deferrals," and without having those catch-up contributions taken into account in applying certain requirements (see ¶ 311).

An applicable employer plan that offers catch-up contributions (and that is otherwise subject to the Code Sec. 401(a)(4) nondiscrimination requirements with respect to benefits, rights, and features) will be treated as failing to meet those requirements unless the plan allows all eligible participants to make the same election with respect to Code Sec. 414(v) catch-up contributions. This is referred to as the "universal availability" requirement. Under this rule, all plans maintained by employers who are treated as a single employer under the controlled group rules are treated as a single plan under the universal availability requirement. (FTC 2d/FIN ¶ H-9240, ¶ H-9248; USTR ¶ 4144.26; TaxDesk ¶ 284,043; PCA ¶ 28,423, ¶ 28,426; PE ¶ 414-4.26)

If a person becomes, or ceases to be, a member of a controlled group, or an affiliated service group, the Code Sec. 410(b) coverage rules will be treated as having been met during a transition period with respect to any plan covering employees of any member of these groups if modified coverage requirements are met. This rule also applies for purposes of the minimum participation rules (under Code Sec. 401(a)(26)). (FTC 2d/FIN ¶ H-5409; USTR ¶ 4104.14; PCA ¶ 23,210; PE ¶ 410-4.14)

Under Prop Reg §1.414(v)-1 (on which taxpayers may rely), an applicable employer plan doesn't fail to comply with the universal availability requirement merely because another applicable employer plan does not provide for catch-up contributions, if: (1) the other applicable employer plan becomes maintained by the employer by reason of a merger, acquisition or similar transaction; and (2) the other applicable employer plan is amended to provide for catch-up contributions as soon as practicable, but no later than by the end of the transition period described in Code Sec. 410(b)(6)(C). (FTC 2d/FIN ¶ H-9240; H-9248.1; USTR ¶ 4144.26; TaxDesk ¶ 284,043; PCA ¶ 28,423; PE ¶ 414-4.26)

New Law. Under the 2002 Act, a plan that becomes, or ceases to be, a member of a controlled group, or an affiliated service group (as described in Code Sec. 410(b)(6)(C)(i)), and which thus can satisfy the coverage requirements by meeting the modified rules of Code Sec. 410(b)(6)(C) during a transition period, won't be treated as a plan of the employer until the end of the expiration of the transition period (as described in Code Sec. 410(b)(6)(C)(ii)) with respect to that plan. (Code Sec. 414(v)(4)(B) as amended by 2002 Act §411(o)(6))

> **observation:** Thus, the universal availability requirement that catch-up contribution elections be available to all of the eligible participants in an employer's controlled group won't be violated if, during a transition period for a plan in a disposition or acquisition to which Code Sec. 410(b)(6)(C) applies, the otherwise eligible participants of that plan are not given the right to make catch-up contributions.

> **observation:** Thus, the 2002 Act takes an approach similar to the proposed regs.

☐ **Effective:** For contributions made in tax years beginning after Dec. 31, 2001. (2002 Act § 411(x))

FTC 2d References are to Federal Tax Coordinator 2d
FIN References are to RIA's Analysis of Federal Taxes: Income
USTR References are to United States Tax Reporter: Income, Estate & Gift, and Excise
PCA References are to the Pension Analysis on Checkpoint and CD-ROM, and in Pension Coordinator
PE References are to the Pension Explanations in Pension and Profit Sharing 2nd
EP References are to the Estate Planning Analysis on Checkpoint and CD-ROM, and in Estate Planning & Taxation Coordinator

¶ 313. Qualified plan distributions that are rolled over are treated as consisting first of taxable amounts

Code Sec. 402(c)(2), as amended by 2002 Act § 411(q)(2)
Generally effective: Distributions made after Dec. 31, 2001.
Committee Reports, see ¶ 5047

For distributions made after Dec. 31, 2001, under changes made by the 2001 Economic Growth and Tax Relief Reconciliation Act (EGTRRA §643), an individual is allowed to roll over the nontaxable portion of an eligible rollover distribution (i.e., the portion that would not be includible in income, even if it was not rolled over) to certain eligible retirement plans, if certain requirements are met. (FTC 2d/FIN ¶ H-11444; USTR ¶ 4024.04; TaxDesk ¶ 144,026; PCA ¶ 32,845; PE ¶ 402-4.04)

> **observation:** Thus, after 2001, if the balance of a participant's plan interest consisted of both taxable and nontaxable amounts, a rollover of an eligible rollover distribution could consist of both amounts that would be includible in income unless rolled over (taxable amounts) and nontaxable amounts. As a result, before the 2002 Act, an allocation between taxable and nontaxable amounts (presumably under the Code Sec. 72 annuity rules) would have been necessary:
>
> ... if there was a distribution of less than the total of the participant's plan interest, even if the entire amount distributed were rolled over; or
>
> ... if there was a distribution, whether of the participant's entire plan interest or only a portion of that interest, and less than the entire amount distributed were rolled over.
>
> If a participant received a distribution of his entire plan interest and rolled over the entire amount of the distribution, then no allocation would have been necessary until a distribution was made from the plan that received the rollover.

> **observation:** The determination of the taxable and nontaxable portion of a rollover, in the absence of a rule indicating that the rollover amount had to be allocated differently to taxable amounts, presumably would have been made on a pro rata basis, under the Code Sec. 72 annuity rules for amounts not received as an annuity. (FTC 2d/FIN ¶ H-11009; H-11026; USTR ¶ 724; 724.17; TaxDesk ¶ 141,006; 141,028; PCA ¶ 32,110; 32,127; PE ¶ 72-4)

> **observation:** Before 2002, if an individual's plan interest consisted of both taxable and nontaxable amounts, and the entire taxable amount was rolled over tax-free to an eligible retirement plan, the balance in the plan (i.e., the portion that was not rolled over) could have been distributed tax-free, since it consisted entirely of nontaxable amounts (e.g., investment in

the contract such as pre-tax employee contributions). And, if less than the entire taxable amount in the plan was distributed and rolled over, it was clear that the amount that was rolled over was from the taxable amount.

New Law. Under the 2002 Act, for amounts that were rolled over that consisted of both (i) amounts that would have been includible in income but for the rollover (taxable amounts), and (ii) amounts that would have not have been includible even if they had not been rolled over (nontaxable amounts), the amount transferred is treated as consisting first of the portion of the distribution that is includible in income (determined without regard to the rollover exclusion). (Code Sec. 402(c)(2) as amended by 2002 Act §411(q)(2))

illustration (1): Pat is a participant in a qualified retirement plan and has a plan interest valued at $100,000 on June 1. Pat had made $20,000 of employee (after-tax) contributions (a nontaxable amount). The balance of $80,000 is a taxable amount. On June 1, Pat receives a distribution of $50,000, which is rolled over to an IRA. Because the $50,000 that is rolled over is less than the taxable amount ($80,000) of Pat's plan interest, the entire $50,000 is treated as a taxable amount. Thus, when Pat receives a distribution from the IRA, the entire amount distributed (attributable to the $50,000 rolled over, plus earnings) will be taxable.

observation: Because the amount transferred from a plan in a rollover is treated as consisting first of taxable amounts, this will affect the basis of remaining amounts in the plan. Specifically, the amount rolled over that is treated as a taxable amount must be subtracted from the balance of the taxable amount remaining in the plan.

illustration (2): Jo Jo is a participant in a qualified retirement plan with a plan interest valued at $100,000 on July 1, with a nontaxable amount of $20,000 and a taxable amount of $80,000. If $60,000 is distributed on July 1 and rolled over tax-free, then the $60,000 distributed is treated as a taxable amount (since it is less than the taxable amount of $80,000 credited to Jo Jo). Thus, the $40,000 remaining in the plan ($100,000 − $60,000) consists of a taxable amount of $20,000 ($80,000 taxable amount − $60,000, the taxable amount distributed and rolled over) and a nontaxable amount of $20,000.

FTC 2d References are to Federal Tax Coordinator 2d

FIN References are to RIA's Analysis of Federal Taxes: Income

USTR References are to United States Tax Reporter: Income, Estate & Gift, and Excise

PCA References are to the Pension Analysis on Checkpoint and CD-ROM, and in Pension Coordinator

PE References are to the Pension Explanations in Pension and Profit Sharing 2nd

EP References are to the Estate Planning Analysis on Checkpoint and CD-ROM, and in Estate Planning & Taxation Coordinator

illustration (3): Gene is a participant (over age 59-1/2) in a qualified retirement plan and has a plan interest valued at $100,000 on Aug. 1. Of this interest, $40,000 is a nontaxable amount and $60,000 is a taxable amount. Gene receives a plan distribution of $50,000 and rolls over $20,000 tax-free to an IRA. The $20,000 rolled over to the IRA is considered to be a taxable amount. The rest of the distribution ($30,000) is currently subject to taxation under the Code Sec. 72 annuity rules. Under these rules, because the distribution is of an amount not received as an annuity, and it is considered received before the annuity starting date (since there *is* no annuity starting date), then the taxable portion of the $30,000 distribution that is not rolled over is $30,000 times the following fraction: $40,000 ($60,000 taxable amount − $20,000, the taxable amount rolled over) ÷ $80,000, the balance after the rollover ($100,000 − $20,000). Thus, $15,000 (($40,000/$80,000) × $30,000) of the distribution that wasn't rolled over ($30,000) is includible in Gene's income.

observation: The rule allocating the amount rolled over as coming first from taxable amounts means that, as under prior law, a distributee can (i) roll over tax-free the amount in a plan that otherwise would have been includible in income when received, and (ii) receive the balance tax-free (as a return of the nontaxable portion in the plan, e.g., employee contributions or other pre-tax amounts that comprise the investment in the contract).

illustration (4): Jamie is a participant in a qualified retirement plan with a plan interest valued at $200,000 on Sept 1. Jamie had made $50,000 of employee (after-tax) contributions (a nontaxable amount). The $150,000 balance in Jamie's plan account was a taxable amount. On Sept. 1, Jamie received a plan distribution of the entire $200,000. $150,000 was rolled over tax-free to an IRA. Because the $150,000 rolled over is treated as a taxable amount (since Jamie's plan interest had a taxable amount of $150,000), the rest of the distribution ($50,000) is tax-free, because it consists entirely of a nontaxable amount (i.e., a return of Jamie's investment of employee contributions).

☐ **Effective:** Distributions made after Dec. 31, 2001. (2002 Act § 411(x))

¶ 314. Direct rollovers of after-tax amounts from qualified retirement plans can be made only to defined contribution plans (and IRAs)

Code Sec. 401(a)(31)(C)(i), as amended by 2002 Act § 411(q)(1)
Generally effective: Distributions made after Dec. 31, 2001
Committee Reports, see ¶ 5047

Under the direct rollover rules, a qualified plan must provide that if a participant who receives an eligible rollover distribution elects to have the distribution paid directly to an "eligible retirement plan," and specifies the plan to which the distribution is to be paid, then the distribution must be made in the form of a direct trustee-to-trustee transfer (i.e., a direct rollover) to the plan specified.

As amended by the 2001 Economic Growth and Tax Relief Reconciliation Act (EGTRRA §643(a)), the direct rollover rules apply to the nontaxable portion of an eligible rollover distribution (as well as to the taxable portion)—but only if the plan to which the distribution is transferred:

(1) agrees to separately account for amounts transferred, including a separate accounting for the portion of the distribution which is includible in gross income and the portion which is not includible in gross income, or

(2) is an IRA.

(FTC 2d/FIN ¶ H-8251; USTR ¶ 4014.27; TaxDesk ¶ 144,037; PCA ¶ 26,652; PE ¶ 401-4.27)

Unlike the direct rollover rules for nontaxable (after-tax) amounts, the regular rollover rules specify that (except for amounts rolled over into an IRA) the nontaxable portion of an eligible rollover distribution can be rolled over (under specified conditions) *only* to a defined contribution plan. (FTC 2d/FIN ¶ H-11444; USTR ¶ 4024.04; TaxDesk ¶ 144,026; PCA ¶ 32,845; PE ¶ 402-4.04)

> *observation:* Apparently, the discrepancy between the rollover rules for eligible rollover distributions and the direct rollover requirements was inadvertent.

New Law. The 2002 Act clarifies that a qualified retirement plan must allow the distributee of an eligible rollover distribution to elect to have the nontaxable portion of the distribution transferred in a direct rollover to a plan that meets the separate accounting requirements, but (unless the transferee plan is a traditional IRA) *only if* the transferee plan is a qualified trust which is part of a plan which is a defined contribution plan. (Code Sec. 401(a)(31)(C)(i) as amended by 2002 Act §411(q)(1))

☐ **Effective:** Distributions made after Dec. 31, 2001. (2002 Act § 411(x))

¶ 315. Small employer pension plan startup costs credit applies to plans that are first effective after 2001, even if adopted before 2002

FTC 2d References are to Federal Tax Coordinator 2d
FIN References are to RIA's Analysis of Federal Taxes: Income
USTR References are to United States Tax Reporter: Income, Estate & Gift, and Excise
PCA References are to the Pension Analysis on Checkpoint and CD-ROM, and in Pension Coordinator
PE References are to the Pension Explanations in Pension and Profit Sharing 2nd
EP References are to the Estate Planning Analysis on Checkpoint and CD-ROM, and in Estate Planning & Taxation Coordinator

Code Sec. 45E, 2002 Act § 411(n)(2)
Generally effective: Qualified employer plans first effective after Dec. 31, 2001
Committee Reports, see ¶ 5044

Under pre-2002 Act law, an eligible employer can claim a credit in an amount equal to 50% of its qualified startup costs in each of the first three years of the plan, up to a $500 per year maximum. See FTC 2d/FIN ¶ L-15691; USTR ¶ 45E4; TaxDesk ¶ 384,061.

The small employer pension plan startup costs credit applied to costs paid or incurred in tax years beginning after Dec. 31, 2001, with respect to qualified employer plans *established* after Dec. 31, 2001. (FTC 2d/FIN ¶ L-15691; USTR ¶ 45E4; TaxDesk ¶ 384,061)

New Law. The 2002 Act provides that the small employer pension plan startup costs credit applies to costs paid or incurred in tax years beginning after Dec. 31, 2001, with respect to qualified employer plans *first effective* (rather than *established*, as under pre-2002 Act law) after Dec. 31, 2001. (2001 Economic Growth and Tax Relief Act § 619(d) as amended by 2002 Act § 411(n)(2))

The 2002 Act clarifies that the small business tax credit for new retirement plan expenses applies in the case of a plan first effective after Dec. 31, 2001, even if adopted on or before Dec. 31, 2001. (Com Rept, see ¶ 5044)

> *recommendation:* Taxpayers who adopted a small employer pension plan on or before Dec. 31, 2001 and are eligible to claim a credit for startup costs, but did not do so, should file an amended return if necessary in order to claim the credit. Calendar year corporate taxpayers generally must file on or before Mar. 15.

☐ **Effective:** Costs paid or incurred in tax years beginning after Dec. 31, 2001, with respect to qualified employer plans first effective after Dec. 31, 2001. (2002 Act § 411(x))

> *observation:* The above provision is effective as if included in 2001 Economic Growth and Tax Relief Act §619. This effective date, as provided in 2001 Economic Growth and Tax Relief Act §619(d), is also affected by 2002 Act §411(n)(2), as discussed above.

¶ 316. Aggregation rules for small employer pension plan startup costs credit are based on affiliated service group rules, not employee leasing rules

Code Sec. 45E(e)(1), as amended by 2002 Act § 411(n)(1)
Generally effective: For costs paid or incurred in tax years beginning after Dec. 31, 2001
Committee Reports, None

Under pre-2002 Act law, an eligible employer can claim a credit in an amount equal to 50% of its qualified startup costs in each of the first three years of the plan, up to a $500 per year maximum. See FTC 2d/FIN ¶ L-15691; USTR ¶ 45E4; TaxDesk ¶ 384,061.

For purposes of this credit, all persons treated as a single employer under Code Sec. 52(a) or Code Sec. 52(b) (which treat employees of certain employers as employed by the same employer for purposes of the work opportunity credit) are treated as one person. In addition, all persons treated as a single employer under Code Sec. 414(n) (dealing with the rules relating to employee leasing, see FTC 2d/FIN ¶ H-5600 *et seq.*; USTR ¶ 4144.19) or Code Sec. 414(o) (dealing with the issuance of regs under Code Sec. 414(n) and Code Sec. 414(m)) were treated as one person. (FTC 2d/FIN ¶ L-15699.1; USTR ¶ 45E4; TaxDesk ¶ 384,069.1)

New Law. For purpose of the aggregation rule applicable to the small employer pension plan startup costs credit, the 2002 Act provides that all persons treated as a single employer under Code Sec. 414(m) (dealing with the affiliated service group rules, see FTC 2d/FIN ¶ H-7950 *et seq.*; USTR ¶ 4144.05), rather than under the employee leasing rules of Code Sec. 414(n), are treated as one person. (Code Sec. 45E(e)(1) as amended by 2002 Act §411(n)(1))

Two or more employers are an "affiliated service group" where certain ownership interests exist and where the employees of one organization perform services for another organization within the group. If an affiliated service group exists, all employees of all members of the affiliated service group are considered employed by a single employer. See FTC 2d/FIN ¶ H-7950 *et seq.*; USTR ¶ 4144.05.

> *observation:* The aggregation rules affect not only whether related employers can each claim separate credits or can only claim one credit, but also whether an employer qualifies as an eligible employer (i.e., an employer that employs 100 or fewer employees who received at least $5,000 of compensation from the employer for the preceding year, see FTC 2d/FIN ¶ L-15692; USTR ¶ 45E4; TaxDesk ¶ 384,062) and can claim any credit.

☐ **Effective:** Costs paid or incurred in tax years beginning after Dec. 31, 2001, with respect to qualified employer plans first effective after Dec. 31, 2001. (2002 Act § 411(x))

> *observation:* The aggregation rule under 2002 Act law discussed above is effective as if included in 2001 Economic Growth and Tax Relief Act § 619. This effective date, as provided in 2001 Economic Growth and Tax

---

FTC 2d References are to Federal Tax Coordinator 2d
FIN References are to RIA's Analysis of Federal Taxes: Income
USTR References are to United States Tax Reporter: Income, Estate & Gift, and Excise
PCA References are to the Pension Analysis on Checkpoint and CD-ROM, and in Pension Coordinator
PE References are to the Pension Explanations in Pension and Profit Sharing 2nd
EP References are to the Estate Planning Analysis on Checkpoint and CD-ROM, and in Estate Planning & Taxation Coordinator

Relief Act § 619(d), is also amended by the 2002 Act, see ¶ 315. The above effective date incorporates this amendment.

¶ 317. Retirement contributions that qualify for saver's credit must be reduced by nontaxable distributions from qualified retirement plans, deferred compensation plans, or traditional IRAs

Code Sec. 25B(d)(2)(A), as amended by 2002 Act § 411(m)
Generally effective: Tax years beginning after Dec. 31, 2001
Committee Reports, see ¶ 5043

Eligible individuals are allowed a tax credit (the "saver's credit") equal to the applicable percentage (10% to 50%, depending on filing status and modified AGI) of up to $2,000 of the individual's qualified retirement savings contributions. (FTC 2d/FIN ¶ A-4701; USTR ¶ 25B4; TaxDesk ¶ 569,201)

The "qualified retirement savings contributions" for which the saver's credit is allowed equals the sum of:

. . . elective contributions to a Code Sec. 401(k) plan (including a SIMPLE 401(k)), a Code Sec. 403(b) annuity, an eligible deferred compensation arrangement of a state or local government (a "governmental 457 plan"), a SIMPLE IRA plan, or a salary reduction SEP;

. . . contributions to a traditional or Roth IRA; and

. . . voluntary after-tax employee contributions to a qualified retirement plan or Code Sec. 403(b) annuity.

(FTC 2d/FIN ¶ A-4703; USTR ¶ 25B4; TaxDesk ¶ 569,203)

Under pre-2002 Act law, with certain exceptions, an individual's qualified retirement savings contributions had to be reduced by the sum of:

. . . any distribution from a qualified retirement plan or eligible deferred compensation plan received by the individual during the testing period that is includible in gross income, and

. . . any distribution from a Roth IRA or a Roth account received by the individual during the testing period that isn't a qualified rollover contribution to a Roth IRA or a rollover to a Roth account.

(FTC 2d/FIN ¶ A-4704; USTR ¶ 25B4; TaxDesk ¶ 569,204)

> ⚟ *observation:* Thus, under pre-2002 Act law, distributions from a qualified retirement plan (including a traditional IRA) or a deferred compensation plan that weren't includible in gross income didn't reduce the amount of the credit.

New Law. The 2002 Act provides that an individual's qualified retirement savings contributions for purposes of the saver's credit must be reduced by the aggregate distributions received by the individual during the testing period from any entity of a type to which qualified contributions may be made. (Code Sec. 25B(d)(2)(A) as amended by 2002 Act §411(m))

> *observation:* This eliminates the requirement that distributions from a qualified retirement plan or deferred compensation plan be includible in gross income in order to reduce the amount of the credit (see below for rollovers).

Thus, contributions that qualify for the credit must be reduced by the amount of a distribution from a qualified retirement plan, an eligible deferred compensation plan, or a traditional IRA that is includible in income or consists of after-tax contributions. (Com Rept, see ¶ 5043)

> *illustration (1):* Taxpayer X makes a $2,000 elective contribution to a 401(k) plan. In the same tax year, X takes a $1,000 distribution from an IRA and doesn't roll it over. Half of the IRA distribution is taxable and half is a nontaxable return of after-tax contributions.
>
> Since an IRA is an entity to which qualified contributions may be made, the entire IRA distribution, including the nontaxable portion, will reduce the amount of the 401(k) contribution that qualifies for the saver's credit.

No reduction is required for the portion of any distribution that isn't includible in gross income by reason of a trustee-to-trustee transfer or a rollover distribution. (Code Sec. 25B(d)(2)(A)) This retains the pre-2002 Act rule that distributions that are rolled over to another retirement plan don't affect the credit. (Com Rept, see ¶ 5043)

> *illustration (2):* Taxpayer Y makes a $2,000 elective contribution to a 401(k) plan. In the same tax year, Y takes a $1,000 distribution from a qualified retirement plan and rolls it over into an IRA. Because the plan distribution was rolled over, it won't reduce the amount of the 401(k) contribution that qualifies for the saver's credit.

☐ **Effective:** Tax years beginning after Dec. 31, 2001. (2002 Act § 411(x))

FTC 2d References are to Federal Tax Coordinator 2d
FIN References are to RIA's Analysis of Federal Taxes: Income
USTR References are to United States Tax Reporter: Income, Estate & Gift, and Excise
PCA References are to the Pension Analysis on Checkpoint and CD-ROM, and in Pension
    Coordinator
PE References are to the Pension Explanations in Pension and Profit Sharing 2nd
EP References are to the Estate Planning Analysis on Checkpoint and CD-ROM, and in
    Estate Planning & Taxation Coordinator

¶ 318. ERISA's enforcement provisions and certain fiduciary responsibility requirements will apply to "deemed IRAs" in a manner similar to SEPs—after 2002

ERISA §4(c), as amended by 2002 Act §411(i)(2)
Generally effective: Plan years beginning after Dec. 31, 2002
Committee Reports, see ¶ 5039

Generally, any pension plan is covered under ERISA if it is an "employee bene-fit plan" established or maintained by an employer, or an employee organization, that is involved with commerce. An "employee benefit plan" is covered under Ti-tle I of ERISA if it is a plan, fund, or program that is established or maintained by an employer or an employee organization, and covers "employees," unless ERISA excludes the plan from coverage (e.g., church plans and government plans). Title I of ERISA includes reporting and disclosure, participation and vesting, funding, and fiduciary requirements, as well as administration and enforcement provisions.

IRAs are exempt from Title I of ERISA, except for IRAs that are considered to be pension plans. An IRA is not considered to be a pension plan covered by Title I of ERISA if certain requirements are met. However, even IRAs that are pension plans are exempt from ERISA's participation, vesting, and funding provisions. In contrast, simplified employee pensions (SEPs) as a rule *are* considered pension plans subject to ERISA. (PCA ¶ 48,108; 48,124; PE ¶ ER3-4.01)

> **observation:** IRAs that are considered pension plans (such as SEP-IRAs) are subject to ERISA's fiduciary responsibility requirements and ERISA's administration and enforcement provisions.

Under pre-2002 Act law, if a pension plan allows an employee to elect to make voluntary employee contributions to "deemed IRAs"—separate accounts and an-nuities that meet the IRA requirements (as provided under Code Sec. 408(q), cre-ated under the 2001 Economic Growth and Tax Relief Reconciliation Act (EGTRRA §602), then those deemed IRAs won't be treated as part of the plan (or as a separate pension plan) for purposes of any provision of Title I of ERISA. Thus, a deemed IRA, including all contributions to it, wouldn't have been subject to the ERISA reporting and disclosure, participation, vesting, funding require-ments—or the ERISA enforcement requirements applicable to the employer plan.

However, deemed IRAs will be subject to ERISA §403(c) (requiring that plan benefits not inure to the benefit of the employer), ERISA §404 (the fiduciary re-sponsibility requirements), and ERISA §405 (providing for co-fiduciary liability). (PCA ¶ 48,075, ¶ 48,115, ¶ 48,124; PE ¶ ER101-4, ¶ ER301-4, ¶ ER401-4.05, ¶ ER403.-4.02, ¶ ER405-4.01)

New Law. For plan years beginning after Dec. 31, 2002, under the 2002 Act, a deemed IRA will also be subject to part 5 of Title I of ERISA, relating to ERISA's administration and enforcement (in addition to being subject to ERISA §403(c) , ERISA §404 , and ERISA §405 , see above). (ERISA §4(c) as amended by 2002 Act §411(i)(2)(A)) The 2002 Act also clarifies that deemed IRAs will be subject to ERISA §403(c) , ERISA §404 , and ERISA §405 in a manner similar to simplified employee pensions (SEPs). (ERISA §4(c))

> *observation:* SEPs are pension plans subject to ERISA even though they are IRAs. Similarly, deemed IRAs will be considered pension plans subject to ERISA's provisions, except where exempted. Presumably, just as the plan administrator of a SEP is subject to ERISA's fiduciary responsibility rules, the plan administrator of a qualified employer plan which allows contributions to a deemed IRA will be subject to ERISA §403(c) , ERISA §404 , and ERISA §405 . Thus, except insofar as a participant exercises control over the assets in his account (as provided for under ERISA §404(c)), the plan administrator presumably will have the duty to prevent plan assets from inuring to the benefit of the employer, and will be subject to the prudent man standard of care to discharge his duties: (i) consistent with the "exclusive purpose" rule, (ii) with the care, skill, prudence, and diligence due under the prevailing circumstances, (iii) to diversify investments so as to minimize risk of large losses, and (iv) to act in accordance with plan documents. Further, the plan administrator of a plan that allows for deemed IRAs will be liable for breaches of fiduciary duty by any co-fiduciary.

☐ **Effective:** Plan years beginning after Dec. 31, 2002. (2002 Act § 411(x))

¶ 319. Types of governmental plans that can provide deemed IRAs are clarified—after 2002

Code Sec. 408(q)(3)(A), as amended by 2002 Act § 411(i)(1)
Generally effective: Plan years beginning after Dec. 31, 2002
Committee Reports, see ¶ 5039

The 2001 Economic Growth and Tax Relief Reconciliation Act (EGTRRA §602(b)) provided that for plan years beginning after Dec. 31, 2002, a separate account or annuity in a "qualified employer plan" (as defined below) will be considered a "deemed IRA," i.e., it will be treated in the same manner as an individual retirement account or annuity (i.e., an IRA) for all purposes of the Code, and not as a qualified employer plan, if, generally:

FTC 2d References are to Federal Tax Coordinator 2d
FIN References are to RIA's Analysis of Federal Taxes: Income
USTR References are to United States Tax Reporter: Income, Estate & Gift, and Excise
PCA References are to the Pension Analysis on Checkpoint and CD-ROM, and in Pension Coordinator
PE References are to the Pension Explanations in Pension and Profit Sharing 2nd
EP References are to the Estate Planning Analysis on Checkpoint and CD-ROM, and in Estate Planning & Taxation Coordinator

(i) the "qualified employer plan" elects to allow employees to make "voluntary employee contributions" (designated as such by the employees) to a separate account or annuity established under the plan, and

(ii) under the terms of the qualified employer plan, the separate account or annuity meets the requirements for a regular IRA or Roth IRA.

Under the "deemed IRA" rules, *contributions* to the separate plan account or annuity (i.e., the deemed IRA) will be treated as contributions to an IRA, and not to the qualified employer plan. And a qualified employer plan that establishes and maintains a deemed IRA program won't fail to meet the Code requirements for a qualified employer plan as a result.

A "qualified employer plan" (which can maintain a deemed IRA program) means:

(a) a Code Sec. 401(a) qualified plan which includes a trust exempt from tax under Code Sec. 501(a);

(b) a Code Sec. 403(a) qualified annuity;

(c) a Code Sec. 403(b) tax-sheltered annuity;

(d) any qualified government plan; and

(e) an otherwise nonqualified plan that is a governmental Code Sec. 457 eligible deferred compensation plan.

(FTC 2d/FIN ¶ H-12280; USTR ¶ 4084.07; TaxDesk ¶ 283,080; PCA ¶ 35,181; PE ¶ 408-4.07)

Under pre-2002 Act law, it wasn't clear what types of government plans were qualified employer plans that could maintain a deemed IRA program.

New Law. The 2002 Act clarifies that, for purposes of the deemed IRA rules, a "qualified employer plan" also includes the following types of plans maintained by a *governmental* employer:

(1) a Code Sec. 401(a) qualified plan which includes a trust exempt from tax under Code Sec. 501(a);

(2) a Code Sec. 403(a) qualified annuity;

(3) a Code Sec. 403(b) tax-sheltered annuity; and

(4) a Code Sec. 457 eligible deferred compensation plan. (Com Rept, see ¶ 5039)

Specifically, a qualified plan will be defined under Code Sec. 72(p)(4)(A)(i) (i.e., the types of plans described in items (1) through (3), above), and in addition, include eligible deferred compensation plans under Code Sec. 457(b) of an eligible employer described in Code Sec. 457(e)(1)(A) (i.e., governmental Code Sec. 457 plans). (Code Sec. 408(q)(3)(A) as amended by 2002 Act §411(i)(1))

> **observation:** While the Technical Explanation of the 2002 Act indicates that various types of qualified governmental plans may be "qualified employer plans," one interpretation of the statutory language indicates that

qualified governmental plans cannot be qualified employer plans. But, since nothing in Code Sec. 72(p)(4)(A)(i) indicates that the plans described in items (1) through (3), above, *cannot* be maintained by a governmental employer, and given the Technical Explanation language, plans of these types that are maintained by governmental employers are qualified employer plans that can maintain a deemed IRA program.

☐ **Effective:** Plan years beginning after Dec. 31, 2002. (2002 Act § 411(x))

¶ 320. Rules applying defined contribution plan limits to Code Sec. 403(b) annuities, Code Sec. 457 plans and church plans are clarified

Code Sec. 403(b), as amended by 2002 Act § 411(p)
Code Sec. 415(c)(7), as amended by 2002 Act § 411(p)(4)
Code Sec. 457(e)(5), as amended by 2002 Act § 411(p)(5)
Generally effective: Years beginning after Dec. 31, 2001
Committee Reports, see ¶ 5046

403(b) annuities. Before the 2001 Economic Growth and Tax Relief Reconciliation Act (EGTRRA), annual contributions to tax-sheltered annuities (403(b) annuities) generally could not have exceeded the lesser of the "exclusion allowance" or the limit for defined contribution plans. The exclusion allowance for a year was equal to 20% of the employee's includible compensation, multiplied by the employee's years of service, minus excludable contributions for prior years under qualified plans, 403(b) annuities, or section 457 plans of the employer. Employees of nonprofit educational institutions, hospitals, home health service agencies, health and welfare service agencies, and churches could irrevocably elect application of one of several special rules that increased the amount of the otherwise permitted contributions. For purposes of determining the contribution limits applicable to 403(b) annuities, includible compensation was the amount of compensation received from the employer for the most recent period that could be counted as a year of service under the exclusion allowance, plus elective deferrals and similar salary reduction amounts.

In EGTRRA § 632, Congress conformed the contribution limits for 403(b) annuities to the limits applicable to other retirement plans to simplify the administration of the pension laws, and to provide more equitable treatment for participants in

---

FTC 2d References are to Federal Tax Coordinator 2d
FIN References are to RIA's Analysis of Federal Taxes: Income
USTR References are to United States Tax Reporter: Income, Estate & Gift, and Excise
PCA References are to the Pension Analysis on Checkpoint and CD-ROM, and in Pension Coordinator
PE References are to the Pension Explanations in Pension and Profit Sharing 2nd
EP References are to the Estate Planning Analysis on Checkpoint and CD-ROM, and in Estate Planning & Taxation Coordinator

similar types of plans. Thus, the exclusion allowance for 403(b) annuities was repealed after 2001 and replaced with the Code Sec. 415 100% of compensation limit that is now applicable to defined contribution plans.

For purposes of calculating the limit on contributions to a 403(b) annuity, includible compensation does not include any amount received by a former employee after the fifth tax year following the tax year in which the former employee was terminated.

Because the treatment of 403(b) annuities and other defined contribution plans was equalized after 2001, the special irrevocable elections available to employees of nonprofit educational institutions, hospitals, home health service agencies, health and welfare service agencies, and churches to increase the amount of their otherwise permitted contributions were repealed. (FTC 2d/FIN ¶ H-12439; USTR ¶ 4034.04; TaxDesk ¶ 280,120; PCA ¶ 36,040; PE ¶ 403-4.04)

> **observation:** EGTRRA did not change the rule, under Code Sec. 403(b)(6), that the limits on contributions to a 403(b) annuity applied at the time contributions became nonforfeitable (i.e., vested).

Church plans. Before EGTRRA, an employee of a church whose adjusted gross income did not exceed $17,000 for a tax year was entitled to an alternative minimum exclusion allowance for purposes of the limit on contributions to 403(b) annuities. The minimum exclusion allowance was the lesser of (1) $3,000 or (2) the employee's includible compensation for the year. For purposes of the limit on annual additions to a defined contribution plan, this minimum exclusion allowance did not violate that limit even if it exceeded 25% of annual compensation. Church employees are also entitled to a special "catch-up" election, which permits the maximum annual plan addition to be an amount not exceeding $10,000, with an aggregate limit of $40,000 for the employee's lifetime. This catch-up election could not be used if the employee had already elected the special year-of-separation-from-service catch-up election under Code Sec. 415(c)(4)(A).

Under EGTRRA, the special minimum exclusion allowance available to church employees whose adjusted gross income did not exceed $17,000 was repealed. And, the special rule providing that this minimum exclusion allowance did not violate the limit on annual additions to a defined contribution plan was also repealed. Further, the year-of-separation-from-service catch-up election was also repealed. However, the $10,000 annual/$40,000-aggregate catch-up election under Code Sec. 415(c)(7) continues to apply. (FTC 2d/FIN ¶ H-12448; USTR ¶ 4034.04; PCA ¶ 36,049; PE ¶ 403-4.04)

Section 457 plans. Before EGTRRA, the maximum permitted annual deferral under an eligible deferred compensation plan of a tax-exempt employer, or state or local government employer (a section 457 plan) was generally the lesser of (1) $8,500 (in 2001), or (2) 33-1/3% of compensation. EGTRRA increased the percentage limit on deferrals to 100% of compensation (the same as for qualified defined contribution plans). (FTC 2d/FIN ¶ H-3317; USTR ¶ 4574; TaxDesk ¶ 135,515; PCA ¶ 40,418; PE ¶ 457-4)

New Law. 403(b) annuities. The 2002 Act clarifies that the contribution limits apply to contributions to a 403(b) annuity in the year that the contributions are made, without regard to when the contributions become nonforfeitable (i.e., vested). (Com Rept, see ¶ 5046) Thus, contributions and additions by an employer to a 403(b) annuity are excluded from an employee's gross income for a tax year to the extent that the aggregate of the contributions and additions (within the meaning of Code Sec. 415(c)(2)) does not exceed the Code Sec. 415 limit. (Code Sec. 403(b)(1) as amended by 2002 Act §411(p)(1)) As a conforming change, Code Sec. 403(b)(6) (describing the treatment for contribution purposes of forfeitable rights that become nonforfeitable) is repealed. (Code Sec. 403(b)(6) repealed by 2002 Act §411(p)(2))

> *observation:* Thus, the rules applicable to 403(b) annuities are the same as those that apply generally to defined contribution plans.

The 2002 Act also clarifies that contributions to a 403(b) annuity, based on includible compensation for the last year of service before retirement, may be made for an employee for up to five years after retirement. (Com Rept, see ¶ 5046) Thus, for purposes of determining the amount of the contribution limit for 403(b) annuities, includible compensation for a tax year is the amount of compensation received from the employer, and includible in the employee's gross income, for the most recent period (which ends not later than the close of the employee's tax year) which can be counted as a full year of service, and *which precedes the taxable year by no more than five years.* Includible compensation does not include any amount contributed by the employer for a 403(b) annuity. (Code Sec. 403(b)(3) as amended by 2002 Act §411(p)(3))

Church plans. The 2002 Act restores special rules for ministers, lay employees of churches and foreign missionaries that Congress says were *inadvertently* eliminated. (Com Rept, see ¶ 5046)

Thus the 2002 Act restores the rule that for purposes of plan contributions by church plans all years of service by a minister, or lay employee, with a church, or with a convention or association of churches, or with a church-related organization are treated as service for one employer. All amounts contributed to the annuity contract by any of these organizations are treated as having been contributed by one employer. (Code Sec. 415(c)(7)(B) as amended by 2002 Act §411(p)(4))

FTC 2d References are to Federal Tax Coordinator 2d
FIN References are to RIA's Analysis of Federal Taxes: Income
USTR References are to United States Tax Reporter: Income, Estate & Gift, and Excise
PCA References are to the Pension Analysis on Checkpoint and CD-ROM, and in Pension Coordinator
PE References are to the Pension Explanations in Pension and Profit Sharing 2nd
EP References are to the Estate Planning Analysis on Checkpoint and CD-ROM, and in Estate Planning & Taxation Coordinator

observation: Before EGTRRA, this rule was found in Code Sec. 403(b)(2)(C).

For ministers and lay employees of churches performing services outside the U.S. (foreign missionaries), there is an alternative minimum contribution allowance. Contributions and additions to a 403(b) annuity when expressed as an annual addition to the employee's account are not treated as exceeding the contribution limit if the annual addition (the sum of employee contributions, employer contributions and forfeitures) is less than the greater of:

(1) $3,000; or

(2) the employee's includible compensation. (Code Sec. 415(c)(7)(C))

observation: This Code Sec. 415(c)(7)(C) rule actually refers to "any individual described in subparagraph (D)." However, subparagraph (D) defines "annual addition." Apparently, consistent with the former Code Sec. 403(b)(2)(D), Congress meant to refer to subparagraph (B)(i), which describes ministers and lay persons employed by churches. Another technical amendment appears to be in order.

observation: Thus the alternative minimum contribution allowance, which, before EGTRRA, was found in Code Sec. 403(b)(2)(D), is restored for *missionaries* only. Before EGTRRA, this allowance applied to *all* church employees making less than $17,001, not to just missionaries.

For purposes of the contribution limits applicable to church plans, the terms "church" and "convention or association of churches" have the same meanings as under Code Sec. 414(e). (Code Sec. 415(c)(7)(E))

observation: Before EGTRRA, this rule was found in Code Sec. 403(b)(2)(C).

Section 457 plans. Under EGTRRA, amounts deferred under a Section 457 plan are generally subject to the same contribution limits as qualified deferred compensation plans. Under the 2002 Act, Congress has conformed the definition of "compensation" used to apply the limits to a Section 457 plan to the definition used for defined contribution plans. (Com Rept, see ¶ 5046) Thus, the term "includible compensation" has the meaning given to the term "participant's compensation" under Code Sec. 415(c)(3). (Code Sec. 457(e)(5) as amended by 2002 Act §411(p)(5))

observation: Before the 2002 Act, includible compensation for 457 plans was limited to compensation for services that was "currently includible in gross income." In contrast, Code Sec. 415(c)(3) defines a participant's compensation as "compensation of the participant from the employer for the year," without actually referring to whether or not the compensation is includible in gross income.

                                    RIA Research Institute of America

☐ **Effective:** For years beginning after Dec. 31, 2001. (2002 Act § 411(x))

¶ 321. Transitional rule allowing defined benefit plans that incorporate Code's plan limits by reference to disregard the anti-cutback rules

Code Sec. None, 2002 Act § 411(j)(3)
Generally effective: Years ending after Dec. 31, 2001.
Committee Reports, see ¶ 5040

The 2001 Economic Growth and Tax Relief Reconciliation Act (EGTRRA) increased the benefit limit applicable to defined benefit plans from $90,000 ($140,000 as indexed for inflation in 2001) to $160,000 (to be indexed for inflation), effective for years ending after Dec. 31, 2001. (FTC 2d/FIN ¶ H-5950; USTR ¶ 4154.02; TaxDesk ¶ 287,002; PCA ¶ 23,701; PE ¶ 415-4.02)

New Law. For some plans that incorporate the benefit limit by reference and that use a plan year other than the calendar year, the increased benefit limits became effective under the plan automatically. According to Congress, this caused unintended benefit increases. (Com Rept, see ¶ 5040)

> *illustration:* Plan A uses a plan year beginning on Feb. 1. Plan A also incorporates by reference the defined benefit limit in Code Sec. 415(b)(1)(A), i.e., the plan refers to the limit under the Code Section rather than specifying a dollar amount ($140,000, for example). For the plan year ending on Jan. 31, 2002, Plan A's year ends *after* Dec. 31, 2002. Thus, Plan A might have unwittingly incorporated the EGTRRA benefit maximum of $160,000, instead of the intended $140,000 (although the $140,000 would have been subject to a pre-EGTRRA cost-of-living adjustment (COLA). If Plan A had been expecting a COLA of less than $20,000 ($160,000 – $140,000), this would have resulted in an unexpected increase in benefit liability for the plan year.

Thus, under the 2002 Act, if, on June 7, 2001 (the date EGTRRA became law), a plan incorporated by reference the defined benefit limit of Code Sec. 415(b)(1)(A), then Code Sec. 411(d)(6) and ERISA §204(g)(1) (the anti-cutback rules) do not apply to a plan amendment that:

(1) is adopted on or before June 30, 2002;

FTC 2d References are to Federal Tax Coordinator 2d
FIN References are to RIA's Analysis of Federal Taxes: Income
USTR References are to United States Tax Reporter: Income, Estate & Gift, and Excise
PCA References are to the Pension Analysis on Checkpoint and CD-ROM, and in Pension Coordinator
PE References are to the Pension Explanations in Pension and Profit Sharing 2nd
EP References are to the Estate Planning Analysis on Checkpoint and CD-ROM, and in Estate Planning & Taxation Coordinator

(2) reduces benefits to the level that would have applied without regard to the benefit increase made by EGTRRA; and

(3) is effective no earlier than years ending after Dec. 31, 2001. (2002 Act § 411(j)(3))

> *illustration:* Thus, in the illustration above, Plan A can amend its plan to reduce the limit from $160,000 to $140,000 without violating the anti-cutback rules.

> *action alert:* Plans must be amended by June 30, 2002, in order to take advantage of the transitional rule permitting a plan to disregard the anti-cutback rules.

> *observation:* Without this transitional rule, if a plan tried to *decrease* accrued benefits (even though here those benefits were the result of a statutory change), it would violate the anti-cutback rule.

☐ **Effective:** For years ending after Dec. 31, 2001. (2002 Act § 411(x))

¶ 322. "Severance from employment" replaces "separation from service" for in-service distributions from top-heavy plans

Code Sec. 416(g)(3)(B), as amended by 2002 Act § 411(k)(2)
Generally effective: For years beginning after Dec. 31, 2001
Committee Reports, see ¶ 5041

Under pre-2002 Act law, in determining the present value of an employee's benefit or the amount of his account, for purposes of the top-heavy plan rules, distributions made to the employee during the one-year period ending on the plan's determination date are taken into account. But—if made for reasons *other than* separation from service, death, or disability—distributions made over the five-year period, rather than the one-year period, ending on the determination date are taken into account. (FTC 2d/FIN ¶ H-8016; USTR ¶ 4164.02; PCA ¶ 26,217; PE ¶ 416-4.02)

Under a provision enacted as part of the 2001 Economic Growth and Tax Relief Reconciliation Act (EGTRRA §646(a)), the rules governing distributions of elective deferrals under Code Sec. 401(k) were modified to allow distributions on the "severance from employment" rather than the "separation from service."

> *observation:* No similar change was made to the top-heavy rules by EGTRRA.

Under pre-EGTRRA law, a separation from service occurred when a participant died, retired, resigned or was discharged, and not when he continued on the same job for a different employer as a result of the liquidation, merger, consolidation or other similar corporate transaction. A severance from employment occurred when a participant ceased to be employed by the employer maintaining the plan. Under the "same desk rule," there was no separation from service if an employee continued on the same job for a different employer following a liquidation, merger, or consolidation of the former employer. Thus, under the EGTRRA amendment, a participant who severed employment could receive a distribution of his 401(k) plan elective deferrals. (FTC 2d/FIN ¶ H-9201.1; USTR ¶ 4014.172; PCA ¶ 28,502.1; PE ¶ 401-4.172)

> **observation:** Before the EGTRRA amendment, a 401(k) plan that made a distribution of elective deferrals to a plan participant before the occurrence of the earlier of the participant's separation from service, death, or disability ran the risk of being disqualified. Generally, participants receiving distributions of elective deferrals before separation from service, death, or disability would have been required to include these amount in income, and were subject to the 10% penalty for early distributions under Code Sec. 72(t).

New Law. The 2002 Act amends the top-heavy rules under Code Sec. 416(g)(3)(B) by replacing the phrase "separation from service" with "severance from employment". (Code Sec. 416(g)(3)(B) as amended by 2002 Act §411(k)(2))

The Technical Explanation of the 2002 Act states that EGTRRA permitted distributions from 401(k) plans, tax-sheltered annuity plans, or eligible deferred compensation plans to be made when the participant has a severance from employment, rather than separation from service. Thus, the provision clarifies that distributions made after severance from employment, rather than separation from service, are taken into account for only one year in determining top-heavy status. (Com Rept, see ¶ 5041)

> **observation:** This change conforms with a similar change made to Code Sec. 416(c)(1)(C)(iii) by EGTRRA (see above) in which "severance from employment" replaced "separation from service" as one of the events (the others are death and disability) whose occurrence permits distributions from 401(k) plans without penalty.

> **illustration:** AlphaCorp has a contract with the Overnite Hotel chain to manage the hotel's computer systems. In 2002, Overnite decides to switch vendors, and BetaCorp replaces AlphaCorp as the manager of the hotel's

---

FTC 2d References are to Federal Tax Coordinator 2d
FIN References are to RIA's Analysis of Federal Taxes: Income
USTR References are to United States Tax Reporter: Income, Estate & Gift, and Excise
PCA References are to the Pension Analysis on Checkpoint and CD-ROM, and in Pension Coordinator
PE References are to the Pension Explanations in Pension and Profit Sharing 2nd
EP References are to the Estate Planning Analysis on Checkpoint and CD-ROM, and in Estate Planning & Taxation Coordinator

computer systems. AlphaCorp terminates all employees who worked on the Overnite engagement. This represents just a small portion of the AlphaCorp workforce, and the company—including its 401(k) plan—continues in existence. As part of the termination, however, the former AlphaCorp employees receive distributions of their 401(k) plan account balances.

Under the "same desk rule," the workers would not have been treated as having separated from service with AlphaCorp., although they would have been treated as having severed employment. Without the 2002 Act change, the 401(k) plan distributions, plus any other distributions made within the *five-year period* ending on the 401(k) plan's determination date, would have to be taken into account in determining the size of the employees' account for top-heavy determination purposes. The 2002 Act amendment ensures that the 401(k) distributions will not be treated as in-service distributions subject to this five-year rule.

☐ **Effective:** For years beginning after Dec. 31, 2001. (2002 Act § 411(x))

¶ 323. Method of determining "defined benefit minimum" for top-heavy plans no longer applies only to frozen plans

Code Sec. 416(c)(1)(C)(iii), as amended by 2002 Act § 411(k)(1)
Generally effective: For years beginning after Dec. 31, 2001
Committee Reports, see ¶ 5041

Top-heavy defined benefit plans (plans in which more than 60% of the accrued benefits in the plan are for key employees) must provide a minimum benefit for non-key employees. This "defined benefit minimum" rule requires that the accrued benefit derived from employer contributions for each participant who is a non-key employee, when expressed as an annual retirement benefit (a benefit payable annually as a single life annuity, with no ancillary benefits, beginning at the normal retirement age under the plan), is at least equal to the product of:

(1) an employee's "average annual compensation" for the period of consecutive years (not exceeding five) during which the employee had the highest aggregate compensation from the employer, multiplied by

(2) the lesser of: (a) 2% per year of service, or (b) 20%.

(FTC 2d/FIN ¶ H-8015; USTR ¶ 4164.01; PCA ¶ 26,216; PE ¶ 416-4.01)

Under pre-2002 Act law, a "frozen plan" (a plan in which benefit accruals have ceased but all assets have not been distributed to participants or their beneficiaries) was subject to a special rule. Under a provision enacted as part of the 2001 Economic Growth and Tax Relief Reconciliation Act (EGTRRA §613(e)), for frozen plans, in determining an employee's years of service with the employer for purposes of the 2% per year provision (2(a), above), service is disregarded it if occurs in a plan year in which the plan does not benefit any key employee or former key employee.

New Law. The 2002 Act amends the heading of Code Sec. 416(c)(1)(C)(iii), changing it from "Exception for frozen plan" to "Exception for plan under which no key employee (or former key employee) benefits for plan year." (Code Sec. 416(c)(1)(C)(iii) as amended by 2002 Act §411(k)(1))

> *observation:* Although the Technical Explanation of the 2002 Act provides no explanation for this change, the change in the subparagraph heading does conform it to the language of the provision itself. By making this change, Congress is clarifying that the exception applies to plans other than just frozen plans.

> *illustration:* Wally, a non-key employee, works for SmallCo, and participates in SmallCo's top-heavy defined benefit plan. Wally has seven years of service, and has averaged $50,000 per year over the past five years. Under the defined benefit minimum rule, Wally's accrued benefit derived from SmallCo's contributions—when expressed as an annual retirement benefit—must be at least:

> (1) $50,000 (average annual compensation for the five-year testing period) multiplied by

> (2) the lesser of: (a) 14% (2% per year of service × seven years of service), or (b) 20%.

> Normally, Wally's defined benefit minimum would have to be at least $7,000 ($50,000 × 14%), when expressed as an annual retirement benefit. However, assuming that the SmallCo plan has not benefitted a key employee or former key employee over the past four years, these four years of service must be disregarded. This reduces Wally's years of service (for purposes of the defined benefit minimum calculation) to 3 years (7 − 4 = 3). Thus, Wally's defined benefit minimum is reduced to $3,000 (2% × 3 years of service × $50,000)

☐ **Effective:** For years beginning after Dec. 31, 2001. (2002 Act § 411(x))

¶ 324. Rollovers may be disregarded in determining the present value of a qualified survivor annuity for cash-out purposes

FTC 2d References are to Federal Tax Coordinator 2d
FIN References are to RIA's Analysis of Federal Taxes: Income
USTR References are to United States Tax Reporter: Income, Estate & Gift, and Excise
PCA References are to the Pension Analysis on Checkpoint and CD-ROM, and in Pension Coordinator
PE References are to the Pension Explanations in Pension and Profit Sharing 2nd
EP References are to the Estate Planning Analysis on Checkpoint and CD-ROM, and in Estate Planning & Taxation Coordinator

Code Sec. 417(e)(1), as amended by 2002 Act § 411(r)(1)(A)
Code Sec. 417(e)(2)(A), as amended by 2002 Act § 411(r)(1)(B)
ERISA §205(g)(1), as amended by 2002 Act §411(r)(2)(A)
ERISA §205(g)(2)(A), as amended by 2002 Act §411(r)(2)(B)
Generally effective: Applies to distributions after Dec. 31, 2001
Committee Reports, see ¶ 5048

A qualified retirement plan may provide for the involuntary cash-out (i.e., the distribution to the participant without the participant's consent) of nonforfeitable accrued retirement benefits with a present value of $5,000 or less. The 2001 Economic Growth and Tax Relief Reconciliation Act (EGTRRA §648) added a provision permitting a qualified retirement plan to provide that the present value of a participant's nonforfeitable accrued benefit may be determined without regard to the portion of the benefit that is attributable to rollover contributions (and any earnings allocable to the rollover contributions). The provision added by EGTRRA applies to distributions after Dec. 31, 2001. (FTC 2d/FIN ¶ H-7510; USTR ¶ 4114.15; PCA ¶ 25,511; PE ¶ 411-4.15)

Similarly, the rules on the involuntary cash-out of benefits in lieu of a qualified survivor annuity (i.e., a qualified joint and survivor annuity (QJSA) or a qualified pre-retirement survivor annuity (QPSA)) also permit a plan to provide for the immediate distribution of the present value of a qualified survivor annuity without the consent of the participant and his spouse if the present value doesn't exceed $5,000. However, before the 2002 Act, there was no provision permitting a plan to disregard rollovers in determining the present value of a qualified survivor annuity. (FTC 2d/FIN ¶ H-8701; USTR ¶ 4174.06; TaxDesk ¶ 145,201; PCA ¶ 27,203; PE ¶ 417-4.06)

New Law. Under the 2002 Act, a qualified retirement plan may provide that the present value of a qualified survivor annuity is determined without regard to the portion of the annuity that is attributable to rollover contributions (and any earnings allocable thereto), for purposes of determining whether the participant and his spouse must consent to the cash-out of the annuity. (Code Sec. 417(e)(1) as amended by 2002 Act §411(r)(1)(A)) (Code Sec. 417(e)(2)(A) as amended by 2002 Act §411(r)(1)(B)) Thus, the 2002 Act clarifies that rollover amounts may be disregarded in determining whether a spouse must consent to the cash-out of a qualified survivor annuity. (Com Rept, see ¶ 5048)

> *illustration:* Cindy Harper is a married participant in the XYZ qualified retirement plan. The present value of Harper's QJSA is $11,000, of which $6,000 is attributable to a rollover contribution. The XYZ plan can cash Harper out of the plan by distributing the $11,000 to her, without her consent or the consent of her husband, since the $6,000 rollover is not taken into account and the remaining $5,000 does not exceed the $5,000 maximum.

The 2002 Act makes similar changes to ERISA §205(g), the parallel provision to Code Sec. 417(e) in the Employee Retirement Income Security Act. (ERISA §205(g)(1) as amended by 2002 Act §411(r)(2)(A)) (ERISA §205(g)(2)(A) as amended by 2002 Act §411(r)(2)(B))

☐ **Effective:** Applies to distributions after Dec. 31, 2001 (2002 Act § 411(x))

¶ 325. Modification of requirements for using prior year's valuation in satisfaction of annual actuarial requirement for defined benefit and money purchase plans

Code Sec. 412(c)(9)(B), as amended by 2002 Act § 411(v)(1)
ERISA §302(c)(9)(B), as amended by 2002 Act §411(v)(2)
Generally effective: Plan years beginning after Dec. 31, 2001
Committee Reports, see ¶ 5052

Defined benefit plans and money purchase plans (including target benefit plans) must meet minimum funding requirements. Under the minimum funding rules, the funding standard account is charged with any net experience loss and credited with any net experience gain.

A determination of experience gains and losses and a valuation of the plan's liability (together, the actuarial valuation) must be made at least once every year, although it may have to be made more often in particular cases under IRS regulations. As a general rule, the required annual actuarial valuation must be made as of a date during the current plan year (or within a month before the beginning of the current plan year).

As an alternative to making the actuarial valuation as of the *current* plan year, the 2001 Economic Growth and Tax Relief Reconciliation Act (EGTRRA § 661(a)) permitted an employer to use the *prior* year's plan valuation, but only if the plan's assets equaled at least 125% of the plan's current liability (determined as of the valuation date for the preceding year). (FTC 2d/FIN ¶ H-7703.1; USTR ¶ 4124.09; PCA ¶ 25,704.1; PE ¶ 412-4.09)

New Law. In order to conform the EGTRRA language described above to match Congressional intent, the 2002 Act modifies the conditions that must be satisfied in order for an employer to use the prior year's plan valuation to satisfy the annual actuarial valuation requirement. (Com Rept, see ¶ 5052) Under the 2002 Act, an employer is permitted to use the prior year's plan valuation, as long as the plan's assets equal at least 100% (vs. 125% under pre-2002 Act law) of the plan's

---

FTC 2d References are to Federal Tax Coordinator 2d
FIN References are to RIA's Analysis of Federal Taxes: Income
USTR References are to United States Tax Reporter: Income, Estate & Gift, and Excise
PCA References are to the Pension Analysis on Checkpoint and CD-ROM, and in Pension Coordinator
PE References are to the Pension Explanations in Pension and Profit Sharing 2nd
EP References are to the Estate Planning Analysis on Checkpoint and CD-ROM, and in Estate Planning & Taxation Coordinator

current liability (determined as of the valuation date for the preceding year). (Code Sec. 412(c)(9)(B)(ii) as amended by 2002 Act §411(v)(1)(A))

The 2002 Act adds that an employer is permitted to *change* the funding method to use a prior year valuation only if the plan's assets equal at least 125% of the plan's current liability (determined as of the valuation date for the preceding year). (Code Sec. 412(c)(9)(B)(iv))

observation: Thus, an employer can *begin* using the prior year's valuation (after having used the current year valuation) as long as the 125% threshold is met. After it has begun using the prior year valuation, the employer can *continue* using the prior year valuation as long as the 100% threshold is met.

illustration: Acme Corporation has maintained a defined benefit pension plan since 1990. Its plan year is the calendar year, and the actuarial valuation has consistently been made as of the date within the plan year to which the valuation relates (i.e., the current year's valuation). For the 2001 plan year, the plan's assets equaled 130% of the plan's current liability. For the 2002 plan year, Acme chose to begin using the prior year valuation. It was entitled to do so because the value of the plan's assets (determined as of the 2001 valuation date) equaled at least 125% of the plan's current liability. Acme can continue using the prior year's valuation as long as the value of the plan's assets equal at least 100% of the plan's current liability (determined as of the valuation date for the preceding year).

observation: Neither the 2002 Act nor the Technical Explanation of the 2002 Act addresses the procedures an employer must follow in order to begin using the prior year's plan valuation. However, in the Committee Report for EGTRRA §661, Congress directed IRS to automatically approve changes in funding method to use a prior year valuation date if the change is made within the first three years that the plan is eligible to make the change. *Presumably,* an employer can make this method change unilaterally, without informing IRS, and without securing IRS permission, as long as it does so within that three year period.

observation: Once an employer begins using the prior year's plan valuation, neither the 2002 Act nor the Technical Explanation of the 2002 Act states whether the employer's decision to use the prior year's valuation can be revoked for reasons other than failing to meet the 100% threshold, and if it can be revoked, whether IRS consent is required.

The 2002 Act makes similar amendments to the parallel ERISA provision concerning use of the prior year plan valuation. (ERISA §302(c)(9)(B) as amended by 2002 Act §411(v)(2))

☐ **Effective:** Plan years beginning after Dec. 31, 2001. (2002 Act § 411(x))

¶ 326. ESOP dividends can be reinvested in company stock without the company losing its dividend deduction; reinvested dividends must be nonforfeitable

Code Sec. 404(k)(4)(B), as amended by 2002 Act § 411(w)(1)(D)
Code Sec. 404(k)(7), as amended by 2002 Act § 411(w)(2)
Generally effective: Tax years beginning after Dec. 31, 2001
Committee Reports, see ¶ 5053

Under Code Sec. 404(k), a Corporation is allowed a deduction (in addition to the deduction allowed under Code Sec. 404(a) for plan contributions) for the amount of the "applicable dividends" paid on applicable employer securities held by an employee stock ownership plan ("ESOP"). ESOPs generally are qualified defined contribution plans (stock bonus or a combination stock bonus and money purchase plans) that invest primarily in securities of the employer.

An "applicable dividend"is any dividend paid in accordance with the plan's provisions that is:

(1) paid in cash to participants in the plan or their beneficiaries,

(2) paid to the plan and distributed in cash to the plan's participants or beneficiaries within 90 days after the plan year of the dividend payment, or

(3) used to make payments on a securities acquisition loan which the ESOP incurred to acquire the securities (whether or not allocated to participants) on which the dividend is paid.

"Applicable employer securities" are employer securities held on the dividend record date by an ESOP which is maintained by the corporation paying the dividend, or a corporation which is a member of its controlled group.

The 2001 Economic Growth and Tax Relief Reconciliation Act (EGTRRA §662(a)) *expanded* the definition of "applicable dividends" (which a corporation is allowed to deduct) to include any dividend which, *at the election* of the participants or beneficiaries is:

(a) payable in cash to participants in the plan or their beneficiaries,

(b) payable to the plan and distributed in cash to the plan's participants or beneficiaries within 90 days after the close of the plan year of the dividend payment, or

(c) paid to the plan and reinvested in "qualifying employer securities."

FTC 2d References are to Federal Tax Coordinator 2d
FIN References are to RIA's Analysis of Federal Taxes: Income
USTR References are to United States Tax Reporter: Income, Estate & Gift, and Excise
PCA References are to the Pension Analysis on Checkpoint and CD-ROM, and in Pension Coordinator
PE References are to the Pension Explanations in Pension and Profit Sharing 2nd
EP References are to the Estate Planning Analysis on Checkpoint and CD-ROM, and in Estate Planning & Taxation Coordinator

observation: The term "qualifying employer securities" (item (c), above) is not specifically defined under Code Sec. 404(k). But Code Sec. 404(a)(9)(A) makes reference to "qualifying employer securities," defining it as described under the Code Sec. 4975(e)(8) excise tax rules on prohibited transactions. Under Code Sec. 4975(e)(8), "qualifying employer securities" are defined under Code Sec. 409(l), which in turn limits qualifying employer securities to common stock (or in specified cases, certain substitutes for common stock).

Under Code Sec. 404(k)(4)(A), the deduction for dividends paid on an applicable dividend is allowed for the corporation's tax year in which the dividend is *paid or distributed* to participants. (FTC 2d/FIN ¶ H-12117; USTR ¶ 4044.14; PCA ¶ 33,218; PE ¶ 404-4.14)

observation: Under pre-2002 Act law, there was no provision specifying that a deduction would be allowed for dividends *paid to the plan and reinvested* in qualifying employer securities at the election of participants.

Under Code Sec. 411(a)(1), a qualified plan must provide that a participant's right to his accrued benefit derived from his own contributions must be fully vested at all times. (FTC 2d/FIN ¶ H-7407; USTR ¶ 4114.25; TaxDesk ¶ 286,028; PCA ¶ 25,408; PE ¶ 411-4.25)

observation: However, pre-2002 Act law did not provide that ESOP participants would be fully vested in dividends they elected to have paid to the plan and reinvested in qualifying employer securities.

New Law. The 2002 Act clarifies that ESOP dividends can be paid to the plan and reinvested without losing the dividend deduction under Code Sec. 404(k). (Com Rept, see ¶ 5053) Thus, under Code Sec. 404(k)(4)(A), an applicable dividend that is *paid to the plan and reinvested* in qualifying employer securities at the election of participants or their beneficiaries is treated as paid in the corporation's tax year in which *the later of* either: (1) the dividend is reinvested *or* (2) the participants' election is made. (Code Sec. 404(k)(4)(B) as amended by 2002 Act §411(w)(1)(D)) In other words, the corporation's deduction for dividends paid that are reinvested in qualifying employer securities at the election of participants or their beneficiaries is allowable for the tax year in which the later of the reinvestment or the election occurs. (Com Rept, see ¶ 5053)

illustration: The Acme Corporation maintains an ESOP for the benefit of its employees. Both Acme's tax year and the ESOP's plan year are the calendar year. On Aug. 31, 2002, the ESOP pays a dividend on behalf of plan participants, who can choose to take the distribution in cash or reinvest the dividend in company stock in the ESOP. As of Dec. 31, 2002, some of the participants accept the cash and some elect to reinvest their dividend in Acme stock. All of the reinvestments in stock occur on Jan. 2, 2003. Acme is entitled to deduct the dividends distributed in cash to participants for its 2002 tax year. However, Acme cannot deduct the rein-vested dividends until its 2003 tax year, since the deduction is allowable for the tax year in which the later of the reinvestment or election occurred.

In addition, the 2002 Act clarifies that dividends that are reinvested in qualify-ing employer securities at the ESOP participant's election must be nonforfeitable. (Com Rept, see ¶ 5053) Specifically, the 2002 Act requires that applicable divi-dends that are paid to the plan and reinvested in qualifying employer securities at the election of participants or their beneficiaries must be fully vested under Code Sec. 411(a)(1). (Code Sec. 404(k)(7) as amended by 2002 Act §411(w)(2))

☐ **Effective:** Tax years beginning after Dec. 31, 2001. (2002 Act § 411(x))

¶ 327. Code Sec. 4980F notice rules apply only to tax qualified defined benefit plans

Code Sec. 4980F(e)(1), as amended by 2002 Act § 411(u)(1)(A)
Code Sec. 4980F(f)(2)(A), as amended by 2002 Act § 411(u)(1)(B)
Code Sec. 4980F(f)(3), as amended by 2002 Act § 411(u)(1)(C)
ERISA §204(h)(9), as amended by 2002 Act §411(u)(2)
Generally effective: For plan amendments taking effect on or after June 7, 2001
Committee Reports, see ¶ 5051

Under rules enacted as part of the 2001 Economic Growth and Tax Relief Rec-onciliation Act (EGTRRA §659), both ERISA §204(h) and Code Sec. 4980F re-quire that defined benefit and defined contribution plans give notice of certain plan amendments to affected parties. Under Code Sec. 4980F, an excise tax is generally imposed on the failure of any "applicable pension plan" (defined as *any* defined benefit plan or an individual account plan subject to Code Sec. 412's funding stan-dards) to provide notice to applicable individuals (plan participants, beneficiaries, etc.), and to employee organizations representing them, when the plan is amended to provide for a "significant reduction in the rate of future benefit accrual." To avoid the excise tax, the plan administrator must provide "written notice" to the applicable individuals, crafted in language that would allow them to understand the effect of the plan amendment. The notice requirements also apply to significant re-ductions in early retirement benefits and retirement-type subsidies. Similar changes were made to the parallel ERISA provisions, except that no excise tax is imposed under ERISA, which however does impose a penalty for "egregious" compliance

FTC 2d References are to Federal Tax Coordinator 2d
FIN References are to RIA's Analysis of Federal Taxes: Income
USTR References are to United States Tax Reporter: Income, Estate & Gift, and Excise
PCA References are to the Pension Analysis on Checkpoint and CD-ROM, and in Pension Coordinator
PE References are to the Pension Explanations in Pension and Profit Sharing 2nd
EP References are to the Estate Planning Analysis on Checkpoint and CD-ROM, and in Estate Planning & Taxation Coordinator

failures that the Code does not. The ERISA penalty generally provides that, for egregious compliance failures, the provisions of the plan would have to be applied as if the plan amendment entitled all applicable individuals to *the greater of:* (i) the benefit to which they would have been entitled without regard to the amendment, *or* (ii) the benefits under the plan as amended. (FTC 2d ¶ H-6272.2; USTR ¶ 49,80F4; PCA ¶ 49,314.2; PE ¶ 49,80F-4)

New Law. The 2002 Act amends the Code Sec. 4980F notice requirements by providing that the notice required to be given to applicable individuals no longer has to be "written" (in the usual sense of the word) but still must be "written" in accordance with already existing Code Sec. 4980F(e)(2), i.e., in a manner designed to be understood by the average plan participant and with sufficient information to allow applicable individuals to understand the amendment's effect. (Code Sec. 4980F(e)(1) as amended by 2002 Act §411(u)(1)(A))

> *observation:* Code Sec. 4980F(g) provides that IRS may, through exercise of its regulatory authority, allow the Code Sec. 4980F notice to be provided using "new technologies," e.g., company-sponsored internet or intranet sites. By eliminating the old "written notice" requirement, the 2002 Act is apparently trying to eliminate the dichotomy between traditional writing techniques and computerized information delivery.

> *observation:* ERISA §204(h)(1) also allows for the provision of notice using "new technologies." However, ERISA §204(h)(1) does not specify that the required notice be "written"; thus, no amendment was needed to the parallel ERISA provision.

The 2002 Act also amends the notice requirements' definition of "applicable pension plan" by changing it from "any defined benefit plan" to "any defined benefit plan described in section 401(a) which includes a trust exempt from tax under section 501(a)." (Code Sec. 4980F(f)(2)(A) as amended by 2002 Act §411(u)(1)(B)) Thus, the 2002 Act clarifies that the notice requirements apply to a defined benefit plan only if the plan is tax qualified. (Com Rept, see ¶ 5051)

> *caution:* The 2002 Act does *not* make a corresponding change to the ERISA §204(h) notice provision (specifically, ERISA §204(h)(8)(B)(i))—the provision that parallels Code Sec. 4980F(f)(2)(A). Thus, *all* defined benefit plans subject to ERISA, not just tax-qualified defined benefit plans, remain subject to the ERISA §204(h) notice requirements. Thus, while the excise tax imposed under Code Sec. 4980F for failing to meet the notice requirements no longer applies to nonqualified defined benefit plans, these plans remain subject to the ERISA §204(h) notice requirements.
>
> Note that for any "egregious failure" to meet the ERISA §204(h) notice requirements, the provisions of the plan would have to be applied as if the plan amendment entitled all applicable individuals to the greater of: (i) the benefit to which they would have been entitled without regard to

the amendment, or (ii) the benefits under the plan as amended (see ERISA §204(h)(6)(A)).

🔻 *illustration:* EndRun Corp., a widget manufacturer, maintains a defined benefit "top hat" plan for its highly compensated employees. In 2002, EndRun suffers immense losses relating to investments in widget derivatives, and decides it must scale back the benefits promised under the top-hat plan. Based on the 2002 Act's technical correction to the definition of defined benefit plan, EndRun assumes the notice requirements do not apply, and amends the plan in a manner that provides for a significant reduction in the rate of future benefit accrual without first giving the required notice.

Result: Because EndRun did not provide the notice required under ERISA §204(h) , and assuming this to be an egregious failure, all applicable individuals are entitled to the benefit to which they would have been entitled without regard to the amendment. That is, the amendment significantly reducing the rate of future benefit accrual under the top hat defined benefit plan cannot take effect.

🔻 *recommendation:* Employers, plan administrators, and plan fiduciaries cannot assume that their company's nonqualified defined benefit plans are no longer subject to the notice rules, and should comply with ERISA §204(h) when amending their defined benefit plans.

The 2002 Act amends the definitional provision governing early retirement benefits and retirement-type subsidies. Before the change, a plan amendment had to "significantly" reduce any early retirement benefit or retirement-type subsidy to be treated as "significantly" reducing the rate of future benefit accrual, thus triggering application of the notice requirements. The 2002 Act removes the word "significantly," so that now a plan amendment that eliminates or reduces any early retirement benefit or retirement-type subsidy is treated as reducing the rate of future benefit accrual. (Code Sec. 4980F(f)(3) as amended by 2002 Act §411(u)(1)(C)) The Technical Explanation of the 2002 Act states that the change clarifies that, for an amendment eliminating an early retirement benefit or retirement-type subsidy, "notice is required only if the early retirement benefit or retirement-type subsidy is significant." (Com Rept, see ¶ 5051)

🔻 *observation:* Before the 2002 Act, a *significant* reduction of any early retirement benefit or retirement-type subsidy was automatically treated as *significantly* reducing the rate of future benefit accrual, thus automatically

FTC 2d References are to Federal Tax Coordinator 2d
FIN References are to RIA's Analysis of Federal Taxes: Income
USTR References are to United States Tax Reporter: Income, Estate & Gift, and Excise
PCA References are to the Pension Analysis on Checkpoint and CD-ROM, and in Pension Coordinator
PE References are to the Pension Explanations in Pension and Profit Sharing 2nd
EP References are to the Estate Planning Analysis on Checkpoint and CD-ROM, and in Estate Planning & Taxation Coordinator

triggering the notice requirements. After the 2002 Act, such a significant reduction of any early retirement benefit or retirement-type subsidy is no automatically treated as *significantly* reducing the rate of future benefit accrual, and so the notice requirements are no longer *automatically* triggered. It would seem then that, even if there is a significant reduction of any early retirement benefit or retirement-type subsidy, there might not necessarily be a significant reduction in the rate of future benefit accrual. Nevertheless, employers and plan administrators would be well advised to consider erring on the side of caution and providing the notice whenever there is a reduction of early retirement benefits or retirement-type subsidies.

The 2002 Act makes a corresponding change to the ERISA §204(h) notice provision that parallels Code Sec. 4980F(f)(3). (ERISA §204(h)(9) as amended by 2002 Act §411(u)(2))

Finally, the 2002 Act modifies a transition rule that appears in EGTRRA §659, but not the Code or ERISA. Under this provision, the Code and ERISA notice provisions did not apply to any plan amendment taking effect on or after June 7, 2001 (EGTRRA's date of enactment) if, before Apr. 15, 2001, notice was provided to plan participants and beneficiaries (*or* their representatives) who were adversely affected by the plan amendment. The 2002 Act provides that, for the transition rule to have applied, notice must have been given to *both* the participants *and* their representatives, not just the participants *or* their representatives. (2002 Act § 411(u)(3))

> **RIA** *action alert:* In light of the retroactive effect of this provision (see effective date provision below) plan sponsors who effected plan amendments subject to the notice rules and who relied on the EGTRRA transition provision, should quickly determine if a revised notice conforming to the Code and ERISA notice requirements should be sent out to applicable individuals and their representatives.

> **RIA** *observation:* Even if it is determined that the plan sponsor erroneously relied on the EGTRRA transition provision, excise taxes should not apply. Code Sec. 4980F(c)(1) provides that no excise tax will be imposed for violations of the notice requirements if IRS determines that the employer sponsoring the plan did not know of the failure and exercised "reasonable diligence" to meet the notice requirements. Relying on the law as it then existed should be considered an exercise of due diligence. In addition, Code Sec. 4980F(c)(4) provides that IRS can waive the excise tax where the failure to comply with the notice requirements is due to reasonable cause and where requiring payment of the excise tax would be inequitable in light of the failure involved. Relying on the law as it then existed should be considered reasonable cause for failing to comply with the notice requirements, making imposition of the excise tax, based on a retroactive law correction, inequitable.

☐ **Effective:** For plan amendments taking effect on or after June 7, 2001. (2002 Act § 411(x))

¶ 328. Mental health parity requirements extended through 2003

Code Sec. 9812(f), as amended by 2002 Act § 610(a)
Generally effective: Plan years beginning after Dec. 31, 2000
Committee Reports, see ¶ 5078

Under Code Sec. 9812, group health plans that provide both medical and surgical benefits and mental health benefits cannot impose aggregate lifetime or annual dollar limits on mental health benefits that are not imposed on substantially all medical and surgical benefits. Under Code Sec. 4980D, an excise tax of $100 per day is imposed on employers sponsoring plans that fail to meet this requirement until the failure is corrected. During a tax year, the maximum tax that can be imposed for failures that are due to reasonable cause, and not willful neglect, cannot exceed the lesser of 10% of an employer's group health plan expenses for the prior year, or $500,000. No tax is imposed if IRS determines that the employer did not know, and by exercising reasonable diligence would not have known, that the failure existed. (FTC 2d/FIN ¶ H-1325.35, ¶ H-1325.46; USTR ¶ 49,80D4, ¶ 98,124; PE ¶ 4980D-4, ¶ 9812-4)

New Law. The mental health parity provisions were initially effective with respect to plan years beginning on or after Jan. 1, 1998, but did not apply to services provided on or after Sept. 30, 2001. Thus, the mental health parity provision had been set to expire for services provided after Sept. 30, 2001. However, Public Law 107-116, § 701(c) (providing appropriations for the Departments of Labor, Health and Human Services, and Education for fiscal year 2002)—which was enacted Jan. 10, 2002—restored the excise tax retroactively to Sept. 30, 2001. But the excise tax did not apply to services provided on or after Dec. 31, 2002. (Com Rept, see ¶ 5078)

The 2002 Act modifies the applicability of the mental health parity requirements so that the rules do *not* apply to services provided:

(1) on or after Sept. 30, 2001 and before Jan. 10, 2002; and

(2) after Dec. 31, 2003. (Code Sec. 9812(f) as amended by 2002 Act §610(a))

FTC 2d References are to Federal Tax Coordinator 2d
FIN References are to RIA's Analysis of Federal Taxes: Income
USTR References are to United States Tax Reporter: Income, Estate & Gift, and Excise
PCA References are to the Pension Analysis on Checkpoint and CD-ROM, and in Pension Coordinator
PE References are to the Pension Explanations in Pension and Profit Sharing 2nd
EP References are to the Estate Planning Analysis on Checkpoint and CD-ROM, and in Estate Planning & Taxation Coordinator

Thus, under the 2002 Act, for services provided on or after Sept. 30, 2001, the excise tax on failures to comply with the mental health parity requirements applies to services provided on or after Jan. 10, 2002, and before Jan. 1, 2004. (Com Rept, see ¶ 5078)

> *observation:* Thus, the 2002 Act leaves a gap period for services provided after Sept. 30, 2001 and before Jan. 10, 2002 during which the excise tax does not apply to services provided. Apparently, Congress did not want to apply the rule retroactively before the enactment of Public Law 107-116 on Jan. 10, 2002.

> *illustration:* Acme Corporation sponsored a group health plan for the benefit of it employees that provided both medical and surgical benefits and mental health benefits. For the 2002 calendar year, the plan imposed an annual limit on mental health benefits provided under the plan, but not on medical and surgical benefits. Thus, the plan failed to satisfy the mental health parity requirements under Code Sec. 9812 and the Code Sec. 4980D $100 per day excise tax applies to Acme. Under the 2002 Act, the excise tax does not apply for failures to comply with Code Sec. 9812 during the gap period described in the observation, above. Here, the $100 per day excise tax does not accrue between Jan. 1, 2002 and Jan. 9, 2002. However, the $100 per day penalty does apply beginning on Jan. 10, 2002, and continues to accrue until the noncompliance with Code Sec. 9812 is remedied.

☐ **Effective:** Plan years beginning after Dec. 31, 2000. (2002 Act § 610(b))

¶ 400. Individual Tax

¶ 401. Nonrefundable personal credits may be used to offset AMT through 2003 (instead of 2001)

Code Sec. 26(a)(2), as amended by 2002 Act § 601(a)
Code Sec. None, 2002 Act § 601(b)(2)
Generally effective: Tax years beginning after Dec. 31, 2001
Committee Reports, see ¶ 5069

Individuals may qualify for a number of nonrefundable personal credits—the dependent care credit, the credit for the elderly and disabled, the adoption credit, the child tax credit, the credit for interest on certain home mortgages, the HOPE Scholarship and Lifetime Learning credits, the D.C. homebuyer's credit and the credit for elective deferrals and IRA contributions (the saver's credit).

The amount of nonrefundable personal credits allowed in a tax year is subject to a limitation based on tax liability—the Code Sec. 26 limitation. For tax years beginning in 2001, all the nonrefundable personal credits were allowed to the extent of the full amount of the individual's regular tax and alternative minimum tax (AMT). Thus, individuals could use these credits to offset AMT liability as well as regular tax liability.

Under pre-2002 Act law, the limitation described above didn't apply in tax years beginning after 2001. The Code Sec. 26 limitation that was in effect after 2001 didn't permit use of the nonrefundable personal credits (other than the adoption credit, child tax credit and saver's credit) as an offset against AMT. (FTC 2d/FIN ¶ L-18101, ¶ L-18102; USTR ¶ 264; TaxDesk ¶ 398,000, ¶ 398,001) The adoption credit, child tax credit and saver's credit were each subject to separate limitations which permitted the AMT offset. (FTC 2d/FIN ¶ A-4403, ¶ A-4604, ¶ A-4705; USTR ¶ 234, ¶ 244.01, ¶ 25B4; TaxDesk ¶ 569,503, ¶ 569,104, ¶ 569,205)

New Law. The 2002 Act allows individuals to offset their entire regular tax liability and AMT liability by the personal nonrefundable credits in 2002 and 2003. (Com Rept, see ¶ 5069)

observation: The 2002 Act thus postpones the effective date for the limitations that, under pre-2002 Act law, applied after 2001. Those limitations (see below) will apply after 2003.

FTC 2d References are to Federal Tax Coordinator 2d
FIN References are to RIA's Analysis of Federal Taxes: Income
USTR References are to United States Tax Reporter: Income, Estate & Gift, and Excise
PCA References are to the Pension Analysis on Checkpoint and CD-ROM, and in Pension Coordinator
PE References are to the Pension Explanations in Pension and Profit Sharing 2nd
EP References are to the Estate Planning Analysis on Checkpoint and CD-ROM, and in Estate Planning & Taxation Coordinator

 Research Institute of America

Specifically, for tax years beginning in 2002 or 2003, the aggregate amount of personal nonrefundable credits may not exceed the sum of:

... the taxpayer's regular tax liability reduced by the foreign tax credit allowable under Code Sec. 27(a), and

... the tax imposed by Code Sec. 55(a)—i.e., the AMT. (Code Sec. 26(a)(2) as amended by 2002 Act §601(a)(2))

> *observation:* Thus, in 2002 and 2003, all of the otherwise allowable nonrefundable personal credits—i.e., not just the adoption credit, child tax credit and saver's credit—may reduce AMT.

> *illustration (1):* K's regular tax bill for 2003 comes to $4,000, and his tentative minimum tax is $4,500. Thus, he must pay a regular tax of $4,000 plus an AMT of $500. He can claim up to $4,500 of nonrefundable personal credits for 2003 ($4,000 regular tax plus $500 excess of tentative minimum tax over regular tax).

Postponed effective date for separate limitations on adoption credit, child tax credit and saver's credit. The 2002 Act also provides that the amendments made by the following sections of the 2001 Economic Growth and Tax Relief Act (EGTRA) won't apply to tax years beginning during 2002 and 2003:

... Sec. 201(b) (which excepts the child tax credit from the Code Sec. 26 limitation and prescribes a specific limitation allowing it to offset AMT, for tax years beginning after 2001),

... Sec. 202(f) (which excepts the adoption credit from the Code Sec. 26 limitation and prescribes a specific limitation allowing it to offset AMT, for tax years beginning after 2001), and

... Sec. 618(b) (which excepts the saver's credit from the Code Sec. 26 limitation and prescribes a specific limitation allowing it to offset AMT, for tax years beginning after 2001). (2002 Act § 601(b)(2))

> *observation:* The 2002 Act extends the period in which *all* of the otherwise allowable nonrefundable personal credits may be used to offset AMT (as well as regular tax) through 2003. Thus, since the above-described EGTRA rules allow an AMT offset in post-2001 tax years for the adoption credit, the child tax credit and the saver's credit, those rules aren't necessary in 2002 and 2003.

> *observation:* For tax years beginning after 2003, the allowance of the nonrefundable personal credits will be limited as follows:

> ... The aggregate amount of *nonrefundable personal credits other than the adoption credit, child tax credit or saver's credit* may not exceed the excess of: (a) the individual's regular tax liability, over (b) the individual's

tentative minimum tax, determined without regard to the AMT foreign tax credit (see FTC 2d/FIN ¶ L-18101; USTR ¶ 264; TaxDesk ¶ 398,000);

... The *adoption credit* may not exceed the excess of: (a) the sum of regular tax liability plus AMT liability, over (b) the sum of nonrefundable personal credits other than the adoption credit, plus the foreign tax credit (see FTC 2d/FIN ¶ A-4403; USTR ¶ 234; TaxDesk ¶ 569,503);

... The *child tax credit* may not exceed the excess of: (a) the sum of regular tax liability and AMT liability, over (b) the sum of nonrefundable personal credits other than the child tax credit, adoption credit and saver's credit, plus the foreign tax credit (see FTC 2d/FIN ¶ A-4604; USTR ¶ 244.01; TaxDesk ¶ 569,104);

... The *saver's credit* may not exceed the excess of: (a) the sum of nonrefundable personal credits other than the saver's credit and adoption credit, plus the foreign tax credit (see FTC 2d/FIN ¶ A-4705; USTR ¶ 25B4; TaxDesk ¶ 569,205).

illustration (2): Assume the facts from Illustration (1), except that it is 2004. K is otherwise entitled to a HOPE credit of $1,000, and no other nonrefundable personal credits. Under the Code Sec. 26 limitation in effect for 2004, K's allowable HOPE credit may not exceed the excess of his regular tax ($4,000) over his tentative minimum tax ($4,500). Since there is no such excess, he can't use any part of the HOPE credit; it can't reduce his regular tax liability or his AMT liability.

observation: The adoption credit, child tax credit and saver's credit are the only nonrefundable personal credits that may reduce AMT liability in tax years beginning after 2003.

observation: The limitations on the adoption credit and child tax credit that will apply after 2003 are similar to those which apply through 2003. Both sets of limitations allow individuals to use the adoption credit and child tax credit to offset their AMT liability. However, the post-2003 limitations have specific ordering rules which may reduce the amount allowable for these credits.

illustration (3): For 2004, H and W, married taxpayers, have a regular tax liability of $2,100, and no AMT liability. Without taking into account any limitations, they are entitled to a child tax credit of $1,200 and a

FTC 2d References are to Federal Tax Coordinator 2d
FIN References are to RIA's Analysis of Federal Taxes: Income
USTR References are to United States Tax Reporter: Income, Estate & Gift, and Excise
PCA References are to the Pension Analysis on Checkpoint and CD-ROM, and in Pension Coordinator
PE References are to the Pension Explanations in Pension and Profit Sharing 2nd
EP References are to the Estate Planning Analysis on Checkpoint and CD-ROM, and in Estate Planning & Taxation Coordinator

HOPE credit of $1,000. The sum of their regular tax plus AMT exceeds the sum of their nonrefundable personal credits other than the child credit by $1,100 ($2,100 − $1,000). They are thus entitled to claim only $1,100 of the child tax credit. They may claim the full $1,000 HOPE credit.

For a discussion of the 2002 Act provision which provides that an individual's foreign tax credit won't be reduced by nonrefundable personal credits until after 2003 (instead of after 2001), see ¶ 402.

☐ **Effective:** Tax years beginning after Dec. 31, 2001. (2002 Act § 601(c)) In other words, tax years beginning in 2002 and 2003. (Com Rept, see ¶ 5069)

¶ 402. Nonrefundable personal credits won't reduce individual's foreign tax credit until after 2003 (instead of after 2001)

Code Sec. 904(h), as amended by 2002 Act § 601(b)(1)
Generally effective: Tax years beginning after Dec. 31, 2001
Committee Reports, see ¶ 5069

The total amount of the foreign tax credit a taxpayer may claim is limited based in part on the taxpayer's U.S. tax liability. For tax years beginning in 2001, an individual's U.S. tax for this purpose was determined without regard to nonrefundable personal credits. For tax years beginning after 2001, pre-2002 Act law provided that for this purpose, U.S. tax was to be reduced by the sum of nonrefundable personal credits (other than the adoption credit, the child tax credit, and the credit for elective deferrals and IRA contributions (the saver's credit)) allowable for the year. (FTC 2d/FIN ¶ O-4401; USTR ¶ 9044.01; TaxDesk ¶ 394,012)

New Law. The 2002 Act adds tax years beginning in 2002 and 2003 to those years in which an individual's U.S. tax liability isn't reduced by nonrefundable personal credits, for purposes of computing the foreign tax credit. (Code Sec. 904(h) as amended by 2002 Act §601(b)(1))

> ✔*observation:* For tax years beginning after 2003, in determining an individual's allowable foreign tax credit, the individual's U.S. tax will be reduced by nonrefundable personal credits (other than the adoption credit, child tax credit and saver's credit).

> ✔*observation:* Any part of the foreign tax that is not used in a tax year because of the limitations on the amount allowable as a foreign tax credit can be carried back two years and forward five years (see FTC 2d/FIN ¶ O-4601; USTR ¶ 9044.02; TaxDesk ¶ 394,030).

For a discussion of the 2002 Act provision which extends the allowance of nonrefundable personal credits as offsets against the alternative minimum tax (AMT) through 2003 (instead of 2001), see ¶ 401.

☐ **Effective:** Tax years beginning after Dec. 31, 2001. (2002 Act § 601(c)) In other words, tax years beginning in 2002 and 2003. (Com Rept, see ¶ 5069)

¶ 403. 2001 rate reduction credit treated as a nonrefundable personal credit

Code Sec. 6428(b), as amended by 2002 Act § 411(a)(1)
Code Sec. 6428(d), as amended by 2002 Act § 411(a)(2)(A)
Code Sec. 6428(e)(2), as amended by 2002 Act § 411(a)(2)(B)
Generally effective: For tax years beginning after Dec. 31, 2000
Committee Reports, see ¶ 5031

Eligible individuals, subject to certain limitations, are allowed a (rate reduction) credit on their 2001 tax returns equal to 5% of their 2001 taxable income up to: $6,000 for singles and marrieds filing separately (i.e., a maximum of $300); $10,000 for heads of household (i.e., a maximum of $500); and $12,000 for marrieds filing jointly (i.e., a maximum of $600). Many taxpayers received a full or partial credit in the form of an advance refund check (computed based on their 2000 tax year). An otherwise allowable 2001 credit must be reduced by the amount of any advance refund received by the taxpayer. See FTC 2d/FIN ¶ A-1105; USTR ¶ 64,284; TaxDesk ¶ 568,205.

In addition, under pre-2002 Act law, the rate reduction credit was subject to a separate limitation based on tax liability similar to the aggregate limitation (the Code Sec. 26(a) limitation) imposed on nonrefundable personal credits for 2001 (see FTC 2d/FIN ¶ L-18101; USTR ¶ 264; TaxDesk ¶ 398,000). The rate reduction credit limitation provided that the credit could not be more than the excess of (1) the sum of a taxpayer's regular income tax liability, plus any alternative minimum tax (AMT) liability, over (2) the sum of the taxpayer's other allowable credits, other than refundable credits. (FTC 2d/FIN ¶ A-1108; USTR ¶ 64,284.01; TaxDesk ¶ 568,208)

The 2001 rate reduction credit was treated as a nonrefundable personal credit for purposes of determining a taxpayer's 2001 estimated tax installments. (FTC 2d/FIN ¶ S-5209; USTR ¶ 64,284; TaxDesk ¶ 571,306)

FTC 2d References are to Federal Tax Coordinator 2d
FIN References are to RIA's Analysis of Federal Taxes: Income
USTR References are to United States Tax Reporter: Income, Estate & Gift, and Excise
PCA References are to the Pension Analysis on Checkpoint and CD-ROM, and in Pension Coordinator
PE References are to the Pension Explanations in Pension and Profit Sharing 2nd
EP References are to the Estate Planning Analysis on Checkpoint and CD-ROM, and in Estate Planning & Taxation Coordinator

New Law. The 2002 Act provides that for purposes of all the Code's income tax provisions, the 2001 rate reduction credit is to be treated as a credit allowable under subpart A of part IV of subchapter A of chapter 1 of the Code (i.e., as a "nonrefundable personal credit"). (Code Sec. 6428(b) as amended by 2002 Act §411(a)(1)) The special rule treating the credit as a nonrefundable personal credit only under the estimated tax installment rules is eliminated. (Code Sec. 6428(d) as amended by 2002 Act §411(a)(2)(A))

> *observation:* The nonrefundable personal credits listed under the above-described subpart of the Code are: the household and dependent care credit (Code Sec. 21); the elderly and disabled credit (Code Sec. 22); the adoption expense credit (Code Sec. 23); the child tax credit (Code Sec. 24) (although partly a refundable credit, see below); the credit for certain home mortgage interest (Code Sec. 25); the HOPE and lifetime learning credits (Code Sec. 25A); and the (post-2001) saver's credit for elective deferrals and IRA contributions (Code Sec. 25B). The DC first-time homebuyer credit (Code Sec. 1400C) is also treated as a nonrefundable personal credit.

In making the change above, the 2002 Act also eliminates the separate limitation based on tax liability that applied for the 2001 rate reduction credit. (Code Sec. 6428(b)) The advance refunds made based on 2000 return information are unaffected by these changes. (Code Sec. 6428(e)(2) as amended by 2002 Act §411(a)(2)(B))

> *observation:* Because the 2001 rate reduction credit is now treated as a nonrefundable personal credit, it is subject to the aggregate Code Sec. 26(a) limitation on such credits. For 2001 tax returns, under that limitation, the aggregate amount of a taxpayer's nonrefundable personal credits may not exceed the sum of: (1) the taxpayer's regular tax liability reduced by the foreign tax credit allowable under Code Sec. 27(a); plus (2) the AMT. (For further discussion of this limitation, which under the 2002 Act is made to apply through 2003, see ¶ 401.)

The Technical Explanation of the 2002 Act says that the 2001 rate reduction credit was made a nonrefundable personal credit so that it would be allowed before the refundable portion of the child tax credit was determined. (Com Rept, see ¶ 5031) (For how to compute the refundable portion of the child tax credit, see ¶ 404.)

☐ **Effective:** For tax years beginning after Dec. 31, 2000. (2002 Act § 411(x))

> *observation:* Despite the wording of the effective date above, because the Code Sec. 6428 rate reduction credit itself only applies for an individual-taxpayer's first tax year beginning in 2001, the above-described 2002 Act change to that credit only has application for an individual's 2001 tax year.

¶ 404. Computation of refundable child tax credit for 2001 to 2003 is based on increase in all refundable credits, not just child tax credit

Code Sec. 24(d)(1)(B), as amended by 2002 Act § 411(b)
Generally effective: Tax years beginning after Dec. 31, 2000
Committee Reports, see ¶ 5032

Taxpayers are allowed a child tax credit of $600 per qualifying child. The credit is generally nonrefundable, but is refundable to the extent of 10% (15% for tax years after 2004) of the taxpayer's earned income in excess of $10,350 (for 2002). For taxpayers with three or more qualifying children, the credit is refundable to the extent the taxpayer's social security taxes exceed the taxpayer's earned income credit, if the refundable amount, computed in this fashion, exceeds the refundable amount computed under the percentage-of-the-excess-over-$10,350 (for 2002) rule.

Under pre-2002 Act law, the refundable portion of the credit was the lesser of:

(1) the child tax credit which would be allowed without regard to this refund provision or the regular tax/AMT limitation that limits the child tax credit to the excess of regular tax (with certain modifications) plus the AMT over the sum of the taxpayer's nonrefundable personal credits (with certain exceptions); or

(2) the amount by which *the amount of child tax credit* (determined without regard to this refund provision) would increase if the regular tax/AMT limitation described at (1) above were increased by the greater of—

(a) 10% of so much of the taxpayer's earned income which is taken into account in computing taxable income for the tax year as exceeds $10,000 (as adjusted for inflation—$10,350 for 2002); or

(b) in the case of a taxpayer with 3 or more qualifying children, the excess (if any) of:

(i) the taxpayer's social security taxes for the tax year, over

(ii) the earned income credit for the tax year. (FTC 2d/FIN ¶ A-4605; USTR ¶ 244.02; TaxDesk ¶ 569,105)

New Law. The 2002 Act clarifies that the portion of the child credit that is refundable is determined by referring to "the aggregate amount of credits allowed by this subpart" rather than the amount of child tax credit (the italicized phrase above). (Code Sec. 24(d)(1)(B) as amended by 2002 Act §411(b)) This would re-

---

FTC 2d References are to Federal Tax Coordinator 2d
FIN References are to RIA's Analysis of Federal Taxes: Income
USTR References are to United States Tax Reporter: Income, Estate & Gift, and Excise
PCA References are to the Pension Analysis on Checkpoint and CD-ROM, and in Pension
    Coordinator
PE References are to the Pension Explanations in Pension and Profit Sharing 2nd
EP References are to the Estate Planning Analysis on Checkpoint and CD-ROM, and in
    Estate Planning & Taxation Coordinator

tain pre-2001 Economic Growth and Tax Relief Act law that was inadvertently changed by the 2001 Act. (Com Rept, see ¶ 5032)

> ⓡ*observation:* The "credits allowed by this subpart" refers to the nonrefundable personal credits allowed under Subpart A of Part IV of Subchapter A of Chapter 1 of Subtitle A of the Code (i.e., Code Sec. 21 through Code Sec. 26, plus any other credits treated as nonrefundable personal credits).

☐ **Effective:** Tax years beginning after Dec. 31, 2000. (2002 Act § 411(x)) The Technical Explanation of the 2002 Act says the change only applies for tax years beginning in 2001. (Com Rept, see ¶ 5032) That's because, for tax years beginning after Dec. 31, 2001, 2001 Economic Growth and Tax Relief Reconciliation Act §201(b)(2)(C)(ii) changes the italicized phrase back to "amount of credit allowed by this section," i.e. the amount of the child tax credit. However, Sec. 601(b)(2) of the 2002 Act provides that the changes made by Sec. 201(b) of the 2001 Act won't apply for tax years beginning during 2002 and 2003, see ¶ 401

> ⓡ*observation:* Therefore, the change described above, determining the refundable child credit based on the "aggregate amount of credits allowed by this subpart," will be in effect for 2001 through 2003.

¶ 405. Elementary and secondary school teachers are allowed an up-to-$250 above-the-line deduction for their out-of-pocket classroom-related expenses for 2002 and 2003

Code Sec. 62(a)(2)(D), as amended by 2002 Act § 406(a)
Code Sec. 62(d), as amended by 2002 Act § 406(b)
Generally effective: Tax years beginning during 2002 and 2003
Committee Reports, see ¶ 5026

Pre-2002 Act law did not provide any above-the-line deduction to elementary or secondary school teachers for the expenses of paying for classroom materials from their own funds. Instead, under pre-2002 Act law, any unreimbursed expenses paid or incurred by elementary or secondary school teachers in connection with their teaching activities were deductible only as unreimbursed employee business expenses—i.e., as below-the-line miscellaneous itemized deductions subject to the 2%-of-AGI floor on such deductions. (FTC 2d/FIN ¶ L-3900 *et seq.*, ¶ L-4108; USTR ¶ 1624.067; TaxDesk ¶ 256,519, ¶ 561,604)

New Law. For tax years beginning during 2002 or 2003, an eligible educator (see below) is allowed an above-the-line deduction (the classroom expense deduction), not in excess of $250 (but subject to the limitation discussed below), for otherwise allowable Code Sec. 162 trade or business expenses paid or incurred by the eligible educator in connection with books, supplies (other than nonathletic supplies for courses of instruction in health or physical education), computer equipment (including related software and services) and other equipment, and supplementary materials used by the eligible educator in the classroom. (Code Sec. 62(a)(2)(D) as amended by 2002 Act §406(a))

illustration (1): During 2002, K, a grade 3 teacher in an elementary school who qualifies as an eligible educator (see below), spends $200 on chalk, crayons, paints, paper and various other supplies for use by K's pupils in the classroom. K is entitled to an above-the-line classroom expense deduction of $200 for her 2002 tax year for these classroom expenses.

illustration (2): The facts are the same as in the above illustration, except that K spends $400 instead of $200. Because the classroom expense deduction is only available for classroom expenses not in excess of $250, K can only take an above-the-line classroom expense deduction for $250 of the $400. The remaining $150 may be claimed as an unreimbursed employee business expense—i.e., as a below-the-line miscellaneous itemized deduction subject to the 2%-of-AGI floor.

illustration (3): M, a high school art teacher who qualifies as an eligible educator, takes the students in her painting classes to a local museum, and spends $56 in the museum cafeteria for snacks for the students. The above-the-line classroom expense deduction is not available for this expense, because the $56 was not for books, supplies, computer equipment, other equipment, or supplementary materials used that M used in the classroom. However, if M can show that the $56 is an ordinary and necessary employee business expense, M can deduct that amount as an unreimbursed employee business expense—i.e., as a below-the-line miscellaneous itemized deduction subject to the 2%-of-AGI floor.

An eligible educator is, with respect to any tax year, an individual who is a kindergarten through grade 12 teacher, instructor, counselor, principal, or aide in a school for at least 900 hours during a school year. (Code Sec. 62(d)(1)(A) as amended by 2002 Act §406(b)) For this purpose, a school is any school which provides elementary education or secondary education (kindergarten through grade 12), as determined under state law. (Code Sec. 62(d)(1)(B))

FTC 2d References are to Federal Tax Coordinator 2d
FIN References are to RIA's Analysis of Federal Taxes: Income
USTR References are to United States Tax Reporter: Income, Estate & Gift, and Excise
PCA References are to the Pension Analysis on Checkpoint and CD-ROM, and in Pension
    Coordinator
PE References are to the Pension Explanations in Pension and Profit Sharing 2nd
EP References are to the Estate Planning Analysis on Checkpoint and CD-ROM, and in
    Estate Planning & Taxation Coordinator

The classroom expense deduction is allowed for expenses only to the extent the amount of those expenses exceeds the amount excludable for the tax year under:

... Code Sec. 135 (excluding from gross income redemption proceeds from U.S. savings bonds redeemed to pay for qualified higher education expenses, see FTC 2d/FIN ¶ J-3051; USTR ¶ 1354; TaxDesk ¶ 157,001);

... Code Sec. 529(c)(1) (excluding from gross income certain distributions from qualified tuition programs for the financing of qualified higher education expenses, see FTC 2d/FIN ¶ J-5401; USTR ¶ 5294.02; TaxDesk ¶ 149,201);

... Code Sec. 530(d)(2) (excluding from gross income certain distributions from Coverdell education savings accounts for qualified education expenses, see FTC 2d/FIN ¶ J-5458; USTR ¶ 5304.01; TaxDesk ¶ 283,808). (Code Sec. 62(d)(2))

□ **Effective:** Tax years beginning after Dec. 31, 2001 (2002 Act § 406(c)), and before Jan. 1, 2004 (Com Rept, see ¶ 5026).

> *observation:* Because the classroom expense deduction is retroactive to tax years beginning after Dec. 31, 2001, the deduction may be claimed for expenses paid or incurred after 2001 and before Mar. 9, 2002 (the date of enactment of the 2002 Act).

¶ 406. Monthly deemed income of spouse under child care credit rules will increase after 2002 to $250 (from $200) with one child, to $500 (from $400) with two or more

Code Sec. 21(d)(2), as amended by 2002 Act § 418(b)
Generally effective: Tax years beginning after Dec. 31, 2002
Committee Reports, see ¶ 5068

Under the child and dependent care credit rules, for a married taxpayer, the employment-related expenses that qualify for the credit may not exceed the lesser of the earned income of the taxpayer or of the taxpayer's spouse. However, the earned income of a spouse who is either a full-time student, or physically or mentally incapable of self-care, is deemed to be not less than:

... $200 for each month that the spouse is a student or incapable of self-care, if there is one qualifying individual (child under 13, etc.), or

... $400 for each month if there are two or more qualifying individuals. (FTC 2d/FIN ¶ A-4307; USTR ¶ 214.06; TaxDesk ¶ 569,308)

New Law. For tax years beginning after Dec. 31, 2002 (2002 Act § 418(c)), the 2002 Act increases the monthly deemed earned income amounts to:

... $250 (from $200) for a taxpayer with one qualifying individual (Code Sec. 21(d)(2)(A) as amended by 2002 Act §418(b)(1)) , or

... $500 (from $400) for a taxpayer with two or more qualifying individuals. (Code Sec. 21(d)(2)(B) as amended by 2002 Act §418(b)(2))

These increases conform the post-2002 dollar limit on deemed earned income of a taxpayer's spouse who is either (1) a full-time student, or (2) physically or mentally incapable of self-care to the previously scheduled post-2002 dollar limits on employment-related expenses applicable in determining the maximum credit amount. (Com Rept, see ¶ 5068)

> *observation:* In other words, after 2002, as a result of the 2002 Act increases in the monthly deemed earned income dollar amounts, the annual deemed earned income of a spouse who is either a full-time student or incapable of self-care will be $3,000 ($250 × 12 months, instead of $2,400, $200 × 12) for one qualifying individual, or $6,000 ($500 × 12 months, instead of $4,800, $400 × 12) for two or more qualifying individuals. These increased amounts will be the same as the scheduled post-2002 annual dollar limits on employment related expense ($3,000 for one qualifying individual, or $6,000 for two or more qualifying individuals, see FTC 2d/FIN ¶ A-4303; USTR ¶ 214.04; TaxDesk ¶ 569,303). This means that the maximum dollar limits on employment-related expenses will apply to taxpayers with such spouses.

> *illustration:* In 2003, a taxpayer and her spouse have one child who is physically incapable of self care. The taxpayer has earned income of $28,000. The taxpayer's spouse is a full-time student and doesn't have any earned income. The taxpayer's spouse is deemed to have earned income of $3,000 (12 × $250) and taxpayer may therefore claim up to the full $3,000 of employment-related expenses for the care of their child.

> *illustration:* Assume the same facts as in the immediately preceding illustration, except the taxpayer and her spouse have three children, all under the age of 10. The taxpayer's spouse is deemed to have earned income of $6,000 (12 × $500) and taxpayer may therefore claim up to the full $6,000 of employment-related expenses for the care of their children.

☐ **Effective:** Tax years beginning after Dec. 31, 2002. (2002 Act § 418(c))

¶ 407. Surviving spouse or head of household filing status allowed with respect to kidnapped child; principal-place-of-abode requirements treated as met

FTC 2d References are to Federal Tax Coordinator 2d
FIN References are to RIA's Analysis of Federal Taxes: Income
USTR References are to United States Tax Reporter: Income, Estate & Gift, and Excise
PCA References are to the Pension Analysis on Checkpoint and CD-ROM, and in Pension Coordinator
PE References are to the Pension Explanations in Pension and Profit Sharing 2nd
EP References are to the Estate Planning Analysis on Checkpoint and CD-ROM, and in Estate Planning & Taxation Coordinator

Code Sec. 151(c)(6)(C), as amended by 2002 Act § 412(b)
Generally effective: Tax years ending after Dec. 21, 2000
Committee Reports, see ¶ 5055

Among the requirements a taxpayer must satisfy with respect to his or her dependents to claim surviving spouse or head of household filing status is the requirement that the taxpayer's household must be the dependent's principal place of abode for more than half the tax year. Pre-2002 Act law didn't specify how the principal-place-of-abode requirements could be met with respect to a dependent child who is kidnapped. (FTC 2d/FIN ¶ A-1702, ¶ A-1406; USTR ¶ 24.02, ¶ 24.03; TaxDesk ¶ 567,002, ¶ 565,511)

The earned income credit (EIC) for taxpayers with qualifying children generally is available only if an otherwise qualifying child has the same principal place of abode as the taxpayer for more than half the tax year (see FTC 2d/FIN ¶ A-4213; USTR ¶ 324.02; TaxDesk ¶ 569,013). In the case of a kidnapped child, the EIC principal-place-of-abode requirements are treated as met if, for the tax year in which the kidnapping occurred, the child had the same principal place of abode as the taxpayer for more than half the portion of the year before the date of the kidnapping. This treatment applies for all tax years during the period that the child is kidnapped. It ends for the first tax year beginning after the year in which the child dies (or, if earlier, would have attained age 18). Under pre-2002 Act law, the principal-place-of-abode rule for kidnapped children applied only for purposes of the EIC. (FTC 2d/FIN ¶ A-4213.1; USTR ¶ 1514.02; TaxDesk ¶ 569,014)

New Law. The 2002 Act makes the principal-place-of-abode rule for kidnapped children that applies for purposes of the EIC applicable for purposes of determining the taxpayer's filing status. An individual who is presumed by law enforcement authorities to have been kidnapped by someone other than the taxpayer or a member of the individual's family, and who had, for the tax year in which the kidnapping occurred, the same principal place of abode as the taxpayer for more than one-half of the portion of the year before the date of the kidnapping, is treated as meeting the principal-place-of-abode requirements of Code Sec. 2(a)(1)(B) (for surviving spouse filing status, see FTC 2d/FIN ¶ A-1702; USTR ¶ 24.02; TaxDesk ¶ 567,002), Code Sec. 2(b)(1)(A) (for head of household filing status, see FTC 2d/FIN ¶ A-1406; USTR ¶ 24.03; TaxDesk ¶ 565,511), and Code Sec. 32(c)(3)(A)(ii) (for the EIC). This treatment applies for all tax years ending during the period that the child is kidnapped. (Code Sec. 151(c)(6)(C) as amended by 2002 Act §412(b)) It ends for the first tax year beginning after the year in which the child dies (or, if earlier, would have attained age 18). (Code Sec. 151(c)(6)(D))

> *observation:* Thus, the 2002 Act provides that in the case of a kidnapped child, the principal-place-of-abode requirements for surviving spouse filing status and for head of household filing status are treated as met, in addition to the principal-place-of-abode requirements for the EIC.

In other words, if a taxpayer met the household maintenance requirement for surviving spouse filing status or head of household filing status, respectively, with respect to his or her dependent child immediately before the kidnapping, then the taxpayer continues to meet that requirement for purposes of the Code Sec. 2 filing status rules until the child would have reached age 18 or is determined to be dead. (Com Rept, see ¶ 5055)

> **✅ *observation:*** Thus, the taxpayer may claim surviving spouse or head of household filing status for the tax year in which the kidnapping occurs, and for each tax year through the year the child is determined to be dead (or, if earlier, would have attained age 18).

> **✅ *observation:*** Surviving spouse filing status generally is only available for two years following the death of the taxpayer's spouse (see FTC 2d/ FIN ¶ A-1702; USTR ¶ 24.02; TaxDesk ¶ 567,002).

☐ **Effective:** Tax years ending after Dec. 21, 2000. (2002 Act § 412(e))

> **✅ *recommendation:*** A taxpayer who didn't claim surviving spouse or head of household filing status for a return for a tax year ending after Dec. 21, 2000, but who is entitled to do so as a result of this 2002 Act provision, should consider filing an amended return.

¶ 408. Advance payments of earned income credit not treated as tax for purposes of any tax credits

Code Sec. 32(g)(2), as amended by 2002 Act § 416(a)(1)
Generally effective: Tax years beginning after Dec. 31, '83
Committee Reports, see ¶ 5061

If any payment of advanced earned income credit is made to an individual by his employer during any calendar year, the individual's income tax for his last tax year beginning in that calendar year is increased by the aggregate amount of those payments. Under pre-2002 Act law, any increase in tax under the above rule wasn't treated as tax for purposes of determining the amount of any credit (other than the earned income credit) allowable under this subpart. (FTC 2d/FIN ¶ H-4855; USTR ¶ 324.03; TaxDesk ¶ 569,028)

FTC 2d References are to Federal Tax Coordinator 2d
FIN References are to RIA's Analysis of Federal Taxes: Income
USTR References are to United States Tax Reporter: Income, Estate & Gift, and Excise
PCA References are to the Pension Analysis on Checkpoint and CD-ROM, and in Pension Coordinator
PE References are to the Pension Explanations in Pension and Profit Sharing 2nd
EP References are to the Estate Planning Analysis on Checkpoint and CD-ROM, and in Estate Planning & Taxation Coordinator

🔵 *observation:* "This subpart" refers to Subpart C of Part IV of Sub-chapter A of Chapter 1 of Subtitle A of the Code (i.e., Code Sec. 31 through Code Sec. 35, which allow the so-called refundable credits).

New Law. The 2002 changes the phrase "this subpart" in Code Sec. 32(g)(2) to "this part." (Code Sec. 32(g)(2) as amended by 2002 Act §416(a)(1)) Thus, the reference is to all tax credits, rather than just the refundable credits. (Com Rept, see ¶ 5061)

🔵 *illustration:* Taxpayer X receives advance earned income payment credits. She is also eligible for lifetime learning credit, a refundable credit that is subject to a limitation based on tax liability. The advance EIC payments that X receives aren't considered tax for purposes of the credit limitation.

☐ **Effective:** Tax years beginning after Dec. 31, '83. (2002 Act § 416(a)(2))

¶ 409. The 10% additional tax on Coverdell ESA distributions doesn't apply to distributions that are includible in income only because a HOPE or Lifetime Learning credit is taken instead

Code Sec. 530(d)(4)(B)(iv), as amended by 2002 Act § 411(f)
Generally effective: For tax years beginning after Dec. 31, 2001
Committee Reports, see ¶ 5036

If an amount distributed from a Coverdell education savings account ("Coverdell ESA," formerly known as an education IRA) is includible in income, an additional tax is imposed. The additional tax is 10% of the amount of the Coverdell ESA distribution which is includible in the distributee's gross income. There are several exceptions to the application of the 10% additional tax, one of which provided (under pre-2002 Act law) that the 10% additional tax did not apply if the distribution was includible in gross income solely because the beneficiary elected to waive the exclusion from income for the Coverdell ESA distribution. FTC 2d/ FIN ¶ J-5459; USTR ¶ 5304.01; TaxDesk ¶ 283,809

A distribution from a Coverdell ESA is included in the gross income of the distributee under the Code Sec. 72 annuity rules. Thus, distributions are considered to consist of a pro-rata share of principal (distributions of which, under all circumstances, are excludable from gross income) and accumulated earnings (distributions of which may be excludable from gross income under the Coverdell ESA rules). If a Coverdell ESA beneficiary's qualified education expenses equal or exceed the total Coverdell ESA distributions for the year, then the distributions are entirely excluded from the beneficiary's gross income. When making the determination whether distributions from a Coverdell ESA exceed the beneficiary's qualified education expenses, the total amount of qualified education expenses for an individual for a tax year must be reduced by the amount of those expenses that were taken into account in determining the Code Sec. 25A HOPE credit and the Lifetime Learning credit allowed to the taxpayer or any other person.

Under the law that applied before the enactment of the 2001 Economic Growth and Tax Relief Reconciliation Act (EGTRRA), taxpayers were permitted to waive an exclusion from income from a Coverdell ESA. This waiver was permitted because, under pre-EGTRRA law, taxpayers could not claim the HOPE or Lifetime Learning credit in the same year that they claimed an exclusion from income for a Coverdell ESA. Thus, taxpayers were permitted to waive the exclusion in order to claim the HOPE or Lifetime Learning credit. Under EGTRRA, after 2001, taxpayers *are* permitted to claim the Coverdell ESA exclusion *and* claim a HOPE or Lifetime Learning credit in the same year, provided they don't claim both for the same expenses. The election to waive the Coverdell ESA exclusion is thus unnecessary, and was dropped by EGTRRA. However, the reference to the election to waive the exclusion was retained in the statutory language relating to the exception from the 10% additional tax on distributions from Coverdell ESAs.

New Law. The reference, in the pre-2002 Act statutory language, to the election to waive the exclusion was intended to preserve the rule that the 10% additional tax doesn't apply for Coverdell ESA earnings that are includible in income solely because the HOPE or Lifetime Learning credit is claimed for those expenses. The 2002 Act clarifies the law to preserve this result. (Com Rept, see ¶ 5036)

The 2002 Act does this by amending the statutory language of the exception to the 10% additional tax by striking the language relating to the election to waive the exclusion from income for a Coverdell ESA. As re-written by the 2002 Act, the exception provides that the 10% additional tax doesn't apply to an amount which is includible in gross income solely by reason of the application of the Code Sec. 530(d)(2)(C)(i)(II) rule that the total amount of qualified education expenses for an individual for a tax year must be reduced by the amount of those expenses that were taken into account in determining the HOPE credit and the Lifetime Learning credits allowed to the taxpayer or any other person. (Code Sec. 530(d)(4)(B)(iv) as amended by 2002 Act §411(f))

This provision prevents the 10% additional tax from applying to a distribution from a Coverdell ESA (or qualified tuition program under Code Sec. 529) that is used to pay qualified education expenses where the taxpayer elects to claim a HOPE or Lifetime Learning credit in lieu of the exclusion under Code Sec. 530 (relating to Coverdell ESAs) or Code Sec. 529 (relating to qualified tuition pro-

---

FTC 2d References are to Federal Tax Coordinator 2d
FIN References are to RIA's Analysis of Federal Taxes: Income
USTR References are to United States Tax Reporter: Income, Estate & Gift, and Excise
PCA References are to the Pension Analysis on Checkpoint and CD-ROM, and in Pension
  Coordinator
PE References are to the Pension Explanations in Pension and Profit Sharing 2nd
EP References are to the Estate Planning Analysis on Checkpoint and CD-ROM, and in
  Estate Planning & Taxation Coordinator

grams). Thus, in that situation, the income distributed from the Coverdell ESA (or qualified tuition program) would be subject to income tax, but not to the 10% additional tax. (Com Rept, see ¶ 5036)

> *illustration:* Smith contributes $50,000 to a Coverdell ESA for his daughter, Mary, when Mary is ten years old. By the time Mary enters college, the amount in the Coverdell ESA is $100,000, of which 50% ($50,000) represents accumulated earnings on the original $50,000 contribution. A distribution of $3,000 is made from the Coverdell ESA to Mary to reimburse her for qualified education expenses which she paid directly. The distribution is considered to consist of principal of $1,500 and accumulated earnings of $1,500. Mary elects to claim a HOPE credit of $1,500 instead of excluding the accumulated earnings portion of the distribution from income under the Coverdell ESA rules. The $1,500 accumulated earnings portion of the distribution is not subject to the 10% additional tax.

☐ **Effective:** For tax years beginning after Dec. 31, 2001 (2002 Act § 411(x))

¶ 410. Additional tax on distributions from Medicare+Choice Archer MSAs not used for qualified medical expenses is not included in a taxpayer's "regular tax liability" for credit purposes

Code Sec. 26(b)(2)(R), as amended by 2002 Act § 415(a)
Generally effective: Tax years beginning after Dec. 31, '98
Committee Reports, see ¶ 5060

For purposes of the rules on credits against income tax (which generally provide that nonrefundable personal credits are allowed only to the extent that the taxpayer's regular tax liability exceeds his tentative minimum tax), "regular tax liability" is the tax imposed by Chapter 1 of the Code. Code Sec. 26(b)(2) contains a list of taxes which are *not* treated as a tax imposed by Chapter 1 for this purpose. One of the taxes listed in Code Sec. 26(b)(2) is the 15% tax on Archer medical savings account (Archer MSA) distributions not used for qualified medical expenses. (FTC 2d/FIN ¶ L-18103; USTR ¶ 264.01; TaxDesk ¶ 398,000)

> *observation:* The impact of having a tax listed in Code Sec. 26(b)(2) is to potentially reduce the amount of any credit against tax that might otherwise be available.

Individuals who are eligible for Medicare are permitted to choose either the traditional Medicare program or a Medicare+Choice Archer medical savings account (Medicare+Choice Archer MSA). A Medicare+Choice Archer MSA is an Archer MSA, but which is designated as a Medicare+Choice Archer MSA by the individual account holder. Distributions from Medicare+Choice Archer MSAs for purposes other than qualified medical expenses are subject to an additional tax if a minimum balance is not maintained. The additional tax is 50% of the excess (if any) of:

(1) the amount of the payment or distribution, over

(2) the excess (if any) of:

(A) the fair market value of the assets of the Medicare+Choice Archer MSA as of the close of the calendar year preceding the calendar year in which the tax year begins, over

(B) an amount equal to 60% of the deductible under the Medicare+Choice Archer MSA plan covering the account holder as of Jan. 1 of the calendar year in which the tax year begins. FTC 2d/FIN ¶ H-1348.4; USTR ¶ 1384.04; TaxDesk ¶ 288,504

New Law. The 2002 Act retroactively adds, to the list of taxes that are not treated as imposed by Chapter 1 for purposes of determining a taxpayer's "regular tax liability," the additional tax on Medicare+Choice Archer MSA distributions not used for qualified medical expenses. (Code Sec. 26(b)(2)(R) as amended by 2002 Act §415(a))

Thus, the 2002 Act conforms the treatment of (1) the additional tax on distributions from Medicare+Choice Archer MSAs not used for qualified medical expenses to (2) the treatment of the additional tax on Archer MSA distributions not used for qualified medical expenses, for purposes of determining whether certain taxes are included in "regular tax liability" under Code Sec. 26(b). (Com Rept, see ¶ 5060)

> *illustration:* Jones has a Medicare+Choice Archer MSA from which he receives a $5,000 distribution. The distribution is used for healthcare expenses that are not qualified medical expenses. Assume that the additional tax that is imposed on the distribution, in accordance with the rules discussed above, is $1,000. Assume also that Jones's regular tax liability for the tax year of the distribution (which does *not* include the $1,000 additional tax, under the above provision of the 2002 Act) is $500. If Jones is entitled to a $750 child and dependent care credit, he may claim a credit of $500 against his regular tax liability (thus reducing his regular tax liability to zero). However, Jones may *not* apply the remaining $250 of the credit against the additional tax on the distribution from his Medicare+Choice Archer MSA.

FTC 2d References are to Federal Tax Coordinator 2d
FIN References are to RIA's Analysis of Federal Taxes: Income
USTR References are to United States Tax Reporter: Income, Estate & Gift, and Excise
PCA References are to the Pension Analysis on Checkpoint and CD-ROM, and in Pension Coordinator
PE References are to the Pension Explanations in Pension and Profit Sharing 2nd
EP References are to the Estate Planning Analysis on Checkpoint and CD-ROM, and in Estate Planning & Taxation Coordinator

☐ **Effective:** Tax years beginning after Dec. 31, '98 (2002 Act § 415(b))

¶ 411. Aggregate expenses for adopting special-needs child after 2002 deemed to be $10,000 for exclusion purposes in year adoption becomes final

Code Sec. 137(a), as amended by 2002 Act § 411(c)(2)(A)
Generally effective: Tax years beginning after Dec. 31, 2002
Committee Reports, see ¶ 5033

Employees can exclude from gross income the qualified adoption expenses paid or reimbursed by an employer under an adoption assistance program. The aggregate amount of amounts paid or expenses incurred that may be taken into account for purposes of the exclusion for all tax years with respect to the adoption of a child by the taxpayer is limited to $10,000.

The 2001 Economic Growth and Tax Relief Act provided that, in the case of an adoption of a child with special needs, an employee could exclude $10,000 of amounts paid or expenses incurred by the employer for adoption expenses furnished under an adoption assistance program, regardless of whether the taxpayer had qualified adoption expenses. This change was to be effective for tax years beginning after Dec. 31, 2002. (FTC 2d/FIN ¶ H-1451; USTR ¶ 1374; TaxDesk ¶ 133,601)

> **observation:** This rule could have been read to mean that the $10,000 exclusion was available in the first year that adoption expenses are incurred, regardless of whether the adoption became final in that year or whether it ever became final.

New Law. Under the 2002 Act, the adoption assistance exclusion is limited to amounts paid or expenses incurred by the employer for qualified adoption expenses. However, in the case of an adoption of a child with special needs, the qualified adoption expenses for tax year in which the adoption becomes final will be increased by an amount equal to the excess (if any) of $10,000 over the actual aggregate qualified adoption expenses with respect to the adoption during that tax year and all prior tax years. (Code Sec. 137(a) as amended by 2002 Act §411(c)(2)(A))

> **observation:** In other words, taxpayers who adopt a child with special needs will be deemed to have qualified adoption expenses in the tax year in which the adoption becomes final in an amount sufficient to bring their total aggregate expenses for the adoption up to $10,000. They can exclude employer-provided adoption assistance up to that amount, whether or not they had $10,000 of actual expenses. In earlier tax years, the taxpayers can exclude employer-provided adoption assistance up to the amount of their actual qualified adoption expenses (subject to the dollar limit).

observation: Taxpayers whose special-needs adoption becomes final after 2002 can take advantage of this provision by requesting adoption assistance from an employer's program in the year it becomes final up to the $10,000 limit.

illustration (1): Taxpayers X and Y receive $2,000 of employer-provided adoption assistance for a special-needs adoption in 2003 and $8,000 in 2004. Their actual qualified adoption expenses are $2,000 in 2003 and $5,000 in 2004. The adoption becomes final in 2004.

In 2003, X and Y can exclude the $2,000 of adoption assistance they receive.

In 2004, X and Y's actual expenses of $5,000 are increased by the excess of $10,000 over their actual aggregate adoption expenses for 2004 and all prior tax years. This amount is $3,000 ($10,000 − ($2,000 + $5,000)).

Thus, X and Y's qualified adoption expenses for 2004 are $8,000 ($5,000 + $3,000), and they can exclude the entire $8,000 they received in 2004. Their total exclusion for the adoption for all years is $10,000.

observation: If a special-needs adoption never becomes final, the taxpayers can exclude employer-provided adoption assistance up to their actual qualified adoption expenses, but they aren't deemed to have had aggregate qualified adoption expenses of $10,000 regardless of actual expenses.

illustration (2): Assume that the adoption in Illustration (1) was never finalized. In that case, X and Y could exclude the employer-provided adoption assistance up to their actual qualified adoption expenses—$2,000 in 2003 and $5,000 in 2004. They wouldn't be deemed to have had an additional $3,000 of qualified expenses in 2004. Their total exclusion for the adoption would have been $7,000.

☐ **Effective:** Tax years beginning after Dec. 31, 2002. (2002 Act § 411(c)(3))

¶ 412. Aggregate expenses for adopting special-needs child after 2002 deemed to be $10,000 for credit purposes in year adoption becomes final

FTC 2d References are to Federal Tax Coordinator 2d
FIN References are to RIA's Analysis of Federal Taxes: Income
USTR References are to United States Tax Reporter: Income, Estate & Gift, and Excise
PCA References are to the Pension Analysis on Checkpoint and CD-ROM, and in Pension Coordinator
PE References are to the Pension Explanations in Pension and Profit Sharing 2nd
EP References are to the Estate Planning Analysis on Checkpoint and CD-ROM, and in Estate Planning & Taxation Coordinator

Code Sec. 23(a)(1), as amended by 2002 Act § 411(c)(1)(A)
Code Sec. 23(a)(2), as amended by 2002 Act § 411(c)(1)(C)
Code Sec. 23(a)(3), as amended by 2002 Act § 411(c)(1)(B)
Generally effective: Tax years beginning after Dec. 31, 2002
Committee Reports, see ¶ 5033

Where qualified adoption expenses are paid or incurred before the tax year the adoption becomes final, the adoption credit is generally allowed in the tax year following the tax year the expenses are paid or incurred. Expenses paid or incurred during or after the tax year in which the adoption becomes final are allowed in the tax year in which the expense is paid or incurred. (FTC 2d/FIN ¶ A-4401.1; USTR ¶ 234; TaxDesk ¶ 569,501.1)

The 2001 Economic Growth and Tax Relief Act provided that, in the case of an adoption of a child with special needs, a $10,000 credit would be allowed regardless of the amount of qualified adoption expenses paid or incurred. This change was to be effective for tax years beginning after Dec. 31, 2002. The 2001 Act also provided, effective for tax years beginning after Dec. 31, 2001, the credit for a special needs adoption is allowed for the tax year in which the adoption became final. (FTC 2d/FIN ¶ A-4401; USTR ¶ 234; TaxDesk ¶ 569,501)

> *observation:* Under this rule, if expenses of a special needs adoption had been paid or incurred over several years, the entire credit would be postponed until the year in which the adoption became final. Also, no credit would be allowed if the adoption was never finalized.

New Law. The 2002 Act eliminates the rule that allowed the credit for a special needs adoption in the tax year in which the adoption became final. (Code Sec. 23(a)(2) as amended by 2002 Act §411(c)(1)(C))

> *observation:* Thus, if expenses of a special needs adoption are paid or incurred over several years, the entire credit isn't postponed until the year in which the adoption becomes final. Instead, expenses paid or incurred before the year in which the adoption becomes final are allowed as a credit in the following year.

Under the Act, the adoption credit allowed is equal to the qualified adoption expenses paid or incurred by the taxpayer. (Code Sec. 23(a)(1) as amended by 2002 Act §411(c)(1)(A)) However, in the case of an adoption of a child with special needs, the taxpayer is treated as having paid qualified adoption expenses during the tax year that the adoption becomes final in an amount equal to the excess (if any) of $10,000 over the aggregate qualified adoption expenses actually paid or incurred by the taxpayer with respect to the adoption during that tax year and all prior tax years. (Code Sec. 23(a)(3) as amended by 2002 Act §411(c)(1)(B))

Thus, the Act clarifies that, for special needs adoptions that become final in tax years beginning after 2002, the adoption expenses taken into account will be increased by the excess (if any) of $10,000 over the aggregate adoption expenses for the tax year the adoption becomes final and all prior tax years. (Com Rept, see ¶ 5033)

> ✒ *illustration (1):* Taxpayers X and Y incurred $2,000 of qualified adoption expenses for a special needs adoption in 2001, $3,000 in 2002, and $4,000 in 2003. The adoption became final in 2003.
>
> In 2002, X and Y can claim a credit for the $2,000 of expenses paid in 2001.
>
> In 2003, X and Y can claim a credit for the $3,000 of expenses paid in 2002 and the $4,000 of expenses paid in 2003. In addition, they can claim a credit for the excess of $10,000 over the aggregate adoption expenses for the tax year the adoption becomes final and all prior tax years. This amount is $1,000 ($10,000 − ($2,000 + $3,000 + $4,000). Thus, their total credit for 2003 is $8,000. Their total credit for all years is $10,000.

> ✒ *observation:* If a special needs adoption is never finalized, the actual expenses paid or incurred can still be claimed as a credit. However, the post-2002 rule allowing a credit for the excess of $10,000 over actual expenses paid or incurred during the current and all prior tax years won't apply.

> ✒ *illustration (2):* Assume the same facts as in Illustration (1), except that the adoption isn't finalized. In that case, X and Y could claim a credit for their actual expenses, but they wouldn't be entitled to an additional credit to bring the total up to $10,000.

For a similar change with respect to the exclusion for employer-provided adoption assistance, see ¶ 411.

☐ **Effective:** Tax years beginning after Dec. 31, 2002, except that the change made by Act §411(c)(1)(C) (eliminating the rule that would have allowed the credit for a special needs adoption in the tax year in which the adoption became final) is effective for tax years beginning after Dec. 31, 2001. (2002 Act § 411(c)(3))

> ✒ *observation:* For tax years beginning after Dec. 31, 2001, the dollar limit on the credit is $10,000 for all adoptions. However, for expenses paid or incurred during tax years beginning before Jan. 1, 2002, that are taken into account in a tax year beginning after Dec. 31, 2001, the dollar limit is $5,000 ($6,000 for special-needs adoptions), see ¶ 413.

FTC 2d References are to Federal Tax Coordinator 2d
FIN References are to RIA's Analysis of Federal Taxes: Income
USTR References are to United States Tax Reporter: Income, Estate & Gift, and Excise
PCA References are to the Pension Analysis on Checkpoint and CD-ROM, and in Pension Coordinator
PE References are to the Pension Explanations in Pension and Profit Sharing 2nd
EP References are to the Estate Planning Analysis on Checkpoint and CD-ROM, and in Estate Planning & Taxation Coordinator

🅡🅘🅐 Research Institute of America   125

For tax years beginning after Dec. 31, 2002, the rule discussed above takes effect, increasing the aggregate qualified adoption expenses of a special-needs adoption to $10,000 in the year that the adoption becomes final.

¶ 413. Qualified adoption expenses paid or incurred before 2002 are subject to pre-2002 dollar limits

Code Sec. None, 2002 Act § 411(c)(1)(F)
Generally effective: Tax years beginning after Dec. 31, 2001
Committee Reports, see ¶ 5033

Where qualified adoption expenses are paid or incurred before the tax year in which the adoption becomes final, the adoption credit is generally allowed in the tax year following the tax year the expenses are paid or incurred. (FTC 2d/FIN ¶ A-4401.1; USTR ¶ 234; TaxDesk ¶ 569,501.1)

The 2001 Economic Growth and Tax Relief Act increased the aggregate amount of adoption expenses that could be taken into account in computing the adoption credit for all tax years with respect to the adoption of a child by the taxpayer from $5,000 ($6,000 in the case of special needs adoptions) to $10,000 for all adoptions. The increase was effective for tax years beginning after Dec. 31, 2001. (FTC 2d/FIN ¶ A-4401; USTR ¶ 234; TaxDesk ¶ 569,501) However, the 2001 Act didn't include a provision describing the dollar limit for amounts paid or incurred during tax years beginning before Jan. 1, 2002, for adoptions that don't become final in those years. (Com Rept, see ¶ 5033)

New Law. The 2002 Act clarifies that expenses paid or incurred during tax years beginning before Jan. 1, 2002, which are taken into account in determining a credit allowed in a tax year beginning after Dec. 31, 2001 (Com Rept, see ¶ 5033), are subject to the $5,000 (or $6,000) dollar cap that was in effect immediately before the enactment of the 2001 Act. (2002 Act § 411(c)(1)(F))

> *illustration (1):* Taxpayers X and Y incurred $8,000 of qualified adoption expenses in 2001 for a non-special-needs adoption. The adoption became final in 2002.
>
> In 2002, X and Y can claim a credit for $5,000 of the expenses paid in 2001. The other $3,000 paid in 2001 can't be claimed, because it exceeds the $5,000 limit in effect for 2001.

> *illustration (2):* Suppose that X and Y also paid $2,000 of qualified adoption expenses for the same adoption in 2002. Those expenses aren't subject to the transitional rule of Act §411(c)(1)(F), because they were paid in a tax year beginning after Dec. 31, 2001. Rather, they are subject to the post-2001 dollar limit on qualified adoption expenses of $10,000 per adoption (see above).

Thus, X and Y can also claim as a credit in 2002 the $2,000 of qualified adoption expenses they paid in 2002. Their total adoption credit for 2002 is $7,000 ($5,000 of 2001 expenses plus $2,000 of 2002 expenses).

☐ **Effective:** Tax years beginning after Dec. 31, 2001. (Com Rept, see ¶ 5033)

¶ 414. Rounding rules provided for inflation adjustments for adoption credit and adoption assistance exclusion

Code Sec. 23(h), as amended by 2002 Act § 418(a)(1)(B)
Code Sec. 137(f), as amended by 2002 Act § 418(a)(2)
Generally effective: Tax years beginning after Dec. 31, 2001
Committee Reports, see ¶ 5067

For tax years beginning after Dec. 31, 2002, all the dollar limits and income limitations relating to the adoption credit (FTC 2d/FIN ¶ A-4402.1; USTR ¶ 234; TaxDesk ¶ 569,502.1) and the adoption assistance exclusion (FTC 2d/FIN ¶ 1452.1; USTR ¶ 1374; TaxDesk ¶ 133,604) will be increased by an amount equal to the dollar amount multiplied by the cost-of-living adjustment determined under Code Sec. 1(f)(3) for the calendar year in which the tax year begins, but using 2001 (rather than 1992) as the base year.

Under pre-2002 Act law, no rounding rule applied to the inflation adjustments, i.e., the post-2002 inflation-adjusted limits would have been exact dollars-and-cents amounts.

New Law. The 2002 Act provides uniform rounding rules for the inflation-adjusted dollar limits and income limitations on the adoption credit and the adoption assistance exclusion. (Com Rept, see ¶ 5067) Any inflation-adjusted amount that isn't a multiple of $10 will be rounded to the nearest multiple of $10. This rule applies for purposes of the adoption credit (Code Sec. 23(h) as amended by 2002 Act §418(a)(1)(B)) and the adoption assistance exclusion. (Code Sec. 137(f) as amended by 2002 Act §418(a)(2))

☐ **Effective:** Tax years beginning after Dec. 31, 2001. (2002 Act § 418(c))

¶ 415. Foster care payments received from taxable (as well as tax-exempt) placement agencies are excludable from foster care provider's gross income

FTC 2d References are to Federal Tax Coordinator 2d
FIN References are to RIA's Analysis of Federal Taxes: Income
USTR References are to United States Tax Reporter: Income, Estate & Gift, and Excise
PCA References are to the Pension Analysis on Checkpoint and CD-ROM, and in Pension Coordinator
PE References are to the Pension Explanations in Pension and Profit Sharing 2nd
EP References are to the Estate Planning Analysis on Checkpoint and CD-ROM, and in Estate Planning & Taxation Coordinator

Code Sec. 131(b)(1), as amended by 2002 Act § 404(a)
Generally effective: Tax years beginning after Dec. 31, 2001
Committee Reports, see ¶ 5024

A foster care provider can exclude qualified foster care payments from gross income. The payment must be for caring for a qualified foster individual, or must be a difficulty of care payment.

Under pre-2002 Act law, a qualified foster care payment had to be paid to the foster care provider by either: (1) a state or political subdivision of a state; or (2) a tax-exempt placement agency described in Code Sec. 501(c)(3). Payments made by placement agencies that were not tax-exempt didn't qualify. There was no requirement that the payments had to be made under a foster care program. (FTC 2d/FIN ¶ J-1502; USTR ¶ 1314.01; TaxDesk ¶ 196,502)

New Law. The 2002 Act expands the definition of qualified foster care payments to include payments by a placement agency that is licensed or certified by a state or local government, or by an entity designated by a state or local government to make payments to providers of foster care. (Com Rept, see ¶ 5024) The requirement that foster care payments paid by placement agencies must be paid by *tax-exempt* placement agencies is removed. Under the Act, the payment can be made by either:

(1) a state or political subdivision of a state (Code Sec. 131(b)(1)(A)(i) as amended by 2002 Act §404(a)) , or

(2) a qualified foster care placement agency (defined below). (Code Sec. 131(b)(1)(A)(ii))

A qualified foster care payment must be made under a foster care program of a state or a political subdivision of a state. (Code Sec. 131(b)(1))

A qualified foster care placement agency is any placement agency which is licensed or certified by the state or political subdivision (Code Sec. 131(b)(3)(A)) , or by an entity designated by the state or political subdivision (Code Sec. 131(b)(3)(B)) , for the foster care program of that state or political subdivision to make foster care payments to providers of foster care. (Code Sec. 131(b)(3))

> *observation:* A qualified foster care placement agency must have the requisite license or certification, but it doesn't have to be tax-exempt.

> *observation:* While the Act expands the list of nongovernmental persons who are eligible to make qualified foster payments by eliminating the requirement that payments made by a placement agency must be made by an agency that's *tax-exempt,* it imposes an additional requirement that the payments must be made under a governmental foster care program.

> *observation:* Although the Act allows state and local governments to employ both tax-exempt and taxable entities to administer their foster care

programs, it doesn't extend the exclusion to payments outside those foster care programs (e.g., payments to a foster care provider from friends or relatives of foster care individuals in its care).

For a discussion of the 2002 Act provision which provides that a qualified foster care individual may be placed in a foster home by a qualified placement agency *regardless* of the individual's age at the time of placement, see ¶ 416.

☐ **Effective:** Tax years beginning after Dec. 31, 2001 (2002 Act § 404(d))

> 🅡 *observation:* Presumably, taxpayers receiving payments for pre-2002 placements from placement agencies that aren't tax-exempt may be able to exclude payments received with respect to these placements after Dec. 31, 2001, if the agency meets the qualified foster care placement agency definition and the payments are made under a foster care program of a state or political subdivision.

> 🅡 *recommendation:* Since this provision applies retroactively to the beginning of 2002, taxpayers whose estimated tax payments for the first quarter of 2002 included amounts attributable to foster care payments that are tax-free as a result of the 2002 Act changes should recalculate their required annual payment for the year and adjust the remaining quarterly installments (see FTC 2d/FIN ¶ S-5230).

¶ 416. Individual placed in foster home by private placement agency can be qualified foster care individual even if not under age 19 at time of placement

Code Sec. 131(b)(2)(B), as amended by 2002 Act § 404(b)
Code Sec. 131(b)(4), redesignated by 2002 Act § 404(b)
Generally effective: Tax years beginning after Dec. 31, 2001
Committee Reports, see ¶ 5024

Amounts paid to a foster care provider for caring, in the foster provider's home, for a qualified foster individual, are excludable from gross income. A qualified foster individual is an individual living in a foster family home in which the individual was placed by an agency of a state or political subdivision of the state. Pre-2002 Act law provided that the placement could also be made by a private placement agency but only if the agency was tax-exempt and the individual was under

---

FTC 2d References are to Federal Tax Coordinator 2d
FIN References are to RIA's Analysis of Federal Taxes: Income
USTR References are to United States Tax Reporter: Income, Estate & Gift, and Excise
PCA References are to the Pension Analysis on Checkpoint and CD-ROM, and in Pension Coordinator
PE References are to the Pension Explanations in Pension and Profit Sharing 2nd
EP References are to the Estate Planning Analysis on Checkpoint and CD-ROM, and in Estate Planning & Taxation Coordinator

🅡 Research Institute of America 129

the age of 19 at the time of placement. (FTC 2d/FIN ¶ J-1503; TaxDesk ¶ 196,503)

New Law. The 2002 Act expands the definition of a qualified foster care individual (Com Rept, see ¶ 5024) by removing the requirement for individuals placed in a foster home by a private placement agency, that the individual had to be under age 19 at the time of placement. Under the Act, a foster care individual includes an individual who was placed in a foster family home by a "qualified foster care placement agency" (generally, a placement agency licensed by a state or political subdivision under its foster care program, see ¶ 415). (Code Sec. 131(b)(2)(B) as amended by 2002 Act §404(b)) Thus, an individual who was placed in a foster family home by a private placement agency may be a qualified foster care individual, regardless of the individual's age at the time of placement. (Com Rept, see ¶ 5024)

> *illustration:* J is living in a foster family home. He was placed there when he was 20 years old, by a child placement agency. The agency is certified by the state, but it's not an agency of the state. J is a qualified foster individual. Under pre-2002 Act law, J wouldn't have qualified, since he wasn't under age 19 when the placement was made.

The Act also removes the requirement for individuals placed by private placement agencies, that the agency had to be *tax-exempt.* (Code Sec. 131(b)(2)(B))

> *observation:* As described at ¶ 415, a private placement agency doesn't have to be tax-exempt to be a qualified foster care placement agency. However, the agency must have the requisite license or certification.

The Act doesn't change the rule that foster care payments (other than "difficulty of care payments") for any period aren't excludable to the extent they are made for more than five qualified foster individuals who are age 19 or older (see FTC 2d/FIN ¶ J-1501; USTR ¶ 1314.01; TaxDesk ¶ 196,501). (Code Sec. 131(b)(4) redesignated by 2002 Act §404(b))

For a discussion of the 2002 Act provision which expands the definition of qualifying private placement agencies to include agencies that are not tax-exempt, see ¶ 415.

☐ **Effective:** Tax years beginning after Dec. 31, 2001 (2002 Act § 404(d))

> *observation:* Presumably, taxpayers receiving payments with respect to individuals who were placed in their homes before 2002 by private placement agencies that aren't tax-exempt—including individuals who were not under age 19 when they were placed—may be able to exclude payments received after Dec. 31, 2001 with respect to these placements, if the agency meets the qualified foster care placement agency definition and the payments otherwise qualify.

recommendation: Since this provision applies retroactively to the beginning of 2002, taxpayers whose estimated tax payments for the first quarter of 2002 included amounts attributable to foster care payments that are tax-free as a result of the 2002 Act changes should recalculate their required annual payment for the year and adjust the remaining quarterly installments (see FTC 2d/FIN ¶ S-5230).

¶ 417. Basic standard deduction for marrieds filing separate will stay at half of amount for marrieds filing joint for 2005 through 2008

Code Sec. 63(c)(2), as amended by 2002 Act § 411(e)(1)
Generally effective: Tax years beginning after Dec. 31, 2004
Committee Reports, see ¶ 5035

Under pre-2002 Act law, for tax years beginning before Jan. 1, 2005, the basic standard deduction for married taxpayers filing separate returns (for 2002, $3,925 as adjusted for inflation) is half the basic standard deduction for married taxpayers filing joint returns and surviving spouses (for 2002, $7,850 as adjusted for inflation). Stated reciprocally, for this period, the basic standard deduction amount for marrieds filing jointly and surviving spouses is twice the basic standard deduction amount for marrieds filing separately.

However, for tax years beginning after Dec. 31, 2004, the basic standard deduction amounts for taxpayers filing jointly and surviving spouses was to become the "applicable percentage" (see below) of the basic standard deduction amount for a category of "in any other case" taxpayers. This "in any other case" category was to include married taxpayers filing separate returns and unmarried individuals filing a single return.

The applicable percentages start at 174% for 2005 and increase to 200% for 2009 and later years, in accord with the following table:

FTC 2d References are to Federal Tax Coordinator 2d
FIN References are to RIA's Analysis of Federal Taxes: Income
USTR References are to United States Tax Reporter: Income, Estate & Gift, and Excise
PCA References are to the Pension Analysis on Checkpoint and CD-ROM, and in Pension
    Coordinator
PE References are to the Pension Explanations in Pension and Profit Sharing 2nd
EP References are to the Estate Planning Analysis on Checkpoint and CD-ROM, and in
    Estate Planning & Taxation Coordinator

For tax years beginning in calendar year:	The applicable percentage is:
2005	174
2006	184
2007	187
2008	190
2009 and thereafter	200

(FTC 2d/FIN ¶ A-2803; USTR ¶ 634; TaxDesk ¶ 562,003)

> *observation:* Thus, under pre-2002 Act law, the basic standard deduction for married taxpayers filing separately was half that of married taxpayers filing jointly until through 2004. Then, from 2005 through 2008, married taxpayers filing separately and unmarried taxpayers filing a single return were (as members of the "in any other case" category) to have a common basic standard deduction, which was more than half of the basic standard deduction for married couples filing jointly and surviving spouses. (The Code stated this relationship in reciprocal terms—i.e., it effectively says that, for this period, the basic standard deduction for marrieds filing jointly and surviving spouses was to be less than twice that of marrieds filing separately and single filers). Then, starting in 2009, the basic standard deduction for marrieds filing separately was again to be half that of joint filers (or, put reciprocally, the basic standard deduction for joint filers would be twice that for marrieds filing separately).

New Law. For tax years beginning after Dec. 31, 2004 ((2002 Act § 411(x))), the 2002 Act creates a basic standard deduction amount specifically for married taxpayers filing separate returns (removing them from the "in any other case" category of taxpayers), and makes that amount one-half the basic standard deduction amount for married taxpayers filing joint returns and surviving spouses. (Code Sec. 63(c)(2)(C) as amended by 2002 Act §411(e)(1)(D))

> *observation:* As discussed above, under pre-2002 Act law, the basic standard deduction for married taxpayers filing separately was half that of married taxpayers filing jointly until through 2004, more than half that of married taxpayers filing jointly from 2005 through 2008, and again half that of married taxpayers filing jointly starting in 2009. The 2002 Act changes above ensure that the basic standard deduction amount for marrieds filing separately will stay equal to one-half the basic standard deduction amount for married filing jointly, without any change in this respect for the period from 2005 through 2008.

The following table shows the basic standard deduction amounts for unmarried individuals (singles), married taxpayers filing joint returns, and married taxpayers filing separate returns, from 2005 through 2009, both as these amounts would be under the 2002 Act, and as they would have been under pre-2002 Act law (prior law), assuming the basic standard deduction amount for singles for 2002 ($4,700 as adjusted for inflation, see above) remains unchanged through 2009. Please note that, for this period, as discussed above, under the 2002 Act, the basic standard deduction for joint filers is a multiple (see the table of "applicable percentages" above) of the basic standard deduction for singles, and the basic standard deduction for marrieds filing separately is one-half the basic standard deduction for joint filers; while under pre-2002 Act law, the basic standard deduction for joint filers was the same multiple of the basic standard deduction for singles, but the basic standard deduction for marrieds filing separately was equal to the basic standard deduction for singles (because both were included in the "in any other case" category of taxpayers).

Phase-in of increased basic standard deduction

Filing status	2005	Prior law	2006	Prior law	2007	Prior law
Single	$4,700*	$4,700*	$4,700*	$4,700*	$4,700*	$4,700*
Joint (or surviving spouse)	× 174% 8,150	× 174% 8,150	× 184% 8,600	× 184% 8,600	× 187% 8,750	× 187% 8,750
Married filing separately	× 50% 4,075	4,700 (same as single)	× 50% 4,300	4,700 (same as single)	× 50% 4,375	4,700 (same as single)

Filing status	2008	Prior law	2009	Prior law
Single	$4,700*	$4,700*	$4,700*	$4,700*
Joint return (or surviving spouse)	× 190% 8,900	× 190% 8,900	× 200% 9,400	× 200% 9,400
Married filing separately	× 50% 4,450	4,700 (same as single)	× 50% 4,700	4,700 (same as single)

*Assumes the basic standard deduction amount for singles for 2002 remains unchanged through 2009.

☐ **Effective:** Tax years beginning after Dec. 31, 2004. (2002 Act § 411(x))

¶ 418. Gain to which mark-to-market election for assets held on Jan. 1, 2001 applies is included in income despite nonrecognition provision

FTC 2d References are to Federal Tax Coordinator 2d
FIN References are to RIA's Analysis of Federal Taxes: Income
USTR References are to United States Tax Reporter: Income, Estate & Gift, and Excise
PCA References are to the Pension Analysis on Checkpoint and CD-ROM, and in Pension Coordinator
PE References are to the Pension Explanations in Pension and Profit Sharing 2nd
EP References are to the Estate Planning Analysis on Checkpoint and CD-ROM, and in Estate Planning & Taxation Coordinator

Code Sec. None, 2002 Act § 414(a)(1)
Generally effective: Tax years ending after May 6, '97
Committee Reports, see ¶ 5059

Taxpayers other than corporations may elect to mark to market any capital asset or property used in a trade or business (as defined in Code Sec. 1231(b)), and held by the taxpayer on Jan. 1, 2001. The asset is treated as having been sold on Jan. 1, 2001, for an amount equal to its fair market value on that date, and reacquired on that date for an amount equal to its fair market value.

Any gain resulting from the above election is treated as received or accrued on the date the asset is treated as sold. Under pre-2002 Act law, the gain was recognized notwithstanding any other Code provision. In Rev Rul 2001-57, IRS held that this means the gain must be recognized even though another Code section (such as Code Sec. 121, which excludes gain on the sale of a principal residence) would entitle the taxpayer to exclude from gross income gain on an actual sale. (FTC 2d/FIN ¶ I-5110.5; USTR ¶ 14.08; TaxDesk ¶ 223,314)

New Law. The 2002 Act clarifies that the gain to which the mark-to-market election applies is included in gross income notwithstanding any other Code provision (rather than merely "recognized"). ('97 Taxpayer Relief Act §311(e)(2)(A) as amended by 2002 Act §414(a)(1))

Thus, the exclusion of gain on the sale of a principal residence under Code Sec. 121 wouldn't apply with respect to an asset for which the mark-to-market election is made. The provision is consistent with the holding of Rev Rul 2001-57. (Com Rept, see ¶ 5059)

> *illustration:* Taxpayer X makes a mark-to-market election with respect to his principal residence on his income tax return for the year including Jan. 1, 2001. On Jan. 1, 2001, the residence had a fair market value that was $250,000 greater than X's basis. If, on that date, X had actually sold the residence for its fair market value, Code Sec. 121 would have entitled X to exclude from gross income the full $250,000 of gain realized on the sale.
>
> In Rev Rul 2001-57, IRS held in this situation that X couldn't exclude from gross income under Code Sec. 121 any of the gain resulting from the deemed sale. The 2002 Act provision now confirms that this holding is correct.

For the effect of the mark-to-market election on passive losses, see ¶ 109.

☐ **Effective:** Tax years ending after May 6, '97. (2002 Act § 414(b))

¶ 500. New York City Relief Provisions

¶ 501. 30% additional first-year depreciation is allowed for, and the AMT depreciation adjustment is not required for, certain buildings placed in service in the New York Liberty Zone after Sept. 10, 2001 and before Jan. 1, 2010, and most other tangible property and computer software placed in service in the New York Liberty Zone after Sept. 10, 2001 and before Jan. 1, 2007

Code Sec. 1400L(b), as added by 2002 Act § 301(a)
Code Sec. 1400L(h), as added by 2002 Act § 301(a)
Generally effective: Property acquired by purchase after, and originally used in the New York Liberty Zone after, Sept. 10, 2001
Committee Reports, see ¶ 5012

Code Sec. 167(a) allows taxpayers a depreciation deduction for the exhaustion of property used in a trade or business or for the production of income, see FTC 2d/FIN ¶ L-7501; USTR ¶ 1674; TaxDesk ¶ 264,501. For most tangible property, the deduction is determined under the modified accelerated cost recovery system (MACRS), see FTC 2d/FIN ¶ L-8101; USTR ¶ 1684; TaxDesk ¶ 266,001.

Depreciable computer software, unless it must be amortized over 15 years under Code Sec. 197, is generally depreciated under Code Sec. 167 using the straight-line method and a 36 month useful life. (FTC 2d/FIN ¶ L-7935; USTR ¶ 1674.033; TaxDesk ¶ 265,434)

For most property (other than buildings) depreciated under MACRS, Code Sec. 56 requires that depreciation deductions are calculated, for purposes of determining alternative minimum taxable income (AMTI) under Code Sec. 55, on the 150% declining balance method. This adjustment is required for alternative minimum tax (AMT) purposes whether or not the property is depreciated on the 150% declining balance method for regular tax purposes. (FTC 2d/FIN ¶ A-8220; USTR ¶ 564.01; TaxDesk ¶ 696,513)

New Law. The 2002 Act provides that, for "qualified New York Liberty Zone property" (defined below), (Code Sec. 1400L(b)(1) as added by 2002 Act §301(a))

... the depreciation deduction under Code Sec. 167(a) for the tax year in which the property is placed in service includes an allowance equal to 30% of the ad-

FTC 2d References are to Federal Tax Coordinator 2d
FIN References are to RIA's Analysis of Federal Taxes: Income
USTR References are to United States Tax Reporter: Income, Estate & Gift, and Excise
PCA References are to the Pension Analysis on Checkpoint and CD-ROM, and in Pension Coordinator
PE References are to the Pension Explanations in Pension and Profit Sharing 2nd
EP References are to the Estate Planning Analysis on Checkpoint and CD-ROM, and in Estate Planning & Taxation Coordinator

justed basis of the qualified New York Liberty Zone property, and (Code Sec. 1400L(b)(1)(A))

... the adjusted basis of the qualified New York Liberty Zone property is reduced by the amount of that deduction before computing the amount otherwise allowable as a depreciation deduction for the tax year and any later tax year. (Code Sec. 1400L(b)(1)(B))

For a taxpayer's right *not* to claim the 30% additional first-year depreciation discussed above, see "Election-out" below.

For the coordination of the 30% additional first-year depreciation discussed above with the 2002 Act provision that provides 30% additional first-year depreciation (referred to below as "168(k) additional first-year depreciation") for many types of property, whether or not the property is qualified New York Liberty Zone property, see "Property not eligible for additional first-year depreciation" below. For definition of "New York Liberty Zone," see below.

> **observation:** Code Sec. 1400L(b)(1) (above) doesn't specify whether the half-year, mid-quarter or mid-month depreciation conventions, see FTC 2d/FIN ¶ L-8103; USTR ¶ 1684.01; TaxDesk ¶ 266,701, apply to the 30% additional first-year depreciation. However, examples in the Technical Explanation of the 2002 Act, reflected in Illustrations (1) and (2) below, indicate that the depreciation conventions *don't* apply; i.e., in each example, the 30% additional first-year depreciation is *not* reduced below 30% (as the use of a convention would have required).

> **caution:** Although, as discussed immediately above, it appears that depreciation conventions don't apply to the 30% additional first-year depreciation itself, the conventions apply to the other first-year depreciation deductions allowed with respect to qualified New York Liberty Zone property. Further, the placement of qualified New York Liberty Zone property into service during the last quarter of a tax year may, in some circumstances, cause the taxpayer to be required to use a mid-quarter convention, rather than a half-year convention, for *all* of the taxpayer's MACRS property (other than buildings and railroad gradings or tunnel bores) placed into service during that tax year, see FTC 2d/FIN ¶ L-8103; USTR ¶ 1684.01; TaxDesk ¶ 266,701.

> *Illustration (1):* On Mar. 1, 2002, T, a calendar year taxpayer, acquires and places in service qualified New York Liberty Zone property that costs $1 million. Assuming that T doesn't make an "election-out" (see below), T is allowed an additional first-year depreciation deduction of $300,000. The remaining $700,000 of adjusted basis is recovered in 2002 and later years under the other depreciation rules of pre-2002 Act law (which are not affected by the 2002 Act). (Com Rept, see ¶ 5012)

observation: Illustration (2) (immediately below) shows that amounts "expensed" under Code Sec. 179 reduce the basis of an asset before the additional first-year depreciation is calculated for the asset and before other depreciation is calculated for the asset.

Illustration (2): On Mar. 1, 2002, W, a calendar year taxpayer, acquires and places in service qualified New York Liberty Zone property that costs $100,000. Assume that the property qualifies for the expensing election under Code Sec. 179, see FTC 2d/FIN ¶ L-9901; USTR ¶ 1794.01; TaxDesk ¶ 268,401. W is first allowed a $59,000 deduction under Code Sec. 179 ($24,000 allowed for section 179 property generally, plus $35,000 allowed for section 179 property that is qualified New York Liberty Zone property, see ¶ 502). W is then allowed an additional first-year depreciation deduction of $12,300 based on an adjusted basis of $41,000 ($100,000 original cost, less the $59,000 deduction). The remaining adjusted basis of $28,700 ($41,000 less $12,300) is recovered in 2002 and later years under the other depreciation rules of pre-2002 Act law (which are not affected by the 2002 Act). (Com Rept, see ¶ 5012)

The additional first-year depreciation deduction is subject to the general rules regarding whether an item is deductible under Code Sec. 162 or subject to capitalization under Code Sec. 263 (the regular capitalization rules, see FTC 2d/FIN ¶ L-5601; USTR ¶ 2634; TaxDesk ¶ 256,201) or Code Sec. 263A (the uniform capitalization, or UNICAP, rules, see FTC 2d/FIN ¶ G-5450; USTR ¶ 263A4; TaxDesk ¶ 456,000). (Com Rept, see ¶ 5012)

"Qualified New York Liberty Zone property" defined. The 2002 Act defines "qualified New York Liberty Zone property" as property which satisfies six specified requirements (which are discussed under the six italicized subheadings below). (Code Sec. 1400L(b)(2))

caution: There are certain types of property which are ineligible to be qualified property even if they satisfy the six requirements of the definition of qualified New York Liberty Zone property, see "Property not eligible for additional first-year depreciation" below.

FTC 2d References are to Federal Tax Coordinator 2d
FIN References are to RIA's Analysis of Federal Taxes: Income
USTR References are to United States Tax Reporter: Income, Estate & Gift, and Excise
PCA References are to the Pension Analysis on Checkpoint and CD-ROM, and in Pension Coordinator
PE References are to the Pension Explanations in Pension and Profit Sharing 2nd
EP References are to the Estate Planning Analysis on Checkpoint and CD-ROM, and in Estate Planning & Taxation Coordinator

Requirement that property be of a certain type. To be qualified New York Liberty Zone property, property must be in one of two categories. (Code Sec. 1400L(b)(2)(A))

One category consists of property described in Code Sec. 168(k)(2)(A)(i) (i.e., property eligible for "168(k) additional first-year depreciation," see above). (Code Sec. 1400L(b)(2)(A)(i)(I))

> 🅡 *observation:* Property described in Code Sec. 168(k)(2)(A)(i) includes the following:
>
> . . . property to which Code Sec. 168 (which provides the MACRS rules) applies, and which has a recovery period of 20 years or less;
>
> . . . computer software (as defined in Code Sec. 167(f)(1)(B)) for which a deduction is allowable under Code Sec. 167(a) without regard to Code Sec. 168(k) (i.e., the rules for additional first year depreciation); thus, additional first-year depreciation isn't available for computer software amortized under Code Sec. 197 (see FTC 2d/FIN ¶ L-7958; USTR ¶ 1974; TaxDesk ¶ 265,434); and
>
> . . . "water utility property" (which is a class of MACRS property defined in Code Sec. 168(e)(5), see FTC 2d/FIN ¶ L-8209.1; USTR ¶ 1684.01; TaxDesk ¶ 266,210).
>
> The property described in Code Sec. 168(k)(2)(A)(i) also includes "qualified leasehold improvement property" (defined as discussed at ¶ 101). However, it would appear that any "qualified leasehold improvement property" that would meet the six requirements for being qualified New York Liberty Zone property would, nevertheless, be excluded from being qualified New York Liberty Zone property because of the exclusion, discussed below, for "qualified New York Liberty Zone leasehold improvement property."

The other category consists of nonresidential real property or residential rental property (buildings and structural components of buildings, see FTC 2d/FIN ¶ L-8203; FTC 2d/FIN ¶ L-8210; USTR ¶ 1684.02; TaxDesk ¶ 266,202; TaxDesk ¶ 266,211) that meets an additional requirement. (Code Sec. 1400L(b)(2)(A)(i)(II)) This requirement is that the nonresidential real property or residential rental property be property that rehabilitates real property damaged, or replaces real property destroyed or condemned, as a result of the Sept. 11, 2001 terrorist attack. For purposes of this requirement, property is treated as replacing real property destroyed or condemned if, as part of an integrated plan, the property replaces real property that is included in a continuous area which includes real property destroyed or condemned. (Code Sec. 1400L(b)(2)(B)) The Technical Explanation says that it is intended by Congress that real property destroyed or condemned only include circumstances in which an entire building or structure was destroyed or condemned as a result of the terrorist attacks. Otherwise, the property is considered damaged real property. For example, if certain structural components (e.g., walls, floors or plumbing fixtures) of a building are damaged or destroyed as a result of the terrorist attacks, but the building isn't destroyed or condemned, then only costs related to replacing the damaged or destroyed components qualify. (Com Rept, see ¶ 5012)

Requirement of active business use in the New York Liberty Zone. To be qualified New York Liberty Zone property, substantially all of the use of the property must be in the New York Liberty Zone ("the Zone"), and in the active conduct of a trade or business by the taxpayer in the Zone. (Code Sec. 1400L(b)(2)(A)(ii))

Original use requirement. To be qualified New York Liberty Zone property, the original use of the property *in the Zone* must begin with the taxpayer after Sept. 10, 2001. (Code Sec. 1400L(b)(2)(A)(iii)) Thus, used property can qualify if it hasn't been previously used within the Zone. (Com Rept, see ¶ 5012)

The Technical Explanation says that Congress intends that additional capital expenditures incurred to recondition or rebuild property, the original use of which in the Zone began with the taxpayer, would satisfy the original use requirement, see Reg §1.48-2, Example 5. (Com Rept, see ¶ 5012)

> **observation:** The Technical Explanation excerpt described immediately above implies that additional capital expenditures incurred to recondition or rebuild property, the original use of which in the Zone, before the reconditioning or rebuilding, did *not* begin with the taxpayer, won't satisfy the original use requirement. However, the example referred to in the Technical Explanation (which is, presumably Reg § 1.48-2*(c)*, Example 5, see FTC 2d/FIN ¶ P-1603) treats a taxpayer's capital expenditures with respect to used property as expenditures made with respect to *new* property for purposes of the pre-'86 investment tax credit. This result implies that capital expenditures to recondition or rebuild property *can* satisfy the original use requirement, *regardless* of the use of the property before the reconditioning or rebuilding. The illustration immediately below follows this more permissive (i.e. more pro-taxpayer) interpretation of original use.

> **illustration (3):** In 2005, Z, a calendar year taxpayer, incurs $5,000 in capital expenditures to recondition a machine that, in 2002, had, for a purchase price of $20,000, been acquired by Z, from R, who had previously used the machine in the Zone. Assuming that Z is the first person, after reconditioning, to use the machine in the Zone, the $5,000 in capital expenditures satisfies the original use requirement.

FTC 2d References are to Federal Tax Coordinator 2d
FIN References are to RIA's Analysis of Federal Taxes: Income
USTR References are to United States Tax Reporter: Income, Estate & Gift, and Excise
PCA References are to the Pension Analysis on Checkpoint and CD-ROM, and in Pension Coordinator
PE References are to the Pension Explanations in Pension and Profit Sharing 2nd
EP References are to the Estate Planning Analysis on Checkpoint and CD-ROM, and in Estate Planning & Taxation Coordinator

Except for the difference discussed under "Property manufactured, constructed, or produced by the taxpayer" below, rules similar to the rules in Code Sec. 168(k)(2)(D) (concerning "168(k) additional first-year depreciation," see ¶ 101) apply to the 30% additional first-year depreciation available for qualified New York Liberty Zone property. (Code Sec. 1400L(b)(2)(D))

> *observation:* Thus, for purposes of the original use requirement, if property (1) is originally placed in service after Sept. 10, 2001 by a person, and (2) is sold and leased back by that person within three months after the date that property was originally placed in service, the property is treated as originally placed in service not earlier than the date on which the property is used under the leaseback, see ¶ 101. (This rule is referred to below as the "sale-leaseback rule.")

Therefore, in the case of any property that is originally placed in service by a person and that is sold to the taxpayer and leased back to that person by the taxpayer within three months after the date that the property was placed in service, the property is treated as originally placed in service by the taxpayer not earlier than the date that the property is used under the leaseback. (Com Rept, see ¶ 5012)

> *observation:* As confirmed by the Technical Explanation's identification of "the taxpayer" as the buyer-lessor (see immediately above), the main effect of the sale-leaseback original use rule is to shift eligibility for additional first-year depreciation from the seller-lessee to the buyer-lessor.

> *illustration (4):* On Oct. 15, 2001, X, a calendar year taxpayer, buys a newly manufactured machine from manufacturer M, and begins to use the machine in the active conduct of X's business in the Zone. On Jan. 10, 2002, X sells the machine to Y, which is a company in the equipment leasing business and is a calendar-year taxpayer. Also, on Jan. 10, 2002, X leases the machine back from Y under a lease, the term of which begins on Jan. 10, 2002. X continues to use the machine in the active conduct of X's business in the Zone. Thus, Jan. 10, 2002 is the date that the machine is first used under the leaseback, and, thus, first satisfies the original use requirement. Therefore, if the machine meets the other requirements for being qualified property, and if Y doesn't make an "election-out" (see below), Y is allowed additional first-year depreciation for the machine in 2002. X is not allowed additional first-year depreciation for the machine in either 2001 or 2002.

> *illustration (5):* The facts are the same as in Illustration (4), except that (1) X acquires the machine and begins to use it in the Zone on Sept. 5, 2001, and (2) the sale and leaseback of the machine occurs on Dec. 1, 2001. The sale and leaseback of the machine occurs within the three-month time period required under the sale-leaseback rule. However, the machine fails the requirement, under the sale-leaseback rule, that property

be originally placed in service after Sept. 10, 2001. Thus, Y isn't allowed additional first-year depreciation for the machine. With respect to X, the machine fails the requirement, in *Code Sec. 1400L(b)(2)(A)(iii)* (above), that the original use of the machine in the Zone must begin with the taxpayer after Sept. 10, 2001. Thus, X also isn't allowed additional first-year depreciation for the machine.

Purchase requirement. To be qualified New York Liberty Zone property, property must be acquired by "purchase" (as defined in Code Sec. 179(d)). (Code Sec. 1400L(b)(2)(A)(iv))

> **✔️ observation:** Under Code Sec. 179(d), a "purchase" is any acquisition of property *other than* an acquisition (1) from a person related to the taxpayer; (2) from another member of a controlled group of corporations; or (3) in which the basis of the acquiring person in the property is (a) in whole or part, a carryover basis, or (b) determined under Code Sec. 1014(a) (concerning property acquired from a decedent), see FTC 2d/FIN ¶ L-9925; USTR ¶ 1794.02; TaxDesk ¶ 268,427.

Timely acquisition requirement. To be qualified New York Liberty Zone property, property must be acquired by the taxpayer after Sept. 10, 2001, and no written binding contract for the acquisition can be in effect before Sept. 11, 2001. (Code Sec. 1400L(b)(2)(A)(iv))

Timely placement into service requirement. To be qualified New York Liberty Zone property, the property must be placed in service by the taxpayer on or before the "termination date." (Code Sec. 1400L(b)(2)(A)(v)) The "termination date" means Dec. 31, 2006 (but, for nonresidential real property and residential rental property, Dec. 31, 2009). (Code Sec. 1400L(b)(2)(A))

> **✔️ observation:** As discussed above (see "Requirement that property be of a certain type"), generally, "nonresidential real property" and "residential rental property" include only buildings and structural components of buildings. Thus, generally, only taxpayers that own qualifying buildings or structural components can take advantage of the Dec. 31, 2009 termination date. Owners of all other property must place the property into service before Jan. 1, 2007.

For the application of the timely placement into service requirement to property manufactured, constructed or produced by the taxpayer, see below.

FTC 2d References are to Federal Tax Coordinator 2d
FIN References are to RIA's Analysis of Federal Taxes: Income
USTR References are to United States Tax Reporter: Income, Estate & Gift, and Excise
PCA References are to the Pension Analysis on Checkpoint and CD-ROM, and in Pension Coordinator
PE References are to the Pension Explanations in Pension and Profit Sharing 2nd
EP References are to the Estate Planning Analysis on Checkpoint and CD-ROM, and in Estate Planning & Taxation Coordinator

Property manufactured, constructed or produced by the taxpayer. Rules similar to the rules in Code Sec. 168(k)(2)(D) (concerning "168(k) additional first-year depreciation," see ¶ 101) apply to the 30% additional first-year depreciation available for qualified New York Liberty Zone property, except that Code Sec. 168(k)(2)(D)(i), see ¶ 101, is applied without regard to "and before Sept. 11, 2004." (Code Sec. 1400L(b)(2)(D))

Thus, property is qualified New York Liberty Zone property if the taxpayer begins the manufacture, construction, or production of the property after Sept. 10, 2001, the property is placed in service on or before the "termination date" (Dec. 31, 2006 or Dec. 31, 2009, as the case may be, see "Timely placement into service requirement" above) and all of the other requirements for qualified New York Liberty Zone property are also met. (Com Rept, see ¶ 5012)

> *illustration (6):* On Aug. 20, 2006, Q, a computer hardware manufacturer and calendar year taxpayer, begins manufacturing 150 desk-top computers for use in Q's business by Q's employees. Assuming that Q doesn't make an "election-out" (see below), Q is allowed 30% additional first-year depreciation for any of the 150 computers that are placed in service before Jan. 1, 2007 (see "Timely placement into service requirement" above) and that meet the other requirements for being qualified New York Liberty Zone property.

> *illustration (7):* The facts are the same as in Illustration (6), except that Q begins manufacturing the 150 computers on Aug. 20, 2001. None of the computers are qualified New York Liberty Zone property.

Property considered manufactured, constructed or produced *by* the taxpayer includes property manufactured, constructed or produced *for* the taxpayer by another person under a contract that is entered into before the manufacture, construction or production of the property. (Com Rept, see ¶ 5012)

Property not eligible for additional first-year depreciation. The property described below isn't eligible for the 30% additional first-year depreciation.

Alternative depreciation system property. "Qualified New York Liberty Zone property" doesn't include any property described in Code Sec. 168(k)(2)(C)(i) (concerning "168(k) additional first-year depreciation," see ¶ 101). (Code Sec. 1400L(b)(2)(C)(ii)) Thus, 30% additional first-year depreciation deduction is precluded for property that is required to be depreciated under the alternative depreciation system (ADS). (Com Rept, see ¶ 5012) For a discussion of the ADS, see FTC 2d/FIN ¶ L-9401; USTR ¶ 1684.03; TaxDesk ¶ 267,501.

> *observation:* Presumably, Code Sec. 1400L(b)(2)(C)(ii) applies the following rules, which apply under Code Sec. 168(k)(2)(C)(i), in determining whether the ADS applies:
>
> (1) the determination is made without regard to Code Sec. 168(g)(7) (relating to elections to have the ADS system apply), and
>
> (2) the determination is made after application of Code Sec. 280F(b) (relating to "listed property" with limited business use, see below).
>
> The effect of rule (1) listed above is that property that is subject to the ADS only because the taxpayer elected to have the ADS apply *is eligible* to be qualified New York Liberty Zone property if it meets all of the other requirements for being qualified New York Liberty Zone property. Thus, property doesn't become ineligible merely because the taxpayer elected ADS under Code Sec. 168(g)(7).
>
> Presumably, the purpose of rule (2) listed above is to clarify that property that isn't mentioned in Code Sec. 168(g)(1), which provides a list of property that is subject to the ADS, is, nevertheless, subject to the ADS, and, thus, *isn't eligible* to be qualified New York Liberty Zone property, if it is property that is covered by the rule in Code Sec. 280F(b). That rule, see FTC 2d/FIN ¶ L-10018; USTR ¶ 280F4; TaxDesk ¶ 267,615, requires that passenger automobiles and certain other types of "listed property," see FTC 2d/FIN ¶ L-10002; USTR ¶ 280F4; TaxDesk ¶ 267,616, be depreciated under the ADS if not used more than 50% of the time in a "qualified business use," see FTC 2d/FIN ¶ L-10025; USTR ¶ 280F4; TaxDesk ¶ 267,621.

Property for which 30% additional first-year depreciation is allowable under Code Sec. 168(k). Qualified New York Liberty Zone property doesn't include property to which Code Sec. 168(k), see ¶ 101, applies. (Code Sec. 1400L(b)(2)(C)(i)) Thus, property is ineligible for additional first-year depreciation under Code Sec. 1400L to the extent that it is eligible for additional first-year depreciation under Code Sec. 168(k) (i.e., property is eligible for only one 30% additional first-year depreciation). (Com Rept, see ¶ 5012)

FTC 2d References are to Federal Tax Coordinator 2d
FIN References are to RIA's Analysis of Federal Taxes: Income
USTR References are to United States Tax Reporter: Income, Estate & Gift, and Excise
PCA References are to the Pension Analysis on Checkpoint and CD-ROM, and in Pension Coordinator
PE References are to the Pension Explanations in Pension and Profit Sharing 2nd
EP References are to the Estate Planning Analysis on Checkpoint and CD-ROM, and in Estate Planning & Taxation Coordinator

Qualified New York Liberty Zone leasehold improvement property. Qualified New York Liberty Zone property doesn't include any "qualified New York Liberty Zone leasehold improvement property" (as defined in Code Sec. 1400L(c)(2), which is discussed in the observation immediately below). (Code Sec. 1400L(b)(2)(C)(iii))

> *observation:* The 2002 Act added to the Code, in Code Sec. 1400L(c)(2), the category of "qualified New York Liberty Zone leasehold improvement property," referred to in the rule immediately above, for the purpose of permitting the cost of that property to be depreciated, generally, over a 5-year period on the straight-line method, see ¶ 503. Thus, it can be presumed that Congress made "qualified New York Liberty Zone leasehold improvement property" ineligible for additional first-year depreciation because it believed that qualified leasehold improvement property shouldn't receive both the benefit of being depreciated over 5 years *and* the benefit of 30% additional first-year depreciation.

Leasehold improvements that don't satisfy the requirements to be treated as qualified New York Liberty Zone leasehold improvement property are eligible for the 30% additional first-year depreciation (assuming all other conditions are met). (Com Rept, see ¶ 5012)

Election-out. Rules similar to the rules in Code Sec. 168(k)(2)(C)(iii) apply for purposes of Code Sec. 1400L(b). (Code Sec. 1400L(b)(2)(C)(iv))

Accordingly, taxpayers are allowed to elect out of the additional first-year depreciation for any class of property for any tax year, see ¶ 101. (Com Rept, see ¶ 5012)

> *observation:* Presumably, property for which the election is made also won't receive the benefit of not being subject to a depreciation adjustment for alternative minimum tax purposes, see "Alternative minimum tax" below.

> *observation:* Presumably there are 10 separate "classes" referred to in the election-out rule, i.e., the 3-year, 5-year, 7-year, 10-year, 15-year and 20-year MACRS classes; the water utility property MACRS class; a class consisting of certain residential rental property; a class consisting of certain nonresidential real property; and a class consisting of most depreciable computer software, see "Requirement that property be of a certain type" under "Qualified New York Liberty Zone property" above. Thus, for example, if a taxpayer makes an election-out with respect to the class consisting of 5-year MACRS property, items of 5-year MACRS property will be ineligible for 30% additional first-year depreciation (and for exemption from the alternative minimum tax depreciation adjustment) even if the ineligibility rules discussed under "Property not eligible for additional first-year depreciation" (above) don't apply to the items.

☑️ observation: Two situations in which a taxpayer might, for a tax year, consider making an election-out for one or more classes, are (1) where the taxpayer has about-to-expire net operating losses and (2) where the taxpayer anticipates being in a higher tax bracket in future years.

Alternative minimum tax. Rules similar to the rules in Code Sec. 168(k)(2)(F) apply for purposes of Code Sec. 1400L(b). (Code Sec. 1400L(b)(2)(E)) Thus, the 30% additional first-year depreciation is allowed for both regular tax and alternative minimum tax purposes for the tax year in which the property is placed in service. (Com Rept, see ¶ 5012) In addition, there is no adjustment to the allowable amount of depreciation for purposes of computing a taxpayer's alternative minimum taxable income for property to which Code Sec. 1400L(b) applies. (Com Rept, see ¶ 5012)

☑️ observation: Thus, presumably, if property is "qualified New York Liberty Zone property" (defined as discussed above), neither the 30% additional first-year depreciation deductions allowable for the property nor any of the other depreciation deductions allowable for the property (in the first year or in later years) are subject to adjustment for alternative minimum tax purposes. This is a significant tax benefit for "qualified New York Liberty Zone property" that is distinct from, and in addition to, the benefit of 30% additional first-year depreciation.

☑️ illustration (8): The facts are the same as in Illustration (1) above. The $300,000 of additional first-year depreciation is fully allowable in 2002 for regular tax and alternative minimum tax purposes. *Additionally*, any other depreciation allowable for regular tax purposes in 2002 or later years is not subject to adjustment for alternative minimum tax purposes.

"New York Liberty Zone" defined. The "New York Liberty Zone" is the area located on or south of Canal Street, East Broadway (east of its intersection with Canal Street), or Grand Street (east of its intersection with East Broadway) in the Borough of Manhattan in New York City. (Code Sec. 1400L(h) as added by 2002 Act §301(a))

☐ **Effective:** Property acquired by purchase after, and originally used in the New York Liberty Zone after, Sept. 10, 2001 (but only if no written binding contract for the acquisition was in effect before Sept. 11, 2001). (Code Sec. 1400L(b)(2)(A))

FTC 2d References are to Federal Tax Coordinator 2d
FIN References are to RIA's Analysis of Federal Taxes: Income
USTR References are to United States Tax Reporter: Income, Estate & Gift, and Excise
PCA References are to the Pension Analysis on Checkpoint and CD-ROM, and in Pension
  Coordinator
PE References are to the Pension Explanations in Pension and Profit Sharing 2nd
EP References are to the Estate Planning Analysis on Checkpoint and CD-ROM, and in
  Estate Planning & Taxation Coordinator

observation: There is no specific effective date provision either in 2002 Act §301, or, as it relates to Code Sec. 1400L(b) and Code Sec. 1400L(h), in the Technical Explanation.

recommendation: Taxpayers eligible for the additional 30% depreciation on qualified New York Liberty Zone property, but who didn't claim the additional depreciation on a tax return already filed, should consider filing an amended return.

¶ 502. Additional first-year expensing in lieu of depreciation is increased by $35,000 for "qualified New York Liberty Zone property" purchased and placed in service by the taxpayer after Sept. 10, 2001 and before Jan. 1, 2007

Code Sec. 1400L(f), as added by 2002 Act § 301(a)
Generally effective: Property purchased and placed in service by the taxpayer after Sept. 10, 2001 and before Jan. 1, 2007
Committee Reports, see ¶ 5016

A taxpayer, other than an estate, trust and certain noncorporate lessors, may elect under Code Sec. 179 to deduct as an expense, rather than to depreciate, up to a specified amount of the cost of purchased new or used tangible personal property placed in service during the tax year in the taxpayer's active trade or business (Code Sec. 179 property, see FTC 2d/FIN ¶ L-9901; USTR ¶ 1794; TaxDesk ¶ 268,411). Under pre-2002 Act law, the maximum deductible amount was $24,000 for 2001 and 2002, and that amount was slated to increase to $25,000 for 2003 and tax years after 2003. (FTC 2d/FIN ¶ L-9907; USTR ¶ 1794.01; TaxDesk ¶ 268,411)

In addition, under pre-2002 Act law, the maximum Code Sec. 179 expensing deduction for any tax year was reduced (but not below zero) by one dollar for every dollar over $200,000 of qualifying property put in service during the tax year. (FTC 2d/FIN ¶ L-9907; USTR ¶ 1794.01; TaxDesk ¶ 268,411)

Additional Code Sec. 179 incentives are provided with respect to "qualified zone property" used by a business in an empowerment zone under Code Sec. 1397A. Those businesses may elect to deduct an additional $20,000 (i.e., a total of $44,000) of the cost of qualified zone property placed in service in 2001. The $20,000 amount is increased to $35,000 for tax years beginning in 2002 and thereafter (see FTC 2d/FIN ¶ L-9951; USTR ¶ 13,97A4; TaxDesk ¶ 268,402). In addition, the phaseout range is applied by taking into account only 50% of the cost of qualified zone property that is Code Sec. 179 property (see FTC 2d/FIN ¶ L-9952; USTR ¶ 13,97A4; TaxDesk ¶ 268,413).

The amount eligible to be expensed for a tax year may not exceed the taxable income for a tax year that is derived from the active conduct of a trade or business (determined without regard to the rules permitting Code Sec. 179 expensing) (see

FTC 2d/FIN ¶ L-9911; USTR ¶ 1794.01; TaxDesk ¶ 268,417). Any amount that is not allowed as a Code Sec. 179 deduction because of the taxable income limitation may be carried forward to succeeding tax years (subject to similar limitations) (see FTC 2d/FIN ¶ L-9917; USTR ¶ 1794.01; TaxDesk ¶ 268,420)

No general business credit under Code Sec. 38 is allowed with respect to any amount for which a deduction is allowed under Code Sec. 179, see FTC 2d/FIN ¶ L-9901; USTR ¶ 1794.01; TaxDesk ¶ 268,401.

New Law. For purposes of Code Sec. 179 (Code Sec. 1400L(f)(1) as added by 2002 Act §301(a)) , the 2002 Act provides that the limitation under Code Sec. 179(b)(1) (rules providing the maximum dollar amounts of Code Sec. 179 property that may be expensed in a tax year, see FTC 2d/FIN ¶ L-9907; USTR ¶ 1794.01; TaxDesk ¶ 268,411) is increased by the *lesser* of: (Code Sec. 1400L(f)(1)(A))

. . . $35,000, or (Code Sec. 1400L(f)(1)(A)(i))

. . . the cost of Code Sec. 179 property which is "qualified New York Liberty Zone property" (see below and ¶ 501) placed in service during the tax year. (Code Sec. 1400L(f)(1)(A)(ii))

The increased expensing available for "qualified New York Liberty Zone property" is in addition to the amount otherwise deductible under pre-2002 Act law. (Com Rept, see ¶ 5016)

> *observation:* Thus, for 2001 and 2002, the maximum amount of section 179 property that is also "qualified New York Liberty Zone property" (see ¶ 501) that may be expensed is $59,000 ($24,000 under Code Sec. 179(b)(1) plus $35,000 under Code Sec. 1400L(f)(1)(A)). In 2003, the maximum amount of property that may be expensed as "qualified New York Liberty Zone property" increases to $60,000 ($25,000 under Code Sec. 179(b)(1) plus $35,000 under Code Sec. 1400L(f)(1)(A)).

> *observation:* One of the requirements for being "qualified New York Liberty Zone property," the property must be placed in service on or before the termination date of Dec. 31, 2006 (Dec. 31, 2009 for nonresidential real property and residential rental property), see below and ¶ 501. Since the Code Sec. 179 deduction only applies to tangible MACRS property (and thus, would not apply to nonresidential real property or residential rental property, see FTC 2d ¶ L-9922; FTC 2d ¶ L-9923; USTR

FTC 2d References are to Federal Tax Coordinator 2d
FIN References are to RIA's Analysis of Federal Taxes: Income
USTR References are to United States Tax Reporter: Income, Estate & Gift, and Excise
PCA References are to the Pension Analysis on Checkpoint and CD-ROM, and in Pension Coordinator
PE References are to the Pension Explanations in Pension and Profit Sharing 2nd
EP References are to the Estate Planning Analysis on Checkpoint and CD-ROM, and in Estate Planning & Taxation Coordinator

¶ 1794.02 ; TaxDesk ¶ 268,425), the additional expensing for "qualified New York Liberty Zone property" will terminate on Dec. 31, 2006.

illustration: On Oct. 1, 2001, X, a calendar year taxpayer, places in service $40,000 of "qualified New York Liberty Zone property." Assuming X doesn't expense more than $19,000 of other property under Code Sec. 179, X can elect to expense the entire $40,000 ($24,000 as Code Sec. 179 property and $16,000 as "qualified New York Liberty Zone property" under Code Sec. 1400L(f)(1)(A)).

illustration: On June 1, 2002, Y, a calendar year taxpayer, places in service $100,000 of "qualified New York Liberty Zone property." Assuming Y expenses no other property under Code Sec. 179, Y can elect to expense $59,000 ($24,000 as Code Sec. 179 property and $35,000 as "qualified New York Liberty Zone property").

For the definition of the "New York Liberty Zone," see ¶ 501.

"Qualified New York Liberty Zone property" defined.   For this purpose, "qualified New York Liberty Zone property" has the meaning given that term by Code Sec. 1400L(b)(2). (Code Sec. 1400L(f)(2))   For a discussion of the definition, see ¶ 501.

Phaseout.   The amount taken into account under Code Sec. 179(b)(2) (which phases out the maximum expensing deduction when a taxpayer places in service more than $200,000 of Code Sec. 179 property during the tax year) for any Code Sec. 179 property which is qualified New York Liberty Zone property is 50% of the cost of the property. (Code Sec. 1400L(f)(1)(B))   As under pre-2002 Act law with respect to empowerment zones (see FTC 2d/FIN ¶ L-9952; USTR ¶ 13,97A4; TaxDesk ¶ 268,413), the phaseout range for the Code Sec. 179 deduction attributable to New York Liberty Zone property is applied by taking into account only 50% of the cost of New York Liberty Zone property that is Code Sec. 179 property. (Com Rept, see ¶ 5016)

observation: For purposes of the increased expensing for empowerment zones, it's not clear whether, in computing the reduced maximum deduction under the phaseout, the cost of Code Sec. 179 property that is qualified zone property is reduced by one-half *before* or *after* application of the $200,000 threshold.

illustration: Z, a calendar year taxpayer, places $250,000 of Code Sec. 179 property that is "qualified New York Liberty Zone property" in service during 2001. Z does not place any Code Sec. 179 property in service outside the New York Liberty Zone.

(1) If the $250,000 of Code Sec. 179 property that is "qualified New York Liberty Zone property" is reduced by one-half *before* application of the $200,000 threshold, then Z's maximum allowable deduction of

$59,000 ($60,000 in 2003) would *not* be reduced under the phaseout. This is because the cost of Code Sec. 179 property that is "qualified New York Liberty Zone property" ($250,000) would be reduced by 50% to $125,000. Since one-half the cost of the Code Sec. 179 property that is "qualified New York Liberty Zone property" does not exceed $200,000, the maximum deduction would *not* be reduced.

(2) On the other hand, if the $250,000 of the Code Sec. 179 property that is "qualified New York Liberty Zone property" is reduced *after* application of the $200,000 threshold, then Z's maximum deduction would be reduced to $34,000, computed as follows:

(a) The cost of Code Sec. 179 property that is "qualified New York Liberty Zone property" ($250,000) would be reduced by the amount of the threshold ($200,000) to $50,000.

(b) Then, $50,000 (from (a)) would be reduced by 50% to $25,000.

(c) Thus, Z's maximum deduction before phaseout ($59,000) would be reduced by $25,000 (from (b)) to $34,000.

Recapture. Rules similar to the rules in Code Sec. 179(d)(10) (see FTC 2d/FIN ¶ L-9935; USTR ¶ 1794.03; TaxDesk ¶ 268,428) apply with respect to any "qualified New York Liberty Zone property" (see ¶ 501) which ceases to be used in the "New York Liberty Zone" (see ¶ 501). (Code Sec. 1400L(f)(3))

> *observation:* Code Sec. 179(d)(10) requires recapture if the property "is not used predominantly in a trade or business" at any time. Thus, a taxpayer will presumably have to recapture any additional expensing for "qualified New York Liberty Zone property" that is not used in a trade or business conducted in the "New York Liberty Zone" (see ¶ 501).

> *observation:* Regs dealing with recapture under Code Sec. 179 provide that the recaptured amount equals the expense deduction taken minus the MACRS depreciation amount that would have been allowed on the expensed amount from the time the property was placed in service up to and including the year of recapture, see FTC 2d/FIN ¶ L-9935; USTR ¶ 1794.03; TaxDesk ¶ 268,428. Presumably, the same rule will apply to determine recapture for "qualified New York Liberty Zone property."

FTC 2d References are to Federal Tax Coordinator 2d
FIN References are to RIA's Analysis of Federal Taxes: Income
USTR References are to United States Tax Reporter: Income, Estate & Gift, and Excise
PCA References are to the Pension Analysis on Checkpoint and CD-ROM, and in Pension Coordinator
PE References are to the Pension Explanations in Pension and Profit Sharing 2nd
EP References are to the Estate Planning Analysis on Checkpoint and CD-ROM, and in Estate Planning & Taxation Coordinator

Effect of expensing on general business credit. As under pre-2002 Act law, no general business credit under Code Sec. 38 is allowed with respect to any amount for which a deduction is allowed under Code Sec. 179, see FTC 2d/FIN ¶ L-9901; USTR ¶ 1794.01; TaxDesk ¶ 268,401. (Com Rept, see ¶ 5016)

☐ **Effective:** Property purchased and placed in service by the taxpayer after Sept. 10, 2001 and before Jan. 1, 2007, but only if no written binding contract for the acquisition was in effect before Sept. 11, 2001. (Code Sec. 1400L(b)(2)(A)(iv)) However, the Technical Explanation of the 2002 Act indicates that the provision is effective for tax years beginning on Dec. 31, 2001 (but, see observation below) and before Jan. 1, 2007. (Com Rept, see ¶ 5016)

> *observation:* The statement from the Technical Explanation appears not to reflect the language of Code Sec. 1400L because it indicates that the increased expensing is *not* available for property purchased and placed in service by the taxpayer for tax years beginning *before* Dec. 31, 2001. Although Code Sec. 1400L(f) doesn't provide a specific effective date for the increased expensing under Code Sec. 179 available for "qualified New York Liberty Zone property", it incorporates by reference the definition of "qualified New York Liberty Zone property" provided in Code Sec. 1400L(b)(2). As indicated at ¶ 501, that definition includes property purchased and placed in service by the taxpayer after Sept. 10, 2001 and before Jan. 1, 2007.

> *recommendation:* Taxpayers eligible for the additional first-year expensing for qualified New York Liberty Zone property, but who didn't make the expensing election on a tax return already filed, should consider filing an amended return.

¶ 503. Qualified New York Liberty Zone leasehold improvement property placed in service after Sept. 10, 2001 and before Jan. 1, 2007 is 5-year property for MACRS depreciation

Code Sec. 1400L(c), as added by 2002 Act § 301(a)
Generally effective: Qualified New York Liberty Zone leasehold improvement property placed in service after Sept. 10, 2001
Committee Reports, see ¶ 5013

Depreciation allowances for property used in a trade or business are generally determined under the modified accelerated cost recovery system (MACRS) based on the recovery period applicable to the particular type of property. Depreciation allowances for improvements made on leased property are determined under MACRS, even if the MACRS recovery period assigned to the property is longer than the term of the lease. Under pre-2002 Act law, if a leasehold improvement constituted an addition or improvement to nonresidential real property already

                            RIA **Research Institute of America**

placed in service, the improvement was depreciated using the straight-line method over a 39-year recovery period, beginning in the month the addition or improvement was placed in service. (FTC 2d/FIN ¶ L-6404, ¶ L-8103, ¶ L-9106; USTR ¶ 1684.02; TaxDesk ¶ 267,020)

> *observation:* Less than a full year's depreciation is allowed for the year the property is placed in service. As a result, depreciation deductions for 39-year recovery property are claimed over 40 years.

The alternative depreciation system (ADS) is required for certain MACRS property and elective for all others. ADS is a straight line depreciation system that has only one depreciation period (generally longer than any other) for each class of MACRS property, see FTC 2d/FIN ¶ L-9401; USTR ¶ 1684.03; TaxDesk ¶ 267,500.

New Law. Under the 2002 Act, for purposes of the Code Sec. 168 MACRS depreciation rules, "5-year property" includes any "qualified New York Liberty Zone leasehold improvement property" ("qualified Zone property") defined below. (Code Sec. 1400L(c)(1) as added by 2002 Act §301(a)) The applicable depreciation method under Code Sec. 168 for qualified Zone property is the straight line method. (Code Sec. 1400L(c)(3))

> *observation:* Making qualified Zone property 5-year property means that the cost will be fully recovered in 6 years; more than 6 times faster than the 40 years under pre-2002 Act rules.

> *observation:* Taxpayers who make leasehold improvements to qualified Zone property under leases that have terms of more than six years to run can recover the cost of the improvements before the end of the lease term.

> *observation:* The general rule that the class life for nonresidential real property is 40 years does not apply to qualified Zone property.

> *illustration:* In 2002, taxpayer pays $150,000 for qualified Zone property. Because this is 5-year recovery property, first year depreciation, under the half-year convention, is $15,000 (10%). For the second year through fifth years, depreciation is $30,000 (20%) per year. For the sixth year, depreciation is $15,000 (1/2 of 20%=10%).

> Under pre-2002 Act law, as 39-year property, if the property was placed in service in month 6, depreciation would have been limited to $2,086

FTC 2d References are to Federal Tax Coordinator 2d
FIN References are to RIA's Analysis of Federal Taxes: Income
USTR References are to United States Tax Reporter: Income, Estate & Gift, and Excise
PCA References are to the Pension Analysis on Checkpoint and CD-ROM, and in Pension Coordinator
PE References are to the Pension Explanations in Pension and Profit Sharing 2nd
EP References are to the Estate Planning Analysis on Checkpoint and CD-ROM, and in Estate Planning & Taxation Coordinator

(1.391%) for the first year, $3,846 (2.564%) for the next 38 years, and $1,766 (1.177%) for year 40.

observation: There is no dollar limit on the amount of qualified Zone property that can qualify as 5-year property.

observation: Congress has indicated that recovery of the costs of certain leasehold improvements should not extend beyond the term of the lease to the extent that the costs do not provide a future benefit beyond that term. Although lease terms differ, lease terms for commercial real estate typically are shorter than the 39-year recovery period for the real estate. By shortening the recovery period for qualified Zone property to 5 years, Congress is ensuring that the cost of most qualified Zone property will be recovered no later than the end of the lease term.

Qualified Zone property has a class life of 9 years for purposes of ADS. (Code Sec. 1400L(c)(4))

"Qualified New York Liberty Zone leasehold improvement property' defined. "Qualified New York Liberty Zone leasehold improvement property" ("qualified Zone property") is qualified leasehold improvement property (as defined in Code Sec. 168(k)(3), see ¶ 101) if: (Code Sec. 1400L(c)(2))

. . . the building is located in the "New York Liberty Zone" (as defined at ¶ 501), (Code Sec. 1400L(c)(2)(A))

. . . the improvement is placed in service after Sept. 10, 2001, and before Jan. 1, 2007, and (Code Sec. 1400L(c)(2)(B))

. . . no written binding contract for the improvement was in effect before Sept. 11, 2001. (Code Sec. 1400L(c)(2)(C))

observation: Owners of buildings within the New York Liberty Zone are likely to factor the value of the faster write off for qualified leasehold improvements into the rental prices they seek for new rentals or renewals of existing leases.

observation: "Qualified property" (as defined at ¶ 101), and "qualified New York Liberty Zone property" (as defined at ¶ 501), for which additional 30% first year depreciation deductions are allowed, do *not* include "qualified New York Liberty Zone leasehold improvement property." Thus, a prospective tenant who has the choice of making qualified leasehold improvements within the New York Liberty Zone or outside the New York Liberty Zone should weigh the relative benefits of the faster write-off for qualified New York Liberty Zone leasehold improvement property versus the 30% additional first-year depreciation deduction for "qualified property" outside the New York Liberty Zone. A tenant who expects to occupy the premises for a relatively short period of time may in some instances do better with space outside the Zone. Taking the time value of money into account can enhance the benefit.

For the additional 30% depreciation deduction allowed for certain "qualified property," see ¶ 101.

For the additional 30% depreciation for qualified New York Liberty Zone property, see ¶ 501.

For the increased Code Sec. 179 expensing election for qualified New York Liberty Zone property, see ¶ 502.

For treatment of qualified New York Liberty Bonds as exempt facility bonds, see ¶ 507.

For extension of the replacement period for certain property involuntarily converted in the New York Liberty Zone, see ¶ 504.

☐ **Effective:** Leasehold improvement property placed in service after Sept. 10, 2001 and before Jan. 1, 2007, unless a binding written contract for the improvement was in effect before Sept. 11, 2001. (Code Sec. 1400L(c)(2))

> 🅥 *recommendation:* Taxpayers who placed qualified New York Liberty Zone leasehold improvement property in service after Sept. 10, 2001, but treated the property as 39 year recovery period property on a tax return which has already been filed, should consider filing an amended return.

¶ 504. The period for replacing certain property involuntarily converted as a result of the terrorist attacks on the World Trade Center in New York City is extended to five years

Code Sec. 1400L(g), as added by 2002 Act § 301(a)
Generally effective: Involuntary conversions in the New York Liberty Zone occurring after Sept. 10, 2001 as a consequence of the terrorist attacks on Sept. 11, 2001
Committee Reports, see ¶ 5017

A property owner who receives insurance proceeds or other compensation for property lost by fire, theft, or condemnation ordinarily must report as income any excess of the compensation received over his adjusted basis of the property lost.

FTC 2d References are to Federal Tax Coordinator 2d
FIN References are to RIA's Analysis of Federal Taxes: Income
USTR References are to United States Tax Reporter: Income, Estate & Gift, and Excise
PCA References are to the Pension Analysis on Checkpoint and CD-ROM, and in Pension Coordinator
PE References are to the Pension Explanations in Pension and Profit Sharing 2nd
EP References are to the Estate Planning Analysis on Checkpoint and CD-ROM, and in Estate Planning & Taxation Coordinator

But he can elect not to report this gain to the extent that he reinvests the compensation in similar property, see FTC 2d/FIN ¶ I-3700; USTR ¶ 10,334.21; TaxDesk ¶ 229,700. If a taxpayer makes this election, gain is recognized only to the extent that the amount realized on the conversion exceeds the cost of the replacement property which must be purchased, see FTC 2d/FIN ¶ I-3701; USTR ¶ 10,334; TaxDesk ¶ 229,701.

In order to elect to defer gain from an involuntary conversion, a taxpayer must replace the converted property by purchasing property similar or related in service or use within a certain time period (the "replacement period") beginning on the earlier of (1) the date on which the property was destroyed, stolen, condemned, etc., or (2) the date on which condemnation or requisition was first threatened or became imminent, and ending two years after the close of the first tax year in which any part of the gain upon the conversion is realized (three years in the case of condemnation or threat of condemnation of real property held for productive use in a trade or business or for investment). IRS has the discretion to grant a later time period subject to IRS's terms and conditions, upon application by the taxpayer, see FTC 2d/FIN ¶ I-3734; USTR ¶ 10,334.26; TaxDesk ¶ 229,724.

There are special rules for conversion of personal residences in the case of a "Presidentially declared disaster." If a compulsory or involuntary conversion of a personal residence occurs because of a "Presidentially declared disaster," the period in which a personal residence can be replaced is extended to four years after the close of the first tax year in which any part of the gain upon conversion is realized, see FTC 2d/FIN ¶ I-3772.1 *et seq.*; USTR ¶ 10,334.40; TaxDesk ¶ 229,750 *et seq.*

New Law. The two-year period during which taxpayers can generally replace involuntarily converted property under Code Sec. 1033(a)(2)(B), see FTC 2d/FIN ¶ I-3734; USTR ¶ 10,334.26; TaxDesk ¶ 229,724, is extended to five years for property that is compulsorily or involuntarily converted as a result of the terrorist attacks on Sept. 11, 2001 in the "New York Liberty Zone" (as defined at ¶ 501), but only if substantially all of the use of the replacement property is in New York City. (Code Sec. 1400L(g) as added by 2002 Act §301(a)) The Technical Explanation of the 2002 Act says that Code Sec. 1400L(g) extends the replacement period to five years for a taxpayer to purchase property to replace property *that was involuntarily converted within the New York Liberty Zone* as a result of the Sept. 11, 2001 terrorist attacks. In all other cases, the pre-2002 Act replacement period rules continue to apply. (Com Rept, see ¶ 5017)

> ⚡*observation:* The Technical Explanation makes it clear that Congress intended that Code Sec. 1400L(g) apply only to property involuntarily converted *within* the New York Liberty Zone. But the wording of Code Sec. 1400L(g) leaves open the possibility that property involuntarily converted (such as by seizure) *outside* the New York Liberty Zone could reap the benefits of Code Sec. 1400L(g) as long as the conversion was *as a result of* the terrorist attacks *within* the New York Liberty Zone on Sept. 11, 2001.

The five-year extension of the replacement period applies notwithstanding Code Sec. 1033(g) or Code Sec. 1033(h). (Code Sec. 1400L(g))

> **❷ observation:** Code Sec. 1033(g)(4) contains a special three-year rule for replacing real property that has been seized or condemned, see FTC 2d/FIN ¶ I-3734; USTR ¶ 10,334.26; TaxDesk ¶ 229,724, and Code Sec. 1033(h)(1)(B) contains a special four-year period for the replacement of principal residences converted in a Presidentially declared disaster area (see FTC 2d/FIN ¶ I-3772.3; USTR ¶ 10,334.40; TaxDesk ¶ 229,751). Presumably, the statement in Code Sec. 1400L(g) that the extension of time for replacing property converted as a result of the World Trade Center terrorist attack to five years applies "notwithstanding" Code Sec. 1033(g) and Code Sec. 1033(h) means that the extension period of Code Sec. 1400L(g) overrides any contrary extension period contained in Code Sec. 1033(g) or Code Sec. 1033(h).

☐ **Effective:** Involuntary conversions in the New York Liberty Zone occurring after Sept. 10, 2001 as a consequence of the terrorist attacks on Sept. 11, 2001. (Com Rept, see ¶ 5017)

¶ 505. Work opportunity tax credit of up to $2,400 per calendar year is allowed for wages paid or incurred to each New York Liberty Zone business employee for work performed during calendar years 2002 or 2003

Code Sec. 1400L(a), as added by 2002 Act § 301(a)
Generally effective: Tax years ending after Dec. 31, 2001 for wages paid or
* incurred for work in calendar years 2002 or 2003*
Committee Reports, see ¶ 5011

The work opportunity tax credit (WOTC) is available on an elective basis for employers hiring individuals from certain targeted groups (see below), see FTC 2d/FIN ¶ L-17775; USTR ¶ 514; TaxDesk ¶ 380,700. The credit is available only if the employee has completed 120 hours of service for the employer, see FTC 2d/FIN ¶ L-17777; USTR ¶ 514; TaxDesk ¶ 380,700. The credit equals 40% (25% for employment of less than 400 hours but at least 120 hours) of qualified wages. Thus, the maximum credit per employee is $2,400 per year (40% of the first $6,000 of qualified first-year wages), see FTC 2d/FIN ¶ L-17778; USTR ¶ 514; TaxDesk ¶ 380,700. With respect to qualified summer youth employees, the maxi-

---

FTC 2d References are to Federal Tax Coordinator 2d
FIN References are to RIA's Analysis of Federal Taxes: Income
USTR References are to United States Tax Reporter: Income, Estate & Gift, and Excise
PCA References are to the Pension Analysis on Checkpoint and CD-ROM, and in Pension
    Coordinator
PE References are to the Pension Explanations in Pension and Profit Sharing 2nd
EP References are to the Estate Planning Analysis on Checkpoint and CD-ROM, and in
    Estate Planning & Taxation Coordinator

mum credit is $1,200 (40% of the first $3,000 of qualified first-year wages per year), see FTC 2d/FIN ¶ L-17779; USTR ¶ 514; TaxDesk ¶ 380,700. Generally, qualified first-year wages are wages attributable to service rendered by a member of a targeted group during the one-year period beginning with the day the individual began work for the employer, see FTC 2d/FIN ¶ L-17783; USTR ¶ 514; TaxDesk ¶ 380,707. The employer's deduction for wages is reduced by the amount of the WOTC credit. See FTC 2d/FIN ¶ L-17780; USTR ¶ 514; TaxDesk ¶ 380,703.

Under pre-2002 Act law, there were eight targeted groups: (1) families eligible to receive benefits under the Temporary Assistance for Needy Families ("TANF") Program; (2) high-risk youths; (3) qualified ex-felons; (4) vocational rehabilitation referrals; (5) qualified summer youth employees; (6) qualified veterans; (7) families receiving food stamps; and (8) persons receiving certain Supplemental Security Income ("SSI") benefits. (FTC 2d/FIN ¶ L-17776; USTR ¶ 514; TaxDesk ¶ 380,701)

New Law. For purposes of the WOTC under Code Sec. 51, a "New York Liberty Zone business employee" (defined below) is treated as a member of a targeted group. (Code Sec. 1400L(a)(1) as added by 2002 Act §301(a)) Thus, the 2002 Act creates a new targeted group for purposes of the WOTC. (Com Rept, see ¶ 5011)

> *observation:* The addition, by the 2002 Act, of the New York Liberty Zone business employees as a targeted group for purposes of the WOTC, is referred to below as the "New York Liberty Zone business employee credit" or as the "credit."

The Technical Explanation of the 2002 Act states that rules that apply to the WOTC (such as the 120 hour minimum employment rule discussed above) apply to the New York Liberty Zone business employee credit. (Com Rept, see ¶ 5011)

> *caution:* However, several of the rules discussed below and at ¶ 506 differ from the rules that generally apply under the WOTC.

> *observation:* Congress has indicated that the credit will encourage a long-term commitment to the New York Liberty Zone by businesses currently located in the Zone and those businesses that were forced to temporarily relocate outside of the Zone. Also, Congress has indicated that the credit will attract some new businesses to the Zone, and create a temporary stimulus necessary to offset any short-term disincentive to operate a business in the Zone.

"New York Liberty Zone business employee" defined. A "New York Liberty Zone business employee" is, for any period, any employee of a "New York Liberty Zone business" (defined below), if substantially all of the services performed during that period by the employee for the New York Liberty Zone business are performed in the "New York Liberty Zone" (defined immediately below). (Code Sec. 1400L(a)(2)(A))

> **observation:** The "New York Liberty Zone" is the area located on or south of Canal Street, East Broadway (east of its intersection with Canal Street), or Grand Street (east of its intersection with East Broadway) in the Borough of Manhattan in New York City, see ¶ 501.

For a special rule providing that the rule limiting the WOTC to new employees doesn't apply to the New York Liberty Zone business employee credit, see below.

The term "New York Liberty Zone business employee" *also* includes, in the case of a New York Liberty Zone business located in New York City outside of the New York Liberty Zone, as a result of the physical destruction or damage of its place of business by the Sept. 11, 2001 terrorist attack, any employee of that business not described in Code Sec. 1400L(a)(2)(A) (above) if substantially all of the services performed during the period by the employee for the business are performed in New York City. (Code Sec. 1400L(a)(2)(B)(i)) However, the number of employees of a business that are treated as New York Liberty Zone business employees on any day by reason of this rule (referred to below as the "non-Liberty Zone employee rule") can't exceed: (Code Sec. 1400L(a)(2)(B)(ii))

(1) the number of employees of that business on Sept. 11, 2001 in the New York Liberty Zone, over (Code Sec. 1400L(a)(2)(B)(ii)(I))

(2) the number of New York Liberty Zone business employees of that business, determined without regard to the non-Liberty Zone employee rule, on the day to which the limitation is being applied. (Code Sec. 1400L(a)(2)(B)(ii)(II))

Thus, for each qualified business that relocated from the New York Liberty Zone elsewhere within New York City due to the physical destruction or damage of their workplaces within the New York Liberty Zone, the number of its employees whose wages are eligible under the new targeted category may not exceed the number of its employees in the New York Liberty Zone on Sept. 11, 2001. Other qualified businesses (e.g., businesses that operate in the New York Liberty Zone both on and after Sept. 11, 2001 and businesses that move into the New York Liberty Zone after Sept. 11, 2001) are not subject to that limitation. (Com Rept, see ¶ 5011)

> **illustration:** XYZ, a business that, as a result of damage to its offices in the New York Liberty Zone by the Sept. 11, 2001 terrorist attack, had to locate elsewhere within New York City, had 40 employees on Sept. 11,

---

FTC 2d References are to Federal Tax Coordinator 2d
FIN References are to RIA's Analysis of Federal Taxes: Income
USTR References are to United States Tax Reporter: Income, Estate & Gift, and Excise
PCA References are to the Pension Analysis on Checkpoint and CD-ROM, and in Pension Coordinator
PE References are to the Pension Explanations in Pension and Profit Sharing 2nd
EP References are to the Estate Planning Analysis on Checkpoint and CD-ROM, and in Estate Planning & Taxation Coordinator

2001. On any day, XYZ can't treat more than 40 of its employees as New York Liberty Zone business employees, whether or not any of its employees continue to perform substantially all of their services for the business in the New York Liberty Zone.

IRS can require any trade or business to have the number described at (1) above verified by the New York State Department of Labor. (Code Sec. 1400L(a)(2)(B)(ii))

For a special rule for determining the number of employees under the non-Liberty Zone employee rule, see "Special rules for determining the credit," below.

observation: The 2002 Act does not provide a definition of or a method for determining what "substantially all" means for purposes of either Code Sec. 1400L(a)(2)(A) or Code Sec. 1400L(a)(2)(B)(i). However, a requirement similar to the requirements imposed by Code Sec. 1400L(a)(2)(A) or Code Sec. 1400L(a)(2)(B)(i) is imposed by Code Sec. 1396(d)(1)(A) (which provides that substantially all of the services performed by a qualified zone employee for the employer have to be performed within an empowerment zone for purposes of the empowerment zone employment credit, see FTC 2d/FIN ¶ L-15637; USTR ¶ 13,964; TaxDesk ¶ 384,026). Thus, it seems likely that IRS would provide in regs, or other guidance under Code Sec. 1400L(a)(2)(A) and Code Sec. 1400L(a)(2)(B)(i), rules similar to the rules provided in regs or other guidance under Code Sec. 1396(d)(1)(A). In that case, whether the requirements in Code Sec. 1400L(a)(2)(A) and Code Sec. 1400L(a)(2)(B)(i) are satisfied would be determined under one of the following two methods: (1) the pay period method (as described in Reg §1.1396-1(b)(1), see FTC 2d/FIN ¶ L-15637.2; USTR ¶ 13,964; TaxDesk ¶ 384,026), or (2) the calendar year method (as described in Reg §1.1396-1(b)(2), see FTC 2d/FIN ¶ L-15637.3; USTR ¶ 13,964; TaxDesk ¶ 384,026).

"New York Liberty Zone Business" defined. A "New York Liberty Zone business" is any trade or business which is: (Code Sec. 1400L(a)(2)(C)(i))

. . . located in the New York Liberty Zone, *or* (Code Sec. 1400L(a)(2)(C)(i)(I))

. . . located in New York City, New York, outside of the New York Liberty Zone, as the result of the physical destruction or damage of the place of business by the Sept. 11, 2001 terrorist attack. (Code Sec. 1400L(a)(2)(C)(i)(II))

Thus, the new targeted group would be individuals who perform substantially all of their services in the New York Liberty Zone for businesses located in the New York Liberty Zone and individuals who perform substantially all of their services in New York City for a business that relocated from the New York Liberty Zone elsewhere within New York City due to the physical destruction or damage of its workplace within the New York Liberty Zone. (Com Rept, see ¶ 5011)

> **☉** *observation:* Thus, the definition of a New York Liberty Zone business does *not* include businesses that relocated *from* the New York Liberty Zone to locations in New Jersey (e.g., Jersey City) or to New York locations outside of New York City (e.g., Westchester County or Long Island). However, the definition of a New York Liberty Zone business includes businesses that relocated *to* the New York Liberty Zone from other areas after Sept. 11, 2001.

It is anticipated that only otherwise qualified businesses that relocate due to *significant* physical damage will be eligible for the credit. (Com Rept, see ¶ 5011)

A New York Liberty Zone business doesn't include any trade or business for any tax year if that trade or business employed an average of more than 200 employees on business days during the tax year. (Code Sec. 1400L(a)(2)(C)(ii)) Thus, no WOTC for the category consisting of New York Liberty Zone business employees is allowed if the otherwise qualifying employer on average employed more than 200 employees during the tax year in question. (Com Rept, see ¶ 5011)

> **☉** *observation:* It is possible that IRS will use aggregation rules, similar to those discussed under "Determining employees for purposes of the non-Liberty Zone employee rule" below, to determine the number of employees for purposes of the 200-employee limitation.

Special rules for determining the credit. For purposes of applying subpart F of part IV of subchapter B of chapter 1 of the Code to wages paid or incurred to any New York Liberty Zone business employee, the special rules discussed below apply. (Code Sec. 1400L(a)(2)(D))

> **☉** *observation:* There appears to be a drafting error in Code Sec. 1400L(a)(2)(D) (as added by 2002 Act §301(a)) since there is no subpart F of part IV of subchapter *B* of chapter 1 in the Code. Presumably, Code Sec. 1400L(a)(2)(D) should refer to subpart F of part IV of subchapter *A* of chapter 1. Subpart F begins with Code Sec. 51 and contains the rules for computing the WOTC.

FTC 2d References are to Federal Tax Coordinator 2d
FIN References are to RIA's Analysis of Federal Taxes: Income
USTR References are to United States Tax Reporter: Income, Estate & Gift, and Excise
PCA References are to the Pension Analysis on Checkpoint and CD-ROM, and in Pension Coordinator
PE References are to the Pension Explanations in Pension and Profit Sharing 2nd
EP References are to the Estate Planning Analysis on Checkpoint and CD-ROM, and in Estate Planning & Taxation Coordinator

Determining employees for purposes of the "non-Liberty Zone employee rule." For purposes of the "non-Liberty Zone employee rule" (above), the rules of Code Sec. 52 apply. (Code Sec. 1400L(a)(2)(D)(ii))

> 🅡 *observation:* The portions of Code Sec. 52 which, presumably, apply to the determination of "employees" under the "non-Liberty Zone employee rule" are those that aggregate employees of controlled groups of corporations under Code Sec. 52(a) and of certain other commonly controlled businesses under Code Sec. 52(b), see FTC 2d/FIN ¶ L-17787; USTR ¶ 514; TaxDesk ¶ 380,718.

Amount of the credit allowed per eligible employee. For purposes of the New York Liberty Zone business employee credit, Code Sec. 51(a) (rule allowing a credit equal to 40% of the "qualified first-year wages", see FTC 2d/FIN ¶ L-17778; USTR ¶ 514; TaxDesk ¶ 380,700) is applied by substituting "qualified wages" (defined below) for "qualified first-year wages." (Code Sec. 1400L(a)(2)(D)(i)) Thus, for the new category, the maximum credit is $2,400 (40% of $6,000 of qualified wages, see **"Qualified wages defined"** below) per qualified employee in each year. (Com Rept, see ¶ 5011)

> 🅡 *observation:* Instead of reading as immediately above, the Technical Explanation states the maximum credit as $2,400 per qualified employee per *tax* year. It seems clear, however, based on the language of Code Sec. 1400L(a)(2)(D)(iv)(II) (discussed below), that the limit is $2,400 per qualified employee per *calendar* year.

> 🅡 *observation:* The employer presumably must reduce his deduction for wages paid to a New York Liberty Zone business employee by the amount of the credit under Code Sec. 280C(a) (which provides that the amount of the WOTC reduces the employer's deduction for wages, see FTC 2d/FIN ¶ L-17780; USTR ¶ 514; TaxDesk ¶ 380,701).

> 🅡 *observation:* For purposes of the WOTC, certain commonly controlled businesses have to apportion the amount of the credit, see FTC 2d/FIN ¶ L-17787; USTR ¶ 514; TaxDesk ¶ 380,718. Presumably, a similar rule applies to commonly controlled New York Liberty Zone businesses.

> Similarly, the credit apportionment rules that apply to estates, trusts, partnerships and S corporations (see FTC 2d/FIN ¶ L-17789; USTR ¶ 514; TaxDesk ¶ 380,718) presumably apply to the New York Liberty Zone business employee credit.

> 🅡 *observation:* Presumably, the New York Liberty Zone business employee credit is also subject to the following rules that apply to the WOTC:

> . . . rules which provide that the WOTC isn't available to most tax-exempt organizations, see FTC 2d/FIN ¶ L-17789A; USTR ¶ 514.

. . . rules limiting the amount of the WOTC that can be claimed by regulated investment companies (RICs) and real estate investment trusts (REITs), see FTC 2d/FIN ¶ L-17789.1; USTR ¶ 514.

For the extent to which an employer's tax liabilities may limit an employer's aggregate New York Liberty Zone business employee credit, see ¶ 506.

"Qualified wages" defined. In determining "qualified wages," the following rules apply in lieu of Code Sec. 51(b) (the definition of qualified wages for purposes of the WOTC, see FTC 2d/FIN ¶ L-17783; USTR ¶ 514; TaxDesk ¶ 380,707): (Code Sec. 1400L(a)(2)(D)(iv))

. . . "qualified wages" are the wages paid or incurred by the employer to individuals who are New York Liberty Zone business employees of the employer for work performed during calendar year 2002 or 2003. (Code Sec. 1400L(a)(2)(D)(iv)(I))

> **☑️ observation:** Presumably, the definition of "wages," for WOTC purposes, provided in Code Sec. 51(c)(1) (generally, "wages" for Federal Unemployment Tax Act (FUTA) purposes, but without regard to the FUTA dollar cap, see FTC 2d/FIN ¶ L-17783; USTR ¶ 514; TaxDesk ¶ 380,707) would apply in determining "qualified wages."

. . . the amount of the qualified wages which may be taken into account with respect to any individual can't exceed $6,000 per calendar year. (Code Sec. 1400L(a)(2)(D)(iv)(II))

> **☑️ illustration:** ABC Corp., a New York Liberty Zone business with a tax year ending June 30 has 100 New York Liberty Zone business employees who began working for ABC on July 1, 2002. ABC paid each of these employees more than $6,000 of qualified wages for work performed between July 1, 2002 and Dec. 31, 2002 and more than $6,000 of qualified wages for work performed between Jan. 1, 2003 and June 30, 2003. ABC's credit with respect to each of the 100 employees for the tax year ending June 30, 2003 is $4,800 ($2,400 [$6,000 × 40%] for work performed in calendar year 2002 plus $2,400 [$6,000 × 40%] for work performed in calendar year 2003). Before taking into account the limitation on the New York Liberty Zone business employee credit described at ¶ 506, ABC's New York Liberty Zone business employee credit for all of its New York Liberty Zone business employees for the tax year ending June 30, 2003 is $480,000 ($4,800 × 100).

FTC 2d References are to Federal Tax Coordinator 2d
FIN References are to RIA's Analysis of Federal Taxes: Income
USTR References are to United States Tax Reporter: Income, Estate & Gift, and Excise
PCA References are to the Pension Analysis on Checkpoint and CD-ROM, and in Pension Coordinator
PE References are to the Pension Explanations in Pension and Profit Sharing 2nd
EP References are to the Estate Planning Analysis on Checkpoint and CD-ROM, and in Estate Planning & Taxation Coordinator

observation: In determining whether wages qualify for the New York Liberty Zone business employee credit, the following rules that apply to the WOTC presumably would also apply for purposes of the New York Liberty Zone business employee credit:

. . . rules that sometimes deny the WOTC for wages paid or incurred to certain employees performing work for a person other than the employer, see FTC 2d/FIN ¶ L-17784.3; USTR ¶ 514.

. . . rules denying a WOTC for wages paid or incurred to an employee for whom the employer is receiving federally funded job training payments or certain related employees, see FTC 2d/FIN ¶ L-17784.2; USTR ¶ 514; TaxDesk ¶ 380,707 and TaxDesk ¶ 380,709.

. . . rules denying a WOTC for wages paid to replacement workers in a labor dispute, see FTC 2d/FIN ¶ L-17783.3; USTR ¶ 514; TaxDesk ¶ 380,707.

Rule limiting the WOTC to new employees doesn't apply to the New York Liberty Zone business employee credit. Code Sec. 51(i)(2) (rules providing that no wages are taken into account for purposes of the WOTC with respect to any individual if, before the hiring date of the individual, the individual had been employed by the employer at any time, see FTC 2d/FIN ¶ L-17784.2; USTR ¶ 514; TaxDesk ¶ 380,701) does not apply. (Code Sec. 1400L(a)(2)(D)(iii)) Thus, unlike the other targeted categories that apply for purposes of the WOTC, the credit for the new targeted group (i.e., New York Liberty Zone business employees) is available for wages paid to both new hires and existing employees. (Com Rept, see ¶ 5011)

Certification of employees not required. According to the Technical Explanation, unlike members of other targeted categories, members of the New York Liberty Zone business employee group won't require certification (under the rules in Code Sec. 51(d)(12), see FTC 2d/FIN ¶ L-17784.1; USTR ¶ 514; TaxDesk ¶ 380,708) for their wages to qualify for the credit. (Com Rept, see ¶ 5011)

Termination date of the WOTC doesn't apply to the New York Liberty Zone business employee credit. Code Sec. 51(c)(4) (rules that, as amended by the 2002 Act, provide that wages don't include any amount paid or incurred to an individual who begins work for the employer (1) after Dec. 31, '94, and before Oct. 1, '96, or (2) after Dec. 31, 2003, see ¶ 202 and FTC 2d/FIN ¶ L-17775; USTR ¶ 514; TaxDesk ¶ 380,700) does not apply. (Code Sec. 1400L(a)(2)(D)(iii))

2002 Act §301(a), which is the 2002 Act provision that provides the New York Liberty Zone business credit, extends the WOTC only for the limited purpose of providing the New York Liberty Zone business employee credit. A separate provision of the 2002 Act (2002 Act §604(a), see ¶ 202) includes a general 2-year extension of the WOTC. (Com Rept, see ¶ 5011)

observation: The general 2-year extension applies to any employee who begins work for the employer before Jan. 1, 2004. However, unlike the credit for wages paid or incurred to members of other targeted groups, the New York Liberty Zone business employee credit is allowed for wages paid or incurred to a New York Liberty Zone business employee who begins work for the employer before Jan. 1, 2004 only for work performed before Jan. 1, 2004.

☐ **Effective:** Tax years ending after Dec. 31, 2001, for wages paid or incurred to qualified individuals for work after Dec. 31, 2001 and before Jan. 1, 2004. (Com Rept, see ¶ 5011)

¶ 506. New York Liberty Zone business employee credit can offset AMT; limitations, carryback, and carryforward rules apply separately to the credit

Code Sec. 38(c)(3), as amended by 2002 Act § 301(b)(1)
Code Sec. 38(c)(2)(A)(ii)(II), as amended by 2002 Act § 301(b)(2)
Generally effective: Tax years ending after Dec. 31, 2001
Committee Reports, see ¶ 5011

Generally, under Code Sec. 38(c)(1), the general business credit, provided by Code Sec. 38, (1) is subject to limits in its offset of a taxpayer's regular income tax liability, and (2) can't be used to offset any of a taxpayer's alternative minimum tax (AMT) liability, see FTC 2d/FIN ¶ L-15202; USTR ¶ 384.02; TaxDesk ¶ 380,502. Carryback and carryforward rules apply to the unused credit, see FTC 2d/FIN ¶ L-15209; USTR ¶ 394.01; TaxDesk ¶ 380,509.

Most of the credits that make up the general business credit are combined for purposes of applying the above rules, see FTC 2d/FIN ¶ L-15202.1, FTC 2d/FIN ¶ L-15209; USTR ¶ 384.02; TaxDesk ¶ 380,503, TaxDesk ¶ 380,509.

Under pre-2002 Act law, the only exceptions to the above rules related to the empowerment zone employment credit and the renewal community employment credit. (FTC 2d/FIN ¶ L-15202, ¶ L-15209; USTR ¶ 384.02, ¶ 394.01; TaxDesk ¶ 380,503, ¶ 380,509)

New Law. The 2002 Act creates the New York Liberty Zone business employee credit as part of the work opportunity tax credit (WOTC), see ¶ 505.

FTC 2d References are to Federal Tax Coordinator 2d
FIN References are to RIA's Analysis of Federal Taxes: Income
USTR References are to United States Tax Reporter: Income, Estate & Gift, and Excise
PCA References are to the Pension Analysis on Checkpoint and CD-ROM, and in Pension Coordinator
PE References are to the Pension Explanations in Pension and Profit Sharing 2nd
EP References are to the Estate Planning Analysis on Checkpoint and CD-ROM, and in Estate Planning & Taxation Coordinator

The 2002 Act also provides the rules, discussed below, that determine how the general business credit limitations, and carryback and carryforward rules, apply to the New York Liberty Zone business employee credit.

Separate limitations on the amount of the credit. For the "New York Liberty Zone business employee credit" (defined below), (Code Sec. 38(c)(3)(A) as amended by 2002 Act §301(b)(1)) the limitations on the general business credit (see above) are applied separately for the credit. (Code Sec. 38(c)(3)(A)(i))

> *observation:* Thus, as is true for the empowerment zone employment credit and the renewal community employment credit, see FTC 2d/FIN ¶ L-15202.1; USTR ¶ 384.02; TaxDesk ¶ 380,509, but not for the WOTC or any of the other credits that make up the general business credit, the limitations on the general business credit are calculated separately (rather than in a combined calculation).

Credit can offset AMT. For the New York Liberty Zone business employee credit, in applying Code Sec. 38(c)(1) to the credit, (Code Sec. 38(c)(3)(A)(ii)) the tentative minimum tax (i.e., the AMT increased by the "regular tax" that was subtracted in arriving at the AMT, see FTC 2d/FIN ¶ A-8100; USTR ¶ 554.01; TaxDesk ¶ 691,000) is treated as being zero. (Code Sec. 38(c)(3)(A)(ii)(I)) Thus, the portion of each employer's WOTC credit attributable to the new targeted group (i.e., employees of New York Liberty Zone businesses) is allowed against the AMT. (Com Rept, see ¶ 5011)

> *observation:* Thus, unlike most other general business credits, the New York Liberty Zone business employee credit can be used against the AMT. Specifically, for purposes of applying the tax liability limitations in Code Sec. 38(c)(1) (see above) to the New York Liberty Zone business employee credit, the credit can't exceed the excess (if any) of the taxpayer's "net income tax" (the taxpayer's regular income tax plus AMT, minus certain credits not included in the general business credit) over the *greater* of: (a) zero (the tentative minimum tax treated as being zero), or (b) 25% of so much of the taxpayer's "net regular tax liability" as exceeds $25,000. The allowable New York Liberty Zone business employee credit is further limited if the taxpayer is allowed other credits that make up the general business credit, see "Ordering rule" below.

> *illustration (1):* In Year 1, taxpayer X, a sole proprietor, before taking into account any credits, has regular income tax liability of $30,000 and tentative minimum tax of $45,000. Before taking into account the limitations on the general business credit, X has a general business credit (other than the New York Liberty Zone business employee credit) of $10,000 and has a New York Liberty Zone business employee credit of $48,000. X has no other tax credits.

X's general business credit (other than the New York Liberty Zone business employee credit) is limited to the excess of $45,000 (X's net income tax for the year [$30,000 plus $15,000 minus $0]) over the greater of (i) X's tentative minimum tax of $45,000, or (ii) $1,250, which is 25% of the excess of $30,000 (X's regular tax liability) over $25,000. Thus, X isn't allowed a general business credit (apart from the New York Liberty Zone business employee credit).

With respect to the New York Liberty Zone business employee credit, the limitation is separately computed. Because X isn't allowed any general business credit (apart from the New York Liberty Zone business employee credit), the limitation is equal to the excess of $45,000 (X's net income tax for the year) over the *greater* of (i) $0 (X's tentative minimum tax treated as being zero), or (ii) $1,250 (25% of the excess of X's regular tax liability of $30,000 over $25,000). Since (ii) is greater than (i), X's net income tax for the year is reduced by $1,250 and the limitation is $43,750 ($45,000 less $1,250). Thus, X can claim $43,750 of the New York Liberty Zone business employee credit against his regular tax liability and AMT liability for Year 1. For how the carryback and carryforward rules apply to X's New York Liberty Zone business employee credit, see illustration (2) below.

 observation: However, if the employer has WOTC attributable to another targeted group, that portion of the WOTC would *not* be allowed against the AMT.

Ordering rule. The limitation under Code Sec. 38(c)(1) (as modified by the rule in Code Sec. 38(c)(3)(A)(ii)(I) that treats the tentative minimum tax as zero) is reduced by the credit allowed under Code Sec. 38(a) for the tax year (other than the New York Liberty Zone business employee credit). (Code Sec. 38(c)(3)(A)(ii)(II))

Also, the 2002 Act amends Code Sec. 38(c)(2)(A)(ii)(II), one of the rules that, for the empowerment zone employment credit and renewal community credit, provides for separate computation of the Code Sec. 38 tax liability limitations (FTC 2d/FIN ¶ L-15202.1; USTR ¶ 384.02; TaxDesk ¶ 380,503) by inserting "or the New York Liberty Zone business employee credit" after "employment credit". (Code Sec. 38(c)(2)(A)(ii)(II) as amended by 2002 Act §301(b)(2))

 observation: There appears to be a drafting error in 2002 Act §301(b)(2) because Code Sec. 38(c)(2)(A)(ii)(II) does not contain the phrase "employment credit", but does contain the phrase "empowerment

---

FTC 2d References are to Federal Tax Coordinator 2d
FIN References are to RIA's Analysis of Federal Taxes: Income
USTR References are to United States Tax Reporter: Income, Estate & Gift, and Excise
PCA References are to the Pension Analysis on Checkpoint and CD-ROM, and in Pension Coordinator
PE References are to the Pension Explanations in Pension and Profit Sharing 2nd
EP References are to the Estate Planning Analysis on Checkpoint and CD-ROM, and in Estate Planning & Taxation Coordinator

zone credit." Congress presumably intended to insert "or the New York Liberty Zone business employee credit" after *"empowerment zone credit."*

observation: Presumably, the effects of Code Sec. 38(c)(3)(A)(ii)(II) and Code Sec. 38(c)(2)(A)(ii)(II) are to require that (1) the taxpayer separately apply the general business credit tax liability limitations on the New York Liberty Zone business employee credit *after* doing the combined calculation required for most other credits that make up the general business credit (the "combined calculation") *and after* the separate calculation required for the empowerment zone employment credit and the renewal community employment credit (the "separate calculation"), and (2) the New York Liberty Zone business employee credit can't exceed the excess (if any) of the taxpayer's "net income tax" (see above) over the *greater of* (a) zero (see above) or (b) 25% of so much of the taxpayer's net regular tax liability as exceeds $25,000, after that excess, of "net income tax" over the greater of (a) or (b), is reduced by the credits allowed under the "combined calculation" and the "separate calculation."

Carryback and forward rules. For the New York Liberty Zone business employee credit, the carryback and carryforward rules that apply to the general business credit (see above) are applied separately with respect to the credit. (Code Sec. 38(c)(3)(A)(i))

observation: Although the carryback and carryforward rules for any unused New York Liberty Zone business employee credits are separately computed, the carryback and carryforward periods (one-year carryback and 20-year carryforward, see FTC 2d/FIN ¶ L-15209; USTR ¶ 394.01; TaxDesk ¶ 380,509) are the same as for other credits that are components of the general business credit.

observation: Thus, as is true for the empowerment zone employment credit and the renewal community employment credit, see FTC 2d/FIN ¶ L-15209; USTR ¶ 384.02; TaxDesk ¶ 380,509, but not for the WOTC or any of the other credits that make up the general business credit, carrybacks and carryforwards are calculated separately (rather than in a combined calculation).

illustration (2): The facts are the same as illustration (1) above. Due to the limitation that applies to X's New York Liberty Zone business employee credit, X can only claim $43,750 of his $48,000 New York Liberty Zone business employee credit and has $4,250 of unused New York Liberty Zone business employee credit. Under the general business credit carryback and carryforward rules, X has to first carry the unused credit to the first available year (in this case, the tax year immediately preceding Year

1). If the credit is still unused, X can carry the unused credit forward for 20 years (in this case, until Year 21).

"New York Liberty Zone business employee credit" defined. For purposes of the limitations on the general business credit under Code Sec. 38(c) (discussed above), the "New York Liberty Zone business employee credit" is the portion of WOTC under Code Sec. 51 determined under Code Sec. 1400L(a). (Code Sec. 38(c)(3)(B))

Redesignation. The 2002 Act redesignates as Code Sec. 38(c)(4) pre-2002 Code Sec. 38(c)(3) (containing special rules relating to how the general business credit applies to married individuals filing separate returns (FTC 2d/FIN ¶ L-15204; USTR ¶ 384.02; TaxDesk ¶ 380,502)), the limitation on the credit for con-trolled groups (FTC 2d/FIN ¶ L-15205; USTR ¶ 384.02; TaxDesk ¶ 380,506), the limitation on the credit for banks, regulated investment companies (RICs) and real estate investment trusts (REITs) (FTC 2d/FIN ¶ L-15206; USTR ¶ 384.02), and the limitation on credit for estates and trusts (FTC 2d/FIN ¶ L-15207; USTR ¶ 384.02; TaxDesk ¶ 380,507). (Code Sec. 38(c)(4) redesignated by 2002 Act §301(b)(1))

☐ **Effective:** Tax years ending after Dec. 31, 2001. (2002 Act § 301(b)(3))

¶ 507. Issuance of up to $8 billion of tax-exempt private activity bonds to finance the rebuilding of portions of New York City is authorized

Code Sec. 1400L(d), as added by 2002 Act § 301(a)
Code Sec. 1400L(i), as added by 2002 Act § 301(a)
Generally effective: Bonds issued after Mar. 9, 2002 and before Jan. 1, 2005
Committee Reports, see ¶ 5014

Interest on debt incurred by state or local governments is excluded from income if the proceeds of the borrowing are used to carry out governmental functions of these entities or the debt is repaid with government funds (see FTC 2d/FIN ¶ J-3000; USTR ¶ 1034; TaxDesk ¶ 158,001). Interest on bonds nominally issued by state or local governments, the proceeds of which directly or indirectly are used by a private person, and the payment of which is derived from the funds of that pri-vate person ("private activity bonds," see FTC 2d/FIN ¶ J-3100; USTR ¶ 1414; TaxDesk ¶ 158,009), is taxable, unless the purpose of the bonds is approved spe-

---

FTC 2d References are to Federal Tax Coordinator 2d
FIN References are to RIA's Analysis of Federal Taxes: Income
USTR References are to United States Tax Reporter: Income, Estate & Gift, and Excise
PCA References are to the Pension Analysis on Checkpoint and CD-ROM, and in Pension Coordinator
PE References are to the Pension Explanations in Pension and Profit Sharing 2nd
EP References are to the Estate Planning Analysis on Checkpoint and CD-ROM, and in Estate Planning & Taxation Coordinator

cifically in the Code or in a non-Code provision of a Revenue Act. Interest on private activity bonds (other than qualified Code Sec. 501(c)(3) bonds) is a tax preference item in calculating the alternative minimum tax (AMT) (see FTC 2d/FIN ¶ A-8201; USTR ¶ 574; TaxDesk ¶ 696,501).

States or local governments may issue tax-exempt "exempt facility bonds" (see FTC 2d/FIN ¶ J-3153; USTR ¶ 1424; TaxDesk ¶ 158,010) to finance property for certain private businesses. Business facilities eligible for this financing include:

... transportation (airports, docks, wharves, local mass commuting and high speed intercity rail facilities);

... privately owned and/or privately operated public works facilities (sewage, solid waste disposal, local district heating or cooling, and hazardous waste disposal facilities);

... privately owned and/or privately operated low-income rental housing; and

... certain private facilities for the local furnishing of electricity or gas.

See FTC 2d/FIN ¶ J-3153; USTR ¶ 1424.

In most cases, the aggregate volume of tax-exempt private activity bonds that may be issued in a state is restricted by annual volume limits. Volume limits for calendar year 2002 are the greater of $75 per state resident or $225 million. After 2002, the volume limits will be indexed annually for inflation. See FTC 2d/FIN ¶ J-3252.1; USTR ¶ 1464.01.

Private activity bonds (other than qualified Code Sec. 501(c)(3) bonds) may not be advance refunded. Governmental and qualified Code Sec. 501(c)(3) bonds may be advance refunded one time. Advance refunding occurs when refunded bonds are not retired within 90 days of issuance of the refunding bonds. See FTC 2d/FIN ¶ J-3660; USTR ¶ 1494.03; TaxDesk ¶ 158,014. Substantial users of property financed with private activity bonds are precluded from owning the bonds to prevent their deducting tax-exempt interest paid to themselves (see FTC 2d/FIN ¶ J-3277; USTR ¶ 1474.02). Owners of most private-activity-bond-financed property are subject to special "change-in-use" penalties if the use of the bond-financed property changes to a use that is not eligible for tax-exempt financing while the bonds are outstanding. See FTC 2d/FIN ¶ J-3151; USTR ¶ 1414.

New Law. The 2002 Act authorizes issuance of an aggregate amount of $8 billion of tax-exempt private activity bonds to finance the construction and rehabilitation of nonresidential and residential real property in a newly designated "Liberty Zone" of New York City. (Com Rept, see ¶ 5014)

> **observation:** The Technical Explanation of the 2002 Act also refers to the New York Liberty Zone as the "New York Recovery Zone." This was a term used in an earlier version of the legislation to refer to the area in the Borough of Manhattan now referred to as the New York Liberty Zone.

For the definition of "New York Liberty Zone," see ¶ 501.

The 2002 Act creates a category of bond called a "qualified New York Liberty Bond" that is treated as an exempt facility bond. (Code Sec. 1400L(d)(1) as added by 2002 Act §301(a))

> *observation:* Private activity bonds that are exempt facility bonds may qualify for tax-exempt status. Certain requirements must be met. Normally, a private activity bond issued by a state or local government is not exempt from federal income tax. However, if a bond is an exempt facility bond, it is a qualified private activity bond, and thus is tax-exempt. Bonds used to finance these specified facilities (see the list above) are tax-exempt only if the facility is available on a regular basis for general public use or is part of a facility so used. Thus, certain bonds used to fund projects that benefit the general public are given favorable tax-exempt status. See FTC 2d/FIN ¶ J-3153; USTR ¶ 1424; TaxDesk ¶ 158,010.

Qualified New York Liberty Bond defined. For purposes of Code Sec. 1400L(d), a qualified New York Liberty Bond is any bond issued as part of an issue if: (Code Sec. 1400L(d)(2))

... at least 95% of the net proceeds (as defined in Code Sec. 150(a)(3)) of the issue will be used for "qualified project costs" (defined below) (Code Sec. 1400L(d)(2)(A)) ;

> *observation:* The term "net proceeds" under Code Sec. 150(a)(3) means the proceeds of an issue of bonds, reduced by amounts in a reasonably required reserve or replacement fund, see FTC 2d/FIN ¶ J-3004.

... the bond is issued by New York State, or any political subdivision of New York State (Code Sec. 1400L(d)(2)(B)) ;

... the bond is designated by the Governor or the Mayor (defined below) for purposes of Code Sec. 1400L (Code Sec. 1400L(d)(2)(C)) ; and

... the bond is issued after Mar. 9, 2002 and before Jan. 1, 2005. (Code Sec. 1400L(d)(2)(D))

Thus, bonds authorized under Code Sec. 1400L(d) may be issued during calendar years 2002, 2003, and 2004. (Com Rept, see ¶ 5014)

> *observation:* The Technical Explanation states "the provision authorizes issuance" of bonds during calendar year 2002, but Code Sec. 1400L(d)(2)(D) makes it clear that in order for a bond to be a quali-

---

FTC 2d References are to Federal Tax Coordinator 2d
FIN References are to RIA's Analysis of Federal Taxes: Income
USTR References are to United States Tax Reporter: Income, Estate & Gift, and Excise
PCA References are to the Pension Analysis on Checkpoint and CD-ROM, and in Pension Coordinator
PE References are to the Pension Explanations in Pension and Profit Sharing 2nd
EP References are to the Estate Planning Analysis on Checkpoint and CD-ROM, and in Estate Planning & Taxation Coordinator

fied New York Liberty Bond, it must be issued *after* Mar. 9, 2002 and before Jan. 1, 2005.

For purposes of Code Sec. 1400L, the terms "Governor" and "Mayor" mean the Governor of New York State and the Mayor of New York City, respectively. (Code Sec. 1400L(i) as added by 2002 Act §301(a))

Amount of bonds authorized. The maximum aggregate face amount of bonds that can be designated under Code Sec. 1400L(d) is $8 billion, of which a maximum of $4 billion may be designated by the Governor and a maximum of $4 billion may be designated by the Mayor. (Code Sec. 1400L(d)(3)(A))

The aggregate face amount of bonds issued is subject to the following limitations for various uses of proceeds:

. . . costs for property located outside the New York Liberty Zone cannot exceed $2 billion; (Code Sec. 1400L(d)(3)(B)(i))

. . . residential rental property cannot exceed $1.6 billion; and (Code Sec. 1400L(d)(3)(B)(ii))

. . . costs for property used for retail sales of tangible property and functionally related and subordinate property cannot exceed $800 million. (Code Sec. 1400L(d)(3)(B)(iii)) Property used for retail sales of tangible property includes department stores and restaurants. (Com Rept, see ¶ 5014)

The above limitations are to be allocated proportionately between the bonds designated by the Governor and those designated by the Mayor, in proportion to the respective amounts each designates. (Code Sec. 1400L(d)(3)(B)) The Technical Explanation indicates that the $1.6 billion limit on the authorized bond amount used to finance residential rental property, and the $800 million limit on property used for retail sales are to be divided equally between the Mayor and the Governor. (Com Rept, see ¶ 5014)

> *observation:* It would appear that the Technical Explanation assumes the Mayor and the Governor would each designate the maximum $4 billion, or an equal amount of bonds, since these would be the only scenarios under which the total limitations of $1.6 billion and $800 million would be divided equally between them.

> *illustration:* If the Mayor designates $4 billion of bonds, and the Governor designates $3.5 billion, the limitations would be allocated $\frac{8}{15}$ and $\frac{7}{15}$, respectively. Thus, the limitation on residential rental property would be ($1.6 billion × $\frac{8}{15}$) or $853,333,333 allocated to the Mayor and the remaining $\frac{7}{15}$, or $746,666,667 allocated to the Governor.

> *illustration:* If the Mayor designates $3.5 billion and the Governor designates $3.5 billion, the limitation on residential rental property would

be allocated $800 million to each, and the limitation on property used for retail sales of tangible property would be allocated $400 million to each.

Current refundings of outstanding bonds issued under Code Sec. 1400L(d) do not count against the $8 billion volume limit to the extent that the principal amount of the refunding bonds does not exceed the outstanding principal amount of the bonds being refunded. The bonds may not be advance refunded. (Com Rept, see ¶ 5014)

No bonds are to be issued for the financing of movable fixtures and equipment. (Code Sec. 1400L(d)(3)(C))

> *observation:* The above limitations by types of property may result in problems in allocation of bond proceeds where buildings are mixed-use, such as office and retail, or retail and residential. The situation could arise in which an office or commercial portion of a building would qualify for the bond funding, while a retail or residential portion may not.

> *illustration:* A building has retail space on the first or ground floor, offices on the second floor, and the remaining floors are residential rental units. If the retail sales property limitation of $800 million, and/or the residential rental property limitation of $1.6 billion have been reached, part of the building will not qualify for the bond financing. There is no mention in the statute or the Technical Explanation about how a building's use is determined.

Qualified project costs. For purposes of Code Sec. 1400L(d), qualified project costs are, with respect to any property located *within* the New York Liberty Zone, the cost of acquisition, construction, reconstruction, and renovation of: (Code Sec. 1400L(d)(4)(A))

. . . nonresidential real property and residential rental property, including fixed tenant improvements associated with that property, (Code Sec. 1400L(d)(4)(A)(i)) i.e., buildings and their structural components, and associated fixed tenant improvements (Com Rept, see ¶ 5014); and

. . . public utility property, as defined in Code Sec. 168(i)(10), i.e., for purposes of MACRS (see FTC 2d/FIN ¶ L-9302). (Code Sec. 1400L(d)(4)(A)(ii)) Examples of public utility property are gas, water, electric and telecommunication lines. (Com Rept, see ¶ 5014)

FTC 2d References are to Federal Tax Coordinator 2d
FIN References are to RIA's Analysis of Federal Taxes: Income
USTR References are to United States Tax Reporter: Income, Estate & Gift, and Excise
PCA References are to the Pension Analysis on Checkpoint and CD-ROM, and in Pension
    Coordinator
PE References are to the Pension Explanations in Pension and Profit Sharing 2nd
EP References are to the Estate Planning Analysis on Checkpoint and CD-ROM, and in
    Estate Planning & Taxation Coordinator

Nonresidential real property includes structural components if a taxpayer treats those components as part of the real property structure for all federal income tax purposes (e.g., cost recovery). (Com Rept, see ¶ 5014)

Fixtures and equipment that can be removed from the New York Liberty Zone for use elsewhere are not eligible for financing with the qualified New York Liberty Bonds. (Com Rept, see ¶ 5014)

> *observation:* Thus, it appears that items such as furniture, computer equipment, window air conditioning units, or removable shelving would not be eligible for financing with the qualified New York Liberty Bonds because they could be removed and used elsewhere outside the New York Liberty Zone. Questions are likely to arise about the permanent or removable nature of certain items since the term "fixed tenant improvements" is not defined in the 2002 Act nor does there appear to be a definition of the term elsewhere in the Code.

> *illustration:* A commercial tenant installs new lighting in the rented space. If this is of a permanent nature, such as fluorescent lighting in a dropped ceiling, this item could be a fixed tenant improvement and not a removable fixture.

Property located outside the New York Liberty Zone. With respect to property located *within* the City of New York, but *outside* the New York Liberty Zone, qualified project costs include the costs of acquisition, construction, reconstruction, and renovation of nonresidential real property, including fixed tenant improvements associated with the property. The property must be part of a project that consists of at least 100,000 square feet of usable office or other commercial space located in a single building or multiple adjacent buildings. (Code Sec. 1400L(d)(4)(B))

> *observation:* It appears that "the City of New York" means all five boroughs, although actual physical damage and destruction from the terrorist attacks was confined to the Borough of Manhattan.

> *observation:* Projects outside the New York Liberty Zone have to provide a certain amount of space in one location for business use; numerous small scattered sites around the City will not qualify for the bond financing.

Public utility property and residential property located outside the New York Liberty Zone cannot be financed with the bonds. (Com Rept, see ¶ 5014)

> *observation:* The only type of property eligible for bond financing outside the New York Liberty Zone (provided proceeds are available) is nonresidential real property. Questions may arise about whether mixed residential and nonresidential use property qualifies for financing, or if an allocation should be made.

observation: The term "commercial space" is not defined in Code Sec. 1400L(d), nor does there appear to be a general definition of the term elsewhere in the Code. Code Sec. 1400L(d)(4)(B) uses both "nonresidential real property" (this term is also not defined in Code Sec. 1400L, but there is some clarification in the Technical Explanation as to what is included) and "commercial space" in explaining what are qualified project costs outside the New York Liberty Zone, but within the City of New York. Questions may arise about property that is clearly nonresidential, but may or may not be considered commercial, such as industrial property, private schools, hospitals, and other properties.

observation: The Technical Explanation says that the tenant targeting rules of Code Sec. 142(d) and Code Sec. 150(b)(2) that apply to exempt facility bonds for residential rental real property (and the corresponding change-in-use penalties for violation of those rules) do not apply to residential rental real property financed with the bonds. (Com Rept, see ¶ 5014) However, the statute does not contain this provision. An earlier version of the legislation had included this item.

Special rules. Code Sec. 146 (relating to volume cap) does not apply to qualified New York Liberty Bonds. (Code Sec. 1400L(d)(5)(A)) Thus, issuance of the bonds is not subject to the aggregate annual state private activity bond volume limits of Code Sec. 146, see FTC 2d/FIN ¶ J-3252.1; USTR ¶ 1464.01. (Com Rept, see ¶ 5014)

Code Sec. 147(d) (relating to acquisition of existing property not permitted) is applied by substituting 50% for 15% each place it appears. (Code Sec. 1400L(d)(5)(B)) For example, the restriction on acquisition of existing property is applied using a minimum requirement of 50% of the cost of acquiring the building being devoted to rehabilitation. See FTC 2d/FIN ¶ J-3276; USTR ¶ 1474.01. (Com Rept, see ¶ 5014)

observation: Thus, the existing property limitations do not apply to bonds used to finance the acquisition of any building if the rehabilitation expenditures with respect to the building are 50% or more of the portion of the cost of acquiring the building financed with the bonds' net proceeds.

FTC 2d References are to Federal Tax Coordinator 2d
FIN References are to RIA's Analysis of Federal Taxes: Income
USTR References are to United States Tax Reporter: Income, Estate & Gift, and Excise
PCA References are to the Pension Analysis on Checkpoint and CD-ROM, and in Pension Coordinator
PE References are to the Pension Explanations in Pension and Profit Sharing 2nd
EP References are to the Estate Planning Analysis on Checkpoint and CD-ROM, and in Estate Planning & Taxation Coordinator

illustration: If a building is purchased for $750,000, tax-exempt bond financing is available if at least $375,000 (50% of $750,000) is spent for rehabilitation of the building.

Code Sec. 148(f)(4)(C) (relating to exception from rebate for certain proceeds to be used to finance construction expenditures) applies to construction proceeds of bonds issued under Code Sec. 1400L(d). (Code Sec. 1400L(d)(5)(C)) Thus, the special arbitrage expenditure rules for certain construction bond proceeds apply to construction proceeds of the qualified New York Liberty Bonds. See FTC 2d/FIN ¶ J-3623; J-3624; USTR ¶ 1484.04. (Com Rept, see ¶ 5014)

Repayments of principal on financing provided by the bond issue:

. . . cannot be used to provide financing. (Code Sec. 1400L(d)(5)(D)(i)) Thus, loan repayments cannot be used to originate new loans. All loan repayments must be used to redeem bonds. (Com Rept, see ¶ 5014)

. . . must be used not later than the close of the first semiannual period beginning after the date of the repayment to redeem bonds that are part of the issue. (Code Sec. 1400L(d)(5)(D)(ii)) This requirement is treated as met with respect to amounts received within 10 years after the date of issuance of the issue (or, in the case of a refunding bond, the date of issuance of the original bond) if those amounts are used by the close of that 10 years to redeem bonds that are part of that issue. (Code Sec. 1400L(d)(5)(D)) This means that redemptions must occur at least semiannually beginning after the expiration of the 10-year period immediately following issuance of the original bonds to which the repayments relate. (Com Rept, see ¶ 5014)

Effect on alternative minimum tax. A qualified New York Liberty Bond is not treated as a specified private activity bond for purposes of Code Sec. 57(a)(5). See FTC 2d/FIN ¶ A-8201; USTR ¶ 574; TaxDesk ¶ 696,501. (Code Sec. 1400L(d)(5)(E)) Thus, interest on these bonds is not a tax preference item for purposes of the AMT preference for private activity bond interest. (Com Rept, see ¶ 5014)

Separate issue election by issuer. Code Sec. 1400L(d) does not apply to the portion of the proceeds of an issue which, if issued as a separate issue, would be treated as a qualified bond or as a bond that is not a private activity bond if the issuer elects to so treat that portion of the proceeds. (Code Sec. 1400L(d)(6))

☐ **Effective:** Bonds issued after Mar. 9, 2002 and before Jan. 1, 2005. (Code Sec. 1400L(d)(2)(D))

¶ 508. Additional advance refunding is allowed for bonds for facilities located in New York City

Code Sec. 1400L(e), as added by 2002 Act § 301(a)
Generally effective: Mar. 9, 2002
Committee Reports, see ¶ 5015

A refunding bond is used to redeem a prior bond issuance, see FTC 2d/FIN ¶ J-3258; USTR ¶ 1504.04; TaxDesk ¶ 158,014. A bond is treated as issued to advance refund another bond if it is issued more than 90 days before the refunding bond is redeemed. In these cases, proceeds of the refunding bonds are invested in an escrow account and held until a future date when the refunded debt is permitted to be redeemed under the terms of the refunded bonds. Under pre-2002 Act law, governmental bonds and qualified Code Sec. 501(c)(3) bonds can be advance refunded one time. However, certain bonds issued before '86 can be advance refunded more than one time in certain cases. (FTC 2d/FIN ¶ J-3660; USTR ¶ 1494.03; TaxDesk ¶ 158,014)

New Law. The 2002 Act allows certain bonds for facilities located in New York City to be advance refunded one additional time. If certain conditions are met, one additional advance refunding is allowed with respect to a bond issued as part of an issue 90% (95% in the case of a bond described in Code Sec. 1400L(e)(2)(C) (a qualified Code Sec. 501(c)(3) bond, see below)) or more of the "net proceeds" of which were used to finance facilities either located within New York City, or property which is functionally related and subordinate to facilities located within New York City for the furnishing of water. For this purpose, "net proceeds" is defined in Code Sec. 150(a)(3), i.e., the proceeds of an issuance of bonds, reduced by amounts in a reasonably required reserve or replacement fund, see FTC 2d/FIN ¶ J-3004. (Code Sec. 1400L(e)(1) as added by 2002 Act §301(a)) In the case of bonds for water facilities issued by the New York Municipal Water Finance Authority, property located outside New York City that is functionally related and subordinate to property located in New York City is deemed to be located in New York City. (Com Rept, see ¶ 5015)

The additional advance refunding is allowed under the applicable rules of Code Sec. 149(d) (dealing with advance refunding, see FTC 2d/FIN ¶ J-3660; USTR ¶ 1494.03; TaxDesk ¶ 158,014) (Code Sec. 1400L(e)(1)) , except with regards to the limit on the number of advance refundings otherwise allowed under those rules. (Com Rept, see ¶ 5015)

A bond to which additional advance refunding applies is one that was outstanding on Sept. 11, 2001 (Code Sec. 1400L(e)(2)) , and is:

(1) A State or local bond (as defined in Code Sec. 103(c)(1)) which is a general obligation of New York City (Code Sec. 1400L(e)(2)(A)) ;

(2) A State or local bond other than a private activity bond (as defined in Code Sec. 141(a), dealing with private activity bonds, see FTC 2d/FIN ¶ J-3101; USTR ¶ 1414; TaxDesk ¶ 158,009) issued by the New York Municipal Water Finance

FTC 2d References are to Federal Tax Coordinator 2d
FIN References are to RIA's Analysis of Federal Taxes: Income
USTR References are to United States Tax Reporter: Income, Estate & Gift, and Excise
PCA References are to the Pension Analysis on Checkpoint and CD-ROM, and in Pension Coordinator
PE References are to the Pension Explanations in Pension and Profit Sharing 2nd
EP References are to the Estate Planning Analysis on Checkpoint and CD-ROM, and in Estate Planning & Taxation Coordinator

Authority or the Metropolitan Transportation Authority of the State of New York (Code Sec. 1400L(e)(2)(B)) ; or

(3) A qualified Code Sec. 501(c)(3) bond (as defined in Code Sec. 145(a), see FTC 2d/FIN ¶ J-3248; USTR ¶ 1454; TaxDesk ¶ 158,010) which is a qualified hospital bond (as defined in Code Sec. 145(c), see FTC 2d/FIN ¶ J-3248.3; USTR ¶ 1454.02) issued by or on behalf of the State of New York or New York City. (Code Sec. 1400L(e)(2)(C))

As a condition for the additional advance refunding, the Governor of New York State (as defined at ¶ 507) or the Mayor of New York City (as defined at ¶ 507) must designate the bond as an advance refunding bond. (Code Sec. 1400L(e)(1)(A)) The maximum aggregate face amount of bonds which may be designated by the Governor cannot exceed $4,500,000,000 and the maximum aggregate face amount of bonds which may be designated by the Mayor can't exceed $4,500,000,000. (Code Sec. 1400L(e)(3)) Thus, up to $4.5 billion of bonds can be designated by each of these officials, and the maximum amount of advance refunding bonds that can be issued is $9 billion. (Com Rept, see ¶ 5015)

In addition, the following requirements must be met with respect to any advance refunding: (Code Sec. 1400L(e)(1)(B))

. . . no advance refundings of the bond would be allowed under any provision of law after Sept. 11, 2001 (Code Sec. 1400L(e)(4)(A)) , i.e., the bond is one for which all advance refunding authority had been exhausted before Sept. 12, 2001; (Com Rept, see ¶ 5015)

. . . the advance refunding bond is the only other outstanding bond with respect to the refunded bond. (Code Sec. 1400L(e)(4)(B)) Thus, at no time after the advance refunding authorized under Code Sec. 1400L(e) occurs can there be more than two sets of bonds outstanding; (Com Rept, see ¶ 5015) and

. . . the requirements of Code Sec. 148 (dealing with arbitrage bonds, see FTC 2d/ FIN ¶ J-3403; USTR ¶ 1484.01; TaxDesk ¶ 158,013) are met with respect to all bonds issued under Code Sec. 1400L(e). (Code Sec. 1400L(e)(4)(C))

To qualify, the additional advance refunding must occur after Mar. 9, 2002 and before Jan. 1, 2005. (Code Sec. 1400L(e)(1))

> *observation:* Other than qualified Code Sec. 501(c)(3) bonds, private activity bonds—e.g., New York Liberty Bonds (see ¶ 507)—can't be advance refunded, see FTC 2d/FIN ¶ J-3660; USTR ¶ 1494.03; TaxDesk ¶ 158,014.

☐ **Effective:** Mar. 9, 2002 and before Jan. 1, 2005. (Com Rept, see ¶ 5015)

¶ 600. Administration

¶ 601. Extension of collection limitations period clarified in cases where installment agreements or offers-in-compromise are considered

Code Sec. 6331(k)(3), as amended by 2002 Act § 416(e)(1)
Generally effective: Mar. 9, 2002
Committee Reports, see ¶ 5060

No IRS levy may be imposed on a person's property or rights to property for any unpaid tax while (1) an offer-in-compromise is pending, (2) an offer to pay those taxes by installment agreement is pending, or (3) an installment agreement is in effect. However, certain exceptions and limitations apply to the above levy prohibition. Those exceptions and limitations are similar to ones that apply under the divisible tax refund rules. Subject to certain exceptions and limitations, the divisible tax refund rules prohibit a levy during an ongoing refund proceeding for FICA, FUTA, or withholding taxes. The running of the statute of limitations on collections (levy generally must be made within 10 years of the tax assessment) is suspended during the period IRS is prohibited from making a levy under the divisible tax refund rules. Under pre-2002 Act law, however, that suspension didn't apply to items (1) through (3) above. (FTC 2d/FIN ¶ V-5104.2; USTR ¶ 63,314.01; TaxDesk ¶ 902,040)

New Law. The 2002 Act provides that the rule suspending the statute of limitations on collections while IRS is prohibited from making a levy applies where a levy is prohibited because an offer-in-compromise is pending (item (1) above) or an offer to pay those taxes by installment agreement is pending (item (2) above). The statute of limitations on collections, however, isn't suspended where an installment agreement is in effect (item (3) above). (Code Sec. 6331(k)(3) as amended by 2002 Act §416(e)(1))

> *observation:* The fact that the new law doesn't suspend the statute of limitations on collections if an installment agreement is in effect may reflect the fact that installment agreements often include provisions extending the collection limitations period.

> *illustration:* A taxpayer requests an installment agreement with IRS at a time when the collection limitations period for the tax liability at issue

---

FTC 2d References are to Federal Tax Coordinator 2d
FIN References are to RIA's Analysis of Federal Taxes: Income
USTR References are to United States Tax Reporter: Income, Estate & Gift, and Excise
PCA References are to the Pension Analysis on Checkpoint and CD-ROM, and in Pension Coordinator
PE References are to the Pension Explanations in Pension and Profit Sharing 2nd
EP References are to the Estate Planning Analysis on Checkpoint and CD-ROM, and in Estate Planning & Taxation Coordinator

will soon run out. While IRS considers the agreement, the statute of limitations on collections is suspended under the 2002 Act provision. After the agreement is in effect, any suspension of the collection limitations period must be by agreement between IRS and the taxpayer.

☐ **Effective:** Mar. 9, 2002. (2002 Act § 416(e)(2))

¶ 602. Information returns for tax years ending after Mar. 9, 2002 related to numerous payments or transactions may be furnished electronically to recipients who have consented to receive the returns electronically

Code Sec. None, 2002 Act § 401
Generally effective: Statements for tax years ending after Mar. 9, 2002
Committee Reports, see ¶ 5021

Information returns concerning transactions with other persons are generally required to be furnished to these persons in writing, generally by Jan. 31 following the close of a year, see FTC 2d/FIN ¶ S-3002; USTR ¶ 60,494; TaxDesk ¶ 811,506. Generally, taxpayer copies of the information returns provided to taxpayers are provided on paper and sent via the U.S. mail. However, a reg allows Form W-2 (Wage and Tax Statement) to be furnished in an electronic format. (FTC 2d/FIN ¶ S-1370; USTR ¶ 60,514) If a recipient has affirmatively consented to receive the statement electronically (and has not withdrawn that consent before the statement is furnished), the payor can furnish the W-2 by posting it on a Web site accessible to the recipient, see FTC 2d/FIN ¶ S-1371; FTC 2d/FIN ¶ S-1375; USTR ¶ 60,514. Under pre-2002 Act law, there was no similar rule permitting other information returns to be furnished electronically.

> ⓡ *observation:* Many publicly held corporations that are required to provide annual reports and other information to shareholders offer to provide those reports and information in an electronic format to consenting shareholders. Among the benefits are reductions in printing and postage costs.

New Law. The 2001 Act permits (except as IRS otherwise provides) any person required to furnish a statement under any section of subpart B of part III of Subchapter A of chapter 61 of the Code (information concerning transactions with other persons) for any tax year ending after Mar. 9, 2002 to electronically furnish the statement to any recipient who has consented to having the statement provided electronically in a manner similar to the one permitted under the Code Sec. 6051 regs (see above) or in such other manner as provided by IRS. (2002 Act § 401) Thus, the 2002 Act removes the statutory impediment to providing copies of specified information returns to taxpayers electronically, thus allowing IRS Form 1099 to be provided to taxpayers electronically, if they have consented to this. (Com Rept, see ¶ 5021)

observation: The authorization for electronic furnishing of statements is not limited to Form 1099. Other forms and statements required by IRS regs, notices, etc., that relate to Code Secs. 6041 through 6050S (for example, Forms 1098-E and 1098-T (used to furnish information required by Code Sec. 6050S)), may also be furnished electronically unless IRS provides otherwise.

observation: The following Code sections are included in subpart B of part III of Subchapter A of chapter 61 of the Code. The forms and returns identified in these sections can thus be furnished electronically to recipients who have consented:

Code Sec. 6041	Information at source.
Code Sec. 6041A	Returns regarding payments of remuneration for services and direct sales.
Code Sec. 6042	Returns regarding payments of dividends and corporate earnings and profits.
Code Sec. 6043	Liquidating, etc., transactions.
Code Sec. 6044	Returns regarding payments of patronage dividends.
Code Sec. 6045	Returns of brokers.
Code Sec. 6046	Returns as to organization or reorganization of foreign corporations and as to acquisitions of their stock.
Code Sec. 6046A	Returns as to interests in foreign partnerships.
Code Sec. 6047	Information relating to certain trusts and annuity plans.
Code Sec. 6048	Information with respect to certain foreign trusts.
Code Sec. 6049	Returns regarding payments of interest.
Code Sec. 6050A	Reporting requirements of certain fishing boat operators.
Code Sec. 6050B	Returns relating to unemployment compensation.
Code Sec. 6050D	Returns relating to energy grants and financing.
Code Sec. 6050E	State and local income tax refunds.
Code Sec. 6050F	Returns relating to social security benefits.
Code Sec. 6050G	Returns relating to certain railroad retirement benefits.
Code Sec. 6050H	Returns relating to mortgage interest received in trade or business from individuals.
Code Sec. 6050I	Returns relating to cash received in trade or business, etc.
Code Sec. 6050J	Returns relating to foreclosures and abandonments of security.
Code Sec. 6050K	Returns relating to exchanges of certain partnership interests.
Code Sec. 6050L	Returns relating to certain dispositions of donated property.
Code Sec. 6050M	Returns relating to persons receiving contracts from Federal executive agencies.
Code Sec. 6050N	Returns regarding payments of royalties.
Code Sec. 6050P	Returns relating to the cancellation of indebtedness by certain entities.
Code Sec. 6050Q	Certain long-term care benefits.
Code Sec. 6050R	Returns relating to certain purchases of fish.
Code Sec. 6050S	Returns relating to higher education tuition and related expenses.

FTC 2d References are to Federal Tax Coordinator 2d
FIN References are to RIA's Analysis of Federal Taxes: Income
USTR References are to United States Tax Reporter: Income, Estate & Gift, and Excise
PCA References are to the Pension Analysis on Checkpoint and CD-ROM, and in Pension Coordinator
PE References are to the Pension Explanations in Pension and Profit Sharing 2nd
EP References are to the Estate Planning Analysis on Checkpoint and CD-ROM, and in Estate Planning & Taxation Coordinator

☐ **Effective:** Statements for any tax year ending after Mar. 9, 2002. (2002 Act § 401)

¶ 603. Partners' settlements with Attorney General given equivalent treatment to settlements with IRS under partnership audit rules

Code Sec. 6224(c)(1), as amended by 2002 Act § 416(d)(1)(A)
Code Sec. 6224(c)(2), as amended by 2002 Act § 416(d)(1)(A)
Code Sec. 6229(f)(2), as amended by 2002 Act § 416(d)(1)(B)
Code Sec. 6231(b)(1)(C), as amended by 2002 Act § 416(d)(1)(C)
Code Sec. 6234(g)(4)(A), as amended by 2002 Act § 416(d)(1)(D)
Generally effective: Settlement agreements entered into after Mar. 9, 2002
Committee Reports, see ¶ 5064

Under pre-2002 Act law, for purposes of the unified partnership audit and review procedures, when the Secretary of the Treasury or his delegate—i.e., IRS or appropriate officials of the Treasury Department—enters into a settlement agreement with a partner with respect to partnership items for a tax year:

... under Code Sec. 6224(c)(1), except as provided by the agreement itself, the agreement binds all the parties to the agreement, as well as certain "indirect partners," with respect to the determination of partnership items for that tax year;

... under Code Sec. 6224(c)(2), the other partners in the partnership have a right to request settlement terms consistent with that agreement;

... under Code Sec. 6229(f)(2), if the settlement agreement settles some partnership items but leaves others in dispute, the limitations period with respect to the disputed items is determined as if the agreement had not been entered into;

... under Code Sec. 6231(b)(1)(C), those items convert to nonpartnership items (which removes the settling partner from ongoing partnership proceeding with respect to the settled items);

... under Code Sec. 6234(g)(4)(A), regarding adjustments to "oversheltered returns," a settlement agreement results in the partnership items being treated as "finally determined," which is one of the prerequisites to the conversion of an oversheltered return proceeding to a deficiency proceeding.

(FTC 2d/FIN ¶ T-2176 *et seq.*, ¶ T-2181.1 *et seq.*, ¶ T-2244, ¶ T-3556, ¶ T-4018.2; USTR ¶ 62,214.03, ¶ 62,214.08; TaxDesk ¶ 825,018, ¶ 825,020, ¶ 825,045)

New Law. The 2002 Act makes the above provisions applicable with respect to settlement agreements entered into by the Attorney General or his delegate, as well as to settlement agreements entered into by the Secretary of the Treasury or his delegate. (Code Sec. 6224(c)(1) as amended by 2002 Act §416(d)(1)(A)) ; (Code Sec. 6224(c)(2) as amended by 2002 Act §416(d)(1)(A)) ; (Code Sec.

6229(f)(2) as amended by 2002 Act §416(d)(1)(B)) ; (Code Sec. 6231(b)(1)(C) as amended by 2002 Act §416(d)(1)(C)) ; (Code Sec. 6234(g)(4)(A) as amended by 2002 Act §416(d)(1)(D))

The intent of the above 2002 Act changes is to avoid the possibility that a partner who enters into a settlement agreement with the Attorney General or his delegate (rather than with the Secretary of the Treasury or his delegate) would inadvertently be bound by the underlying partnership proceedings rather than by that settlement agreement. (Com Rept, see ¶ 5064)

☐ **Effective:** Settlement agreements entered into after Mar. 9, 2002. (2002 Act § 416(d)(2))

¶ 604. Social Security Administration must disclose return information to federal child support agency

Code Sec. 6103(l)(8)(A), as amended by 2002 Act § 416(c)
Generally effective: Mar. 9, 2002
Committee Reports, see ¶ 5063

Under pre-2002 Act law, the Social Security Administration, in response to a written request, was required to disclose certain return information directly to officers and employees of a state or local child support enforcement agency. The return information that must be disclosed is from returns with respect to social security account numbers, net earnings from self-employment, wages, and payments of retirement income which have been disclosed to the Social Security Administration under Code Sec. 6103(l)(1) or Code Sec. 6103(l)(5). (FTC 2d/FIN ¶ S-6360; USTR ¶ 61,034.01)

New Law. The 2002 Act provides that the Social Security Administration must also disclose the return information directly to officers and employees of a federal child support enforcement agency. (Code Sec. 6103(l)(8)(A) as amended by 2002 Act §416(c))

Thus, the 2002 Act allows the Social Security Administration to make disclosures directly to the Office of Child Support Enforcement (OCSE), which is a federal agency that oversees child support enforcement at the federal level and acts as a coordinator for most programs involved with child support enforcement. The OCSE would make disclosures to the state and local child support enforcement agencies, thus acting as a conduit for the disclosure of tax information from IRS to

---

FTC 2d References are to Federal Tax Coordinator 2d
FIN References are to RIA's Analysis of Federal Taxes: Income
USTR References are to United States Tax Reporter: Income, Estate & Gift, and Excise
PCA References are to the Pension Analysis on Checkpoint and CD-ROM, and in Pension Coordinator
PE References are to the Pension Explanations in Pension and Profit Sharing 2nd
EP References are to the Estate Planning Analysis on Checkpoint and CD-ROM, and in Estate Planning & Taxation Coordinator

the various state and local child support enforcement agencies. (Com Rept, see ¶ 5063)

☐ **Effective:** Mar. 9, 2002.

¶ 700. Miscellaneous

¶ 701. Amount of REIT's "redetermined rents" and "redetermined deductions" to which 100% tax applies clarified

Code Sec. 857(b)(7)(B)(i), as amended by 2002 Act § 413(a)(1)
Code Sec. 857(b)(7)(C), as amended by 2002 Act § 413(a)(2)
Generally effective: Tax years beginning after Dec. 31, 2000
Committee Reports, see ¶ 5058

A 100% tax is imposed on certain amounts not determined at arm's length between a REIT and its taxable REIT subsidiary. Amounts subject to the 100% tax include "redetermined rents" and "redetermined deductions."

> *observation:* This is to prevent a REIT from shifting income earned by a taxable REIT subsidiary, which is subject to the corporate tax, to the REIT, which is not taxed on income that is passed through to its shareholders.

Under pre-2002 Act law, redetermined rents were a REIT's rents from real property "the amount of which" would be reduced by applying the principles of Code Sec. 482 to clearly reflect income as a result of services furnished to a REIT tenant by its taxable REIT subsidiary. Redetermined deductions were the deductions of a taxable REIT subsidiary (other than redetermined rents) "if the amount of such deductions" would be decreased by applying the principles of Code Sec. 482 to clearly reflect income between the REIT and the subsidiary.

> *observation:* Code Sec. 482 sets the standard for an arm's-length amount, but the 100% tax applies in lieu of an actual Code Sec. 482 reallocation of income or deductions.

> *illustration (1):* A REIT which owns an office building has a taxable REIT subsidiary that furnishes services to the tenants of the REIT's building that are ordinarily not provided by building owners. IRS determines that the taxable REIT subsidiary's charge to tenants for the services was below the market rate for such services and that a portion of the rents paid by tenants to the REIT was really a payment for the services provided to the tenants by the taxable REIT subsidiary. IRS also determines that cer-

---

FTC 2d References are to Federal Tax Coordinator 2d
FIN References are to RIA's Analysis of Federal Taxes: Income
USTR References are to United States Tax Reporter: Income, Estate & Gift, and Excise
PCA References are to the Pension Analysis on Checkpoint and CD-ROM, and in Pension Coordinator
PE References are to the Pension Explanations in Pension and Profit Sharing 2nd
EP References are to the Estate Planning Analysis on Checkpoint and CD-ROM, and in Estate Planning & Taxation Coordinator

tain of the taxable REIT subsidiary's employees provide services to the REIT without any payment by the REIT. Since a portion of the rent was really a payment for the taxable REIT subsidiary's services there is a redetermined rent subject to the 100% tax. Since the taxable REIT subsidiary's deduction for the compensation paid to its employees must be reduced there is a redetermined deduction subject to the 100% tax.

(FTC 2d/FIN ¶ E-6615.1; USTR ¶ 8574.01)

New Law. Under the 2002 Act, redetermined rents are the amount by which rents would be reduced by applying the principles of Code Sec. 482 to clearly reflect services furnished to a REIT tenant by its taxable REIT subsidiary. (Code Sec. 357(b)(7)(B)(i) as amended by 2002 Act §413(a)(1)) Redetermined deductions are the amount by which the other deductions of a taxable REIT subsidiary would be reduced by applying the principles of Code Sec. 482 to clearly reflect income between the REIT and the subsidiary. (Code Sec. 857(b)(7)(C))

The 2002 Act clarifies that redetermined rents are the excess of the amount treated by the REIT as rents from real property over the amount that would be so treated after reduction under Code Sec. 482 to clearly reflect income as a result of services rendered by a taxable REIT subsidiary of the REIT to a tenant of the REIT. Similarly, redetermined deductions are the excess of the amount treated by the taxable REIT subsidiary as other deductions over the amount that would be so treated after reduction under Code Sec. 482. (Com Rept, see ¶ 5058)

> *observation:* Under pre-2002 Act law, if a REIT's rents from a tenant were overstated because they reflected an amount that the REIT's taxable subsidiary undercharged for services performed for the tenant, literally read, the entire amount of rent from the tenant was redetermined rent subject to 100% tax. Similarly, if the taxable REIT subsidiary did not charge an arm's length amount for services performed for the REIT, literally read, the entire amount of the taxable subsidiary's deductions (other than redetermined rent) were redetermined deductions. The 2002 Act makes clear that the amount subject to the 100% tax is limited to the amount of the misallocation.

> *illustration (2):* Assume that in illustration (1) above, the REIT received $300,000 of rent from a tenant that included $5,000 by which the taxable REIT subsidiary's charges to the tenant for services were understated. The 2002 Act makes clear that only the $5,000 is redetermined rent. Under pre-2002 Act law, literally read, the entire $300,000 of rent would be redetermined rent.

☐ **Effective:** For tax years beginning after Dec. 31, 2000. (2002 Act § 413(b))

¶ 702. Provision governing transfers to non-grantor trusts after 2009 clarified; these transfers will be treated as transfers of property by gift

Code Sec. 2511(c), as amended by 2002 Act § 411(g)(1)
Generally effective: For gifts made after Dec. 31, 2009
Committee Reports, see ¶ 5037

The Economic Growth and Tax Relief Reconciliation Act of 2001 (EGTRRA, PL 107-16) repealed the estate and generation-skipping transfer (GST) taxes after 2009, but EGTRRA did not repeal the gift tax. After 2009, the top gift tax rate will be the same as the top individual income tax rate. FTC 2d ¶s R-1000.1, R-9500.1, Q-8003.1; USTR ¶s 22,104, 26,644, 25,024; TaxDesk ¶s 751,000.1, 791,000.1; EP ¶s 43,051.1, 46,031.1, 48,554A

> *observation:* Presumably, the gift tax has been left in place to discourage taxpayers from making income-splitting transfers—i.e., transfers to related taxpayers in lower income tax brackets.

EGTRRA also amended the Code to provide for the post-2009 treatment of transfers in trust. Under pre-2002 Act law, a transfer in trust was to be treated (except as provided by regs) as a "taxable gift under section 2503", unless the trust was treated as wholly owned by the donor or the donor's spouse under the grantor trust rules—i.e., unless all of the income of the trust was taxed to the grantor or the grantor's spouse. (FTC 2d ¶ Q-3000.1; USTR Estate & Gift Taxes ¶ 25,114; EP ¶ 47,651.1)

> *observation:* Presumably, this provision treating transfers to non-grantor trusts as gifts was intended to discourage taxpayers from making income-splitting transfers in trust after the repeal of the estate and GST taxes after 2009. However, before the 2002 Act made the technical correction discussed below, the scope of the provision was uncertain. For example, it was unclear whether transfers to non-grantor trusts that constituted incomplete gifts before 2010 would be treated as completed gifts after 2009.

The term "taxable gift" is defined as the total amount of gifts made during the calendar year, reduced by the charitable and marital deductions and the gift tax annual exclusion. FTC 2d ¶ Q-8011; USTR ¶ 25,034; TaxDesk ¶ 731,000; EP

FTC 2d References are to Federal Tax Coordinator 2d
FIN References are to RIA's Analysis of Federal Taxes: Income
USTR References are to United States Tax Reporter: Income, Estate & Gift, and Excise
PCA References are to the Pension Analysis on Checkpoint and CD-ROM, and in Pension Coordinator
PE References are to the Pension Explanations in Pension and Profit Sharing 2nd
EP References are to the Estate Planning Analysis on Checkpoint and CD-ROM, and in Estate Planning & Taxation Coordinator

¶ 48,561 A charitable deduction is allowed for an interest transferred for charitable purposes where a donor transfers an interest in property for charitable purposes and an interest in the same property is retained by the donor, provided the transfer is made in a qualifying trust. FTC 2d ¶ Q-6034; USTR ¶ 25,224; TaxDesk ¶ 733,006; EP ¶ 48,336 A marital deduction is allowed where a donor transfers by gift an interest in property to an individual who is the donor's spouse at the time of the gift. FTC 2d ¶ Q-6101; USTR ¶ 25,234; TaxDesk ¶ 734,000; EP ¶ 48,402 For purposes of the per donee annual exclusion from gift tax, in the case of a gift in trust, the donee is not the trust, but each beneficiary with a present interest in the trust. FTC 2d ¶ Q-5005; USTR ¶ 25,034; TaxDesk ¶ 731,005; EP ¶ 48,206

Under pre-2002 Act law, a gift in trust was taxable only if it was a "completed gift". The essence of a completed gift in trust was the trust grantor's abandonment of control over the property put in trust. What was to be abandoned was the donor's economic dominion and control over the property. The gift was complete as to any property (or part of the property transferred, or interest in the property) of which the donor had so parted with dominion and control as to leave in him no power to change its disposition, whether for his own benefit or for the benefit of another. But if the donor reserved a power to change his disposition, the gift would be incomplete—either entirely or partially, depending on all the facts and circumstances. (FTC 2d ¶ Q-3004; USTR Estate & Gift Taxes ¶ 25,114.01; TaxDesk ¶ 715,004; EP ¶ 47,655)

New Law. The 2002 Act replaces the phrase "taxable gift under section 2503" with the phrase "transfer of property by gift" in the provision treating transfers to non-grantor trusts as gifts after 2009. (Code Sec. 2511(c) as amended by 2002 Act §411(g)(1))

Thus, the provision clarifies that the effect of the EGTRRA amendment is to treat certain transfers in trust as transfers of property by gift. The result of the clarification is that the gift tax annual exclusion and the marital and charitable deductions may apply to these transfers. (Com Rept, see ¶ 5037)

Under the provision as clarified, certain amounts transferred in trust will be treated as transfers of property by gift, despite the fact that the transfers would be regarded as incomplete gifts before 2010. (Com Rept, see ¶ 5037)

> *Illustration:* In 2010, Taxpayer transfers property in trust to pay the income to one person for life, remainder to such persons and in such portions as Taxpayer may decide. Under gift tax regs in effect before 2010, the transfer of the remainder interest in the trust would not be treated as a completed gift. Under the 2002 Act, however, the entire value of the property will be treated as being transferred by gift. (Com Rept, see ¶ 5037)

Under the provision as clarified, certain amounts transferred in trust will be treated as transfers of property by gift, despite the fact that the transfers would not be treated as transferred under the law applicable to gifts made before 2010. (Com Rept, see ¶ 5037)

Illustration: In 2010, Taxpayer transfers property in trust to pay the income to one person for life, and makes no transfer of a remainder interest. Under the 2002 Act, the entire value of the property will be treated as being transferred by gift. (Com Rept, see ¶ 5037)

observation: Thus, the scope of the provision as clarified is very broad. To preserve the integrity of the income tax, all transfers to non-grantor trusts will be treated as gifts. Presumably, however, Congress does not view transfers to non-grantor trusts with spousal and charitable beneficiaries as income-splitting devices, and so the marital and charitable deductions may be available to mitigate the gift tax consequences of such a broad provision. Annual exclusions may also be available with respect to transfers to non-grantor trusts, presumably even if the trust beneficiaries are in income tax brackets that are lower than the donor's bracket.

☐ **Effective:** For gifts made after Dec. 31, 2009 (2002 Act § 411(x))

¶ 703. Mandate that terminal operators offer both dyed and undyed diesel fuel or kerosene after 2001 is retroactively repealed

Code Sec. 4101(e), repealed by 2002 Act § 615(a)
Generally effective: Jan. 1, 2002
Committee Reports, see ¶ 5083

Under pre-2002 Act law, beginning after Dec. 31, 2001, a diesel fuel or kerosene terminal would not qualify as an approved facility (i.e., could not be a registered terminal) permitted to receive and store non-tax-paid diesel fuel, or kerosene (i.e., fuel that hasn't yet been subject to excise tax), unless the terminal operator offered for removal both dyed and undyed versions of the diesel fuel or kerosene, respectively. (Fuels are dyed to qualify for exemption from tax where they are to be sold for a specified nontaxable use, e.g., as heating oil.) The requirement didn't apply to any terminal providing only aviation-grade kerosene by pipeline to an airport. (FTC 2d ¶ W-1530.1; USTR Excise Taxes ¶ 41,014)

New Law. The 2002 Act retroactively repeals the requirement that terminal operators offer both dyed and undyed versions of diesel fuel or kerosene to qualify a terminal as an approved facility. (Code Sec. 4101(e) repealed by 2002 Act §615(a))

FTC 2d References are to Federal Tax Coordinator 2d
FIN References are to RIA's Analysis of Federal Taxes: Income
USTR References are to United States Tax Reporter: Income, Estate & Gift, and Excise
PCA References are to the Pension Analysis on Checkpoint and CD-ROM, and in Pension Coordinator
PE References are to the Pension Explanations in Pension and Profit Sharing 2nd
EP References are to the Estate Planning Analysis on Checkpoint and CD-ROM, and in Estate Planning & Taxation Coordinator

observation: Thus, terminals can determine what fuel(s) to carry based on their market demands.

☐ **Effective:** Jan. 1, 2002. (2002 Act § 615(b))

¶ 704. Securities futures contract rules are clarified

Code Sec. 1234A, as amended by 2002 Act § 412(d)(1)(A)
Code Sec. 1234B(a)(1), as amended by 2002 Act § 412(d)(1)(B)(i)
Code Sec. 1234B(b), as amended by 2002 Act § 412(d)(1)(B)(i)
Code Sec. 1091(e), as amended by 2002 Act § 412(d)(2)
Code Sec. 1233(e)(2)(E), as amended by 2002 Act § 412(d)(3)(A)
Code Sec. 1234B(b), as amended by 2002 Act § 412(d)(3)(B)
Generally effective: Dec. 21, 2000
Committee Reports, see ¶ 5057

Gain or loss on the sale or exchange of securities futures contracts that are capital assets is treated as gain or loss from the sale or exchange of property having the same character as the property to which the contract relates has in the hands of the taxpayer. If the gain or loss is capital gain or loss and the straddle rules do not apply, it is treated as short-term capital gain or loss. A termination of a securities futures contracts that is a capital asset is treated as a sale or exchange of the contract. (FTC 2d/FIN ¶ I-6281, ¶ I-6282; USTR ¶ 12,34A4, ¶ 12,34B4; TaxDesk ¶ 250,201, ¶ 250,202)

The wash sale rules which disallow losses realized within the period beginning 30 days before and ending 30 days after a purchase of substantially identical stock or securities apply to losses on the closing of a short sale where substantially identical stock or securities are sold or another short sale of substantially identical stock or securities is entered into. The wash sale provisions apply to securities futures contracts, even though the contracts are settled in cash, rather than in the underlying property. (FTC 2d/FIN ¶ I-3905, ¶ I-3905.1; USTR ¶ 10,914; TaxDesk ¶ 227,006, ¶ 227,007)

The short sale rules provide that the closing of a short sale generates short-term capital gain to the extent substantially identical property was held for not more than one year before the short sale or was acquired while the short sale was open. In addition, the holding period of substantially identical property is delayed while the short sale is open and the substantially identical property is held. Losses on short sales are long-term capital loss to the extent substantially identical property was held by the taxpayer for more than one year on the date of the short sale. For this purpose, a securities futures contract to acquire substantially identical property is treated as substantially identical property. (FTC 2d/FIN ¶ I-7710, ¶ I-7712.1, ¶ I-7714, ¶ I-7720; USTR ¶ 12,334.09; TaxDesk ¶ 228,907, ¶ 228,911, ¶ 228,913, ¶ 228,919)

New Law. The 2002 Act provides that gain or loss on the termination of a securities futures contract has the same character as gain or loss from the sale or exchange of the property to which the contract relates has or would have in the hands of the taxpayer. (Code Sec. 1234B(a)(1) as amended by 2002 Act §412(d)(1)(B)(i)) Also, the rule that capital gain or loss on a sale or exchange of a securities futures contract is treated as short-term gain or loss also applies to a termination of a securities futures contract, except as provided under the straddle rules or the short sale rules (see below). (Code Sec. 1234B(b) as amended by 2002 Act §412(d)(1)(B)(i)) ; (Code Sec. 1234B(b) as amended by 2002 Act §412(d)(3)(B)) Thus, gain or loss on a termination of a securities futures contract is treated in the same fashion as a sale or exchange of the securities futures contract. (Com Rept, see ¶ 5057) The rule that the gain or loss on a termination of a securities futures contract that was a capital asset was treated as capital gain or loss is repealed. (Code Sec. 1234A as amended by 2002 Act §412(d)(1)(A))

The 2002 Act provides that the wash sale rules apply to losses from the sale, exchange, or termination of a securities futures contract (Code Sec. 1091(e) as amended by 2002 Act §412(d)(2)(B)) , if within the relevant period, substantially identical stock or securities are sold, a short sale of substantially identical stock or securities is entered into, or a securities futures contract to sell substantially identical stock or securities is entered into. (Code Sec. 1091(e)(2) as amended by 2002 Act §412(d)(2)(C)) For this purpose, a securities futures contract is defined in Code Sec. 1234B(c). (Code Sec. 1091(e) as amended by 2002 Act §412(d)(2)(D)) Thus, the wash sale rules apply to losses from the sale, exchange, or termination of a securities futures contract in a manner similar to the way they apply to the closing of a short sale. (Com Rept, see ¶ 5057)

The 2002 Act provides that entering into a securities futures contract to sell is treated as a short sale for purposes of the special holding period rules described above (that recharacterize capital gains as short-term capital gains and capital losses as long-term capital loss, and that delay the beginning of the holding periods while a short sale is open). In addition, for purposes of these rules the settlement of a securities futures contract is treated as the closing of the short sale. (Code Sec. 1233(e)(2)(E) as amended by 2002 Act §412(d)(3)(A))

The above provisions are described by the Technical Explanation of the 2002 Act as clarifications. (Com Rept, see ¶ 5057)

> *observation:* The above provisions conform the tax treatment of entering into a securities futures contract to sell to that of a short sale, since the two are economically similar.

☐ **Effective:** Dec. 21, 2000. (2002 Act § 412(e))

FTC 2d References are to Federal Tax Coordinator 2d
FIN References are to RIA's Analysis of Federal Taxes: Income
USTR References are to United States Tax Reporter: Income, Estate & Gift, and Excise
PCA References are to the Pension Analysis on Checkpoint and CD-ROM, and in Pension Coordinator
PE References are to the Pension Explanations in Pension and Profit Sharing 2nd
EP References are to the Estate Planning Analysis on Checkpoint and CD-ROM, and in Estate Planning & Taxation Coordinator

¶ 705. Unnecessary reference to "the old contract" is deleted from rules on whether a life insurance contract is a modified endowment contract if there is a material change to the contract

Code Sec. 7702A(c)(3)(A)(ii), as amended by 2002 Act § 416(f)
Generally effective: Applies to contracts entered into after June 20, '88
Committee Reports, see ¶ 5066

To discourage the purchase of life insurance as a tax-sheltered investment vehicle, favorable tax treatment is denied to amounts (other than death benefits) received under a class of life insurance contracts called "modified endowment contracts." A contract is treated as a modified endowment contract if it meets the Code Sec. 7702 definition of a life insurance contract, but fails a "7-pay test." If there is a material change in the benefits or other terms of a contract that was not reflected in any previous determination under the 7-pay test, the contract is treated as a new contract entered into on the day the change takes place. In addition, pre-2002 Act law provided that, if there is a material change to the contract, appropriate adjustments must be made in determining whether the contract meets the 7-pay test to take into account the cash surrender value under "the old contract." FTC 2d/FIN ¶ J-5072; USTR ¶ 77,02A4.01; EP ¶ 42,770.3

New Law. The 2002 Act deletes the word "old" from the statutory language quoted in the preceding sentence. The 2002 Act accomplishes this by retroactively repealing §318(a)(2) of the Community Renewal Tax Relief Act of 2000 (P.L. 106-554), which substituted the phrase "the old contract" for the phrase "the contract." The 2002 Act also provides that the rule on making adjustments to determine whether a contract meets the 7-pay test after a material change shall be read and applied as if the amendment made by §318(a)(2) of the Community Renewal Tax Relief Act of 2000 had not been enacted. (Code Sec. 7702A(c)(3)(A)(ii) as amended by 2002 Act §416(f))

Thus, the 2002 Act clarifies that, for purposes of determining whether a life insurance contract is a modified endowment contract, if there is a material change to the contract, appropriate adjustments are made in determining whether the contract meets the 7-pay test to take into account the cash surrender value under the contract. No reference is needed to the cash surrender under the "old contract" because the law provides a definition of cash surrender value for this purpose by cross reference to Code Sec. 7702(f)(2)(A).

The Technical Explanation of the 2002 Act says that the rule on making adjustments to determine whether a contract meets the 7-pay test after a material change to the contract occurs is not intended to permit a policyholder to engage in a series of "material changes" to circumvent the premium limitations in the modified endowment contract rules. Thus, if there is a material change to a life insurance contract, it is intended that the fair market value of the contract be used as the cash surrender value under the provision, if the amount of the putative cash surrender value of the contract is artificially depressed. (Com Rept, see ¶ 5066)

> *illustration:* The face amount of a modified endowment contract is increased from $1 million to $1.5 million. This increase is a material change to the contract. As a result of the change, there is an artificial or temporary reduction of $X in the cash surrender value of the contract. This $X amount is not taken into account in determining whether the contract meets the 7-pay test. Instead, the fair market value of the contract is used as the cash surrender value for this purpose.

Further, in applying the 7-pay test to any premiums paid under a contract that has been materially changed, the 7-pay premium for each of the first 7 contract years after the change is to be reduced by the product of (1) the cash surrender value of the contract as of the date that the material change takes effect (determined without regard to any increase in the cash surrender value that is attributable to the amount of the premium payment that is not necessary), and (2) a fraction, the numerator of which equals the 7-pay premium for the future benefits under the contract, and the denominator of which equals the net single premium for such benefits computed using the same assumptions used in determining the 7-pay premium. (Com Rept, see ¶ 5066)

☐ **Effective:** Applies to contracts entered into after June 20, '88. (2002 Act § 412(e))

¶ 706. Basis reduction rule where basis exceeds fair market value and liabilities are not taken into account clarified

Code Sec. 358(h)(1)(A), as amended by 2002 Act § 412(c)
Generally effective: Assumptions of liabilities after Oct. 18, '99
Committee Reports, see ¶ 5056

When one or more transferors (T) transfer property to a controlled corporation (C) in exchange for its stock no gain or loss is recognized by the transferors if only C stock (other than certain preferred stock) is received, see FTC 2d/FIN ¶ F-1501; USTR ¶ 3514.01; TaxDesk ¶ 231,000. C's assumption of T liabilities is not treated as taxable boot (e.g., money) unless the T liabilities exceed the basis of the transferred property or a tax-avoidance rule applies. However, C's assumption of a T liability is treated as money solely for the purpose of reducing T's basis in the C stock.

FTC 2d References are to Federal Tax Coordinator 2d
FIN References are to RIA's Analysis of Federal Taxes: Income
USTR References are to United States Tax Reporter: Income, Estate & Gift, and Excise
PCA References are to the Pension Analysis on Checkpoint and CD-ROM, and in Pension Coordinator
PE References are to the Pension Explanations in Pension and Profit Sharing 2nd
EP References are to the Estate Planning Analysis on Checkpoint and CD-ROM, and in Estate Planning & Taxation Coordinator

> ⚡ *illustration (1):* T's basis for a property is $500,000. T transfers the property to C in exchange for all of C's common stock, and C assumes $100,000 of T's liabilities. T recognizes no gain or loss and has a $400,000 basis for the C stock.

A liability is not taken into account for purposes of reducing basis to the extent that the payment of the liability would give rise to a deduction (or is a partnership liability that will give rise to a deduction or its equivalent under the rules for Code Sec. 736(a) liquidating payments to a partner that are treated as a distributive share of income to the recipient, or a guaranteed payment). IRS has ruled that a liability that would give rise to an increase in basis, rather than a deduction, also is not taken into account. FTC 2d/FIN ¶ F-1803; USTR ¶ 3584.04; TaxDesk ¶ 231,904

> ⚡ *illustration (2):* T transfers his cash-basis business to C for all of the stock of C (worth $1,000,000). The basis of the transferred assets is $1,000,000, and C assumes $1,500,000 of accounts payable, which will be deductible when they are paid. T recognizes no gain and has a $1,000,000 basis for the C stock.

A basis-reduction rule (Basis Reduction Rule) applies to a transferor of property to a controlled corporation or to a transferor or exchanging shareholder in a reorganization where the basis of property received (after applying the other basis rules) exceeds its fair market value and a liability assumed in exchange for the property does not reduce the property's basis. The basis reduction is the amount (determined as of the date of the exchange) of any liability:

(1) which is assumed in exchange for the property, and

(2) does not otherwise reduce the basis of the property. (FTC 2d/FIN ¶ F-1803.1; USTR ¶ 3584.042; TaxDesk ¶ 231,905)

> ⚡ *illustration (3):* T transfers assets with an adjusted basis and fair market value of $100 to T's wholly-owned corporation, C, and C assumes $50 of T's liabilities. The payment of these liabilities would give rise to a deduction. The value of the C stock received by T is $50. Under the earlier basis rules, the liabilities are not taken into account because they will give rise to a deduction. However, under the Basis Reduction Rule, the basis of the C stock T receives is reduced to its fair market value of $50.

> ⚡ *observation:* If not for the Basis Reduction Rule, T and C (in Illustration (3) above) could in effect deduct the same amount. C would deduct the $50 when it is incurred and, because T's basis would not reflect the $50 liability, T would have a built-in loss that he could recognize at any time. Thus, T could immediately sell the C stock for $50 and recognize a loss, perhaps years before C paid the liability.

A liability for purposes of the Basis Reduction Rule includes any fixed or contingent obligation to make payment, without regard to whether the obligation is otherwise taken into account for income tax purposes. (FTC 2d/FIN ¶ F-1803.1; USTR ¶ 3584.042; TaxDesk ¶ 231,905)

 observation: The Basis Reduction Rule applies to the liabilities described above that are not treated as assumed. The Basis Reduction Rule should also apply to a liability which is not taken into account at the time of the transfer for basis purposes because it is contingent but which nevertheless reduces currently the value of the transferee's stock.

IRS is to issue rules for partnership transactions to prevent the acceleration or duplication of losses through the assumption of (or transfer of assets subject to) liabilities. IRS may also provide for adjustments for S corporations.

New Law. The 2002 Act clarifies that only a liability which is assumed by another person as part of the exchange can bring about a reduction of basis under the Basis Reduction Rule. (Code Sec. 358(h)(1)(A) as amended by 2002 Act §412(c))

Thus, the Basis Reduction Rule of Code Sec. 358(h) gives rise to a basis reduction in the amount of any liability that is assumed by another party as part of the exchange in which the property (whose basis exceeds its fair market value) is received, so long as the other requirements under Code Sec. 358(h) apply. (Com Rept, see ¶ 5056)

 observation: Absent the technical amendment, the Basis Reduction Rule could be read as literally applying where the taxpayer receives stock with a basis in excess of its fair market value which is subject to a liability.

 observation: The Basis Reduction Rule was intended to apply in situations such as illustration (3) where the basis of property received by the taxpayer exceeded its fair market value and a liability assumed by the transferee did not reduce the basis of the property under the basis reduction section of the Code (Code Sec. 358(d)(1)) because of the exception for liabilities whose payment would give rise to a deduction. These liabilities were described as liabilities to which Code Sec. 358(d)(1) did not apply. However, Code Sec. 358(d)(1) also wouldn't apply to liabilities assumed by the taxpayer. Thus, literally read, where the basis of property received by the taxpayer exceeded its fair market value and it was *the taxpayer* that assumed the liability as part of the exchange, the Basis Reduction Rule could be read as applying.

FTC 2d References are to Federal Tax Coordinator 2d
FIN References are to RIA's Analysis of Federal Taxes: Income
USTR References are to United States Tax Reporter: Income, Estate & Gift, and Excise
PCA References are to the Pension Analysis on Checkpoint and CD-ROM, and in Pension Coordinator
PE References are to the Pension Explanations in Pension and Profit Sharing 2nd
EP References are to the Estate Planning Analysis on Checkpoint and CD-ROM, and in Estate Planning & Taxation Coordinator

illustration (4): In a transfer to a controlled corporation (or in a reorganization), T transfers property with a basis of $100 and receives stock of C with a fair market value of $50. As part of the exchange, T assumes a liability of $10. Under pre-2002 Act law, literally read, T's basis could be reduced by the amount of the liability. The 2002 Act clarifies that T's basis is not reduced by the $10 liability.

☐ **Effective:**   For assumptions of liabilities after Oct. 18, '99, or in the case of rules that IRS prescribes for partnership or S corporation transactions, such later date as may be provided in those rules. (2002 Act § 412(e))

¶ 800. Client Letters

¶ 801. Overview of tax changes in the Job Creation and Worker Assistance Act of 2002

> **To the practitioner:** You can use the following client letter to provide clients with an overview of the Job Creation and Worker Assistance Act of 2002.

Dear Client,

I am writing to tell you that there's a new law on the books carrying a number of important tax changes. The "Job Creation and Worker Assistance Act of 2002," signed into law by the President on March 9, mostly benefits businesses and professional practices. What's more, several changes are retroactively effective and may affect returns that have already been filed as well as those that are about to be filed for tax year 2001. There are several changes affecting individuals as well.

Here's what you need to know right now about this important new legislation:

Tax breaks for businesses and professional practices include the following changes:

. . . An additional 30% first-year depreciation writeoff for most types of new nonrealty property acquired after Sept. 10, 2001 and before Sept. 11, 2004. For example, if a business or practice bought a new qualifying $10,000 machine normally depreciated over five years, the first-year writeoff under the new law is $4,400. Under prior law, the maximum first-year writeoff is only $2,000. The extra 30% first-year writeoff also applies to certain types of interior improvements to leased nonresidential realty (such as an office building or factory).

. . . The first-year depreciation dollar cap on new luxury autos bought for business purposes is boosted by $4,600, effective for autos acquired after Sept. 10, 2001 and before Sept. 11, 2004. For qualifying autos bought after Sept. 10,

---

FTC 2d References are to Federal Tax Coordinator 2d
FIN References are to RIA's Analysis of Federal Taxes: Income
USTR References are to United States Tax Reporter: Income, Estate & Gift, and Excise
PCA References are to the Pension Analysis on Checkpoint and CD-ROM, and in Pension Coordinator
PE References are to the Pension Explanations in Pension and Profit Sharing 2nd
EP References are to the Estate Planning Analysis on Checkpoint and CD-ROM, and in Estate Planning & Taxation Coordinator

2001 and before 2003, that means a maximum first year writeoff of $7,660 (the regular $3,060 first year dollar cap plus $4,600). The extra writeoff applies only if the auto is used more than 50% for business, and is fully available only if the auto is used 100% for business. The net result is a larger up-front deduction for those who buy new autos for use in their business or practice.

. . . The net operating loss (NOL) carryback period is increased from two or three years to five years, for NOLs arising in tax years ending in 2001 or 2002. This change could create additional refunds for businesses suffering losses. Related changes help businesses with NOLs avoid alternative minimum tax problems.

. . . Many tax breaks that expired at the end of 2001 are retroactively reinstated and extended for two years. These include the work opportunity tax credit and the welfare-to-work credit.

. . . Businesses operating in lower Manhattan that suffered as a result of the Sept. 11 terrorist attacks are given a package of five new tax breaks.

Tax changes for individuals include the following provisions:

. . . A two-year reprieve from an onerous rule that would have reduced an individual's personal nonrefundable credits (such as education credits) because of the alternative minimum tax (or AMT). Under the new law, for 2002 and 2003, you'll be able to use your personal nonrefundable credits to offset both your regular tax liability and your AMT liability.

. . . A crackdown on S corporation shareholders prevents them from increasing the basis of their stock in the entity (and thereby being able to deduct suspended losses) by debt that's forgiven and excluded from the corporation's income when the entity is bankrupt or insolvent.

. . . A number of changes, mostly favorable, deal with the enhanced retirement savings opportunities created by the 2001 tax law. For example, a change makes it clear that a person can make "catch-up" contributions any time during the year he or she turns age 50, not just after the calendar date he or she attains age 50.

. . . For 2002 and 2003, there's a new up-to-$250 deduction for educators below the college level who spend their own money on books and other materials they use in the classroom. The new deduction is available to itemizers and non-itemizers.

Please keep in mind that I've described only the highlights of the most important changes in the new law. Give me a call at your earliest convenience for more details on how you may be affected, and whether immediate action is needed to take advantage of the new law's tax breaks.

Very truly yours,

RIA Research Institute of America

¶ 802. Retroactively effective depreciation changes in the Job Creation and Worker Assistance Act of 2002

> **To the practitioner:** This letter can be sent to business and professional clients to tell them about the retroactively effective depreciation changes provided for in the Job Creation and Worker Assistance Act of 2002. For analysis of the 30% first-year depreciation provisions, see ¶ 101 and ¶ 102.

Dear Client:

I am writing to tell you of important changes for business and professional clients in the recently enacted Job Creation and Worker Assistance Act of 2002. In an effort to stimulate the economy, Congress is giving taxpayers an extra 30% first-year depreciation writeoff for most new capital assets (other than buildings) acquired after Sept. 10, 2001, and before Sept. 11, 2004, and placed in service before 2005 (before 2006, for certain property with longer production periods). In effect, this additional writeoff means that you can recover more of the cost of a business asset in the year you place it in service.

What qualifies for the extra 30% depreciation writeoff? Most types of new, nonrealty assets, such as business machines, computers, most types of computer software, many types of production equipment, trucks, trailers, and business furniture.

New business autos also qualify for a bigger first year writeoff. The first-year depreciation dollar cap on new autos bought for business purposes is boosted by $4,600, effective for autos acquired after Sept. 10, 2001 and before Sept. 11, 2004. For qualifying autos bought after Sept. 10, 2001 and before 2003, that means a maximum first year writeoff of $7,660 (the regular $3,060 first year dollar cap plus $4,600). The extra writeoff applies only if the auto is used more than 50% for business, and is fully available only if the auto is used 100% for business.

Taxpayers also are entitled to an extra 30% depreciation writeoff for qualified leasehold improvements. In general, these are interior improvements made under a lease to commercial property (such as an office building or warehouse), and placed in service more than three years after the building was first placed in service. Certain structural improvements don't qualify, and neither do expansions. Additionally, the improvements generally must be acquired after Sept. 10, 2001, and before Sept. 11, 2004, and placed in service before 2005.

These depreciation changes are retroactively effective (that is, they apply to qualifying new property acquired after Sept. 10, 2001). As a result, returns that have already been filed for tax year 2001 (as well as 2000 returns of some fiscal-year businesses) will have to be amended to take advantage of the additional writeoff. However, under some circumstances, a taxpayer may be better off not claiming the extra first-year depreciation deduction. Finally, note that our firm may have to file extensions for some 2001 returns, in order to give us time to analyze how our clients can make the most of the new law changes.

Please contact our offices for more details on how you are affected by the Job Creation and Worker Assistance Act of 2002.

Very truly yours,

¶ 803. NOL carryback lengthened under the Job Creation and Worker Assistance Act of 2002

> **To the practitioner:** For analysis of NOL carryback rules, see ¶ 103, ¶ 104.

Dear Client,

As you probably know, Congress has recently passed an "economic stimulus" package called the "Job Creation and Worker Assistance Act of 2002." The Act is a combination of business economic stimulus provisions, relief provisions for lower-Manhattan businesses affected by the 9/11 terrorist attacks, a 13-week extension of unemployment benefits, extensions for expired or soon-to-expire tax breaks, and technical corrections.

An important business provision in the 2002 Act temporarily extends the carryback period for 2001 and 2002 net operating losses (NOLs) to five years. This extension is intended to assist companies that had high tax liabilities during the high-growth years of the late 1990s, but are going through harder times now. Carrying back the loss to a profitable year can generate an immediate tax refund. A related provision temporarily eases a restriction on the use of NOLs against alternative minimum tax.

The purpose of this letter is to provide you with a brief overview of the new NOL carryback and carryforward provisions. If you would like to discuss how these new provisions affect your business situation, please do not hesitate to contact my office.

General rules for NOL carrybacks and carryforwards

A net operating loss ("NOL") is, generally, the amount by which a taxpayer's allowable deductions exceed the taxpayer's gross income. A carryback of an NOL generally results in the refund of Federal income tax for the carryback year. A carryforward of an NOL reduces Federal income tax for the carryforward year.

FTC 2d References are to Federal Tax Coordinator 2d
FIN References are to RIA's Analysis of Federal Taxes: Income
USTR References are to United States Tax Reporter: Income, Estate & Gift, and Excise
PCA References are to the Pension Analysis on Checkpoint and CD-ROM, and in Pension Coordinator
PE References are to the Pension Explanations in Pension and Profit Sharing 2nd
EP References are to the Estate Planning Analysis on Checkpoint and CD-ROM, and in Estate Planning & Taxation Coordinator

In general, an NOL may be carried back two years and carried forward 20 years to offset taxable income in the earlier years. A three-year carryback applies for NOLs arising from casualty or theft losses of individuals, or attributable to Presidentially declared disasters for farmers or small businesses. The carryback period may be waived.

Temporary increase in NOL carryback period

The 2002 Act increases the usual two and three year carryback periods to five years for NOLs arising in tax years ending in 2001 or 2002.

A taxpayer may elect to forgo the five-year carryback period and instead carry the NOL back 2 years (or 3 years, if applicable) and forward 20 years. Such an election must be made by the due date of the return (including extensions) for the year of the loss, and, once made, is irrevocable. Taxpayers should bear in mind that a waiver of the carryback period also applies for alternative minimum tax purposes.

Consideration should be given to waiving the 5-year carryback period if the taxpayer was in a low bracket in the fifth, fourth and third years back and expects to be in higher brackets going forward. A taxpayer in this situation should also consider waiving the 2-year (or 3-year) carryback period if the taxpayer was in a low bracket in the preceding 2 or 3 years.

Temporary easing of restriction on use of NOLs against AMT

Under the alternative minimum tax rules, an alternative tax net operating loss deduction (ATNOL) cannot reduce a taxpayer's alternative minimum taxable income ("AMTI") by more than 90 percent. Under the 2002 Act, an ATNOL attributable to (1) NOL carrybacks arising in tax years ending in 2001 or 2002, or (2) NOL carryforwards to 2001 and 2002 tax years, may offset 100% of a taxpayer's AMTI. Thus, for example, under the Act, a calendar year taxpayer's ATNOL consisting exclusively of a carryback arising in 2001 would be carried back to '96 (under the Act's 5-year rule discussed above) and could fully offset the taxpayer's AMTI for '96.

We can handle all the paperwork to take advantage of these new provisions to generate any tax refund that may be due to your business. Please telephone for a consultation.

Very truly yours,

¶ 804. How the Job Creation and Worker Assistance Act of 2002 affects 2001 returns

> **To the practitioner:** This letter can be sent to clients to give them an overview of the Job Creation & Worker Assistance Act of 2002, signed into law on Mar. 9, 2002. For analysis of the provision allowing additional first year depreciation for property placed in service after Sept. 10, 2001, see ¶ 101. For analysis of the provision increasing the first year depreciation amount for automobiles, see ¶ 102. For analysis of the provisions providing New York Liberty Zone tax relief, see ¶ 501, ¶ 502, ¶ 503, ¶ 504, ¶ 505, ¶ 506, and ¶ 507. For analysis of the provision extending the NOL carryback to five years for NOLs in 2001 and 2002, see ¶ 103. For analysis of the provision waiving the limitation on the use of NOLs against the alternative minimum tax for years 2001 and 2002, see ¶ 104. For analysis of the provision precluding an S corporation's cancellation of indebtedness income from increasing shareholder basis, see ¶ 105. For analysis of the provision clarifying the deemed sale and repurchase election for 5-year capital gain property, see ¶ 109. For analysis of the extension of the work opportunity tax credit, see ¶ 202. For analysis of the extension of the welfare-to-work tax credit, see ¶ 201. For analysis of the extension of the credit for production of electricity from renewable resources, ¶ 205. For analysis of the extension of the credit for purchasing electric vehicles, see ¶ 211.

Dear Client,

As you probably know, Congress has recently passed an "economic stimulus" package called the "Job Creation and Worker Assistance Act of 2002." The Act is a combination of business economic stimulus provisions, relief

---

FTC 2d References are to Federal Tax Coordinator 2d
FIN References are to RIA's Analysis of Federal Taxes: Income
USTR References are to United States Tax Reporter: Income, Estate & Gift, and Excise
PCA References are to the Pension Analysis on Checkpoint and CD-ROM, and in Pension Coordinator
PE References are to the Pension Explanations in Pension and Profit Sharing 2nd
EP References are to the Estate Planning Analysis on Checkpoint and CD-ROM, and in Estate Planning & Taxation Coordinator

provisions for lower-Manhattan businesses affected by the 9/11 terrorist attacks, a 13-week extension of unemployment benefits, extensions for expired or soon-to-expire tax breaks, and technical corrections.

An important fact to know about the 2002 Act is that it includes several retroactive tax breaks for both individuals and businesses. For example, the Act contains significant retroactive depreciation changes that may affect returns that have already been filed, or are about to be filed. Other changes that may affect 2001 returns include an increased net operating loss (NOL) carryback period, a change for S corporation debt discharge income, and several technical corrections dealing with the deemed sale-and-repurchase election for five-year gain.

Following is a brief overview of the provisions in the Act that may affect 2001 tax returns. Please call me if you would like to discuss how these changes affect your situation.

Additional first year depreciation allowance

Effective for new property placed in service after Sept. 10, 2001, the 2002 Act allows taxpayers to claim an additional first-year depreciation deduction equal to 30% of the adjusted basis of qualified property. This is property that meets the following conditions:

... It is MACRS-eligible property with a recovery period of 20 years or less; certain water utility property; most computer software; or qualified leasehold improvement property (generally a non-structural, non-expansion improvement to an interior portion of an existing nonresidential building, provided certain requirements are met).

... The property generally must be acquired after Sept. 10, 2001, and before Sept. 11, 2004, and be placed in service before 2005 (before 2006, for certain property with longer production periods).

The additional first-year depreciation deduction is allowed for both regular tax and AMT purposes for the tax year in which the property is placed in service. The basis of the property is reduced by the additional first-year depreciation allowance, and regular MACRS depreciation allowances are adjusted to reflect the additional first-year depreciation deduction. In addition, if a taxpayer claims the additional first-year depreciation for qualified property, the taxpayer's entire depreciation deduction (not just the additional first-year depreciation deduction) for that property is allowed for AMT purposes.

If Code Sec. 179 expensing is claimed on qualified property, the amount expensed comes off the top before the additional 30% first-year depreciation allowance is computed. Then the taxpayer computes regular first-year depreciation (and depreciation for future years) with reference to the adjusted basis remaining after expensing and after the additional 30% first-year allowance.

The additional first-year depreciation allowance is not available for:

... property that must be depreciated under the alternative depreciation system (e.g., tangible personal property used predominantly outside the U.S.);

... listed property (such as a passenger auto) that isn't used more than 50% for business; and

... New York Liberty Zone qualified leasehold improvement property (see discussion below).

Increased first year depreciation dollar cap for luxury autos

The maximum first-year depreciation dollar cap for a business auto that is qualified property (defined above) is increased by $4,600 generally for business autos purchased after Sept. 10, 2001 and before Sept. 11, 2004. The regular first-year depreciation allowance is capped at $3,060 for autos placed in service in 2001 or 2002, so under the Act the combined first-year allowance for a luxury auto that is qualified property is $7,660.

New York Liberty Zone tax breaks

A number of retroactively effective tax breaks apply for the New York Liberty Zone, in lower Manhattan. Here is a brief summary:

(1) Additional 30% first-year depreciation for certain nonresidential or residential realty (only to the extent it rehabilitates realty damaged, or replaces realty destroyed or condemned, as a result of the Sept. 11, 2001 terrorist attack). Note that this property isn't eligible for the regular 30% additional first-year depreciation allowance (described above) because the recovery period for realty exceeds 20 years.

(2) Straight line depreciation over 5 years (9 years under the alternative depreciation system, or ADS) for qualified leasehold improvement property (generally a non-structural, non-expansion improvement to an interior portion of an existing nonresidential building, provided certain requirements are met) that is NYLZ property.

(3) The regular maximum expensing allowance under Code Sec. 179 ($24,000 for eligible property placed in service in tax years beginning in 2001

FTC 2d References are to Federal Tax Coordinator 2d
FIN References are to RIA's Analysis of Federal Taxes: Income
USTR References are to United States Tax Reporter: Income, Estate & Gift, and Excise
PCA References are to the Pension Analysis on Checkpoint and CD-ROM, and in Pension Coordinator
PE References are to the Pension Explanations in Pension and Profit Sharing 2nd
EP References are to the Estate Planning Analysis on Checkpoint and CD-ROM, and in Estate Planning & Taxation Coordinator

or 2002, $25,000 after 2002) is increased by $35,000 for qualified NYLZ property.

(4) The Code Sec. 1033 replacement period for property involuntarily converted in the NYLZ as a result of the 9/11 terrorist attack is extended from two years to five years, but only if substantially all of the replacement property is in New York City.

(5) The Act creates a new targeted group of work opportunity credit (WOTC) eligible individuals, namely those who work in the NYLZ (or elsewhere in New York City, if their business was forced to relocate because of the 9/11 terrorist attack) for a business employing an average of 200 or fewer employees. For the new targeted group, the maximum credit is $2,400 (40% of up to $6,000 of qualified wages) per qualified employee per year. These new rules apply for work performed in calendar years 2002 and 2003.

Temporary increase in NOL carryback period

The 2002 Act increases the two and three year NOL carryback periods to five years for NOLs arising in tax years ending in 2001 or 2002. A taxpayer may elect to forgo the five-year carryback period and instead carry the NOL back 2 years (or 3 years, if applicable) and forward 20 years.

Temporary waiver of limitation on use of NOLs against AMT

Under the alternative minimum tax rules, an alternative tax net operating loss deduction (ATNOL) cannot reduce a taxpayer's alternative minimum taxable income ("AMTI") by more than 90 percent of the AMTI. Under the 2002 Act, an ATNOL attributable to (1) NOL carrybacks arising in tax years ending in 2001 or 2002, or (2) NOL carryforwards to 2001 and 2002 tax years, may offset 100% of a taxpayer's AMTI.

Retroactively effective extenders

The Act extends a number of tax breaks that expired at the end of 2001 or were soon to expire, including:

... The work opportunity tax credit (WOTC) and the welfare-to-work tax credit, for two years.

... The credit for production of electricity from wind, closed-loop biomass, and poultry litter, for qualified facilities placed in service before 2004.

... The 10% credit for the purchase of electric vehicles is fully available for qualified purchases made in 2002 and 2003, and phases down over 2004-2006.

Please call our offices at your earliest convenience to discuss how your business is affected by these important changes. Of course, we can handle all the paperwork to take advantage of any of these new provisions to generate any tax refund that may be due to your business.

Very truly yours,

FTC 2d References are to Federal Tax Coordinator 2d
FIN References are to RIA's Analysis of Federal Taxes: Income
USTR References are to United States Tax Reporter: Income, Estate & Gift, and Excise
PCA References are to the Pension Analysis on Checkpoint and CD-ROM, and in Pension Coordinator
PE References are to the Pension Explanations in Pension and Profit Sharing 2nd
EP References are to the Estate Planning Analysis on Checkpoint and CD-ROM, and in Estate Planning & Taxation Coordinator

 Research Institute of America

¶ 805. Extensions of expired or soon-to-expire tax breaks in the Job Creation and Worker Assistance Act of 2002

To the practitioner: This letter outlines the extender provisions in the Job Creation and Worker Assistance Act of 2002. For analysis of the work opportunity credit extender provision, see ¶ 202. For analysis of the welfare-to-work credit extender, see ¶ 201. For analysis of the 2002 Act provision extending the Code Sec. 45 credit for the production of energy from alternative sources, see ¶ 205. For analysis of the provision extending the credit for purchase of electric vehicles, see ¶ 211. For analysis of the 2002 Act provision deferring the phaseout of the maximum deduction for the lost of qualified clean-fuel vehicles, see ¶ 209. For analysis of the provision allowing individuals to offset their entire regular tax liability and alternative minimum tax liability by the personal nonrefundable credits in 2002 and 2003, see ¶ 401. For analysis of the provision extending the suspension of the rule limiting the amount of a taxpayer's percentage depletion deduction to 100 percent of the net income from marginal oil or gas wells, see ¶ 206. For analysis of the provision allowing the issuance of qualified zone academy bonds through 2002 and 2003, see ¶ 213. For analysis of the provision extending the Archer MSA program through 2003, see ¶ 214. For analysis of the provisions extending the Indian employment credit and the accelerated depreciation rules for property on Indian reservations, see ¶ 215 and ¶ 216. For analysis of the provisions extending the temporary exclusion from Subpart F income for certain income from the active conduct of a banking, financing, or similar business, or in the conduct of an insurance business, see ¶ 203 and ¶ 204.

FTC 2d References are to Federal Tax Coordinator 2d
FIN References are to RIA's Analysis of Federal Taxes: Income
USTR References are to United States Tax Reporter: Income, Estate & Gift, and Excise
PCA References are to the Pension Analysis on Checkpoint and CD-ROM, and in Pension Coordinator
PE References are to the Pension Explanations in Pension and Profit Sharing 2nd
EP References are to the Estate Planning Analysis on Checkpoint and CD-ROM, and in Estate Planning & Taxation Coordinator

Dear Client,

As you probably know, Congress has recently passed an "economic stimulus" package called the "Job Creation and Worker Assistance Act of 2002." The Act is a combination of business economic stimulus provisions, relief provisions for lower-Manhattan businesses affected by the Sept. 11 terrorist attacks, a 13-week extension of unemployment benefits, extensions for expired or soon-to-expire tax breaks, and technical corrections.

The purpose of this letter is to provide you with a brief overview of the provisions of the Act that extend expired or soon-to-expire tax breaks. Several of the tax breaks expired at the end of 2001. Thus, their extension may immediately impact fiscal-year taxpayers (e.g, fiscal-year business with a year ending Jan. 31, 2002). Please call me if you would like to discuss how these changes affect your personal and business situation.

Work opportunity tax credit and welfare-to-work tax credit

The work opportunity tax credit (WOTC) and the welfare-to-work tax credit both are retroactively extended for two years, for wages paid or incurred to a qualified individual who begins work for an employer after 2001 and before 2004.

Credit for production of electricity from certain sources

The credit for production of electricity from wind, closed-loop biomass, and poultry litter, is extended for two years to apply to qualified facilities placed in service before 2004.

Credit for purchase of electric vehicle

Under pre-Act law, the 10% credit for the purchase of electric vehicles was to have been phased out over 2002-2004. Effective for property placed in service after 2001, the Act makes the full 10% credit available for qualified purchases made in 2002 and 2003, and phases down the credit over 2004-2006.

Deductions for qualified clean-fuel vehicle and clean-fuel vehicle refueling property

Under pre-Act law, the deduction for qualified clean-fuel vehicle property and clean-fuel vehicle refueling property was to have been phased out over 2002-2004. Effective for property placed in service after 2001, the Act makes the full amount of the deduction available for qualified vehicles placed in service in 2002 and 2003, and phases down the deduction over 2004-2006. The Act also makes the deduction for clean-fuel vehicle refueling property available for property placed in service prior to January 1, 2007.

Alternative minimum tax relief for individuals

RIA Research Institute of America

The 2002 Act allows an individual to offset the entire regular tax liability and alternative minimum tax liability by the personal nonrefundable credits (including the dependent care credit, the credit for the elderly and disabled, the adoption credit, the child tax credit, the credit for interest on certain home mortgages, the HOPE Scholarship and Lifetime Learning credits, the IRA credit, and the D.C. homebuyer's credit) in 2002 and 2003.

Taxable income limit on percentage depletion for marginal production

Under pre-Act law, the rule limiting the amount of a taxpayer's percentage depletion deduction to 100 percent of the net income from an oil- or gas-producing property was suspended for production from marginal wells for taxable years beginning after 1997 and before 2002. The Act extends the period when the 100-percent net-income limit is suspended to include taxable years beginning in 2002 and 2003.

Extension of authority to issue qualified zone academy bonds

Under pre-Act law, a total of $400 million of qualified zone academy bonds could be issued annually in calendar years 1998 through 2001. The Act authorizes issuance of up to $400 million of qualified zone academy bonds annually in calendar years 2002 and 2003.

Extension of Archer medical savings accounts ("MSAs")

The Act extends the Archer MSA program for another year, through December 31, 2003.

Extension of tax incentives for investment on Indian reservations

The Act extends for one year (i.e., through December 31, 2004) the Indian employment credit and the accelerated depreciation rules for property on Indian reservations.

Subpart F exceptions for active financing income

Under pre-Act law, temporary exceptions from foreign personal holding company income, foreign base company services income, and insurance income applied for subpart F purposes for certain income that was derived in the active conduct of a banking, financing, or similar business, or in the conduct of an insurance business (so-called "active financing income"). The exceptions did not apply for tax years beginning after 2001. The Act extends

FTC 2d References are to Federal Tax Coordinator 2d
FIN References are to RIA's Analysis of Federal Taxes: Income
USTR References are to United States Tax Reporter: Income, Estate & Gift, and Excise
PCA References are to the Pension Analysis on Checkpoint and CD-ROM, and in Pension Coordinator
PE References are to the Pension Explanations in Pension and Profit Sharing 2nd
EP References are to the Estate Planning Analysis on Checkpoint and CD-ROM, and in Estate Planning & Taxation Coordinator

these temporary exceptions for 5 years so that they apply for tax years of foreign corporations beginning after Dec. 31, 2001, and before Jan. 1, 2007, and for tax years of U.S. shareholders with or within which such foreign corporation tax years end. While the Act generally retains prior rules as to how an insurance company's reserve for a life insurance or annuity contract is determined under the exceptions, it permits a taxpayer in certain circumstances, subject to approval by IRS, to establish that the reserve for contracts is the amount taken into account in determining the foreign statement reserve for the contracts (reduced by catastrophe, equalization, or deficiency reserves or any similar reserves).

This letter gives you the high points of the extender provisions in the 2002 Act. Please call our offices and we'll set up an appointment to discuss in detail how the changes affect you, your family, and your business.

Very truly yours,

¶ 806. New York City tax incentives in the Job Creation and Worker Assistance Act of 2002

To the practitioner: This letter is designed to be sent to clients with business or property interests in lower Manhattan. For more details on the New York Liberty Zone tax breaks, see ¶ 501, ¶ 502, ¶ 503, ¶ 504, ¶ 505, ¶ 506, ¶ 507, and ¶ 508. For analysis of the provision allowing 30% additional first-year depreciation for New York Liberty Zone property, see ¶ 501. For analysis of the provision allowing additional first-year expensing in lieu of depreciation for New York Liberty Zone property, see ¶ 502. For analysis of the provision treating New York Liberty Zone leasehold improvements as 5-year property for MACRS depreciation, see ¶ 503. For analysis of the provision extending the period for replacing certain involuntarily converted New York Liberty Zone property, see ¶ 504. For analysis of the provisions extending the work opportunity tax credit to New York Liberty Zone employees, see ¶ 505 and ¶ 506. For analysis of the provision authoring the issuance of tax-exempt private activity bonds to finance the rebuilding of New York City, see ¶ 507. For analysis of the provision allowing additional advance refunding for bonds for New York City facilities, see ¶ 508.

Dear Client,

As you probably know, Congress has recently passed an "economic stimulus" package called the "Job Creation and Worker Assistance Act of 2002." The Act is a combination of business economic stimulus provisions, relief provisions for lower-Manhattan businesses affected by the 9/11 terrorist attacks, a 13-week extension of unemployment benefits, extensions for expired or soon-to-expire tax breaks, and technical corrections.

FTC 2d References are to Federal Tax Coordinator 2d
FIN References are to RIA's Analysis of Federal Taxes: Income
USTR References are to United States Tax Reporter: Income, Estate & Gift, and Excise
PCA References are to the Pension Analysis on Checkpoint and CD-ROM, and in Pension Coordinator
PE References are to the Pension Explanations in Pension and Profit Sharing 2nd
EP References are to the Estate Planning Analysis on Checkpoint and CD-ROM, and in Estate Planning & Taxation Coordinator

The purpose of this letter is to provide you with a brief overview of the Act's relief provisions for lower-Manhattan businesses affected by the 9/11 terrorist attacks. If you have any questions about any of these New York City tax incentive provisions, or any other aspect of the new Act, please do not hesitate to contact my office.

Geographical scope of relief provisions

The new provisions apply for the New York Liberty Zone, which is the area located on or south of Canal street, East Broadway (east of its intersection with Canal Street), or Grand Street (east of its intersection with East Broadway) in the Borough of Manhattan, New York, New York.

Enhanced first-year depreciation

The 2002 Act allows an additional 30% first-year depreciation deduction for depreciable qualified New York Liberty Zone property; the bonus depreciation allowance applies for both regular and alternative minimum tax purposes. Taxpayers may elect out of the additional first-year depreciation for any class of property for any tax year.

To qualify, property must be depreciable under MACRS rules (i.e., not property that must be depreciated under the alternative depreciation system (ADS) of MACRS on a straight-line basis over its ADS useful life), and that:

(a) has a recovery period of 20 years or less; or

(b) is water utility property; or

(c) is certain nonresidential real property and residential rental property; or

(d) is computer software other than software with a 15-year cost recovery period under Code Sec. 197.

The property generally must be acquired by purchase by the taxpayer after Sept. 10, 2001, and be placed in service before Jan. 1, 2007 (before Jan. 1, 2010 for qualifying real property). In addition, the property's first use in the Liberty Zone must begin with the taxpayer after Sept. 10, 2001 (used property may qualify), and substantially all of its use must be in the Liberty Zone. Improvements to recondition or rebuild property in the Liberty Zone satisfy the original-use requirement.

Nonresidential real property and residential rental property qualifies for the bonus depreciation only to the extent that it rehabilitates real property damaged, or replaces real property destroyed or condemned, as a result of the terrorist attacks of Sept. 11, 2001.

Rapid depreciation for qualified New York Liberty Zone leasehold improvements

RIA Research Institute of America

The 2002 Act allows the cost of qualified leasehold improvement property (generally a non-structural, non-expansion improvement to an interior portion of an existing nonresidential building, provided certain requirements are met) that is Liberty Zone property to be depreciated on a straight line basis over 5 years (9 years under the alternative depreciation system (ADS)). The property must be located in the New York Liberty Zone and be placed in service after Sept. 10, 2001, and before 2007.

Increased expensing for Liberty Zone property

Under the 2002 Act, the regular maximum expensing allowance under Code Sec. 179 ($24,000 for eligible property placed in service in tax years beginning in 2001 or 2002, $25,000 after 2002) is increased by $35,000 for qualified New York Liberty Zone property. The original use of the property in the New York Liberty Zone must commence with the taxpayer after Sept. 10, 2001; the property must be acquired by the taxpayer by purchase after Sept. 10, 2001, and must be placed in service before 2007. Substantially all of the use of the property must be in the Liberty Zone in the active conduct of the trade or business of a taxpayer in that zone.

Extended replacement period for involuntarily converted Liberty Zone property

Under the 2002 Act, the Code Sec. 1033 tax-free replacement period for property involuntarily converted in the New York Liberty Zone as a result of the 9/11 terrorist attack is extended to five years from the usual two, three, or four years, but only if substantially all of the replacement property is in New York City.

Expansion of work opportunity tax credit targeted categories to include certain employees in New York City

The 2002 Act creates a new targeted group of work opportunity credit (WOTC) eligible individuals, namely those who work in the New York Liberty Zone (or elsewhere in New York City, if their business was forced to relocate because of the 9/11 terrorist attack) for a business employing an average of 200 or fewer employees. For the new targeted group, the maximum credit is $2,400 (40% of up to $6,000 of qualified wages) per qualified employee per year. These new rules apply for work performed in calendar years 2002 and 2003.

Private activity bond authorization for rebuilding the New York Liberty Zone

The 2002 Act authorizes issuance during calendar years 2002, 2003, and 2004 of an aggregate amount of $8 billion of tax-exempt private activity bonds to finance the construction and rehabilitation of certain nonresidential real property and residential rental real property in the Liberty Zone.

As you can see, the 2002 Act provides significant tax incentives for business and investment in lower Manhattan. Please call me to discuss how your business can benefit from these opportunities.

Very truly yours,

[¶ 3000]   *Code As Amended*

This section reproduces new law enacted by P.L. 107-147, the Job Creation and Worker Assistance Act of 2002. Code sections appear as amended, added or repealed starting at ¶ 3001. They are in Code section order. New matter is shown in italics. All changes and effective dates are shown in the endnotes.

[¶ 3001]

Code Sec. 21.   **Expenses for household and dependent care services necessary for gainful employment.**

* * * * * * * * * * *

(d) Earned income limitation.

(1) In general. Except as otherwise provided in this subsection, the amount of the employment-related expenses incurred during any taxable year which may be taken into account under subsection (a) shall not exceed—

(A) in the case of an individual who is not married at the close of such year, such individual's earned income for such year, or

(B) in the case of an individual who is married at the close of such year, the lesser of such individual's earned income or the earned income of his spouse for such year.

(2) Special rule for spouse who is a student or incapable of caring for himself. In the case of a spouse who is a student or a qualifying individual described in subsection (b)(1)(C), for purposes of paragraph (1), such spouse shall be deemed for each month during which such spouse is a full-time student at an educational institution, or is such a qualifying individual, to be gainfully employed and to have earned income of not less than—

(A) [1]*$250* if subsection (c)(1) applies for the taxable year, or

(B) [2]*$500* if subsection (c)(2) applies for the taxable year.

In the case of any husband and wife, this paragraph shall apply with respect to only one spouse for any one month.

* * * * * * * * * * *

[For Analysis, see ¶ 406. For Committee Reports, see ¶ 5068.]

[Endnote Code Sec. 21]

Matter in *italics* in Code Sec. 21(d)(2)(A) and Code Sec. 21(d)(2)(B) was added by Sec. 418(b)(1) and (2) of the Job Creation and Worker Assistance Act of 2002, P.L. 107-147, 3/9/2002, which struck out:

1. "$200"
2. "$400"

Effective Date (Sec. 418(c), P.L. 107-147, 3/9/2002) effective for tax. yrs. begin. after 12/31/2002.

[¶ 3002]

Code Sec. 23.   **Adoption expenses.**

(a) Allowance of credit.

[1]*(1) In general. In the case of an individual, there shall be allowed as a credit against the tax imposed by this chapter the amount of the qualified adoption expenses paid or incurred by the taxpayer.*

(2) Year credit allowed. The credit under paragraph (1) with respect to any expense shall be allowed—

(A) in the case of any expense paid or incurred before the taxable year in which such adoption becomes final, for the taxable year following the taxable year during which such expense is paid or incurred, and

(B) in the case of an expense paid or incurred during or after the taxable year in which such adoption becomes final, for the taxable year in which such expense is paid or incurred.[2]

[3]*(3) $10,000 credit for adoption of child with special needs regardless of expenses. In the case of an adoption of a child with special needs which becomes final during a taxable year, the taxpayer shall be treated as having paid during such year qualified adoption expenses with respect to such adoption in an amount equal to the excess (if any) of $10,000 over the aggregate qualified adoption expenses actually paid or incurred by the taxpayer with respect to such adoption during such taxable year and all prior taxable years.*

(b) Limitations.

(1) Dollar limitation. The aggregate amount of qualified adoption expenses which may be taken into account under [4]*subsection (a)* for all taxable years with respect to the adoption of a child by the taxpayer shall not exceed $10,000.

* * * * * * * * * * *

(h) Adjustments for inflation. In the case of a taxable year beginning after December 31, 2002, each of the dollar amounts in [5]*subsection (a)(3)* and paragraphs (1) and (2)(A)(i) of subsection (b) shall be increased by an amount equal to—

(1) such dollar amount, multiplied by

(2) the cost-of-living adjustment determined under section 1(f)(3) for the calendar year in which the taxable year begins, determined by substituting "calendar year 2001" for "calendar year 1992" in subparagraph (B) thereof.

[6]*If any amount as increased under the preceding sentence is not a multiple of $10, such amount shall be rounded to the nearest multiple of $10.*

* * * * * * * * * * *

(i) Regulations. The Secretary shall prescribe such regulations as may be appropriate to carry out this section and section 137, including regulations which treat unmarried individuals who pay or incur qualified adoption expenses with respect to the same child as 1 taxpayer for purposes of applying [7]*the dollar amounts in subsections (a)(3) and (b)(1)* of this section and in section 137(b)(1).

[For Analysis, see ¶412, ¶414. For Committee Reports, see ¶5033, ¶5067.]

[Endnote Code Sec. 23]

Code Sec. 23(a)(1), in *italics*, was added by Sec. 411(c)(1)(A) of the Job Creation and Worker Assistance Act of 2002, P.L. 107-147, 3/9/2002, which struck out:

1. "(1) In general. In the case of an individual, there shall be allowed as a credit against the tax imposed by this chapter—

"(A) in the case of an adoption of a child other than a child with special needs, the amount of the qualified adoption expenses paid or incurred by the taxpayer, and

"(B) in the case of an adoption of a child with special needs, $10,000."

Effective Date (Sec. 411(x), P.L. 107-147, 3/9/2002) effective for tax. yrs. begin. after 12/31/2002.

In Code Sec. 23(a)(2), Sec. 411(c)(1)(C), P.L. 107-147, 3/9/2002, struck out:

2. "In the case of the adoption of a child with special needs, the credit allowed under paragraph (1) shall be allowed for the taxable year in which the adoption becomes final."

Effective Date (Sec. 411(x), P.L. 107-147, 3/9/2002) effective for tax. yrs. begin. after 12/31/2001.

Code Sec. 23(a)(3), in *italics*, was added by Sec. 411(c)(1)(B), P.L. 107-147, 3/9/2002.

3. added para. (a)(3)

Effective Date (Sec. 411(x), P.L. 107-147, 3/9/2002) effective for tax. yrs. begin. after 12/31/2002.

Matter in *italics* in Code Sec. 23(b)(1) was added by Sec. 411(c)(1)(D), P.L. 107-147, 3/9/2002, which struck out:

4. "subsection (a)(1)(A)"

Effective Date (Sec. 411(x), P.L. 107-147, 3/9/2002) effective for tax. yrs. begin. after 12/31/2001.

Matter in *italics* in Code Sec. 23(h) was added by Sec. 418(a)(1)(A) and (B), P.L. 107-147, 3/9/2002, which struck out:

5. "subsection (a)(1)(B)"

6. added matter in subsec. (h)
Effective Date (Sec. 418(c), P.L. 107-147, 3/9/2002) effective for tax. yrs. begin. after 12/31/2001.

Matter in *italics* in Code Sec. 23(i) was added by Sec. 411(c)(1)(E), P.L. 107-147, 3/9/2002, which struck out:
7. "the dollar limitation in subsection (b)(1)"
Effective Date (Sec. 411(x), P.L. 107-147, 3/9/2002) effective for tax. yrs. begin. after 12/31/2002.

Note Sec. 601(b)(2), P.L. 107-147, following, provides rules for applying amendments made by Secs. 201(b) and 202(f) of P.L. 107-16. Sec. 601(b)(2) reads as follows:
"(2) The amendments made by sections 201(b), 202(f), and 618(b) of the Economic Growth and Tax Relief Reconciliation Act of 2001 [P.L. 107-16] shall not apply to taxable years beginning during 2002 and 2003."
Note The amendments made by Secs. 201(b) and 202(f), P.L. 107-16, are as follows:
Sec. 201(b)(2)(E) substituted "and sections 24 and 1400C" for "and section 1400C" in subsec. (c) [prior to amendment by Sec. 202(f)(2)(A)(i)-(ii), see below.]
Sec. 202(f)(1) added para. (b)(4).
Sec. 202(f)(2)(A)(i) substituted "subsection (b)(4)" for "section 26(a)" in subsec. (c) [as amended by Sec. 201(b)(2)(E), see above].
Sec. 202(f)(2)(A)(ii) deleted "reduced by the sum of the credits allowable under this subpart (other than this section and sections 24 and 1400C)" before ", such excess shall be carried" in subsec. (c) [as amended by Sec. 201(b)(2)(E), see above].

[¶ 3003]
Code Sec. 24.   Allowance of credit.

* * * * * * * * * * * *

(d) Portion of credit refundable.

(1) In general. The aggregate credits allowed to a taxpayer under subpart C shall be increased by the lesser of—

(A) the credit which would be allowed under this section without regard to this subsection and the limitation under section 26(a), or

(B) the amount by which the [1]*aggregate amount of credits allowed by this subpart* (determined without regard to this subsection) would increase if the limitation imposed by section 26(a) were increased by the greater of—

(i) 15 percent (10 percent in the case of taxable years beginning before January 1, 2005) of so much of the taxpayer's earned income (within the meaning of section 32) which is taken into account in computing taxable income for the taxable year as exceeds $10,000, or

(ii) in the case of a taxpayer with 3 or more qualifying children, the excess (if any) of—

(I) the taxpayer's social security taxes for the taxable year, over

(II) the credit allowed under section 32 for the taxable year.
The amount of the credit allowed under this subsection shall not be treated as a credit allowed under this subpart and shall reduce the amount of credit otherwise allowable under subsection (a) without regard to section 26(a).

* * * * * * * * * * * *

[For Analysis, see ¶ 404. For Committee Reports, see ¶ 5032

[Endnote Code Sec. 24]
Matter in *italics* in Code Sec. 24(d)(1)(B) was added by Sec. 411(b) of the Job Creation and Worker Assistance Act of 2002, P.L. 107-147, 3/9/2002, which struck out:
1. "amount of credit allowed by this section"
Effective Date (Sec. 411(x), P.L. 107-147, 3/9/2002) effective as if included by the amendments made by Sec. 201, P.L. 107-16. Sec. 201(e), P.L. 107-16, which provides effective dates, reads as follows:
"(e) Effective dates.
"(1) In general. Except as provided in paragraph (2), the amendments made by this section shall apply to taxable years beginning after December 31, 2000.
"(2) Subsection (b). The amendments made by subsection (b) shall apply to taxable years beginning after December 31, 2001.

Note Sec. 601(b)(2), P.L. 107-147, 3/9/2002, following, provides rules for applying amendments made by Sec. 201(b), 202(f) and 618(b) of P.L. 107-16. Sec. 601(b)(2), P.L. 107-147, reads as follows:

"(2) The amendments made by sections 201(b), 202(f), and 618(b) of the Economic Growth and Tax Relief Reconciliation Act of 2001 [P.L. 107-16] shall not apply to taxable years beginning during 2002 and 2003."

Note The amendments made by Secs. 201(b), 202(f) and 618(b) are as follows:

Sec. 201(b)(1) added para. (b)(3).

Sec. 201(b)(2)(A) substituted "Limitations." for "Limitation based on adjusted gross income." in the heading of subsec. (b)

Sec. 201(b)(2)(B) substituted "Limitation based on adjusted gross income." for "In general." in the heading of para. (b)(1)

Sec. 201(b)(2)(C)(i) substituted "subsection (b)(3)" for "section 26(a)" each place it appeared in subsec. (d).

Sec. 201(b)(2)(C)(ii) substituted "amount of credit allowed by this section" for "aggregate amount of credits allowed by this subpart"

Sec. 202(f)(2)(B) substituted "this section and section 23" for "this section" in subpara. (b)(3)(B)

Sec. 618(b)(2)(A) substituted "sections 23 and 25B" for "section 23" in subpara. (b)(3)(B)

[¶ 3004]

Code Sec. 25.   Interest on certain home mortgages.

* * * * * * * * * * * *

[Endnote Code Sec. 25]

Note Sec. 601(b)(2), P.L. 107-147, 3/9/2002, following, provides rules for applying amendments made by Sec. 201(b), 202(f) and 618(b) of P.L. 107-16. Sec. 601(b)(2), P.L. 107-147, reads as follows:

"(2) The amendments made by sections 201(b), 202(f), and 618(b) of the Economic Growth and Tax Relief Reconciliation Act of 2001 [P.L. 107-16] shall not apply to taxable years beginning during 2002 and 2003."

Note The amendments made by Secs. 201(b) and 618(b), P.L. 107-16, are as follows:

Sec. 201(b)(2)(F) added ", 24," after "sections 23" in subpara. (e)(1)(C).

Sec. 618(b)(2)(B) added "25B," after "24," in subpara. (e)(1)(C) [as amended by Sec. 201(b)(2)(F), see above.]

[¶ 3005]

Code Sec. 25B.   Elective deferrals and IRA contributions by certain individuals.

* * * * * * * * * * * *

(d) Qualified retirement savings contributions.

* * * * * * * * * * * *

(2) Reduction for certain distributions.

[1]*(A) In general. The qualified retirement savings contributions determined under paragraph (1) shall be reduced (but not below zero) by the aggregate distributions received by the individual during the testing period from any entity of a type to which contributions under paragraph (1) may be made. The preceding sentence shall not apply to the portion of any distribution which is not includible in gross income by reason of a trustee-to-trustee transfer or a rollover distribution.*

(B) Testing period. For purposes of subparagraph (A), the testing period, with respect to a taxable year, is the period which includes —

(i) such taxable year,

(ii) the 2 preceding taxable years, and

(iii) the period after such taxable year and before the due date (including extensions) for filing the return of tax for such taxable year.

(C) Excepted distributions. There shall not be taken into account under subparagraph (A)—

(i) any distribution referred to in section 72(p), 401(k)(8), 401(m)(6), 402(g)(2), 404(k), or 408(d)(4), and

(ii) any distribution to which section 408A(d)(3) applies.

(D) Treatment of distributions received by spouse of individual. For purposes of determining distributions received by an individual under subparagraph (A) for any taxable year, any distribution received by the spouse of such individual shall be treated as received by such individual if such individual and spouse file a joint return for such taxable year and for the taxable year during which the spouse receives the distribution.

* * * * * * * * * * * *

²*(h)* **Termination.** This section shall not apply to taxable years beginning after December 31, 2006.

[For Analysis, see ¶ 317. For Committee Reports, see ¶ 5043.]

[Endnote Code Sec. 25B]

Code Sec. 25B(d)(2)(A), in *italics*, was added by Sec. 411(m) of the Job Creation and Worker Assistance Act of 2002, P.L. 107-147, 3/9/2002, which struck out:

1. "(A) In general. The qualified retirement savings contributions determined under paragraph (1) shall be reduced (but not below zero) by the sum of—

"(i) any distribution from a qualified retirement plan (as defined in section 4974(c)), or from an eligible deferred compensation plan (as defined in section 457(b)), received by the individual during the testing period which is includible in gross income, and

"(ii) any distribution from a Roth IRA or a Roth account received by the individual during the testing period which is not a qualified rollover contribution (as defined in section 408A(e)) to a Roth IRA or a rollover under section 402(c)(8)(B) to a Roth account."

Effective Date (Sec. 411(x), P.L. 107-147, 3/9/2002) effective for tax. yrs. begin. after 12/31/2001.

Matter in *italics* in Code Sec. 25B(h) was added by Sec. 417(1), P.L. 107-147, 3/9/2002, which struck out:

2. "(g)"

Effective Date effective 3/9/2002.

Note Sec. 601(b)(2), P.L. 107-147, 3/9/2002, following, provides rules for applying amendment made by Sec. 618(b) of P.L. 107-16. Sec. 601(b)(2), P.L. 107-147, reads as follows:

"(2) The amendments made by sections 201(b), 202(f), and 618(b) of the Economic Growth and Tax Relief Reconciliation Act of 2001 [P.L. 107-16] shall not apply to taxable years beginning during 2002 and 2003."

Note The amendment made by Sec. 618(b), P.L. 107-16, is as follows:

Sec. 618(b)(1) added subsec. (g), relating to "Limitation based on amount of tax".

[¶ 3006]
Code Sec. 26.   Limitation based on tax liability; definition of tax liability.
(a) Limitation based on amount of tax.

* * * * * * * * * * * *

(2) Special ¹*rule for 2000, 2001, 2002, and 2003.* For purposes of any taxable year beginning ²*during 2000, 2001, 2002, or 2003,* the aggregate amount of credits allowed by this subpart for the taxable year shall not exceed the sum of—

(A) the taxpayer's regular tax liability for the taxable year reduced by the foreign tax credit allowable under section 27(a), and

(B) the tax imposed by section 55(a) for the taxable year.

(b) Regular tax liability. For purposes of this part—

(1) In general. The term "regular tax liability" means the tax imposed by this chapter for the taxable year.

(2) Exception for certain taxes.

* * * * * * * * * * * *

(P) section 860K (relating to treatment of transfers of high-yield interests to disqualified holders),³

(Q) section 220(f)(4) (relating to additional tax on Archer MSA distributions not used for qualified medical expenses)⁴, *and*

⁵*(R) section 138(c)(2) (relating to penalty for distributions from Medicare+Choice MSA not used for qualified medical expenses if minimum balance not maintained).*

* * * * * * * * * * * *

[For Analysis, see ¶ 401, ¶ 410. For Committee Reports, see ¶ 5060, ¶ 5069.]

[Endnote Code Sec. 26]

Matter in *italics* in Code Sec. 26(a)(2) was added by Sec. 601(a)(1) and (2) of the Job Creation and Worker Assistance Act of 2002, P.L. 107-147, 3/9/2002, which struck out:

1. "Rule for 2000 and 2001."
2. "during 2000 or 2001,"

Effective Date (Sec. 601(c), P.L. 107-147, 3/9/2002) effective for tax. yrs. begin. after 12/31/2001.

Matter in *italics* in Code Sec. 26(b)(2)(P), Code Sec. 26(b)(2)(Q) and Code Sec. 26(b)(2)(R) added by Sec. 415(a), P.L. 107-147, 3/9/2002, which struck out:

3. "and"
4. "."
5. added subpara. (b)(2)(R)

Effective Date (Sec. 415(b), P.L. 107-147, 3/9/2002) effective for tax. yrs. begin. after 12/31/98.

Note Sec. 601(b)(2), P.L. 107-147, 3/9/2002, following, provides rules for applying amendments made by Sec. 201(b), 202(f) and 618(b) of P.L. 107-16. Sec. 601(b)(2), P.L. 107-147, reads as follows:

"(2) The amendments made by sections 201(b), 202(f), and 618(b) of the Economic Growth and Tax Relief Reconciliation Act of 2001 [P.L. 107-16] shall not apply to taxable years beginning during 2002 and 2003."

Note The amendments made by Secs. 201(b), 202(f) and 618(b), P.L. 107-16, are as follows:

Sec. 201(b)(2)(D) added "(other than section 24)" after "this subpart" in para. (a)(1).

Sec. 202(f)(2)(C) substituted "sections 23 and 24" for "section 24" in para. (a)(1) [as amended by Sec. 201(b)(2)(D), see above].

Sec. 618(b)(2)(C) substituted ", 24, and 25B" for "and 24" in para. (a)(1) [as amended by Secs. 201(b)(2)(D) and 202(f)(2)(C), see above].

[¶ 3007]
Code Sec. 30.   Credit for qualified electric vehicles.

* * * * * * * * * * * *

(2) Phaseout. In the case of any qualified electric vehicle placed in service after [1]*December 31, 2003*, the credit otherwise allowable under subsection (a) (determined after the application of paragraph (1)) shall be reduced by—

(A) 25 percent in the case of property placed in service in calendar year [2]*2004*,
(B) 50 percent in the case of property placed in service in calendar year [3]*2005*, and
(C) 75 percent in the case of property placed in service in calendar year [4]*2006*.

* * * * * * * * * * * *

(e) Termination. This section shall not apply to any property placed in service after [5]*December 31, 2006*.

[For Analysis, see ¶ 211. For Committee Reports, see ¶ 5070.]

[Endnote Code Sec. 30]

Matter in *italics* in Code Sec. 30(b)(2) and Code Sec. 30(e) was added by Sec. 602(a) of the Job Creation and Worker Assistance Act of 2002, P.L. 107-147, 3/9/2002, which struck out:

1. "December 31, 2001,"
2. "2002"
3. "2003"
4. "2004"
5. "December 31, 2004"

Effective Date (Sec. 602(c), P.L. 107-147, 3/9/2002) effective for property placed in service after 12/31/2001.

[¶ 3008]
Code Sec. 32.   Earned income.

* * * * * * * * * * *

(g) Coordination with advance payments of earned income credit.

(1) Recapture of excess advance payments. If any payment is made to the individual by an employer under section 3507 during any calendar year, then the tax imposed by this chapter for the individual's last taxable year beginning in such calendar year shall be increased by the aggregate amount of such payments.

(2) Reconciliation of payments advanced and credit allowed. Any increase in tax under paragraph (1) shall not be treated as tax imposed by this chapter for purposes of determining the amount of any credit (other than the credit allowed by subsection (a)) allowable under this [1]*part.*

* * * * * * * * * * *

[For Analysis, see ¶ 408. For Committee Reports, see ¶ 5061.]

[Endnote Code Sec. 32]

Matter in *italics* in Code Sec. 32(g)(2) added by Sec. 416(a)(1) of the Job Creation and Worker Assistance Act of 2002, P.L. 107-147, 3/9/2002, which struck out:

1. "subpart"

Effective Date (Sec. 416(a)(2), P.L. 107-147, 3/9/2002) effective for tax. yrs. begin. after 12/31/83, and to carrybacks from such years.

[¶ 3009]
Code Sec. 38.   General business credit.

* * * * * * * * * * *

(b) Current year business credit. For purposes of this subpart, the amount of the current year business credit is the sum of the following credits determined for the taxable year:

(1) the investment credit determined under section 46,

(2) the work opportunity credit determined under section 51(a),

(3) the alcohol fuels credit determined under section 40(a),

(4) the research credit determined under section 41(a),

(5) the low-income housing credit determined under section 42(a),

(6) the enhanced oil recovery credit under section 43(a),

(7) in the case of an eligible small business (as defined in section 44(b)), the disabled access credit determined under section 44(a),

(8) the renewable electricity production credit under section 45(a),

(9) the empowerment zone employment credit determined under section 1396(a),

(10) the Indian employment credit as determined under section 45A(a),

(11) the employer social security credit determined under section 45B(a),

(12) the orphan drug credit determined under section 45C(a),

(13) the new markets tax credit determined under section 45D(a),

(14) in the case of an eligible employer (as defined in section 45E(c)), the small employer pension plan startup cost credit determined under section 45E(a), plus

(15) the employer-provided child care credit determined under [1]*section 45F(a).*

(c) Limitation based on amount of tax.

* * * * * * * * * * *

(2) Empowerment zone employment credit may offset 25 percent of minimum tax.

(A) In general. In the case of the empowerment zone employment credit credit—

(i) this section and section 39 shall be applied separately with respect to such credit, and

(ii) for purposes of applying paragraph (1) to such credit—

(I) 75 percent of the tentative minimum tax shall be substituted for the tentative minimum tax under subparagraph (A) thereof, and

(II) the limitation under paragraph (1) (as modified by subclause (I)) shall be reduced by the credit allowed under subsection (a) for the taxable year (other than the empowerment zone employment credit [2]*or the New York Liberty Zone business employee credit).*

(B) Empowerment zone employment credit. For purposes of this paragraph, the term "empowerment zone employment credit" means the portion of the credit under subsection (a) which is attributable to the credit determined under section 1396 (relating to empowerment zone employment credit).

[3]*(3) Special rules for New York Liberty Zone business employee credit.*

(A) In general. In the case of the New York Liberty Zone business employee credit—

(i) this section and section 39 shall be applied separately with respect to such credit, and

(ii) in applying paragraph (1) to such credit—

(I) the tentative minimum tax shall be treated as being zero, and

(II) the limitation under paragraph (1) (as modified by subclause (I)) shall be reduced by the credit allowed under subsection (a) for the taxable year (other than the New York Liberty Zone business employee credit).

(B) New York Liberty Zone business employee credit. For purposes of this subsection, the term "New York Liberty Zone business employee credit" means the portion of work opportunity credit under section 51 determined under section 1400L(a).

[4]*(4) Special rules.*

(A) Married individuals. In the case of a husband or wife who files a separate return, the amount specified under subparagraph (B) of paragraph (1) shall be $12,500 in lieu of $25,000. This subparagraph shall not apply if the spouse of the taxpayer has no business credit carryforward or carryback to, and has no current year business credit for, the taxable year of such spouse which ends within or with the taxpayer's taxable year.

(B) Controlled groups. In the case of a controlled group, the $25,000 amount specified under subparagraph (B) of paragraph (1) shall be reduced for each component member of such group by apportioning $25,000 among the component members of such group in such manner as the Secretary shall by regulations prescribe. For purposes of the preceding sentence, the term "controlled group" has the meaning given to such term by section 1563(a).

(C) Limitations with respect to certain persons. In the case of a person described in subparagraph (A) or (B) of section 46(e)(1) (as in effect on the day before the date of the enactment of the Revenue Reconciliation Act of 1990), the $25,000 amount specified under subparagraph (B) of paragraph (1) shall equal such person's ratable share (as determined under section 46(e)(2) (as so in effect)) of such amount.

(D) Estates and trusts. In the case of an estate or trust, the $25,000 amount specified under subparagraph (B) of paragraph (1) shall be reduced to an amount which bears the same ratio to $25,000 as the portion of the income of the estate or trust which is not allocated to beneficiaries bears to the total income of the estate or trust.

* * * * * * * * * * * *

[For Analysis, see ¶ 506. For Committee Reports, see ¶ 5011.]

[Endnote Code Sec. 38]

Matter in *italics* in Code Sec. 38(b)(15) was added by Sec. 411(d)(2) of the Job Creation and Worker Assistance Act of 2002, P.L. 107-147, 3/9/2002, which struck out:

1. "45F"

Effective Date (Sec. 411(x), P.L. 107-147, 3/9/2002) effective for tax. yrs. begin. after 12/31/2001.

Matter in *italics* in Code Sec. 38(c)(2)(A)(ii)(II), Code Sec. 38(c)(3) and Code Sec. 38(c)(4) added by Sec. 301(b)(1) and (2), P.L. 107-147, 3/9/2002, which struck out:

2. added matter in subclause (c)(2)(A)(ii)(II)
3. added para. (c)(3)
4. "(3)"
Effective Date (Sec. 301(b)(3), P.L. 107-147, 3/9/2002) effective for tax. yrs. end. after 12/31/2001.

[¶ 3010]
Code Sec. 42.   Low-income housing credit.

* * * * * * * * * * *

(h) Limitation on aggregate credit allowable with respect to projects located in a state.

* * * * * * * * * * *

(3) Housing credit dollar amount for agencies.

* * * * * * * * * * *

(C) State housing credit ceiling. The State housing credit ceiling applicable to any State for any calendar year shall be an amount equal to the sum of—
(i) the unused State housing credit ceiling (if any) of such State for the preceding calendar year,
(ii) the greater of—
(I) $1.75 ($1.50 for 2001) multiplied by the State population, or
(II) $2,000,000,
(iii) the amount of State housing credit ceiling returned in the calendar year, plus
(iv) the amount (if any) allocated under subparagraph (D) to such State by the Secretary.
For purposes of clause (i), the unused State housing credit ceiling for any calendar year is the excess (if any) of the sum of [1]*the amounts described in clauses (ii) through (iv) over the aggregate housing credit dollar amount allocated for such year.* For purposes of clause (iii), the amount of State housing credit ceiling returned in the calendar year equals the housing credit dollar amount previously allocated within the State to any project which fails to meet the 10 percent test under paragraph (1)(E)(ii) on a date after the close of the calendar year in which the allocation was made or which does not become a qualified low-income housing project within the period required by this section or the terms of the allocation or to any project with respect to which an allocation is cancelled by mutual consent of the housing credit agency and the allocation recipient.

* * * * * * * * * * *

(m) Responsibilities of housing credit agencies.

* * * * * * * * * * *

(1) Plans for allocation of credit among projects.

* * * * * * * * * * *

(B) Qualified allocation plan. For purposes of this paragraph, the term "qualified allocation plan" means any plan—
(i) which sets forth selection criteria to be used to determine housing priorities of the housing credit agency which are appropriate to local conditions,
(ii) which also gives preference in allocating housing credit dollar amounts among selected projects to—
(I) projects serving the lowest income tenants,
(II) projects obligated to serve qualified tenants for the longest periods, and[2]
(III) projects which are located in qualified census tracts (as defined in subsection (d)(5)(C)) and the development of which contributes to a concerted community revitalization plan, [3]*and*
(iii) which provides a procedure that the agency (or an agent or other private contractor of such agency) will follow in monitoring for noncompliance with the provisions of

this section and in notifying the Internal Revenue Service of such noncompliance which such agency becomes aware of and in monitoring for noncompliance with habitability standards through regular site visits.

* * * * * * * * * * *

[Endnote Code Sec. 42]

Matter in *italics* in Code Sec. 42(h)(3)(C) and Code Sec. 42(m)(1)(B)(ii) was added by Sec. 417(2) and (3) of the Job Creation and Worker Assistance Act of 2002, P.L. 107-147, 3/9/2002, which struck out:

1. "the amounts described in clauses (i) [(ii)] through (iv) over the aggregate housing credit dollar amount allocated for such year."

2. "and"

3. added matter in subclause (m)(1)(B)(ii)(III)

Effective Date effective 3/9/2002.

[¶ 3011]

Code Sec. 45.   Electricity produced from certain renewable resources.

* * * * * * * * * * *

(c) **Definitions.** For purposes of this section —

(1) **Qualified energy resources.** The term "qualified energy resources" means —

(A) wind,

(B) closed-loop biomass, and

(C) poultry waste.

(2) **Closed-loop biomass.** The term "closed-loop biomass" means any organic material from a plant which is planted exclusively for purposes of being used at a qualified facility to produce electricity.

(3) **Qualified facility.**

(A) Wind facility. In the case of a facility using wind to produce electricity, the term "qualified facility" means any facility owned by the taxpayer which is originally placed in service after December 31, 1993, and before January 1, [1]*2004.*

(B) Closed-loop biomass facility. In the case of a facility using closed-loop biomass to produce electricity, the term "qualified facility" means any facility owned by the taxpayer which is originally placed in service after December 31, 1992, and before January 1, [2]*2004.*

(C) Poultry waste facility. In the case of a facility using poultry waste to produce electricity, the term "qualified facility" means any facility of the taxpayer which is originally placed in service after December 31, 1999, and before January 1, [3]*2004.*

* * * * * * * * * * *

[For Analysis, see ¶ 205. For Committee Reports, see ¶ 5071.]

[Endnote Code Sec. 45]

Matter in *italics* in Code Sec. 45(c)(3)(A)-(C) was added by Sec. 603(a) of the Job Creation and Worker Assistance Act of 2002, P.L. 107-147, 3/9/2002, which struck out:

1. "2002"

2. "2002"

3. "2002"

Effective Date (Sec. 603(b), P.L. 107-147, 3/9/2002) effective for facilities placed in service after 12/21/2001.

[¶ 3012]
Code Sec. 45A.   Indian employment credit.

* * * * * * * * * * * *

(f) Termination. This section shall not apply to taxable years beginning after [1]*December 31, 2004.*

[For Analysis, see ¶ 215. For Committee Reports, see ¶ 5081.]

[Endnote Code Sec. 45A]

Matter in *italics* in Code Sec. 45A(f) was added by Sec. 613(a) of the Job Creation and Worker Assistance Act of 2002, P.L. 107-147, 3/9/2002, which struck out:

1. "December 31, 2003"

Effective Date effective 3/9/2002.

[¶ 3013]
Code Sec. 45E.   Small employer pension plan startup costs.

* * * * * * * * * * * *

(e) Special rules. For purposes of this section—

(1) Aggregation rules. All persons treated as a single employer under subsection (a) or (b) of section 52, or subsection [1]*(m)* or (o) of section 414, shall be treated as one person. All eligible employer plans shall be treated as 1 eligible employer plan.

(2) Disallowance of deduction. No deduction shall be allowed for that portion of the qualified startup costs paid or incurred for the taxable year which is equal to the credit determined under subsection (a).

(3) Election not to claim credit. This section shall not apply to a taxpayer for any taxable year if such taxpayer elects to have this section not apply for such taxable year.

[For Analysis, see ¶ 315, ¶ 316. For Committee Reports, see ¶ 5044.]

[Endnote Code Sec. 45E]

Matter in *italics* in Code Sec. 45E(e)(1) was added by Sec. 411(n)(1) of the Job Creation and Worker Assistance Act of 2002, P.L. 107-147, 3/9/2002, which struck out:

1. "(n)"

Effective Date (Sec. 411(x), P.L. 107-147, 3/9/2002) effective for costs paid or incurred in tax. yrs. begin. after 12/31/2001, with respect to qualified employer plans first effective after 12/31/2001.

[¶ 3014]
Code Sec. 45F.   Employer-provided child care credit.

* * * * * * * * * * * *

(d) Recapture of acquisition and construction credit.

* * * * * * * * * * * *

(4) Special rules.

* * * * * * * * * * * *

(B) No credits against tax. Any increase in tax under this subsection shall not be treated as a tax imposed by this chapter for purposes of determining the amount of any credit under [1]*this chapter or for purposes of section 55.*

* * * * * * * * * * * *

[For Analysis, see ¶ 108. For Committee Reports, see ¶ 5034.]

[Endnote Code Sec. 45F]

Matter in *italics* in Code Sec. 45F(d)(4)(B) was added by Sec. 411(d)(1) of the Job Creation and Worker Assistance Act of 2002, P.L. 107-147, 3/9/2002, which struck out:

1. "subpart A, B, or D of this part"

Effective Date (Sec. 411(x), P.L. 107-147, 3/9/2002) effective for tax. yrs. begin. after 12/31/2001.

[¶ 3015]
Code Sec. 51.　　Amount of credit.

* * * * * * * * * * *

(c) Wages defined. For purposes of this subpart—

* * * * * * * * * * *

(4) Termination. The term "wages" shall not include any amount paid or incurred to an individual who begins work for the employer—

(A) after December 31, 1994, and before October 1, 1996, or

(B) after December 31, [1]*2003.*

* * * * * * * * * * *

[For Analysis, see ¶ 202. For Committee Reports, see ¶ 5072.]

[Endnote Code Sec. 51]

Matter in *italics* in Code Sec. 51(c)(4)(B) was added by Sec. 604(a) of the Job Creation and Worker Assistance Act of 2002, P.L. 107-147, 3/9/2002, which struck out:

1. "2001"

Effective Date (Sec. 604(b), P.L. 107-147, 3/9/2002) effective for individuals who begin work for the employer after 12/31/2001.

[¶ 3016]
Code Sec. 51A.　　Temporary incentives for employing long-term family assistance recipients.

* * * * * * * * * * *

(c) Long-term family assistance recipients. For purposes of this section—

(1) In general. The term "long-term family assistance recipient" means any individual who is certified by the designated local agency (as defined in section [1]*51(d)(11))*—

(A) as being a member of a family receiving assistance under a IV-A program (as defined in section 51(d)(2)(B)) for at least the 18-month period ending on the hiring date,

(B) (i) as being a member of a family receiving such assistance for 18 months beginning after the date of the enactment of this section, and

(ii) as having a hiring date which is not more than 2 years after the end of the earliest such 18-month period, or

(C) (i) as being a member of a family which ceased to be eligible after the date of the enactment of this section for such assistance by reason of any limitation imposed by Federal or State law on the maximum period such assistance is payable to a family, and

(ii) as having a hiring date which is not more than 2 years after the date of such cessation.

* * * * * * * * * * *

(f) Termination. This section shall not apply to individuals who begin work for the employer after December 31, [2]*2003.*

[For Analysis, see ¶ 201. For Committee Reports, see ¶ 5073.]

[Endnote Code Sec. 51A]

Matter in Code Sec. 51A(c)(1) was added by Sec. 417(4) of the Job Creation and Worker Assistance Act of 2002, P.L. 107-147, 3/9/2002, which struck out:
   1. "51(d)(10)"
Effective Date effective 3/9/2002.

Matter in *italics* in Code Sec. 51A(f) was added by Sec. 605(a), P.L. 107-147, 3/9/2002, which struck out:
   2. "2001"
Effective Date (Sec. 605(b), P.L. 107-147, 3/9/2002) effective for individuals who begin work for the employer after 12/31/2001.

[¶ 3017]
Code Sec. 56.   **Adjustments in computing alternative minimum taxable income.**

  (a) Adjustments applicable to all taxpayers. In determining the amount of the alternative minimum taxable income for any taxable year the following treatment shall apply (in lieu of the treatment applicable for purposes of computing the regular tax):

   (1) Depreciation.

    (A) In general.

     (i) Property other than certain personal property. Except as provided in clause (ii), the depreciation deduction allowable under section 167 with respect to any tangible property placed in service after December 31, 1986, shall be determined under the alternative system of section 168(g). In the case of property placed in service after December 31, 1998, the preceding sentence shall not apply but clause (ii) shall continue to apply.

     (ii) 150-percent declining balance method for certain property. The method of depreciation used shall be—

      (I) the 150 percent declining balance method,

      (II) switching to the straight line method for the 1st taxable year for which using the straight line method with respect to the adjusted basis as of the beginning of the year will yield a higher allowance.

    The preceding sentence shall not apply to any section 1250 property (as defined in section 1250(c)) (and the straight line method shall be used for [1]*such section 1250* property) or to any other property if the depreciation deduction determined under section 168 with respect to such other property for purposes of the regular tax is determined by using the straight line method.

* * * * * * * * * * * *

  (d) Alternative tax net operating loss deduction defined.

   (1) In general. For purposes of subsection (a)(4), the term "alternative tax net operating loss deduction" means the net operating loss deduction allowable for the taxable year under section 172, except that—

   [2]*(A) the amount of such deduction shall not exceed the sum of—*

    (i) the lesser of—

     (I) the amount of such deduction attributable to net operating losses (other than the deduction attributable to carryovers described in clause (ii)(I)), or

     (II) 90 percent of alternative minimum taxable income determined without regard to such deduction, plus

    (ii) the lesser of—

     (I) the amount of such deduction attributable to the sum of carrybacks of net operating losses for taxable years ending during 2001 or 2002 and carryforwards of net operating losses to taxable years ending during 2001 and 2002, or

     (II) alternative minimum taxable income determined without regard to such deduction reduced by the amount determined under clause (i), and

* * * * * * * * * * * *

[For Analysis, see ¶ 104. For Committee Reports, see ¶ 5002.]

[Endnote Code Sec. 56]

Matter in *italics* in Code Sec. 56(a)(1)(A) was added by Sec. 417(5) of the Job Creation and Worker Assistance Act of 2002, P.L. 107-147, 3/9/2002, which struck out:

1. "such 1250"

Effective Date effective 3/9/2002.

Code Sec. 56(d)(1)(A), in *italics*, was added by Sec. 102(c)(1), P.L. 107-147, 3/9/2002, which struck out:

2. "(A) the amount of such deduction shall not exceed 90 percent of alternate minimum taxable income determined without regard to such deduction, and"

Effective Date (Sec. 102(c)(2), P.L. 107-147, 3/9/2002) effective for tax. yrs. end. before 1/1/2003.

[¶ 3018]
Code Sec. 62.   Adjusted gross income defined.

(a) General rule. For purposes of this subtitle, the term "adjusted gross income" means, in the case of an individual, gross income minus the following deductions:

* * * * * * * * * * * *

(2) Certain trade and business deductions of employees.

* * * * * * * * * * * *

[1]*(D) Certain expenses of elementary and secondary school teachers. In the case of taxable years beginning during 2002 or 2003, the deductions allowed by section 162 which consist of expenses, not in excess of $250, paid or incurred by an eligible educator in connection with books, supplies (other than nonathletic supplies for courses of instruction in health or physical education), computer equipment (including related software and services) and other equipment, and supplementary materials used by the eligible educator in the classroom.*

* * * * * * * * * * * *

[2]*(d) Definition; special rules.*

(1) Eligible educator.

(A) In general. For purposes of subsection (a)(2)(D), the term "eligible educator" means, with respect to any taxable year, an individual who is a kindergarten through grade 12 teacher, instructor, counselor, principal, or aide in a school for at least 900 hours during a school year.

(B) School. The term "school" means any school which provides elementary education or secondary education (kindergarten through grade 12), as determined under State law.

(2) Coordination with exclusions. A deduction shall be allowed under subsection (a)(2)(D) for expenses only to the extent the amount of such expenses exceeds the amount excludable under section 135, 529(c)(1), or 530(d)(2) for the taxable year.

[For Analysis, see ¶ 405. For Committee Reports, see ¶ 5026.]

[Endnote Code Sec. 62]

Code Sec. 62(a)(2)(D) and Code Sec. 62(d), in *italics*§, was added by Sec. 406(a) and (b) of the Job Creation and Worker Assistance Act of 2002, P.L. 107-147, 3/9/2002.

1. added subpara. (a)(2)(D)

2. added subsec. (d)

Effective Date (Sec. 406(c), P.L. 107-147, 3/9/2002) effective for tax. yrs. begin. after 12/31/2001.

[¶ 3019]
Code Sec. 63.   Taxable income defined.

* * * * * * * * * * *

(c) Standard deduction. For purposes of this subtitle—

(1) In general. Except as otherwise provided in this subsection, the term "standard deduction" means the sum of—

(A) the basic standard deduction, and

(B) the additional standard deduction.

(2) Basic standard deduction. For purposes of paragraph (1), the basic standard deduction is—

(A) the applicable percentage of the dollar amount in effect under [1]*subparagraph (D)* for the taxable year in the case of—

(i) a joint return, or

(ii) a surviving spouse (as defined in section 2(a)),

(B) $4,400 in the case of a head of household (as defined in section 2(b)),[2]

[3]*(C) one-half of the amount in effect under subparagraph (A) in the case of a married individual filing a separate return, or*

[4]*(D) $3,000 in any other case.*

[5]*If any amount determined under subparagraph (A) is not a multiple of $50, such amount shall be rounded to the next lowest multiple of $50.*

(3) Additional standard deduction for aged and blind. For purposes of paragraph (1), the additional standard deduction is the sum of each additional amount to which the taxpayer is entitled under subsection (f).

(4) Adjustments for inflation. In the case of any taxable year beginning in a calendar year after 1988, each dollar amount contained in [6]*paragraph (2)(B), (2)(D), or (5)* or subsection (f) shall be increased by an amount equal to—

(A) such dollar amount, multiplied by

(B) the cost-of-living adjustment determined under section 1(f)(3) for the calendar year in which the taxable year begins, by substituting for "calendar year 1992" in subparagraph (B) thereof—

(i) "calendar year 1987" in the case of the dollar amounts contained in [7]*paragraph (2)(B), (2)(D), or (5)(A)* or subsection (f), and

(ii) "calendar year 1997" in the case of the dollar amount contained in paragraph (5)(B).[8]

* * * * * * * * * * *

[For Analysis, see ¶ 417. For Committee Reports, see ¶ 5035.]

[Endnote Code Sec. 63]

Matter in *italics* in Code Sec. 63(c)(2) and Code Sec. 63(c)(4) was added by Sec. 411(e)(1)(A)-(E) and (e)(2)(A)-(C) of the Job Creation and Worker Assistance Act of 2002, P.L. 107-147, 3/9/2002, which struck out:

1. "subparagraph (C)"
2. "or"
3. added subpara. (c)(2)(C)
4. "(C)"
5. added matter in para. (c)(2)
6. "paragraph (2) or (5)"
7. "paragraph (2)"
8. "The preceding sentence shall not apply to the amount referred to in paragraph (2)(A)."

Effective Date (Sec. 411(x), P.L. 107-147, 3/9/2002) effective for tax. yrs. begin. after 12/31/2004.

 Research Institute of America   **315**

[¶ 3020]
Code Sec. 108.   Income from discharge of indebtedness.

* * * * * * * * * * *

(d) Meaning of terms; special rules relating to certain provisions.

* * * * * * * * * * *

(7) Special rules for S corporation.

(A) Certain provisions to be applied at corporate level. In the case of an S corporation, subsections (a), (b), (c), and (g) shall be applied at the corporate level [1], *including by not taking into account under section 1366(a) any amount excluded under subsection (a) of this section.*

* * * * * * * * * * *

[For Analysis, see ¶ 105. For Committee Reports, see ¶ 5022.]

[Endnote Code Sec. 108]
Matter in *italics* in Code Sec. 108(d)(7)(A) was added by Sec. 402(a) of the Job Creation and Worker Assistance Act of 2002, P.L. 107-147, 3/9/2002.
  1. added matter in subpara. (d)(7)(A)
Effective Date (Sec. 402(b), P.L. 107-147, 3/9/2002) effective for discharges of indebtedness after 10/11/2001, in tax. yrs. end. after 10/11/2001, except as provided in Sec 402(b)(2) of this Act, which reads as follows:
  "(2) Exception. The amendment made by this section shall not apply to any discharge of indebtedness before March 1, 2002, pursuant to a plan of reorganization filed with a bankruptcy court on or before October 11, 2001."

[¶ 3021]
Code Sec. 131.   Certain foster care payments.

* * * * * * * * * * *

(b) Qualified foster care payment defined. For purposes of this section
  [1]*(1) In general. The term "qualified foster care payment" means any payment made pursuant to a foster care program of a State or political subdivision thereof—*
    (A) which is paid by—
      (i) a State or political subdivision thereof, or
      (ii) a qualified foster care placement agency, and
    (B) which is—
      (i) paid to the foster care provider for caring for a qualified foster individual in the foster care provider's home, or
      (ii) a difficulty of care payment.
  (2) Qualified foster individual. The term "qualified foster individual" means any individual who is living in a foster family home in which such individual was placed by—
    (A) an agency of a State or political subdivision thereof, or
    [2]*(B) a qualified foster care placement agency.*
  [3]*(3) Qualified foster care placement agency. The term "qualified foster care placement agency" means any placement agency which is licensed or certified by—*
    (A) a State or political subdivision thereof, or
    (B) an entity designated by a State or political subdivision thereof,
  for the foster care program of such State or political subdivision to make foster care payments to providers of foster care.
  [4]*(4)* **Limitation based on number of individuals over the age of 18.** In the case of any foster home in which there is a qualified foster care individual who has attained age 19, foster care payments (other than difficulty of care payments) for any period to which such payments

relate shall not be excludable from gross income under subsection (a) to the extent such payments are made for more than 5 such qualified foster individuals.

* * * * * * * * * * * *

[For Analysis, see ¶ 415, ¶ 416. For Committee Reports, see ¶ 5024.]

[Endnote Code Sec. 131]

Matter in *italics* in Code Sec. 131(b)(1), Code Sec. 131(b)(2)(B), Code Sec. 131(b)(3) and Code Sec. 131(b)(4) was added by Sec. 404(a)-(c) of the Job Creation and Worker Assistance Act of 2002, P.L. 107-147, 3/9/2002, which struck out:

1. "(1) In general. The term 'qualified foster care payment' means any amount—
"(A) which is paid by a State or political subdivision thereof or by a placement agency which is described in section 501(c)(3) and exempt from tax under section 501(a), and"
2. "(B) in the case of an individual who has not attained age 19, an organization which is licensed by a State (or political subdivision thereof) as a placement agency and which is described in section 501(c)(3) and exempt from tax under section 501(a)."
3. added para. (b)(3)
4. "(3)"

Effective Date (Sec. 404(c), P.L. 107-147, 3/9/2002) effective for tax. yrs. begin. after 12/31/2001.

[¶ 3022]
Code Sec. 137.   Adoption assistance programs.

¹*(a) Exclusion.*

(1) In general. Gross income of an employee does not include amounts paid or expenses incurred by the employer for qualified adoption expenses in connection with the adoption of a child by an employee if such amounts are furnished pursuant to an adoption assistance program.

(2) $10,000 Exclusion for adoption of child with special needs regardless of expenses. In the case of an adoption of a child with special needs which becomes final during a taxable year, the qualified adoption expenses with respect to such adoption for such year shall be increased by an amount equal to the excess (if any) of $10,000 over the actual aggregate qualified adoption expenses with respect to such adoption during such taxable year and all prior taxable years.

(b) Limitations.

(1) Dollar limitation. The aggregate of the amounts paid or expenses incurred which may be taken into account under ²*subsection (a)* for all taxable years with respect to the adoption of a child by the taxpayer shall not exceed $10,000.

(2) Income limitation. The amount excludable from gross income under subsection (a) for any taxable year shall be reduced (but not below zero) by an amount which bears the same ratio to the amount so excludable (determined without regard to this paragraph but with regard to paragraph (1)) as—

(A) the amount (if any) by which the taxpayer's adjusted gross income exceeds $150,000, bears to

(B) $40,000.

* * * * * * * * * * * *

(3) Determination of adjusted gross income. For purposes of paragraph (2), adjusted gross income shall be determined—

(A) without regard to this section and sections 221, 222, 911, 931, and 933, and

(B) after the application of sections 86, 135, 219, and 469.

* * * * * * * * * * * *

(f) Adjustments for inflation. In the case of a taxable year beginning after December 31, 2002, each of the dollar amounts in subsection (a)(2) and paragraphs (1) and (2)(A) of subsection (b) shall be increased by an amount equal to—

(1) such dollar amount, multiplied by

(2) the cost-of-living adjustment determined under section 1(f)(3) for the calendar year in which the taxable year begins, determined by substituting "calendar year 2001" for "calendar year 1992" in subparagraph (B) thereof.

³*If any amount as increased under the preceding sentence is not a multiple of $10, such amount shall be rounded to the nearest multiple of $10.*

[For Analysis, see ¶411, ¶414. For Committee Reports, see ¶5033, ¶5067.]

[Endnote Code Sec. 137]

Code Sec. 137(a), in *italics*, was added by Sec. 411(c)(2)(A) of the Job Creation and Worker Assistance Act of 2002, P.L. 107-147, 3/9/2002, which struck out:

1. "(a) In general.

"Gross income of an employee does not include amounts paid or expenses incurred by the employer for adoption expenses in connection with the adoption of a child by an employee if such amounts are furnished pursuant to an adoption assistance program. The amount of the exclusion shall be—

"(1) in the case of an adoption of a child other than a child with special needs, the amount of the qualified adoption expenses paid or incurred by the taxpayer, and

"(2) in the case of an adoption of a child with special needs, $10,000."

Effective Date (Sec. 411(c)(3), P.L. 107-147, 3/9/2002) effective for tax. yrs. begin. after 12/31/2002.

Matter in *italics* in Code Sec. 137(b)(2) [sic (1)] was added by Sec. 411(c)(2)(B), P.L. 107-147, 3/9/2002, which struck out:

2. "subsection (a)(1)"

Effective Date (Sec. 411(c)(3), P.L. 107-147, 3/9/2002) effective for tax. yrs. begin. after 12/31/2001.

Matter in *italics* in Code Sec. 137(f) was added by Sec. 418(a)(2), P.L. 107-147, 3/9/2002.

3. added matter in subsec. (f)

Effective Date (Sec. 418(c), P.L. 107-147, 3/9/2002) effective for tax. yrs. begin. after 12/31/2001.

[¶3023]
Code Sec. 151.   Allowance of deductions for personal exemptions.

* * * * * * * * * * * *

(c) Additional exemption for dependents.

* * * * * * * * * * * *

(6) Treatment of missing children.

(A) In general. Solely for the purposes referred to in subparagraph (B), a child of the taxpayer—

(i) who is presumed by law enforcement authorities to have been kidnapped by someone who is not a member of the family of such child or the taxpayer, and

(ii) who was (without regard to this paragraph) the dependent of the taxpayer for the portion of the taxable year before the date of the kidnapping,

shall be treated as a dependent of the taxpayer for all taxable years ending during the period that the child is kidnapped.

(B) Purposes. Subparagraph (A) shall apply solely for purposes of determining—

(i) the deduction under this section,

(ii) the credit under section 24 (relating to child tax credit), and

(iii) whether an individual is a surviving spouse or a head of a household (¹*as such terms are defined in section 2*).

(C) Comparable treatment ²*for principal place of abode requirements. An* individual—

(i) who is presumed by law enforcement authorities to have been kidnapped by someone who is not a member of the family of such individual or the taxpayer, and

(ii) who had, for the taxable year in which the kidnapping occurred, the same principal place of abode as the taxpayer for more than one-half of the portion of such year before the date of the kidnapping,

shall be treated as meeting the ³*principal place of abode requirements of section 2(a)(1)(B), section 2(b)(1)(A), and section 32(c)(3)(A)(ii)* with respect to a taxpayer for all taxable years ending during the period that the individual is kidnapped.

(D) Termination of treatment. Subparagraphs (A) and (C) shall cease to apply as of the first taxable year of the taxpayer beginning after the calendar year in which there is a determination that the child is dead (or, if earlier, in which the child would have attained age 18).

* * * * * * * * * * * *

[For Analysis, see ¶ 407. For Committee Reports, see ¶ 5055.]

[Endnote Code Sec. 151]
Matter in *italics* in Code Sec. 151(c)(6)(B)(iii) was added by Sec. 417(6) of the Job Creation and Worker Assistance Act of 2002, P.L. 107-147, 3/9/2002.
1. added matter in clause (c)(6)(B)(iii)
Effective Date effective 3/9/2002.

Matter in *italics* in Code Sec. 151(c)(6)(C) was added by Sec. 412(b)(1) and (2), P.L. 107-147, 3/9/2002, which struck out:
2. "for earned income credit. For purposes of section 32, an"
3. "requirement of section 32(c)(3)(A)(ii)"
Effective Date (Sec. 102(c)(2), P.L. 107-147, 3/9/2002) effective for tax. yrs. end. after 12/21/2000.

[¶ 3024]
Code Sec. 168.   Accelerated cost recovery system.

* * * * * * * * * * * *

(j) Property on Indian reservations.

* * * * * * * * * * * *

(8) Termination. This subsection shall not apply to property placed in service after [1]December 31, 2004.

[2]*(k) Special allowance for certain property acquired after September 10, 2001, and before September 11, 2004.*
(1) Additional allowance. In the case of any qualified property—
(A) the depreciation deduction provided by section 167(a) for the taxable year in which such property is placed in service shall include an allowance equal to 30 percent of the adjusted basis of the qualified property, and
(B) the adjusted basis of the qualified property shall be reduced by the amount of such deduction before computing the amount otherwise allowable as a depreciation deduction under this chapter for such taxable year and any subsequent taxable year.
(2) Qualified property. For purposes of this subsection—
(A) In general. The term "qualified property" means property—
(i) (I) to which this section applies which has a recovery period of 20 years or less,
(II) which is computer software (as defined in section 167(f)(1)(B)) for which a deduction is allowable under section 167(a) without regard to this subsection,
(III) which is water utility property, or
(IV) which is qualified leasehold improvement property,
(ii) the original use of which commences with the taxpayer after September 10, 2001,
(iii) which is—
(I) acquired by the taxpayer after September 10, 2001, and before September 11, 2004, but only if no written binding contract for the acquisition was in effect before September 11, 2001, or
(II) acquired by the taxpayer pursuant to a written binding contract which was entered into after September 10, 2001, and before September 11, 2004, and
(iv) which is placed in service by the taxpayer before January 1, 2005, or, in the case of property described in subparagraph (B), before January 1, 2006.
(B) Certain property having longer production periods treated as qualified property.

(i) In general. The term "qualified property" includes property—

(I) which meets the requirements of clauses (i), (ii), and (iii) of subparagraph (A),

(II) which has a recovery period of at least 10 years or is transportation property, and

(III) which is subject to section 263A by reason of clause (ii) or (iii) of subsection (f)(1)(B) thereof.

(ii) Only pre-September 11, 2004, basis eligible for additional allowance. In the case of property which is qualified property solely by reason of clause (i), paragraph (1) shall apply only to the extent of the adjusted basis thereof attributable to manufacture, construction, or production before September 11, 2004.

(iii) Transportation property. For purposes of this subparagraph, the term "transportation property" means tangible personal property used in the trade or business of transporting persons or property.

(C) Exceptions.

(i) Alternative depreciation property. The term "qualified property" shall not include any property to which the alternative depreciation system under subsection (g) applies, determined—

(I) without regard to paragraph (7) of subsection (g) (relating to election to have system apply), and

(II) after application of section 280F(b) (relating to listed property with limited business use).

(ii) Qualified New York Liberty Zone leasehold improvement property. The term "qualified property" shall not include any qualified New York Liberty Zone leasehold improvement property (as defined in section 1400L(c)(2)).

(iii) Election out. If a taxpayer makes an election under this clause with respect to any class of property for any taxable year, this subsection shall not apply to all property in such class placed in service during such taxable year.

(D) Special rules.

(i) Self-constructed property. In the case of a taxpayer manufacturing, constructing, or producing property for the taxpayer's own use, the requirements of clause (iii) of subparagraph (A) shall be treated as met if the taxpayer begins manufacturing, constructing, or producing the property after September 10, 2001, and before September 11, 2004.

(ii) Sale-leasebacks. For purposes of subparagraph (A)(ii), if property—

(I) is originally placed in service after September 10, 2001, by a person, and

(II) sold and leased back by such person within 3 months after the date such property was originally placed in service,

such property shall be treated as originally placed in service not earlier than the date on which such property is used under the leaseback referred to in subclause (II).

(E) Coordination with section 280F. For purposes of section 280F—

(i) Automobiles. In the case of a passenger automobile (as defined in section 280F(d)(5)) which is qualified property, the Secretary shall increase the limitation under section 280F(a)(1)(A)(i) by $4,600.

(ii) Listed property. The deduction allowable under paragraph (1) shall be taken into account in computing any recapture amount under section 280F(b)(2).

(F) Deduction allowed in computing minimum tax. For purposes of determining alternative minimum taxable income under section 55, the deduction under subsection (a) for qualified property shall be determined under this section without regard to any adjustment under section 56.

(3) Qualified leasehold improvement property. *For purposes of this subsection—*

(A) In general. The term "qualified leasehold improvement property" means any improvement to an interior portion of a building which is nonresidential real property if—

(i) such improvement is made under or pursuant to a lease (as defined in subsection (h)(7))—

(I) by the lessee (or any sublessee) of such portion, or

(II) by the lessor of such portion,

(ii) such portion is to be occupied exclusively by the lessee (or any sublessee) of such portion, and

(iii) such improvement is placed in service more than 3 years after the date the building was first placed in service.

(B) Certain improvements not included. Such term shall not include any improvement for which the expenditure is attributable to—

(i) the enlargement of the building,

(ii) any elevator or escalator,

(iii) any structural component benefiting a common area, and

(iv) the internal structural framework of the building.

(C) Definitions and special rules. For purposes of this paragraph—

(i) Commitment to lease treated as lease. A commitment to enter into a lease shall be treated as a lease, and the parties to such commitment shall be treated as lessor and lessee, respectively.

(ii) Related persons. A lease between related persons shall not be considered a lease. For purposes of the preceding sentence, the term "related persons" means—

(I) members of an affiliated group (as defined in section 1504), and

(II) persons having a relationship described in subsection (b) of section 267; except that, for purposes of this clause, the phrase "80 percent or more" shall be substituted for the phrase "more than 50 percent" each place it appears in such subsection.

[For Analysis, see ¶101, ¶102, ¶216. For Committee Reports, see ¶5001, ¶5081.]

[Endnote Code Sec. 168]

Matter in *italics* in Code Sec. 168(j)(8) was added by Sec. 613(b) of the Job Creation and Worker Assistance Act of 2002, P.L. 107-147, 3/9/2002, which struck out:

1. "December 31, 2003"

Effective Date effective 3/9/2002.

Code Sec. 168(k), in *italics*, was added by Sec. 101(a), P.L. 107-147, 3/9/2002.

2. added subsec. (k)

Effective Date (Sec. 101(b), P.L. 107-147, 3/9/2002) effective for property placed in service after 9/10/2001, in tax. yrs. end. after 9/10/2001.

[¶3025]
Code Sec. 170.   Charitable, etc., contributions and gifts.

* * * * * * * * * * * *

(e) Certain contributions of ordinary income and capital gain property.

* * * * * * * * * * * *

(6) Special rule for contributions of computer technology and equipment for educational purposes.

* * * * * * * * * * * *

(B) Qualified computer contribution. For purposes of this paragraph, the term "qualified computer contribution" means a charitable contribution by a corporation of any computer technology or equipment, but only if —

(i) the contribution is to—

(I) an educational organization described in subsection (b)(1)(A)(ii),

(II) an entity described in section 501(c)(3) and exempt from tax under section 501(a) other than an entity described in subclause (I)) that is organized primarily for purposes of supporting elementary and secondary education, or

(III) a public library (within the meaning of section 213(2)(A) of the Library Services and Technology Act (20 U.S.C. 9122(2)(A)), as in effect on the date of the enactment of the Community Renewal Tax Relief Act of [1]*2000),* established and maintained by an entity described in subsection (c)(1),

* * * * * * * * * * * *

[Endnote Code Sec. 170]

Matter in *italics* in Code Sec. 170(e)(6)(B)(i)(III) was added by Sec. 417(7) of the Job Creation and Worker Assistance Act of 2002, P.L. 107-147, 3/9/2002, which struck out:

1. "2000,"

Effective Date effective 3/9/2002.

[¶ 3026]
Code Sec. 172.   Net operating loss deduction.

* * * * * * * * * * * *

(b) Net operating loss carrybacks and carryovers.

(1) Years to which loss may be carried.

(A) General rule. Except as otherwise provided in this paragraph, a net operating loss for any taxable year—

(i) shall be a net operating loss carryback to each of the 2 taxable years preceding the taxable year of such loss, and

(ii) shall be a net operating loss carryover to each of the 20 taxable years following the taxable year of the loss.

* * * * * * * * * * * *

(F) Retention of 3-year carryback in certain cases.

(i) In general. Subparagraph (A)(i) shall be applied by substituting "[1]*3 taxable years*" for "[2]*2 taxable years*" with respect to the portion of the net operating loss for the taxable year which is an eligible loss with respect to the taxpayer.

(ii) Eligible loss. For purposes of clause (i), the term "eligible loss" means—

(I) in the case of an individual, losses of property arising from fire, storm, shipwreck, or other casualty, or from theft,

(II) in the case of a taxpayer which is a small business, net operating losses attributable to Presidentially declared disasters (as defined in section 1033(h)(3)), and

(III) in the case of a taxpayer engaged in the trade or business of farming (as defined in section 263A(e)(4)), net operating losses attributable to such Presidentially declared disasters.

Such term shall not include any farming loss (as defined in subsection (i)).

(iii) Small business. For purposes of this subparagraph, the term "small business" means a corporation or partnership which meets the gross receipts test of section 448(c) for the taxable year in which the loss arose (or, in the case of a sole proprietorship, which would meet such test if such proprietorship were a corporation).

(iv) Coordination with paragraph (2). For purposes of applying paragraph (2), an eligible loss for any taxable year shall be treated in a manner similar to the manner in which a specified liability loss is treated.

* * * * * * * * * * * *

[3]*(H) In the case of a taxpayer which has a net operating loss for any taxable year ending during 2001 or 2002, subparagraph (A)(i) shall be applied by substituting "5" for "2" and subparagraph (F) shall not apply.*

* * * * * * * * * * * *

[4]*(j) Election to disregard 5-year carryback for certain net operating losses. Any taxpayer entitled to a 5-year carryback under subsection (b)(1)(H) from any loss year may elect to have*

the carryback period with respect to such loss year determined without regard to subsection (b)(1)(H). Such election shall be made in such manner as may be prescribed by the Secretary and shall be made by the due date (including extensions of time) for filing the taxpayer's return for the taxable year of the net operating loss. Such election, once made for any taxable year, shall be irrevocable for such taxable year.

⁵*(k)* **Cross references.**

(1) For treatment of net operating loss carryovers in certain corporate acquisitions, see section 381.

(2) For special limitation on net operating loss carryovers in case of a corporate change of ownership, see section 382.

[For Analysis, see ¶ 103. For Committee Reports, see ¶ 5002.]

[Endnote Code Sec. 172]

Matter in *italics* in Code Sec. 172(b)(1)(F)(i) was added by Sec. 417(8)(A) and (B) of the Job Creation and Worker Assistance Act of 2002, P.L. 107-147, 3/9/2002, which struck out:

1. "3 years"
2. "2 years"

Effective Date effective 3/9/2002.

Matter in *italics* in Code Sec. 172(b)(1)(H), Code Sec. 172(j) and Code Sec. 172(k) added by Sec. 102(a) and (b), P.L. 107-147, 3/9/2002, which struck out:

3. added subpara. (b)(1)(H)
4. added subsec. (j)
5. "(j)"

Effective Date (Sec. 102(d), P.L. 107-147, 3/9/2002) effective for net operating losses for tax. yrs. end. after 12/31/2000.

[¶ 3027]
Code Sec. 179A.   Deduction for clean-fuel vehicles and certain refueling property.

* * * * * * * * * * * *

(b) Limitations.

(1) Qualified clean-fuel vehicle property.

(A) In general. The cost which may be taken into account under subsection (a)(1)(A) with respect to any motor vehicle shall not exceed—

(i) in the case of a motor vehicle not described in clause (ii) or (iii), $2,000,

(ii) in the case of any truck or van with a gross vehicle weight rating greater than 10,000 pounds but not greater than 26,000 pounds, $5,000, or

(iii) $50,000 in the case of—

(I) a truck or van with a gross vehicle weight rating greater than 26,000 pounds, or

(II) any bus which has a seating capacity of at least 20 adults (not including the driver).

(B) Phaseout. In the case of any qualified clean-fuel vehicle property placed in service after ¹*December 31, 2003*, the limit otherwise applicable under subparagraph (A) shall be reduced by—

(i) 25 percent in the case of property placed in service in calendar year ²*2004*,

(ii) 50 percent in the case of property placed in service in calendar year ³*2005*, and

(iii) 75 percent in the case of property placed in service in calendar year ⁴*2006*.

* * * * * * * * * * * *

(f) Termination. This section shall not apply to any property placed in service after ⁵*December 31, 2006*.

[For Analysis, see ¶ 209, ¶ 210. For Committee Reports, see ¶ 5074.]

[Endnote Code Sec. 179A]

Matter in *italics* in Code Sec. 179A(b)(1)(B) and Code Sec. 179A(f) was added by Sec. 606(a)(1) and (2) of the Job Creation and Worker Assistance Act of 2002, P.L. 107-147, 3/9/2002, which struck out:

1. "December 31, 2001,"
2. "2002"
3. "2003"
4. "2004"
5. "December 31, 2004"

Effective Date (Sec. 606(b), P.L. 107-147, 3/9/2002) effective for property placed in service after 12/31/2001.

[¶ 3028]
Code Sec. 220.   Archer MSAs.

* * * * * * * * * * * *

(i) Limitation on number of taxpayers having Archer MSAs.

(1) In general. Except as provided in paragraph (5), no individual shall be treated as an eligible individual for any taxable year beginning after the cut-off year unless—

(A) such individual was an active MSA participant for any taxable year ending on or before the close of the cut-off year, or

(B) such individual first became an active MSA participant for a taxable year ending after the cut-off year by reason of coverage under a high deductible health plan of an MSA-participating employer.

(2) Cut-off year. For purposes of paragraph (1), the term "cut-off year" means the earlier of—

(A) calendar year [1]*2003*, or

(B) the first calendar year before [2]*2003* for which the Secretary determines under subsection (j) that the numerical limitation for such year has been exceeded.

(3) Active MSA participant. For purposes of this subsection—

(A) In general. The term "active MSA participant" means, with respect to any taxable year, any individual who is the account holder of any Archer MSA into which any contribution was made which was excludable from gross income under section 106(b), or allowable as a deduction under this section, for such taxable year.

(B) Special rule for cut-off years before [3]*2003*. In the case of a cut-off year before [4]*2003*—

(i) an individual shall not be treated as an eligible individual for any month of such year or an active MSA participant under paragraph (1)(A) unless such individual is, on or before the cut-off date, covered under a high deductible health plan, and

(ii) an employer shall not be treated as an MSA-participating employer unless the employer, on or before the cut-off date, offered coverage under a high deductible health plan to any employee.

(C) Cut-off date. For purposes of subparagraph (B)—

(i) In general. Except as otherwise provided in this subparagraph, the cut-off date is October 1 of the cut-off year.

(ii) Employees with enrollment periods after October 1. In the case of an individual described in subclause (I) of subsection (c)(1)(A)(iii), if the regularly scheduled enrollment period for health plans of the individual's employer occurs during the last 3 months of the cut-off year, the cut-off date is December 31 of the cut-off year.

(iii) Self-employed individuals. In the case of an individual described in subclause (II) of subsection (c)(1)(A)(iii), the cut-off date is November 1 of the cut-off year.

(iv) Special rules for 1997. If 1997 is a cut-off year by reason of subsection (j)(1)(A)—

(I) each of the cut-off dates under clauses (i) and (iii) shall be 1 month earlier than the date determined without regard to this clause, and

(II) clause (ii) shall be applied by substituting "4 months" for "3 months".

* * * * * * * * * * * *

         RIA Research Institute of America

(j) Determination of whether numerical limits are exceeded.

* * * * * * * * * * * *

(2) Determination of whether limit exceeded for [5]***1998, 1999, 2001, or 2002.***

(A) In general. The numerical limitation for [6]*1998, 1999, 2001, or 2002* is exceeded if the sum of—

(i) the number of MSA returns filed on or before April 15 of such calendar year for taxable years ending with or within the preceding calendar year, plus

(ii) the Secretary's estimate (determined on the basis of the returns described in clause (i)) of the number of MSA returns for such taxable years which will be filed after such date,

exceeds 750,000 (600,000 in the case of 1998). For purposes of the preceding sentence, the term "MSA return" means any return on which any exclusion is claimed under section 106(b) or any deduction is claimed under this section.

(B) Alternative computation of limitation. The numerical limitation for [7]*1998, 1999, 2001, or 2002* is also exceeded if the sum of—

(i) 90 percent of the sum determined under subparagraph (A) for such calendar year, plus

(ii) the product of 2.5 and the number of Archer MSAs established during the portion of such year preceding July 1 (based on the reports required under paragraph (4)) for taxable years beginning in such year,

exceeds 750,000.

(C) No limitation for 2000. The numerical limitation shall not apply for 2000.

* * * * * * * * * * * *

(4) Reporting by MSA trustees.

(A) In general. Not later than August 1 of 1997, 1998, 1999, [8]*2001, and 2002*, each person who is the trustee of an Archer MSA established before July 1 of such calendar year shall make a report to the Secretary (in such form and manner as the Secretary shall specify) which specifies—

(i) the number of Archer MSAs established before such July 1 (for taxable years beginning in such calendar year) of which such person is the trustee,

(ii) the name and TIN of the account holder of each such account, and

(iii) the number of such accounts which are accounts of previously uninsured individuals.

* * * * * * * * * * * *

[For Analysis, see ¶ 214. For Committee Reports, see ¶ 5080.]

[Endnote Code Sec. 220]

Matter in *italics* in Code Sec. 220(i)(2), Code Sec. 220(i)(3)(B), Code Sec. 220(j)(2) and Code Sec. 220(j)(4)(A) was added by Sec. 612(a) and (b) of the Job Creation and Worker Assistance Act of 2002, P.L. 107-147, 3/9/2002, which struck out:

1. "2002"
2. "2002"
3. "2002"
4. "2002"
5. "1998, 1999, or 2001"
6. "1998, 1999, or 2001"
7. "1998, 1999, or 2001"
8. "and 2001"

Effective Date (Sec. 612(c), P.L. 107-147, 3/9/2002) effective 1/1/2002.

[¶ 3029]
Code Sec. 280F.   Limitation on depreciation for luxury automobiles; limitation where certain property used for personal purposes.
  (a) Limitation on amount of depreciation for luxury automobiles.
    (1) Depreciation.

* * * * * * * * * * * *

(C) Special rule for certain clean-fuel passenger automobiles.

(i) Modified automobiles. In the case of a passenger automobile which is propelled by a fuel which is not a clean-burning fuel to which is installed qualified clean-fuel vehicle property (as defined in section 179A(c)(1)(A)) for purposes of permitting such vehicle to be propelled by a clean burning fuel (as defined in section 179A(e)(1)), subparagraph (A) shall not apply to the cost of the installed qualified clean burning vehicle property.

(ii) Purpose built passenger vehicles. In the case of a purpose built passenger vehicle (as defined in section 4001(a)(2)(C)(ii)), each of the annual limitations specified in sub-paragraphs (A) and (B) shall be tripled.

[1]*(iii) Application of subparagraph. This subparagraph shall apply to property placed in service after August 5, 1997, and before January 1, 2007.*

* * * * * * * * * * * *

[For Analysis, see ¶ 207, ¶ 208. For Committee Reports, see ¶ 5070.]

[Endnote Code Sec. 280F]
  Code Sec. 280F(a)(1)(C)(iii), in *italics*, was added by Sec. 602(b)(1) of the Job Creation and Worker Assistance Act of 2002, P.L. 107-147, 3/9/2002.
  1. added clause (a)(1)(C)(iii)
Effective Date (Sec. 602(c), P.L. 107-147, 3/9/2002) effective for property placed in service after 12/31/2001.

[¶ 3030]
Code Sec. 351.   Transfer to corporation controlled by transferor.

* * * * * * * * * * * *

  (h) Cross references.
    (1) For special rule where another party to the exchange assumes a liability[1], see section 357.

* * * * * * * * * * * *

[Endnote Code Sec. 351]
  Matter in *italics* in Code Sec. 351(h)(1) was added by Sec. 417(9) of the Job Creation and Worker Assistance Act of 2002, P.L. 107-147, 3/9/2002.
  1. added matter in para. (h)(1)
Effective Date Effective 3/9/2002.

[¶ 3031]
Code Sec. 358.   Basis to distributees.

* * * * * * * * * * * *

  (h) Special rules for assumption of liabilities to which subsection (d) does not apply.
    (1) In general. If, after application of the other provisions of this section to an exchange or series of exchanges, the basis of property to which subsection (a)(1) applies exceeds the

℞ℐ𝒜 Research Institute of America

fair market value of such property, then such basis shall be reduced (but not below such fair market value) by the amount (determined as of the date of the exchange) of any liability—

[1](A) which is assumed by another person as part of the exchange, and

(B) with respect to which subsection (d)(1) does not apply to the assumption.

* * * * * * * * * * * *

[For Analysis, see ¶ 706. For Committee Reports, see ¶ 5056.]

[Endnote Code Sec. 358]

Matter in *italics* in Code Sec. 358(h)(1)(A) was added by Sec. 412(c) of the Job Creation and Workers Assistance Act of 2002, P.L. 107-147, 3/9/2002, which struck out:

1. "(A) which is assumed in exchange for such property, and"

Effective Date (Sec. 412(e), P.L. 107-147, 3/9/2002) effective for assumptions of liability after 10/18/99.

[¶ 3032]
Code Sec. 401.   Qualified pension, profit-sharing, and stock bonus plans.
(a) Requirements for qualification.

* * * * * * * * * * * *

(30) Limitations on elective deferrals. In the case of a trust which is part of a plan under which elective deferrals (within the meaning of section 402(g)(3)) may be made with respect to any individual during a calendar year, such trust shall not constitute a qualified trust under this subsection unless the plan provides that the amount of such deferrals under such plan and all other plans, contracts, or arrangements of an employer maintaining such plan may not exceed the amount of the limitation in effect under [1]402(g)(1)(A) for taxable years beginning in such calendar year.

(31) Direct transfer of eligible rollover distributions.

(A) In general. A trust shall not constitute a qualified trust under this section unless the plan of which such trust is a part provides that if the distributee of any eligible rollover distribution—

(i) elects to have such distribution paid directly to an eligible retirement plan, and

(ii) specifies the eligible retirement plan to which such distribution is to be paid (in such form and at such time as the plan administrator may prescribe),

such distribution shall be made in the form of a direct trustee-to-trustee transfer to the eligible retirement plan so specified.

(B) Certain mandatory distributions.

(i) In general. In case of a trust which is part of an eligible plan, such trust shall not constitute a qualified trust under this section unless the plan of which such trust is a part provides that if—

(I) a distribution described in clause (ii) in excess of $1,000 is made, and

(II) the distributee does not make an election under subparagraph (A) and does not elect to receive the distribution directly,

the plan administrator shall make such transfer to an individual retirement plan of a designated trustee or issuer and shall notify the distributee in writing (either separately or as part of the notice under section 402(f)) that the distribution may be transferred to another individual retirement plan.

(ii) Eligible plan. For purposes of clause (i) the term "eligible plan" means a plan which provides that any nonforfeitable accrued benefit for which the present value (as determined under section 411(a)(11)) does not exceed $5,000 shall be immediately distributed to the participant.

(C) Limitation. Subparagraphs (A) and (B) shall apply only to the extent that the eligible rollover distribution would be includible in gross income if not transferred as provided in subparagraph (A) (determined without regard to sections 402(c), 403(a)(4), 403(b)(8), and 457(e)(16)). The preceding sentence shall not apply to such distribution if the plan to which such distribution is transferred—

(i) [2]*is a qualified trust which is part of a plan which is a defined contribution plan and* agrees to separately account for amounts so transferred, including separately accounting for the portion of such distribution which is includible in gross income and the portion of such distribution which is not so includible, or

(ii) is an eligible retirement plan described in clause (i) or (ii) of section 402(c)(8)(B).

(D) Eligible rollover distribution. For purposes of this paragraph, the term "eligible rollover distribution" has the meaning given such term by section 402(f)(2)(A).

(E) Eligible retirement plan. For purposes of this paragraph, the term "eligible retirement plan" has the meaning given such term by section 402(c)(8)(B), except that a qualified trust shall be considered an eligible retirement plan only if it is a defined contribution plan, the terms of which permit the acceptance of rollover distributions.

* * * * * * * * * * *

[For Analysis, see ¶ 314. For Committee Reports, see ¶ 5047.]

[Endnote Code Sec. 401]

Matter in *italics* in Code Sec. 401(a)(30) was added by Sec. 411(o)(2) of the Job Creation and Worker Assistance Act of 2002, P.L. 107-147, 3/9/2002, which struck out:

1. "402(g)(1)"

Effective Date (Sec. 411(x), P.L. 107-147, 3/9/2002) effective for contributions in tax. yrs. begin. after 12/31/2001.

Matter in *italics* in Code Sec. 401(a)(31)(C)(i) (as amended by Sec. 657, P.L. 107-16) was added by Sec. 411(q)(1) of the Job Creation and Worker Assistance Act of 2002, P.L. 107-147, 3/9/2002.

2. added matter in clause (a)(31)(C)(i)

Effective Date (Sec. 411(x), P.L. 107-147, 3/9/2002) effective for distributions made after 12/31/2001.

Note The amendments made by Sec. 657, P.L. 107-16 are effective for distributions made after final regulations implementing Sec. 657(c)(2)(A), P.L. 107-16 are prescribed. Sec. 657(c)(2) of P.L. 107-16 provides:

"(2) Regulations.

"(A) Automatic rollover safe harbor. Not later than 3 years after the date of enactment of this Act, the Secretary of Labor shall prescribe regulations providing for safe harbors under which the designation of an institution and investment of funds in accordance with section 401(a)(31)(B) of the Internal Revenue Code of 1986 is deemed to satisfy the fiduciary requirements of section 404(a) of the Employee Retirement Income Security Act of 1974 (29 U.S.C. 1104(a)).

"(B) Use of low-cost individual retirement plans. The Secretary of the Treasury and the Secretary of Labor may provide, and shall give consideration to providing, special relief with respect to the use of low-cost individual retirement plans for purposes of transfers under section 401(a)(31)(B) of the Internal Revenue Code of 1986 and for other uses that promote the preservation of assets for retirement income purposes."

[¶ 3033]
Code Sec. 402.   Taxability of beneficiary of employees' trust.

* * * * * * * * * * *

(c) Rules applicable to rollovers from exempt trusts.

* * * * * * * * * * *

(2) Maximum amount which may be rolled over. In the case of any eligible rollover distribution, the maximum amount transferred to which paragraph (1) applies shall not exceed the portion of such distribution which is includible in gross income (determined without regard to paragraph (1)). The preceding sentence shall not apply to such distribution to the extent—

(A) such portion is transferred in a direct trustee-to-trustee transfer to a qualified trust which is part of a plan which is a defined contribution plan and which agrees to separately account for amounts so transferred, including separately accounting for the portion of such distribution which is includible in gross income and the portion of such distribution which is not so includible, or

(B) such portion is transferred to an eligible retirement plan described in clause (i) or (ii) of paragraph (8)(B).

[1]*In the case of a transfer described in subparagraph (A) or (B), the amount transferred shall be treated as consisting first of the portion of such distribution that is includible in gross income (determined without regard to paragraph (1)).*

* * * * * * * * * * * *

(g) Limitation on exclusion for elective deferrals.

(1) In general.

(A) Limitation. Notwithstanding subsections (e)(3) and (h)(1)(B), the elective deferrals of any individual for any taxable year shall be included in such individual's gross income to the extent the amount of such deferrals for the taxable year exceeds the applicable dollar amount. The preceding sentence shall not apply the portion of such excess as does not exceed the designated Roth contributions of the individual for the taxable year.

(B) Applicable dollar amount. For purposes of subparagraph (A), the applicable dollar amount shall be the amount determined in accordance with the following table:

For taxable years beginning in calendar year:	The applicable dollar amount:
2002	$11,000
2003	$12,000
2004	$13,000
2005	$14,000
2006 or thereafter	$15,000

[2]*(C) Catch-up contributions. In addition to subparagraph (A), in the case of an eligible participant (as defined in section 414(v)), gross income shall not include elective deferrals in excess of the applicable dollar amount under subparagraph (B) to the extent that the amount of such elective deferrals does not exceed the applicable dollar amount under section 414(v)(2)(B)(i) for the taxable year (without regard to the treatment of the elective deferrals by an applicable employer plan under section 414(v)).*

* * * * * * * * * * * *

(7) Special rule for certain organizations.

(A) In general. In the case of a qualified employee of a qualified organization, with respect to employer contributions described in paragraph (3)(C) made by such organization, the limitation of paragraph (1) for any taxable year shall be increased by whichever of the following is the least:

(i) $3,000,

(ii) $15,000 reduced by amounts not included in gross income for prior taxable years by reason of this paragraph, or

(iii) the excess of $5,000 multiplied by the number of years of service of the employee with the qualified organization over the employer contributions described in paragraph (3) made by the organization on behalf of such employee for prior taxable years (determined in the manner prescribed by the Secretary).

(B) Qualified organization. For purposes of this paragraph, the term "qualified organization" means any educational organization, hospital, home health service agency, health and welfare service agency, church, or convention or association of churches. Such term includes any organization described in section 414(e)(3)(B)(ii). Terms used in this subparagraph shall have the same meaning as when used in section 415(c)(4) (as in effect before the enactment of the Economic Growth and Tax Relief Reconciliation Act of [3]*2001).*

(C) Qualified employee. For purposes of this paragraph, the term "qualified employee" means any employee who has completed 15 years of service with the qualified organization.

(D) Years of service. For purposes of this paragraph, the term "years of service" has the meaning given such term by section 403(b).

* * * * * * * * * * * *

(h) Special rules for simplified employee pensions. For purposes of this chapter—

(1) In general. Except as provided in paragraph (2), contributions made by an employer on behalf of an employee to an individual retirement plan pursuant to a simplified employee pension (as defined in section 408(k))—

(A) shall not be treated as distributed or made available to the employee or as contributions made by the employee, and

(B) if such contributions are made pursuant to an arrangement under section 408(k)(6) under which an employee may elect to have the employer make contributions to the simplified employee pension on behalf of the employee, shall not be treated as distributed or made available or as contributions made by the employee merely because the simplified employee pension includes provisions for such election.

(2) Limitations on employer contributions. Contributions made by an employer to a simplified employee pension with respect to an employee for any year shall be treated as distributed or made available to such employee and as contributions made by the employee to the extent such contributions exceed the lesser of—

(A) [4]*25 percent* of the compensation (within the meaning of section 414(s)) from such employer includible in the employee's gross income for the year (determined without regard to the employer contributions to the simplified employee pension), or

(B) the limitation in effect under section 415(c)(1)(A), reduced in the case of any highly compensated employee (within the meaning of section 414(q)) by the amount taken into account with respect to such employee under section 408(k)(3)(D).

(3) Distributions. Any amount paid or distributed out of an individual retirement plan pursuant to a simplified employee pension shall be included in gross income by the payee or distributee, as the case may be, in accordance with the provisions of section 408(d).

* * * * * * * * * * * *

[For Analysis, see ¶ 301, ¶ 308, ¶ 313. For Committee Reports, see ¶ 5042, ¶ 5045, ¶ 5047.]

[Endnote Code Sec. 402]

Matter in *italics* in Code Sec. 402(c)(2) was added by Sec. 411(q)(2) of the Job Creation and Worker Assistance Act of 2002, P.L. 107-147, 3/9/2002.
  1. added matter in para. (c)(2)
Effective Date (Sec. 411(x), P.L. 107-147, 3/9/2002) effective for distributions made after 12/31/2001.

Code Sec. 402(g)(1)(C), in *italics*, was added by Sec. 411(o)(1), P.L. 107-147, 3/9/2002.
  2. added subpara. (g)(1)(C)
Effective Date (Sec. 411(x), P.L. 107-147, 3/9/2002) effective for contributions in tax. yrs. begin. after 12/31/2001.

Matter in *italics* in Code Sec. 402(g)(7)(B) was added by Sec. 411(p)(6), P.L. 107-147, 3/9/2002, which struck out:
  3. "2001."
Effective Date (Sec. 411(x), P.L. 107-147, 3/9/2002) effective for yrs. begin. after 12/31/2001.

Matter in *italics* in Code Sec. 402(h)(2)(A) was added by Sec. 411(l)(3), P.L. 107-147, 3/9/2002, which struck out:
  4. "15 percent"
Effective Date (Sec. 411(x), P.L. 107-147, 3/9/2002) effective for yrs. begin. after 12/31/2001.

[¶ 3034]
Code Sec. 403.   Taxation of employee annuities.

* * * * * * * * * * * *

(b) Taxability of beneficiary under annuity purchased by section 501(c)(3) organization or public school.

(1) General rule. If—

(A) an annuity contract is purchased—

(i) for an employee by an employer described in section 501(c)(3) which is exempt from tax under section 501(a),

(ii) for an employee (other than an employee described in clause (i)), who performs services for an educational organization described in section 170(b)(1)(A)(ii), by an employer which is a State, a political subdivision of a State, or an agency or instrumentality of any one or more of the foregoing, or

(iii) for the minister described in section 414(e)(5)(A) by the minister or by an employer,

(B) such annuity contract is not subject to subsection (a),

(C) the employee's rights under the contract are nonforfeitable, except for failure to pay future premiums,

(D) except in the case of a contract purchased by a church, such contract is purchased under a plan which meets the nondiscrimination requirements of paragraph (12), and

(E) in the case of a contract purchased under a salary reduction agreement, the contract meets the requirements of section 401(a)(30),

[1]*then contributions and other additions by such employer for such annuity contract shall be excluded from the gross income of the employee for the taxable year to the extent that the aggregate of such contributions and additions (when expressed as an annual addition (within the meaning of section 415(c)(2)) does not exceed the applicable limit under section 415. The amount actually distributed to any distributee under such contract shall be taxable to the distributee (in the year in which so distributed) under section 72 (relating to annuities). For purposes of applying the rules of this subsection to contributions and other additions by an employer for a taxable year, amounts transferred to a contract described in this paragraph by reason of a rollover contribution described in paragraph (8) of this subsection or section 408(d)(3)(A)(ii) shall not be considered contributed by such employer.*

* * * * * * * * * * *

(3) Includible compensation. For purposes of this subsection, the term "includible compensation" means, in the case of any employee, the amount of compensation which is received from the employer described in paragraph (1)(A), and which is includible in gross income (computed without regard to section 911) for the most recent period (ending not later than the close of the taxable year) which under paragraph (4) may be counted as one year of service [2], *and which precedes the taxable year by no more than five years.* Such term does not include any amount contributed by the employer for any annuity contract to which this subsection applies[3]. Such term includes—

(A) any elective deferral (as defined in section 402(g)(3)), and

(B) any amount which is contributed or deferred by the employer at the election of the employee and which is not includible in the gross income of the employee by reason of section 125, 132(f)(4), or 457.

* * * * * * * * * * *

[4]*(6) Repealed.*

* * * * * * * * * * *

[For Analysis, see ¶ 320. For Committee Reports, see ¶ 5046.]

[Endnote Code Sec. 403]

Matter in *italics* in Code Sec. 403(b)(1), Code Sec. 403(b)(3) and Code Sec. 403(b)(6) added by Sec. 411(p)(1), (2), (3)(A) and (B) of the Job Creation and Worker Assistance Act of 2002, P.L. 107-147, 3/9/2002, which struck out:

1. "then amounts contributed by such employer for such annuity contract on or after such rights become nonforfeitable shall be excluded from the gross income of the employee for the taxable year to the extent that the aggregate of such amounts does not exceed the applicable limit under section 415. The amount actually distributed to any distributee under such contract shall be taxable to the distributee (in the year in which so distributed) under section 72 (relating to annuities). For purposes of applying the rules of this subsection to amounts contributed by an employer for a taxable year, amounts transferred to a contract described in this paragraph by reason of a rollover contribution described in paragraph (8) of this subsection or section 408(d)(3)(A)(ii) shall not be considered contributed by such employer."

2. added matter in para. (b)(3)

3. "or any amount received by a former employee after the fifth taxable year following the taxable year in which such employee was terminated"

4. "(6) Forfeitable rights which become nonforfeitable. For purposes of this subsection and section 72(f) (relating to special rules for computing employees' contributions to annuity contracts), if rights of the employee under an annuity contract described in subparagraphs (A) and (B) of paragraph (1) change from forfeitable to nonforfeitable rights, then the amount (determined without regard to this subsection) includible in gross income by reason of such change shall be treated as an amount contributed by the employer for such annuity contract as of the time such rights become nonforfeitable."

Effective Date (Sec. 411(x), P.L. 107-147, 3/9/2002) effective for yrs. begin. after 12/31/2001.

[¶ 3035]
Code Sec. 404.   Deduction for contributions of an employer to an employees' trust or annuity plan and compensation under a deferred-payment plan.

(a) General rule. If contributions are paid by an employer to or under a stock bonus, pension, profit-sharing, or annuity plan, or if compensation is paid or accrued on account of any employee under a plan deferring the receipt of such compensation, such contributions or compensation shall not be deductible under this chapter; but, if they would otherwise be deductible, they shall be deductible under this section, subject, however, to the following limitations as to the amounts deductible in any year:

(1) Pension trusts.

* * * * * * * * * * * *

(D) Special rule in case of certain plans.

(i) In general. In the case of any defined benefit plan, except as provided in regulations, the maximum amount deductible under the limitations of this paragraph shall not be less than the unfunded current liability determined under section 412(l).

* * * * * * * * * * * *

(iv) [1]*Special rule for terminating plans.* In the case of a plan which, subject to section 4041 of the Employee Retirement Income Security Act of 1974, terminates during the plan year, clause (i) shall be applied by substituting for unfunded current liability the amount required to make the plan sufficient for benefit liabilities (within the meaning of section 4041(d) of such Act).

* * * * * * * * * * * *

(7) Limitation on deductions where combination of defined contribution plan and defined benefit plan.

* * * * * * * * * * * *

[2]*(C) Paragraph not to apply in certain cases.*

(i) Beneficiary test. This paragraph shall not have the effect of reducing the amount otherwise deductible under paragraphs (1), (2), and (3), if no employee is a beneficiary under more than 1 trust or under a trust and an annuity plan.

(ii) Elective deferrals. If, in connection with 1 or more defined contribution plans and 1 or more defined benefit plans, no amounts (other than elective deferrals (as defined in section 402(g)(3))) are contributed to any of the defined contribution plans for the taxable year, then subparagraph (A) shall not apply with respect to any of such defined contribution plans and defined benefit plans.

* * * * * * * * * * * *

(k) Deduction for dividends paid on certain employer securities.

(1) General rule. In the case of a C corporation, there shall be allowed as a deduction for a taxable year the amount of any applicable dividend paid in cash by such corporation[4] with respect to applicable employer securities. Such deduction shall be in addition to the deductions allowed under subsection (a).

(2) Applicable dividend. For purposes of this subsection—

(A) In general. The term "applicable dividend" means any dividend which, in accordance with the plan provisions—

(i) is paid in cash to the participants in the plan or their beneficiaries,

(ii) is paid to the plan and is distributed in cash to participants in the plan or their beneficiaries not later than 90 days after the close of the plan year in which paid,

(iii) is, at the election of such participants or their beneficiaries—

(I) payable as provided in clause (i) or (ii), or

(II) paid to the plan and reinvested in qualifying employer securities, or

(iv) is used to make payments on a loan described in subsection (a)(9) the proceeds of which were used to acquire the employer securities (whether or not allocated to participants) with respect to which the dividend is paid.

(B) Limitation on certain dividends. A dividend described in subparagraph [5]*(A)(iv)* which is paid with respect to any employer security which is allocated to a participant shall not be treated as an applicable dividend unless the plan provides that employer securities with a fair market value of not less than the amount of such dividend are allocated to such participant for the year which (but for subparagraph (A)) such dividend would have been allocated to such participant.

* * * * * * * * * * * *

(4) Time for deduction.

(A) In general. The deduction under paragraph (1) shall be allowable in the taxable year of the corporation in which the dividend is paid or distributed to a participant or his beneficiary.

[6]*(B) Reinvestment dividends. For purposes of subparagraph (A), an applicable dividend reinvested pursuant to clause (iii)(II) of paragraph (2)(A) shall be treated as paid in the taxable year of the corporation in which such dividend is reinvested in qualifying employer securities or in which the election under clause (iii) of paragraph (2)(A) is made, whichever is later.*

[7]*(C)* Repayment of loans. In the case of an applicable dividend described in clause [8]*(iv)* of paragraph (2)(A), the deduction under paragraph (1) shall be allowable in the taxable year of the corporation in which such dividend is used to repay the loan described in such clause.

* * * * * * * * * * * *

(6) Definitions. For purposes of this subsection—

(A) Employer securities. The term "employer securities" has the meaning given such term by section 409(l).

(B) Employee stock ownership plan. The term "employee stock ownership plan" has the meaning given such term by section 4975(e)(7). Such term includes a tax credit employee stock ownership plan (as defined in section 409).

[9]*(7) Full vesting. In accordance with section 411, an applicable dividend described in clause (iii)(II) of paragraph (2)(A) shall be subject to the requirements of section 411(a)(1).*

* * * * * * * * * * * *

(n) Elective deferrals not taken into account for purposes of deduction limits. Elective deferrals (as defined in section 402(g)(3)) shall not be subject to any limitation contained in paragraph (3), (7), or (9) of [10]*subsection (a) or paragraph (1)(C) of subsection (h)* and such elective deferrals shall not be taken into account in applying any such limitation to any other contributions.

[For Analysis, see ¶ 303, ¶ 304, ¶ 305, ¶ 326. For Committee Reports, see ¶ 5042, ¶ 5053.]

[Endnote Code Sec. 404]

Matter in *italics* in Code Sec. 404(a)(1)(D)(iv) was added by Sec. 411(s) of the Job Creation and Worker Assistance Act of 2002, P.L. 107-147, 3/9/2002, which struck out:

1. "Plans maintained by professional service employers"

Effective Date (Sec. 411(x), P.L. 107-147, 3/9/2002) effective for plan yrs. begin. after 12/31/2001.

Matter in *italics* in Code Sec. 404(a)(7)(C) and Code Sec. 404(a)(12) was added by Sec. 411(l)(1) and (4), P.L. 107-147, 3/9/2002, which struck out:

2. "(C) Paragraph not to apply in certain cases. This paragraph shall not have the effect of reducing the amount otherwise deductible under paragraphs (1), (2), and (3), if no employee is a beneficiary under more than 1 trust or under a trust and an annuity plan."

3. "(9),"

Effective Date (Sec. 411(x), P.L. 107-147, 3/9/2002) effective for yrs. begin. after 12/31/2001.

Matter in *italics* in Code Sec. 404(k)(1), Code Sec. 404(k)(2)(B), Code Sec. 404(k)(4)(B), Code Sec. 404(k)(4)(C) and Code Sec. 404(k)(7) added by Sec. 411(w)(1)(A)-(D) and (w)(2), P.L. 107-147, 3/9/2002, which struck out:

4. "during the taxable year"
5. "(A)(iii)"
6. added subpara. (k)(4)(B)
7. "(B)"
8. "(iii)"
9. added para. (k)(7)
Effective Date (Sec. 411(x), P.L. 107-147, 3/9/2002) effective for tax. yrs. begin. after 12/31/2001.

Matter in *italics* in Code Sec. 404(n) was added by Sec. 411(l)(2), P.L. 107-147, 3/9/2002, which struck out:
10. "subsection (a),"
Effective Date (Sec. 411(x), P.L. 107-147, 3/9/2002) effective for yrs. begin. after 12/31/2001.

[¶ 3036]
Code Sec. 408.   Individual retirement accounts.

* * * * * * * * * * *

(k) Simplified employee pension defined.

* * * * * * * * * * *

(2) **Participation requirements.** This paragraph is satisfied with respect to a simplified employee pension for a year only if for such year the employer contributes to the simplified employee pension of each employee who—

(A) has attained age 21,

(B) has performed service for the employer during at least 3 of the immediately preceding 5 years, and

(C) received at least [1]*$450* in compensation (within the meaning of section 414(q)(4)) from the employer for the year.

For purposes of this paragraph, there shall be excluded from consideration employees described in subparagraph (A) or (C) of section 410(b)(3). For purposes of any arrangement described in subsection (k)(6), any employee who is eligible to have employer contributions made on the employee's behalf under such arrangement shall be treated as if such a contribution was made.

* * * * * * * * * * *

(8) **Cost-of-living adjustment.** The Secretary shall adjust the [2]*$450* amount in paragraph (2)(C) at the same time and in the same manner as under section 415(d) and shall adjust the $200,000 amount in paragraphs (3)(C) and (6)(D)(ii) at the same time, and by the same amount, as any adjustment under section 401(a)(17)(B); except that any increase in the [3]*$450* amount which is not a multiple of $50 shall be rounded to the next lowest multiple of $50.

* * * * * * * * * * *

(q) Deemed IRAs under qualified employer plans.

(1) **General rule.** If—

(A) a qualified employer plan elects to allow employees to make voluntary employee contributions to a separate account or annuity established under the plan, and

(B) under the terms of the qualified employer plan, such account or annuity meets the applicable requirements of this section or section 408A for an individual retirement account or annuity,

then such account or annuity shall be treated for purposes of this title in the same manner as an individual retirement plan and not as a qualified employer plan (and contributions to such account or annuity as contributions to an individual retirement plan and not to the qualified employer plan). For purposes of subparagraph (B), the requirements of subsection (a)(5) shall not apply.

(2) **Special rules for qualified employer plans.** For purposes of this title, a qualified employer plan shall not fail to meet any requirement of this title solely by reason of establishing and maintaining a program described in paragraph (1).

RIA **Research Institute of America**

(3) Definitions. For purposes of this subsection—

[4](A) *Qualified employer plan. The term "qualified employer plan" has the meaning given such term by section 72(p)(4)(A)(i); except that such term shall also include an eligible deferred compensation plan (as defined in section 457(b)) of an eligible employer described in section 457(e)(1)(A).*

(B) Voluntary employee contribution. The term "voluntary employee contribution" means any contribution (other than a mandatory contribution within the meaning of section 411(c)(2)(C))—

(i) which is made by an individual as an employee under a qualified employer plan which allows employees to elect to make contributions described in paragraph (1), and

(ii) with respect to which the individual has designated the contribution as a contribution to which this subsection applies.

* * * * * * * * * * * *

[For Analysis, see ¶ 302, ¶ 319. For Committee Reports, see ¶ 5039, ¶ 5040.]

[Endnote Code Sec. 408]

Matter in *italics* in Code Sec. 408(k)(2)(C) and Code Sec. 408(k)(8) was added by Sec. 411(j)(1)(A) and (B) of the Job Creation and Worker Assistance Act of 2002, P.L. 107-147, 3/9/2002, which struck out:

1. "$300"
2. "$300"
3. "$300"

Effective Date (Sec. 411(x), P.L. 107-147, 3/9/2002) effective for yrs. begin. after 12/31/2001.

Code Sec. 408(q)(3)(A), in *italics*, was added by Sec. 411(i)(1), P.L. 107-147, 3/9/2002, which struck out:

4. "(A) Qualified employer plan. The term 'qualified employer plan' has the meaning given such term by section 72(p)(4); except such term shall not include a government plan which is not a qualified plan unless the plan is an eligible deferred compensation plan (as defined in section 457(b))."

Effective Date (Sec. 411(x), P.L. 107-147, 3/9/2002) effective for plan yrs. begin. after 12/31/2002.

[¶ 3037]
Code Sec. 409.   Qualifications for tax credit employee stock ownership plans.

* * * * * * * * * * * *

(o) Distribution and payment requirements. A plan meets the requirements of this subsection if—

(1) Distribution requirement.

(A) In general. The plan provides that, if the participant and, if applicable pursuant to sections 401(a)(11) and 417, with the consent of the participant's spouse elects, the distribution of the participant's account balance in the plan will commence not later than 1 year after the close of the plan year—

(i) in which the participant separates from service by reason of the attainment of normal retirement age under the plan, disability, or death, or

(ii) which is the 5th plan year following the plan year in which the participant otherwise separates from service, except that this clause shall not apply if the participant is reemployed by the employer before distribution is required to begin under this clause.

(B) Exception for certain financed securities. For purposes of this subsection, the account balance of a participant shall not include any employer securities acquired with the proceeds of the loan described in section 404(a)(9) until the close of the plan year in which such loan is repaid in full.

(C) Limited distribution period. The plan provides that, unless the participant elects otherwise, the distribution of the participant's account balance will be in substantially equal periodic payments (not less frequently than annually) over a period not longer than the greater of—

(i) 5 years, or

(ii) in the case of a participant with an account balance in excess of [1]*$800,000,* 5 years plus 1 additional year (but not more than 5 additional years) for each [2]*$160,000* or fraction thereof by which such balance exceeds [3]*$800,000.*

* * * * * * * * * * * *

[For Analysis, see ¶ 302. For Committee Reports, see ¶ 5040.]

[Endnote Code Sec. 409]

Matter in *italics* in Code Sec. 409(o)(1)(C)(ii) was added by Sec. 411(j)(2)(A) and (B) of the Job Creation and Worker Assistance Act of 2002, P.L. 107-147, 3/9/2002, which struck out:
1. "$500,000"
2. "$100,000"
3. "$500,000"

Effective Date (Sec. 411(x), P.L. 107-147, 3/9/2002) effective for yrs. begin. after 12/31/2001.

[¶ 3038]

Code Sec. 412.   Minimum funding standards.

* * * * * * * * * * * *

(c) Special rules.

* * * * * * * * * * * *

(9) Annual valuation.

(A) In general. For purposes of this section, a determination of experience gains and losses and a valuation of the plan's liability shall be made not less frequently than once every year, except that such determination shall be made more frequently to the extent required in particular cases under regulations prescribed by the Secretary.

(B) Valuation date.

(i) Current year. Except as provided in clause (ii), the valuation referred to in subparagraph (A) shall be made as of a date within the plan year to which the valuation refers or within one month prior to the beginning of such year.

(ii) Use of prior year valuation. The valuation referred to in subparagraph (A) may be made as of a date within the plan year prior to the year to which the valuation refers if, as of such date, the value of the assets of the plan are not less than [1]*100 percent* of the plan's current liability (as defined in paragraph (7)(B)).

(iii) Adjustments. Information under clause (ii) shall, in accordance with regulations, be actuarially adjusted to reflect significant differences in participants.

[2]*(iv) Limitation. A change in funding method to use a prior year valuation, as provided in clause (ii), may not be made unless as of the valuation date within the prior plan year, the value of the assets of the plan are not less than 125 percent of the plan's current liability (as defined in paragraph (7)(B)).*

* * * * * * * * * * * *

(l) Additional funding requirements for plans which are not multiemployer plans.

* * * * * * * * * * * *

(7) Current liability. For purposes of this subsection—

(A) In general. The term "current liability" means all liabilities to employees and their beneficiaries under the plan.

(B) Treatment of unpredictable contingent event benefits.

(i) In general. For purposes of subparagraph (A), any unpredictable contingent event benefit shall not be taken into account until the event on which the benefit is contingent occurs.

(ii) Unpredictable contingent event benefit. The term "unpredictable contingent event benefit" means any benefit contingent on an event other than—

(I) age, service, compensation, death, or disability, or

 **Research Institute of America**

(II) an event which is reasonably and reliably predictable (as determined by the Secretary).

(C) Interest rate and mortality assumptions used. Effective for plan years beginning after December 31, 1994—

(i) Interest rate.

(I) In general. The rate of interest used to determine current liability under this subsection shall be the rate of interest used under subsection (b)(5), except that the highest rate in the permissible range under subparagraph (B)(ii) thereof shall not exceed the specified percentage under subclause (II) of the weighted average referred to in such subparagraph.

(II) Specified percentage. For purposes of subclause (I), the specified percentage shall be determined as follows:

In the case of plan years beginning in calendar year:	The specified percentage is:
1995	109
1996	108
1997	107
1998	106
1999 and thereafter	105

[3]*(III) Special rule for 2002 and 2003. For a plan year beginning in 2002 or 2003, notwithstanding subclause (I), in the case that the rate of interest used under subsection (b)(5) exceeds the highest rate permitted under subclause (I), the rate of interest used to determine current liability under this subsection may exceed the rate of interest otherwise permitted under subclause (I); except that such rate of interest shall not exceed 120 percent of the weighted average referred to in subsection (b)(5)(B)(ii).*

(m) Quarterly contributions required.

* * * * * * * * * * * *

[4]*(7) **Special rules for 2002 and 2004.** In any case in which the interest rate used to determine current liability is determined under subsection (l)(7)(C)(i)(III)—*

(A) 2002. For purposes of applying paragraphs (1) and (4)(B)(ii) for plan years beginning in 2002, the current liability for the preceding plan year shall be redetermined using 120 percent as the specified percentage determined under subsection (l)(7)(C)(i)(II).

(B) 2004. For purposes of applying paragraphs (1) and (4)(B)(ii) for plan years beginning in 2004, the current liability for the preceding plan year shall be redetermined using 105 percent as the specified percentage determined under subsection (l)(7)(C)(i)(II).

* * * * * * * * * * * *

[For Analysis, see ¶306, ¶325. For Committee Reports, see ¶5025, ¶5052.]

[Endnote Code Sec. 412]

Matter in *italics* in Code Sec. 412(c)(9)(B)(ii) and Code Sec. 412(c)(9)(B)(iv) added by Sec. 411(v)(1)(A) and (B) of the Job Creation and Worker Assistance Act of 2002, P.L. 107-147, 3/9/2002, which struck out:

1. "125 percent"
2. added clause (c)(9)(B)(iv)

Effective Date (Sec. 411(x), P.L. 107-147, 3/9/2002) effective for plan yrs. begin. after 12/31/2001.

Code Sec. 412(l)(7)(C)(i)(III) and Code Sec. 412(m)(7), in *italics* were added by Sec. 405(a)(1) and (2), P.L. 107-147, 3/9/2002.

3. added subclause (l)(7)(C)(i)(III)
4. added para. (m)(7)

Enacted 3/9/2002.

Code Sec. 414.   Definitions and special rules.

* * * * * * * * * * * *

(v) Catch-up contributions for individuals age 50 or over.

(1) In general. An applicable employer plan shall not be treated as failing to meet any requirement of this title solely because the plan permits an eligible participant to make additional elective deferrals in any plan year.

(2) Limitation on amount of additional deferrals.

(A) In general. A plan shall not permit additional elective deferrals under paragraph (1) for any year in an amount greater than the lesser of—

(i) the applicable dollar amount, or

(ii) the excess (if any) of—

(I) the participant's compensation (as defined in section 415(c)(3)) for the year, over

(II) any other elective deferrals of the participant for such year which are made without regard to this subsection.

(B) Applicable dollar amount. For purposes of this paragraph—

(i) In the case of an applicable employer plan other than a plan described in section 401(k)(11) or 408(p), the applicable dollar amount shall be determined in accordance with the following table:

For taxable years beginning in:	The applicable dollar amount is:
2002	$1,000
2003	$2,000
2004	$3,000
2005	$4,000
2006 and thereafter	$5,000.

(ii) In the case of an applicable employer plan described in section 401(k)(11) or 408(p), the applicable dollar amount shall be determined in accordance with the following table:

For taxable years beginning in:	The applicable dollar amount is:
2002	$500
2003	$1,000
2004	$1,500
2005	$2,000
2006 and thereafter	$2,500.

(C) Cost-of-living adjustment. In the case of a year beginning after December 31, 2006, the Secretary shall adjust annually the $5,000 amount in subparagraph (B)(i) and the $2,500 amount in subparagraph (B)(ii) for increases in the cost-of-living at the same time and in the same manner as adjustments under section 415(d); except that the base period taken into account shall be the calendar quarter beginning July 1, 2005, and any increase under this subparagraph which is not a multiple of $500 shall be rounded to the next lower multiple of $500.

[1](D) Aggregation of plans. For purposes of this paragraph, plans described in clauses (i), (ii), and (iv) of paragraph (6)(A) that are maintained by the same employer (as determined under subsection (b), (c), (m) or (o)) shall be treated as a single plan, and plans described in clause (iii) of paragraph (6)(A) that are maintained by the same employer shall be treated as a single plan.

(3) Treatment of contributions. In the case of any contribution to a plan under paragraph (1)—

(A) such contribution shall not, with respect to the year in which the contribution is made—

RIA Research Institute of America

(i) be subject to any otherwise applicable limitation contained in [2]*section 401(a)(30), 402(h), 403(b), 408, 415(c), and 457(b)(2) (determined without regard to section 457(b)(3))*, or

(ii) be taken into account in applying such limitations to other contributions or benefits under such plan or any other such plan, and

(B) except as provided in paragraph (4), such plan shall not be treated as failing to meet the requirements of [3]*section 401(a)(4), 401(k)(3), 401(k)(11), 403(b)(12), 408(k), 410(b), or 416* by reason of the making of (or the right to make) such contribution.

(4) Application of nondiscrimination rules.

(A) In general. An applicable employer plan shall be treated as failing to meet the non-discrimination requirements under section 401(a)(4) with respect to benefits, rights, and features unless the plan allows all eligible participants to make the same election with respect to the additional elective deferrals under this subsection.

(B) Aggregation. For purposes of subparagraph (A), all plans maintained by employers who are treated as a single employer under subsection (b), (c), (m), or (o) of section 414 shall be treated as 1 plan[4], *except that a plan described in clause (i) of section 410(b)(6)(C) shall not be treated as a plan of the employer until the expiration of the transition period with respect to such plan (as determined under clause (ii) of such section).*

(5) Eligible participant. For purposes of this subsection, the term "eligible participant" means[5] a participant in a plan—

[6]*(A) who would attain age 50 by the end of the taxable year,*

(B) with respect to whom no other elective deferrals may (without regard to this subsection) be made to the plan for the [7]*plan (or other applicable) year* by reason of the application of any limitation or other restriction described in paragraph (3) or comparable limitation or restriction contained in the terms of the plan.

(6) Other definitions and rules. For purposes of this subsection—

(A) Applicable employer plan. The term "applicable employer plan" means—

(i) an employees' trust described in section 401(a) which is exempt from tax under section 501(a),

(ii) a plan under which amounts are contributed by an individual's employer for an annuity contract described in section 403(b),

(iii) an eligible deferred compensation plan under section 457 of an eligible employer described in section 457(e)(1)(A), and

(iv) an arrangement meeting the requirements of section 408(k) or (p).

(B) Elective deferral. The term "elective deferral" has the meaning given such term by subsection (u)(2)(C).

[8]*(C) Exception for section 457 plans. This subsection shall not apply to a participant for any year for which a higher limitation applies to the participant under section 457(b)(3).*
[For Analysis, see ¶ 307, ¶ 309, ¶ 310, ¶ 311, ¶ 312. For Committee Reports, see ¶ 5045.]

[Endnote Code Sec. 414]

Matter in *italics* in Code Sec. 414(v)(2)(D), Code Sec. 414(v)(3)(A)(i), Code Sec. 414(v)(3)(B), Code Sec. 414(v)(4)(B), Code Sec. 414(v)(5) and Code Sec. 414(v)(6)(C) added by Sec. 411(o)(3)-(8) of the Job Creation and Worker Assistance Act of 2002, P.L. 107-147, 3/9/2002, which struck out:

1. added subpara. (v)(2)(D)
2. "section 402(g), 402(h), 403(b), 404(a), 404(h), 408(k), 408(p), 415, or 457"
3. "section 401(a)(4), 401(a)(26), 401(k)(3), 401(k)(11), 401(k)(12), 403(b)(12), 408(k), 408(p), 408B, 410(b), or 416"
4. added matter in subpara. (v)(4)(B)
5. ", with respect to any plan year,"
6. "(A) who has attained the age of 50 before the close of the plan year, and"
7. "plan year"
8. "(C) Exception for section 457 plans. This subsection shall not apply to an applicable employer plan described in subparagraph (A)(iii) for any year to which section 457(b)(3) applies."

Effective Date (Sec. 411(x), P.L. 107-147, 3/9/2002) effective for contributions in tax. yrs. begin. after 12/31/2001.

[¶ 3040]
Code Sec. 415.   **Limitations on benefits and contributions under qualified plans.**

* * * * * * * * * * * *

(c) Limitation for defined contribution plans.

* * * * * * * * * * * *

[1]*(7) Special rules relating to church plans.*

(A) Alternative contribution limitation.

(i) In general. Notwithstanding any other provision of this subsection, at the election of a participant who is an employee of a church or a convention or association of churches, including an organization described in section 414(e)(3)(B)(ii), contributions and other additions for an annuity contract or retirement income account described in section 403(b) with respect to such participant, when expressed as an annual addition to such participant's account, shall be treated as not exceeding the limitation of paragraph (1) if such annual addition is not in excess of $10,000.

(ii) $40,000 aggregate limitation. The total amount of additions with respect to any participant which may be taken into account for purposes of this subparagraph for all years may not exceed $40,000.

(B) Number of years of service for duly ordained, commissioned, or licensed ministers or lay employees. For purposes of this paragraph—

(i) all years of service by—

(I) a duly ordained, commissioned, or licensed minister of a church, or

(II) a lay person,

as an employee of a church, a convention or association of churches, including an organization described in section 414(e)(3)(B)(ii), shall be considered as years of service for 1 employer, and

(ii) all amounts contributed for annuity contracts by each such church (or convention or association of churches) or such organization during such years for such minister or lay person shall be considered to have been contributed by 1 employer.

(C) Foreign missionaries. In the case of any individual described in subparagraph (D) performing services outside the United States, contributions and other additions for an annuity contract or retirement income account described in section 403(b) with respect to such employee, when expressed as an annual addition to such employee's account, shall not be treated as exceeding the limitation of paragraph (1) if such annual addition is not in excess of the greater of $3,000 or the employee's includible compensation determined under section 403(b)(3).

(D) Annual addition. For purposes of this paragraph, the term "annual addition" has the meaning given such term by paragraph (2).

(E) Church, convention or association of churches. For purposes of this paragraph, the terms "church" and "convention or association of churches" have the same meaning as when used in section 414(e).

* * * * * * * * * * * *

[For Analysis, see ¶ 320. For Committee Reports, see ¶ 5046.]

[Endnote Code Sec. 415]

Code Sec. 415(c)(7), in *italics*, was added by Sec. 411(p)(4) of the Job Creation and Worker Assistance Act of 2002, P.L. 107-147, 3/9/2002, which struck out:

1. "(7) Certain contributions by church plans not treated as exceeding limit.

"(A) In general. Notwithstanding any other provision of this subsection, at the election of a participant who is an employee of a church or a convention or association of churches, including an organization described in section 414(e)(3)(B)(ii), contributions and other additions for an annuity contract or retirement income account described in section

403(b) with respect to such participant, when expressed as an annual addition to such participant's account, shall be treated as not exceeding the limitation of paragraph (1) if such annual addition is not in excess of $10,000.

"(B) $40,000 aggregate limitation. The total amount of additions with respect to any participant which may be taken into account for purposes of this subparagraph for all years may not exceed $40,000.

"(C) Annual addition. For purposes of this paragraph, the term 'annual addition' has the meaning given such term by paragraph (2)."

Effective Date Sec. 411(x), P.L. 107-147, 3/9/2002) effective for yrs. begin. after 12/31/2001.

Note Sec. 411(j)(3), P.L. 107-147, 3/9/2002 added Sec. 611(i)(3) of P.L. 107-16 which provides:

"(3) Special rule. In the case of plan that, on June 7, 2001, incorporated by reference the limitation of section 415(b)(1)(A) of the Internal Revenue Code of 1986, section 411(d)(6) of such Code and section 204(g)(1) of the Employee Retirement Income Security Act of 1974 do not apply to a plan amendment that—

"(A) is adopted on or before June 30, 2002,

"(B) reduces benefits to the level that would have applied without regard to the amendments made by subsection (a) of this section, and

"(C) is effective no earlier than the years described in paragraph (2)."

[¶3041]
Code Sec. 416.   Special rules for top-heavy plans.

* * * * * * * * * * * *

(c) Plan must provide minimum benefits.
(1) Defined benefit plans.

(A) In general. A defined benefit plan meets the requirements of this subsection if the accrued benefit derived from employer contributions of each participant who is a non-key employee, when expressed as an annual retirement benefit, is not less than the applicable percentage of the participant's average compensation for years in the testing period.

(B) Applicable percentage. For purposes of subparagraph (A), the term "applicable percentage" means the lesser of—

(i) 2 percent multiplied by the number of years of service with the employer, or

(ii) 20 percent.

(C) Years of service. For purposes of this paragraph—

(i) In general. Except as provided in clause (ii) or (iii), years of service shall be determined under the rules of paragraphs (4), (5), and (6) of section 411(a).

(ii) Exception for years during which plan was not top-heavy. A year of service with the employer shall not be taken into account under this paragraph if—

(I) the plan was not a top-heavy plan for any plan year ending during such year of service, or

(II) such year of service was completed in a plan year beginning before January 1, 1984.

(iii) [1]*Exception for plan under which no key employee (or former key employee) benefits for plan year.* For purposes of determining an employee's years of service with the employer, any service with the employer shall be disregarded to the extent that such service occurs during a plan year when the plan benefits (within the meaning of section 410(b)) no key employee or former key employee.

(D) Average compensation for high 5 years. For purposes of this paragraph—

(i) In general. A participant's testing period shall be the period of consecutive years (not exceeding 5) during which the participant had the greatest aggregate compensation from the employer.

(ii) Year must be included in year of service. The years taken into account under clause (i) shall be properly adjusted for years not included in a year of service.

(iii) Certain years not taken into account. Except to the extent provided in the plan, a year shall not be taken into account under clause (i) if—

(I) such year ends in a plan year beginning before January 1, 1984, or

(II) such year begins after the close of the last year in which the plan was a top-heavy plan.

(E) Annual retirement benefit. For purposes of this paragraph, the term "annual retirement benefit" means a benefit payable annually in the form of a single life annuity (with no ancillary benefits) beginning at the normal retirement age under the plan.

* * * * * * * * * * *

(g) **Top-heavy plan defined.** For purposes of this section—

* * * * * * * * * * *

(3) **Distributions during last year before determination date taken into account.**
(A) In general. For purposes of determining—
(i) the present value of the cumulative accrued benefit for any employee, or
(ii) the amount of the account of any employee,
such present value or amount shall be increased by the aggregate distributions made with respect to such employee under the plan during the 1-year period ending on the determination date. The preceding sentence shall also apply to distributions under a terminated plan which if it had not been terminated would have been required to be included in an aggregation group.

(B) 5-year period in case of in-service distribution. In the case of any distribution made for a reason other than [2]*severance from employment*, death, or disability, subparagraph (A) shall be applied by substituting "5-year period" for "1-year period."

* * * * * * * * * * *

[For Analysis, see ¶322, ¶323. For Committee Reports, see ¶5041.]

[Endnote Code Sec. 416]

Matter in *italics* in Code Sec. 416(c)(1)(C)(iii) and Code Sec. 416(g)(3)(B) was added by Sec. 411(k)(1) and (2) of the Job Creation and Worker Assistance Act of 2002, P.L. 107-147, 3/9/2002, which struck out:
1. "Exception for frozen plan"
2. "separation from service"
Effective Date (Sec. 411(x), P.L. 107-147, 3/9/2002) effective for yrs. begin. after 12/31/2001.

[¶3042]
Code Sec. 417.   Definitions and special rules for purposes of minimum survivor annuity requirements.

* * * * * * * * * * *

(e) **Restrictions on cash-outs.**
(1) **Plan may require distribution if present value not in excess of dollar limit.** A plan may provide that the present value of a qualified joint and survivor annuity or a qualified preretirement survivor annuity will be immediately distributed if such value does not [1]*exceed the amount that can be distributed without the participant's consent under section 411(a)(11).* No distribution may be made under the preceding sentence after the annuity starting date unless the participant and the spouse of the participant (or where the participant has died, the surviving spouse) consents in writing to such distribution.

(2) **Plan may distribute benefit in excess of dollar limit only with consent.** If—
(A) the present value of the qualified joint and survivor annuity or the qualified preretirement survivor annuity [2]*exceeds the amount that can be distributed without the participant's consent under section 411(a)(11)*, and
(B) the participant and the spouse of the participant (or where the participant has died, the surviving spouse) consent in writing to the distribution,
the plan may immediately distribute the present value of such annuity.

* * * * * * * * * * *

[For Analysis, see ¶324. For Committee Reports, see ¶5048.]

[Endnote Code Sec. 417]

Matter in *italics* in Code Sec. 417(e)(1) and Code Sec. 417(e)(2)(A) was added by Sec. 411(r)(1)(A) and (B) of the Job Creation and Worker Assistance Act of 2002, P.L. 107-147, 3/9/2002, which struck out:

1. "exceed the dollar limit under section 411(a)(11)(A)"

2. "exceeds the dollar limit under section 411(a)(11)(A)"

Effective Date (Sec. 411(x), P.L. 107-147, 3/9/2002) effective for distributions after 12/31/2001.

[¶ 3043]

Code Sec. 448.   Limitation on use of cash method of accounting.

* * * * * * * * * * * *

(d) Definitions and special rules. For purposes of this section—

* * * * * * * * * * * *

¹*(5) Special rule for certain services.*

(A) In general. In the case of any person using an accrual method of accounting with respect to amounts to be received for the performance of services by such person, such person shall not be required to accrue any portion of such amounts which (on the basis of such person's experience) will not be collected if—

(i) such services are in fields referred to in paragraph (2)(A), or

(ii) such person meets the gross receipts test of subsection (c) for all prior taxable years.

(B) Exception. This paragraph shall not apply to any amount if interest is required to be paid on such amount or there is any penalty for failure to timely pay such amount.

(C) Regulations. The Secretary shall prescribe regulations to permit taxpayers to determine amounts referred to in subparagraph (A) using computations or formulas which, based on experience, accurately reflect the amount of income that will not be collected by such person. A taxpayer may adopt, or request consent of the Secretary to change to, a computation or formula that clearly reflects the taxpayer's experience. A request under the preceding sentence shall be approved if such computation or formula clearly reflects the taxpayer's experience.

* * * * * * * * * * * *

[For Analysis, see ¶ 106. For Committee Reports, see ¶ 5023.]

[Endnote Code Sec. 448]

Code Sec. 448(d)(5), in *italics*, was added by Sec. 403(a) of the Job Creation and Worker Assistance Act of 2002, P.L. 107-147, 3/9/2002, which struck out:

1. "(5) Special rule for services. In the case of any person using an accrual method of accounting with respect to amounts to be received for the performance of services by such person, such person shall not be required to accrue any portion of such amounts which (on the basis of experience) will not be collected. This paragraph shall not apply to any amount if interest is required to be paid on such amount or there is any penalty for failure to timely pay such amount."

Effective Date (Sec. 403(b), P.L. 107-147, 3/9/2002) effective for tax. yrs. end. after 3/9/2002. Sec. 403(b)(2) of this Act, relating to change in method of accounting, reads as follows:

"(2) Change in method of accounting. In the case of any taxpayer required by the amendments made by this section to change its method of accounting for its first taxable year ending after the date of the enactment of this Act—

"(A) such change shall be treated as initiated by the taxpayer,

"(B) such change shall be treated as made with the consent of the Secretary of the Treasury, and

"(C) the net amount of the adjustments required to be taken into account by the taxpayer under section 481 of the Internal Revenue Code of 1986 shall be taken into account over a period of 4 years (or if less, the number of taxable years that the taxpayer used the method permitted under section 448(d)(5) of such Code as in effect before the date of the enactment of this Act) beginning with such first taxable year."

[¶ 3044]

Code Sec. 457.   Deferred compensation plans of state and local governments and tax-exempt organizations.

* * * * * * * * * * *

(e) Other definitions and special rules. For purposes of this section—

* * * * * * * * * * *

[1]**(5) Includible compensation.** *The term "includible compensation" has the meaning given to the term "participant's compensation" by section 415(c)(3).*

* * * * * * * * * * *

[2]**(18) Coordination with catch-up contributions for individuals age 50 or older.** *In the case of an individual who is an eligible participant (as defined by section 414(v)) and who is a participant in an eligible deferred compensation plan of an employer described in paragraph (1)(A), subsections (b)(3) and (c) shall be applied by substituting for the amount otherwise determined under the applicable subsection the greater of—*

(A) the sum of—

(i) the plan ceiling established for purposes of subsection (b)(2) (without regard to subsection (b)(3)), plus

(ii) the applicable dollar amount for the taxable year determined under section 414(v)(2)(B)(i), or

(B) the amount determined under the applicable subsection (without regard to this paragraph).

* * * * * * * * * * *

[For Analysis, see ¶ 310, ¶ 320. For Committee Reports, see ¶ 5045, ¶ 5046.]

[Endnote Code Sec. 457]

Code Sec. 457(e)(5), in *italics*, was added by Sec. 411(p)(5) of the Job Creation and Workers Assistance Act of 2002, P.L. 107-147, 3/9/2002, which struck out:

1. "(5) Includible compensation. The term 'includible compensation' means compensation for service performed for the employer which (taking into account the provisions of this section and other provisions of this chapter) is currently includible in gross income."

Effective Date (Sec. 411(x), P.L. 107-147, 3/9/2002) effective for yrs. begin. after 12/31/2001.

Code Sec. 457(e)(18), in *italics*, was added by Sec. 411(o)(9), P.L. 107-147, 3/9/2002.

2. added para. (e)(18)

Effective Date (Sec. 411(x), P.L. 107-147, 3/9/2002) effective for contributions in tax yrs. begin. after 12/31/2001.

[¶ 3045]
Code Sec. 469.   Passive activity losses and credits limited.

* * * * * * * * * * *

(i) $25,000 offset for rental real estate activities.

* * * * * * * * * * *

(3) Phase-out of exemption.

(A) In general. In the case of any taxpayer, the $25,000 amount under paragraph (2) shall be reduced (but not below zero) by 50 percent of the amount by which the adjusted gross income of the taxpayer for the taxable year exceeds $100,000.

(B) Special phase-out of rehabilitation credit. In the case of any portion of the passive activity credit for any taxable year which is attributable to the rehabilitation credit determined under section 47, subparagraph (A) shall be applied by substituting "$200,000" for "$100,000".

 Research Institute of America

(C) Exception for commercial revitalization deduction. Subparagraph (A) shall not apply to any portion of the passive activity loss for any taxable year which is attributable to the commercial revitalization deduction under section 1400I.

(D) Exception for low-income housing credit. Subparagraph (A) shall not apply to any portion of the passive activity credit for any taxable year which is attributable to any credit determined under section 42.

(E) Ordering rules to reflect exceptions and separate phase-outs. If subparagraph (B), (C), or (D) applies for a taxable year, paragraph (1) shall be applied—

(i) first to the portion of the passive activity loss to which subparagraph (C) does not apply,

¹*(ii) second to the portion of such loss to which subparagraph (C) applies,*

²*(iii) third to the portion of the passive activity credit to which subparagraph (B) or (D) does not apply,*

³*(iv) fourth to the portion of such credit to which subparagraph (B) applies, and*

(v) then to the portion of such credit to which subparagraph (D) applies.

* * * * * * * * * * * *

[For Analysis, see ¶ 107. For Committee Reports, see ¶ 5054.]

[Endnote Code Sec. 469]

Code Sec. 469(i)(3)(E)(ii), Code Sec. 469(i)(3)(E)(iii) and Code Sec. 469(i)(3)(E)(iv), in *italics*, was added by Sec. 412(a) of the Job Creation and Worker Assistance Act of 2002, P.L. 107-147, 3/9/2002, which struck out:

1. "(ii) second to the portion of the passive activity credit to which subparagraph (B) or (D) does not apply,"
2. "(iii) third to the portion of such credit to which subparagraph (B) applies,"
3. "(iv) fourth to the portion of such loss to which subparagraph (C) applies, and"

Effective Date (Sec. 412(e), P.L. 107-147, 3/9/2002) effective as if included in the amendments made by Sec. 101, of the Community Renewal Tax Relief Act of 2000, P.L. 106-554, enacted 12/21/2000.

[¶ 3046]
Code Sec. 475.   Mark to market accounting method for dealers in securities.

* * * * * * * * * * * *

(g) Regulatory authority. The Secretary shall prescribe such regulations as may be necessary or appropriate to carry out the purposes of this section, including rules—

(1) to prevent the use of year-end transfers, related parties, or other arrangements to avoid the provisions of this section,

(2) to provide for the application of this section to any security which is a hedge which cannot be identified with a specific security, position, right to income, or liability, and

(3) to prevent the use by taxpayers of subsection (c)(4) to avoid the application of this section to a receivable that is inventory in the hands of the taxpayer (or a person who bears a relationship to the taxpayer described in ¹*section* 267(b) or 707(b)).

[Endnote Code Sec. 475]

Matter in *italics* in Code Sec. 475(g)(3) was added by Sec. 417(10) of the Job Creation and Worker Assistance Act of 2002, P.L. 107-147, 3/9/2002, which struck out:

1. "sections"

Effective Date effective 3/9/2002.

[¶ 3047]
Code Sec. 529.   Qualified tuition programs.

* * * * * * * * * * * *

(e) Other definitions and special rules. For purposes of this section—

* * * * * * * * * * * *

(3) Qualified higher education expenses.

(A) In general. The term "qualified higher education expenses" means—

(i) tuition, fees, books, supplies, and equipment required for the enrollment or attendance of a designated beneficiary at an eligible educational institution; and

(ii) expenses for special needs services in the case of a special needs beneficiary which are incurred in connection with such enrollment or attendance.

(B) Room and board included for students who are at least half-time.

(i) In general. In the case of an individual who is an eligible student (as defined in section 25A(b)(3)) for any academic period, such term shall also include reasonable costs for such period (as determined under the qualified tuition program) incurred by the designated beneficiary for room and board while attending such institution. For purposes of *subsection (b)(6)*, a designated beneficiary shall be treated as meeting the requirements of this clause.

(ii) Limitation. The amount treated as qualified higher education expenses by reason of clause (i) shall not exceed—

(I) the allowance (applicable to the student) for room and board included in the cost of attendance (as defined in section 472 of the Higher Education Act of 1965 (20 U.S.C. 1087ll), as in effect on the date of the enactment of the Economic Growth and Tax Relief Reconciliation Act of 2001) as determined by the eligible educational institution for such period, or

(II) if greater, the actual invoice amount the student residing in housing owned or operated by the eligible educational institution is charged by such institution for room and board costs for such period.

* * * * * * * * * * *

[Endnote Code Sec. 529]

Matter in *italics* in Code Sec. 529(e)(3)(B)(i) was added by Sec. 417(11) of the Job Creation and Worker Assistance Act of 2002, P.L. 107-147, 3/9/2002, which struck out:

1. "subsection (b)(7)"

Effective Date effective 3/9/2002.

[¶3048]
Code Sec. 530.   Coverdell education savings accounts.

* * * * * * * * * * *

(d) Tax treatment of distributions.

* * * * * * * * * * *

(4) Additional tax for distributions not used for educational expenses.

(A) In general. The tax imposed by this chapter for any taxable year on any taxpayer who receives a payment or distribution from a Coverdell education savings account which is includible in gross income shall be increased by 10 percent of the amount which is so includible.

(B) Exceptions. Subparagraph (A) shall not apply if the payment or distribution is—

(i) made to a beneficiary (or to the estate of the designated beneficiary) on or after the death of the designated beneficiary,

(ii) attributable to the designated beneficiary's being disabled (within the meaning of section 72(m)(7)),

(iii) made on account of a scholarship, allowance, or payment described in section 25A(g)(2) received by the account holder to the extent the amount of the payment or distribution does not exceed the amount of the scholarship, allowance, or payment, or

(iv) an amount which is includible in gross income solely *by application of paragraph (2)(C)(i)(II)* for the taxable year.

* * * * * * * * * * *

[For Analysis, see ¶ 409. For Committee Reports, see ¶ 5036.]

[Endnote Code Sec. 530]

Matter in *italics* in Code Sec. 530(d)(4)(B)(iv) was added by Sec. 411(f) of the Job Creation and Worker Assistance Act of 2002, P.L. 107-147, 3/9/2002, which struck out:

1. "because the taxpayer elected under paragraph (2)(C) to waive the application of paragraph (2)"

Effective Date (Sec. 411(x), P.L. 107-147, 3/9/2002) effective for tax. yrs. begin. after 12/31/2001.

[¶ 3049]

Code Sec. 613A.   Limitations on percentage depletion in case of oil and gas wells.

* * * * * * * * * * * *

(c) Exemption for independent producers and royalty owners.

* * * * * * * * * * * *

(6) Oil and natural gas produced from marginal properties.

* * * * * * * * * * * *

(H) Temporary suspension of taxable income limit with respect to marginal production. The second sentence of subsection (a) of section 613 shall not apply to so much of the allowance for depletion as is determined under subparagraph (A) for any taxable year beginning after December 31, 1997, and before January 1, [1]*2004.*

* * * * * * * * * * * *

[For Analysis, see ¶ 206. For Committee Reports, see ¶ 5075.]

[Endnote Code Sec. 613A]

Matter in *italics* in Code Sec. 613A(c)(6)(H) was added by Sec. 607(a) of the Job Creation and Worker Assistance Act of 2002, P.L. 107-147, 3/9/2002, which struck out:

1. "2002"

Effective Date (Sec. 607(b), P.L. 107-147, 3/9/2002) effective for tax. yrs. begin. after 12/31/2001.

[¶ 3050]

Code Sec. 741.   Recognition and character of gain or loss on sale or exchange.

In the case of a sale or exchange of an interest in a partnership, gain or loss shall be recognized to the transferor partner. Such gain or loss shall be considered as gain or loss from the sale or exchange of a capital asset, except as otherwise provided in section 751 (relating to unrealized receivables and inventory items[1]).

[Endnote Code Sec. 741]

In Code Sec. 741, Sec. 417(12) of the Job Creation and Worker Assistance Act of 2002, P.L. 107-147, 3/9/2002, struck out:

1. "which have appreciated substantially in value"

Effective Date effective 3/9/2002.

[¶ 3051]

Code Sec. 809.   Reduction in certain deductions of mutual life insurance companies.

* * * * * * * * * * * *

[1]*(j) Differential earnings rate treated as zero for certain years.* Notwithstanding subsection (c) or (f), the differential earnings rate shall be treated as zero for purposes of computing both the differential earnings amount and the recomputed differential earnings amount for a mutual life insurance company's taxable years beginning in 2001, 2002, or 2003.

 Research Institute of America   347

[For Analysis, see ¶ 212. For Committee Reports, see ¶ 5079.]

[Endnote Code Sec. 809]

Code Sec. 809(j), in *italics*, was added by Sec. 611(a) of the Job Creation and Workers Assistance Act of 2002, P.L. 107-147, 3/9/2002.

1. added subsec. (j)

Effective Date (Sec. 611(b), P.L. 107-147, 3/9/2002) effective for tax. yrs. begin. after 12/31/2000.

[¶ 3052]

Code Sec. 857.   Taxation of real estate investment trusts and their beneficiaries.

* * * * * * * * * * *

(b) **Method of taxation of real estate investment trusts and holders of shares or certificates of beneficial interest.**

* * * * * * * * * * *

(7) **Income from redetermined rents, redetermined deductions, and excess interest.**

(A) Imposition of tax. There is hereby imposed for each taxable year of the real estate investment trust a tax equal to 100 percent of redetermined rents, redetermined deductions, and excess interest.

(B) Redetermined rents.

(i) In general. The term "redetermined rents" means rents from real property (as defined in ¹*section 856(d))* ²*to the extent the amount of the rents* would (but for subparagraph (E)) be reduced on distribution, apportionment, or allocation under section 482 to clearly reflect income as a result of services furnished or rendered by a taxable REIT subsidiary of the real estate investment trust to a tenant of such trust.

(ii) Exception for certain amounts. Clause (i) shall not apply to amounts received directly or indirectly by a real estate investment trust—

(I) for services furnished or rendered by a taxable REIT subsidiary that are described in paragraph (1)(B) of section 856(d), or

(II) from a taxable REIT subsidiary that are described in paragraph (7)(C)(ii) of such section.

(iii) Exception for de minimis amounts. Clause (i) shall not apply to amounts described in section 856(d)(7)(A) with respect to a property to the extent such amounts do not exceed the one percent threshold described in section 856(d)(7)(B) with respect to such property.

(iv) Exception for comparably priced services. Clause (i) shall not apply to any service rendered by a taxable REIT subsidiary of a real estate investment trust to a tenant of such trust if—

(I) such subsidiary renders a significant amount of similar services to persons other than such trust and tenants of such trust who are unrelated (within the meaning of section 856(d)(8)(F)) to such subsidiary, trust, and tenants, but

(II) only to the extent the charge for such service so rendered is substantially comparable to the charge for the similar services rendered to persons referred to in subclause (I).

(v) Exception for certain separately charged services. Clause (i) shall not apply to any service rendered by a taxable REIT subsidiary of a real estate investment trust to a tenant of such trust if—

(I) the rents paid to the trust by tenants (leasing at least 25 percent of the net leasable space in the trust's property) who are not receiving such service from such subsidiary are substantially comparable to the rents paid by tenants leasing comparable space who are receiving such service from such subsidiary, and

(II) the charge for such service from such subsidiary is separately stated.

(vi) Exception for certain services based on subsidiary's income from the services. Clause (i) shall not apply to any service rendered by a taxable REIT subsidiary of a real estate investment trust to a tenant of such trust if the gross income of such subsidiary from such service is not less than 150 percent of such subsidiary's direct cost in furnishing or rendering the service.

(vii) Exceptions granted by Secretary. The Secretary may waive the tax otherwise imposed by subparagraph (A) if the trust establishes to the satisfaction of the Secretary that rents charged to tenants were established on an arms' length basis even though a taxable REIT subsidiary of the trust provided services to such tenants.

(C) Redetermined deductions. The term "redetermined deductions" means deductions (other than redetermined rents) of a taxable REIT subsidiary of a real estate investment trust ³*to the extent the amount* of such deductions would (but for subparagraph (E)) be decreased on distribution, apportionment, or allocation under section 482 to clearly reflect income as between such subsidiary and such trust.

(D) Excess interest. The term "excess interest" means any deductions for interest payments by a taxable REIT subsidiary of a real estate investment trust to such trust to the extent that the interest payments are in excess of a rate that is commercially reasonable.

(E) Coordination with section 482. The imposition of tax under subparagraph (A) shall be in lieu of any distribution, apportionment, or allocation under section 482.

(F) Regulatory authority. The Secretary shall prescribe such regulations as may be necessary or appropriate to carry out the purposes of this paragraph. Until the Secretary prescribes such regulations, real estate investment trusts and their taxable REIT subsidiaries may base their allocations on any reasonable method.

* * * * * * * * * * * *

[For Analysis, see ¶ 701. For Committee Reports, see ¶ 5058.]

[Endnote Code Sec. 857]

Matter in *italics* in Code Sec. 857(b)(7)(B)(i) was added by Sec. 417(13) of the Job Creation and Worker Assistance Act of 2002, P.L. 107-147, 3/9/2002, which struck out:

1. "subsection 856(d)"

Effective Date effective 3/9/2002.

Matter in *italics* in Code Sec. 857(b)(7)(B)(i) and Code Sec. 857(b)(7)(C) was added by Sec. 413(a)(1) and (2), P.L. 107-147, 3/9/2002, which struck out:

2. "the amount of which"
3. "if the amount"

Effective Date (Sec. 413(b), P.L. 107-147, 3/9/2002) effective for tax. yrs. begin. after 12/31/2000.

[¶ 3053]
Code Sec. 904.   Limitation on credit.

* * * * * * * * * * * *

(h) Coordination with nonrefundable personal credits. In the case of an individual, for purposes of subsection (a), the tax against which the credit is taken is such tax reduced by the sum of the credits allowable under subpart A of part IV of subchapter A of this chapter (other than sections 23, 24, and 25B). This subsection shall not apply to taxable years beginning ¹*during 2000, 2001, 2002, or 2003.*

* * * * * * * * * * * *

[For Analysis, see ¶ 402. For Committee Reports, see ¶ 5069.]

[Endnote Code Sec. 904]

Matter in *italics* in Code Sec. 904(h) was added by Sec. 601(b)(1) of the Job Creation and Worker Assistance Act of 2002, P.L. 107-147, 3/9/2002, which struck out:

1. "during 2000 or 2001"

Effective Date (Sec. 601(c), P.L. 107-147, 3/9/2002) effective for tax. yrs. begin. after 12/31/2001.

Note Sec. 601(b)(2), P.L. 107-147, 3/9/2002, following, provides rules for applying amendments made by Secs. 201(b), 202(f) and 618(b) of P.L. 107-16. Sec. 601(b)(2) reads as follows:

"(2) The amendments made by sections 201(b), 202(f), and 618(b) of the Economic Growth and Tax Relief Reconciliation Act of 2001 [P.L. 107-16] shall not apply to taxable years beginning during 2002 and 2003."

Note The amendments made by Secs. 201(b), 202(f) and 618(b) are as follows:

Sec. 201(b)(2)(G) added "(other than section 24)" after "chapter" in subsec. (h).

Sec. 202(f)(2)(C) substituted "sections 23 and 24" for "section 24" in subsec. (h) [as amended by Sec. 201(b)(2)(G) of this Act, see above].

Sec. 618(b)(2)(D) substituted ", 24, and 25B" for "and 24" in subsec. (h) [as amended by Sec. 201(b)(2)(G) and Sec. 202(f)(2)(C) of this Act, see above].

[¶ 3054]
Code Sec. 943.   Other definitions and special rules.

* * * * * * * * * * *

(e) Election to be treated as domestic corporation.

* * * * * * * * * * *

(4) Special rules.

(A) Requirements. This subsection shall not apply to an applicable foreign corporation if such corporation fails to meet the requirements (if any) which the Secretary may prescribe to ensure that the taxes imposed by this chapter on such corporation are paid.

(B) Effect of election, revocation, and termination.

(i) Election. For purposes of section 367, a foreign corporation making an election under this subsection shall be treated as transferring (as of the first day of the first taxable year to which the election applies) all of its assets to a domestic corporation in connection with an exchange to which section 354 applies.

(ii) Revocation and termination. For purposes of section 367, if—

(I) an election is made by a corporation under paragraph (1) for any taxable year, and

(II) such election ceases to apply for any subsequent taxable year,

[1]*such corporation shall be treated as a domestic corporation transferring (as of the 1st day of the first such subsequent taxable year to which such election ceases to apply) all of its property to a foreign corporation in connection with an exchange to which section 354 applies.*

(C) Eligibility for election. The Secretary may by regulation designate one or more classes of corporations which may not make the election under this subsection.

* * * * * * * * * * *

[Endnote Code Sec. 943]

In Code Sec. 943(e)(4)(B), Sec. 417(14) of the Job Creation and Worker Assistance Act of 2002, P.L. 107-147, 3/9/2002, adjusted the margin of the flush language beginning with "such corporation" and ending with "section 354 applies" so that it is flush with subpara. (e)(4)(A), rather than with clause (e)(4)(B)(ii).

[¶ 3055]
Code Sec. 953.   Insurance income.

* * * * * * * * * * *

(e) Exempt insurance income. For purposes of this section—

* * * * * * * * * * *

(10) Application. This subsection and section 954(i) shall apply only to taxable years of a foreign corporation beginning after December 31, 1998, and before [1]*January 1, 2007*, and to taxable years of United States shareholders with or within which any such taxable year of such foreign corporation ends. If this subsection does not apply to a taxable year of a foreign corporation beginning after [2]*December 31, 2006* (and taxable years of United States shareholders ending with or within such taxable year), then, notwithstanding the preceding sentence, subsection (a) shall be applied to such taxable years in the same manner as it would if the taxable year of the foreign corporation began in 1998.

* * * * * * * * * * * *

[For Analysis, see ¶ 203, ¶ 204. For Committee Reports, see ¶ 5082.]

[Endnote Code Sec. 953]
Matter in *italics* in Code Sec. 953(e)(10) was added by Sec. 614(a)(1)(A) and (B) of the Job Creation and Worker Assistance Act of 2002, P.L. 107-147, 3/9/2002, which struck out:
  1. "January 1, 2002"
  2. "December 31, 2001"
Effective Date (Sec. 614(c), P.L. 107-147, 3/9/2002) effective for tax. yrs. begin. after 12/31/2001.

[¶ 3056]
Code Sec. 954.   Foreign base company income.

* * * * * * * * * * * *

(h) Special rule for income derived in the active conduct of banking, financing, or similar businesses.

* * * * * * * * * * * *

(9) Application. This subsection, subsection (c)(2)(C)(ii), and the last sentence of subsection (e)(2) shall apply only to taxable years of a foreign corporation beginning after December 31, 1998, and before [1]*January 1, 2007,* and to taxable years of United States shareholders with or within which any such taxable year of such foreign corporation ends.

(i) Special rule for income derived in the active conduct of insurance business.

* * * * * * * * * * * *

(4) Methods for determining unearned premiums and reserves. For purposes of paragraph (2)(A)—

(A) Property and casualty contracts. The unearned premiums and reserves of a qualifying insurance company or a qualifying insurance company branch with respect to property, casualty, or health insurance contracts shall be determined using the same methods and interest rates which would be used if such company or branch were subject to tax under subchapter L, except that—

(i) the interest rate determined for the functional currency of the company or branch, and which, except as provided by the Secretary, is calculated in the same manner as the Federal mid-term rate under section 1274(d), shall be substituted for the applicable Federal interest rate, and

(ii) such company or branch shall use the appropriate foreign loss payment pattern.

[2]*(B) Life insurance and annuity contracts.*

(i) In general. Except as provided in clause (ii), the amount of the reserve of a qualifying insurance company or qualifying insurance company branch for any life insurance or annuity contract shall be equal to the greater of—

(I) the net surrender value of such contract (as defined in section 807(e)(1)(A)), or

(II) the reserve determined under paragraph (5).

(ii) Ruling request, etc. The amount of the reserve under clause (i) shall be the foreign statement reserve for the contract (less any catastrophe, deficiency, equalization, or similar reserves), if, pursuant to a ruling request submitted by the taxpayer or as provided in published guidance, the Secretary determines that the factors taken into account in determining the foreign statement reserve provide an appropriate means of measuring income.

* * * * * * * * * * * *

[For Analysis, see ¶ 203, ¶ 204. For Committee Reports, see ¶ 5082.]

[Endnote Code Sec. 954]

 Research Institute of America

Matter in *italics* in Code Sec. 954(h)(9) and Code Sec. 954(i)(4)(B) was added by Sec. 614(a)(2) and (b)(1) of the Job Creation and Worker Assistance Act of 2002, P.L. 107-147, 3/9/2002, which struck out:

1. "January 1, 2002"

2. "(B) Life insurance and annuity contracts. The amount of the reserve of a qualifying insurance company or qualifying insurance company branch for any life insurance or annuity contract shall be equal to the greater of—

"(i) the net surrender value of such contract (as defined in section 807(e)(1)(A)), or

"(ii) the reserve determined under paragraph (5)."

Effective Date (Sec. 614(c), P.L. 107-147, 3/9/2002) effective for tax. yrs. begin. after 12/31/2001.

[¶ 3057]

Code Sec. 995.   Taxation of DISC income to shareholders.

* * * * * * * * * * *

(b) Deemed distributions.

* * * * * * * * * * *

(3) Taxable income attributable to military property.

(A) In general. For purposes of paragraph (1)(D), taxable income of a DISC for the taxable year attributable to military property shall be determined by only taking into account—

(i) the gross income of the DISC for the taxable year which is attributable to military property, and

(ii) the deductions which are properly apportioned or allocated to such income.

(B) Military property. For purposes of subparagraph (A), the term "military property" means any property which is an arm, ammunition, or implement of war designated in the munitions list published pursuant to section 38 of the [1]*Arms Export Control Act* (22 U.S.C. 2778).

* * * * * * * * * * *

[Endnote Code Sec. 995]

Matter in *italics* in Code Sec. 995(b)(3)(B) was added by Sec. 417(15) of the Job Creation and Worker Assistance Act of 2002, P.L. 107-147, 3/9/2002, which struck out:

1. "International Security Assistance and Arms Export Control Act of 1976"

Effective Date effective 3/9/2002.

[¶ 3058]

Code Sec. 1091.   Loss from wash sales of stock or securities.

* * * * * * * * * * *

(e) Certain short sales of stock or [1]*securities and securities futures contracts to sell.* Rules similar to the rules of subsection (a) shall apply to any loss realized on the closing of a short sale of [2]*(or the sale, exchange, or termination of a securities futures contract to sell)* stock or securities if, within a period beginning 30 days before the date of such closing and ending 30 days after such date—

(1) substantially identical stock or securities were sold, or

(2) another short sale of [3]*(or securities futures contracts to sell)* substantially identical stock or securities was entered into.

[4]*For purposes of this subsection, the term "securities futures contract" has the meaning provided by section 1234B(c).*

* * * * * * * * * * *

[For Analysis, see ¶ 704. For Committee Reports, see ¶ 5057.]

[Endnote Code Sec. 1091]

Matter in *italics* in Code Sec. 1091(e) was added by Sec. 412(d)(2)(A)-(D) of the Job Creation and Worker Assistance Act of 2002, P.L. 107-147, 3/9/2002, which struck out:

1. "securities."

 Research Institute of America

2. added matter in subsec. (e)
3. added matter in para. (e)(2)
4. added a flush sentence at the end of subsec. (e)
Effective Date (Sec. 412(e), P.L. 107-147, 3/9/2002) effective 12/21/2000.

[¶ 3059]
Code Sec. 1221.   Capital asset defined.

* * * * * * * * * * *

(b) Definitions and special rules.

(1) Commodities derivative financial instruments. For purposes of subsection (a)(6)—

(A) Commodities derivatives dealer. The term "commodities derivatives dealer" means a person which regularly offers to enter into, assume, offset, assign, or terminate positions in commodities derivative financial instruments with customers in the ordinary course of a trade or business.

(B) Commodities derivative financial instrument.

(i) In general. The term "commodities derivative financial instrument" means any contract or financial instrument with respect to commodities (other than a share of stock in a corporation, a beneficial interest in a partnership or trust, a note, bond, debenture, or other evidence of indebtedness, or a section 1256 contract (as defined in section [1]1256(b))), the value or settlement price of which is calculated by or determined by reference to a specified index.

* * * * * * * * * * *

[Endnote Code Sec. 1221]
Matter in *italics* in Code Sec. 1221(b)(1)(B)(i) was added by Sec. 417(20) of the Job Creation and Worker Assistance Act of 2002, P.L. 107-147, 3/9/2002, which struck out:
1. "1256(b))"
Effective Date effective 3/9/2002.

[¶ 3060]
Code Sec. 1233.   Gains and losses from short sales.

* * * * * * * * * * *

(e) Rules for application of section.

* * * * * * * * * * *

(2) For purposes of subsections (b) and (d)—

(A) the term "property" includes only stocks and securities (including stocks and securities dealt with on a "when issued" basis), and commodity futures, which are capital assets in the hands of the taxpayer, but does not include any position to which section 1092(b) applies;

(B) in the case of futures transactions in any commodity on or subject to the rules of a board of trade or commodity exchange, a commodity future requiring delivery in 1 calendar month shall not be considered as property substantially identical to another commodity future requiring delivery in a different calendar month;

(C) in the case of a short sale of property by an individual, the term "taxpayer", in the application of this subsection and subsections (b) and (d), shall be read as "taxpayer or his spouse"; but an individual who is legally separated from the taxpayer under a decree of divorce or of separate maintenance shall not be considered as the spouse of the taxpayer; [1]

(D) a securities futures contract (as defined in section 1234B) to acquire substantially identical property shall be treated as substantially identical property[2]*; and*

³*(E) entering into a securities futures contract (as so defined) to sell shall be considered to be a short sale, and the settlement of such contract shall be considered to be the closing of such short sale.*

* * * * * * * * * * *

[For Analysis, see ¶ 704. For Committee Reports, see ¶ 5057.]

[Endnote Code Sec. 1233]

Matter in *italics* in Code Sec. 1233(e)(2)(C), Code Sec. 1233(e)(2)(D) and Code Sec. 1233(e)(2)(E) was added by Sec. 412(d)(3)(A) of the Job Creation and Worker Assistance Act of 2002, P.L. 107-147, 3/9/2002, which struck out:

1. "and"
2. "."
3. added subpara. (e)(2)(E)

Effective Date (Sec. 412(e), P.L. 107-147, 3/9/2002) effective 12/21/2000.

[¶ 3061]
Code Sec. 1234A.   Gains or losses from certain terminations.
Gain or loss attributable to the cancellation, lapse, expiration, or other termination of—

(1) a right or obligation (other than a securities futures contract, as defined in section 1234B) with respect to property which is (or on acquisition would be) a capital asset in the hands of the taxpayer, ¹*or*

(2) a section 1256 contract (as defined in section 1256) not described in paragraph (1) which is a capital asset in the hands of the taxpayer, ²

³*(3) Repealed.*

shall be treated as gain or loss from the sale of a capital asset. The preceding sentence shall not apply to the retirement of any debt instrument (whether or not through a trust or other participation agreement).

[For Analysis, see ¶ 704. For Committee Reports, see ¶ 5057.]

[Endnote Code Sec. 1234A]

Matter in *italics* in Code Sec. 1234A(1), Code Sec. 1234A(2) and Code Sec. 1234A(3) was added by Sec. 412(d)(1)(A) of the Job Creation and Worker Assistance Act of 2002, P.L. 107-147, 3/9/2002, which struck out:

1. added matter in para. (1)
2. "or"
3. "(3) a securities futures contract (as so defined) which is a capital asset in the hands of the taxpayer,"

Effective Date (Sec. 412(e), P.L. 107-147, 3/9/2002) effective 12/21/2000.

[¶ 3062]
Code Sec. 1234B.   Gains or losses from securities futures contracts.
(a) Treatment of gain or loss.

(1) In general. Gain or loss attributable to the ¹*sale, exchange, or termination* of a securities futures contract shall be considered gain or loss from the sale or exchange of property which has the same character as the property to which the contract relates has in the hands of the taxpayer (or would have in the hands of the taxpayer if acquired by the taxpayer).

* * * * * * * * * * *

(b) Short-term gains and losses. Except as provided in the regulations under section 1092(b) or this section, ²*or in section 1233,* if gain or loss on the ³*sale, exchange, or termination* of a securities futures contract to sell property is considered as gain or loss from the sale or exchange of a capital asset, such gain or loss shall be treated as short-term capital gain or loss.

* * * * * * * * * * *

⁴*(f) Cross reference. For special rules relating to dealer securities futures contracts, see section 1256.*

Research Institute of America

[For Analysis, see ¶ 704. For Committee Reports, see ¶ 5057.]

[Endnote Code Sec. 1234B]

Matter in *italics* in Code Sec. 1234B(a)(1), Code Sec. 1234B(b) and Code Sec. 1234B(f) added by Sec. 412(d)(1)(B)(i), (ii) and (d)(3)(B) of the Job Creation and Worker Assistance Act of 2002, P.L. 107-147, 3/9/2002, which struck out:

    1. "sale or exchange"

    2. added matter in subsec. (b)

    3. "sale or exchange"

    4. added subsec. (f)

Effective Date (Sec. 412(e), P.L. 107-147, 3/9/2002) effective 12/21/2000.

[¶ 3063]

Code Sec. 1256.   Section 1256 contracts marked to market.

* * * * * * * * * * * *

(f) Special rules.

* * * * * * * * * * * *

    [1]*(5) **Special rule related to losses.** Section 1091 (relating to loss from wash sales of stock or securities) shall not apply to any loss taken into account by reason of paragraph (1) of subsection (a).*

* * * * * * * * * * * *

[Endnote Code Sec. 1256]

Code Sec. 1256(f)(5), in *italics*, was added by Sec. 416(b)(1) of the Job Creation and Worker Assistance Act of 2002, P.L. 107-147, 3/9/2002.

    1. added para. (f)(5)

Effective Date (Sec. 416(b)(2), P.L. 107-147, 3/9/2002) effective for any sale after 11/10/88, in tax. yrs. end. after 11/10/88.

[¶ 3064]

Code Sec. 1394.   Tax-exempt enterprise zone facility bonds.

* * * * * * * * * * * *

(c) Limitation on amount of bonds.

    (1) In general. Subsection (a) shall not apply to any issue if the aggregate amount of outstanding enterprise zone facility bonds allocable to any person (taking into account such issue) exceeds—

        (A) $3,000,000 with respect to any 1 empowerment zone or enterprise community, or

        (B) $20,000,000 with respect to all empowerment zones and enterprise communities.

    (2) Aggregate enterprise zone facility bond benefit. For purposes of [1]*paragraph (1)*, the aggregate amount of outstanding enterprise zone facility bonds allocable to any person shall be determined under rules similar to the rules of section 144(a)(10), taking into account only bonds to which subsection (a) applies.

* * * * * * * * * * * *

[Endnote Code Sec. 1394]

Matter in *italics* in Code Sec. 1394(c)(2) was added by Sec. 417(16) of the Job Creation and Worker Assistance Act of 2002, P.L. 107-147, 3/9/2002, which struck out:

    1. "subparagraph (A)"

Effective Date effective 3/9/2002.

[¶ 3065]

Code Sec. 1397E.   Credit to holders of qualified zone academy bonds.

* * * * * * * * * * *

(e) Limitation on amount of bonds designated.

(1) National limitation. There is a national zone academy bond limitation for each calendar year. Such limitation is $400,000,000 for 1998, 1999, [1]*2000, 2001, 2002, and 2003* and, except as provided in paragraph (4), zero thereafter.

* * * * * * * * * * *

[For Analysis, see ¶ 213. For Committee Reports, see ¶ 5076.]

[Endnote Code Sec. 1397E]

Matter in *italics* in Code Sec. 1397E(e)(1) was added by Sec. 608(a) of the Job Creation and Worker Assistance Act of 2002, P.L. 107-147, 3/9/2002, which struck out:

1. "2000, and 2001"

Effective Date (Sec. 608(b), P.L. 107-147, 3/9/2002) effective for obligations issued after 3/9/2002.

[¶ 3066]
Code Sec. 1400C.   First-time homebuyer credit for District of Columbia.

* * * * * * * * * * *

[Endnote Code Sec. 1400C]

Note Sec. 601(b)(2), P.L. 107-147, 3/9/2002, following, provides rules for applying amendments made by Sec. 201(b), 202(f) and 618(b) of P.L. 107-16. Sec. 601(b)(2), P.L. 107-147, reads as follows:

"(2) The amendments made by sections 201(b), 202(f), and 618(b) of the Economic Growth and Tax Relief Reconciliation Act of 2001 [P.L. 107-16] shall not apply to taxable years beginning during 2002 and 2003."

Note The amendments made by Secs. 201(b), 202(f) and 618(b), P.L. 107-16, are as follows:

Sec. 201(b)(2)(H) added "and section 24" after "this section" in subsec. (d), effective for tax. yrs. begin. after 12/31/2001.

Sec. 202(f)(2)(C) substituted "sections 23 and 24" for "section 24" in subsec. (d), [as amended by Sec. 201(b)(2)(H), see above].

Sec. 618(b)(2)(E) substituted ", 24, and 25B" for "and 24" in subsec. (d), [as amended by Sec. 201(b)(2)(H) and Sec. 202(f)(2)(C), see above].

[¶ 3067]
Code Sec.[1] 1400L.   *Tax benefits for New York Liberty Zone.*

(a) *Expansion of work opportunity tax credit.*

(1) *In general.* *For purposes of section 51, a New York Liberty Zone business employee shall be treated as a member of a targeted group.*

(2) *New York Liberty Zone business employee.* *For purposes of this subsection—*

(A) In general. The term "New York Liberty Zone business employee" means, with respect to any period, any employee of a New York Liberty Zone business if substantially all the services performed during such period by such employee for such business are performed in the New York Liberty Zone.

(B) Inclusion of certain employees outside the New York Liberty Zone.

(i) In general. In the case of a New York Liberty Zone business described in subclause (II) of subparagraph (C)(i), the term "New York Liberty Zone business employee" includes any employee of such business (not described in subparagraph (A)) if substantially all the services performed during such period by such employee for such business are performed in the City of New York, New York.

(ii) Limitation. The number of employees of such a business that are treated as New York Liberty Zone business employees on any day by reason of clause (i) shall not exceed the excess of—

(I) the number of employees of such business on September 11, 2001, in the New York Liberty Zone, over

(II) the number of New York Liberty Zone business employees (determined without regard to this subparagraph) of such business on the day to which the limitation is being applied.

The Secretary may require any trade or business to have the number determined under subclause (I) verified by the New York State Department of Labor.

(C) New York Liberty Zone business.

(i) In general. The term "New York Liberty Zone business" means any trade or business which is—

(I) located in the New York Liberty Zone, or

(II) located in the City of New York, New York, outside the New York Liberty Zone, as a result of the physical destruction or damage of such place of business by the September 11, 2001, terrorist attack.

(ii) Credit not allowed for large businesses. The term "New York Liberty Zone business" shall not include any trade or business for any taxable year if such trade or business employed an average of more than 200 employees on business days during the taxable year.

(D) Special rules for determining amount of credit. For purposes of applying subpart F of part IV of subchapter B of this chapter to wages paid or incurred to any New York Liberty Zone business employee—

(i) section 51(a) shall be applied by substituting "qualified wages" for "qualified first-year wages",

(ii) the rules of section 52 shall apply for purposes of determining the number of employees under subparagraph (B),

(iii) subsections (c)(4) and (i)(2) of section 51 shall not apply, and

(iv) in determining qualified wages, the following shall apply in lieu of section 51(b):

(I) Qualified wages. The term "qualified wages" means wages paid or incurred by the employer to individuals who are New York Liberty Zone business employees of such employer for work performed during calendar year 2002 or 2003.

(II) Only first $6,000 of wages per calendar year taken into account. The amount of the qualified wages which may be taken into account with respect to any individual shall not exceed $6,000 per calendar year.

(b) Special allowance for certain property acquired after September 10, 2001.

(1) Additional allowance. In the case of any qualified New York Liberty Zone property—

(A) the depreciation deduction provided by section 167(a) for the taxable year in which such property is placed in service shall include an allowance equal to 30 percent of the adjusted basis of such property, and

(B) the adjusted basis of the qualified New York Liberty Zone property shall be reduced by the amount of such deduction before computing the amount otherwise allowable as a depreciation deduction under this chapter for such taxable year and any subsequent taxable year.

(2) Qualified New York Liberty Zone property. For purposes of this subsection—

(A) In general. The term "qualified New York Liberty Zone property" means property—

(i) (I) which is described in section 168(k)(2)(A)(i), or

(II) which is nonresidential real property, or residential rental property, which is described in subparagraph (B),

(ii) substantially all of the use of which is in the New York Liberty Zone and is in the active conduct of a trade or business by the taxpayer in such Zone,

(iii) the original use of which in the New York Liberty Zone commences with the taxpayer after September 10, 2001,

(iv) which is acquired by the taxpayer by purchase (as defined in section 179(d)) after September 10, 2001, but only if no written binding contract for the acquisition was in effect before September 11, 2001, and

(v) which is placed in service by the taxpayer on or before the termination date.

The term "termination date" means December 31, 2006 (December 31, 2009, in the case of nonresidential real property and residential rental property).

(B) Eligible real property. Nonresidential real property or residential rental property is described in this subparagraph only to the extent it rehabilitates real property damaged, or replaces real property destroyed or condemned, as a result of the September 11, 2001, terrorist attack. For purposes of the preceding sentence, property shall be treated as replacing real property destroyed or condemned if, as part of an integrated plan, such property replaces real property which is included in a continuous area which includes real property destroyed or condemned.

(C) Exceptions.

(i) 30 percent additional allowance property. Such term shall not include property to which section 168(k) applies.

(ii) Alternative depreciation property. The term "qualified New York Liberty Zone property" shall not include any property described in section 168(k)(2)(C)(i).

(iii) Qualified New York Liberty Zone leasehold improvement property. Such term shall not include any qualified New York Liberty Zone leasehold improvement property.

(iv) Election out. For purposes of this subsection, rules similar to the rules of section 168(k)(2)(C)(iii) shall apply.

(D) Special rules. For purposes of this subsection, rules similar to the rules of section 168(k)(2)(D) shall apply, except that clause (i) thereof shall be applied without regard to "and before September 11, 2004".

(E) Allowance against alternative minimum tax. For purposes of this subsection, rules similar to the rules of section 168(k)(2)(F) shall apply.

(c) 5-year recovery period for depreciation of certain leasehold improvements.

(1) In general. For purposes of section 168, the term "5-year property" includes any qualified New York Liberty Zone leasehold improvement property.

(2) Qualified New York Liberty Zone leasehold improvement property. For purposes of this section, the term "qualified New York Liberty Zone leasehold improvement property" means qualified leasehold improvement property (as defined in section 168(k)(3)) if—

(A) such building is located in the New York Liberty Zone,

(B) such improvement is placed in service after September 10, 2001, and before January 1, 2007, and

(C) no written binding contract for such improvement was in effect before September 11, 2001.

(3) Requirement to use straight line method. The applicable depreciation method under section 168 shall be the straight line method in the case of qualified New York Liberty Zone leasehold improvement property.

(4) 9-year recovery period under alternative system. For purposes of section 168(g), the class life of qualified New York Liberty Zone leasehold improvement property shall be 9 years.

(d) Tax-exempt bond financing.

(1) In general. For purposes of this title, any qualified New York Liberty Bond shall be treated as an exempt facility bond.

(2) Qualified New York Liberty Bond. For purposes of this subsection, the term "qualified New York Liberty Bond" means any bond issued as part of an issue if—

(A) 95 percent or more of the net proceeds (as defined in section 150(a)(3)) of such issue are to be used for qualified project costs,

(B) such bond is issued by the State of New York or any political subdivision thereof,

(C) the Governor or the Mayor designates such bond for purposes of this section, and

(D) such bond is issued after the the date of the enactment of this section and before January 1, 2005.

(3) Limitations on amount of bonds.

(A) Aggregate amount designated. The maximum aggregate face amount of bonds which may be designated under this subsection shall not exceed $8,000,000,000, of which not to exceed $4,000,000,000 may be designated by the Governor and not to exceed $4,000,000,000 may be designated by the Mayor.

(B) *Specific limitations.* The aggregate face amount of bonds issued which are to be used for—

(i) costs for property located outside the New York Liberty Zone shall not exceed $2,000,000,000,

(ii) residential rental property shall not exceed $1,600,000,000, and

(iii) costs with respect to property used for retail sales of tangible property and functionally related and subordinate property shall not exceed $800,000,000.

The limitations under clauses (i), (ii), and (iii) shall be allocated proportionately between the bonds designated by the Governor and the bonds designated by the Mayor in proportion to the respective amounts of bonds designated by each.

(C) *Movable property.* No bonds shall be issued which are to be used for movable fixtures and equipment.

(4) Qualified project costs. For purposes of this subsection—

(A) *In general.* The term "qualified project costs" means the cost of acquisition, construction, reconstruction, and renovation of—

(i) nonresidential real property and residential rental property (including fixed tenant improvements associated with such property) located in the New York Liberty Zone, and

(ii) public utility property (as defined in section 168(i)(10)) located in the New York Liberty Zone.

(B) *Costs for certain property outside zone included.* Such term includes the cost of acquisition, construction, reconstruction, and renovation of nonresidential real property (including fixed tenant improvements associated with such property) located outside the New York Liberty Zone but within the City of New York, New York, if such property is part of a project which consists of at least 100,000 square feet of usable office or other commercial space located in a single building or multiple adjacent buildings.

(5) Special rules. In applying this title to any qualified New York Liberty Bond, the following modifications shall apply:

(A) Section 146 (relating to volume cap) shall not apply.

(B) Section 147(d) (relating to acquisition of existing property not permitted) shall be applied by substituting "50 percent" for "15 percent" each place it appears.

(C) Section 148(f)(4)(C) (relating to exception from rebate for certain proceeds to be used to finance construction expenditures) shall apply to the available construction proceeds of bonds issued under this section.

(D) Repayments of principal on financing provided by the issue—

(i) may not be used to provide financing, and

(ii) must be used not later than the close of the 1st semiannual period beginning after the date of the repayment to redeem bonds which are part of such issue.

The requirement of clause (ii) shall be treated as met with respect to amounts received within 10 years after the date of issuance of the issue (or, in the case of a refunding bond, the date of issuance of the original bond) if such amounts are used by the close of such 10 years to redeem bonds which are part of such issue.

(E) Section 57(a)(5) shall not apply.

(6) Separate issue treatment of portions of an issue. This subsection shall not apply to the portion of an issue which (if issued as a separate issue) would be treated as a qualified bond or as a bond that is not a private activity bond (determined without regard to paragraph (1)), if the issuer elects to so treat such portion.

(e) Advance refundings of certain tax-exempt bonds.

(1) In general. With respect to a bond described in paragraph (2) issued as part of an issue 90 percent (95 percent in the case of a bond described in paragraph (2)(C)) or more of the net proceeds (as defined in section 150(a)(3)) of which were used to finance facilities located within the City of New York, New York (or property which is functionally related and subordinate to facilities located within the City of New York for the furnishing of water), one additional advanced refunding after the date of the enactment of this section and before January 1, 2005, shall be allowed under the applicable rules of section 149(d) if—

(A) the Governor or the Mayor designates the advance refunding bond for purposes of this subsection, and

(B) the requirements of paragraph (4) are met.

(2) Bonds described. A bond is described in this paragraph if such bond was outstanding on September 11, 2001, and is—

(A) a State or local bond (as defined in section 103(c)(1)) which is a general obligation of the City of New York, New York,

(B) a State or local bond (as so defined) other than a private activity bond (as defined in section 141(a)) issued by the New York Municipal Water Finance Authority or the Metropolitan Transportation Authority of the State of New York, or

(C) a qualified 501(c)(3) bond (as defined in section 145(a)) which is a qualified hospital bond (as defined in section 145(c)) issued by or on behalf of the State of New York or the City of New York, New York.

(3) Aggregate limit. For purposes of paragraph (1), the maximum aggregate face amount of bonds which may be designated under this subsection by the Governor shall not exceed $4,500,000,000 and the maximum aggregate face amount of bonds which may be designated under this subsection by the Mayor shall not exceed $4,500,000,000.

(4) Additional requirements. The requirements of this paragraph are met with respect to any advance refunding of a bond described in paragraph (2) if—

(A) no advance refundings of such bond would be allowed under any provision of law after September 11, 2001,

(B) the advance refunding bond is the only other outstanding bond with respect to the refunded bond, and

(C) the requirements of section 148 are met with respect to all bonds issued under this subsection.

(f) Increase in expensing under section 179.

(1) In general. For purposes of section 179—

(A) the limitation under section 179(b)(1) shall be increased by the lesser of—

(i) $35,000, or

(ii) the cost of section 179 property which is qualified New York Liberty Zone property placed in service during the taxable year, and

(B) the amount taken into account under section 179(b)(2) with respect to any section 179 property which is qualified New York Liberty Zone property shall be 50 percent of the cost thereof.

(2) Qualified New York Liberty Zone property. For purposes of this subsection, the term "qualified New York Liberty Zone property" has the meaning given such term by subsection (b)(2).

(3) Recapture. Rules similar to the rules under section 179(d)(10) shall apply with respect to any qualified New York Liberty Zone property which ceases to be used in the New York Liberty Zone.

(g) Extension of replacement period for nonrecognition of gain. Notwithstanding subsections (g) and (h) of section 1033, clause (i) of section 1033(a)(2)(B) shall be applied by substituting "5 years" for "2 years" with respect to property which is compulsorily or involuntarily converted as a result of the terrorist attacks on September 11, 2001, in the New York Liberty Zone but only if substantially all of the use of the replacement property is in the City of New York, New York.

(h) New York Liberty Zone. For purposes of this section, the term "New York Liberty Zone" means the area located on or south of Canal Street, East Broadway (east of its intersection with Canal Street), or Grand Street (east of its intersection with East Broadway) in the Borough of Manhattan in the City of New York, New York.

(i) References to Governor and Mayor. For purposes of this section, the terms "Governor" and "Mayor" mean the Governor of the State of New York and the Mayor of the City of New York, New York, respectively.

[For Analysis, see ¶ 501, ¶ 502, ¶ 503, ¶ 504, ¶ 505, ¶ 507, ¶ 508. For Committee Reports, see ¶ 5011, ¶ 5012, ¶ 5013, ¶ 5014, ¶ 5015, ¶ 5016, ¶ 5017.]

[Endnote Code Sec. 1400L]

Code Sec. 1400L, in *italics*, was added by Sec. 301(a) of the Job Creation and Worker Assistance Act of 2002, P.L. 107-147, 3/9/2002.

1. added Code Sec. 1400L

Enacted 3/9/2002.

[¶ 3068]
Code Sec. 2016.   Recovery of taxes claimed as credit.

If any tax claimed as a credit under section 2014 is recovered from any foreign country, [1]the executor, or any other person or persons recovering such amount, shall give notice of such recovery to the Secretary at such time and in such manner as may be required by regulations prescribed by him, and the Secretary shall (despite the provisions of section 6501) redetermine the amount of the tax under this chapter and the amount, if any, of the tax due on such redetermination, shall be paid by the executor or such person or persons, as the case may be, on notice and demand. No interest shall be assessed or collected on any amount of tax due on any redetermination by the Secretary resulting from a refund to the executor of tax claimed as a credit under section 2014, for any period before the receipt of such refund, except to the extent interest was paid by the foreign country on such refund.

[Endnote Code Sec. 2016]

In Code Sec. 2016, Sec. 411(h) of the Job Creation and Worker Assistance Act of 2002, P.L. 107-147, 3/9/2002, struck out:

1. "any State, any possession of the United States, or the District of Columbia,"

Effective Date (Sec. 411(x), P.L. 107-147, 3/9/2002) effective for estates of decedents dying, and generation-skipping transfers, after 12/31/2004.

[¶ 3069]
Code Sec. 2101.   Tax imposed.

* * * * * * * * * * * *

(b) Computation of tax. The tax imposed by this section shall be the amount equal to the excess (if any) of—

    (1) a tentative tax computed under section 2001(c) on the sum of—

        (A) the amount of the taxable estate, and

        (B) the amount of the adjusted taxable gifts, over

    (2) a tentative tax computed under section 2001(c) on the amount of the adjusted taxable gifts.[1]

* * * * * * * * * * * *

[Endnote Code Sec. 2101]

In Code Sec. 2101(b), Sec. 411(g)(2) of the Job Creation and Worker Assistance Act of 2002, P.L. 107-147, 3/9/2002, struck out:

1. "For purposes of the preceding sentence, there shall be appropriate adjustments in the application of section 2001(c)(2) to reflect the difference between the amount of the credit provided under section 2102(c) and the amount of the credit provided under section 2010."

Effective Date (Sec. 411(x), P.L. 107-147, 3/9/2002) effective for estates of decedents dying, and gifts made, after 12/31/2001.

 Research Institute of America

[¶ 3070]
Code Sec. 2511.   Transfers in general.

* * * * * * * * * * * *

(c) **Treatment of certain transfers in trust.** Notwithstanding any other provision of this section and except as provided in regulations, a transfer in trust shall be treated as a [1]*transfer of property by gift,* unless the trust is treated as wholly owned by the donor or the donor's spouse under subpart E of part I of subchapter J of chapter 1.

[For Analysis, see ¶ 702. For Committee Reports, see ¶ 5037.]

[Endnote Code Sec. 2511]
  Matter in *italics* in Code Sec. 2511(c) was added by Sec. 411(g)(1) of the Job Creation and Worker Assistance Act of 2002, P.L. 107-147, 3/9/2002, which struck out:
  1. "taxable gift under section 2503,"
Effective Date (Sec. 411(x), P.L. 107-147, 3/9/2002) effective for gifts made after 12/31/2009.

[¶ 3071]
Code Sec. 3304.   Approval of State laws.

(a) **Requirements.** The Secretary of Labor shall approve any State law submitted to him, within 30 days of such submission, which he finds provides that—

(1) all compensation is to be paid through public employment offices or such other agencies as the Secretary of Labor may approve;

(2) no compensation shall be payable with respect to any day of unemployment occurring within 2 years after the first day of the first period with respect to which contributions are required;

(3) all money received in the unemployment fund shall (except for refunds of sums erroneously paid into such fund and except for refunds paid in accordance with the provisions of section 3305(b)) immediately upon such receipt be paid over to the Secretary of the Treasury to the credit of the Unemployment Trust Fund established by section 904 of the Social Security Act (42 U.S.C. 1104);

(4) all money withdrawn from the unemployment fund of the State shall be used solely in the payment of unemployment compensation, exclusive of expenses of administration, and for refunds of sums erroneously paid into such fund and refunds paid in accordance with the provisions of section 3305(b); except that—

(A) an amount equal to the amount of employee payments into the unemployment fund of a State may be used in the payment of cash benefits to individuals with respect to their disability, exclusive of expenses of administration;

(B) the amounts specified by section 903(c)(2) [1]*or 903(d)(4)* of the Social Security Act may, subject to the conditions prescribed in such section, be used for expenses incurred by the State for administration of its unemployment compensation law and public employment offices;

(C) nothing in this paragraph shall be construed to prohibit deducting an amount from unemployment compensation otherwise payable to an individual and using the amount so deducted to pay for health insurance, or the withholding of Federal, State, or local individual income tax, if the individual elected to have such deduction made and such deduction was made under a program approved by the Secretary of Labor;

(D) amounts may be deducted from unemployment benefits and used to repay overpayments as provided in section 303(g) of the Social Security Act; and

(E) amounts may be withdrawn for the payment of short-time compensation under a plan approved by the Secretary of Labor.

 Research Institute of America

* * * * * * * * * * *

[Endnote Code Sec. 3304]

Matter in *italics* in Code Sec. 3304(a)(4)(B) was added by Sec. 209(d)(1) of the Job Creation and Worker Assistance Act of 2002, P.L. 107-147, 3/9/2002.

1. added matter in subpara. (a)(4)(B)

Effective Date effective 3/9/2002.

[¶ 3072]
Code Sec. 3306.   Definitions.

* * * * * * * * * * *

(f) Unemployment fund. For purposes of this chapter, the term "unemployment fund" means a special fund, established under a State law and administered by a State agency, for the payment of compensation. Any sums standing to the account of the State agency in the Unemployment Trust Fund established by section 904 of the Social Security Act, as amended (42 U.S.C. 1104), shall be deemed to be a part of the unemployment fund of the State, and no sums paid out of the Unemployment Trust Fund to such State agency shall cease to be a part of the unemployment fund of the State until expended by such State agency. An unemployment fund shall be deemed to be maintained during a taxable year only if throughout such year, or such portion of the year as the unemployment fund was in existence, no part of the moneys of such fund was expended for any purpose other than the payment of compensation (exclusive of expenses of administration) and for refunds of sums erroneously paid into such fund and refunds paid in accordance with the provisions of section 3305(b); except that—

(1) an amount equal to the amount of employee payments into the unemployment fund of a State may be used in the payments of cash benefits to individuals with respect to their disability, exclusive of expenses of administration;

(2) the amounts specified by section 903(c)(2) [1]*or 903(d)(4)* of the Social Security Act may, subject to the conditions prescribed in such section, be used for expenses incurred by the State for administration of its unemployment compensation law and public employment offices,

(3) nothing in this subsection shall be construed to prohibit deducting any amount from unemployment compensation otherwise payable to an individual and using the amount so deducted to pay for health insurance, or the withholding of Federal, State, or local individual income tax, if the individual elected to have such deduction made and such deduction was made under a program approved by the Secretary of Labor;

(4) amounts may be deducted from unemployment benefits and used to repay overpayments as provided in section 303(g) of the Social Security Act; and

(5) amounts may be withdrawn for the payment of short-time compensation under a plan approved by the Secretary of Labor.

* * * * * * * * * * *

[Endnote Code Sec. 3306]

Matter in *italics* in Code Sec. 3306(f)(2) was added by Sec. 209(d)(1) of the Job Creation and Worker Assistance Act of 2002, P.L. 107-147, 3/9/2002.

1. added matter in para. (f)(2)

Effective Date effective 3/9/2002.

[¶ 3073]
Code Sec. 4101.   Registration and bond.
  (a) Registration.

* * * * * * * * * * *

¹*(e) Repealed.*
[For Analysis, see ¶ 703. For Committee Reports, see ¶ 5083.]

[Endnote Code Sec. 4101]
    Code Sec. 4101(e) was deleted by Sec. 615(a) of the Job Creation and Worker Assistance Act of 2002, P.L. 107-147, 3/9/2002. Prior to deletion, subsec. (e) read as follows:
    1. "(e) Certain approved terminals of registered persons required to offer dyed diesel fuel and kerosene for nontaxable purposes.
    "(1) In general. A terminal for kerosene or diesel fuel may not be an approved facility for storage of non-tax-paid diesel fuel or kerosene under this section unless the operator of such terminal offers such fuel in a dyed form for removal for nontaxable use in accordance with section 4082(a).
    "(2) Exception. Paragraph (1) shall not apply to any terminal exclusively providing aviation grade kerosene by pipeline to an airport."
Effective Date (Sec. 615(b), P.L. 107-147, 3/9/2002) effective 1/1/2002.

[¶ 3074]
Code Sec.¹ 4980E.   *Failure of employer to make comparable Archer MSA contributions.*

* * * * * * * * * * *

[Endnote Code Sec. 4980E]
    Matter in *italics* in the heading of Code Sec. 4980E added by Sec. 417(17)(A) of the Job Creation and Worker Assistance Act of 2002, P.L. 107-147, 3/9/2002, which struck out:
    1. "Sec. 4980E. Failure of employer to make comparable medical savings account contributions."
Effective Date effective 3/9/2002.

[¶ 3075]
Code Sec. 4980F.   Failure of applicable plans reducing benefit accruals to satisfy notice requirements.

* * * * * * * * * * *

(e) Notice requirements for plans significantly reducing benefit accruals.

(1) In general. If an applicable pension plan is amended to provide for a significant reduction in the rate of future benefit accrual, the plan administrator shall provide ¹*the notice described in paragraph (2)* to each applicable individual (and to each employee organization representing applicable individuals).

(2) Notice. The notice required by paragraph (1) shall be written in a manner calculated to be understood by the average plan participant and shall provide sufficient information (as determined in accordance with regulations prescribed by the Secretary) to allow applicable individuals to understand the effect of the plan amendment. The Secretary may provide a simplified form of notice for, or exempt from any notice requirement, a plan—

    (A) which has fewer than 100 participants who have accrued a benefit under the plan, or

    (B) which offers participants the option to choose between the new benefit formula and the old benefit formula.

(3) Timing of notice. Except as provided in regulations, the notice required by paragraph (1) shall be provided within a reasonable time before the effective date of the plan amendment.

(4) Designees. Any notice under paragraph (1) may be provided to a person designated, in writing, by the person to which it would otherwise be provided.

(5) Notice before adoption of amendment. A plan shall not be treated as failing to meet the requirements of paragraph (1) merely because notice is provided before the adoption of the plan amendment if no material modification of the amendment occurs before the amendment is adopted.

Research Institute of America

(f) Definitions and special rules. For purposes of this section—

(1) Applicable individual. The term "applicable individual" means, with respect to any plan amendment—

(A) each participant in the plan, and

(B) any beneficiary who is an alternate payee (within the meaning of section 414(p)(8)) under an applicable qualified domestic relations order (within the meaning of section 414(p)(1)(A)),

whose rate of future benefit accrual under the plan may reasonably be expected to be significantly reduced by such plan amendment.

(2) Applicable pension plan. The term "applicable pension plan" means—

[2]*(A) any defined benefit plan described in section 401(a) which includes a trust exempt from tax under section 501(a), or*

(B) an individual account plan which is subject to the funding standards of section 412.

Such term shall not include a governmental plan (within the meaning of section 414(d)) or a church plan (within the meaning of section 414(e)) with respect to which the election provided by section 410(d) has not been made.

(3) Early retirement. A plan amendment which eliminates or [3] reduces any early retirement benefit or retirement-type subsidy (within the meaning of section 411(d)(6)(B)(i)) shall be treated as having the effect of [4] reducing the rate of future benefit accrual.

* * * * * * * * * * * *

[For Analysis, see ¶327. For Committee Reports, see ¶5051.]

[Endnote Code Sec. 4980F]

Matter in *italics* in Code Sec. 4980F(e)(1), Code Sec. 4980F(f)(2)(A) and Code Sec. 4980F(f)(3) added by Sec. 411(u)(1)(A)-(C) of of the Job Creation and Worker Assistance Act of 2002, P.L. 107-147, 3/9/2002, which struck out:

1. "written notice"
2. "(A) any defined benefit plan, or"
3. "significantly"
4. "significantly"

Effective Date (Sec. 411(x), P.L. 107-147, 3/9/2002) effective for plan amendments taking effect on or after 6/7/2001. For transitional rules, see Sec. 659(c)(2) and (3) of P.L. 107-16 which reads as follows:

"(2) Transition. Until such time as the Secretary of the Treasury issues regulations under sections 4980F(e)(2) and (3) of the Internal Revenue Code of 1986, and section 204(h) of the Employee Retirement Income Security Act of 1974, as added by the amendments made by this section, a plan shall be treated as meeting the requirements of such sections if it makes a good faith effort to comply with such requirements.

"(3) Special notice rule.

"(A) In general. The period for providing any notice required by the amendments made by this section shall not end before the date which is 3 months after the date of the enactment of this Act.

"(B) Reasonable notice. The amendments made by this section shall not apply to any plan amendment taking effect on or after the date of the enactment of this Act if, before April 25, 2001, notice was provided to participants and beneficiaries adversely affected by the plan amendment (or their representatives) which was reasonably expected to notify them of the nature and effective date of the plan amendment."

[¶3076]
Code Sec. 6103.   Confidentiality and disclosure of returns and return information.

* * * * * * * * * * * *

(l) Disclosure of returns and return information for purposes other than tax administration.

* * * * * * * * * * * *

(8) Disclosure of certain return information by Social Security Administration to [1]*Federal, State, and local* child support enforcement agencies.

(A) In general. Upon written request, the Commissioner of Social Security shall disclose directly to officers and employees of a [2]*Federal or* State or local child support enforcement agency return information from returns with respect to social security account numbers, net earnings from self-employment (as defined in section 1402), wages (as defined in section

3121(a) or 3401(a)), and payments of retirement income which have been disclosed to the Social Security Administration as provided by paragraph (1) or (5) of this subsection.

* * * * * * * * * * *

[For Analysis, see ¶ 604. For Committee Reports, see ¶ 5063.]

[Endnote Code Sec. 6103]

Matter in *italics* in Code Sec. 6103(l)(8) was added by Sec. 416(c)(1)(A) and (B) of the Job Creation and Worker Assistance Act of 2002, P.L. 107-147, 3/9/2002, which struck out:
1. "State and local"
2. added matter in subpara. (l)(8)(A)

Effective Date (Sec. 416(c)(2), P.L. 107-147, 3/9/2002) effective 3/9/2002.

[¶ 3077]
Code Sec. 6105.   Confidentiality of information arising under treaty obligations.

* * * * * * * * * * *

(c) Definitions. For purposes of this section—
   (1) Tax convention information. The term "tax convention information" means any—
      (A) agreement entered into with the competent authority of one or more foreign governments pursuant to a tax convention,
      (B) application for relief under a tax convention,
      (C) [1] background information related to such agreement or application,
      (D) document implementing such agreement, and
      (E) [2] other information exchanged pursuant to a tax convention which is treated as confidential or secret under the tax convention.

* * * * * * * * * * *

[Endnote Code Sec. 6105]

Matter in Code Sec. 6105(c)(1)(C) and Code Sec. 6105(c)(1)(E) deleted by Sec. 417(18) of the Job Creation and Worker Assistance Act of 2002, P.L. 107-147, 3/9/2002, which struck out:
1. "any"
2. "any"

Effective Date effective 3/9/2002.

[¶ 3078]
Code Sec. 6224.   Participation in administrative proceedings; waivers; agreements.

* * * * * * * * * * *

(c) Settlement agreement. In the absence of a showing of fraud, malfeasance, or misrepresentation of fact—
   (1) Binds all parties. A settlement agreement between the Secretary [1]*or the Attorney General (or his delegate)* and 1 or more partners in a partnership with respect to the determination of partnership items for any partnership taxable year shall (except as otherwise provided in such agreement) be binding on all parties to such agreement with respect to the determination of partnership items for such partnership taxable year. An indirect partner is bound by any such agreement entered into by the pass-thru partner unless the indirect partner has been identified as provided in section 6223(c)(3).
   (2) Other partners have right to enter into consistent agreements. If the Secretary [2]*or the Attorney General (or his delegate)* enters into a settlement agreement with any partner with respect to partnership items for any partnership taxable year, the Secretary [3]*or the Attorney General (or his delegate)* shall offer to any other partner who so requests settlement terms for the partnership taxable year which are consistent with those contained in such settlement agreement. Except in the case of an election under paragraph (2) or (3) of section 6223(e) to

have a settlement agreement described in this paragraph apply, this paragraph shall apply with respect to a settlement agreement entered into with a partner before notice of a final partnership administrative adjustment is mailed to the tax matters partner only if such other partner makes the request before the expiration of 150 days after the day on which such notice is mailed to the tax matters partner.

* * * * * * * * * * *

[For Analysis, see ¶ 603. For Committee Reports, see ¶ 5064.]

[Endnote Code Sec. 6224]
   Matter in *italics* in Code Sec. 6224(c)(1) and Code Sec. 6224(c)(2) was added by Sec. 416(d)(1)(A) of the Job Creation and Workers Assistance Act of 2002, P.L. 107-147, 3/9/2002.
   1. added matter in para. (c)(1)
   2. added matter in para. (c)(2)
   3. added matter in para. (c)(2)
Effective Date (Sec. 416(d)(2), P.L. 107-147, 3/9/2002) effective for settlement agreements entered into after 3/9/2002.

[¶ 3079]
Code Sec. 6227.   Administrative adjustment requests.

* * * * * * * * * * *

   (d) Other requests. If any partner files a request for an administrative adjustment (other than a request described in [1]*subsection (c)*), the Secretary may—
      (1) process the request in the same manner as a claim for credit or refund with respect to items which are not partnership items,
      (2) assess any additional tax that would result from the requested adjustments,
      (3) mail to the partner, under subparagraph (A) of section 6231(b)(1) (relating to items becoming nonpartnership items), a notice that all partnership items of the partner for the partnership taxable year to which such request relates shall be treated as nonpartnership items, or
      (4) conduct a partnership proceeding.

[Endnote Code Sec. 6227]
   Matter in *italics* in Code Sec. 6227(d) was added by Sec. 417(19)(A) of the Job Creation and Workers Assistance Act of 2002, P.L. 107-147, 3/9/2002, which struck out:
   1. "subsection (b)"
Effective Date effective 3/9/2002.

[¶ 3080]
Code Sec. 6228.   Judicial review where administrative adjustment request is not allowed in full.
   (a) Request on behalf of partnership.
      (1) In general. If any part of an administrative adjustment request filed by the tax matters partner under [1]*subsection (c) of section 6227* is not allowed by the Secretary, the tax matters partner may file a petition for an adjustment with respect to the partnership items to which such part of the request relates with—
         (A) the Tax Court,
         (B) the district court of the United States for the district in which the principal place of business of the partnership is located, or
         (C) the Claims Court.

* * * * * * * * * * *

   (3) Coordination with administrative adjustment.
      (A) Administrative adjustment before filing of petition. No petition may be filed under this subsection after the Secretary mails to the tax matters partner a notice of final partner-

ship administrative adjustment for the partnership taxable year to which the request under [2]section 6227 relates.

* * * * * * * * * * *

(b) Other requests.

(1) Notice providing that items become nonpartnership items. If the Secretary mails to a partner, under subparagraph (A) of section 6231(b)(1) (relating to items ceasing to be partnership items), a notice that all partnership items of the partner for the partnership taxable year to which a timely request for administrative adjustment under [3]*subsection (d) of section 6227* relates shall be treated as nonpartnership items—

(A) such request shall be treated as a claim for credit or refund of an overpayment attributable to nonpartnership items, and

(B) the partner may bring an action under section 7422 with respect to such claim at any time within 2 years of the mailing of such notice.

(2) Other cases.

(A) In general. If the Secretary fails to allow any part of an administrative adjustment request filed under [4]*subsection (d) of section 6227* by a partner and paragraph (1) does not apply—

(i) such partner may, pursuant to section 7422, begin a civil action for refund of any amount due by reason of the adjustments described in such part of the request, and

(ii) on the beginning of such civil action, the partnership items of such partner for the partnership taxable year to which such part of such request relates shall be treated as nonpartnership items for purposes of this subchapter.

* * * * * * * * * * *

[Endnote Code Sec. 6228]

Matter in *italics* in Code Sec. 6228(a)(1), Code Sec. 6228(a)(3)(A), Code Sec. 6228(b)(1) and Code Sec. 6228(b)(2)(A) added by Sec. 417(19)(B)(i)-(iii) of the Job Creation and Worker Assistance Act of 2002, P.L. 107-147, 3/9/2002, which struck out:

1. "subsection (b) of section 6227"
2. "subsection (b) of"
3. "subsection (c) of section 6227"
4. "subsection (c) of section 6227"

Effective Date effective 3/9/2002.

[¶ 3081]
Code Sec. 6229.   Period of limitations for making assessments.

* * * * * * * * * * *

(f) Special rules.

* * * * * * * * * * *

(2) Special rule for partial settlement agreements. If a partner enters into a settlement agreement with the Secretary [1]*or the Attorney General (or his delegate)* with respect to the treatment of some of the partnership items in dispute for a partnership taxable year but other partnership items for such year remain in dispute, the period of limitations for assessing any tax attributable to the settled items shall be determined as if such agreement had not been entered into.

* * * * * * * * * * *

[For Analysis, see ¶ 603. For Committee Reports, see ¶ 5064.]

[Endnote Code Sec. 6229]

Matter in *italics* in Code Sec. 6229(f)(2) was added by Sec. 416(d)(1)(B) of the Job Creation and Worker Assistance Act of 2002, P.L. 107-147, 3/9/2002.

1. added matter in para. (f)(2)

Effective Date (Sec. 416(d)(2), P.L. 107-147, 3/9/2002) effective for settlement agreements entered into after 3/9/2002.

RIA Research Institute of America

[¶ 3082]
Code Sec. 6231.   Definitions and special rules.

* * * * * * * * * * * *

(b) Items cease to be partnership items in certain cases.

(1) In general. For purposes of this subchapter, the partnership items of a partner for a partnership taxable year shall become nonpartnership items as of the date—

(A) the Secretary mails to such partner a notice that such items shall be treated as nonpartnership items,

(B) the partner files suit under section 6228(b) after the Secretary fails to allow an administrative adjustment request with respect to any of such items,

(C) the Secretary [1]*or the Attorney General (or his delegate)* enters into a settlement agreement with the partner with respect to such items, or

(D) such change occurs under subsection (e) of section 6223 (relating to effect of Secretary's failure to provide notice) or under subsection (c) of this section.

(2) Circumstances in which notice is permitted. The Secretary may mail the notice referred to in subparagraph (A) of paragraph (1) to a partner with respect to partnership items for a partnership taxable year only if—

(A) such partner—

(i) has complied with subparagraph (B) of section 6222(b)(1) (relating to notification of inconsistent treatment) with respect to one or more of such items, and

(ii) has not, as of the date on which the Secretary mails the notice, filed a request for administrative adjustments which would make the partner's treatment of the item or items with respect to which the partner complied with subparagraph (B) of section 6222(b)(1) consistent with the treatment of such item or items on the partnership return, or

(B)

(i) such partner has filed a request under [2]*section 6227(d)* for administrative adjustment of one or more of such items, and

(ii) the adjustments requested would not make such partner's treatment of such items consistent with the treatment of such items on the partnership return.

* * * * * * * * * * * *

[For Analysis, see ¶ 603. For Committee Reports, see ¶ 5064.]

[Endnote Code Sec. 6231]
   Matter in *italics* in Code Sec. 6231(b)(1)(C) was added by Sec. 416(d)(1)(C) of the Job Creation and Worker Assistance Act of 2002, P.L. 107-147, 3/9/2002.
   1. added matter in subpara. (b)(1)(C)
Effective Date (Sec. 416(d)(2), P.L. 107-147, 3/9/2002) effective for settlement agreements entered into after 3/9/2002.

   Matter in *italics* in Code Sec. 6231(b)(2)(B)(i) was added by Sec. 417(19)(C), P.L. 107-147, 3/9/2002, which struck out:
   2. "section 6227(c)"
Effective Date effective 3/9/2002.

[¶ 3083]
Code Sec. 6234.   Declaratory judgment relating to treatment of items other than partnership items with respect to an oversheltered return.

* * * * * * * * * * * *

(g) Coordination with other proceedings under this subchapter.

* * * * * * * * * * * *

(4) Finally determined. For purposes of this subsection, the treatment of partnership items shall be treated as finally determined if—

(A) the Secretary [1]*or the Attorney General (or his delegate)* enters into a settlement agreement (within the meaning of section 6224) with the taxpayer regarding such items,

(B) a notice of final partnership administrative adjustment has been issued and—

(i) no petition has been filed under section 6226 and the time for doing so has expired, or

(ii) a petition has been filed under section 6226 and the decision of the court has become final, or

(C) the period within which any tax attributable to such items may be assessed against the taxpayer has expired.

* * * * * * * * * * * *

[For Analysis, see ¶ 603. For Committee Reports, see ¶ 5064.]

[Endnote Code Sec. 6234]

Matter in *italics* in Code Sec. 6234(g)(4)(A) was added by Sec. 416(d)(1)(D) of the Job Creation and Worker Assistance Act of 2002, P.L. 107-147, 3/9/2002.

1. added matter in subpara. (g)(4)(A)

Effective Date (Sec. 416(d)(2), P.L. 107-147, 3/9/2002) effective for settlement agreements entered into after 3/9/2002.

[¶ 3084]
Code Sec. 6331.   Levy and distraint.

* * * * * * * * * * * *

(k) No levy while certain offers pending or installment agreement pending or in effect.

* * * * * * * * * * * *

[1]*(3) Certain rules to apply. Rules similar to the rules of—*

(A) paragraphs (3) and (4) of subsection (i), and

(B) except in the case of paragraph (2)(C), paragraph (5) of subsection (i),

shall apply for purposes of this subsection.

* * * * * * * * * * * *

[For Analysis, see ¶ 601. For Committee Reports, see ¶ 5060.]

[Endnote Code Sec. 6331]

Code Sec. 6331(k)(3), in *italics*, added by Sec. 416(e)(1) of the Job Creation and Worker Assistance Act of 2002, P.L. 107-147, 3/9/2002, which struck out:

1. "(3) Certain rules to apply. Rules similar to the rules of paragraphs (3) and (4) of subsection (i) shall apply for purposes of this subsection."

Effective Date (Sec. 416(e)(2), P.L. 107-147, 3/9/2002) effective 3/9/2002.

[¶ 3085]
Code Sec. 6428.   Acceleration of 10 percent income tax rate bracket benefit for 2001.

* * * * * * * * * * * *

[1]*(b) Credit treated as nonrefundable personal credit. For purposes of this title, the credit allowed under this section shall be treated as a credit allowable under subpart A of part IV of subchapter A of chapter 1.*

* * * * * * * * * * * *

²*(d) Coordination with advance refunds of credit.*

(1) In general. The amount of credit which would (but for this paragraph) be allowable under this section shall be reduced (but not below zero) by the aggregate refunds and credits made or allowed to the taxpayer under subsection (e). Any failure to so reduce the credit shall be treated as arising out of a mathematical or clerical error and assessed according to section 6213(b)(1).

(2) Joint returns. In the case of a refund or credit made or allowed under subsection (e) with respect to a joint return, half of such refund or credit shall be treated as having been made or allowed to each individual filing such return.

(e) Advance refunds of credit based on prior year data.

* * * * * * * * * * *

³*(2) Advance refund amount.* For purposes of paragraph (1), the advance refund amount is the amount that would have been allowed as a credit under this section for such first taxable year if—

(A) this section (other than subsections (b) and (d) and this subsection) had applied to such taxable year, and

(B) the credit for such taxable year were not allowed to exceed the excess (if any) of—

(i) the sum of the regular tax liability (as defined in section 26(b)) plus the tax imposed by section 55, over

(ii) the sum of the credits allowable under part IV of subchapter A of chapter 1 (other than the credits allowable under subpart C thereof, relating to refundable credits).

* * * * * * * * * * *

[For Analysis, see ¶ 403. For Committee Reports, see ¶ 5031.]

[Endnote Code Sec. 6428]

Matter in *italics* Code Sec. 6428(b), Code Sec. 6428(d) and Code Sec. 6428(e)(2), in *italics* was added by Sec. 411(a)(1), (a)(2)(A) and (B) of the Job Creation and Worker Assistance Act of 2002, P.L. 107-147, 3/9/2002, which struck out:

1. "(b) Limitation based on amount of tax. "The credit allowed by subsection (a) shall not exceed the excess (if any) of—

"(1) the sum of the regular tax liability (as defined in section 26(b) plus the tax imposed by section 55, over

"(2) the sum of the credits allowable under part IV of subchapter A of chapter 1 (other than the credits allowable under subpart C thereof, relating to refundable credits)."

2. "(d) Special rules.

"(1) Coordination with advance refunds of credit.

"(A) In general. The amount of credit which would (but for this paragraph) be allowable under this section shall be reduced (but not below zero) by the aggregate refunds and credits made or allowed to the taxpayer under subsection (e). Any failure to so reduce the credit shall be treated as arising out of a mathematical or clerical error and assessed according to section 6213(b)(1).

"(B) Joint returns. In the case of a refund or credit made or allowed under subsection (e) with respect to a joint return, half of such refund or credit shall be treated as having been made or allowed to each individual filing such return.

"(2) Coordination with estimated tax.

"The credit under this section shall be treated for purposes of section 6654(f) in the same manner as a credit under subpart A of part IV of subchapter A of chapter 1."

3. "(2) Advance refund amount.

"For purposes of paragraph (1), the advance refund amount is the amount that would have been allowed as a credit under this section for such first taxable year if this section (other than subsection (d) and this subsection) had applied to such taxable year."

Effective Date (Sec. 411(x), P.L. 107-147, 3/9/2002) effective for tax. yrs. begin. after 12/31/2000.

[¶ 3086]

Code Sec. 7652.   Shipments to the United States.

* * * * * * * * * * *

(f) Limitation on cover over of tax on distilled spirits. For purposes of this section, with respect to taxes imposed under section 5001 or this section on distilled spirits, the amount covered into the treasuries of Puerto Rico and the Virgin Islands shall not exceed the lesser of the rate of—

 Research Institute of America

(1) $10.50 ($13.25 in the case of distilled spirits brought into the United States after June 30, 1999, and before [1]*January 1, 2004*), or

(2) the tax imposed under section 5001(a)(1), on each proof gallon.

* * * * * * * * * * * *

[Endnote Code Sec. 7652]

Matter in *italics* in Code Sec. 7652(f)(1) was added by Sec. 609(a) of the Job Creation and Worker Assistance Act of 2002, P.L. 107-147, 3/9/2002, which struck out:

1. "January 1, 2002"

Effective Date (Sec. 609(b), P.L. 107-147, 3/9/2002) effective for articles brought into the United States after 12/31/2001.

[¶3087]

Code Sec. 7702A.   Modified endowment contract defined.

* * * * * * * * * * * *

(c) Computational rules.

* * * * * * * * * * * *

(3) Treatment of material changes.

(A) In general. If there is a material change in the benefits under (or in other terms of) the contract which was not reflected in any previous determination under this section, for purposes of this section—

(i) such contract shall be treated as a new contract entered into on the day on which such material change takes effect, and

(ii) appropriate adjustments shall be made in determining whether such contract meets the 7-pay test of subsection (b) to take into account the cash surrender value [1]*under the contract.*

* * * * * * * * * * * *

[For Analysis, see ¶705. For Committee Reports, see ¶5066.]

[Endnote Code Sec. 7702A]

Matter in *italics* in Code Sec. 7702A(c)(3)(A)(ii) reinstated by Sec. 416(f), P.L. 107-147, 3/9/2002, which repealed Sec. 318(a)(2) of the Community Renewal Tax Relief Act of 2000, P.L. 106-554, as if it had never been enacted. Sec. 318(a)(2) of such Act substituted "under the old contract" for "under the contract" in Code Sec. 7702A(c)(3)(A)(ii).

1. "under the old contract"

[¶3088]

Code Sec. 9812.   Parity in the application of certain limits to mental health benefits.

* * * * * * * * * * * *

[1]*(f) Application of section. This section shall not apply to benefits for services furnished—*

(1) on or after September 30, 2001, and before January 10, 2002, and

(2) after December 31, 2003.

[For Analysis, see ¶328. For Committee Reports, see ¶5078.]

[Endnote Code Sec. 9812]

Matter in *italics* in Code Sec. 9812(f) was added by Sec. 610(a) of the Job Creation and Worker Assistance Act of 2002, P.L. 107-147, 3/9/2002, which struck out:

1. "(f) Sunset. This section shall not apply to benefits for services furnished on or after December 31, 2002."

Effective Date (Sec. 610(b), P.L. 107-147, 3/9/2002) effective for plan yrs. begin. after 12/31/2000.

Research Institute of America

2002 Tax Legislation
One Hundred Seventh Congress
2nd Session
P.L. 107-147

Act Sections of the Job Creation and Worker Assistance Act of 2002, P.L. 107-147, or portions thereof, that do not amend specific Code Sections follow. Sections of the Code as amended by P.L. 107-147 are reproduced at Code as Amended.

[¶ 4001] **Sec. 1. SHORT TITLE; ETC.**

(a) SHORT TITLE.

(b) REFERENCES TO INTERNAL REVENUE CODE OF 1986. Except as otherwise expressly provided, whenever in this Act an amendment or repeal is expressed in terms of an amendment to, or repeal of, a section or other provision, the reference shall be considered to be made to a section or other provision of the Internal Revenue Code of 1986.

(c) TABLE OF CONTENTS. Sec. 1. Short title; etc.

[¶ 4002] **Sec. 101. SPECIAL DEPRECIATION ALLOWANCE FOR CERTAIN PROPERTY ACQUIRED AFTER SEPTEMBER 10, 2001, AND BEFORE SEPTEMBER 11, 2004.**

* * * * * * * * * * *

(b) EFFECTIVE DATE. The amendments made by this section shall apply to property placed in service after September 10, 2001, in taxable years ending after such date.

[¶ 4003] **Sec. 102. CARRYBACK OF CERTAIN NET OPERATING LOSSES ALLOWED FOR 5 YEARS; TEMPORARY SUSPENSION OF 90 PERCENT AMT LIMIT.**

* * * * * * * * * * *

(c) TEMPORARY SUSPENSION OF 90 PERCENT LIMIT ON CERTAIN NOL CARRYOVERS.

* * * * * * * * * * *

(2) EFFECTIVE DATE. The amendment made by this subsection shall apply to taxable years ending before January 1, 2003.

(d) EFFECTIVE DATE. Except as provided in subsection (c), the amendments made by this section shall apply to net operating losses for taxable years ending after December 31, 2000.

[¶ 4004] **Sec. 201. SHORT TITLE.**

This title may be cited as the "Temporary Extended Unemployment Compensation Act of 2002".

[¶ 4005] **Sec. 202. FEDERAL-STATE AGREEMENTS.**

(a) IN GENERAL. Any State which desires to do so may enter into and participate in an agreement under this title with the Secretary of Labor (in this title referred to as the "Secretary"). Any State which is a party to an agreement under this title may, upon providing 30 days' written notice to the Secretary, terminate such agreement.

(b) PROVISIONS OF AGREEMENT. Any agreement under subsection (a) shall provide that the State agency of the State will make payments of temporary extended unemployment compensation to individuals who—

(1) have exhausted all rights to regular compensation under the State law or under Federal law with respect to a benefit year (excluding any benefit year that ended before March 15, 2001);

(2) have no rights to regular compensation or extended compensation with respect to a week under such law or any other State unemployment compensation law or to compensation under any other Federal law;

(3) are not receiving compensation with respect to such week under the unemployment compensation law of Canada; and

(4) filed an initial claim for regular compensation on or after March 15, 2001.

(c) EXHAUSTION OF BENEFITS. For purposes of subsection (b)(1), an individual shall be deemed to have exhausted such individual's rights to regular compensation under a State law when—

(1) no payments of regular compensation can be made under such law because such individual has received all regular compensation available to such individual based on employment or wages during such individual's base period; or

(2) such individual's rights to such compensation have been terminated by reason of the expiration of the benefit year with respect to which such rights existed.

(d) WEEKLY BENEFIT AMOUNT, ETC. For purposes of any agreement under this title—

(1) the amount of temporary extended unemployment compensation which shall be payable to any individual for any week of total unemployment shall be equal to the amount of the regular compensation (including dependents' allowances) payable to such individual during such individual's benefit year under the State law for a week of total unemployment;

(2) the terms and conditions of the State law which apply to claims for regular compensation and to the payment thereof shall apply to claims for temporary extended unemployment compensation and the payment thereof, except—

(A) that an individual shall not be eligible for temporary extended unemployment compensation under this title unless, in the base period with respect to which the individual exhausted all rights to regular compensation under the State law, the individual had 20 weeks of full-time insured employment or the equivalent in insured wages, as determined under the provisions of the State law implementing section 202(a)(5) of the Federal-State Extended Unemployment Compensation Act of 1970 (26 U.S.C. 3304 note); and

(B) where otherwise inconsistent with the provisions of this title or with the regulations or operating instructions of the Secretary promulgated to carry out this title; and

(3) the maximum amount of temporary extended unemployment compensation payable to any individual for whom a temporary extended unemployment compensation account is established under section 203 shall not exceed the amount established in such account for such individual.

(e) ELECTION BY STATES. Notwithstanding any other provision of Federal law (and if State law permits), the Governor of a State that is in an extended benefit period may provide for the payment of temporary extended unemployment compensation in lieu of extended compensation to individuals who otherwise meet the requirements of this section. Such an election shall not require a State to trigger off an extended benefit period.

[¶ 4006] Sec. 203. TEMPORARY EXTENDED UNEMPLOYMENT COMPENSATION ACCOUNT.

(a) IN GENERAL. Any agreement under this title shall provide that the State will establish, for each eligible individual who files an application for temporary extended unemployment compensation, a temporary extended unemployment compensation account with respect to such individual's benefit year.

(b) AMOUNT IN ACCOUNT.

(1) IN GENERAL. The amount established in an account under subsection (a) shall be equal to the lesser of—

(A) 50 percent of the total amount of regular compensation (including dependents' allowances) payable to the individual during the individual's benefit year under such law, or

(B) 13 times the individual's average weekly benefit amount for the benefit year.

(2) WEEKLY BENEFIT AMOUNT. For purposes of this subsection, an individual's weekly benefit amount for any week is the amount of regular compensation (including dependents' allowances) under the State law payable to such individual for such week for total unemployment.

(c) SPECIAL RULE.

(1) IN GENERAL. Notwithstanding any other provision of this section, if, at the time that the individual's account is exhausted, such individual's State is in an extended benefit period (as determined under paragraph (2)), then, such account shall be augmented by an amount equal to the amount originally established in such account (as determined under subsection (b)(1)).

(2) EXTENDED BENEFIT PERIOD. For purposes of paragraph (1), a State shall be considered to be in an extended benefit period if, at the time of exhaustion (as described in paragraph (1))—

(A) such a period is then in effect for such State under the Federal-State Extended Unemployment Compensation Act of 1970; or

(B) such a period would then be in effect for such State under such Act if section 203(d) of such Act were applied as if it had been amended by striking "5" each place it appears and inserting "4".

[¶ 4007] Sec. 204. PAYMENTS TO STATES HAVING AGREEMENTS FOR THE PAYMENT OF TEMPORARY EXTENDED UNEMPLOYMENT COMPENSATION.

(a) GENERAL RULE. There shall be paid to each State that has entered into an agreement under this title an amount equal to 100 percent of the temporary extended unemployment compensation paid to individuals by the State pursuant to such agreement.

(b) TREATMENT OF REIMBURSABLE COMPENSATION. No payment shall be made to any State under this section in respect of any compensation to the extent the State is entitled to reimbursement in respect of such compensation under the provisions of any Federal law other than this title or chapter 85 of title 5, United States Code. A State shall not be entitled to any reimbursement under such chapter 85 in respect of any compensation to the extent the State is entitled to reimbursement under this title in respect of such compensation.

(c) DETERMINATION OF AMOUNT. Sums payable to any State by reason of such State having an agreement under this title shall be payable, either in advance or by way of reimbursement (as may be determined by the Secretary), in such amounts as the Secretary estimates the State will be entitled to receive under this title for each calendar month, reduced or increased, as the case may be, by any amount by which the Secretary finds that the Secretary's estimates for any prior calendar month were greater or less than the amounts which should have been paid to the State. Such estimates may be made on the basis of such statistical, sampling, or other method as may be agreed upon by the Secretary and the State agency of the State involved.

[¶ 4008] **Sec. 205. FINANCING PROVISIONS.**

(a) IN GENERAL. Funds in the extended unemployment compensation account (as established by section 905(a) of the Social Security Act (42 U.S.C. 1105(a)) of the Unemployment Trust Fund (as established by section 904(a) of such Act (42 U.S.C. 1104(a)) shall be used for the making of payments to States having agreements entered into under this title.

(b) CERTIFICATION. The Secretary shall from time to time certify to the Secretary of the Treasury for payment to each State the sums payable to such State under this title. The Secretary of the Treasury, prior to audit or settlement by the General Accounting Office, shall make payments to the State in accordance with such certification, by transfers from the extended unemployment compensation account (as so established) to the account of such State in the Unemployment Trust Fund (as so established).

(c) ASSISTANCE TO STATES. There are appropriated out of the employment security administration account (as established by section 901(a) of the Social Security Act (42 U.S.C. 1101(a)) of the Unemployment Trust Fund, without fiscal year limitation, such funds as may be necessary for purposes of assisting States (as provided in title III of the Social Security Act (42 U.S.C. 501 et seq.)) in meeting the costs of administration of agreements under this title.

(d) APPROPRIATIONS FOR CERTAIN PAYMENTS. There are appropriated from the general fund of the Treasury, without fiscal year limitation, to the extended unemployment compensation account (as so established) of the Unemployment Trust Fund (as so established) such sums as the Secretary estimates to be necessary to make the payments under this section in respect of—
  (1) compensation payable under chapter 85 of title 5, United States Code; and
  (2) compensation payable on the basis of services to which section 3309(a)(1) of the Internal Revenue Code of 1986 applies.
Amounts appropriated pursuant to the preceding sentence shall not be required to be repaid.

[¶ 4009] **Sec. 206. FRAUD AND OVERPAYMENTS.**

(a) IN GENERAL. If an individual knowingly has made, or caused to be made by another, a false statement or representation of a material fact, or knowingly has failed, or caused another to fail, to disclose a material fact, and as a result of such false statement or representation or of such nondisclosure such individual has received an amount of temporary extended unemployment compensation under this title to which he was not entitled, such individual—

(1) shall be ineligible for further temporary extended unemployment compensation under this title in accordance with the provisions of the applicable State unemployment compensation law relating to fraud in connection with a claim for unemployment compensation; and

(2) shall be subject to prosecution under section 1001 of title 18, United States Code.

(b) REPAYMENT. In the case of individuals who have received amounts of temporary extended unemployment compensation under this title to which they were not entitled, the State shall require such individuals to repay the amounts of such temporary extended unemployment compensation to the State agency, except that the State agency may waive such repayment if it determines that—

(1) the payment of such temporary extended unemployment compensation was without fault on the part of any such individual; and

(2) such repayment would be contrary to equity and good conscience.

(c) RECOVERY BY STATE AGENCY.

(1) IN GENERAL. The State agency may recover the amount to be repaid, or any part thereof, by deductions from any temporary extended unemployment compensation payable to such individual under this title or from any unemployment compensation payable to such individual under any Federal unemployment compensation law administered by the State agency or under any other Federal law administered by the State agency which provides for the payment of any assistance or allowance with respect to any week of unemployment, during the 3-year period after the date such individuals received the payment of the temporary extended unemployment compensation to which they were not entitled, except that no single deduction may exceed 50 percent of the weekly benefit amount from which such deduction is made.

(2) OPPORTUNITY FOR HEARING. No repayment shall be required, and no deduction shall be made, until a determination has been made, notice thereof and an opportunity for a fair hearing has been given to the individual, and the determination has become final.

(d) REVIEW. Any determination by a State agency under this section shall be subject to review in the same manner and to the same extent as determinations under the State unemployment compensation law, and only in that manner and to that extent.

[¶ 4010] **Sec. 207. DEFINITIONS.** In this title, the terms "compensation", "regular compensation", "extended compensation", "additional compensation", "benefit year", "base period", "State", "State agency", "State law", and "week" have the respective meanings given such terms under section 205 of the Federal-State Extended Unemployment Compensation Act of 1970 (26 U.S.C. 3304 note).

[¶ 4011] **Sec. 208. APPLICABILITY.** An agreement entered into under this title shall apply to weeks of unemployment—

(1) beginning after the date on which such agreement is entered into; and

(2) ending before January 1, 2003.

[¶ 4012] **Sec. 209. SPECIAL REED ACT TRANSFER IN FISCAL YEAR 2002.**

Research Institute of America

(a) REPEAL OF CERTAIN PROVISIONS ADDED BY THE BALANCED BUDGET ACT OF 1997.

(1) IN GENERAL. The following provisions of section 903 of the Social Security Act (42 U.S.C. 1103) are repealed:

(A) Paragraph (3) of subsection (a).

(B) The last sentence of subsection (c)(2).

(2) SAVINGS PROVISION. Any amounts transferred before the date of enactment of this Act under the provision repealed by paragraph (1)(A) shall remain subject to section 903 of the Social Security Act, as last in effect before such date of enactment.

(b) SPECIAL TRANSFER IN FISCAL YEAR 2002. Section 903 of the Social Security Act is amended by adding at the end the following:

"Special Transfer in Fiscal Year 2002

"(d)(1) The Secretary of the Treasury shall transfer (as of the date determined under paragraph (5)) from the Federal unemployment account to the account of each State in the Unemployment Trust Fund the amount determined with respect to such State under paragraph (2).

"(2)(A) The amount to be transferred under this subsection to a State account shall (as determined by the Secretary of Labor and certified by such Secretary to the Secretary of the Treasury) be equal to—

"(i) the amount which would have been required to have been transferred under this section to such account at the beginning of fiscal year 2002 if—

"(I) section 209(a)(1) of the Temporary Extended Unemployment Compensation Act of 2002 had been enacted before the close of fiscal year 2001, and

"(II) section 5402 of Public Law 105-33 (relating to increase in Federal unemployment account ceiling) had not been enacted, minus

"(ii) the amount which was in fact transferred under this section to such account at the beginning of fiscal year 2002.

"(B) Notwithstanding the provisions of subparagraph (A)—

"(i) the aggregate amount transferred to the States under this subsection may not exceed a total of $8,000,000,000; and

"(ii) all amounts determined under subparagraph (A) shall be reduced ratably, if and to the extent necessary in order to comply with the limitation under clause (i).

"(3)(A) Except as provided in paragraph (4), amounts transferred to a State account pursuant to this subsection may be used only in the payment of cash benefits—

"(i) to individuals with respect to their unemployment, and

"(ii) which are allowable under subparagraph (B) or (C).

"(B)(i) At the option of the State, cash benefits under this paragraph may include amounts which shall be payable as—

"(I) regular compensation, or

"(II) additional compensation, upon the exhaustion of any temporary extended unemployment compensation (if such State has entered into an agreement under the Temporary Extended Unemployment Compensation Act of 2002), for individuals eligible for regular compensation under the unemployment compensation law of such State.

"(ii) Any additional compensation under clause (i) may not be taken into account for purposes of any determination relating to the amount of any extended compensation for which an individual might be eligible.

"(C)(i) At the option of the State, cash benefits under this paragraph may include amounts which shall be payable to 1 or more categories of individuals not otherwise eligible for regular compensation under the unemployment compensation law of such State, including those described in clause (iii).

"(ii) The benefits paid under this subparagraph to any individual may not, for any period of unemployment, exceed the maximum amount of regular compensation authorized under the unemployment compensation law of such State for that same period, plus any additional compensation (described in subparagraph (B)(i)) which could have been paid with respect to that amount.

"(iii) The categories of individuals described in this clause include the following:

"(I) Individuals who are seeking, or available for, only part-time (and not full-time) work.

"(II) Individuals who would be eligible for regular compensation under the unemployment compensation law of such State under an alternative base period.

"(D) Amounts transferred to a State account under this subsection may be used in the payment of cash benefits to individuals only for weeks of unemployment beginning after the date of enactment of this subsection.

"(4) Amounts transferred to a State account under this subsection may be used for the administration of its unemployment compensation law and public employment offices (including in connection with benefits described in paragraph (3) and any recipients thereof), subject to the same conditions as set forth in subsection (c)(2) (excluding subparagraph (B) thereof, and deeming the reference to 'subsections (a) and (b)' in subparagraph (D) thereof to include this subsection).

"(5) Transfers under this subsection shall be made within 10 days after the date of enactment of this paragraph.".

(c) LIMITATIONS ON TRANSFERS. Section 903(b) of the Social Security Act shall apply to transfers under section 903(d) of such Act (as amended by this section). For purposes of the preceding sentence, such section 903(b) shall be deemed to be amended as follows:

(1) By substituting "the transfer date described in subsection (d)(5)" for "October 1 of any fiscal year".

(2) By substituting "remain in the Federal unemployment account" for "be transferred to the Federal unemployment account as of the beginning of such October 1".

(3) By substituting "fiscal year 2002 (after the transfer date described in subsection (d)(5))" for "the fiscal year beginning on such October 1".

(4) By substituting "under subsection (d)" for "as of October 1 of such fiscal year".

(5) By substituting "(as of the close of fiscal year 2002)" for "(as of the close of such fiscal year)".

(d) TECHNICAL AMENDMENTS.
* * * * * * * * * * * *

(2) Section 303(a)(5) of the Social Security Act is amended in the second proviso by inserting "or 903(d)(4)" after "903(c)(2)".

(e) REGULATIONS. The Secretary of Labor may prescribe any operating instructions or regulations necessary to carry out this section and the amendments made by this section.

[¶ 4013] Sec. 301. TAX BENEFITS FOR AREA OF NEW YORK CITY DAMAGED IN TERRORIST ATTACKS ON SEPTEMBER 11, 2001.
* * * * * * * * * * * *

(b) CREDIT ALLOWED AGAINST REGULAR AND MINIMUM TAX.
* * * * * * * * * * * *

(3) EFFECTIVE DATE. The amendments made by this subsection shall apply to taxable years ending after December 31, 2001.

(c) CLERICAL AMENDMENT. The table of subchapters for chapter 1 is amended by adding at the end the following new item:

Research Institute of America

"Subchapter Y—New York Liberty Zone Benefits.".

[¶ 4014] **Sec. 401. ALLOWANCE OF ELECTRONIC 1099'S.**

Any person required to furnish a statement under any section of subpart B of part III of subchapter A of chapter 61 of the Internal Revenue Code of 1986 for any taxable year ending after the date of the enactment of this Act, may electronically furnish such statement (without regard to any first class mailing requirement) to any recipient who has consented to the electronic provision of the statement in a manner similar to the one permitted under regulations issued under section 6051 of such Code or in such other manner as provided by the Secretary.

[¶ 4015] **Sec. 402. EXCLUDED CANCELLATION OF INDEBTEDNESS INCOME OF S CORPORATION NOT TO RESULT IN ADJUSTMENT TO BASIS OF STOCK OF SHAREHOLDERS.**

* * * * * * * * * *

(b) EFFECTIVE DATE.

(1) IN GENERAL. Except as provided in paragraph (2), the amendment made by this section shall apply to discharges of indebtedness after October 11, 2001, in taxable years ending after such date.

(2) EXCEPTION. The amendment made by this section shall not apply to any discharge of indebtedness before March 1, 2002, pursuant to a plan of reorganization filed with a bankruptcy court on or before October 11, 2001.

[¶ 4016] **Sec. 403. LIMITATION ON USE OF NONACCRUAL EXPERIENCE METHOD OF ACCOUNTING.**

* * * * * * * * * *

(b) EFFECTIVE DATE.

(1) IN GENERAL. The amendments made by this section shall apply to taxable years ending after the date of the enactment of this Act.

(2) CHANGE IN METHOD OF ACCOUNTING. In the case of any taxpayer required by the amendments made by this section to change its method of accounting for its first taxable year ending after the date of the enactment of this Act—

(A) such change shall be treated as initiated by the taxpayer,

(B) such change shall be treated as made with the consent of the Secretary of the Treasury, and

(C) the net amount of the adjustments required to be taken into account by the taxpayer under section 481 of the Internal Revenue Code of 1986 shall be taken into account over a period of 4 years (or if less, the number of taxable years that the taxpayer used the method permitted under section 448(d)(5) of such Code as in effect before the date of the enactment of this Act) beginning with such first taxable year.

[¶ 4017] **Sec. 404. EXCLUSION FOR FOSTER CARE PAYMENTS TO APPLY TO PAYMENTS BY QUALIFIED PLACEMENT AGENCIES.**

* * * * * * * * * *

(d) EFFECTIVE DATE. The amendments made by this section shall apply to taxable years beginning after December 31, 2001.

[¶ 4018] **Sec. 405. INTEREST RATE RANGE FOR ADDITIONAL FUNDING REQUIREMENTS.**

* * * * * * * * * *

(b) AMENDMENTS TO THE EMPLOYEE RETIREMENT INCOME SECURITY ACT OF 1974.

(1) SPECIAL RULE. Clause (i) of section 302(d)(7)(C) of such Act (29 U.S.C. 1082(d)(7)(C)) is amended by adding at the end the following new subclause:

"(III) SPECIAL RULE FOR 2002 AND 2003.—For a plan year beginning in 2002 or 2003, notwithstanding subclause (I), in the case that the rate of interest used under subsection (b)(5) exceeds the highest rate permitted under subclause (I), the rate of interest used to determine current liability under this subsection may exceed the rate of interest otherwise permitted under subclause (I); except that such rate of interest shall not exceed 120 percent of the weighted average referred to in subsection (b)(5)(B)(ii).".

(2) QUARTERLY CONTRIBUTIONS. Subsection (e) of section 302 of such Act (29 U.S.C. 1082) is amended by adding at the end the following new paragraph:

"(7) SPECIAL RULES FOR 2002 AND 2004.—In any case in which the interest rate used to determine current liability is determined under subsection (d)(7)(C)(i)(III)—

"(A) 2002.—For purposes of applying paragraphs (1) and (4)(B)(ii) for plan years beginning in 2002, the current liability for the preceding plan year shall be redetermined using 120 percent as the specified percentage determined under subsection (d)(7)(C)(i)(II).

"(B) 2004.—For purposes of applying paragraphs (1) and (4)(B)(ii) for plan years beginning in 2004, the current liability for the preceding plan year shall be redetermined using 105 percent as the specified percentage determined under subsection (d)(7)(C)(i)(II).".

(c) PBGC. Clause (iii) of section 4006(a)(3)(E) of the Employee Retirement Income Security Act of 1974 (29 U.S.C. 1306(a)(3)(E)) is amended by adding at the end the following new subclause:

"(IV) In the case of plan years beginning after December 31, 2001, and before January 1, 2004, subclause (II) shall be applied by substituting '100 percent' for '85 percent'. Subclause (III) shall be applied for such years without regard to the preceding sentence. Any reference to this clause by any other sections or subsections shall be treated as a reference to this clause without regard to this subclause.".

[¶ 4019] **Sec. 406. ADJUSTED GROSS INCOME DETERMINED BY TAKING INTO ACCOUNT CERTAIN EXPENSES OF ELEMENTARY AND SECONDARY SCHOOL TEACHERS.**

* * * * * * * * * * *

(c) EFFECTIVE DATE. The amendments made by this section shall apply to taxable years beginning after December 31, 2001.

[¶ 4020] **Sec. 411. AMENDMENTS RELATED TO ECONOMIC GROWTH AND TAX RELIEF RECONCILIATION ACT OF 2001.**

* * * * * * * * * * *

(c) AMENDMENTS RELATED TO SECTION 202 OF THE ACT.

(1) CORRECTIONS TO CREDIT FOR ADOPTION EXPENSES.

* * * * * * * * * * *

(F) Expenses paid or incurred during any taxable year beginning before January 1, 2002, may be taken into account in determining the credit under section 23 of the Internal Revenue Code of 1986 only to the extent the aggregate of such expenses does not exceed the applicable limitation under section 23(b)(1) of such Code as in effect on the day before the date of the enactment of the Economic Growth and Tax Relief Reconciliation Act of 2001.

* * * * * * * * * * *

(3) EFFECTIVE DATE. The amendments made by this subsection shall apply to taxable years beginning after December 31, 2002; except that the amendments made by paragraphs (1)(C), (1)(D), and (2)(B) shall apply to taxable years beginning after December 31, 2001.

* * * * * * * * * * *

(i) AMENDMENTS RELATING TO SECTION 602 OF THE ACT.

(2) Section 4(c) of Employee Retirement Income Security Act of 1974 is amended—

(A) by inserting "and part 5 (relating to administration and enforcement)" before the period at the end, and

(B) by adding at the end the following new sentence: "Such provisions shall apply to such accounts and annuities in a manner similar to their application to a simplified employee pension under section 408(k) of the Internal Revenue Code of 1986.".

* * * * * * * * * * *

(j) AMENDMENTS RELATING TO SECTION 611 OF THE ACT.

* * * * * * * * * * * *

(3) Section 611(i) of the Economic Growth and Tax Relief Reconciliation Act of 2001 is amended by adding at the end the following new paragraph:

"(3) SPECIAL RULE.—In the case of plan that, on June 7, 2001, incorporated by reference the limitation of section 415(b)(1)(A) of the Internal Revenue Code of 1986, section 411(d)(6) of such Code and section 204(g)(1) of the Employee Retirement Income Security Act of 1974 do not apply to a plan amendment that—

"(A) is adopted on or before June 30, 2002,

"(B) reduces benefits to the level that would have applied without regard to the amendments made by subsection (a) of this section, and

"(C) is effective no earlier than the years described in paragraph (2).".

* * * * * * * * * * *

(n) AMENDMENTS RELATING TO SECTION 619 OF THE ACT.

* * * * * * * * * * *

(2) Section 619(d) of the Economic Growth and Tax Relief Reconciliation Act of 2001 is amended by striking "established" and inserting "first effective".

* * * * * * * * * * *

(r) AMENDMENTS RELATING TO SECTION 648 OF THE ACT.

* * * * * * * * * * * *

(2) Section 205(g) of the Employee Retirement Income Security Act of 1974 is amended—

(A) in paragraph (1) by striking "exceed the dollar limit under section 203(e)(1)" and inserting "exceed the amount that can be distributed without the participant's consent under section 203(e)", and

(B) in paragraph (2)(A) by striking "exceeds the dollar limit under section 203(e)(1)" and inserting "exceeds the amount that can be distributed without the participant's consent under section 203(e)".

* * * * * * * * * * *

(t) AMENDMENTS RELATING TO SECTION 657 OF THE ACT. Section 404(c)(3) of the Employee Retirement Income Security Act of 1974 is amended—

* * * * * * * * * * *

(1) by striking "the earlier of" in subparagraph (A) the second place it appears, and

(2) by striking "if the transfer" and inserting "a transfer that".

(u) AMENDMENTS RELATING TO SECTION 659 OF THE ACT.

* * * * * * * * * * *

(2) Section 204(h)(9) of the Employee Retirement Income Security Act of 1974 is amended by striking "significantly" both places it appears.

(3) Section 659(c)(3)(B) of the Economic Growth and Tax Relief Reconciliation Act of 2001 is amended by striking "(or" and inserting "(and".

(v) AMENDMENTS RELATING TO SECTION 661 OF THE ACT.

* * * * * * * * * * *

(2) Section 302(c)(9)(B) of the Employee Retirement Income Security Act of 1974 is amended—

(A) in clause (ii) by striking "125 percent" and inserting "100 percent", and

(B) by adding at the end the following new clause:

"(iv) A change in funding method to use a prior year valuation, as provided in clause (ii), may not be made unless as of the valuation date within the prior plan year, the value of the assets of the plan are not less than 125 percent of the plan's current liability (as defined in paragraph (7)(B)).".

* * * * * * * * * * *

(x) EFFECTIVE DATE. Except as provided in subsection (c), the amendments made by this section shall take effect as if included in the provisions of the Economic Growth and Tax Relief Reconciliation Act of 2001 to which they relate.

[¶ 4021] Sec. 412. AMENDMENTS RELATED TO COMMUNITY RENEWAL TAX RELIEF ACT OF 2000.

* * * * * * * * * * *

(e) EFFECTIVE DATE. The amendments made by this section shall take effect as if included in the provisions of the Community Renewal Tax Relief Act of 2000 to which they relate.

[¶ 4022] Sec. 413. AMENDMENTS RELATED TO THE TAX RELIEF EXTENSION ACT OF 1999.

* * * * * * * * * * *

(b) EFFECTIVE DATE. The amendments made by this section shall take effect as if included in section 545 of the Tax Relief Extension Act of 1999.

[¶ 4023] Sec. 414. AMENDMENTS RELATED TO THE TAXPAYER RELIEF ACT OF 1997.

(a) AMENDMENTS RELATED TO SECTION 311 OF THE ACT.

(1) in paragraph (2)(A), by striking "recognized" and inserting "included in gross income", and

(2) by adding at the end the following new paragraph:

"(5) DISPOSITION OF INTEREST IN PASSIVE ACTIVITY.—Section 469(g)(1)(A) of the Internal Revenue Code of 1986 shall not apply by reason of an election made under paragraph (1).".

(b) EFFECTIVE DATE. The amendments made by this section shall take effect as if included in section 311 of the Taxpayer Relief Act of 1997.

[¶ 4024] Sec. 415. AMENDMENT RELATED TO THE BALANCED BUDGET ACT OF 1997.

* * * * * * * * * * *

(b) EFFECTIVE DATE. The amendment made by this section shall take effect as if included in section 4006 of the Balanced Budget Act of 1997.

[¶ 4025] **Sec. 416. OTHER TECHNICAL CORRECTIONS.**

(a) COORDINATION OF ADVANCED PAYMENTS OF EARNED INCOME CREDIT.
* * * * * * * * * * *

(2) The amendment made by this subsection shall take effect as if included in section 474 of the Tax Reform Act of 1984.

(b) SPECIAL RULE RELATED TO WASH SALE LOSSES.
* * * * * * * * * * *

(2) The amendment made by this subsection shall take effect as if included in section 5075 of the Technical and Miscellaneous Revenue Act of 1988.

(c) DISCLOSURE BY SOCIAL SECURITY ADMINISTRATION TO FEDERAL CHILD SUPPORT AGENCIES.
* * * * * * * * * * *

(2) The amendments made by this subsection shall take effect on the date of the enactment of this Act.

(d) TREATMENT OF SETTLEMENTS UNDER PARTNERSHIP AUDIT RULES.
* * * * * * * * * * *

(2) The amendments made by this subsection shall apply with respect to settlement agreements entered into after the date of the enactment of this Act.

(e) AMENDMENT RELATED TO PROCEDURE AND ADMINISTRATION.
* * * * * * * * * * *

(2) The amendment made by this subsection shall take effect on the date of the enactment of this Act.

(f) MODIFIED ENDOWMENT CONTRACTS. Paragraph (2) of section 318(a) of the Community Renewal Tax Relief Act of 2000 (114 Stat. 2763A-645) is repealed, and clause (ii) of section 7702A(c)(3)(A) shall read and be applied as if the amendment made by such paragraph had not been enacted.

[¶ 4026] **Sec. 417. CLERICAL AMENDMENTS.**
* * * * * * * * * * *

(21) Section 159 of the Community Renewal Tax Relief Act of 2000 (114 Stat. 2763A-624) is amended by striking "fuctions" and inserting "functions".
* * * * * * * * * * *

(24) (A) Section 525 of the Ticket to Work and Work Incentives Improvement Act of 1999 (Public Law 106-170; 113 Stat. 1928) is amended by striking "7200" and inserting "7201".

[¶ 4027] **Sec. 418. ADDITIONAL CORRECTIONS.**
* * * * * * * * * * *

(c) EFFECTIVE DATE. The amendments made by this section shall take effect as if included in the provisions of the Economic Growth and Tax Relief Reconciliation Act of 2001 to which they relate.

[¶ 4028] **Sec. 501. NO IMPACT ON SOCIAL SECURITY TRUST FUNDS.**

(a) IN GENERAL. Nothing in this Act (or an amendment made by this Act) shall be construed to alter or amend title II of the Social Security Act (or any regulation promulgated under that Act).

(b) TRANSFERS.

(1) ESTIMATE OF SECRETARY. The Secretary of the Treasury shall annually estimate the impact that the enactment of this Act has on the income and balances of the trust funds established under section 201 of the Social Security Act (42 U.S.C. 401).

(2) TRANSFER OF FUNDS. If, under paragraph (1), the Secretary of the Treasury estimates that the enactment of this Act has a negative impact on the income and balances of the trust funds established under section 201 of the Social Security Act (42 U.S.C. 401), the Secretary shall transfer, not less frequently than quarterly, from the general revenues of the Federal Government an amount sufficient so as to ensure that the income and balances of such trust funds are not reduced as a result of the enactment of this Act.

[¶ 4029] **Sec. 502. EMERGENCY DESIGNATION.** Congress designates as emergency requirements pursuant to section 252(e) of the Balanced Budget and Emergency Deficit Control Act of 1985 the following amounts:

(1) An amount equal to the amount by which revenues are reduced by this Act below the recommended levels of Federal revenues for fiscal year 2002, the total of fiscal years 2002 through 2006, and the total of fiscal years 2002 through 2011, provided in the conference report accompanying H. Con. Res. 83, the concurrent resolution on the budget for fiscal year 2002.

(2) Amounts equal to the amounts of new budget authority and outlays provided in this Act in excess of the allocations under section 302(a) of the Congressional Budget Act of 1974 to the Committee on Finance of the Senate for fiscal year 2002, the total of fiscal years 2002 through 2006, and the total of fiscal years 2002 through 2011.

[¶ 4030] **Sec. 601. ALLOWANCE OF NONREFUNDABLE PERSONAL CREDITS AGAINST REGULAR AND MINIMUM TAX LIABILITY.**
* * * * * * * * * * * *

(b) CONFORMING AMENDMENTS.
* * * * * * * * * * * *

(2) The amendments made by sections 201(b), 202(f), and 618(b) of the Economic Growth and Tax Relief Reconciliation Act of 2001 shall not apply to taxable years beginning during 2002 and 2003.

(c) EFFECTIVE DATE. The amendments made by this section shall apply to taxable years beginning after December 31, 2001.

[¶ 4031] **Sec. 602. CREDIT FOR QUALIFIED ELECTRIC VEHICLES.**
* * * * * * * * * * * *

(b) CONFORMING AMENDMENTS.
* * * * * * * * * * * *

(2) Subsection (b) of section 971 of the Taxpayer Relief Act of 1997 is amended by striking "and before January 1, 2005".

(c) EFFECTIVE DATE. The amendments made by this section shall apply to property placed in service after December 31, 2001.

[¶ 4032] **Sec. 603. CREDIT FOR ELECTRICITY PRODUCED FROM CERTAIN RE-NEWABLE RESOURCES.**

* * * * * * * * * * *

(b) EFFECTIVE DATE. The amendments made by subsection (a) shall apply to facilities placed in service after December 31, 2001.

[¶ 4033] **Sec. 604. WORK OPPORTUNITY CREDIT.**

* * * * * * * * * * *

(b) EFFECTIVE DATE. The amendment made by subsection (a) shall apply to individuals who begin work for the employer after December 31, 2001.

[¶ 4034] **Sec. 605. WELFARE-TO-WORK CREDIT.**

* * * * * * * * * * *

(b) EFFECTIVE DATE. The amendment made by subsection (a) shall apply to individuals who begin work for the employer after December 31, 2001.

[¶ 4035] **Sec. 606. DEDUCTION FOR CLEAN-FUEL VEHICLES AND CERTAIN RE-FUELING PROPERTY.**

* * * * * * * * * * *

(b) EFFECTIVE DATE. The amendments made by subsection (a) shall apply to property placed in service after December 31, 2001.

[¶ 4036] **Sec. 607. TAXABLE INCOME LIMIT ON PERCENTAGE DEPLETION FOR OIL AND NATURAL GAS PRODUCED FROM MARGINAL PROPERTIES.**

* * * * * * * * * * *

(b) EFFECTIVE DATE. The amendment made by subsection (a) shall apply to taxable years beginning after December 31, 2001.

[¶ 4037] **Sec. 608. QUALIFIED ZONE ACADEMY BONDS.**

* * * * * * * * * * *

(b) EFFECTIVE DATE. The amendment made by subsection (a) shall apply to obligations issued after the date of the enactment of this Act.

[¶ 4038] **Sec. 609. COVER OVER OF TAX ON DISTILLED SPIRITS.**

* * * * * * * * * * *

(b) EFFECTIVE DATE. The amendment made by subsection (a) shall apply to articles brought into the United States after December 31, 2001.

[¶ 4039] **Sec. 610. PARITY IN THE APPLICATION OF CERTAIN LIMITS TO MENTAL HEALTH BENEFITS.**

* * * * * * * * * * *

(b) EFFECTIVE DATE. The amendment made by subsection (a) shall apply to plan years beginning after December 31, 2000.

[¶ 4040] **Sec. 611. TEMPORARY SPECIAL RULES FOR TAXATION OF LIFE IN-SURANCE COMPANIES.**

* * * * * * * * * * *

(b) EFFECTIVE DATE. The amendment made by this section shall apply to taxable years beginning after December 31, 2000.

[¶ 4041] Sec. 612. AVAILABILITY OF MEDICAL SAVINGS ACCOUNTS.
* * * * * * * * * * * *

(c) EFFECTIVE DATE. The amendments made by this section shall take effect on January 1, 2002.

[¶ 4042] Sec. 614. SUBPART F EXEMPTION FOR ACTIVE FINANCING.
* * * * * * * * * * * *

(c) EFFECTIVE DATE. The amendments made by this section shall apply to taxable years beginning after December 31, 2001.

[¶ 4043] Sec. 615. REPEAL OF REQUIREMENT FOR APPROVED DIESEL OR KEROSENE TERMINALS.
* * * * * * * * * * * *

(b) EFFECTIVE DATE. The amendment made by subsection (a) shall take effect on January 1, 2002.

[¶ 4044] Sec. 616. REAUTHORIZATION OF TANF SUPPLEMENTAL GRANTS FOR POPULATION INCREASES FOR FISCAL YEAR 2002. Section 403(a)(3) of the Social Security Act (42 U.S.C. 603(a)(3)) is amended by adding at the end the following:

"(H) REAUTHORIZATION OF GRANTS FOR FISCAL YEAR 2002.—Notwithstanding any other provision of this paragraph—

"(i) any State that was a qualifying State under this paragraph for fiscal year 2001 or any prior fiscal year shall be entitled to receive from the Secretary for fiscal year 2002 a grant in an amount equal to the amount required to be paid to the State under this paragraph for the most recent fiscal year in which the State was a qualifying State;

"(ii) subparagraph (G) shall be applied as if '2002' were substituted for '2001'; and

"(iii) out of any money in the Treasury of the United States not otherwise appropriated, there are appropriated for fiscal year 2002 such sums as are necessary for grants under this subparagraph.".

[¶ 4045] Sec. 617. 1-YEAR EXTENSION OF CONTINGENCY FUND UNDER THE TANF PROGRAM. Section 403(b) of the Social Security Act (42 U.S.C. 603(b)) is amended—

(1) in paragraph (2), by striking "and 2001" and inserting "2001, and 2002"; and

(2) in paragraph (3)(C)(ii), by striking "2001" and inserting "2002".

[¶ 5000] Joint Committee on Taxation Technical Explanation of the Job Creation and Worker Assistance Act of 2002

No official Committee Reports have been issued for H.R. 3090, the Job Creation and Worker Assistance Act of 2002, which was signed into law on Mar. 9, 2002 (P.L. 107-147, 3/9/2002). Thus, this section reproduces all relevant parts of the Joint Committee on Taxation Technical Explanation of the Job Creation and Worker Assistance Act of 2002 (JCX-12-02), 3/6/2002.

[¶ 5001]   Section 101.   Special depreciation allowance for certain property acquired after September 10, 2001, and before September 11, 2004.

(Code Sec. 168)

[Joint Committee on Taxation Report]

Present Law

Depreciation deductions

A taxpayer is allowed to recover, through annual depreciation deductions, the cost of certain property used in a trade or business or for the production of income. The amount of the depreciation deduction allowed with respect to tangible property for a taxable year is determined under the modified accelerated cost recovery system ("MACRS"). Under MACRS, different types of property generally are assigned applicable recovery periods and depreciation methods. The recovery periods applicable to most tangible personal property (generally tangible property other than residential rental property and nonresidential real property) range from 3 to 25 years. The depreciation methods generally applicable to tangible personal property are the 200-percent and 150-percent declining balance methods, switching to the straight-line method for the taxable year in which the depreciation deduction would be maximized.

Section 280F limits the annual depreciation deductions with respect to passenger automobiles to specified dollar amounts, indexed for inflation.

Section 167(f)(1) provides that capitalized computer software costs, other than computer software to which section 197 applies, are recovered ratably over 36 months.

In lieu of depreciation, a taxpayer with a sufficiently small amount of annual investment generally may elect to deduct up to $24,000 (for taxable years beginning in 2001 or 2002) of the cost of qualifying property placed in service for the taxable year (sec. 179). This amount is increased to $25,000 for taxable years beginning in 2003 and thereafter. In general, qualifying property is defined as depreciable tangible personal property that is purchased for use in the active conduct of a trade or business.

Explanation of Provision

The provision allows an additional first-year depreciation deduction equal to 30 percent of the adjusted basis of qualified property. The additional first-year depreciation deduction is allowed for both regular tax and alternative minimum tax purposes for the taxable year in which the property is placed in service.[2] The basis of the property and the depreciation allowances in the year of purchase and later years are appropriately adjusted to reflect the additional first-year depreciation deduction. In addition, the provision provides that there would be no adjustment to the allowable amount of depreciation for purposes of computing a taxpayer's alternative minimum taxable income with respect to property to which the pro-

---

2. The additional first-year depreciation deduction is subject to the general rules regarding whether an item is deductible under section 162 or subject to capitalization under section 263 or section 263A.

 Research Institute of America

vision applies. A taxpayer is allowed to elect out of the additional first-year depreciation for any class of property for any taxable year.

In order for property to qualify for the additional first-year depreciation deduction it must meet all of the following requirements. First, the property must be property to which the general rules of MACRS[3] apply with (1) an applicable recovery period of 20 years or less, (2) water utility property (as defined in section 168(e)(5)), (3) computer software other than computer software covered by section 197, or (4) qualified leasehold improvement property[4]. Second, the original use[5] of the property must commence with the taxpayer on or after September 11, 2001.[6] Third, the taxpayer must purchase the property within the applicable time period. Finally, the property must be placed in service before January 1, 2005. An extension of the place in service date of one year (i.e., January 1, 2006) is provided for certain property with a recovery period of ten years or longer and certain transportation property.[7] Transportation property is defined as tangible personal property used in the trade or business of transporting persons or property.

The applicable time period for acquired property is (1) after September 10, 2001 and before September 11, 2004, and no binding written contract for the acquisition is in effect before September 11, 2001 or (2) pursuant to a binding written contract which was entered into after September 10, 2001, and before September 11, 2004. With respect to property that is manufactured, constructed, or produced by the taxpayer for use by the taxpayer, the taxpayer must begin the manufacture, construction, or production of the property after September 10, 2001, and before September 11, 2004. Property that is manufactured, constructed, or produced for the taxpayer by another person under a contract that is entered into prior to the manufacture, construction, or production of the property is considered to be manufactured, constructed, or produced by the taxpayer. For property eligible for the extended placed in service date, a special rule limits the amount of costs eligible for the additional first year depreciation. With respect to such property, only the portion of the basis that is properly attributable to the costs incurred before September 11, 2004 ("progress expenditures") shall be eligible for the additional first year depreciation.[8]

---

3. A special rule precludes the additional first-year depreciation deduction for property that is required to be depreciated under the alternative depreciation system of MACRS.
4. Qualified leasehold improvement property is any improvement to an interior portion of a building that is nonresidential real property, provided certain requirements are met. The improvement must be made under or pursuant to a lease either by the lessee (or sublessee) of that portion of the building, or by the lessor of that portion of the building. That portion of the building is to be occupied exclusively by the lessee (or any sublessee). The improvement must be placed in service more than three years after the date the building was first placed in service.

   Qualified leasehold improvement property does not include any improvement for which the expenditure is attributable to the enlargement of the building, any elevator or escalator, any structural component benefiting a common area, or the internal structural framework of the building.

   For purposes of the provision, a binding commitment to enter into a lease would be treated as a lease, and the parties to the commitment would be treated as lessor and lessee. A lease between related persons would not be considered a lease for this purpose.

   Finally, New York Liberty Zone qualified leasehold improvement property is not eligible for the additional first year depreciation deduction.
5. The term "original use" means the first use to which the property is put, whether or not such use corresponds to the use of such property by the taxpayer. It is intended that, when evaluating whether property qualifies as "original use," the factors used to determine whether property qualified as "new section 38 property" for purposes of the investment tax credit would apply. See Treasury Regulation 1.48-2. Thus, it is intended that additional capital expenditures incurred to recondition or rebuild acquired property (or owned property) would satisfy the "original use" requirement. However, the cost of reconditioned or rebuilt property acquired by the taxpayer would not satisfy the "original use" requirement. For example, if on February 1, 2002, a taxpayer buys from X for $20,000 a machine that has been previously used by X. Prior to September 11, 2004, the taxpayer makes an expenditure on the property of $5,000 of the type that must be capitalized. Regardless of whether the $5,000 is added to the basis of such property or is capitalized as a separate asset, such amount would be treated as satisfying the "original use" requirement and would be qualified property (assuming all other conditions are met). No part of the $20,000 purchase price would qualify for the additional first year depreciation.
6. A special rule applies in the case of certain leased property. In the case of any property that is originally placed in service by a person and that is sold to the taxpayer and leased back to such person by the taxpayer within three months after the date that the property was placed in service, the property would be treated as originally placed in service by the taxpayer not earlier than the date that the property is used under the leaseback.
7. In order for property to qualify for the extended placed in service date, the property is required to have a production period exceeding two years or an estimated production period exceeding one year and a cost exceeding $1 million.
8. For purposes of determining the amount of eligible progress expenditures, it is intended that rules similar to sec. 46(d)(3) as in effect prior to the Tax Reform Act of 1986 shall apply.

The limitation on the amount of depreciation deductions allowed with respect to certain passenger automobiles (sec. 280F of the Code) is increased in the first year by $4,600 for automobiles that qualify (and do not elect out of the increased first year deduction). The $4,600 increase is not indexed for inflation.

The following examples illustrate the operation of the provision.

EXAMPLE 1. — Assume that on March 1, 2002, a calendar year taxpayer acquires and places in service qualified property that costs $1 million. Under the provision, the taxpayer is allowed an additional first-year depreciation deduction of $300,000. The remaining $700,000 of adjusted basis is recovered in 2002 and subsequent years pursuant to the depreciation rules of present law.

EXAMPLE 2. — Assume that on March 1, 2002, a calendar year taxpayer acquires and places in service qualified property that costs $50,000. In addition, assume that the property qualifies for the expensing election under section 179. Under the provision, the taxpayer is first allowed a $24,000 deduction under section 179. The taxpayer then is allowed an additional first-year depreciation deduction of $7,800 based on $26,000 ($50,000 original cost less the section 179 deduction of $24,000) of adjusted basis. Finally, the remaining adjusted basis of $18,200 ($26,000 adjusted basis less $7,800 additional first-year depreciation) is to be recovered in 2002 and subsequent years pursuant to the depreciation rules of present law.

Effective Date

The provision applies to property placed in service after September 10, 2001.

[¶ 5002]   Section 102.   Carryback of certain net operating losses allowed for 5 years; temporary suspension of 90 percent AMT limit.

(Code Sec. 56, 172)

[Joint Committee on Taxation Report]

Present Law

A net operating loss ("NOL") is, generally, the amount by which a taxpayer's allowable deductions exceed the taxpayer's gross income. A carryback of an NOL generally results in the refund of Federal income tax for the carryback year. A carryforward of an NOL reduces Federal income tax for the carryforward year.

In general, an NOL may be carried back two years and carried forward 20 years to offset taxable income in such years. Different rules apply with respect to NOLs arising in certain circumstances. For example, a three-year carryback applies with respect to NOLs (1) arising from casualty or theft losses of individuals, or (2) attributable to Presidentially declared disasters for taxpayers engaged in a farming business or a small business. A five-year carryback period applies to NOLs from a farming loss (regardless of whether the loss was incurred in a Presidentially declared disaster area). Special rules also apply to real estate investment trusts (no carryback), specified liability losses (10-year carryback), and excess interest losses (no carryback to any year preceding a corporate equity reduction transaction).

The alternative minimum tax rules provide that a taxpayer's NOL deduction cannot reduce the taxpayer's alternative minimum taxable income ("AMTI") by more than 90 percent of the AMTI.

 Research Institute of America   503

Explanation of Provision

The provision temporarily extends the general NOL carryback period to five years (from two years) for NOLs arising in taxable years ending in 2001 and 2002.[9] In addition, the five-year carryback period applies to NOLs from these years that qualify under present law for a three-year carryback period (i.e., NOLs arising from casualty or theft losses of individuals or attributable to certain Presidentially declared disaster areas).

A taxpayer can elect to forgo the five-year carryback period. The election to forgo the five-year carryback period is made in the manner prescribed by the Secretary of the Treasury and must be made by the due date of the return (including extensions) for the year of the loss. The election is irrevocable. If a taxpayer elects to forgo the five-year carryback period, then the losses are subject to the rules that otherwise would apply under section 172 absent the provision.

The provision also allows an NOL deduction attributable to NOL carrybacks arising in taxable years ending in 2001 and 2002, as well as NOL carryforwards to these taxable years, to offset 100 percent of a taxpayer's AMTI.[10]

Effective Date

The 5-year carryback provision is effective for net operating losses generated in taxable years ending after December 31, 2000.

The provision allowing the use of NOL carrybacks and carryforwards to offset 100 percent of AMTI is effective for taxable years ending before January 1, 2003.

[¶ 5011]   Section 301.   Tax benefits for area of New York City damaged in terrorist attacks on September 11, 2001; expansion of work opportunity credit.

(Code Sec. 1400L(a))

[Joint Committee on Taxation Report]

Present Law

In general

The work opportunity tax credit ("WOTC") is available on an elective basis for employers hiring individuals from one or more of eight targeted groups. The credit equals 40 percent (25 percent for employment of less than 400 hours) of qualified wages. Generally, qualified wages are wages attributable to service rendered by a member of a targeted group during the one-year period beginning with the day the individual began work for the employer.

The maximum credit per employee is $2,400 (40 percent of the first $6,000 of qualified first-year wages). With respect to qualified summer youth employees, the maximum credit is $1,200 (40 percent of the first $3,000 of qualified first-year wages).

For purposes of the credit, wages are generally defined as under the Federal Unemployment Tax Act, without regard to the dollar cap.

---

9. The provision does not affect the terms and conditions that the Internal Revenue Service may impose on a taxpayer seeking approval for a change in its annual accounting period. *See e.g.*, Rev. Proc. 2000-11, 2000-1 C.B. 309, sec. 5.06 ("If the corporation (or consolidated group) has a NOL (or consolidated NOL) in the short period required to effect the change, the NOL may not be carried back but must be carried over in accordance with the provisions of sec. 172 beginning with the first taxable year after the short period. However, the short period NOL (or consolidated NOL) is carried back or carried over in accordance with sec. 172 if it is either: (a) $50,000 or less, or (b) results from a short period of 9 months or longer and is less than the NOL (or the consolidated NOL) for a full 12-month period beginning with the first day of the short period.")

10. Section 172(b)(2) should be appropriately applied in computing AMTI to take proper account of the order that the NOL carryovers and carrybacks are used as a result of this provision. *See* section 56(d)(1)(B)(ii).

RIA **Research Institute of America**

Targeted groups eligible for the credit

The eight targeted groups are: (1) families eligible to receive benefits under the Temporary Assistance for Needy Families ("TANF") Program; (2) high-risk youth; (3) qualified ex-felons; (4) vocational rehabilitation referrals; (5) qualified summer youth employees; (6) qualified veterans; (7) families receiving food stamps; and (8) persons receiving certain Supplemental Security Income ("SSI") benefits.

The employer's deduction for wages is reduced by the amount of the credit.

Expiration date

The credit is effective for wages paid or incurred to a qualified individual who began work for an employer before January 1, 2002.

Explanation of Provision

The bill creates a new targeted group for the WOTC and extends WOTC only for this purpose.[11] Generally, the new targeted group is individuals who perform substantially all their services in the recovery zone for a business located on or south of Canal Street, East Broadway (east of its intersection with Canal Street), or Grand Street (east of its intersection with East Broadway) in the Borough of Manhattan, New York, New York (the "New York Liberty Zone"). The new targeted group also includes individuals who perform substantially all their services in New York City for a business that relocated from the New York Liberty Zone elsewhere within New York City due to the physical destruction or damage of their workplaces within the New York Liberty Zone by the September 11, 2001 terrorist attack. It is anticipated that only otherwise qualified businesses that relocate due to significant physical damage will be eligible for the credit.

Generally qualified wages for purposes of this targeted group are wages paid or incurred for work performed in the New York Liberty Zone after December 31, 2001 and before January 1, 2004 by such qualified individuals. Also, in the case of otherwise qualified businesses that relocated due to the destruction or damage of their workplaces by the September 11, 2001 terrorist attack, the credit can be claimed for work performed outside of the zone but within New York City subject to the dates specified above. Other rules like the minimum employment periods (sec. 51(i)(3)) of the WOTC apply.

Unlike the other targeted categories, the credit for the new targeted group is available for wages paid to both new hires and existing employees. For each qualified business that relocated from the New York Liberty Zone elsewhere within New York City due to the physical destruction or damage of their workplaces within the New York Liberty Zone, the number of that employer's employees whose wages are eligible under the new targeted category may not exceed the number of its employees in the New York Liberty Zone on September 11, 2001. Other qualified businesses (e.g., businesses that operate in the New York Liberty Zone both on and after Sept. 11, 2001 and businesses that move into the New York Liberty Zone after September 11, 2001) would not be subject to that limitation.

No credit for this new category of workers is allowed if the otherwise qualifying employer on average employed more than 200 employees during the taxable year in question.

Unlike the other targeted categories, members of this targeted group will not require certification for their wages to qualify for the credit.

For the new category, the maximum credit is $2,400 (40 percent of $6,000 of qualified wages) per qualified employee in each taxable year.

The portion of each employer's WOTC credit attributable to the new targeted group is allowed against the alternative minimum tax.

---

11. A separate provision of this bill includes a general 2-year extension of WOTC.

Effective Date

The provision is effective in taxable years ending after December 31, 2001 (for wages paid or incurred to qualified individuals for work after December 31, 2001 and before January 1, 2004).

[¶ 5012]   Section 301.   Tax benefits for area of New York City damaged in terrorist attacks on September 11, 2001; special allowance for certain property acquired after September 10, 2001.

(Code Sec. 1400L(b))

[Joint Committee on Taxation Report]

Present Law

Depreciation deductions

A taxpayer is allowed to recover, through annual depreciation deductions, the cost of certain property used in a trade or business or for the production of income. The amount of the depreciation deduction allowed with respect to tangible property for a taxable year is determined under the modified accelerated cost recovery system ("MACRS"). Under MACRS, different types of property generally are assigned applicable recovery periods and depreciation methods. The recovery periods applicable to most tangible personal property (generally tangible property other than residential rental property and nonresidential real property) range from 3 to 25 years. The depreciation methods generally applicable to tangible personal property are the 200-percent and 150-percent declining balance methods, switching to the straight-line method for the taxable year in which the depreciation deduction would be maximized. In lieu of depreciation, a taxpayer with a sufficiently small amount of annual investment generally may elect to deduct up to $24,000 (for taxable years beginning in 2001 or 2002) of the cost of qualifying property placed in service for the taxable year (sec. 179). For taxable years beginning in 2003 and thereafter, the amount deductible under section 179 is increased to $25,000.

Section 167(f)(1) provides that capitalized computer software costs, other than computer software to which section 197 applies, are recovered ratably over 36 months.

Explanation of Provision

The provision allows an additional first-year depreciation deduction equal to 30 percent of the adjusted basis of qualified New York Liberty Zone ("Liberty Zone") property. The additional first-year depreciation deduction is allowed for both regular tax and alternative minimum tax purposes for the taxable year in which the property is placed in service.[12] The basis of the property and the depreciation allowances in the year of purchase and later years are appropriately adjusted to reflect the additional first-year depreciation deduction. In addition, the provision provides that there would be no adjustment to the allowable amount of depreciation for purposes of computing a taxpayer's alternative minimum taxable income with respect to property to which the provision applies. A taxpayer is allowed to elect out of the additional first-year depreciation for any class of property for any taxable year.

In order for property to qualify for the additional first-year depreciation deduction it must meet all of the following requirements. First, the property must be property to which the general rules of MACRS[13] apply with (1) an applicable recovery period of 20 years or less, (2) water utility property (as defined in section 168(e)(5)), (3) certain nonresidential real property and residential rental property, or (4) computer software other than computer software covered by section 197. A special rule precludes the additional first year deprecia-

---

12. The additional first-year depreciation deduction is subject to the general rules regarding whether an item is deductible under section 162 or subject to capitalization under section 263 or section 263A.
13. A special rule precludes the additional first-year depreciation deduction for property that is required to be depreciated under the alternative depreciation system of MACRS.

                                 RIA Research Institute of America

tion under this provision for (1) qualified New York Liberty Zone leasehold improvement property[14] and, (2) property eligible for the additional first year depreciation under section 168(k) (i.e., property is eligible for only one 30% additional first year depreciation). Second, substantially all of the use of such property must be in the Liberty Zone. Third, the original use[15] of the property in the Liberty Zone must commence with the taxpayer on or after September 11, 2001.[16] Finally, the property must be acquired by purchase[17] by the taxpayer (1) after September 10, 2001 and placed in service on or before December 31, 2006. For qualifying nonresidential real property and residential rental property the property must be placed in service on or before December 31, 2009 in lieu of December 31, 2006. Property will not qualify if a binding written contract for the acquisition of such property is in effect before September 11, 2001.

Nonresidential real property and residential rental property is eligible for the additional first-year depreciation only to the extent such property rehabilitates real property damaged, or replaces real property destroyed or condemned as a result of the terrorist attacks of September 11, 2001. Property shall be treated as replacing destroyed property, if as part of an integrated plan, such property replaces real property which is included in a continuous area which includes real property destroyed or condemned. For purposes of this provision, it is intended that real property destroyed (or condemned) only include circumstances in which an entire building or structure was destroyed (or condemned) as a result of the terrorist attacks. Otherwise, such property is considered damaged real property. For example, if certain structural components (e.g., walls, floors, or plumbing fixtures) of a building are damaged or destroyed as a result of the terrorist attacks but the building is not destroyed (or condemned), then only costs related to replacing the damaged or destroyed components qualifies for the provision.

Property that is manufactured, constructed, or produced by the taxpayer for use by the taxpayer qualifies if the taxpayer begins the manufacture, construction, or production of the property after September 10, 2001, and the property is placed in service on or before December 31, 2006[18] (and all other requirements are met). Property that is manufactured, constructed, or produced for the taxpayer by another person under a contract that is entered into prior to the manufacture, construction, or production of the property is considered to be manufactured, constructed, or produced by the taxpayer.

The Liberty Zone means the area located on or south of Canal Street, East Broadway (east of its intersection with Canal Street), or Grand Street (east of its intersection with East Broadway) in the Borough of Manhattan in the City of New York, New York.

The following examples illustrate the operation of the provision.

EXAMPLE 1. — Assume that on March 1, 2002, a calendar year taxpayer acquires and places in service qualified property in the Liberty Zone that costs $1 million. Under the provision, the taxpayer is allowed an additional first-year depreciation deduction of $300,000. The remaining $700,000 of adjusted basis is recovered in 2002 and subsequent years pursuant to the depreciation rules of present law.

---

14. Qualified New York Liberty Zone leasehold improvement property is defined in another provision of the bill. Leasehold improvements that do not satisfy the requirements to be treated as "qualified New York Liberty Zone leasehold improvement property" are eligible for the 30 percent additional first-year depreciation deduction (assuming all other conditions are met).
15. Thus, used property may constitute qualified property so long as it has not previously been used within the Liberty Zone. In addition, it is intended that additional capital expenditures incurred to recondition or rebuild property the original use of which in the Liberty Zone began with the taxpayer would satisfy the "original use" requirement. See Treasury Regulation 1.48-2 Example 5.
16. A special rule applies in the case of certain leased property. In the case of any property that is originally placed in service by a person and that is sold to the taxpayer and leased back to such person by the taxpayer within three months after the date that the property was placed in service, the property would be treated as originally placed in service by the taxpayer not earlier than the date that the property is used under the leaseback.
17. For purposes of this provision, purchase is defined under section 179(d).
18. December 31, 2009 with respect to nonresidential real property and residential rental property.

EXAMPLE 2. — Assume that on March 1, 2002, a calendar year taxpayer acquires and places in service qualified property in the Liberty Zone that costs $100,000. In addition, assume that the property qualifies for the expensing election under section 179. Under the provision, the taxpayer is first allowed a $59,000 deduction under section 179.[19] The taxpayer then is allowed an additional first-year depreciation deduction of $12,300 based on $41,000 ($100,000 original cost less the section 179 deduction of $59,000) of adjusted basis. Finally, the remaining adjusted basis of $28,700 ($41,000 adjusted basis less $12,300 additional first-year depreciation) is to be recovered in 2002 and subsequent years pursuant to the depreciation rules of present law.

[¶ 5013]   Section 301.   Tax benefits for area of New York City damaged in terrorist attacks on September 11, 2001; 5-year recovery period for depreciation of certain leasehold improvements.

(Code Sec. 1400L(c))

[Joint Committee on Taxation Report]

Present Law

Depreciation of leasehold improvements

Depreciation allowances for property used in a trade or business generally are determined under the modified Accelerated Cost Recovery System ("MACRS") of section 168. Depreciation allowances for improvements made on leased property are determined under MACRS, even if the MACRS recovery period assigned to the property is longer than the term of the lease (sec. 168(i)(8)).[38] This rule applies regardless whether the lessor or lessee places the leasehold improvements in service.[39] If a leasehold improvement constitutes an addition or improvement to nonresidential real property already placed in service, the improvement is depreciated using the straight-line method over a 39-year recovery period, beginning in the month the addition or improvement was placed in service (secs. 168(b)(3), (c)(1), (d)(2), and (i)(6)).[40]

Treatment of dispositions of leasehold improvements

A lessor of leased property that disposes of a leasehold improvement which was made by the lessor for the lessee of the property may take the adjusted basis of the improvement into account for purposes of determining gain or loss if the improvement is irrevocably disposed of or abandoned by the lessor at the termination of the lease.[41] This rule conforms the treatment of lessors and lessees with respect to leasehold improvements disposed of at the end of a term of lease. For purposes of applying this rule, it is expected that a lessor must be able to separately account for the adjusted basis of the leasehold improvement that is irrevocably disposed of or abandoned. This rule does not apply to the extent section

---

19. Section 301 provides that property in the Liberty Zone is eligible for an additional $35,000 of expensing under section 179.

38. The Tax Reform Act of 1986 modified the Accelerated Cost Recovery System ("ACRS") to institute MACRS. Prior to the adoption of ACRS by the Economic Recovery Act of 1981, taxpayers were allowed to depreciate the various components of a building as separate assets with separate useful lives. The use of component depreciation was repealed upon the adoption of ACRS. The Tax Reform Act of 1986 also denied the use of component depreciation under MACRS.

39. Former Code sections 168(f)(6) and 178 provided that in certain circumstances, a lessee could recover the cost of leasehold improvements made over the remaining term of the lease. These provisions were repealed by the Tax Reform Act of 1986.

40. If the improvement is characterized as tangible personal property, ACRS or MACRS depreciation is calculated using the shorter recovery periods and accelerated methods applicable to such property. The determination of whether certain improvements are characterized as tangible personal property or as nonresidential real property often depends on whether or not the improvements constitute a "structural component" of a building (as defined by Treas. Reg. sec. 1.48-1(e)(1)). See, for example, *Metro National Corp.*, 52 TCM 1440 (1987); *King Radio Corp.*, 486 F.2d 1091 (10th Cir., 1973); *Mallinckrodt, Inc.*, 778 F.2d 402 (8th Cir., 1985) (with respect various leasehold improvements).

41. The conference report describing this provision mistakenly states that the provision applies to improvements that are irrevocably disposed of or abandoned by the *lessee* (rather than the *lessor*) at the termination of the lease.

280B applies to the demolition of a structure, a portion of which may include leasehold improvements.[42]

Explanation of Provision

The provision provides that 5-year property for purposes of the depreciation rules of section 168 includes qualified New York Liberty Zone leasehold improvement property ("qualified NYLZ leasehold improvement property"). The term qualified NYLZ leasehold improvement property means property defined in section 168(e)(6)[43] that is placed in service after September 10, 2001 and before January 1, 2007 (and not subject to a binding contract on September 10, 2001) in the New York Liberty Zone. The straight-line method is required to be used with respect to qualified NYLZ leasehold improvement property. A 9-year period is specified as the class life of qualified NYLZ leasehold improvement property for purposes of the alternative depreciation system.

[¶5014]   Section 301.   Tax benefits for area of New York City damaged in terrorist attacks on September 11, 2001; tax-exempt bond financing.

(Code Sec. 1400L(d))

[Joint Committee on Taxation Report]

Present Law

Rules governing issuance of tax-exempt bonds

In general

Interest on debt incurred by States or local governments is excluded from income if the proceeds of the borrowing are used to carry out governmental functions of those entities or the debt is repaid with governmental funds (sec. 103). Interest on bonds that nominally are issued by States or local governments, but the proceeds of which are used (directly or indirectly) by a private person and payment of which is derived from funds of such a private person is taxable unless the purpose of the borrowing is approved specifically in the Code or in a non-Code provision of a revenue Act. These bonds are called "private activity bonds."[20] The term "private person" includes the Federal Government and all other individuals and entities other than States or local governments.

Private activities eligible for financing with tax-exempt private activity bonds

Present law includes several exceptions permitting States or local governments to act as conduits providing tax-exempt financing for private activities. Both capital expenditures and limited working capital expenditures of charitable organizations described in section 501(c)(3) of the Code ("qualified 501(c)(3) bonds") may be financed with tax-exempt bonds.

States or local governments may issue tax-exempt "exempt-facility bonds" to finance property for certain private businesses. Business facilities eligible for this financing include transportation (airports, ports, local mass commuting, and high speed intercity rail facilities); privately owned and/or privately operated public works facilities (sewage, solid waste disposal, local district heating or cooling, and hazardous waste disposal facilities); privately owned and/or operated low-income rental housing;[21] and certain private facilities for the local furnishing of electricity or gas. A further provision allows tax-exempt financing for "environmental enhancements of hydro-electric generating facilities." Tax-exempt financing also is authorized for capital expenditures for small manufacturing facilities and land and equipment for first-time farmers ("qualified small-issue bonds"), local redevelopment activ-

---

42. Under present law, section 280B denies a deduction for any loss sustained on the demolition of any structure.
43. Section 168(e)(6) regarding qualified leasehold improvement property is added by section 205 of the bill.
20. Interest on private activity bonds (other than qualified 501(c)(3) bonds) is a preference item in calculating the alternative minimum tax.
21. Residential rental projects must satisfy low-income tenant occupancy requirements for a minimum period of 15 years.

ities ("qualified redevelopment bonds"), and eligible empowerment zone and enterprise community businesses.

Tax-exempt private activity bonds also may be issued to finance limited non-business purposes: certain student loans and mortgage loans for owner-occupied housing ("qualified mortgage bonds" and "qualified veterans' mortgage bonds"). Purchasers of houses financed with qualified mortgage bonds must be first-time homebuyers satisfying prescribed income limits, the purchase prices of the houses is limited, the amount by which interest rates charged to homebuyers may exceed the interest paid by issuers is restricted, and a recapture provision applies to target the benefit to purchasers having longer-term need for the subsidy provided by the bonds. Qualified veterans' mortgage bonds are not subject to these limitations, but these bonds may only be issued by five States and may only be used to finance mortgage loans to veterans who served on active duty before January 1, 1977.

With the exception of qualified 501(c)(3) bonds, private activity bonds may not be issued to finance working capital requirements of private businesses.

In most cases, the aggregate volume of tax-exempt private activity bonds that may be issued in a State is restricted by annual volume limits. These annual volume limits are equal to $62.50 per resident of the State, or $187.5 million if greater. The volume limits are scheduled to increase to the greater of $75 per resident of the State or $225 million in calendar year 2002. After 2002, the volume limits will be indexed annually for inflation.

Arbitrage restrictions on tax-exempt bonds

The Federal income tax does not apply to the income of States and local governments that is derived from the exercise of an essential governmental function. To prevent these tax-exempt entities from issuing more Federally subsidized tax-exempt bonds than is necessary for the activity being financed or from issuing such bonds earlier than needed for the purpose of the borrowing, the Code includes arbitrage restrictions limiting the ability to profit from investment of tax-exempt bond proceeds. In general, arbitrage profits may be earned only during specified periods (e.g., defined "temporary periods" before funds are needed for the purpose of the borrowing) or on specified types of investments (e.g., "reasonably required reserve or replacement funds"). Subject to limited exceptions, profits that are earned during these periods or on such investments must be rebated to the Federal Government. Governmental bonds are subject to less restrictive arbitrage rules that most private activity bonds.

Miscellaneous additional restrictions on tax-exempt bonds

Several additional restrictions apply to the issuance of tax-exempt bonds. First, private activity bonds (other than qualified 501(c)(3) bonds) may not be advance refunded. Governmental bonds and qualified 501(c)(3) bonds may be advance refunded one time. An advance refunding occurs when the refunded bonds are not retired within 90 days of issuance of the refunding bonds.

Issuance of private activity bonds is subject to restrictions on use of proceeds for the acquisition of land and existing property, use of proceeds to finance certain specified facilities, (e.g., airplanes, skyboxes, other luxury boxes, health club facilities, gambling facilities, and liquor stores) and use of proceeds to pay costs of issuance (e.g., bond counsel and underwriter fees). Additionally, the term of the bonds generally may not exceed 120 percent of the economic life of the property being financed and certain public approval requirements (similar to requirements that typically apply under State law to issuance of governmental debt) apply under Federal law to issuance of private activity bonds. Present law precludes substantial users of property financed with private activity bonds from owning the bonds to prevent their deducting tax-exempt interest paid to themselves. Finally, owners of most private-activity-bond-financed property are subject to special "change-in-use" penalties if the use of the bond-financed property changes to a use that is not eligible for tax-exempt financing while the bonds are outstanding.

RIA **Research Institute of America**

Explanation of Provision

In general

The provision authorizes issuance during calendar years 2002, 2003, and 2004 of an aggregate amount of $8 billion of tax-exempt private activity bonds to finance the construction and rehabilitation of nonresidential real property[22] and residential rental real property[23] in a newly designated "Liberty Zone" (the "Zone") of New York City.[24] Property eligible for financing with these bonds includes buildings and their structural components, fixed tenant improvements,[25] and public utility property (e.g., gas, water, electric and telecommunication lines). All business addresses located on or south of Canal Street, East Broadway (east of its intersection with Canal Street), or Grand Street (east of its intersection with East Broadway) in the Borough of Manhattan are considered to be located within the New York Recovery Zone. Issuance of bonds authorized under the provision is limited to projects approved by the Mayor of New York City or the Governor of New York State, each of whom may designate up to $4 billion of the bonds authorized under the bill.

If the Mayor or the Governor determines that it is not feasible to use all of the authorized bond proceeds which he is authorized to designate for property located in the Zone, up to $1 billion of bond proceeds may designated by each to be used for the acquisition, construction, and rehabilitation of commercial real property (including fixed tenant improvements) located outside the Zone and within New York City.[26] Bond-financed property located outside the Zone must meet the additional requirements that the project have at least 100,000 square feet of usable office or other commercial space in a single building or multiple adjacent buildings.

Subject to the following exceptions and modifications, issuance of these tax-exempt bonds is subject to the general rules applicable to issuance of exempt-facility private activity bonds:

(1) Issuance of the bonds is not subject to the aggregate annual State private activity bond volume limits (sec. 146);

(2) The restriction on acquisition of existing property is applied using a minimum requirement of 50 percent of the cost of acquiring the building being devoted to rehabilitation (sec. 147(d));

(3) The special arbitrage expenditure rules for certain construction bond proceeds apply to available construction proceeds of the bonds (sec. 148(f)(4)(C));

(4) The tenant targeting rules applicable to exempt-facility bonds for residential rental property (and the corresponding change in use penalties for violation of those rules) do not apply to such property financed with the bonds (secs. 142(d) and 150(b)(2));

(5) Repayments of bond-financed loans may not be used to make additional loans, but rather must be used to retire outstanding bonds (with the first such retirement occurring 10 years after issuance of the bonds);[27] and

(6) Interest on the bonds is not a preference item for purposes of the alternative minimum tax preference for private activity bond interest (sec. 57(a)(5)).

---

22. No more than $800 million of the authorized bond amount may be used to finance property used for retail sales of tangible property (e.g., department stores, restaurants, etc.) and functionally related and subordinate property. The term nonresidential real property includes structural components of such property if the taxpayer treats such components as part of the real property structure for all Federal income tax purposes (e.g., cost recovery). The $800 million limit is divided equally between the Mayor and the Governor.
23. No more than $1.6 billion of the authorized bond amount may be used to finance residential rental property. The $1.6 billion limit is divided equally between the Mayor and the Governor.
24. Current refundings of outstanding bonds issued under the provision do not count against the $8 billion volume limit to the extent that the principal amount of the refunding bonds does not exceed the outstanding principal amount of the bonds being refunded. The bonds may not be advance refunded.
25. Fixtures and equipment that could be removed from the designated zone for use elsewhere are not eligible for financing with these bonds.
26. Public utility property and residential property located outside the Zone cannot be financed with the bonds.
27. It is intended that redemptions will occur at least semi-annually beginning at the end of 10 years after the bonds are issued; however, amounts of less than $250,000 are not to be required to be used to redeem bonds at such intervals.

Effective Date

The provision is effective for bonds issued after the date of enactment and before January 1, 2005.

[¶ 5015]   Section 301.   Tax benefits for area of New York City damaged in terrorist attacks on September 11, 2001; advance refundings of certain tax-exempt bonds.

(Code Sec. 1400L(e))

[Joint Committee on Taxation Report]

Present Law

Interest on bonds issued by States or local governments is excluded from income if the proceeds of the borrowing are used to carry out governmental functions of those entities or the debt is repaid with governmental funds (sec. 103). Interest on bonds that nominally are issued by States or local governments, but the proceeds of which are used (directly or indirectly) by a private person and payment of which is derived from funds of such a private person is taxable unless the purpose of the borrowing is approved specifically in the Code or in a non-Code provision of a revenue Act. These bonds are called private activity bonds. Present law includes several exceptions permitting States or local governments to act as conduits providing tax-exempt financing for private activities. One such exception is the provision of financing for activities of charitable organizations described in section 501(c)(3) of the Code ("qualified 501(c)(3) bonds").

A refunding bond is used to redeem a prior bond issuance. The Code contains different rules for "current" as opposed to "advance" refunding bonds. Tax-exempt bonds may be refunded currently an indefinite number of times. A current refunding occurs when the refunded debt is redeemed within 90 days of issuance of the refunding bonds. Governmental bonds and qualified 501(c)(3) bonds also may be advance refunded one time (sec. 149(d)).[28] An advance refunding occurs when the refunded debt is not redeemed within 90 days after the refunding bonds are issued. Rather, proceeds of the refunding bonds are invested in an escrow account and held until a future date when the refunded debt may be redeemed until the terms of the refunded bonds.

Explanation of Provision

The bill permits certain bonds for facilities located in New York City to be advance refunded one additional time. These bonds include only bonds for which all present-law advance refunding authority was exhausted before September 12, 2001, and with respect to which the advance refunding bonds authorized under present law were outstanding on September 11, 2001.[29] Further, to be eligible for the additional advance refunding, at least 90 percent of the refunded bonds must have been used to finance facilities located in New York City,[30][31] and the bonds must be —

(1) Governmental general obligation bonds of New York City;

(2) Governmental bonds issued by the Metropolitan Transportation Authority of the State of New York;

(3) Governmental bonds issued by the New York Municipal Water Finance Authority; or

---

28. Bonds issued before 1986 and pursuant to certain transition rules contained in the Tax Reform Act of 1986 may be advance refunded more than one time in certain cases.
29. Thus, at no time after the advance refunding authorized under the provision occurs may there be more than two sets of bonds outstanding.
30. This requirement is 95 percent in the case of eligible qualified 501(c)(3) bonds.
31. In the case of bonds for water facilities issued by the New York Municipal Water Finance Authority, property located outside New York City that is functionally related and subordinate to property located in the city is deemed to be located in the city.

(4) Qualified 501(c)(3) bonds issued by or on behalf of New York State or New York City to finance hospital facilities (as defined in section 145(c).

The maximum amount of advance refunding bonds that may be issued pursuant to this provision is $9 billion. Eligible advance refunding bonds must be designated as such by the Mayor of New York City or the Governor of New York State. Up to $4.5 billion of bonds may be designated by each of these officials. Advance refunding bonds issued under the provision must satisfy all requirements of section 148 and 149(d) except for the limit on the number of advance refundings allowed under section 149(d).

Effective Date

The provision is effective on the date of enactment and before January 1, 2005.

[¶ 5016]   Section 301.   Tax benefits for area of New York City damaged in terrorist attacks on September 11, 2001; increase in expensing under section 179.

(Code Sec. 1400L(f))

[Joint Committee on Taxation Report]

Present Law

Present law provides that, in lieu of depreciation, a taxpayer with a sufficiently small amount of annual investment may elect to deduct up to $24,000 (for taxable years beginning in 2001 or 2002) of the cost of qualifying property placed in service for the taxable year (sec. 179). This amount is increased to $25,000 of the cost of qualified property placed in service for taxable years beginning in 2003 and thereafter. The $24,000 ($25,000 for taxable years beginning in 2003 and thereafter) amount is phased-out (but not below zero) by the amount by which the cost of qualifying property placed in service during the taxable year exceeds $200,000.

Additional section 179 incentives are provided with respect to a qualified zone property used by a business in an empowerment zone (sec. 1397A). Such a business may elect to deduct an additional $20,000 of the cost of qualified zone property placed in service in year 2001. The $20,000 amount is increased to $35,000 for taxable years beginning in 2002 and thereafter. In addition, the phase-out range is applied by taking into account only 50 percent of the cost of qualified zone property that is section 179 property.

The amount eligible to be expensed for a taxable year may not exceed the taxable income for a taxable year that is derived from the active conduct of a trade or business (determined without regard to this provision). Any amount that is not allowed as a deduction because of the taxable income limitation may be carried forward to succeeding taxable years (subject to similar limitations). No general business credit under section 38 is allowed with respect to any amount for which a deduction is allowed under section 179.

Explanation of Provision

The provision increases the amount a taxpayer can deduct under section 179 for qualifying property used in the New York Liberty Zone.[32] Specifically, the provision increases the maximum dollar amount that may be deducted under section 179 by the lesser of (1) $35,000 or (2) the cost of qualifying property placed in service during the taxable year. This amount is in addition to the amount otherwise deductible under section 179.

Qualifying property means section 179 property[33] purchased and placed in service by the taxpayer after September 10, 2001 and before January 1, 2007, where (1) substantially all of its use is in the New York Liberty Zone in the active conduct of a trade or business by

---

32. The "New York Liberty Zone" means the area located on or south of Canal Street, East Broadway (east of its intersection with Canal Street), or Grand Street (east of its intersection with East Broadway) in the Borough of Manhattan in the City of New York, New York.
33. As defined in section 179(d)(1).

the taxpayer in the zone, and (2) the original use of which in the New York Liberty Zone commences with the taxpayer after September 10, 2001.

As under present law with respect to empowerment zones, the phase-out range for the section 179 deduction attributable to New York Liberty Zone property is applied by taking into account only 50 percent of the cost of New York Liberty Zone property that is section 179property. Also, no general business credit under section 38 is allowed with respect to any amount for which a deduction is allowed under section 179.

Effective Date

The provision is effective for taxable years beginning on December 31, 2001 and before January 1, 2007.

[¶ 5017]   Section 301.   Tax benefits for area of New York City damaged in terrorist attacks on September 11, 2001; extension of replacement period for nonrecognition of gain.

(Code Sec. 1400L(g))

[Joint Committee on Taxation Report]

Present Law

A taxpayer may elect not to recognize gain with respect to property that is involuntarily converted if the taxpayer acquires within an applicable period (the "replacement period") property similar or related in service or use (sec. 1033). If the taxpayer does not replace the converted property with property similar or related in service or use, then gain generally is recognized. If the taxpayer elects to apply the rules of section 1033, gain on the converted property is recognized only to the extent that the amount realized on the conversion exceeds the cost of the replacement property. In general, the replacement period begins with the date of the disposition of the converted property and ends two years after the close of the first taxable year in which any part of the gain upon conversion is realized.[34] The replacement period is extended to three years if the converted property is real property held for the productive use in a trade or business or for investment.[35]

Special rules apply for property converted in a Presidentially declared disaster.[36] With respect to a principal residence that is converted in a Presidentially declared disaster, no gain is recognized by reason of the receipt of insurance proceeds for unscheduled personal property that was part of the contents of such residence. In addition, the replacement period for the replacement of such a principal residence is extended to four years after the close of the first taxable year in which any part of the gain upon conversion is realized. With respect to investment or business property that is converted in a Presidentially declared disaster, any tangible property acquired and held for productive use in a business is treated as similar or related in service or use to the converted property.

Explanation of Provision

The provision extends the replacement period to five years for a taxpayer to purchase property to replace property that was involuntarily converted within the New York Liberty Zone[37] as a result of the terrorist attacks that occurred on September 11, 2001. However, the five-year period is available only if substantially all of the use of the replacement property is in New York City. In all other cases, the present-law replacement period rules continue to apply.

---

34. Section 1033(a)(2)(B).
35. Section 1033(g)(4).
36. Section 1033(h). For this purpose, a "Presidentially declared disaster" means any disaster which, with respect to the area in which the property is located, resulted in a subsequent determination by the President that such area warrants assistance by the Federal Government under the Disaster Relief and Emergency Assistance Act.
37. The "New York Liberty Zone" has the same definition throughout this bill.

Effective Date

The provision is effective for involuntary conversions in the New York Liberty Zone occurring on or after September 11, 2001, as a consequence of the terrorist attacks on such date.

[¶ 5021]   Section 401.   Allowance of electronic 1099's.

(Code Sec. 6051)

[Joint Committee on Taxation Report]

Present Law

Many provisions in the Code require entities to file information returns with the IRS and to provide copies to taxpayers. For example, employers are required to provide information with respect to wages paid to employees, and entities (such as banks and credit unions) that pay interest to individuals are also required to provide information with respect to those payments. In general, the copies of the information returns that are provided to taxpayers are provided on paper via the U.S. mail.

Temporary regulations allow Form W-2 to be furnished electronically on a voluntary basis. Under Temp. Treas. Reg. §31.6051-1T(j), a recipient must have affirmatively consented to receive the statement electronically and must not have withdrawn that consent before the statement is furnished. A similar rule cannot be implemented administratively with respect to some information returns, because the Code requires that the copies furnished to individuals must be furnished either in person or in a statement sent by first-class mail in a specified format.[44]

IRS Form 5498 is used to report contributions to an Archer MSA, an Individual Retirement Account, or a Coverdell education savings accounts. In addition, distributions from these accounts are reported on IRS Form 1099. Under present law, the Secretary has the authority to issue rules under which Forms 5498 and 1099 related to these accounts may be provided electronically.

Explanation of Provision

The provision removes the statutory impediment to providing copies of specified information returns to taxpayers electronically. Accordingly, these copies may be furnished electronically to a recipient who has consented to this; the copies may be furnished in a manner similar to the one permitted with respect to Form W-2 or in another manner provided by the Secretary.

Effective Date

The provision is effective on date of enactment.

[¶ 5022]   Section 402.   Excluded cancellation of indebtedness income of S corporation not to result in adjustment to basis of stock of shareholders.

(Code Sec. 108)

[Joint Committee on Taxation Report]

Present Law

In general, an S corporation is not subject to the corporate income tax on its items of income and loss. Instead, an S corporation passes through its items of income and loss to its shareholders. Each shareholder takes into account separately his or her pro rata share of these items on their individual income tax returns. To prevent double taxation of these

---

44. See 6042(c), 6044(e) and 6049(c)(2).

items, each shareholder's basis in the stock of the S corporation is increased by the amount included in income (including tax-exempt income) and is decreased by the amount of any losses (including nondeductible losses) taken into account. A shareholder may deduct losses only to the extent of a shareholder's basis in his or her stock in the S corporation plus the shareholder's adjusted basis in any indebtedness of the corporation to the shareholder. Any loss that is disallowed by reason of lack of basis is "suspended" at the corporate level and is carried forward and allowed in any subsequent year in which the shareholder has adequate basis in the stock or debt.

In general, gross income includes income from the discharge of indebtedness. However, income from the discharge of indebtedness of a taxpayer in a bankruptcy case or when the taxpayer is insolvent (to the extent of the insolvency) is excluded from income.[45] The taxpayer is required to reduce tax attributes, such as net operating losses, certain carryovers, and basis in assets, to the extent of the excluded income.

In the case of an S corporation, the eligibility for the exclusion and the attribute reduction are applied at the corporate level. For this purpose, a shareholder's suspended loss is treated as a tax attribute that is reduced. Thus, if the S corporation is in bankruptcy or is insolvent, any income from the discharge of indebtedness by a creditor of the S corporation is excluded from the corporation's income, and the S corporation reduces its tax attributes (including any suspended losses).

To illustrate these rules, assume that a sole shareholder of an S corporation has zero basis in its stock of the corporation. The S corporation borrows $100 from a third party and loses the entire $100. Because the shareholder has no basis in its stock, the $100 loss is "suspended" at the corporate level. If the $100 debt is forgiven when the corporation is in bankruptcy or is insolvent, the $100 income from the discharge of indebtedness is excluded from income, and the $100 "suspended" loss should be eliminated in order to achieve a tax result that is consistent with the economics of the transactions in that the shareholder has no economic gain or loss from these transactions.

Notwithstanding the economics of the overall transaction, the United States Supreme Court ruled in the case of *Gitlitz v. Commissioner*[46] that, under present law, income from the discharge of indebtedness of an S corporation that is excluded from income is treated as an item of income which increases the basis of a shareholder's stock in the S corporation and allows the suspended corporate loss to pass thru to a shareholder. Thus, under the decision, an S corporation shareholder is allowed to deduct a loss for tax purposes that it did not economically incur.

Explanation of Provision

The provision provides that income from the discharge of indebtedness of an S corporation that is excluded from the S corporation's income is not taken into account as an item of income by any shareholder and thus does not increase the basis of any shareholder's stock in the corporation.

Effective Date

The provision generally applies to discharges of indebtedness after October 11, 2001. The provision does not apply to any discharge of indebtedness before March 1, 2002, pursuant to a plan of reorganization filed with a bankruptcy court on or before October 11, 2001.

---

45. Special rules also apply to certain real estate debt and farm debt.
46. 531 U.S. 206 (2001).

[¶ 5023]   Section 403.   Limitation on use of nonaccrual experience method of accounting.

(Code Sec. 448)

[Joint Committee on Taxation Report]

Present Law

An accrual method taxpayer generally must recognize income when all the events have occurred that fix the right to receive the income and the amount of the income can be determined with reasonable accuracy. An accrual method taxpayer may deduct the amount of any receivable that was previously included in income that becomes worthless during the year.

Accrual method taxpayers are not required to include in income amounts to be received for the performance of services which, on the basis of experience, will not be collected (the "non-accrual experience method"). The availability of this method is conditioned on the taxpayer not charging interest or a penalty for failure to timely pay the amount charged.

Generally, a cash method taxpayer is not required to include an amount in income until received. A taxpayer generally may not use the cash method if purchase, production, or sale of merchandise is an income producing factor. Such taxpayers generally are required to keep inventories and use an accrual method of accounting. In addition, corporations (and partnerships with corporate partners) generally may not use the cash method of accounting if their average annual gross receipts years exceed $5 million. An exception to this $5 million rule is provided for qualified personal service corporations. A qualified personal service corporation is a corporation (1) substantially all of whose activities involve the performance of services in the fields of health, law, engineering, architecture, accounting, actuarial science, performing arts or consulting and (2) substantially all of the stock of which is owned by current or former employees performing such services, their estates or heirs. Qualified personal service corporations are allowed to use the cash method without regard to whether their average annual gross receipts exceed $5 million.

Explanation of Provision

Under the provision, the non-accrual experience method of accounting is available only for amounts to be received for the performance of qualified services and for services provided by certain small businesses. Amounts to be received for all other services are subject to the general rule regarding inclusion in income. Qualified services are services in the fields of health, law, engineering, architecture, accounting, actuarial science, performing arts or consulting. As under present law, the availability of this method is conditioned on the taxpayer not charging interest or a penalty for failure to timely pay the amount charged.

Under a special rule, the non-accrual experience method of accounting continues to be available for the performance of non-qualified services if the average annual gross receipts (as defined in sec. 448(c)) of the taxpayer (or any predecessor) does not exceed $5 million. The rules of paragraph (2) and (3) of section 448(c) (i.e., the rules regarding the aggregation of related taxpayers, taxpayers not in existence for the entire three year period, short taxable years, definition of gross receipts, and treatment of predecessors) apply for purposes of determining the average annual gross receipts test.

The provision requires that the Secretary of the Treasury prescribe regulations to permit a taxpayer to use alternative computations or formulas if such alternative computations or formulas accurately reflect, based on experience, the amount of its year-end receivables that will not be collected. It is anticipated that the Secretary of the Treasury will consider providing safe harbors in such regulations that ma y be relied upon by taxpayers. In addition, the provision also provides that the Secretary of the Treasury permit taxpayers to adopt, or request consent of the Secretary of the Treasury to change to, an alternative computation or formula that clearly reflects the taxpayer's experience. The provision requires the Secretary of Treasury to approve a request provided that the alternative computation or formula clearly reflects the taxpayer's experience.

Effective Date

The provision is effective for taxable years ending after date of enactment. Any change in the taxpayer's method of accounting required as a result of the limitation on the use of the non-accrual experience method is treated as a voluntary change initiated by the taxpayer with the consent of the Secretary of the Treasury. Any resultant section 481(a) adjustment is to be taken into account over a period not to exceed the lesser of the number of years the taxpayer has used the non-accrual experience method of accounting or four years under principles consistent with those in Rev. Proc. 99-49.[47]

[¶ 5024]   Section 404.   Exclusion for foster care payments to apply to payments by qualified placement agencies.

(Code Sec. 131)

[Joint Committee on Taxation Report]

Present Law

If certain requirements are satisfied, an exclusion from gross income is provided for qualified foster care payments paid to a foster care provider by either (1) a State or local government; or (2) a tax-exempt placement agency. Qualified foster care payments are amounts paid for caring for a qualified foster care individual in the foster care provider's home and difficulty of care payments.[48] A qualified foster care individual is an individual living in a foster care family home in which the individual was placed by: (1) an agency of the State or local government (regardless of the individual's age at the time of placement); or (2) a tax-exempt placement agency licensed by the State or local government (if such individual was under the age of 19 at the time of placement).

Explanation of Provision

The bill makes two modifications to the present-law exclusion for qualified foster care payments. First, the bill expands the definition of qualified foster care payments to include payments by any placement agency that is licensed or certified by a State or local government, or an entity designated by a State or local government to make payments to providers of foster care. Second, the bill expands the definition of a qualified foster care individual by including foster care individuals placed by a qualified foster care placement agency (regardless of the individual's age at the time of placement).

Effective Date

The provision is effective for taxable years beginning after December 31, 2001.

---

47. 1999-2 C.B. 725
48. A difficulty of care payment is a payment designated by the person making such payment as compensation for providing the additional care of a qualified foster care individual in the home of the foster care provider which is required by reason of a physical, mental, or emotional handicap of such individual and with respect to which the State has determined that there is a need for additional compensation.

RIA Research Institute of America

[¶ 5025]   Section 405.   Interest rate range for additional funding requirements.

(Code Sec. 412)

[Joint Committee on Taxation Report]

Present Law

In general

ERISA and the Code impose both minimum and maximum[49] funding requirements with respect to defined benefit pension plans. The minimum funding requirements are designed to provide at least a certain level of benefit security by requiring the employer to make certain minimum contributions to the plan. The amount of contributions required for a plan year is generally the amount needed to fund benefits earned during that year plus that year's portion of other liabilities that are amortized over a period of years, such as benefits resulting from a grant of past service credit.

Additional contributions for underfunded plans

Additional contributions are required under a special funding rule if a single-employer defined benefit pension plan is underfunded.[50] Under the special rule, a plan is considered underfunded for a plan year if the value of the plan assets is less than 90 percent of the plan's current liability.[51] The value of plan assets as a percentage of current liability is the plan's "funded current liability percentage."

If a plan is underfunded, the amount of additional required contributions is based on certain elements, including whether the plan has an unfunded liability related to benefits accrued before 1988 or 1995 or to changes in the mortality table used to determine contributions, and whether the plan provides for unpredictable contingent event benefits (that is, benefits that depend on contingencies that are not reliably and reasonably predictable, such as facility shutdowns or reductions in workforce). However, the amount of additional contributions cannot exceed the amount needed to increase the plan's funded current liability percentage to 100 percent.

Required interest rate

In general, a plan's current liability means all liabilities to employees and their beneficiaries under the plan. The interest rate used to determine a plan's current liability must be within a permissible range of the weighted average of the interest rates on 30-year Treasury securities for the four-year period ending on the last day before the plan year begins.[52] The permissible range is from 90 percent to 105 percent. As a result of debt reduction, the Department of the Treasury does not currently issue 30-year Treasury securities.

Timing of plan contributions

In general, plan contributions required to satisfy the funding rules must be made within 8 1/2 months after the end of the plan year. If the contribution is made by such due date, the contribution is treated as if it were made on the last day of the plan year.

In the case of a plan with a funded current liability percentage of less than 100 percent for the preceding plan year, estimated contributions for the current plan year must be made in quarterly installments during the current plan year. The amount of each required installment is 25 percent of the lesser of (1) 90 percent of the amount required to be contributed

---

49. The maximum funding requirement for a defined benefit plan is referred to as the full funding limitation. Additional contributions are not required if a plan has reached the full funding limitation.
50. Plans with no more than 100 participants on any day in the preceding plan year are not subject to the special funding rule. Plans with more than 100 but not more than 150 participants are generally subject to lower contribution requirements under the special funding rule.
51. Under an alternative test, a plan is not considered underfunded if (1) the value of the plan assets is at least 80 percent of current liability and (2) the value of the plan assets was at least 90 percent of current liability for each of the two immediately preceding years or each of the second and third immediately preceding years.
52. The interest rate used under the plan must be consistent with the assumptions which reflect the purchase rates which would be used by insurance companies to satisfy the liabilities under the plan (section 412(b)(5)(B)(iii)(II)).

for the current plan year or (2) 100 percent of the amount required to be contributed for the preceding plan year.[53]

PBGC premiums

Because benefits under a defined benefit pension plan may be funded over a period of years, plan assets may not be sufficient to provide the benefits owed under the plan to employees and their beneficiaries if the plan terminates before all benefits are paid. In order to protect employees and their beneficiaries, the Pension Benefit Guaranty Corporation ("PBGC") generally insures the benefits owed under defined benefit pension plans. Employers pay premiums to the PBGC for this insurance coverage.

In the case of an underfunded plan, additional PBGC premiums are required based on the amount of unfunded vested benefits. These premiums are referred to as "variable rate premiums." In determining the amount of unfunded vested benefits, the interest rate used is 85 percent of the interest rate on 30-year Treasury securities for the month preceding the month in which the plan year begins.

Explanation of Provision

Additional contributions

The provision expands the permissible range of the statutory interest rate used in calculating a plan's current liability for purposes of applying the additional contribution requirements for plan years beginning after December 31, 2001, and before January 1, 2004. Under the provision, the permissible range is from 90 percent to 120 percent for these years. Use of a higher interest rate under the expanded range will affect the plan's current liability, which may in turn affect the need to make additional contributions and the amount of any additional contributions.

Because the quarterly contributions requirements are based on current liability for the preceding plan year, the provision also provides special rules for applying these requirements for plans years beginning in 2002 (when the expanded range first applies) and 2004 (when the expanded range no longer applies). In each of those years ("present year"), current liability for the preceding year is redetermined, using the permissible range applicable to the present year. This redetermined current liability will be used for purposes of the plan's funded current liability percentage for the preceding year, which may affect the need to make quarterly contributions and for purposes of determining the amount of any quarterly contributions in the present year, which is based in part on the preceding year.

PBGC variable rate premiums

Under the provision, the interest rate used in determining the amount of unfunded vested benefits for variable rate premium purposes is increased to 100 percent of the interest rate on 30-year Treasury securities for the month preceding the month in which the plan year begins.

Effective Date

The provision is effective with respect to plan contributions and PBGC variable rate premiums for plan years beginning after December 31, 2001, and before January 1, 2004.

---

53. No additional quarterly contributions are due once the plan's funded current liability percentage for the plan year reaches 100 percent.

RIA Research Institute of America

[¶ 5026]   Section 406.   Adjusted gross income determined by taking into account certain expenses of elementary and secondary school teachers.

(Code Sec. 62)

[Joint Committee on Taxation Report]

Present Law

In general, ordinary and necessary business expenses are deductible (sec. 162). However, unreimbursed employee business expenses are deductible only as an itemized deduction and only to the extent that the individual's total miscellaneous deductions (including employee business expenses) exceed two percent of adjusted gross income.

An individual's otherwise allowable itemized deductions may be further limited by the overall limitation on itemized deductions, which reduces itemized deductions for taxpayers with adjusted gross income in excess of $137,300 (for 2002).[54] In addition, miscellaneous itemized deductions are not allowable under the alternative minimum tax.

Explanation of Provision

The bill provides an above-the-line deduction for up to $250 annually of expenses paid or incurred by an eligible educator for books, supplies (other than nonathletic supplies for courses of instruction in health or physical education), computer equipment (including related software and services) and other equipment, and supplementary materials used by the eligible educator in the classroom. To be eligible for this deduction, the expenses must be otherwise deductible under 162 as a trade or business expense.

An eligible educator is a kindergarten through grade 12 teacher, instructor, counselor, or principal in a school for at least 900 hours during a school year. A school means any school which provides elementary education or secondary education, as determined under State law.

Effective Date

The provision is effective for taxable years beginning after December 31, 2001, and before January 1, 2004.

[¶ 5031]   Section 411(a).   Amendments related to Economic Growth and Tax Relief Reconciliation Act of 2001.

(Code Sec. 6428)

[Joint Committee on Taxation Report]

Section 6428 credit interaction with refundable child tax credit. The provision treats the section 6428 credit (rate reduction) like a nonrefundable personal credit, thus allowing it prior to determining the refundable child credit.

[¶ 5032]   Section 411(b).   Amendments related to Economic Growth and Tax Relief Reconciliation Act of 2001.

(Code Sec. 24)

[Joint Committee on Taxation Report]

Child tax credit. The provision clarifies that for taxable years beginning in 2001, the portion of the child credit that is refundable is determined by referring in Code section 24(d)(1)(B) to "the aggregate amount of credits allowed by this subpart." This would retain prior law that was inadvertently changed by the Act.

---

54. The effect of this overall limitation is phased down beginning in 2006, and is repealed for 2010.

[¶ 5033]   Section 411(c).   Amendments related to Economic Growth and Tax Relief Reconciliation Act of 2001.

(Code Sec. 23, 137)

[Joint Committee on Taxation Report]

Transition rule for adoption tax credit. Under prior law, the maximum amount of adoption expenses which could be taken into account in computing the adoption tax credit for any child was $5,000 ($6,000 in the case of special needs adoptions). Under prior and present law, the credit generally is allowed in the taxable year following the taxable year the expenses are paid or incurred where expenses are paid or incurred before the taxable year the adoption becomes final. The Act increased the maximum amount of expenses to $10,000 for taxable years beginning after 2001, but did not include a provision describing the dollar limit for amounts paid or incurred during taxable years beginning before January 1, 2002, for adoptions that do not become final in those years. The provision clarifies that amount of expenses paid or incurred during taxable years beginning before January 1, 2002, which are taken into account in determining a credit allowed in a taxable year beginning after December 31, 2001, are subject to the $5,000 (or $6,000) dollar cap in effect immediately prior to the enactment of the Act.

Dollar amount of credit for special needs adoptions. The provision clarifies that, for special needs adoptions that become final in taxable years beginning after 2002, the adoption expenses taken into account shall be increased by the excess (if any) of $10,000 over the aggregate adoption expenses for the taxable year the adoption becomes final and all prior taxable years.

Employer-provided adoption assistance exclusion with respect to special needs adoptions. The provision clarifies that, for taxable years beginning after 2002, the amount of adoption expenses taken into account in determining the exclusion for employer-provided adoption assistance in the case of a special needs adoption is increased by the excess (if any) of $10,000 over the aggregate qualified adoption expenses with respect to the adoption for the taxable year the adoption becomes final and all prior taxable years.

[¶ 5034]   Section 411(d).   Amendments related to Economic Growth and Tax Relief Reconciliation Act of 2001.

(Code Sec. 45F)

[Joint Committee on Taxation Report]

Credit for employer expenses for child care assistance. The provision clarifies that recapture tax with respect to this credit is treated like recapture taxes with respect to other credits under chapter 1 of the Code. Thus, it would not be treated as a tax for purposes of determining the amounts of other credits or determining the amount of alternative minimum tax.

[¶ 5035]   Section 411(e).   Amendments related to Economic Growth and Tax Relief Reconciliation Act of 2001.

(Code Sec. 63)

[Joint Committee on Taxation Report]

Elimination of marriage penalty in standard deduction. The provision provides rules that were inadvertently omitted providing for separate returns and rounding rules for the standard deduction for the transition period years.

RIA **Research Institute of America**

[¶5036]   Section 411(f).   Amendments related to Economic Growth and Tax Relief Reconciliation Act of 2001.

(Code Sec. 530)

[Joint Committee on Taxation Report]

Education IRAs; non-application of 10-percent additional tax with respect to amounts for which HOPE credit is claimed. Under the law prior to the Act, taxpayers could not claim the HOPE (or Lifetime learning) credit in the same year that they claimed an exclusion from income from an education IRA. Taxpayers were permitted to waive the exclusion in order to claim the HOPE (or Lifetime learning) credit. For taxpayers electing the waiver, earnings from amounts withdrawn from education IRAs and attributable to education expenses for which a HOPE (or Lifetime learning) credit was claimed were includable in income, but the additional ten percent tax was not applied. Under the Act, taxpayers are permitted to claim the education IRA exclusion and claim a HOPE (or Lifetime learning) credit in the same year, provided they do not claim both with respect to the same educational expenses. The election to waive the education IRA exclusion was thus unnecessary, and was dropped. However, a reference to the election was retained (sec. 530(d)(4)(b)(iv)). The reference to the election was intended to preserve the rule relating to the non-application of the 10-percent additional tax for education IRA earnings that are includable in income solely because the HOPE (or Lifetime learning) credit is claimed for those expenses. The provision clarifies the present-law rules to reflect this result.

The provision prevents the 10-percent additional tax from applying to a distribution from an education IRA (or qualified tuition program) that is used to pay qualified higher education expenses, but the taxpayer elects to claim a HOPE or Lifetime Learning credit in lieu of the exclusion under section 530 or 529. Thus, the income distributed from the education IRA (or qualified tuition program) would be subject to income tax, but not to the 10-percent additional tax.

[¶5037]   Section 411(g).   Amendments related to Economic Growth and Tax Relief Reconciliation Act of 2001.

(Code Sec. 2511)

[Joint Committee on Taxation Report]

Transfers in trust. The provision clarifies that the effect of section 511(e) of the Act (effective for gifts made after 2009) is to treat certain transfers in trust as transfers of property by gift. The result of the clarification is that the gift tax annual exclusion and the marital and charitable deductions may apply to such transfers. Under the provision as clarified, certain amounts transferred in trust will be treated as transfers of property by gift, despite the fact that such transfers would be regarded as incomplete gifts or would not be treated as transferred under the law applicable to gifts made prior to 2010. For example, if in 2010 an individual transfers property in trust to pay the income to one person for life, remainder to such persons and in such portions as the settlor may decide, then the entire value of the property will be treated as being transferred by gift under the provision, even though the transfer of the remainder interest in the trust would not be treated as a completed gift under current Treas. Reg. sec. 25.2511-2(c). Similarly, if in 2010 an individual transfers property in trust to pay the income to one person for life, and makes no transfer of a remainder interest, the entire value of the property will be treated as being transferred by gift under the provision.

[¶5038]   Section 411(h).   Amendments related to Economic Growth and Tax Relief Reconciliation Act of 2001.

(Code Sec. 2016)

[Joint Committee on Taxation Report]

Recovery of taxes claimed as credit (State death tax credit). The provision eliminates as deadwood a reference to the State death tax credit.

[¶ 5039]   Section 411(i).   Amendments related to Economic Growth and Tax Relief Reconciliation Act of 2001.

(Code Sec. 408)

[Joint Committee on Taxation Report]

Individual Retirement Arrangements ("IRAs"). Under the Act, a qualified employer plan may provide for voluntary employee contributions to a separate account that is deemed to be an IRA. The provision clarifies that, for purposes of deemed IRAs, the term "qualified employer plan" includes the following types of plans maintained by a governmental employer: a qualified retirement plan under section 401(a), a qualified annuity plan under section 403(a), a tax-sheltered annuity plan under section 403(b), and an eligible deferred compensation plan under section 457(b). The provision also clarifies that the Employee Retirement Income Security Act ("ERISA") is intended to apply to a deemed IRA in a manner similar to a simplified employee pension ("SEP").

[¶ 5040]   Section 411(j).   Amendments related to Economic Growth and Tax Relief Reconciliation Act of 2001.

(Code Sec. 408, 409)

[Joint Committee on Taxation Report]

Increase in benefit and contribution limits. Under the Act, the benefit and contribution limits that apply to qualified retirement plans are increased. These increases are generally effective for years beginning after December 31, 2001, but the increase in the limit on benefits under a defined benefit plan is effective for years ending after December 31, 2001. In the case of some plans that incorporate the benefit limits by reference and that use a plan year other than the calendar year, the increased benefit limits became effective under the plan automatically, causing unintended benefit increases. The provision permits an employer to amend such a plan by June 30, 2002, to reduce benefits to the level that applied before enactment of the Act without violating the anticutback rules that generally apply to plan amendments.

In connection with the increases in the benefit and contribution limits under the Act, a new base period applies in indexing the 2002 dollar amounts for future cost-of-living adjustments. The same indexing method applies to the dollar amounts used to determine eligibility to participate in a SEP and to determine the proper period for distributions from an employee stock ownership plan ("ESOP"). The provision changes these dollar amounts to the 2002 indexed amounts so that future indexing will operate properly.

[¶ 5041]   Section 411(k).   Amendments related to Economic Growth and Tax Relief Reconciliation Act of 2001.

(Code Sec. 416)

[Joint Committee on Taxation Report]

Modification of top-heavy rules. Under the Act, in determining whether a plan is top-heavy, distributions made because of separation from service, death, or disability are taken into account for one year after distribution. Other distributions are taken into account for five years. The Act also permits distributions from a section 401(k) plan, a tax-sheltered annuity plan, or an eligible deferred compensation plan to be made when the participant has a severance from employment (rather than separation from service). The provision clarifies that distributions made after severance from employment (rather than separation from service) are taken into account for only one year in determining top-heavy status.

[¶ 5042]   Section 411(l).   Amendments related to Economic Growth and Tax Relief Reconciliation Act of 2001.

(Code Sec. 404)

[Joint Committee on Taxation Report]

Elective deferrals not taken into account for deduction limits. The provision clarifies that elective deferrals to a SEP are not subject to the deduction limits and are not taken into account in applying the limits to other SEP contributions. The provision also clarifies that the combined deduction limit of 25 percent of compensation for qualified defined benefit and defined contribution plans does not apply if the only amounts contributed to the defined contribution plan are elective deferrals.

Deduction limits. Under present law, contributions to a SEP are included in an employee's income to the extent they exceed the lesser of 15 percent of compensation or $40,000 (for 2002), subject to a reduction in some cases. Under prior law, the annual limitation on the amount of deductible contributions to a SEP was 15 percent of compensation. Under the Act, the annual limitation on the amount of deductible contributions that can be made to a SEP is increased from 15 percent of compensation to 25 percent of compensation. The provision makes a conforming change to the rule that limits the amount of SEP contributions that may be made for a particular employee. Under the provision, contributions are included in an employee's income to the extent they exceed the lesser of 25 percent of compensation or $40,000 (for 2002), subject to a reduction in some cases.

Under present law, the Secretary of the Treasury has the authority to require an employer who makes contributions to a SEP to provide simplified reports with respect to such contributions. Consistent with present law and the provision, such reports could appropriately include information as to compliance with the requirements that apply to SEPs, including the contribution limits.

[¶ 5043]   Section 411(m).   Amendments related to Economic Growth and Tax Relief Reconciliation Act of 2001.

(Code Sec. 25B)

[Joint Committee on Taxation Report]

Nonrefundable credit for certain individuals for elective deferrals and IRA contributions. The provision clarifies that the amount of contributions taken into account in determining the credit for elective deferrals and IRA contributions is reduced by the amount of a distribution from a qualified retirement plan, an eligible deferred compensation plan, or a traditional IRA that is includible in income or that consists of after-tax contributions. The provision retains the rule that distributions that are rolled over to another retirement plan do not affect the credit.

[¶ 5044]   Section 411(n).   Amendments related to Economic Growth and Tax Relief Reconciliation Act of 2001.

(Code Sec. 45E)

[Joint Committee on Taxation Report]

Small business tax credit for new retirement plan expenses. The provision clarifies that the small business tax credit for new retirement plan expenses applies in the case of a plan first effective after December 31, 2001, even if adopted on or before that date.

[¶5045]   Section 411(o).   Amendments related to Economic Growth and Tax Relief Reconciliation Act of 2001.

(Code Sec. 402, 414, 457)

[Joint Committee on Taxation Report]

Additional salary reduction catch-up contributions. Under the Act, an individual aged 50 or over may make additional elective deferrals ("catch-up contributions") to certain retirement plans, up to a specified limit. A plan may not permit catch-up deferrals in excess of this limit. The provision clarifies that, for this purpose, the limit applies to all qualified retirement plans, tax-sheltered annuity plans, SEPs and SIMPLE plans maintained by the same employer on an aggregated basis, as if all plans were a single plan. The limit applies also to all eligible deferred compensation plans of a government employer on an aggregated basis.

Under the Act, catch-up contributions up to the specified limit are excluded from an individual's income. The provision also clarifies that the total amount that an individual may exclude from income as catch-up contributions for a year cannot exceed the catch-up contribution limit for that year (and for that type of plan), without regard to whether the individual made catch-up contributions under plans maintained by the more than one employer.

The provision clarifies that an individual who will attain age 50 by the end of the taxable year is an eligible participant as of the beginning of the taxable year rather than only at the attainment of age 50. The provision also clarifies that a participant in an eligible deferred compensation plan of a government employer may make catch-up contributions in an amount equal to the greater of the amount permitted under the new catch-up rule and the amount permitted under the special catch-up rule for eligible deferred compensation plans.

The provision revises the lists of requirements that do not apply to catch-up contributions to reflect other statutory amendments made by the Act and to reflect the fact that catch-up contributions can be made only to a qualified defined contribution plan, not to a qualified defined benefit plan. The provision also clarifies that the special nondiscrimination rule for mergers and acquisitions applies for purposes of the nondiscrimination requirement applicable to catch-up contributions.

[¶5046]   Section 411(p).   Amendments related to Economic Growth and Tax Relief Reconciliation Act of 2001.

(Code Sec. 403, 415, 457)

[Joint Committee on Taxation Report]

Equitable treatment for contributions of employees to defined contribution plans. Under prior law, the limits on contributions to a tax-sheltered annuity plan applied at the time contributions became vested. Under the Act, tax-sheltered annuity plans are generally subject to the same contribution limits as qualified defined contribution plans, but certain special rules were retained.

The provision clarifies that the limits apply to contributions to a tax-sheltered annuity plan in the year the contributions are made without regard to when the contributions become vested. The provision also clarifies that contributions may be made for an employee for up to five years after retirement, based on includible compensation for the last year of service before retirement. The provision also restores special rules for ministers and lay employees of churches and for foreign missionaries that were inadvertently eliminated.

Under the Act, amounts deferred under an eligible deferred compensation plan are generally subject to the same contribution limits as qualified defined contribution plans. The provision conforms the definition of compensation used in applying the limits to an eligible deferred compensation plan to the definition used for defined contribution plans.

[¶ 5047]   Section 411(q).   Amendments related to Economic Growth and Tax Relief Reconciliation Act of 2001.

(Code Sec. 401, 402)

[Joint Committee on Taxation Report]

Rollovers of retirement plan and IRA distributions. Under prior law and under the Act, a qualified retirement plan must provide for the rollover of certain distributions directly to a qualified defined contribution plan, a qualified annuity plan, a tax-sheltered annuity plan, a governmental eligible deferred compensation plan, or a traditional IRA, if the participant elects a direct rollover. The provision clarifies that a qualified retirement plan must provide for the direct rollover of after-tax contributions only to a qualified defined contribution plan or a traditional IRA. The provision also clarifies that, if a distribution includes both pretax and after-tax amounts, the portion of the distribution that is rolled over is treated as consisting first of pretax amounts.

[¶ 5048]   Section 411(r).   Amendments related to Economic Growth and Tax Relief Reconciliation Act of 2001.

(Code Sec. 401, 402)

[Joint Committee on Taxation Report]

Employers may disregard rollovers for purposes of cash-out amounts. Under prior and present law, if a participant in a qualified retirement plan ceases to be employed with the employer maintaining the plan, the plan may distribute the participant's nonforfeitable accrued benefit without the consent of the participant and, if applicable, the participant's spouse, if the present value of the benefit does not exceed $5,000. Under the Act, a plan may provide that the present value of the benefit is determined without regard to the portion of the benefit that is attributable to rollover contributions (and any earnings allocable thereto) for purposes of determining whether the participant must consent to the cash-out of the benefit. The provision clarifies that rollover amounts may be disregarded also in determining whether a spouse must consent to the cash-out of the benefit.

[¶ 5051]   Section 411(u).   Amendments related to Economic Growth and Tax Relief Reconciliation Act of 2001.

(Code Sec. 4980F)

[Joint Committee on Taxation Report]

Notice of significant reduction in plan benefit accruals. Under the Act, notice must be provided to participants if a defined benefit plan is amended to provide for a significant reduction in the future rate of benefit accrual, including any elimination or reduction of an early retirement benefit or retirement-type subsidy. The provision clarifies that the notice requirement applies to a defined benefit plan only if the plan is qualified. The provision further clarifies that, in the case of an amendment that eliminates an early retirement benefit or retirement-type subsidy, notice is required only if the early retirement benefit or retirement-type subsidy is significant. The provision also eliminates inconsistencies in the statutory language.

[¶ 5052]   Section 411(v).   Amendments related to Economic Growth and Tax Relief Reconciliation Act of 2001.

(Code Sec. 412)

[Joint Committee on Taxation Report]

Modification of timing of plan valuations. Under the Act, a plan valuation may be made as of any date in the immediately preceding plan year if, as of such date, plan assets are not less than 100 percent of the plan's current liability. Under the Act, a change in funding method to use a valuation date in the prior year generally may not be made unless, as of such date, plan assets are not less than 125 percent of the plan's current liability. The provision conforms the statutory language to Congressional intent as reflected in the Statement of Managers.

[¶ 5053]   Section 411(w).   Amendments related to Economic Growth and Tax Relief Reconciliation Act of 2001.

(Code Sec. 404)

[Joint Committee on Taxation Report]

ESOP dividends may be reinvested without loss of dividend deduction. Under prior and present law, a deduction is permitted for a dividend paid with respect to employer stock held in an ESOP if the dividend is (1) paid in cash directly to participants or (2) paid to the plan and subsequently distributed to the participants in cash no later than 90 days after the close of the plan year in which the dividend is paid to the plan. The deduction is allowable for the taxable year of the corporation in which the dividend is paid or distributed to the participants.

Under the Act, in addition to the deductions permitted under present law, a deduction is permitted for a dividend paid with respect to employer stock that, at the election of the participants, is payable in cash directly to participants or paid to the plan and subsequently distributed to the participants in cash no later than 90 days after the close of the plan year in which the dividend is paid to the plan, or paid to the plan and reinvested in qualifying employer securities. Under the provision, the deduction for dividends that are reinvested in qualifying employer securities at the election of participants is allowable for the taxable year in which the later of the reinvestment or the election occurs. The provision also clarifies that a dividend that is reinvested in qualifying employer securities at the participant's election must be nonforfeitable.

[¶ 5054]   Section 412(a).   Amendments related to Community Renewal Tax Relief Act of 2000.

(Code Sec. 469)

[Joint Committee on Taxation Report]

Phaseout of $25,000 amount for certain rental real estate under passive loss rules. Present law provides for a phaseout of the $25,000 amount allowed in the case of certain deductions and certain credits with respect to rental real estate activities, for taxpayers with adjusted gross income exceeding $100,000. The phaseout rule does not apply, or applies separately, in the case of the rehabilitation credit, the low-income housing credit, and the commercial revitalization deduction. The provision clarifies the operation of the ordering rules to reflect the exceptions and separate phaseout rules for these items.

[¶ 5055]   Section 412(b).   Amendments related to Community Renewal Tax Relief Act of 2000.

(Code Sec. 151)

[Joint Committee on Taxation Report]

Treatment of missing children. Present law provides that in the case of a dependent child of the taxpayer that is kidnapped, the taxpayer may continue to treat the child as a dependent for purposes of the dependency exemption, child credit, surviving spouse filing status, and head of household filing status. A similar rule applies under the earned income credit. The provision clarifies that, if a taxpayer met the household maintenance requirement of the surviving spouse filing status or the head of household filing status, respectively, with respect to his or her dependent child immediately before the kidnapping, then the taxpayer would be deemed to continue to meet that requirement for purposes of the filing status rule of section 2 of the Code until the child would have reached age 18 or is determined to be dead.

[¶ 5056]   Section 412(c).   Amendments related to Community Renewal Tax Relief Act of 2000.

(Code Sec. 358)

[Joint Committee on Taxation Report]

Basis of property in an exchange by a corporation involving assumption of liabilities. The provision clarifies that the basis reduction rule of section 358(h) of the Code gives rise to a basis reduction in the amount of any liability that is assumed by another party as part of the exchange in which the property (whose basis exceeds its fair market value) is received, so long as the other requirements under section 358(h) apply.

[¶ 5057]   Section 412(d).   Amendments related to Community Renewal Tax Relief Act of 2000.

(Code Sec. 1091, 1233, 1234A, 1234B)

[Joint Committee on Taxation Report]

Tax treatment of securities futures contracts. The provision clarifies that the termination of a securities contract is treated in a manner similar to a sale or exchange of a securities futures contract for purposes of determining the character of any gain or loss from a termination of a securities futures contract. Under the provision, any gain or loss from the termination of a securities futures contract (other than a dealer securities futures contract) is treated as gain or loss from the sale or exchange of property that has the same character as the property to which the contract relates has (or would have) in the hands of the taxpayer.

The provision also clarifies that losses from the sale, exchange, or termination of a securities futures contract (other than a dealer securities futures contract) to sell generally are treated in the same manner as losses from the closing of a short sale for purposes of applying the wash sale rules. Thus, the wash sale rules apply to any loss from the sale, exchange, or termination of a securities futures contract (other than dealer securities futures contract) if, within a period beginning 30 days before the date of such sale, exchange, or termination and ending 30 days after such date: (1) stock that is substantially identical to the stock to which the contract relates is sold; (2) a short sale of substantially identical stock is entered into; or (3) another securities futures contract to sell substantially identical stock is entered into.

The provision clarifies that a securities futures contract to sell generally is treated in a manner similar to a short sale for purposes of the special holding period rules in section 1233. Thus, subsections (b) and (d) of section 1233 may apply to characterize certain capital gains as short-term capital gain and certain capital losses as long-term capital loss, and to determine holding periods where certain securities futures contracts to sell are entered into while holding the substantially identical stock.

[¶ 5058]   Section 413.   Amendments related to the Tax Relief Extension Act of 1999.

(Code Sec. 857)

[Joint Committee on Taxation Report]

Taxable REIT subsidiaries - 100 percent tax on improperly allocated amounts. The provision clarifies that redetermined rents, to which the excise tax applies, are the excess of the amount treated by the REIT as rents from real property under Code section 856(d) over the amount that would be so treated after reduction under Code section 482 to clearly reflect income as a result of services furnished or rendered by a taxable REIT subsidiary of the REIT to a tenant of the REIT. Similarly, redetermined deductions are the excess of the amount treated by the taxable REIT subsidiary as other deductions over the amount that would be so treated after reduction under Code section 482.

[¶ 5059]   Section 414.   Amendments related to the Taxpayer Relief Act of 1997.

(Code Sec. 469)

[Joint Committee on Taxation Report]

Election to recognize gain on assets held on January 1, 2001; treatment of gain on sale of principal residence. The provision clarifies that the gain to which the mark-to-market election applies is included in gross income. Thus, the exclusion of gain on the sale of a principal residence under Code section 121 would not apply with respect to an asset for which the election to mark to market is made. The provision is consistent with the holding of Rev. Rul. 2001-57.

Election to recognize gain on assets held on January 1, 2001; treatment of disposition of interest in passive activity. The provision clarifies that the election to mark to market an interest in a passive activity does not result in the deduction of suspended losses by reason of section 469(g)(1)(A). Any gain taken into account by reason of an election with respect to any interest in a passive activity is taken into account in determining the passive activity loss for the taxable year (as defined in section 469(d)(1)). Section 469(g)(1)(A) may apply to a subsequent disposition of the interest in the activity by the taxpayer.

[¶ 5060]   Section 415.   Amendment related to the Balanced Budget Act of 1997.

(Code Sec. 26)

[Joint Committee on Taxation Report]

Medicare+Choice MSA. The provision conforms the treatment of the additional tax on Medicare+Choice MSAs distributions not used for qualified medical expenses if a minimum balance is not maintained to the treatment of the additional tax on Archer MSA distributions not used for qualified medical expenses, for purposes of determining whether certain taxes are included within regular tax liability under Code section 26(b).

[¶ 5061]   Section 416(a).   Other technical corrections.

(Code Sec. 32)

[Joint Committee on Taxation Report]

Advance payments of earned income credit. The provision corrects a reference in section 32(g)(2) to refer to credits allowable under this part (i.e., all tax credits) rather than under this subpart (i.e., the refundable credits). The provision is effective as if included in section 474 of the Tax Reform Act of 1984.

[¶ 5062]   Section 416(b).   Other technical corrections.

(Code Sec. 1256)

[Joint Committee on Taxation Report]

Coordination of wash sale rules and section 1256 contracts. The bill clarifies that the wash sale rules do not apply to any loss arising from a section 1256 contract. This rule is similar to the rule in present-law section 475 applicable to securities that are marked to market under that section. The provision is effective as if included in section 5075 of the Technical and Miscellaneous Revenue Act of 1988.

RIA Research Institute of America

[¶ 5063]   Section 416(c).   Other technical corrections.

(Code Sec. 6103)

[Joint Committee on Taxation Report]

Disclosure by the Social Security Administration to Federal child support enforcement agencies. Section 6103(l)(8) permits the Social Security Administration (SSA) to disclose certain tax information in its possession to State child support enforcement agencies. The Office of Child Support Enforcement (OCSE), a Federal agency, oversees child support enforcement at the Federal level and acts as a coordinator for most programs involved with child support enforcement. OCSE acts as a conduit for the disclosure of tax information from the Internal Revenue Service to the various State and local child support enforcement agencies. The change to section 6103(l)(8) permits SSA to make disclosures directly to OCSE, which in turn would make the disclosures to the State and local child support enforcement agencies. The provision is effective on the date of enactment.

[¶ 5064]   Section 416(d).   Other technical corrections.

(Code Sec. 6224, 6229, 6231, 6234)

[Joint Committee on Taxation Report]

Treatment of settlements under partnership audit rules. The provision clarifies that the partnership audit procedures that apply to settlement agreements entered into by the Secretary also apply to settlement agreements entered into by the Attorney General. Under present law, when the Secretary enters into a settlement agreement with a partner with respect to partnership items, those items convert to nonpartnership items, and the other partners in the partnership have a right to request consistent settlement terms. The conversion of the settling partner's partnership items to nonpartnership items is the mechanism by which the settling partner is removed from the ongoing partnership proceeding. If these rules did not apply to settlement agreements entered into by the Attorney General (or his delegate), it is possible that a settling partner would inadvertently be bound by the outcome of the partnership proceeding rather than the settlement agreement entered into with the Attorney General (or his delegate) (sec. 6224(c)(2)). Similar changes are made to related provisions with respect to settlement agreements. The provision is effective for settlement agreements entered into after the date of enactment.

[¶ 5065]   Section 416(e).   Other technical corrections.

(Code Sec. 6331)

[Joint Committee on Taxation Report]

Clarification of permissible extension of limitations period for installment agreements. Uncertainty existed as to whether the permissible extension of the period of limitations in the context of installment agreements is governed by reference to an agreement of the parties pursuant to section 6502 or by reference to the period of time during which the installment agreement is in effect pursuant to sections 6331(k)(3) and (i)(5). A 2000 technical correction clarified that the permissible extension of the period of limitations in the context of installment agreements is governed by the pertinent provisions of section 6502. The provision further clarifies that the elimination of the application of the section 6331(i)(5) rules applies only to section 6331(k)(2)(C). The provision modifies section 313(b)(3) of H.R. 5662, the Community Renewal Tax Relief Act of 2000 (Pub. Law No. 106-554). This is the further technical correction referred to in footnote 185a, Joint Committee on Taxation, *General Explanation of Tax Legislation Enacted in the 106th Congress* (JCS-2-01), April 19, 2001, page 162. The provision is effective on the date of enactment.

[¶ 5066]   Section 416(f).   Other technical corrections.

(Code Sec. 7702A)

[Joint Committee on Taxation Report]

Determination of whether a life insurance contract is a modified endowment contract. The provision clarifies that, for purposes of determining whether a life insurance contract is a modified endowment contract, if there is a material change to the contract, appropriate adjustments are made in determining whether the contract meets the 7-pay test to take into account the cash surrender value under the contract. No reference is needed to the cash surrender under the "old contract" (as was provided under section 318(a)(2) of H.R. 5662, the Community Renewal Tax Relief Act of 2000 (Pub. Law No. 106-554)) because prior and present law provide a definition of cash surrender value for this purpose (by cross reference to section 7702(f)(2)(A)). It is reiterated that Code section 7702A(c)(3)(ii) is not intended to permit a policyholder to engage in a series of "material changes" to circumvent the premium limitations in section 7702A. Thus, if there is a material change to a life insurance contract, it is intended that the fair market value of the contract be used as the cash surrender value under the provision, if the amount of the putative cash surrender value of the contract is artificially depressed. For example, if there is a material change because of an increase in the face amount of the contract, any artificial or temporary reduction in the cash surrender value of the contract is not to be taken into account, but rather, it is intended that the fair market value of the contract be used as cash surrender value, so that the substance rather than the form of the transaction is reflected. Further, as stated in the 1988 Act legislative history to section 7702A,[55] in applying the 7-pay test to any premiums paid under a contract that has been materially changed, the 7-pay premium for each of the first 7 contract years after the change is to be reduced by the product of (1) the cash surrender value of the contract as of the date that the material change takes effect (determined without regard to any increase in the cash surrender value that is attributable to the amount of the premium payment that is not necessary), and (2) a fraction the numerator of which equals the 7-pay premium for the future benefits under the contract, and the denominator of which equals the net single premium for such benefits computed using the same assumptions used in determining the 7-pay premium. The provision is effective as if section 318(a) of the Community Renewal Tax Relief Act of 2000 (114. Stat. 2763A-645) had not been enacted.

[¶ 5067]   Section 418(a).   Additional corrections.

(Code Sec. 23, 137)

[Joint Committee on Taxation Report]

Adoption credit and employer-provided adoption assistance exclusion rounding rules. The provision provides uniform rounding rules (to the nearest multiple of $10) for the inflation-adjusted dollar limits and income limitations in the adoption credit and the employer-provided adoption assistance exclusion. The provision is effective as if included in the provision of the Economic Growth and Tax Reform Reconciliation Act of 2001 to which it relates.

[¶ 5068]   Section 418(b).   Additional corrections.

(Code Sec. 21)

[Joint Committee on Taxation Report]

Dependent care credit. The provision conforms the dollar limit on deemed earned income of a taxpayer's spouse who is either (1) a full-time student, or (2) physically or men-

---

55. Conference Report to accompany H.R. 4333, the "Technical and Miscellaneous Revenue Act of 1988" (H. Rep. No. 100-1104), Oct. 21, 1988, vol. II, p. 105.

tally incapable of caring for himself, to the dollar limit on employment-related expenses applicable in determining the maximum credit amount. The 2001 Act increased the dollar limit on employer-related expenses to $3,000 for one qualifying individual or $6,000 for two or more qualifying individuals annually but did not conform the dollar limit on deemed earned income of a spouse. The provision is effective as if included in the provision of the Economic Growth and Tax Reform Reconciliation Act of 2001 to which it relates.

[¶ 5069]   Section 601.   Allowance of nonrefundable personal credits against regular and minimum tax liability.

(Code Sec. 26, 904)

[Joint Committee on Taxation Report]

Present Law

Present law provides for certain nonrefundable personal tax credits (i.e., the dependent care credit, the credit for the elderly and disabled, the adoption credit, the child tax credit[56], the credit for interest on certain home mortgages, the HOPE Scholarship and Lifetime Learning credits, the IRA credit, and the D.C. homebuyer's credit). For taxable years beginning after 2001, these credits (other than the adoption credit, child credit and IRA credit) are allowed only to the extent that the individual's regular income tax liability exceeds the individual's tentative minimum tax, determined without regard to the minimum tax foreign tax credit. The adoption credit, child credit, and IRA credit are allowed to the full extent of the individual's regular tax and alternative minimum tax.

For taxable years beginning in 2001, all the nonrefundable personal credits are allowed to the extent of the full amount of the individual's regular tax and alternative minimum tax.

The alternative minimum tax is the amount by which the tentative minimum tax exceeds the regular income tax. An individual's tentative minimum tax is an amount equal to (1) 26 percent of the first $175,000 ($87,500 in the case of a married individual filing a separate return) of alternative minimum taxable income ("AMTI") in excess of a phased-out exemption amount and (2) 28 percent of the remaining AMTI. The maximum tax rates on net capital gain used in computing the tentative minimum tax are the same as under the regular tax. AMTI is the individual's taxable income adjusted to take account of specified preferences and adjustments. The exemption amounts are: (1) $45,000 ($49,000 in taxable years beginning before 2005) in the case of married individuals filing a joint return and surviving spouses; (2) $33,750 ($35,750 in taxable years beginning before 2005) in the case of other unmarried individuals; (3) $22,500 ($24,500 in taxable years beginning before 2005) in the case of married individuals filing a separate return; and (4) $22,500 in the case of an estate or trust. The exemption amounts are phased out by an amount equal to 25 percent of the amount by which the individual's AMTI exceeds (1) $150,000 in the case of married individuals filing a joint return and surviving spouses, (2) $112,500 in the case of other unmarried individuals, and (3) $75,000 in the case of married individuals filing separate returns or an estate or a trust. These amounts are not indexed for inflation.

Explanation of Provision

The provision allows an individual to offset the entire regular tax liability and alternative minimum tax liability by the personal nonrefundable credits in 2002 and 2003.

Effective Date

The provision is effective for taxable years beginning in 2002 and 2003.

---

56. A portion of the child credit may be refundable.

 Research Institute of America

[¶ 5070]   Section 602.   Credit for qualified electric vehicles.

(Code Sec. 30, 280F)

[Joint Committee on Taxation Report]

Present Law

A 10-percent tax credit is provided for the cost of a qualified electric vehicle, up to a maximum credit of $4,000 (sec. 30). A qualified electric vehicle is a motor vehicle that is powered primarily by an electric motor drawing current from rechargeable batteries, fuel cells, or other portable sources of electrical current, the original use of which commences with the taxpayer, and that is acquired for the use by the taxpayer and not for resale. The full amount of the credit is available for purchases prior to 2002. The credit phases down in the years 2002 through 2004, and is unavailable for purchases after December 31, 2004.[57]

Explanation of Provision

The bill defers the phase down of the credit for two years. Taxpayers may claim the full amount of the credit for qualified purchases made in 2002 and 2003. Under the bill, the phase down of the credit value commences in 2004 and the credit is unavailable for purchases after December 31, 2006. A conforming modification is made to section 280F.

Effective Date

The provision is effective for property placed in service after December 31, 2001.

[¶ 5071]   Section 603.   Credit for electricity produced from certain renewable resources.

(Code Sec. 45)

[Joint Committee on Taxation Report]

Present Law

An income tax credit is allowed for the production of electricity from either qualified wind energy, qualified "closed-loop" biomass, or qualified poultry waste facilities (sec. 45).

The credit applies to electricity produced by a wind energy facility placed in service after December 31, 1993, and before January 1, 2002, to electricity produced by a closed-loop biomass facility placed in service after December 31, 1992, and before January 1, 2002, and to a poultry waste facility placed in service after December 31, 1999, and before January 1, 2002. The credit is allowable for production during the 10-year period after a facility is originally placed in service. In order to claim the credit, a taxpayer must own the facility and sell the electricity produced by the facility to an unrelated party. In the case of a poultry waste facility, the taxpayer may claim the credit as a lessee/operator of a facility owned by a governmental unit.

Closed-loop biomass is plant matter, where the plants are grown for the sole purpose of being used to generate electricity. It does not include waste materials (including, but not limited to, scrap wood, manure, and municipal or agricultural waste). The credit also is not available to taxpayers who use standing timber to produce electricity. Poultry waste means poultry manure and litter, including wood shavings, straw, rice hulls, and other bedding material for the disposition of manure.

---

57. The amount the taxpayer may claim as a depreciation deduction for any passenger automobile is limited (sec. 280F). In the case of a passenger vehicle designed to be propelled primarily by electricity and built by an original equipment manufacturer, the otherwise applicable limitation amounts are tripled. These exceptions from sec. 280F apply to vehicles placed in service prior to January 1, 2005.

The credit for electricity produced from wind, closed-loop biomass, or poultry waste is a component of the general business credit (sec. 38(b)(8)). The credit, when combined with all other components of the general business credit, generally may not exceed for any taxable year the excess of the taxpayer's net income tax over the greater of (1) 25 percent of net regular tax liability above $25,000, or (2) the tentative minimum tax. For credits arising in taxable years beginning after December 31, 1997, an unused general business credit generally may be carried back one year and carried forward 20 years (sec. 39). To coordinate the carryback with the period of application for this credit, the credit for electricity produced from closed-loop biomass facilities may not be carried back to a tax year ending before 1993 and the credit for electricity produced from wind energy may not be carried back to a tax year ending before 1994 (sec. 39).

Explanation of Provision

The bill extends the placed in service date for qualified facilities by two years to include those facilities placed in service prior to January 1, 2004.

Effective Date

The provision is effective for facilities placed in service after December 31, 2001.

[¶ 5072]   Section 604.   Work opportunity credit.

(Code Sec. 51)

[Joint Committee on Taxation Report]

Present Law

In general

The work opportunity tax credit ("WOTC") is available on an elective basis for employers hiring individuals from one or more of eight targeted groups. The credit equals 40 percent (25 percent for employment of less than 400 hours) of qualified wages. Generally, qualified wages are wages attributable to service rendered by member of a targeted group during the one-year period beginning with the day the individual began work for the employer.

The maximum credit per employee is $2,400 (40 percent of the first $6,000 of qualified first-year wages). With respect to qualified summer youth employees, the maximum credit is $1,200 (40 percent of the first $3,000 of qualified first-year wages).

For purposes of the credit, wages are generally defined as under the Federal Unemployment Tax Act, without regard to the dollar cap.

Targeted groups eligible for the credit

The eight targeted groups are: (1) families eligible to receive benefits under the Temporary Assistance for Needy Families ("TANF") Program; (2) high-risk youth; (3) qualified ex-felons; (4) vocational rehabilitation referrals; (5) qualified summer youth employees; (6) qualified veterans; (7) families receiving food stamps; and (8) persons receiving certain Supplemental Security Income ("SSI") benefits.

The employer's deduction for wages is reduced by the amount of the credit.

Expiration date

The credit is effective for wages paid or incurred to a qualified individual who began work for an employer before January 1, 2002.

Explanation of Provision

The bill extends the work opportunity tax credit for two years (through December 31, 2003).

Effective Date

The provision is effective for wages paid or incurred to a qualified individual who begins work for an employer on or after January 1, 2002, and before January 1, 2004.

[¶ 5073]   Section 605.   Welfare-to-work credit.

(Code Sec. 51A)

[Joint Committee on Taxation Report]

Present Law

In general

The welfare-to-work tax credit is available on an elective basis for employers for the first $20,000 of eligible wages paid to qualified long-term family assistance recipients during the first two years of employment. The credit is 35 percent of the first $10,000 of eligible wages in the first year of employment and 50 percent of the first $10,000 of eligible wages in the second year of employment. The maximum credit is $8,500 per qualified employee.

Qualified long-term family assistance recipients are: (1) members of a family that has received family assistance for at least 18 consecutive months ending on the hiring date; (2) members of a family that has received family assistance for a total of at least 18 months (whether or not consecutive) after the date of enactment of this credit if they are hired within 2 years after the date that the 18-month total is reached; and (3) members of a family that is no longer eligible for family assistance because of either Federal or State time limits, if they are hired within two years after the Federal or State time limits made the family ineligible for family assistance. Family assistance means benefits under the Temporary Assistance to Needy Families ("TANF") program.

For purposes of the credit, wages are generally defined under the Federal Unemployment Tax Act, without regard to the dollar amount. In addition, wages include the following: (1) educational assistance excludable under a section 127 program; (2) the value of excludable health plan coverage but not more than the applicable premium defined under section 4980B(f)(4); and (3) dependent care assistance excludable under section 129.

The employer's deduction for wages is reduced by the amount of the credit.

Expiration date

The welfare to work credit is effective for wages paid or incurred to a qualified individual who began work for an employer before January 1, 2002.

Explanation of Provision

The bill extends the welfare to work credit for two years (through December 31, 2003).

Effective Date

The provision is effective for wages paid or incurred to a qualified individual who begins work for an employer on or after January 1, 2002, and before January 1, 2004.

[¶ 5074]   Section 606.   Deduction for clean-fuel vehicles and certain refueling property.

(Code Sec. 179A)

[Joint Committee on Taxation Report]

Present Law

Certain costs of qualified clean-fuel vehicle property and clean-fuel vehicle refueling property may be expensed and deducted when such property is placed in service (sec. 179A).[58] Qualified clean-fuel vehicle property includes motor vehicles that use certain clean-burning fuels (natural gas, liquefied natural gas, liquefied petroleum gas, hydrogen, electricity and any other fuel at least 85 percent of which is methanol, ethanol, any other alcohol or ether). The maximum amount of the deduction is $50,000 for a truck or van with a gross vehicle weight over 26,000 pounds or a bus with seating capacities of at least 20 adults; $5,000 in the case of a truck or van with a gross vehicle weight between 10,000 and 26,000 pounds; and $2,000 in the case of any other motor vehicle. Qualified electric vehicles do not qualify for the clean-fuel vehicle deduction.

Clean-fuel vehicle refueling property comprises property for the storage or dispensing of a clean-burning fuel, if the storage or dispensing is the point at which the fuel is delivered into the fuel tank of a motor vehicle. Clean-fuel vehicle refueling property also includes property for the recharging of electric vehicles, but only if the property is located at a point where the electric vehicle is recharged. Up to $100,000 of such property at each location owned by the taxpayer may be expensed with respect to that location.

The deduction for clean-fuel vehicle property phases down in the years 2002 through 2004, and is unavailable for purchases after December 31, 2004. The deduction for clean-fuel vehicle refueling property is unavailable for property placed in service after December 31, 2004.

Explanation of Provision

The bill defers the phase down of the deduction for clean-fuel vehicle property by two years. Taxpayers may claim the full amount of the deduction for qualified vehicles placed in service in 2002 and 2003. Under the bill, the phase down of the deduction for clean-fuel vehicles commences in 2004 and the deduction is unavailable for purchases after December 31, 2006. A conforming modification is made to section 280F.

The provision extends the placed in service date for clean-fuel vehicle refueling property by two years. The deduction for clean-fuel vehicle refueling property is available for property placed in service prior to January 1, 2007.

Effective Date

The provision is effective for property placed in service after December 31, 2001.

---

58. The amount the taxpayer may claim as a depreciation deduction for any passenger automobile is limited (sec. 280F). In the case of a qualified clean-burning fuel vehicle, the limitation of sec. 280F applies only to that portion of the vehicle's cost not represented by the installed qualified clean-burning fuel property. The taxpayer may claim an amount otherwise allowable as a depreciation deduction on the installed qualified clean-burning fuel property, without regard to the limitation. These exceptions from sec. 280F apply to vehicles placed in service prior to January 1, 2005.

[¶ 5075]   Section 607.   Taxable income limit on percentage depletion for oil and natural gas produced from marginal properties.

(Code Sec. 613A)

[Joint Committee on Taxation Report]

Present Law

In general

Depletion, like depreciation, is a form of capital cost recovery. In both cases, the taxpayer is allowed a deduction in recognition of the fact that an asset — in the case of depletion for oil or gas interests, the mineral reserve itself — is being expended in order to produce income. Certain costs incurred prior to drilling an oil or gas property are recovered through the depletion deduction. These include costs of acquiring the lease or other interest in the property and geological and geophysical costs (in advance of actual drilling). Depletion is available to any person having an economic interest in a producing property.

Two methods of depletion are allowable under the Code: (1) the cost depletion method, and (2) the percentage depletion method (secs. 611-613). Under the cost depletion method, the taxpayer deducts that portion of the adjusted basis of the depletable property which is equal to the ratio of units sold from that property during the taxable year to the number of units remaining as of the end of taxable year plus the number of units sold during the taxable year. Thus, the amount recovered under cost depletion may never exceed the taxpayer's basis in the property.

Under the percentage depletion method, generally, 15 percent of the taxpayer's gross income from an oil- or gas-producing property is allowed as a deduction in each taxable year (sec. 613A(c)). The amount deducted generally may not exceed 100 percent of the net income from that property in any year (the "net-income limitation") (sec. 613(a)). The Taxpayer Relief Act of 1997 suspended the 100-percent-of-net-income limitation for production from marginal wells for taxable years beginning after December 31, 1997, and before January 1, 2000. The limitation subsequently was extended to include taxable years beginning before January 1, 2002. Additionally, the percentage depletion deduction for all oil and gas properties may not exceed 65 percent of the taxpayer's overall taxable income (determined before such deduction and adjusted for certain loss carrybacks and trust distributions) (sec. 613A(d)(1)).[59] Because percentage depletion, unlike cost depletion, is computed without regard to the taxpayer's basis in the depletable property, cumulative depletion deductions may be greater than the amount expended by the taxpayer to acquire or develop the property.

A taxpayer is required to determine the depletion deduction for each oil or gas property under both the percentage depletion method (if the taxpayer is entitled to use this method) and the cost depletion method. If the cost depletion deduction is larger, the taxpayer must utilize that method for the taxable year in question (sec. 613(a)).

Limitation of oil and gas percentage depletion to independent producers and royalty owners

Generally, only independent producers and royalty owners (as contrasted to integrated oil companies) are allowed to claim percentage depletion. Percentage depletion for eligible taxpayers is allowed only with respect to up to 1,000 barrels of average daily production of domestic crude oil or an equivalent amount of domestic natural gas (sec. 613A(c)). For producers of both oil and natural gas, this limitation applies on a combined basis.

In addition to the independent producer and royalty owner exception, certain sales of natural gas under a fixed contract in effect on February 1, 1975, and certain natural gas from geopressured brine, are eligible for percentage depletion, at rates of 22 percent and 10 percent, respectively. These exceptions apply without regard to the 1,000-barrel-per-day limitation and regardless of whether the producer is an independent producer or an integrated oil company.

---

59. Amounts disallowed as a result of this rule may be carried forward and deducted in subsequent taxable years, subject to the 65-percent taxable income limitation for those years.

RIA **Research Institute of America**

Explanation of Provision

The provision extends the period when the 100-percent net-income limit is suspended to include taxable years beginning in 2002 and 2003.

Effective Date

The provision is effective for taxable years beginning after December 31, 2001 and before January 1, 2004.

[¶ 5076]   Section 608.   Qualified zone academy bonds.

(Code Sec. 1397E)

[Joint Committee on Taxation Report]

Present Law

Tax-exempt bonds

Interest on State and local governmental bonds generally is excluded from gross income for Federal income tax purposes if the proceeds of the bonds are used to finance direct activities of these governmental units or if the bonds are repaid with revenues of the governmental units. Activities that can be financed with these tax-exempt bonds include the financing of public schools (sec. 103).

Qualified zone academy bonds

As an alternative to traditional tax-exempt bonds, States and local governments are given the authority to issue "qualified zone academy bonds" ("QZABs") (sec. 1397E). A total of $400 million of qualified zone academy bonds may be issued annually in calendar years 1998 through 2001. The $400 million aggregate bond cap is allocated each year to the States according to their respective populations of individuals below the poverty line. Each State, in turn, allocates the credit authority to qualified zone academies within such State.

Financial institutions that hold qualified zone academy bonds are entitled to a nonrefundable tax credit in an amount equal to a credit rate multiplied by the face amount of the bond. A taxpayer holding a qualified zone academy bond on the credit allowance date is entitled to a credit. The credit is includable in gross income (as if it were a taxable interest payment on the bond), and may be claimed against regular income tax and AMT liability.

The Treasury Department sets the credit rate at a rate estimated to allow issuance of qualified zone academy bonds without discount and without interest cost to the issuer. The maximum term of the bond is determined by the Treasury Department, so that the present value of the obligation to repay the bond is 50 percent of the face value of the bond.

"Qualified zone academy bonds" are defined as any bond issued by a State or local government, provided that (1) at least 95 percent of the proceeds are used for the purpose of renovating, providing equipment to, developing course materials for use at, or training teachers and other school personnel in a "qualified zone academy" and (2) private entities have promised to contribute to the qualified zone academy certain equipment, technical assistance or training, employee services, or other property or services with a value equal to at least 10 percent of the bond proceeds.

A school is a "qualified zone academy" if (1) the school is a public school that provides education and training below the college level, (2) the school operates a special academic program in cooperation with businesses to enhance the academic curriculum and increase graduation and employment rates, and (3) either (a) the school is located in an empowerment zones enterprise community designated under the Code, or (b) it is reasonably expected that at least 35 percent of the students at the school will be eligible for free or reduced-cost lunches under the school lunch program established under the National School Lunch Act.

Explanation of Provision

The provision authorizes issuance of up to $400 million of qualified zone academy bonds annually in calendar years 2002 and 2003.

Effective Date

The provision is effective for obligations issued after the date of enactment.

[¶ 5077]   Section 609.   Cover over of tax on distilled spirits.

(Code Sec. 7652)

[Joint Committee on Taxation Report]

Present Law

A $13.50 per proof gallon[60] excise tax is imposed on distilled spirits produced in, or imported or brought into, the United States. The excise tax does not apply to distilled spirits that are exported from the United States or to distilled spirits that are consumed in U.S. possessions (e.g., Puerto Rico and the Virgin Islands).

The Code provides for coverover (payment) of $13.25 per proof gallon of the excise tax imposed on rum imported (or brought) into the United States (without regard to the country of origin) to Puerto Rico and the Virgin Islands during the period July 1, 1999 through December 31, 2001. Effective on January 1, 2002, the coverover rate is scheduled to return to its permanent level of $10.50 per proof gallon.

Amounts covered over to Puerto Rico and the Virgin Islands are deposited into the treasuries of the two possessions for use as those possessions determine.

Explanation of Provision

The provision extends the $13.25-per-proof-gallon coverover rate for two additional years, through December 31, 2003.

Effective Date

The provision is effective for articles brought into the United States after December 31, 2001.

[¶ 5078]   Section 610.   Parity in the application of certain limits to mental health benefits.

(Code Sec. 9812)

[Joint Committee on Taxation Report]

Prior Law

The Mental Health Parity Act of 1996 amended ERISA and the Public Health Service Act to provide that group health plans that provide both medical and surgical benefits and mental health benefits cannot impose aggregate lifetime or annual dollar limits on mental health benefits that are not imposed on substantially all medical and surgical benefits. The provisions of the Mental Health Parity Act are effective with respect to plan years beginning on or after January 1, 1998, but do not apply to benefits for services furnished on or after September 30, 2001.

---

60. A proof gallon is a liquid gallon consisting of 50 percent alcohol.

The Taxpayer Relief Act of 1997 added to the Internal Revenue Code the requirements imposed under the Mental Health Parity Act, and imposed an excise tax on group health plans that fail to meet the requirements. The excise tax is equal to $100 per day during the period of noncompliance and is imposed on the employer sponsoring the plan if the plan fails to meet the requirements. The maximum tax that can be imposed during a taxable year cannot exceed the lesser of 10 percent of the employer's group health plan expenses for the prior year or $500,000. No tax is imposed if the Secretary determines that the employer did not know, and exercising reasonable diligence would not have known, that the failure existed.

The excise tax is applicable with respect to plan years beginning on or after January 1, 1998, and expired with respect to benefits for services provided on or after September 30, 2001.

Section 701 of Public Law 107-116 (providing appropriations for the Departments of Labor, Health and Human Services, and Education for fiscal year 2002), which was enacted January 10, 2002, restored the excise tax retroactively to September 30, 2001. The excise tax will expire with respect to benefits provided for services on or after December 31, 2002.

Explanation of Provision

With respect to services provided on or after September 30, 2001, the excise tax on failures to comply with mental health parity requirements is amended to apply to benefits for such services provided on or after January 10, 2002, and before January 1, 2004.

Effective Date

The provision is effective with respect to plan years beginning after December 31, 2000.

[¶ 5079]   Section 611.   Temporary special rules for taxation of life insurance companies.

(Code Sec. 809)

[Joint Committee on Taxation Report]

Prior and Present Law

In general, a corporation may not deduct amounts distributed to shareholders with respect to the corporation's stock. The Deficit Reduction Act of 1984 added a provision to the rules governing insurance companies that was intended to remedy the failure of prior law to distinguish between amounts returned by mutual life insurance companies to policyholders as customers, and amounts distributed to them as owners of the mutual company.

Under the provision, section 809, a mutual life insurance company is required to reduce its deduction for policyholder dividends by the company's differential earnings amount. If the company's differential earnings amount exceeds the amount of its deductible policyholder dividends, the company is required to reduce its deduction for changes in its reserves by the excess of its differential earnings amount over the amount of its deductible policyholder dividends. The differential earnings amount is the product of the differential earnings rate and the average equity base of a mutual life insurance company.

The differential earnings rate is based on the difference between the average earnings rate of the 50 largest stock life insurance companies and the earnings rate of all mutual life insurance companies. The mutual earnings rate applied under the provision is the rate for the second calendar year preceding the calendar year in which the taxable year begins. Under present law, the differential earnings rate cannot be a negative number.

A company's equity base equals the sum of: (1) its surplus and capital increased by 50 percent of the amount of any provision for policyholder dividends payable in the following taxable year; (2) the amount of its nonadmitted financial assets; (3) the excess of its statutory reserves over its tax reserves; and (4) the amount of any mandatory security valuation reserves, deficiency reserves, and voluntary reserves. A company's average equity base is the average of the company's equity base at the end of the taxable year and its equity base at the end of the preceding taxable year.

A recomputation or "true-up" in the succeeding year is required if the differential earnings amount for the taxable year either exceeds, or is less than, the recomputed differential earnings amount. The recomputed differential earnings amount is calculated taking into account the average mutual earnings rate for the calendar year (rather than the second preceding calendar year, as above). The amount of the true-up for any taxable year is added to, or deducted from, the mutual company's income for the succeeding taxable year.

Explanation of Provision

The provision provides a zero rate for both the differential earnings rate and recomputed differential earnings rate ("true-up") for a life insurance company's taxable years beginning in 2001, 2002, or 2003, under the rules requiring reduction in certain deductions of mutual life insurance companies (sec. 809).

Effective Date

The provision is effective for taxable years beginning after December 31, 2000.

[¶ 5080]   Section 612.   Availability of medical savings accounts.

(Code Sec. 220)

[Joint Committee on Taxation Report]

Present Law

In general

Within limits, contributions to a an Archer medical savings account ("MSA") are deductible in determining adjusted gross income if made by an eligible individual and are excludable from gross income and wages for employment tax purposes if made by the employer of an eligible individual. Earnings on amounts in an Archer MSA are not currently taxable. Distributions from an Archer MSA for medical expenses are not taxable. Distributions not used for medical expenses are taxable. In addition, distributions not used for medical expenses are subject to an additional 15-percent tax unless the distribution is made after age 65, death, or disability.

Eligible individuals

Archer MSAs are available to employees covered under an employer-sponsored high deductible plan of a small employer and self-employed individuals covered under a high deductible health plan.[61] An employer is a small employer if it employed, on average, no more than 50 employees on business days during either the preceding or the second preceding year. An individual is not eligible for an Archer MSA if they are covered under any other health plan in addition to the high deductible plan.

Tax treatment of and limits on contributions

Individual contributions to an Archer MSA are deductible (within limits) in determining adjusted gross income (i.e., "above the line"). In addition, employer contributions are excludable from gross income and wages for employment tax purposes (within the same limits), except that this exclusion does not apply to contributions made through a cafeteria

---

61. Self-employed individuals include more than 2-percent shareholders of S corporations who are treated as partners for purposes of fringe benefit rules pursuant to section 1372.

plan. In the case of an employee, contributions can be made to an Archer MSA either by the individual or by the individual's employer.

The maximum annual contribution that can be made to an Archer MSA for a year is 65 percent of the deductible under the high deductible plan in the case of individual coverage and 75 percent of the deductible in the case of family coverage.

Definition of high deductible plan

A high deductible plan is a health plan with an annual deductible of at least $1,600 and no more than $2,400 in the case of individual coverage and at least $3,200 and no more than $4,800 in the case of family coverage. In addition, the maximum out-of-pocket expenses with respect to allowed costs (including the deductible) must be no more than $3,200 in the case of individual coverage and no more than $5,850 in the case of family coverage.[62] A plan does not fail to qualify as a high deductible plan merely because it does not have a deductible for preventive care as required by State law. A plan does not qualify as a high deductible health plan if substantially all of the coverage under the plan is for permitted coverage (as described above). In the case of a self-insured plan, the plan must in fact be insurance (e.g., there must be appropriate risk shifting) and not merely a reimbursement arrangement.

Taxation of distributions

Distributions from an Archer MSA for the medical expenses of the individual and his or her spouse or dependents generally are excludable from income.[63] However, in any year for which a contribution is made to an Archer MSA, withdrawals from an Archer MSA maintained by that individual generally are excludable from income only if the individual for whom the expenses were incurred was covered under a high deductible plan for the month in which the expenses were incurred.[64] For this purpose, medical expenses are defined as under the itemized deduction for medical expenses, except that medical expenses do not include expenses for insurance other than long-term care insurance, premiums for health care continuation coverage, and premiums for health care coverage while an individual is receiving unemployment compensation under Federal or State law.

Distributions that are not used for medical expenses are includible in income. Such distributions are also subject to an additional 15-percent tax unless made after age 65, death, or disability.

Cap on taxpayers utilizing Archer MSAs

The number of taxpayers benefiting annually from an Archer MSA contribution is limited to a threshold level (generally 750,000 taxpayers). If it is determined in a year that the threshold level has been exceeded (called a "cut-off" year) then, in general, for succeeding years during the pilot period 1997-2002, only those individuals who (1) made an Archer MSA contribution or had an employer Archer MSA contribution for the year or a preceding year (i.e., are active Archer MSA participants) or (2) are employed by a participating employer, those individuals are eligible for an Archer MSA contribution. In determining whether the threshold for any year has been exceeded, Archer MSAs of individuals who were not covered under a health insurance plan for the six month period ending on the date on which coverage under a high deductible plan commences would not be taken into account.[65] However, if the threshold level is exceeded in a year, previously uninsured individuals are subject to the same restriction on contributions in succeeding years as other individuals. That is, they would not be eligible for an Archer MSA contribution for a year following a cut-off year unless they are an active Archer MSA participant (i.e., had an

---

62. These dollar amounts are for 2001. These amounts are indexed for inflation in $50 increments.
63. This exclusion does not apply to expenses that are reimbursed by insurance or otherwise.
64. The exclusion still applies to expenses for continuation coverage or coverage while the individual is receiving unemployment compensation, even for an individual who is not an eligible individual.
65. Permitted coverage, as described above, does not constitute coverage under a health insurance plan for this purpose.

Archer MSA contribution for the year or a preceding year) or are employed by a participating employer.

The number of Archer MSAs established has not exceeded the threshold level.

End of Archer MSA pilot program

After 2002, no new contributions may be made to Archer MSAs except by or on behalf of individuals who previously had Archer MSA contributions and employees who are employed by a participating employer. An employer is a participating employer if (1) the employer made any Archer MSA contributions for any year to an Archer MSA on behalf of employees or (2) at least 20 percent of the employees covered under a high deductible plan made Archer MSA contributions of at least $100 in the year 2001.

Self-employed individuals who made contributions to an Archer MSA during the period 1997-2002 also may continue to make contributions after 2002.

Explanation of Provision

The provision extends the Archer MSA program for another year, through December 31, 2003.

Effective Date

The provision is effective on the January 1, 2002.

[¶ 5081]   Section 613.   Incentives for Indian employment and property on Indian reservations.

(Code Sec. 45A, 168)

[Joint Committee on Taxation Report]

Present Law

Present law provides the following tax incentives in order to encourage investment on Indian reservations.

Indian employment credit

A general business credit is available for an employer of qualified employees that work on an Indian reservation.[66] The credit is equal to 20 percent of the excess of qualified wages and health insurance costs paid to qualified employees in the current year over the amount paid in 1993, up to a maximum of $20,000. Wages for which the work opportunity credit is available are not qualified wages and are not eligible for the credit.

Employees generally are qualified employees if they (or their spouse) are enrolled in an Indian tribe and live on or near the Indian reservation where they work, perform services that are all or substantially all within an Indian reservation, and do not receive wages greater than $30,000 (adjusted for inflation after 1994) for the taxable year. The credit is not available for employees involved in certain gaming activities or who work in a building that houses certain gaming activities.

The Indian employment credit is not available after December 31, 2003.

Accelerated depreciation of property on Indian reservations

A special depreciation recovery period is available to qualified Indian reservation property.[67] In general, qualified Indian reservation property is property used predominantly in the active conduct of a trade or business within an Indian reservation, which is not used

---

66. Section 45A.
67. Section 168(j).

outside the reservation on a regular basis and was not acquired from a related person. Property used to conduct or house certain gaming activities is not qualified Indian reservation property.

The applicable recovery period for qualified Indian reservation property is as follows:

In the case of:	The applicable recovery period is:
3 year property	2 years
5 year property	3 years
7 year property	4 years
10 year property	6 years
15 year property	9 years
20 year property	12 years
Nonresidential real property	22 years

Accelerated depreciation of property on Indian reservations is not available for property placed in service after December 31, 2003.

Explanation of Provision

The provision extends for one year (i.e., through December 31, 2004) the Indian employment credit and the accelerated depreciation rules for property on Indian reservations.

Effective Date

The provision is effective on the date of enactment.

[¶5082]   Section 614.   Subpart F exemption for active financing.

(Code Sec. 953, 954)

[Joint Committee on Taxation Report]

Present Law

Under the subpart F rules, 10-percent U.S. shareholders of a controlled foreign corporation ("CFC") are subject to U.S. tax currently on certain income earned by the CFC, whether or not such income is distributed to the shareholders. The income subject to current inclusion under the subpart F rules includes, among other things, foreign personal holding company income and insurance income. In addition, 10-percent U.S. shareholders of a CFC are subject to current inclusion with respect to their shares of the CFC's foreign base company services income (i.e., income derived from services performed for a related person outside the country in which the CFC is organized).

Foreign personal holding company income generally consists of the following: (1) dividends, interest, royalties, rents, and annuities; (2) net gains from the sale or exchange of (a) property that gives rise to the preceding types of income, (b) property that does not give rise to income, and (c) interests in trusts, partnerships, and REMICs; (3) net gains from commodities transactions; (4) net gains from foreign currency transactions; (5) income that is equivalent to interest; (6) income from notional principal contracts; and (7) payments in lieu of dividends.

Insurance income subject to current inclusion under the subpart F rules includes any income of a CFC attributable to the issuing or reinsuring of any insurance or annuity contract in connection with risks located in a country other than the CFC's country of organization. Subpart F insurance income also includes income attributable to an insurance contract in connection with risks located within the CFC's country of organization, as the result of an arrangement under which another corporation receives a substantially equal amount of consideration for insurance of other country risks. Investment income of a CFC that is allocable to any insurance or annuity contract related to risks located outside the CFC's country of organization is taxable as subpart F insurance income (Prop. Treas. Reg. sec. 1.953-1(a)).

Temporary exceptions from foreign personal holding company income, foreign base company services income, and insurance income apply for subpart F purposes for certain income that is derived in the active conduct of a banking, financing, or similar business, or in the conduct of an insurance business (so-called "active financing income").[68]

With respect to income derived in the active conduct of a banking, financing, or similar business, a CFC is required to be predominantly engaged in such business and to conduct substantial activity with respect to such business in order to qualify for the exceptions. In addition, certain nexus requirements apply, which provide that income derived by a CFC or a qualified business unit ("QBU") of a CFC from transactions with customers is eligible for the exceptions if, among other things, substantially all of the activities in connection with such transactions are conducted directly by the CFC or QBU in its home country, and such income is treated as earned by the CFC or QBU in its home country for purposes of such country's tax laws. Moreover, the exceptions apply to income derived from certain cross border transactions, provided that certain requirements are met. Additional exceptions from foreign personal holding company income apply for certain income derived by a securities dealer within the meaning of section 475 and for gain from the sale of active financing assets.

In the case of insurance, in addition to a temporary exception from foreign personal holding company income for certain income of a qualifying insurance company with respect to risks located within the CFC's country of creation or organization, certain temporary exceptions from insurance income and from foreign personal holding company income apply for certain income of a qualifying branch of a qualifying insurance company with respect to risks located within the home country of the branch, provided certain requirements are met under each of the exceptions. Further, additional temporary exceptions from insurance income and from foreign personal holding company income apply for certain income of certain CFCs or branches with respect to risks located in a country other than the United States, provided that the requirements for these exceptions are met.

In the case of a life insurance or annuity contract, reserves for such contracts are determined as follows for purposes of these provisions. The reserves equal the greater of: (1) the net surrender value of the contract (as defined in sec. 807(e)(1)(A)), including in the case of pension plan contracts; or (2) the amount determined by applying the tax reserve method that would apply if the qualifying life insurance company were subject to tax under Subchapter L of the Code, with the following modifications. First, there is substituted for the applicable Federal interest rate an interest rate determined for the functional currency of the qualifying insurance company's home country, calculated (except as provided by the Treasury Secretary in order to address insufficient data and similar problems) in the same manner as the mid-term applicable Federal interest rate (within the meaning of sec. 1274(d)). Second, there is substituted for the prevailing State assumed rate the highest assumed interest rate permitted to be used for purposes of determining statement reserves in the foreign country for the contract. Third, in lieu of U.S. mortality and morbidity tables, mortality and morbidity tables are applied that reasonably reflect the current mortality and morbidity risks in the foreign country. Fourth, the Treasury Secretary may provide that the interest rate and mortality and morbidity tables of a qualifying insurance company may be used for one or more of its branches when appropriate. In no event may the reserve for any contract at any time exceed the foreign statement reserve for the contract, reduced by any catastrophe, equalization, or deficiency reserve or any similar reserve.

---

68. Temporary exceptions from the subpart F provisions for certain active financing income applied only for taxable years beginning in 1998. Those exceptions were modified and extended for one year, applicable only for taxable years beginning in 1999. The Tax Relief Extension Act of 1999 (P.L. No. 106-170) clarified and extended the temporary exceptions for two years, applicable only for taxable years beginning after 1999 and before 2002.

Present law also provides a temporary exception from foreign personal holding company income for income from investment of assets equal to 10 percent of reserves (determined for purposes of the provision) for contracts regulated in the country in which sold as life insurance or annuity contracts. This exception does not apply to investment income with respect to excess surplus.

Explanation of Provision

The provision extends for five years the present-law temporary exceptions from subpart F foreign personal holding company income, foreign base company services income, and insurance income for certain income that is derived in the active conduct of a banking, financing, or similar business, or in the conduct of an insurance business.

The provision generally retains present law with respect to the determination of an insurance company's reserve for a life insurance or annuity contract under these exceptions. The provision does, however, permit a taxpayer in certain circumstances, subject to approval by the IRS through the ruling process or in published guidance, to establish that the reserve for such contracts is the amount taken into account in determining the foreign statement reserve for the contract (reduced by catastrophe, equalization, or deficiency reserve or any similar reserve). IRS approval is to be based on whether the method, the interest rate, the mortality and morbidity assumptions, and any other factors taken into account in determining foreign statement reserves (taken together or separately) provide an appropriate means of measuring income for Federal income tax purposes. In seeking a ruling, the taxpayer is required to provide the IRS with necessary and appropriate information as to the method, interest rate, mortality and morbidity assumptions and other assumptions under the foreign reserve rules so that a comparison can be made to the reserve amount determined by applying the tax reserve method that would apply if the qualifying insurance company were subject to tax under Subchapter L of the Code (with the modifications provided under present law for purposes of these exceptions). The IRS also may issue published guidance indicating its approval. Present law continues to apply with respect to reserves for any life insurance or annuity contract for which the IRS has not approved the use of the foreign statement reserve. An IRS ruling request under this provision is subject to the present-law provisions relating to IRS user fees.

Effective Date

The provision is effective for taxable years of foreign corporations beginning after December 31, 2001, and before January 1, 2007, and for taxable years of U.S. shareholders with or within which such taxable years of such foreign corporations end.

[¶ 5083]   Section 615.   Repeal of requirement for approved diesel or kerosene terminals.

(Code Sec. 4101)

[Joint Committee on Taxation Report]

Present Law

Excise taxes are imposed on highway motor fuels, including gasoline, diesel fuel, and kerosene, to finance the Highway Trust Fund programs. Subject to limited exceptions, these taxes are imposed on all such fuels when they are removed from registered pipeline or barge terminal facilities, with any tax-exemptions being accomplished by means of refunds to consumers of the fuel.[69] One such exception allows removal of diesel fuel or kerosene without payment of tax if the fuel is destined for a nontaxable use (e.g., use as heating oil) and is indelibly dyed.

---

69. Tax is imposed before that point if the motor fuel is transferred (other than in bulk) from a refinery or if the fuel is sold to an unregistered party while still held in the refinery or bulk distribution system (e.g., in a pipeline or terminal facility).

Terminal facilities are not permitted to receive and store non-tax-paid motor fuels unless they are registered with the Internal Revenue Service. Under present law, a prerequisite to registration is that if the terminal offers for sale diesel fuel, it must offer both dyed and undyed diesel fuel. Similarly, if the terminal offers for sale kerosene, it must offer both dyed and undyed kerosene. This "dyed-fuel mandate" was enacted in 1997, to be effective on July 1, 1998. Subsequently, the effective date was delayed until July 1, 2000, and later until January 1, 2002.

Explanation of Provision

The diesel fuel and kerosene dyeing mandate is repealed.

Effective Date

The provision is effective on January 1, 2002.

¶ 6000. Act Section Cross-Reference Table

Act §	Code §	Topic	Generally effective date	Analysis ¶	Com Rep ¶
101(a)	168(k)	30% additional first-year depreciation is allowed for, and the AMT depreciation adjustment is not required for, most new tangible personal property and computer software and certain leasehold improvements acquired after Sept. 10, 2001, if acquired or contracted for before Sept. 11, 2004 and placed in service within certain time limits	Property placed in service after Sept. 10, 2001, in tax years ending after Sept. 10, 2001	101	5001
101(a)	168(k)(2)(E)(i)	First-year depreciation limit for passenger automobiles is raised by $4,600 for most new automobiles that are predominantly used in a business and acquired after Sept. 10, 2001, if acquired or contracted for before Sept. 11, 2004 and placed in service before Jan. 1, 2005	Property placed in service after Sept. 10, 2001, in tax years ending after Sept. 10, 2001	102	5001
102(a)	172(b)(1)(H)	NOL carryback period extended to five years for NOLs in 2001 and 2002	NOLs for tax years ending after Dec. 31, 2000	103	5002
102(b)	172(j)	NOL carryback period extended to five years for NOLs in 2001 and 2002	NOLs for tax years ending after Dec. 31, 2000	103	5002
102(c)(1)	56(d)(1)(A)	Alternative tax net operating loss (NOL) deduction increased from 90% to 100% for NOL carrybacks from and NOL carryforwards to tax years ending during 2001 and 2002	Tax years ending before Jan. 1, 2003	104	5002

Act §	Code §	Topic	Generally effective date	Analysis ¶	Com Rep ¶
301(a)	1400L(a)	Work opportunity tax credit of up to $2,400 per calendar year is allowed for wages paid or incurred to each New York Liberty Zone business employee for work performed during calendar years 2002 or 2003	Tax years ending after Dec. 31, 2001 for wages paid or incurred for work in calendar years 2002 or 2003	505	5011
301(a)	1400L(b)	30% additional first-year depreciation is allowed for, and the AMT depreciation adjustment is not required for, certain buildings placed in service in the New York Liberty Zone after Sept. 10, 2001 and before Jan. 1, 2010, and most other tangible property and computer software placed in service in the New York Liberty Zone after Sept. 10, 2001 and before Jan. 1, 2007	Property acquired by purchase after, and originally used in the New York Liberty Zone after, Sept. 10, 2001	501	5012
301(a)	1400L(c)	Qualified New York Liberty Zone leasehold improvement property placed in service after Sept. 10, 2001 and before Jan. 1, 2007 is 5-year property for MACRS depreciation	Qualified New York Liberty Zone leasehold improvement property placed in service after Sept. 10, 2001	503	5013
301(a)	1400L(d)	Issuance of up to $8 billion of tax-exempt private activity bonds to finance the rebuilding of portions of New York City is authorized	Bonds issued after Mar. 9, 2002 and before Jan. 1, 2005	507	5014
301(a)	1400L(e)	Additional advance refunding is allowed for bonds for facilities located in New York City	Mar. 9, 2002	508	5015

Act §	Code §	Topic	Generally effective date	Analysis ¶	Com Rep ¶
301(a)	1400L(f)	Additional first-year expensing in lieu of depreciation is increased by $35,000 for "qualified New York Liberty Zone property" purchased and placed in service by the taxpayer after Sept. 10, 2001 and before Jan. 1, 2007	Property purchased and placed in service by the taxpayer after Sept. 10, 2001 and before Jan. 1, 2007	502	5016
301(a)	1400L(g)	The period for replacing certain property involuntarily converted as a result of the terrorist attacks on the World Trade Center in New York City is extended to five years	Involuntary conversions in the New York Liberty Zone occurring after Sept. 10, 2001 as a consequence of the terrorist attacks on Sept. 11, 2001	504	5017
301(a)	1400L(h)	30% additional first-year depreciation is allowed for, and the AMT depreciation adjustment is not required for, certain buildings placed in service in the New York Liberty Zone after Sept. 10, 2001 and before Jan. 1, 2010, and most other tangible property and computer software placed in service in the New York Liberty Zone after Sept. 10, 2001 and before Jan. 1, 2007	Property acquired by purchase after, and originally used in the New York Liberty Zone after, Sept. 10, 2001	501	5012
301(a)	1400L(i)	Issuance of up to $8 billion of tax-exempt private activity bonds to finance the rebuilding of portions of New York City is authorized	Bonds issued after Mar. 9, 2002 and before Jan. 1, 2005	507	5014

Act §	Code §	Topic	Generally effective date	Analysis ¶	Com Rep ¶
301(b)(1)	38(c)(3)	New York Liberty Zone business employee credit can offset AMT; limitations, carryback, and carryforward rules apply separately to the credit	Tax years ending after Dec. 31, 2001	506	5011
301(b)(2)	38(c)(2)(A)(ii)(II)	New York Liberty Zone business employee credit can offset AMT; limitations, carryback, and carryforward rules apply separately to the credit	Tax years ending after Dec. 31, 2001	506	5011
401	None	Information returns for tax years ending after Mar. 9, 2002 related to numerous payments or transactions may be furnished electronically to recipients who have consented to receive the returns electronically	Statements for tax years ending after Mar. 9, 2002	602	5021
402(a)	108(d)(7)(A)	S corporation cancellation of indebtedness income doesn't increase shareholder basis	Discharges of debt after Oct. 11, 2001	105	5022
403(a)	448(d)(5)	Use of nonaccrual experience method of accounting is available only for amounts received for performing certain qualified personal services, or for amounts received for services by taxpayers with average annual gross receipts of $5 million or less	Tax years ending after Mar. 9, 2002	106	5023
404(a)	131(b)(1)	Foster care payments received from taxable (as well as tax-exempt) placement agencies are excludable from foster care provider's gross income	Tax years beginning after Dec. 31, 2001	415	5024

 Research Institute of America

Act §	Code §	Topic	Generally effective date	Analysis ¶	Com Rep ¶
404(b)	131(b)(2)(B)	Individual placed in foster home by private placement agency can be qualified foster care individual even if not under age 19 at time of placement	Tax years beginning after Dec. 31, 2001	416	5024
404(b)	131(b)(4)	Individual placed in foster home by private placement agency can be qualified foster care individual even if not under age 19 at time of placement	Tax years beginning after Dec. 31, 2001	416	5024
405(a)(1)	412(l)(7)(C)(i)(III)	Temporary relief from low yields on 30-year bonds provided for additional funding requirements and for determining PBGC variable rate premiums	Plan years beginning after Dec. 31, 2001 and before Jan. 1, 2004	306	5025
405(a)(2)	412(m)(7)	Temporary relief from low yields on 30-year bonds provided for additional funding requirements and for determining PBGC variable rate premiums	Plan years beginning after Dec. 31, 2001 and before Jan. 1, 2004	306	5025
406(a)	62(a)(2)(D)	Elementary and secondary school teachers are allowed an up-to-$250 above-the-line deduction for their out-of-pocket classroom-related expenses for 2002 and 2003	Tax years beginning during 2002 and 2003	405	5026
406(b)	62(d)	Elementary and secondary school teachers are allowed an up-to-$250 above-the-line deduction for their out-of-pocket classroom-related expenses for 2002 and 2003	Tax years beginning during 2002 and 2003	405	5026
411(a)(1)	6428(b)	2001 rate reduction credit treated as a nonrefundable personal credit	For tax years beginning after Dec. 31, 2000	403	5031

Act §	Code §	Topic	Generally effective date	Analysis ¶	Com Rep ¶
411(a)(2)(A)	6428(d)	2001 rate reduction credit treated as a nonrefundable personal credit	For tax years beginning after Dec. 31, 2000	403	5031
411(a)(2)(B)	6428(e)(2)	2001 rate reduction credit treated as a nonrefundable personal credit	For tax years beginning after Dec. 31, 2000	403	5031
411(b)	24(d)(1)(B)	Computation of refundable child tax credit for 2001 to 2003 is based on increase in all refundable credits, not just child tax credit	Tax years beginning after Dec. 31, 2000	404	5032
411(c)(1)(A)	23(a)(1)	Aggregate expenses for adopting special-needs child after 2002 deemed to be $10,000 for credit purposes in year adoption becomes final	Tax years beginning after Dec. 31, 2002	412	5033
411(c)(1)(B)	23(a)(3)	Aggregate expenses for adopting special-needs child after 2002 deemed to be $10,000 for credit purposes in year adoption becomes final	Tax years beginning after Dec. 31, 2002	412	5033
411(c)(1)(C)	23(a)(2)	Aggregate expenses for adopting special-needs child after 2002 deemed to be $10,000 for credit purposes in year adoption becomes final	Tax years beginning after Dec. 31, 2001	412	5033
411(c)(1)(F)	None	Qualified adoption expenses paid or incurred before 2002 are subject to pre-2002 dollar limits	Tax years beginning after Dec. 31, 2001	413	5033
411(c)(2)(A)	137(a)	Aggregate expenses for adopting special-needs child after 2002 deemed to be $10,000 for exclusion purposes in year adoption becomes final	Tax years beginning after Dec. 31, 2002	411	5033

Act §	Code §	Topic	Generally effective date	Analysis ¶	Com Rep ¶
411(d)(1)	45F(d)(4)(B)	Treatment of the employer-provided child care assistance credit recapture "tax" as not being a tax is confirmed and clarified	Tax years beginning after Dec. 31, 2001	108	5034
411(e)(1)	63(c)(2)	Basic standard deduction for marrieds filing separate will stay at half of amount for marrieds filing joint for 2005 through 2008	Tax years beginning after Dec. 31, 2004	417	5035
411(f)	530(d)(4)(B)(iv)	The 10% additional tax on Coverdell ESA distributions doesn't apply to distributions that are includible in income only because a HOPE or Lifetime Learning credit is taken instead	For tax years beginning after Dec. 31, 2001	409	5036
411(g)(1)	2511(c)	Provision governing transfers to non-grantor trusts after 2009 clarified; these transfers will be treated as transfers of property by gift	For gifts made after Dec. 31, 2009	702	5037
411(i)(1)	408(q)(3)(A)	Types of governmental plans that can provide deemed IRAs are clarified—after 2002	Plan years beginning after Dec. 31, 2002	319	5039
411(j)(1)	408(k)	Dollar limits for SEP eligibility, and for determining the distribution period from an ESOP, are increased to permit proper inflation indexing	Years beginning after Dec. 31, 2001	302	5040
411(j)(2)	409(o)(1)(C)(ii)	Dollar limits for SEP eligibility, and for determining the distribution period from an ESOP, are increased to permit proper inflation indexing	Years beginning after Dec. 31, 2001	302	5040
411(j)(3)	None	Transitional rule allowing defined benefit plans that incorporate Code's plan limits by reference to disregard the anti-cutback rules	Years ending after Dec. 31, 2001.	321	5040

Act §	Code §	Topic	Generally effective date	Analysis ¶	Com Rep ¶
411(k)(1)	416(c)(1)(C)(iii)	Method of determining "defined benefit minimum" for top-heavy plans no longer applies only to frozen plans	For years beginning after Dec. 31, 2001	323	5041
411(k)(2)	416(g)(3)(B)	"Severance from employment" replaces "separation from service" for in-service distributions from top-heavy plans	For years beginning after Dec. 31, 2001	322	5041
411(l)(1)	404(a)(12)	"Compensation" for purposes of determining deduction limits for contributions to SEPs includes salary reduction amounts	Years beginning after Dec. 31, 2001	304	5042
411(l)(2)	404(n)	Elective deferrals are no longer taken into account in applying SEP deduction limits for employer contributions	For years beginning after Dec. 31, 2001	303	5042
411(l)(3)	402(h)(2)(A)	Limitation on deductible contributions to SEPs increased from 15% to 25% of compensation	For years beginning after Dec. 31, 2001	301	5042
411(l)(4)	404(a)(7)(C)	Deduction limit for combined plans doesn't apply if defined contribution plan receives only elective deferrals	For years beginning after Dec. 31, 2001	305	5042
411(m)	25B(d)(2)(A)	Retirement contributions that qualify for saver's credit must be reduced by nontaxable distributions from qualified retirement plans, deferred compensation plans, or traditional IRAs	Tax years beginning after Dec. 31, 2001	317	5043
411(n)(1)	45E(e)(1)	Aggregation rules for small employer pension plan startup costs credit are based on affiliated service group rules, not employee leasing rules	For costs paid or incurred in tax years beginning after Dec. 31, 2001	316	None

Act §	Code §	Topic	Generally effective date	Analysis ¶	Com Rep ¶
411(n)(2)	45E	Small employer pension plan startup costs credit applies to plans that are first effective after 2001, even if adopted before 2002	Qualified employer plans first effective after Dec. 31, 2001	315	5044
411(o)(1)	402(g)(1)(C)	Additional elective deferrals that don't exceed catch-up contribution limit are excludable from eligible participant's income	For contributions made in tax years beginning after Dec. 31, 2001	308	5045
411(o)(3)	414(v)(2)(D)	Plan's catch-up contribution limit must be applied on an aggregate basis, applying the controlled group rules	For contributions made in tax years beginning after Dec. 31, 2001	309	5045
411(o)(4)	414(v)(3)(A)(i)	List of qualification requirements that don't apply to catch-up contribution is revised	For contributions made in tax years beginning after Dec. 31, 2001	311	5045
411(o)(5)	414(v)(3)(B)	List of qualification requirements that don't apply to catch-up contribution is revised	For contributions made in tax years beginning after Dec. 31, 2001	311	5045
411(o)(6)	414(v)(4)(B)	Plans in transition period under nondiscrimination rules for certain dispositions and acquisitions are not subject to universal availability requirement for catch-up contributions	For contributions made in tax years beginning after Dec. 31, 2001	312	5045
411(o)(7)	414(v)(5)	Individuals who reach age 50 by the end of the tax year are eligible to make catch-up contributions as of the beginning of the year	For contributions made in tax years beginning after Dec. 31, 2001	307	5045
411(o)(8)	414(v)(6)(C)	Governmental section 457 plan participants can make catch-up contributions equal to the greater of the amount allowed under Code Sec. 414(v) or under Code Sec. 457	For contributions made in tax years beginning after Dec. 31, 2001	310	5045

Act §	Code §	Topic	Generally effective date	Analysis ¶	Com Rep ¶
411(o)(9)	457(e)(18)	Governmental section 457 plan participants can make catch-up contributions equal to the greater of the amount allowed under Code Sec. 414(v) or under Code Sec. 457	For contributions made in tax years beginning after Dec. 31, 2001	310	5045
411(p)	403(b)	Rules applying defined contribution plan limits to Code Sec. 403(b) annuities, Code Sec. 457 plans and church plans are clarified	Years beginning after Dec. 31, 2001	320	5046
411(p)(4)	415(c)(7)	Rules applying defined contribution plan limits to Code Sec. 403(b) annuities, Code Sec. 457 plans and church plans are clarified	Years beginning after Dec. 31, 2001	320	5046
411(p)(5)	457(e)(5)	Rules applying defined contribution plan limits to Code Sec. 403(b) annuities, Code Sec. 457 plans and church plans are clarified	Years beginning after Dec. 31, 2001	320	5046
411(q)(1)	401(a)(31)(C)(i)	Direct rollovers of after-tax amounts from qualified retirement plans can be made only to defined contribution plans (and IRAs)	Distributions made after Dec. 31, 2001	314	5047
411(q)(2)	402(c)(2)	Qualified plan distributions that are rolled over are treated as consisting first of taxable amounts	Distributions made after Dec. 31, 2001.	313	5047
411(r)(1)(A)	417(e)(1)	Rollovers may be disregarded in determining the present value of a qualified survivor annuity for cash-out purposes	Applies to distributions after Dec. 31, 2001	324	5048
411(r)(1)(B)	417(e)(2)(A)	Rollovers may be disregarded in determining the present value of a qualified survivor annuity for cash-out purposes	Applies to distributions after Dec. 31, 2001	324	5048

Act §	Code §	Topic	Generally effective date	Analysis ¶	Com Rep ¶
411(u)(1)(A)	4980F(e)(1)	Code Sec. 4980F notice rules apply only to tax qualified defined benefit plans	For plan amendments taking effect on or after June 7, 2001	327	5051
411(u)(1)(B)	4980F(f)(2)(A)	Code Sec. 4980F notice rules apply only to tax qualified defined benefit plans	For plan amendments taking effect on or after June 7, 2001	327	5051
411(u)(1)(C)	4980F(f)(3)	Code Sec. 4980F notice rules apply only to tax qualified defined benefit plans	For plan amendments taking effect on or after June 7, 2001	327	5051
411(v)(1)	412(c)(9)(B)	Modification of requirements for using prior year's valuation in satisfaction of annual actuarial requirement for defined benefit and money purchase plans	Plan years beginning after Dec. 31, 2001	325	5052
411(w)(1)(D)	404(k)(4)(B)	ESOP dividends can be reinvested in company stock without the company losing its dividend deduction; reinvested dividends must be non-forfeitable	Tax years beginning after Dec. 31, 2001	326	5053
411(w)(2)	404(k)(7)	ESOP dividends can be reinvested in company stock without the company losing its dividend deduction; reinvested dividends must be non-forfeitable	Tax years beginning after Dec. 31, 2001	326	5053
412(a)	469(i)(3)(E)	Commercial revitalization deduction for renewal communities is given a higher priority under the rule that determines the order in which deductions and credits are applied against the up-to-$25,000 of passive losses (or credit equivalents) permitted for certain real estate activities	Buildings placed in service in renewal communities after Dec. 31, 2001 and before Jan. 1, 2010	107	5054

Act §	Code §	Topic	Generally effective date	Analysis ¶	Com Rep ¶
412(b)	151(c)(6)(C)	Surviving spouse or head of household filing status allowed with respect to kidnapped child; principal-place-of-abode requirements treated as met	Tax years ending after Dec. 21, 2000	407	5055
412(c)	358(h)(1)(A)	Basis reduction rule where basis exceeds fair market value and liabilities are not taken into account clarified	Assumptions of liabilities after Oct. 18, '99	706	5056
412(d)(1)(A)	1234A	Securities futures contract rules are clarified	Dec. 21, 2000	704	5057
412(d)(1)(B)(i)	1234B(a)(1)	Securities futures contract rules are clarified	Dec. 21, 2000	704	5057
412(d)(1)(B)(i)	1234B(b)	Securities futures contract rules are clarified	Dec. 21, 2000	704	5057
412(d)(2)	1091(e)	Securities futures contract rules are clarified	Dec. 21, 2000	704	5057
412(d)(3)(A)	1233(e)(2)(E)	Securities futures contract rules are clarified	Dec. 21, 2000	704	5057
412(d)(3)(B)	1234B(b)	Securities futures contract rules are clarified	Dec. 21, 2000	704	5057
413(a)(1)	857(b)(7)(B)(i)	Amount of REIT's "redetermined rents" and "redetermined deductions" to which 100% tax applies clarified	Tax years beginning after Dec. 31, 2000	701	5058
413(a)(2)	857(b)(7)(C)	Amount of REIT's "redetermined rents" and "redetermined deductions" to which 100% tax applies clarified	Tax years beginning after Dec. 31, 2000	701	5058
414(a)(1)	None	Gain to which mark-to-market election for assets held on Jan. 1, 2001 applies is included in income despite nonrecognition provision	Tax years ending after May 6, '97	418	5059
414(a)(2)	None	Mark-to-market election for assets held on Jan. 1, 2001 doesn't trigger deduction of suspended passive losses	Tax years ending after May 6, '97	109	5059

 Research Institute of America

Act §	Code §	Topic	Generally effective date	Analysis ¶	Com Rep ¶
415(a)	26(b)(2)(R)	Additional tax on distributions from Medicare+Choice Archer MSAs not used for qualified medical expenses is not included in a taxpayer's "regular tax liability" for credit purposes	Tax years beginning after Dec. 31, '98	410	5060
416(a)(1)	32(g)(2)	Advance payments of earned income credit not treated as tax for purposes of any tax credits	Tax years beginning after Dec. 31, '83	408	5061
416(c)	6103(l)(8)(A)	Social Security Administration must disclose return information to federal child support agency	Mar. 9, 2002	604	5063
416(d)(1)(A)	6224(c)(1)	Partners' settlements with Attorney General given equivalent treatment to settlements with IRS under partnership audit rules	Settlement agreements entered into after Mar. 9, 2002	603	5064
416(d)(1)(A)	6224(c)(2)	Partners' settlements with Attorney General given equivalent treatment to settlements with IRS under partnership audit rules	Settlement agreements entered into after Mar. 9, 2002	603	5064
416(d)(1)(B)	6229(f)(2)	Partners' settlements with Attorney General given equivalent treatment to settlements with IRS under partnership audit rules	Settlement agreements entered into after Mar. 9, 2002	603	5064
416(d)(1)(C)	6231(b)(1)(C)	Partners' settlements with Attorney General given equivalent treatment to settlements with IRS under partnership audit rules	Settlement agreements entered into after Mar. 9, 2002	603	5064
416(d)(1)(D)	6234(g)(4)(A)	Partners' settlements with Attorney General given equivalent treatment to settlements with IRS under partnership audit rules	Settlement agreements entered into after Mar. 9, 2002	603	5064

Act §	Code §	Topic	Generally effective date	Analysis ¶	Com Rep ¶
416(e)(1)	6331(k)(3)	Extension of collection limitations period clarified in cases where installment agreements or offers-in-compromise are considered	Mar. 9, 2002	601	5060
416(f)	7702A(c)(3)(A)(ii)	Unnecessary reference to "the old contract" is deleted from rules on whether a life insurance contract is a modified endowment contract if there is a material change to the contract	Applies to contracts entered into after June 20, '88	705	5066
418(a)(1)(B)	23(h)	Rounding rules provided for inflation adjustments for adoption credit and adoption assistance exclusion	Tax years beginning after Dec. 31, 2001	414	5067
418(a)(2)	137(f)	Rounding rules provided for inflation adjustments for adoption credit and adoption assistance exclusion	Tax years beginning after Dec. 31, 2001	414	5067
418(b)	21(d)(2)	Monthly deemed income of spouse under child care credit rules will increase after 2002 to $250 (from $200) with one child, to $500 (from $400) with two or more	Tax years beginning after Dec. 31, 2002	406	5068
601(a)	26(a)(2)	Nonrefundable personal credits may be used to offset AMT through 2003 (instead of 2001)	Tax years beginning after Dec. 31, 2001	401	5069
601(b)(1)	904(h)	Nonrefundable personal credits won't reduce individual's foreign tax credit until after 2003 (instead of after 2001)	Tax years beginning after Dec. 31, 2001	402	5069
601(b)(2)	None	Nonrefundable personal credits may be used to offset AMT through 2003 (instead of 2001)	Tax years beginning after Dec. 31, 2001	401	5069

 Research Institute of America

Act §	Code §	Topic	Generally effective date	Analysis ¶	Com Rep ¶
602(a)(1)(A)	30(b)(2)	Two-year deferral of the phaseout of the qualified electric vehicle credit permits taxpayers to claim a full credit in 2002 and 2003; credit is extended to apply to property placed in service before Jan. 1, 2007	Property placed in service after Dec. 31, 2001	211	5070
602(a)(1)(B)	30(b)(2)(A)	Two-year deferral of the phaseout of the qualified electric vehicle credit permits taxpayers to claim a full credit in 2002 and 2003; credit is extended to apply to property placed in service before Jan. 1, 2007	Property placed in service after Dec. 31, 2001	211	5070
602(a)(1)(B)	30(b)(2)(B)	Two-year deferral of the phaseout of the qualified electric vehicle credit permits taxpayers to claim a full credit in 2002 and 2003; credit is extended to apply to property placed in service before Jan. 1, 2007	Property placed in service after Dec. 31, 2001	211	5070
602(a)(1)(B)	30(b)(2)(C)	Two-year deferral of the phaseout of the qualified electric vehicle credit permits taxpayers to claim a full credit in 2002 and 2003; credit is extended to apply to property placed in service before Jan. 1, 2007	Property placed in service after Dec. 31, 2001	211	5070
602(a)(2)	30(e)	Two-year deferral of the phaseout of the qualified electric vehicle credit permits taxpayers to claim a full credit in 2002 and 2003; credit is extended to apply to property placed in service before Jan. 1, 2007	Property placed in service after Dec. 31, 2001	211	5070

Act §	Code §	Topic	Generally effective date	Analysis ¶	Com Rep ¶
602(b)(1)	280F(a)(1)(C)(iii)	Exemption for qualified clean-fuel vehicle property from the depreciation and expense deduction limits is extended for two years to property placed in service before Jan. 1, 2007	Property placed in service after Dec. 31, 2001	207	5070
602(b)(1)	280F(a)(1)(C)(iii)	Tripling of automobile depreciation and expense deduction limits for electric vehicles is extended for two years to vehicles placed in service before Jan. 1, 2007	Property placed in service after Dec. 31, 2001	208	5070
603(a)	45(c)(3)	Credit for electricity produced from renewable resources is extended for two years to include qualified facilities placed in service before Jan. 1, 2004	Facilities placed in service after Dec. 31, 2001	205	5071
604(a)	51(c)(4)(B)	Work opportunity credit is extended for two years through Dec. 31, 2003 and retroactively restored to Jan. 1, 2002	Individuals who begin work for an employer after Dec. 31, 2001	202	5072
605(a)	51A(f)	Welfare-to-work credit is extended for two years through Dec. 31, 2003 and retroactively restored to Jan. 1, 2002	Individuals who begin work for an employer after Dec. 31, 2001	201	5073
606(a)(1)(A)	179A(b)(1)(B)	Phaseout of maximum deduction for cost of qualified clean-fuel vehicles is deferred for two years so that a full deduction is available for cost of qualified vehicles placed in service in 2002 and 2003; deduction is extended to apply to property placed in service before Jan. 1, 2007	Property placed in service after Dec. 31, 2001	209	5074

Act §	Code §	Topic	Generally effective date	Analysis ¶	Com Rep ¶
606(a)(1)(B)	179A(b)(1)(B)(i)	Phaseout of maximum deduction for cost of qualified clean-fuel vehicles is deferred for two years so that a full deduction is available for cost of qualified vehicles placed in service in 2002 and 2003; deduction is extended to apply to property placed in service before Jan. 1, 2007	Property placed in service after Dec. 31, 2001	209	5074
606(a)(1)(B)	179A(b)(1)(B)(ii)	Phaseout of maximum deduction for cost of qualified clean-fuel vehicles is deferred for two years so that a full deduction is available for cost of qualified vehicles placed in service in 2002 and 2003; deduction is extended to apply to property placed in service before Jan. 1, 2007	Property placed in service after Dec. 31, 2001	209	5074
606(a)(1)(B)	179A(b)(1)(B)(iii)	Phaseout of maximum deduction for cost of qualified clean-fuel vehicles is deferred for two years so that a full deduction is available for cost of qualified vehicles placed in service in 2002 and 2003; deduction is extended to apply to property placed in service before Jan. 1, 2007	Property placed in service after Dec. 31, 2001	209	5074
606(a)(2)	179A(f)	Deduction for cost of clean-fuel vehicle refueling property is extended two years to property placed in service before Jan. 1, 2007	Property placed in service after Dec. 31, 2001	210	5074

Act §	Code §	Topic	Generally effective date	Analysis ¶	Com Rep ¶
606(a)(2)	179A(f)	Phaseout of maximum deduction for cost of qualified clean-fuel vehicles is deferred for two years so that a full deduction is available for cost of qualified vehicles placed in service in 2002 and 2003; deduction is extended to apply to property placed in service before Jan. 1, 2007	Property placed in service after Dec. 31, 2001	209	5074
607(a)	613A(c)(6)(H)	Suspension of taxable income limitation on percentage depletion from marginal oil and gas wells is extended for two years to include tax years beginning before 2004	Tax years beginning after Dec. 31, 2001	206	5075
608(a)	1397E(e)(1)	Authorization for issuance of qualified zone academy bonds of up to $400 million per year is extended for two years to include calendar years 2002 and 2003	Obligations issued after Mar. 9, 2002	213	5076
610(a)	9812(f)	Mental health parity requirements extended through 2003	Plan years beginning after Dec. 31, 2000	328	5078
611(a)	809(j)	Reduction of deductions for mutual life insurance companies is suspended for tax years beginning in 2001, 2002, or 2003	Tax years beginning after Dec. 31, 2000	212	5079
612(a)	220(i)(2)	Archer MSA program is extended through 2003	Jan. 1, 2002	214	5080
613(a)	45A(f)	Indian employment credit for wages paid to qualified Indians is extended through 2004	Mar. 9, 2002	215	5081
613(b)	168(j)(8)	Depreciation tax breaks for qualified Indian reservation property are extended through 2004	Mar. 9, 2002	216	5081

 Research Institute of America

Act §	Code §	Topic	Generally effective date	Analysis ¶	Com Rep ¶
614(a)(1)	953(e)(10)	Exceptions under Subpart F for active banking, financing and insurance income expiring in 2001 extended through 2006	Tax years beginning after Dec. 31, 2001	203	5082
614(a)(1)	953(e)(10)	Special rule for determining life insurance and annuity contract reserves of a qualifying insurance company or branch modified and extended through 2006	Tax years beginning after Dec. 31, 2001	204	5082
614(a)(2)	954(h)(9)	Exceptions under Subpart F for active banking, financing and insurance income expiring in 2001 extended through 2006	Tax years beginning after Dec. 31, 2001	203	5082
614(b)	954(i)(4)(B)	Special rule for determining life insurance and annuity contract reserves of a qualifying insurance company or branch modified and extended through 2006	Tax years beginning after Dec. 31, 2001	204	5082
615(a)	4101(e)	Mandate that terminal operators offer both dyed and undyed diesel fuel or kerosene after 2001 is retroactively repealed	Jan. 1, 2002	703	5083

¶ 6001. Code Section Cross-Reference Table

Code §	Act §	Topic	Generally effective date	Analysis ¶	Com Rep ¶
21(d)(2)	418(b)	Monthly deemed income of spouse under child care credit rules will increase after 2002 to $250 (from $200) with one child, to $500 (from $400) with two or more	Tax years beginning after Dec. 31, 2002	406	5068
23(a)(1)	411(c)(1)(A)	Aggregate expenses for adopting special-needs child after 2002 deemed to be $10,000 for credit purposes in year adoption becomes final	Tax years beginning after Dec. 31, 2002	412	5033
23(a)(2)	411(c)(1)(C)	Aggregate expenses for adopting special-needs child after 2002 deemed to be $10,000 for credit purposes in year adoption becomes final	Tax years beginning after Dec. 31, 2001	412	5033
23(a)(3)	411(c)(1)(B)	Aggregate expenses for adopting special-needs child after 2002 deemed to be $10,000 for credit purposes in year adoption becomes final	Tax years beginning after Dec. 31, 2002	412	5033
23(h)	418(a)(1)(B)	Rounding rules provided for inflation adjustments for adoption credit and adoption assistance exclusion	Tax years beginning after Dec. 31, 2001	414	5067
24(d)(1)(B)	411(b)	Computation of refundable child tax credit for 2001 to 2003 is based on increase in all refundable credits, not just child tax credit	Tax years beginning after Dec. 31, 2000	404	5032
25B(d)(2)(A)	411(m)	Retirement contributions that qualify for saver's credit must be reduced by nontaxable distributions from qualified retirement plans, deferred compensation plans, or traditional IRAs	Tax years beginning after Dec. 31, 2001	317	5043

Code Section Table

Code §	Act §	Topic	Generally effective date	Analysis ¶	Com Rep ¶
26(a)(2)	601(a)	Nonrefundable personal credits may be used to off-set AMT through 2003 (instead of 2001)	Tax years beginning after Dec. 31, 2001	401	5069
26(b)(2)(R)	415(a)	Additional tax on distributions from Medicare+Choice Archer MSAs not used for qualified medical expenses is not included in a taxpayer's "regular tax liability" for credit purposes	Tax years beginning after Dec. 31, '98	410	5060
30(b)(2)	602(a)(1)(A)	Two-year deferral of the phaseout of the qualified electric vehicle credit permits taxpayers to claim a full credit in 2002 and 2003; credit is extended to apply to property placed in service before Jan. 1, 2007	Property placed in service after Dec. 31, 2001	211	5070
30(b)(2)(A)	602(a)(1)(B)	Two-year deferral of the phaseout of the qualified electric vehicle credit permits taxpayers to claim a full credit in 2002 and 2003; credit is extended to apply to property placed in service before Jan. 1, 2007	Property placed in service after Dec. 31, 2001	211	5070
30(b)(2)(B)	602(a)(1)(B)	Two-year deferral of the phaseout of the qualified electric vehicle credit permits taxpayers to claim a full credit in 2002 and 2003; credit is extended to apply to property placed in service before Jan. 1, 2007	Property placed in service after Dec. 31, 2001	211	5070
30(b)(2)(C)	602(a)(1)(B)	Two-year deferral of the phaseout of the qualified electric vehicle credit permits taxpayers to claim a full credit in 2002 and 2003; credit is extended to apply to property placed in service before Jan. 1, 2007	Property placed in service after Dec. 31, 2001	211	5070

 Research Institute of America

Code §	Act §	Topic	Generally effective date	Analysis ¶	Com Rep ¶
30(e)	602(a)(2)	Two-year deferral of the phaseout of the qualified electric vehicle credit permits taxpayers to claim a full credit in 2002 and 2003; credit is extended to apply to property placed in service before Jan. 1, 2007	Property placed in service after Dec. 31, 2001	211	5070
32(g)(2)	416(a)(1)	Advance payments of earned income credit not treated as tax for purposes of any tax credits	Tax years beginning after Dec. 31, '83	408	5061
38(c)(2)(A)(ii)(II)	301(b)(2)	New York Liberty Zone business employee credit can offset AMT; limitations, carryback, and carryforward rules apply separately to the credit	Tax years ending after Dec. 31, 2001	506	5011
38(c)(3)	301(b)(1)	New York Liberty Zone business employee credit can offset AMT; limitations, carryback, and carryforward rules apply separately to the credit	Tax years ending after Dec. 31, 2001	506	5011
45(c)(3)	603(a)	Credit for electricity produced from renewable resources is extended for two years to include qualified facilities placed in service before Jan. 1, 2004	Facilities placed in service after Dec. 31, 2001	205	5071
45A(f)	613(a)	Indian employment credit for wages paid to qualified Indians is extended through 2004	Mar. 9, 2002	215	5081
45E	411(n)(2)	Small employer pension plan startup costs credit applies to plans that are first effective after 2001, even if adopted before 2002	Qualified employer plans first effective after Dec. 31, 2001	315	5044
45E(e)(1)	411(n)(1)	Aggregation rules for small employer pension plan startup costs credit are based on affiliated service group rules, not employee leasing rules	For costs paid or incurred in tax years beginning after Dec. 31, 2001	316	None

Code §	Act §	Topic	Generally effective date	Analysis ¶	Com Rep ¶
45F(d)(4)(B)	411(d)(1)	Treatment of the employer-provided child care assistance credit recapture "tax" as not being a tax is confirmed and clarified	Tax years beginning after Dec. 31, 2001	108	5034
51(c)(4)(B)	604(a)	Work opportunity credit is extended for two years through Dec. 31, 2003 and retroactively restored to Jan. 1, 2002	Individuals who begin work for an employer after Dec. 31, 2001	202	5072
51A(f)	605(a)	Welfare-to-work credit is extended for two years through Dec. 31, 2003 and retroactively restored to Jan. 1, 2002	Individuals who begin work for an employer after Dec. 31, 2001	201	5073
56(d)(1)(A)	102(c)(1)	Alternative tax net operating loss (NOL) deduction increased from 90% to 100% for NOL carrybacks from and NOL carryforwards to tax years ending during 2001 and 2002	Tax years ending before Jan. 1, 2003	104	5002
62(a)(2)(D)	406(a)	Elementary and secondary school teachers are allowed an up-to-$250 above-the-line deduction for their out-of-pocket classroom-related expenses for 2002 and 2003	Tax years beginning during 2002 and 2003	405	5026
62(d)	406(b)	Elementary and secondary school teachers are allowed an up-to-$250 above-the-line deduction for their out-of-pocket classroom-related expenses for 2002 and 2003	Tax years beginning during 2002 and 2003	405	5026
63(c)(2)	411(e)(1)	Basic standard deduction for marrieds filing separate will stay at half of amount for marrieds filing joint for 2005 through 2008	Tax years beginning after Dec. 31, 2004	417	5035
108(d)(7)(A)	402(a)	S corporation cancellation of indebtedness income doesn't increase shareholder basis	Discharges of debt after Oct. 11, 2001	105	5022

Code §	Act §	Topic	Generally effective date	Analysis ¶	Com Rep ¶
131(b)(1)	404(a)	Foster care payments received from taxable (as well as tax-exempt) placement agencies are excludable from foster care provider's gross income	Tax years beginning after Dec. 31, 2001	415	5024
131(b)(2)(B)	404(b)	Individual placed in foster home by private placement agency can be qualified foster care individual even if not under age 19 at time of placement	Tax years beginning after Dec. 31, 2001	416	5024
131(b)(4)	404(b)	Individual placed in foster home by private placement agency can be qualified foster care individual even if not under age 19 at time of placement	Tax years beginning after Dec. 31, 2001	416	5024
137(a)	411(c)(2)(A)	Aggregate expenses for adopting special-needs child after 2002 deemed to be $10,000 for exclusion purposes in year adoption becomes final	Tax years beginning after Dec. 31, 2002	411	5033
137(f)	418(a)(2)	Rounding rules provided for inflation adjustments for adoption credit and adoption assistance exclusion	Tax years beginning after Dec. 31, 2001	414	5067
151(c)(6)(C)	412(b)	Surviving spouse or head of household filing status allowed with respect to kidnapped child; principal-place-of-abode requirements treated as met	Tax years ending after Dec. 21, 2000	407	5055
168(j)(8)	613(b)	Depreciation tax breaks for qualified Indian reservation property are extended through 2004	Mar. 9, 2002	216	5081

Code §	Act §	Topic	Generally effective date	Analysis ¶	Com Rep ¶
168(k)	101(a)	30% additional first-year depreciation is allowed for, and the AMT depreciation adjustment is not required for, most new tangible personal property and computer software and certain leasehold improvements acquired after Sept. 10, 2001, if acquired or contracted for before Sept. 11, 2004 and placed in service within certain time limits	Property placed in service after Sept. 10, 2001, in tax years ending after Sept. 10, 2001	101	5001
168(k)(2)(E)(i)	101(a)	First-year depreciation limit for passenger automobiles is raised by $4,600 for most new automobiles that are predominantly used in a business and acquired after Sept. 10, 2001, if acquired or contracted for before Sept. 11, 2004 and placed in service before Jan. 1, 2005	Property placed in service after Sept. 10, 2001, in tax years ending after Sept. 10, 2001	102	5001
172(b)(1)(H)	102(a)	NOL carryback period extended to five years for NOLs in 2001 and 2002	NOLs for tax years ending after Dec. 31, 2000	103	5002
172(j)	102(b)	NOL carryback period extended to five years for NOLs in 2001 and 2002	NOLs for tax years ending after Dec. 31, 2000	103	5002
179A(b)(1)(B)	606(a)(1)(A)	Phaseout of maximum deduction for cost of qualified clean-fuel vehicles is deferred for two years so that a full deduction is available for cost of qualified vehicles placed in service in 2002 and 2003; deduction is extended to apply to property placed in service before Jan. 1, 2007	Property placed in service after Dec. 31, 2001	209	5074

Research Institute of America

Code §	Act §	Topic	Generally effective date	Analysis ¶	Com Rep ¶
179A(b)(1)(B)(i)	606(a)(1)(B)	Phaseout of maximum deduction for cost of qualified clean-fuel vehicles is deferred for two years so that a full deduction is available for cost of qualified vehicles placed in service in 2002 and 2003; deduction is extended to apply to property placed in service before Jan. 1, 2007	Property placed in service after Dec. 31, 2001	209	5074
179A(b)(1)(B)(ii)	606(a)(1)(B)	Phaseout of maximum deduction for cost of qualified clean-fuel vehicles is deferred for two years so that a full deduction is available for cost of qualified vehicles placed in service in 2002 and 2003; deduction is extended to apply to property placed in service before Jan. 1, 2007	Property placed in service after Dec. 31, 2001	209	5074
179A(b)(1)(B)(iii)	606(a)(1)(B)	Phaseout of maximum deduction for cost of qualified clean-fuel vehicles is deferred for two years so that a full deduction is available for cost of qualified vehicles placed in service in 2002 and 2003; deduction is extended to apply to property placed in service before Jan. 1, 2007	Property placed in service after Dec. 31, 2001	209	5074
179A(f)	606(a)(2)	Deduction for cost of clean-fuel vehicle refueling property is extended two years to property placed in service before Jan. 1, 2007	Property placed in service after Dec. 31, 2001	210	5074
179A(f)	606(a)(2)	Phaseout of maximum deduction for cost of qualified clean-fuel vehicles is deferred for two years so that a full deduction is available for cost of qualified vehicles placed in service in 2002 and 2003; deduction is extended to apply to property placed in service before Jan. 1, 2007	Property placed in service after Dec. 31, 2001	209	5074

Code §	Act §	Topic	Generally effective date	Analysis ¶	Com Rep ¶
220(i)(2)	612(a)	Archer MSA program is extended through 2003	Jan. 1, 2002	214	5080
280F(a)(1)(C)(iii)	602(b)(1)	Exemption for qualified clean-fuel vehicle property from the depreciation and expense deduction limits is extended for two years to property placed in service before Jan. 1, 2007	Property placed in service after Dec. 31, 2001	207	5070
280F(a)(1)(C)(iii)	602(b)(1)	Tripling of automobile depreciation and expense deduction limits for electric vehicles is extended for two years to vehicles placed in service before Jan. 1, 2007	Property placed in service after Dec. 31, 2001	208	5070
358(h)(1)(A)	412(c)	Basis reduction rule where basis exceeds fair market value and liabilities are not taken into account clarified	Assumptions of liabilities after Oct. 18, '99	706	5056
401(a)(31)(C)(i)	411(q)(1)	Direct rollovers of after-tax amounts from qualified retirement plans can be made only to defined contribution plans (and IRAs)	Distributions made after Dec. 31, 2001	314	5047
402(c)(2)	411(q)(2)	Qualified plan distributions that are rolled over are treated as consisting first of taxable amounts	Distributions made after Dec. 31, 2001.	313	5047
402(g)(1)(C)	411(o)(1)	Additional elective deferrals that don't exceed catch-up contribution limit are excludable from eligible participant's income	For contributions made in tax years beginning after Dec. 31, 2001	308	5045
402(h)(2)(A)	411(l)(3)	Limitation on deductible contributions to SEPs increased from 15% to 25% of compensation	For years beginning after Dec. 31, 2001	301	5042
403(b)	411(p)	Rules applying defined contribution plan limits to Code Sec. 403(b) annuities, Code Sec. 457 plans and church plans are clarified	Years beginning after Dec. 31, 2001	320	5046
404(a)(7)(C)	411(l)(4)	Deduction limit for combined plans doesn't apply if defined contribution plan receives only elective deferrals	For years beginning after Dec. 31, 2001	305	5042

Code §	Act §	Topic	Generally effective date	Analysis ¶	Com Rep ¶
404(a)(12)	411(l)(1)	"Compensation" for purposes of determining deduction limits for contributions to SEPs includes salary reduction amounts	Years beginning after Dec. 31, 2001	304	5042
404(k)(4)(B)	411(w)(1)(D)	ESOP dividends can be reinvested in company stock without the company losing its dividend deduction; reinvested dividends must be nonforfeitable	Tax years beginning after Dec. 31, 2001	326	5053
404(k)(7)	411(w)(2)	ESOP dividends can be reinvested in company stock without the company losing its dividend deduction; reinvested dividends must be nonforfeitable	Tax years beginning after Dec. 31, 2001	326	5053
404(n)	411(l)(2)	Elective deferrals are no longer taken into account in applying SEP deduction limits for employer contributions	For years beginning after Dec. 31, 2001	303	5042
408(k)	411(j)(1)	Dollar limits for SEP eligibility, and for determining the distribution period from an ESOP, are increased to permit proper inflation indexing	Years beginning after Dec. 31, 2001	302	5040
408(q)(3)(A)	411(i)(1)	Types of governmental plans that can provide deemed IRAs are clarified—after 2002	Plan years beginning after Dec. 31, 2002	319	5039
409(o)(1)(C)(ii)	411(j)(2)	Dollar limits for SEP eligibility, and for determining the distribution period from an ESOP, are increased to permit proper inflation indexing	Years beginning after Dec. 31, 2001	302	5040
412(c)(9)(B)	411(v)(1)	Modification of requirements for using prior year's valuation in satisfaction of annual actuarial requirement for defined benefit and money purchase plans	Plan years beginning after Dec. 31, 2001	325	5052

Code §	Act §	Topic	Generally effective date	Analysis ¶	Com Rep ¶
412(l)(7)(C)(i)(III)	405(a)(1)	Temporary relief from low yields on 30-year bonds provided for additional funding requirements and for determining PBGC variable rate premiums	Plan years beginning after Dec. 31, 2001 and before Jan. 1, 2004	306	5025
412(m)(7)	405(a)(2)	Temporary relief from low yields on 30-year bonds provided for additional funding requirements and for determining PBGC variable rate premiums	Plan years beginning after Dec. 31, 2001 and before Jan. 1, 2004	306	5025
414(v)(2)(D)	411(o)(3)	Plan's catch-up contribution limit must be applied on an aggregate basis, applying the controlled group rules	For contributions made in tax years beginning after Dec. 31, 2001	309	5045
414(v)(3)(A)(i)	411(o)(4)	List of qualification requirements that don't apply to catch-up contribution is revised	For contributions made in tax years beginning after Dec. 31, 2001	311	5045
414(v)(3)(B)	411(o)(5)	List of qualification requirements that don't apply to catch-up contribution is revised	For contributions made in tax years beginning after Dec. 31, 2001	311	5045
414(v)(4)(B)	411(o)(6)	Plans in transition period under nondiscrimination rules for certain dispositions and acquisitions are not subject to universal availability requirement for catch-up contributions	For contributions made in tax years beginning after Dec. 31, 2001	312	5045
414(v)(5)	411(o)(7)	Individuals who reach age 50 by the end of the tax year are eligible to make catch-up contributions as of the beginning of the year	For contributions made in tax years beginning after Dec. 31, 2001	307	5045
414(v)(6)(C)	411(o)(8)	Governmental section 457 plan participants can make catch-up contributions equal to the greater of the amount allowed under Code Sec. 414(v) or under Code Sec. 457	For contributions made in tax years beginning after Dec. 31, 2001	310	5045

Code §	Act §	Topic	Generally effective date	Analysis ¶	Com Rep ¶
415(c)(7)	411(p)(4)	Rules applying defined contribution plan limits to Code Sec. 403(b) annuities, Code Sec. 457 plans and church plans are clarified	Years beginning after Dec. 31, 2001	320	5046
416(c)(1)(C)(iii)	411(k)(1)	Method of determining "defined benefit minimum" for top-heavy plans no longer applies only to frozen plans	For years beginning after Dec. 31, 2001	323	5041
416(g)(3)(B)	411(k)(2)	"Severance from employment" replaces "separation from service" for in-service distributions from top-heavy plans	For years beginning after Dec. 31, 2001	322	5041
417(e)(1)	411(r)(1)(A)	Rollovers may be disregarded in determining the present value of a qualified survivor annuity for cash-out purposes	Applies to distributions after Dec. 31, 2001	324	5048
417(e)(2)(A)	411(r)(1)(B)	Rollovers may be disregarded in determining the present value of a qualified survivor annuity for cash-out purposes	Applies to distributions after Dec. 31, 2001	324	5048
448(d)(5)	403(a)	Use of nonaccrual experience method of accounting is available only for amounts received for performing certain qualified personal services, or for amounts received for services by taxpayers with average annual gross receipts of $5 million or less	Tax years ending after Mar. 9, 2002	106	5023
457(e)(5)	411(p)(5)	Rules applying defined contribution plan limits to Code Sec. 403(b) annuities, Code Sec. 457 plans and church plans are clarified	Years beginning after Dec. 31, 2001	320	5046
457(e)(18)	411(o)(9)	Governmental section 457 plan participants can make catch-up contributions equal to the greater of the amount allowed under Code Sec. 414(v) or under Code Sec. 457	For contributions made in tax years beginning after Dec. 31, 2001	310	5045

Code Section Table

Code §	Act §	Topic	Generally effective date	Analysis ¶	Com Rep ¶
469(i)(3)(E)	412(a)	Commercial revitalization deduction for renewal communities is given a higher priority under the rule that determines the order in which deductions and credits are applied against the up-to-$25,000 of passive losses (or credit equivalents) permitted for certain real estate activities	Buildings placed in service in renewal communities after Dec. 31, 2001 and before Jan. 1, 2010	107	5054
530(d)(4)(B)(iv)	411(f)	The 10% additional tax on Coverdell ESA distributions doesn't apply to distributions that are includible in income only because a HOPE or Lifetime Learning credit is taken instead	For tax years beginning after Dec. 31, 2001	409	5036
613A(c)(6)(H)	607(a)	Suspension of taxable income limitation on percentage depletion from marginal oil and gas wells is extended for two years to include tax years beginning before 2004	Tax years beginning after Dec. 31, 2001	206	5075
809(j)	611(a)	Reduction of deductions for mutual life insurance companies is suspended for tax years beginning in 2001, 2002, or 2003	Tax years beginning after Dec. 31, 2000	212	5079
857(b)(7)(B)(i)	413(a)(1)	Amount of REIT's "redetermined rents" and "redetermined deductions" to which 100% tax applies clarified	Tax years beginning after Dec. 31, 2000	701	5058
857(b)(7)(C)	413(a)(2)	Amount of REIT's "redetermined rents" and "redetermined deductions" to which 100% tax applies clarified	Tax years beginning after Dec. 31, 2000	701	5058
904(h)	601(b)(1)	Nonrefundable personal credits won't reduce individual's foreign tax credit until after 2003 (instead of after 2001)	Tax years beginning after Dec. 31, 2001	402	5069

 Research Institute of America

Code §	Act §	Topic	Generally effective date	Analysis ¶	Com Rep ¶
953(e)(10)	614(a)(1)	Exceptions under Subpart F for active banking, financing and insurance income expiring in 2001 extended through 2006	Tax years beginning after Dec. 31, 2001	203	5082
953(e)(10)	614(a)(1)	Special rule for determining life insurance and annuity contract reserves of a qualifying insurance company or branch modified and extended through 2006	Tax years beginning after Dec. 31, 2001	204	5082
954(h)(9)	614(a)(2)	Exceptions under Subpart F for active banking, financing and insurance income expiring in 2001 extended through 2006	Tax years beginning after Dec. 31, 2001	203	5082
954(i)(4)(B)	614(b)	Special rule for determining life insurance and annuity contract reserves of a qualifying insurance company or branch modified and extended through 2006	Tax years beginning after Dec. 31, 2001	204	5082
1091(e)	412(d)(2)	Securities futures contract rules are clarified	Dec. 21, 2000	704	5057
1233(e)(2)(E)	412(d)(3)(A)	Securities futures contract rules are clarified	Dec. 21, 2000	704	5057
1234A	412(d)(1)(A)	Securities futures contract rules are clarified	Dec. 21, 2000	704	5057
1234B(a)(1)	412(d)(1)(B)(i)	Securities futures contract rules are clarified	Dec. 21, 2000	704	5057
1234B(b)	412(d)(1)(B)(i)	Securities futures contract rules are clarified	Dec. 21, 2000	704	5057
1234B(b)	412(d)(3)(B)	Securities futures contract rules are clarified	Dec. 21, 2000	704	5057
1397E(e)(1)	608(a)	Authorization for issuance of qualified zone academy bonds of up to $400 million per year is extended for two years to include calendar years 2002 and 2003	Obligations issued after Mar. 9, 2002	213	5076

Code §	Act §	Topic	Generally effective date	Analysis ¶	Com Rep ¶
1400L(a)	301(a)	Work opportunity tax credit of up to $2,400 per calendar year is allowed for wages paid or incurred to each New York Liberty Zone business employee for work performed during calendar years 2002 or 2003	Tax years ending after Dec. 31, 2001 for wages paid or incurred for work in calendar years 2002 or 2003	505	5011
1400L(b)	301(a)	30% additional first-year depreciation is allowed for, and the AMT depreciation adjustment is not required for, certain buildings placed in service in the New York Liberty Zone after Sept. 10, 2001 and before Jan. 1, 2010, and most other tangible property and computer software placed in service in the New York Liberty Zone after Sept. 10, 2001 and before Jan. 1, 2007	Property acquired by purchase after, and originally used in the New York Liberty Zone after, Sept. 10, 2001	501	5012
1400L(c)	301(a)	Qualified New York Liberty Zone leasehold improvement property placed in service after Sept. 10, 2001 and before Jan. 1, 2007 is 5-year property for MACRS depreciation	Qualified New York Liberty Zone leasehold improvement property placed in service after Sept. 10, 2001	503	5013
1400L(d)	301(a)	Issuance of up to $8 billion of tax-exempt private activity bonds to finance the rebuilding of portions of New York City is authorized	Bonds issued after Mar. 9, 2002 and before Jan. 1, 2005	507	5014
1400L(e)	301(a)	Additional advance refunding is allowed for bonds for facilities located in New York City	Mar. 9, 2002	508	5015

Code §	Act §	Topic	Generally effective date	Analysis ¶	Com Rep ¶
1400L(f)	301(a)	Additional first-year expensing in lieu of depreciation is increased by $35,000 for "qualified New York Liberty Zone property" purchased and placed in service by the taxpayer after Sept. 10, 2001 and before Jan. 1, 2007	Property purchased and placed in service by the taxpayer after Sept. 10, 2001 and before Jan. 1, 2007	502	5016
1400L(g)	301(a)	The period for replacing certain property involuntarily converted as a result of the terrorist attacks on the World Trade Center in New York City is extended to five years	Involuntary conversions in the New York Liberty Zone occurring after Sept. 10, 2001 as a consequence of the terrorist attacks on Sept. 11, 2001	504	5017
1400L(h)	301(a)	30% additional first-year depreciation is allowed for, and the AMT depreciation adjustment is not required for, certain buildings placed in service in the New York Liberty Zone after Sept. 10, 2001 and before Jan. 1, 2010, and most other tangible property and computer software placed in service in the New York Liberty Zone after Sept. 10, 2001 and before Jan. 1, 2007	Property acquired by purchase after, and originally used in the New York Liberty Zone after, Sept. 10, 2001	501	5012
1400L(i)	301(a)	Issuance of up to $8 billion of tax-exempt private activity bonds to finance the rebuilding of portions of New York City is authorized	Bonds issued after Mar. 9, 2002 and before Jan. 1, 2005	507	5014
2511(c)	411(g)(1)	Provision governing transfers to non-grantor trusts after 2009 clarified; these transfers will be treated as transfers of property by gift	For gifts made after Dec. 31, 2009	702	5037

Code §	Act §	Topic	Generally effective date	Analysis ¶	Com Rep ¶
4101(e)	615(a)	Mandate that terminal operators offer both dyed and undyed diesel fuel or kerosene after 2001 is retroactively repealed	Jan. 1, 2002	703	5083
4980F(e)(1)	411(u)(1)(A)	Code Sec. 4980F notice rules apply only to tax qualified defined benefit plans	For plan amendments taking effect on or after June 7, 2001	327	5051
4980F(f)(2)(A)	411(u)(1)(B)	Code Sec. 4980F notice rules apply only to tax qualified defined benefit plans	For plan amendments taking effect on or after June 7, 2001	327	5051
4980F(f)(3)	411(u)(1)(C)	Code Sec. 4980F notice rules apply only to tax qualified defined benefit plans	For plan amendments taking effect on or after June 7, 2001	327	5051
6103(l)(8)(A)	416(c)	Social Security Administration must disclose return information to federal child support agency	Mar. 9, 2002	604	5063
6224(c)(1)	416(d)(1)(A)	Partners' settlements with Attorney General given equivalent treatment to settlements with IRS under partnership audit rules	Settlement agreements entered into after Mar. 9, 2002	603	5064
6224(c)(2)	416(d)(1)(A)	Partners' settlements with Attorney General given equivalent treatment to settlements with IRS under partnership audit rules	Settlement agreements entered into after Mar. 9, 2002	603	5064
6229(f)(2)	416(d)(1)(B)	Partners' settlements with Attorney General given equivalent treatment to settlements with IRS under partnership audit rules	Settlement agreements entered into after Mar. 9, 2002	603	5064
6231(b)(1)(C)	416(d)(1)(C)	Partners' settlements with Attorney General given equivalent treatment to settlements with IRS under partnership audit rules	Settlement agreements entered into after Mar. 9, 2002	603	5064

Code §	Act §	Topic	Generally effective date	Analysis ¶	Com Rep ¶
6234(g)(4)(A)	416(d)(1)(D)	Partners' settlements with Attorney General given equivalent treatment to settlements with IRS under partnership audit rules	Settlement agreements entered into after Mar. 9, 2002	603	5064
6331(k)(3)	416(e)(1)	Extension of collection limitations period clarified in cases where installment agreements or offers-in-compromise are considered	Mar. 9, 2002	601	5060
6428(b)	411(a)(1)	2001 rate reduction credit treated as a nonrefundable personal credit	For tax years beginning after Dec. 31, 2000	403	5031
6428(d)	411(a)(2)(A)	2001 rate reduction credit treated as a nonrefundable personal credit	For tax years beginning after Dec. 31, 2000	403	5031
6428(e)(2)	411(a)(2)(B)	2001 rate reduction credit treated as a nonrefundable personal credit	For tax years beginning after Dec. 31, 2000	403	5031
7702A(c)(3)(A)(ii)	416(f)	Unnecessary reference to "the old contract" is deleted from rules on whether a life insurance contract is a modified endowment contract if there is a material change to the contract	Applies to contracts entered into after June 20, '88	705	5066
9812(f)	610(a)	Mental health parity requirements extended through 2003	Plan years beginning after Dec. 31, 2000	328	5078
None	401	Information returns for tax years ending after Mar. 9, 2002 related to numerous payments or transactions may be furnished electronically to recipients who have consented to receive the returns electronically	Statements for tax years ending after Mar. 9, 2002	602	5021
None	411(c)(1)(F)	Qualified adoption expenses paid or incurred before 2002 are subject to pre-2002 dollar limits	Tax years beginning after Dec. 31, 2001	413	5033

Code §	Act §	Topic	Generally effective date	Analysis ¶	Com Rep ¶
None	411(j)(3)	Transitional rule allowing defined benefit plans that incorporate Code's plan limits by reference to disregard the anti-cutback rules	Years ending after Dec. 31, 2001.	321	5040
None	414(a)(1)	Gain to which mark-to-market election for assets held on Jan. 1, 2001 applies is included in income despite nonrecognition provision	Tax years ending after May 6, '97	418	5059
None	414(a)(2)	Mark-to-market election for assets held on Jan. 1, 2001 doesn't trigger deduction of suspended passive losses	Tax years ending after May 6, '97	109	5059
None	601(b)(2)	Nonrefundable personal credits may be used to offset AMT through 2003 (instead of 2001)	Tax years beginning after Dec. 31, 2001	401	5069

¶ 6002. Act Section ERISA Cross-Reference Table

Act §	ERISA §	Topic	Generally effective date	Analysis ¶	Com Rep ¶
405(b)(1)	302(d)(7)(C)(i)(III)	Temporary relief from low yields on 30-year bonds provided for additional funding requirements and for determining PBGC variable rate premiums	Plan years beginning after Dec. 31, 2001 and before Jan. 1, 2004	306	5025
405(b)(2)	302(e)(7)	Temporary relief from low yields on 30-year bonds provided for additional funding requirements and for determining PBGC variable rate premiums	Plan years beginning after Dec. 31, 2001 and before Jan. 1, 2004	306	5025
405(c)	4006(a)(3)(E)(iii)(IV)	Temporary relief from low yields on 30-year bonds provided for additional funding requirements and for determining PBGC variable rate premiums	Plan years beginning after Dec. 31, 2001 and before Jan. 1, 2004	306	5025
411(i)(2)	4(c)	ERISA's enforcement provisions and certain fiduciary responsibility requirements will apply to "deemed IRAs" in a manner similar to SEPs—after 2002	Plan years beginning after Dec. 31, 2002	318	5039
411(r)(2)(A)	205(g)(1)	Rollovers may be disregarded in determining the present value of a qualified survivor annuity for cash-out purposes	Applies to distributions after Dec. 31, 2001	324	5048
411(r)(2)(B)	205(g)(2)(A)	Rollovers may be disregarded in determining the present value of a qualified survivor annuity for cash-out purposes	Applies to distributions after Dec. 31, 2001	324	5048
411(u)(2)	204(h)(9)	Code Sec. 4980F notice rules apply only to tax qualified defined benefit plans	For plan amendments taking effect on or after June 7, 2001	327	5051

Act §	ERISA §	Topic	Generally effective date	Analysis ¶	Com Rep ¶
411(v)(2)	302(c)(9)(B)	Modification of requirements for using prior year's valuation in satisfaction of annual actuarial requirement for defined benefit and money purchase plans	Plan years beginning after Dec. 31, 2001	325	5052

¶ 6003. ERISA Section Cross-Reference Table

ERISA §	Act §	Topic	Generally effective date	Analysis ¶	Com Rep ¶
4(c)	411(i)(2)	ERISA's enforcement provisions and certain fiduciary responsibility requirements will apply to "deemed IRAs" in a manner similar to SEPs—after 2002	Plan years beginning after Dec. 31, 2002	318	5039
204(h)(9)	411(u)(2)	Code Sec. 4980F notice rules apply only to tax qualified defined benefit plans	For plan amendments taking effect on or after June 7, 2001	327	5051
205(g)(1)	411(r)(2)(A)	Rollovers may be disregarded in determining the present value of a qualified survivor annuity for cash-out purposes	Applies to distributions after Dec. 31, 2001	324	5048
205(g)(2)(A)	411(r)(2)(B)	Rollovers may be disregarded in determining the present value of a qualified survivor annuity for cash-out purposes	Applies to distributions after Dec. 31, 2001	324	5048
302(c)(9)(B)	411(v)(2)	Modification of requirements for using prior year's valuation in satisfaction of annual actuarial requirement for defined benefit and money purchase plans	Plan years beginning after Dec. 31, 2001	325	5052
302(d)(7)(C)(i)(III)	405(b)(1)	Temporary relief from low yields on 30-year bonds provided for additional funding requirements and for determining PBGC variable rate premiums	Plan years beginning after Dec. 31, 2001 and before Jan. 1, 2004	306	5025
302(e)(7)	405(b)(2)	Temporary relief from low yields on 30-year bonds provided for additional funding requirements and for determining PBGC variable rate premiums	Plan years beginning after Dec. 31, 2001 and before Jan. 1, 2004	306	5025

ERISA §	Act §	Topic	Generally effective date	Analysis ¶	Com Rep ¶
4006(a)(3)(E)(iii)(IV)	405(c)	Temporary relief from low yields on 30-year bonds provided for additional funding requirements and for determining PBGC variable rate premiums	Plan years beginning after Dec. 31, 2001 and before Jan. 1, 2004	306	5025

            RIA Research Institute of America

¶ 6004. Code Sections Amended by 2002 Act
(including conforming amendments)

Code Sec.	Act Sec.	Code Sec.	Act Sec.
21(d)(2)(A)	418(b)(1)	42(h)(3)(C)	417(2)
21(d)(2)(B)	418(b)(2)	42(m)(1)(B)(ii)(II)	417(3)
23	411(c)(1)(F)	42(m)(1)(B)(ii)(III)	417(3)
23(a)(1)	411(c)(1)(A)	45(c)(3)(A)	603(a)
23(a)(2)	411(c)(1)(C)	45(c)(3)(B)	603(a)
23(a)(3)	411(c)(1)(B)	45(c)(3)(C)	603(a)
23(b)(1)	411(c)(1)(D)	45A(f)	613(a)
23(h)	418(a)(1)(A)	45F(d)(4)(B)	411(d)(1)
23(h)	418(a)(1)(B)	51(c)(4)(B)	604(a)
23(i)	411(c)(1)(E)	51A(c)(1)	417(4)
24(d)(1)(B)	411(b)	51A(f)	605(a)
25B(d)(2)(A)	411(m)	56(a)(1)(A)(ii)	417(5)
25B(g)	417(1)	56(d)(1)(A)	102(c)(1)
25B(h)	417(1)	62(a)(2)(D)	406(a)
26(a)(2)	601(a)(1)	62(d)	406(b)
26(a)(2)	601(a)(2)	63(c)(2)	411(e)(1)(E)
26(b)(2)(P)	415(a)	63(c)(2)(A)	411(e)(1)(A)
26(b)(2)(Q)	415(a)	63(c)(2)(B)	411(e)(1)(B)
26(b)(2)(R)	415(a)	63(c)(2)(C)	411(e)(1)(C)
30(b)(2)	602(a)(1)(A)	63(c)(2)(D)	411(e)(1)(C)
30(b)(2)(A)	602(a)(1)(A)	63(c)(4)	411(e)(2)(A)
30(b)(2)(B)	602(a)(1)(A)	63(c)(4)	411(e)(2)(C)
30(b)(2)(C)	602(a)(1)(A)	63(c)(4)(B)(i)	411(e)(2)(B)
30(e)	602(a)(2)	108(d)(7)(A)	402(a)
32(g)(2)	416(a)(1)	131(b)(1)	404(a)
38(b)(15)	411(d)(2)	131(b)(2)(B)	404(b)
38(c)(2)(A)(ii)(II)	301(b)(2)	131(b)(3)	404(c)
38(c)(3)	301(b)(1)	131(b)(4)	404(c)
38(c)(3)	301(b)(1)	137(a)	411(c)(2)(A)
38(c)(3)	301(b)(1)	137(b)(2)[sic(1)]	411(c)(2)(B)
38(c)(4)	301(b)(1)	137(f)	418(a)(2)

Code Sec.	Act Sec.	Code Sec.	Act Sec.
151(c)(6)(B)(iii)	417(6)	403(b)(6)	411(p)(2)
151(c)(6)(C)	412(b)(1)	404(a)(1)(D)(iv)	411(s)
151(c)(6)(C)	412(b)(2)	404(a)(12)	411(l)(1)
168(j)(8)	613(b)	404(a)(7)(C)	411(l)(4)
168(k)	101(a)	404(k)(1)	411(w)(1)(A)
170(e)(6)(B)(i)(III)	417(7)	404(k)(2)(B)	411(w)(1)(B)
172(b)(1)(F)(i)	417(8)(A)	404(k)(4)(B)	411(w)(1)(C)
172(b)(1)(F)(i)	417(8)(B)	404(k)(4)(B)	411(w)(1)(D)
172(b)(1)(H)	102(a)	404(k)(4)(C)	411(w)(1)(D)
172(j)	102(b)	404(k)(7)	411(w)(2)
172(k)	102(b)	404(n)	411(l)(2)
179A(b)(1)(B)	606(a)(1)(A)	408(k)(2)(C)	411(j)(1)(A)
179A(b)(1)(B)(i)	606(a)(1)(B)	408(k)(8)	411(j)(1)(B)
179A(b)(1)(B)(ii)	606(a)(1)(B)	408(q)(3)(A)	411(i)(1)
179A(b)(1)(B)(iii)	606(a)(1)(B)	409(o)(1)(C)(ii)	411(j)(2)(A)
179A(f)	606(a)(2)	409(o)(1)(C)(ii)	411(j)(2)(B)
220(i)(2)	612(a)	412(c)(9)(B)(ii)	411(v)(1)(A)
220(i)(3)(B)	612(a)	412(c)(9)(B)(iv)	411(v)(1)(B)
220(j)(2)	612(b)(1)	412(l)(7)(C)(i)(III)	405(a)(1)
220(j)(4)(A)	612(b)(2)	412(m)(7)	405(a)(2)
45E(e)(1)	411(n)(1)	414(v)(2)(D)	411(o)(3)
280F(a)(1)(C)(iii)	602(b)(1)	414(v)(3)(A)(i)	411(o)(4)
351(h)(1)	417(9)	414(v)(3)(B)	411(o)(5)
358(h)(1)(A)	412(c)	414(v)(4)(B)	411(o)(6)
401(a)(30)	411(o)(2)	414(v)(5)	411(o)(7)(A)
401(a)(31)(C)(i)	411(q)(1)	414(v)(5)(A)	411(o)(7)(B)
402(c)(2)	411(q)(2)	414(v)(5)(B)	411(o)(7)(C)
402(g)(1)(C)	411(o)(1)	414(v)(6)(C)	411(o)(8)
402(g)(7)(B)	411(p)(6)	415(c)(7)	411(p)(4)
402(h)(2)(A)	411(l)(3)	416(c)(1)(C)(iii)	411(k)(1)
403(b)(1)	411(p)(1)	416(g)(3)(B)	411(k)(2)
403(b)(3)	411(p)(3)(A)	417(e)(1)	411(r)(1)(A)
403(b)(3)	411(p)(3)(B)	417(e)(2)(A)	411(r)(1)(B)

                             RIA **Research Institute of America**

Code Sec.	Act Sec.	Code Sec.	Act Sec.
448(d)(5)	403(a)	1234A(1)	412(d)(1)(A)
457(e)(18)	411(o)(9)	1234A(2)	412(d)(1)(A)
457(e)(5)	411(p)(5)	1234A(3)	412(d)(1)(A)
469(i)(3)(E)(ii)	412(a)	1234B(a)(1)	412(d)(1)(B)(i)
469(i)(3)(E)(ii)	412(a)	1234B(b)	412(d)(1)(B)(i)
469(i)(3)(E)(iii)	412(a)	1234B(b)	412(d)(3)(B)
469(i)(3)(E)(iii)	412(a)	1234B(f)	412(d)(1)(B)(ii)
469(i)(3)(E)(iv)	412(a)	1256(f)(5)	416(b)(1)
469(i)(3)(E)(iv)	412(a)	1394(c)(2)	417(16)
475(g)(3)	417(10)	1397E(e)(1)	608(a)
529(e)(3)(B)(i)	417(11)	1400L	301(a)
530(d)(4)(B)(iv)	411(f)	2016	411(h)
613A(c)(6)(H)	607(a)	2101(b)	411(g)(2)
741	417(12)	2511(c)	411(g)(1)
809(j)	611(a)	3304(a)(4)(B)	209(d)(1)
857(b)(7)(B)(i)	413(a)(1)	3306(f)(2)	209(d)(1)
857(b)(7)(B)(i)	417(13)	4101(e)	615(a)
857(b)(7)(C)	413(a)(2)	4980E	417(17)(A)
904(h)	601(b)(1)	4980F(e)(1)	411(u)(1)(A)
943(e)(4)(B)	417(14)	4980F(f)(2)(A)	411(u)(1)(B)
953(e)(10)	614(a)(1)(A)	4980F(f)(3)	411(u)(1)(C)
953(e)(10)	614(a)(1)(B)	6103(l)(8)	416(c)(1)(A)
954(h)(9)	614(a)(2)	6103(l)(8)(A)	416(c)(1)(B)
954(i)(4)(B)	614(b)(1) [sic (b)]	6105(c)(1)(C)	417(18)
995(b)(3)(B)	417(15)	6105(c)(1)(E)	417(18)
1091(e)	412(d)(2)(D)	6224(c)(1)	416(d)(1)(A)
1091(e)	412(d)(2)(B)	6224(c)(2)	416(d)(1)(A)
1091(e)	412(d)(2)(A)	6227(d)	417(19)(A)
1091(e)(2)	412(d)(2)(C)	6228(a)(1)	417(19)(B)(i)
1221(b)(1)(B)(i)	417(20)	6228(a)(3)(A)	417(19)(B)(ii)
1233(e)(2)(C)	412(d)(3)(A)	6228(b)(1)	417(19)(B)(iii)
1233(e)(2)(D)	412(d)(3)(A)	6228(b)(2)(A)	417(19)(B)(iii)
1233(e)(2)(E)	412(d)(3)(A)	6229(f)(2)	416(d)(1)(B)

Code Sec.	Act Sec.	Code Sec.	Act Sec.
6231(b)(1)(C)	416(d)(1)(C)	29USC1054(h)(9)	411(u)(2)
6231(b)(2)(B)(i)	417(19)(C)	29USC1055(g)(1)	411(r)(2)(A)
6234(g)(4)(A)	416(d)(1)(D)	29USC1055(g)(2)(A)	411(r)(2)(B)
6331(k)(3)	416(e)(1)	29USC1082(c)(9)(B)(ii)	411(v)(2)(A)
6428(b)	411(a)(1)	29USC1082(c)(9)(B)(iv)	411(v)(2)(B)
6428(d)	411(a)(2)(A)	29USC1082(d)(7)(C)(i)(III)	405(b)(1)
6428(e)(2)	411(a)(2)(B)	29USC1082(e)(7)	405(b)(2)
7652(f)(1)	609(a)	29USC1103(c)	411(i)(2)(B)
7702A(c)(3)(A)(ii)	416(f)	29USC1104(c)(3)	411(t)(2)
9812(f)	610(a)	29USC1104(c)(3)(A)	411(t)(1)
29USC1003(c)	411(i)(2)(A)	29USC1306(a)(3)(E)(iii)(IV)	405(c)

Research Institute of America

¶ 6005. 2002 Act Sections Amending Code
(including conforming amendments and changes to ERISA in Title 29 USC)

Act Sec.	Code Sec.	Act Sec.	Code Sec.
101(a)	168(k)	411(c)(1)(C)	23(a)(2)
102(a)	172(b)(1)(H)	411(c)(1)(D)	23(b)(1)
102(b)	172(j) redes. (k)	411(c)(1)(E)	23(i)
102(b)	172(j)	411(c)(1)(F)	23
102(c)(1)	56(d)(1)(A)	411(c)(2)(A)	137(a)
209(d)(1)	3304(a)(4)(B)	411(c)(2)(B)	137(b)(2)[sic(1)]
209(d)(1)	3306(f)(2)	411(d)(1)	45F(d)(4)(B)
301(a)	1400L	411(d)(2)	38(b)(15)
301(b)(1)	38(c)(3)	411(e)(1)(A)	63(c)(2)(A)
301(b)(1)	38(c)(4)	411(e)(1)(B)	63(c)(2)(B)
301(b)(2)	38(c)(2)(A)(ii)(II)	411(e)(1)(C)	63(c)(2)(C)
402(a)	108(d)(7)(A)	411(e)(1)(D)	63(c)(2)(D)
403(a)	448(d)(5)	411(e)(1)(E)	63(c)(2)
404(a)	131(b)(1)	411(e)(2)(A)	63(c)(4)
404(b)	131(b)(2)(B)	411(e)(2)(B)	63(c)(4)(B)(i)
404(c)	131(b)(3)	411(e)(2)(C)	63(c)(4)
404(c)	131(b)(4)	411(f)	530(d)(4)(B)(iv)
405(a)(1)	412(l)(7)(C)(i)(III)	411(g)(1)	2511(c)
405(a)(2)	412(m)(7)	411(g)(2)	2101(b)
405(b)(1)	29USC1082(d)(7)(C)(i)(III)	411(h)	2016
405(b)(2)	29USC1082(e)(7)	411(i)(1)	408(q)(3)(A)
405(c)	29USC1306(a)(3)(E)(iii)(IV)	411(i)(2)(A)	29USC1003(c)
406(a)	62(a)(2)(D)	411(i)(2)(B)	29USC1103(c)
406(b)	62(d)	411(j)(1)(A)	408(k)(2)(C)
411(a)(1)	6428(b)	411(j)(1)(B)	408(k)(8)
411(a)(2)(A)	6428(d)	411(j)(2)(A)	409(o)(1)(C)(ii)
411(a)(2)(B)	6428(e)(2)	411(j)(2)(B)	409(o)(1)(C)(ii)
411(b)	24(d)(1)(B)	411(k)(1)	416(c)(1)(C)(iii)
411(c)(1)(A)	23(a)(1)	411(k)(2)	416(g)(3)(B)
411(c)(1)(B)	23(a)(3)	411(l)(1)	404(a)(12)
		411(l)(2)	404(n)

Act Sec.	Code Sec.	Act Sec.	Code Sec.
411(l)(3)	402(h)(2)(A)	411(u)(1)(C)	4980F(f)(3)
411(l)(4)	404(a)(7)(C)	411(u)(2)	29USC1054(h)(9)
411(m)	25B(d)(2)(A)	411(v)(1)(A)	412(c)(9)(B)(ii)
411(n)(1)	45E(e)(1)	411(v)(1)(B)	412(c)(9)(B)(iv)
411(o)(1)	402(g)(1)(C)	411(v)(2)(A)	29USC1082(c)(9)(B)(ii)
411(o)(2)	401(a)(30)	411(v)(2)(B)	29USC1082(c)(9)(B)(iv)
411(o)(3)	414(v)(2)(D)	411(w)(1)(A)	404(k)(1)
411(o)(4)	414(v)(3)(A)(i)	411(w)(1)(B)	404(k)(2)(B)
411(o)(5)	414(v)(3)(B)	411(w)(1)(C)	404(k)(4)(B)
411(o)(6)	414(v)(4)(B)	411(w)(1)(D)	404(k)(4)(B)
411(o)(7)(A)	414(v)(5)	411(w)(1)(D)	404(k)(4)(C)
411(o)(7)(B)	414(v)(5)(A)	411(w)(2)	404(k)(7)
411(o)(7)(C)	414(v)(5)(B)	412(a)	469(i)(3)(E)(ii)
411(o)(8)	414(v)(6)(C)	412(a)	469(i)(3)(E)(iii)
411(o)(9)	457(e)(18)	412(a)	469(i)(3)(E)(iv)
411(p)(1)	403(b)(1)	412(a)	469(i)(3)(E)(ii)
411(p)(2)	403(b)(6)	412(a)	469(i)(3)(E)(iii)
411(p)(3)(A)	403(b)(3)	412(a)	469(i)(3)(E)(iv)
411(p)(3)(B)	403(b)(3)	412(b)(1)	151(c)(6)(C)
411(p)(4)	415(c)(7)	412(b)(2)	151(c)(6)(C)
411(p)(5)	457(e)(5)	412(c)	358(h)(1)(A)
411(p)(6)	402(g)(7)(B)	412(d)(1)(A)	1234A(1)
411(q)(1)	401(a)(31)(C)(i)	412(d)(1)(A)	1234A(2)
411(q)(2)	402(c)(2)	412(d)(1)(A)	1234A(3)
411(r)(1)(A)	417(e)(1)	412(d)(1)(B)(i)	1234B(a)(1)
411(r)(1)(B)	417(e)(2)(A)	412(d)(1)(B)(i)	1234B(b)
411(r)(2)(A)	29USC1055(g)(1)	412(d)(1)(B)(ii)	1234B(f)
411(r)(2)(B)	29USC1055(g)(2)(A)	412(d)(2)(A)	1091(e)
411(s)	404(a)(1)(D)(iv)	412(d)(2)(B)	1091(e)
411(t)(1)	29USC1104(c)(3)(A)	412(d)(2)(C)	1091(e)(2)
411(t)(2)	29USC1104(c)(3)	412(d)(2)(D)	1091(e)
411(u)(1)(A)	4980F(e)(1)	412(d)(3)(A)	1233(e)(2)(C)
411(u)(1)(B)	4980F(f)(2)(A)	412(d)(3)(A)	1233(e)(2)(D)

Act Sec.	Code Sec.	Act Sec.	Code Sec.
412(d)(3)(A)	1233(e)(2)(E)	417(13)	857(b)(7)(B)(i)
412(d)(3)(B)	1234B(b)	417(14)	943(e)(4)(B)
413(a)(1)	857(b)(7)(B)(i)	417(15)	995(b)(3)(B)
413(a)(2)	857(b)(7)(C)	417(16)	1394(c)(2)
415(a)	26(b)(2)(P)	417(17)(A)	4980E
415(a)	26(b)(2)(Q)	417(18)	6105(c)(1)(C)
415(a)	26(b)(2)(R)	417(18)	6105(c)(1)(E)
416(a)(1)	32(g)(2)	417(19)(A)	6227(d)
416(b)(1)	1256(f)(5)	417(19)(B)(i)	6228(a)(1)
416(c)(1)(A)	6103(l)(8)	417(19)(B)(ii)	6228(a)(3)(A)
416(c)(1)(B)	6103(l)(8)(A)	417(19)(B)(iii)	6228(b)(1)
416(d)(1)(A)	6224(c)(1)	417(19)(B)(iii)	6228(b)(2)(A)
416(d)(1)(A)	6224(c)(2)	417(19)(C)	6231(b)(2)(B)(i)
416(d)(1)(B)	6229(f)(2)	417(20)	1221(b)(1)(B)(i)
416(d)(1)(C)	6231(b)(1)(C)	418(a)(1)(A)	23(h)
416(d)(1)(D)	6234(g)(4)(A)	418(a)(1)(B)	23(h)
416(e)(1)	6331(k)(3)	418(a)(2)	137(f)
416(f)	7702A(c)(3)(A)(ii)	418(b)(1)	21(d)(2)(A)
417(1)	25B(g)	418(b)(2)	21(d)(2)(B)
417(1)	25B(h)	601(a)(1)	26(a)(2)
417(2)	42(h)(3)(C)	601(a)(2)	26(a)(2)
417(3)	42(m)(1)(B)(ii)(II)	601(b)(1)	904(h)
417(3)	42(m)(1)(B)(ii)(III)	602(a)(1)(A)	30(b)(2)
417(4)	51A(c)(1)	602(a)(1)(A)	30(b)(2)(A)
417(5)	56(a)(1)(A)(ii)	602(a)(1)(A)	30(b)(2)(B)
417(6)	151(c)(6)(B)(iii)	602(a)(1)(A)	30(b)(2)(C)
417(7)	170(e)(6)(B)(i)(III)	602(a)(2)	30(e)
417(8)(A)	172(b)(1)(F)(i)	602(b)(1)	280F(a)(1)(C)(iii)
417(8)(B)	172(b)(1)(F)(i)	603(a)	45(c)(3)(A)
417(9)	351(h)(1)	603(a)	45(c)(3)(B)
417(10)	475(g)(3)	603(a)	45(c)(3)(C)
417(11)	529(e)(3)(B)(i)	604(a)	51(c)(4)(B)
417(12)	741	605(a)	51A(f)

Act Sec.	Code Sec.	Act Sec.	Code Sec.
606(a)(1)(A)	179A(b)(1)(B)	612(a)	220(i)(3)(B)
606(a)(1)(B)	179A(b)(1)(B)(i)	612(b)(1)	220(j)(2)
606(a)(1)(B)	179A(b)(1)(B)(ii)	612(b)(2)	220(j)(4)(A)
606(a)(1)(B)	179A(b)(1)(B)(iii)	613(a)	45A(f)
606(a)(2)	179A(f)	613(b)	168(j)(8)
607(a)	613A(c)(6)(H)	614(a)(1)(A)	953(e)(10)
608(a)	1397E(e)(1)	614(a)(1)(B)	953(e)(10)
609(a)	7652(f)(1)	614(a)(2)	954(h)(9)
610(a)	9812(f)	614(b)(1) [sic (b)]	954(i)(4)(B)
611(a)	809(j)	615(a)	4101(e)
612(a)	220(i)(2)		

¶ 6006. ERISA Sections Amended by 2002 Act
(including conforming amendments)

ERISA Sec.	Act Sec.	ERISA Sec.	Act Sec.
4(c)	411(i)(2)(B)	302(c)(9)(B)(ii)	411(v)(2)(A)
4(c)	411(i)(2)(A)	302(c)(9)(B)(iv)	411(v)(2)(B)
45E(e)(1)	411(n)(1)	302(d)(7)(C)(i)(III)	405(b)(1)
204	411(j)(3)	302(e)(7)	405(b)(2)
204(h)(9)	411(u)(2)	404(c)(3)	411(t)(2)
205(g)(1)	411(r)(2)(A)	404(c)(3)(A)	411(t)(1)
205(g)(2)(A)	411(r)(2)(B)	4006(a)(3)(E)(iii)(IV)	405(c)

¶ 6007. 2002 Act Sections Amending ERISA
(including conforming amendments)

Act Sec.	ERISA Sec.	Act Sec.	ERISA Sec.
405(b)(1)	302(d)(7)(C)(i)(III)	411(r)(2)(A)	205(g)(1)
405(b)(2)	302(e)(7)	411(r)(2)(B)	205(g)(2)(A)
405(c)	4006(a)(3)(E)(iii)(IV)	411(t)(1)	404(c)(3)(A)
411(i)(2)(A)	4(c)	411(t)(2)	404(c)(3)
411(i)(2)(B)	4(c)	411(u)(2)	204(h)(9)
411(j)(3)	204	411(v)(2)(A)	302(c)(9)(B)(ii)
411(n)(1)	45E(e)(1)	411(v)(2)(B)	302(c)(9)(B)(iv)

RIA Research Institute of America

¶ 6008. FTC 2d ¶s affected by 2002 Act

FTC 2d ¶	Analysis ¶	FTC 2d ¶	Analysis ¶	FTC 2d ¶	Analysis ¶
1452.1	414	H-9152	303, 305	L-8103	503
A-1108	403	H-9201.1	322	L-8202	216
A-1406	407	H-9240	307, 309,	L-8806	216
A-1702	407		310, 311,	L-8807	216
A-2803	417		312	L-9106	503
A-4213.1	407	H-9241	307	L-9907	502
A-4303	406	H-9244	309	L-10003.1	207
A-4307	406	H-9247	311	L-10004	102
A-4401	412, 413	H-9247.1	311	L-10004.1	208
A-4401.1	412, 413	H-9248	312	L-15202	506
A-4402.1	414	H-9327	302	L-15202.1	506
A-4403	401	H-10120	305	L-15204	506
A-4604	401	H-11444	313, 314	L-15205	506
A-4605	404	H-12117	326	L-15206	506
A-4704	317	H-12280	319	L-15207	506
A-4705	401	H-12305	302	L-15209	506
A-8212	104	H-12311	303, 304	L-15645.12	213
A-8220	101, 501	H-12315	301, 303,	L-15671	215
D-1765	105		304	L-15691	315
D-1863	105	H-12319.1	301	L-15699.1	316
E-5201	212	H-12439	320	L-17752	205
E-6615.1	701	H-12448	320	L-17753	205
F-1803.1	706	I-3905	704	L-17775	202
G-2502	106	I-3905.1	704	L-17776	505
G-2503	106	I-5110.5	109, 418	L-17835	201
H-1325.35	328	I-6281	704	L-17878	108
H-1325.46	328	I-6282	704	L-18010	208
H-1342.2	214	I-7710	704	L-18011	211
H-1348.4	410	I-7712.1	704	L-18013	211
H-1451	411	I-7714	704	L-18101	401
H-3317	320	I-7720	704	L-18102	401
H-3320	310	J-1502	415	L-18103	410
H-4855	408	J-1503	416	M-4300	103
H-5950	321	J-3051	405	M-4301	103
H-6272.2	327	J-3660	508	M-4305.1	103
H-7407	326	J-5072	705	M-4305.2	103
H-7629.1	306	J-5401	405	M-5144	107
H-7632	306	J-5458	405	M-5701	109
H-7634	306	J-5459	409	N-2729	206
H-7635	306	J-7416	105	O-2423.1	203
H-7703.1	325	K-7001	210	O-2480.3	203
H-8015	323	K-7005	209	O-2480.16	203
H-8016	322	L-3900 et seq.	405	O-2480.18	203
H-8251	314	L-4108	405	O-2480.19	204
H-8701	324	L-6404	503	O-2494	203
H-9151	308	L-7935	101, 501	O-4401	402

FTC 2d ¶	Analysis ¶	FTC 2d ¶	Analysis ¶	FTC 2d ¶	Analysis ¶
Q-3000.1	702	T-2176 *et seq.*	603	T-4018.2	603
Q-3004	702	T-2181.1 *et seq.*	603	V-5104.2	601
S-1370	602			W-1530.1	703
S-5209	403	T-2244	603		
S-6360	604	T-3556	603		

¶ 6009. USTR ¶ s affected by 2002 Act

USTR ¶	Analysis ¶	USTR ¶	Analysis ¶	USTR ¶	Analysis ¶
10,914	704	264	401	4024.04	313, 314
12,34A4	704			4034.04	320
12,34B4	704	264.01	410	4044.09	305
12,334.09	704	280F4	102, 207, 208	4044.14	326
13,97E4.01	213			4044.15	301, 303, 304
		304	208, 211		
13,664	105	324.03	408		
14.08	109, 418	384.02	506	4084.05	302
24.02	407			4084.07	319
24.03	407	394.01	506	4094.11	302
25,114	702	454	205	4114.25	326
		514	202, 505	4124.07	306
25,114.01	702	564.01	101, 104, 501		
25B4	317, 401			4124.09	325
41,014	703	613A4	206	4124.10	306
45A4	215			4144.22	303, 304
45E4	315, 316	634	417	4144.26	307, 309, 310, 311, 312
		1084.03	105		
45F4.01	108	1314.01	415		
49,80D4	328	1354	405		
49,80F4	327	1374	411, 414	4154.02	321
51A4	201				
60,514	602	1384.04	410	4164.01	323
		1494.03	508	4164.02	322
61,034.01	604	1514.02	407	4174.06	324
62,214.03	603	1624.067	405	4484	106
62,214.08	603	1674.033	101, 501	4574	310, 320
63,314.01	601				
64,284	403	1684.01	216	4694.32	109
		1684.02	503	4694.60	107
64,284.01	403	1724	103	5294.02	405
77,02A4.01	705	1724.30	103	5304.01	405, 409
98,124	328	1794.01	502	6134.009	206
179A4	209, 210				
214.04	406	2204.02	214	8094	212
		3584.042	706	8574.01	701
214.06	406	4014.27	314	9044.01	402
234	401, 412, 413, 414	4014.172	322	9534.01	203, 204
		4024	303, 305, 308	9544.02	203
244.01	401				
244.02	404				

¶ 6010. TaxDesk ¶s affected by 2002 Act

TaxDesk ¶	Analysis ¶	TaxDesk ¶	Analysis ¶	TaxDesk ¶	Analysis ¶
133,601	411	282,307	301	397,001	208, 211
133,604	414	282,309	301, 303,	397,003	211
135,515	320		304	398,000	401, 410
135,516	310	283,080	319	398,001	401
144,026	313, 314	283,808	405	413,614	107
144,037	314	283,809	409	417,501	109
145,201	324	284,025	308	440,823	106
149,201	405	284,026	303, 305	561,604	405
157,001	405	284,043	307, 309,	562,003	417
158,014	508		310, 311,	565,511	407
188,028	105		312	567,002	407
196,502	415	284,045	311	568,208	403
196,503	416	286,028	326	569,014	407
223,314	109, 418	287,002	321	569,028	408
227,006	704	288,147	214	569,104	401
227,007	704	288,504	410	569,105	404
228,907	704	307,001	209, 210	569,204	317
228,911	704	356,000	103	569,205	401
228,913	704	356,001	103	569,303	406
228,919	704	356,010	103	569,308	406
231,905	706	356,011	103	569,501	412, 413
250,201	704	380,502	506	569,501.1	412, 413
250,202	704	380,503	506	569,502.1	414
256,519	405	380,506	506	569,503	401
265,434	101, 501	380,507	506	571,306	403
267,007	216	380,509	506	614,704	105
267,020	503	380,700	202	617,001	105
267,601	102	380,701	505	696,001	104
267,602	208	381,300	201	696,513	101, 501
267,604	207	382,108	108	715,004	702
268,411	502	384,039	215	825,018	603
271,001	206	384,054	205	825,020	603
280,120	320	384,061	315	825,045	603
281,015	305	384,069.1	316	902,040	601
282,007	303, 304	394,012	402		
282,302	302				

¶ 6011. PCA ¶s affected by 2002 Act

PCA ¶	Analysis ¶	PCA ¶	Analysis ¶	PCA ¶	Analysis ¶
23,701	321	28,423	307, 309,	35,516	301, 303,
25,408	326		310, 311,		304
25,630.1	306		312	35,520.1	301
25,633	306	28,425	311	36,040	320
25,635	306	28,426	312	36,049	320
25,636	306	28,502.1	322	40,418	320
25,704.1	325	28,628	302	40,421	310
26,216	323	30,221	305		
26,217	322	32,845	313, 314	48,075	318
26,652	314	33,218	326	48,115	318
27,203	324	35,181	319	48,124	318
28,402	308	35,506	302	49,314.2	327
28,403	303, 305	35,512	303, 304	58,307	306

¶ 6012. PE ¶s affected by 2002 Act

PE ¶	Analysis ¶	PE ¶	Analysis ¶	PE ¶	Analysis ¶
49,80F-4	327	408-4.07	319	416-4.02	322
401-4.27	314	409-4.11	302	417-4.06	324
401-4.172	322	411-4.25	326	457-4	310, 320
402-4	303, 305, 308	412-4.07	306	4980D-4	328
		412-4.09	325	9812-4	328
402-4.04	313, 314	412-4.10	306	ER101-4	318
403-4.04	320	414-4.22	303, 304	ER301-4	318
404-4.09	305	414-4.26	307, 309, 310, 311, 312	ER401-4.05	318
404-4.14	326			ER403.-4.02	318
404-4.15	301, 303, 304	415-4.02	321	ER405-4.01	318
408-4.05	302	416-4.01	323	ER4006-4.01	306

¶ 6013. EP ¶ s affected by 2002 Act

EPTC/EPA ¶	Analysis ¶	EPTC/EPA ¶	Analysis ¶	EPTC/EPA ¶	Analysis ¶
42,770.3	705	47,651.1	702	47,655	702

¶ 6014. Table of Action Alert Items

Date	Action	Topic	Analysis ¶
June 7, 2001	In light of the retroactive effect of this provision (see Date) plan sponsors who effected plan amendments subject to the notice rules and who relied on the EGTRRA transition provision, should quickly determine if a revised notice conforming to the Code and ERISA notice requirements should be sent out to applicable individuals and their representatives.	Code Sec. 4980F notice rules apply only to tax qualified defined benefit plans	327
June 30, 2002	Plans must be amended by June 30, 2002, in order to take advantage of the transitional rule permitting a plan to disregard the anti-cutback rules.	Transitional rule allowing defined benefit plans that incorporate Code's plan limits by reference to disregard the anti-cutback rules	321

INDEX

References are to paragraph numbers

Research Institute of America

Research Institute of America

M

N